Ebenezer Sibley's

Clavis or Key to the Mysteries of Magic

Sourceworks of Ceremonial Magic Series

In the same series:

Volume I – The Practical Angel Magic of John Dee's Enochian Tables - ISBN 978-0-9547639-0-9

Volume II – The Keys to the Gateway of Magic: Summoning the Solomonic Archangels & Demonic Princes – ISBN 978-0-9547639-1-6

Volume III – The Goetia of Dr Rudd: The Angels & Demons of *Liber Malorum Spirituum seu Goetia* – ISBN 978-0-9547639-2-3

Volume IV – The Veritable Key of Solomon – ISBN 978-0-7378-1453-0 (cloth) - ISBN 978-0-9547639-8-5 (limited leather)

Volume V – The grimoire of Saint Cyprian: *Clavis Inferni* - ISBN 978-0-9557387-1-5 (cloth) – ISBN 978-0-9557387-4-6 (limited leather)

Volume VI – *Sepher Raziel: Liber Salomonis* – ISBN 978-0-9557387-3-9 (cloth) – ISBN 978-0-9557387-5-3 (limited leather)

Volume VII – *Liber Lunæ & Sepher ha-Levanah* - ISBN 978-0-9557387-2-1 (cloth) - ISBN 978-0-9557387-3-8 (limited leather)

Volume VIII - The Magical Treatise of Solomon, or *Hygromanteia*- ISBN 978-0-9568285-0-7 (cloth) - ISBN 978-0-9568285-1-4 (limited leather)

Volume IX – A Cunning Man's Grimoire: the Secret of Secrets – ISBN 978-0-9932042-7-2 (cloth) – ISBN 978-0-9932042-8-9 (limited leather)

Volume X – Clavis or Key to the Mysteries of Magic – Rabbi Solomon - Ebenezer Sibley – ISBN 978-1912212-08-8 (cloth) – ISBN 978-1912212-09-5 (limited leather)

For further details of forthcoming volumes in this series edited from classic magical manuscripts see www.GoldenHoard.com

Figure 01: The wyvern from the Evocation of the Spirit Birto in Sloane MS 3824, f.1. With kind permission of the Trustees of the British Library.

The Clavis or Key to Unlock the

Mysteries of Magic

by Rabbi Solomon - translated by Ebenezer Sibley
Introduction by Dr Stephen Skinner & Daniel Clark

with additional texts by Frederick Hockley

GOLDEN HOARD

2018

Published by Golden Hoard Press Pte Ltd
PO Box 1073 Robinson Road
Singapore, 902123.

www.GoldenHoard.com

First Edition

ISBN: 978-1912212-08-8   *Cloth Edition*

ISBN: 978-1912212-09-5   *Limited Leather Edition*   Copy number..........

Printed in Malaysia

Acknowledgements

To Myra Mapili for the initial transcription of the original handwriting in the manuscript of this grimoire in the shortest possible time. And to Navaneeta Das for help with historical research. Acknowledgements to Daniel Clark for his great work in restoring and digitally cleaning up this and so many other manuscript grimoires.

Frederick Hockley has to be acknowledged for his tireless copying of rare manuscripts on magic which helped to assure their survival. For example Hockley's manuscript copy of the 'Four Experiments of the Spirits Birto, Agares, Bealpharos & Vassago' in Wellcome MS 2842 written in 1829 was probably the immediate source of Part 3 of the present manuscript. He in turn derived it from Elias Ashmole's 1649 Sloane MS 3824.

In his preface Hockley writes a very significant paragraph:

> "That these are true Experiments is apparent and that these Spirits have been by the Great Diligence and constant perseverance of Learned and intelligible [Intelligent] Magicians brought to obedience and fellowship is manifestly true by the Obligations hereafter given – besides what myself have seen and therefore I have not any doubt of the truth of them."

In this he confirms his own practical involvement, and hints at one of the keys of practical magic.

We wish also to acknowledge the National Library of Israel for allowing us access to Yar. Var. MS 18. We would also like to thank the many other librarians who allowed us access to their copies of this and other manuscripts, and in particular a special thank you to the staff of the Library of the University of Utah special collections for their help, patience and understanding.

Contents

List of Figures

Preface

Ebenezer Sibley, a name familiar to the astrologers and occultists of polite Georgian and Victorian society, is largely unknown today. Sibley's life was dedicated to the esoteric, the scientific and the fringe medical. In the course of a busy life, he published a number of works on astrology, medicine and magic (some over 1000 pages long). The present text is his most complete work devoted to magic, never published in full before. After his death, at the encouragement of John Denley an occult bookseller, a number of copies were made. Although Hockley did not pen the present manuscript, he was a major part of the constellation of copyists who did, and he also provided other magical texts that were later added in to the *Clavis*. The current whereabouts of Sibley's original manuscript has yet to be discovered, but it maybe that this work has only survived because of the dedication of copyists like Hockley.

Sibley's *Clavis* would continue to be copied by a variety of different scribes passing through the hands of both collectors and practitioners of magic. The manuscript that you now hold (MS 18) eventually found its way from the auction houses of London to its current resting place in the National Library of Israel.

The *Clavis* was clearly a well-respected and sort-after work in its day. Great care and long hours must have been spent labouring over its creation. One thing that rapidly becomes apparent when comparing this manuscript with the other exemplars is its beauty. Grimoires were not often thought of in terms of their aesthetic appeal, their readers usually being more concerned with the practical techniques embedded in them. From its ornate title pages and borders to its spectacular illustration of the many Seals and Pentacles, the entire work is inked in the most vibrant of colours, both a manual of practical magic and a shining example of Victorian calligraphy and imagination, which amazingly has not faded over time.

We have taken the unusual step of placing the Introduction *after* the main text, in order to ensure that the printed page numbers match those of the manuscript, at least for the first 108 pages.[1] After that the manuscript pages are no longer in sync with the printed page numbers, because the numbering sequences in the manuscript are irregular and restart with every new Part. Nevertheless no page is missing, and all page references in the Introduction and transcription refer to the printed page number.

Go direct to page 273 if you wish to read the Introduction next.

---

[1] Page number 90 was skipped in the original manuscript by the scribe, but no content is missing.

1. 2. The two Seals of the Earth, without which no Spirit will appear. 3. Magic Wands & Sword.
4. A Great Character, 5. The Greatest Character. 6. Magic Circle. 7. Magic Knife reversed.
8. Engraving Tools.   9. Seal, Whosoever beareth this sign all Spirits will do him Homage.
10. Seal, Whosoever beareth this sign need fear no foe.

The
Clavis or Key
To Unlock The Mysteries
OF
MAGIC
OF
RABBI SOLOMON
Translated From The Hebrew Into French and from the
French Rendered into English with Additions.
By Ebenezer Sibley, MD.
Fellow of the Harmoniac Philosophical Society at Paris & author
of the Complete Illustration of Astrology, Editor of Culpep-
per's Complete Herbal, Placidus De Titus on Elementary Philo-
-sophy &c.   The whole Enriched with Coloured Figures.
Talismans, Pentacles, Circles, Characters &c. —————

1

Preface

The Doctrine of Spirits was universally believed in throughout all ages, both by Philosophers, Patriarchs, Apostles, and Prophets, and approved of by the greatest men the World ever produced. The Testimony of Jacob Behmen the Tutonick Philosopher is not the least in Vindication of the truth thereof, viz, in his <u>Book of the Forty Questions on the Soul</u>, where he saith, when speaking on the spontaneous appearing of Spirits departed: "That those Souls "which have not attained Heaven, and so stick in the source in the prin- "-ciple, in the Birth, those have yet the human form and Essence with the "works in them, they diligently search out the cause of their Retention, and "therefore many of them come again with the Astral Spirits, and wander "up and down in their Houses, and places of abode, appear in human shape, "and desire this and that, and oftimes take care about their Wills and Testa- "ments, and also think to procure the blessing of the saints, that they may "rest, and if their Earthly Affairs do stick in them, they care many "times about their Children and Friends. This condition of theirs con- "-tinueth so long till they fall into their Rest, and till their Astral Spirits "be consumed, then all such doings, care, and perplexities are at an "End, and they have then no more knowledge thereof, but see them "only in wonders of the <u>Magic Art</u>." He saith also when speaking of the possibility of raising the Spirits of Deceased Persons, "that a living Man hath such power, that he is also able with his Spirit

3

2

"to go into Heaven to the separated or departed Souls, and stir them up
"about some Question by a hearty Desire, but it must be earnest, it must
"be faith that can break open a principle, and this we see in Samuel
"the Prophet, whom the King of Israel raised up." But he that would
accomplish any of these great things, must take away as much as possible
Corporeity from things, or else he must add Spirit to the Body, or awaken
the sleepy Spirit, or join his Imagination to the Imagination of the
Soul of the World, he will never do any great things.   Behmen, in his
Clavis, (page 21) saith, "The Spirit of the World is hidden in the four
"Elements, as the Soul is in the Body, and is nothing else but an Effluence
"and Working power, proceeding from the Sun and Stars. Its dwelling from
"whence it worketh, is spiritually encompassed with the four Elements,
"therefore, he that knoweth how to infuse the propitious Influx of the Stars
"into things, or the mixture of things may perform wonders, for as the Stars
"do tie the Vital Spirits to the Bodies, by Light and Heat, so by the same means
"do they infuse it into the Body."   It is therefore necessary, He that would
wish to work in any Magical Operations, that he knows, that neither Soul,
Spirit, nor Intelligence can be worked with, but by the means of some living
Spirit, for two extreems cannot be joined together without a mean, there —
— fore Demons appear not but after Sacrifices used &c. which must be the
Effusion of Human, or some Blood of Black Cattle, for they are allured by
the Vital Spirits of living Creatures — So they are put to flight, where
sharp and venomous things are used, thus wonderful things in
Nature are performed by a due Application of Actives to passives,
thereunto disposed, and Jacob Behmen saith in his Threefold Life
(Page 192). After he has finished Speaking of External things. "That Heaven,
Earth, and Everything Lie in Man."   This is clear if we consider
the Materials of which we are composed, as first, our Body is of the

earth, Dead, inert and heavy and has no feeling. Second, but Life which is Light, quickeneth, moveth, and giveth sense to it, and the Heavens are the sole spring of this Light. Third, The Soul is the Spirit of God being the free Will, or understanding, in this is Power, and from which three considerations, we find the Reason of this joining or connection found in a living man where-by he receives such great Power, for the Body void of itself, is joined to Light and through Light or Heat to the Heavens, and by the Heavens to a thin spiritual substance which is the first mover and put in motion the Heavens by which we see in what order things are Created and knit together, Body and Soul being very far substances, very far distant one from another and have need of a mean or Bond to join such distant substances together and for this purpose, is that thin and Spiritual mean which the Philosopher call Spirit. This Copulating Spirit is more excellent than the Elements, and even answers to Heaven. Aristotle speaks of the proportion thus, "Like as the Virtue of the Heavens is conveyed to the Earth by the "Vehicle of Light, so all the faculties of the Soul, viz. Light, Motion, "and Sense, are by the help of this bright Spirit conveyed and transferred "to the Terrene Body," for the passage from a common Life unto a Magical is no other but a sleep from this Life, and awaking to that." For those things which happen to the willing and knowing Magician, is the same which happen to the Ignorant and Unwise Men in their falling to sleep, only the Magician by his knowledge doth know when his mind doth meditate of himself, therefore it is he deliberateth, reasoneth, and determineth what is to be done. He observeth when his cogita-tions proceed from a Divine and separate Essence, and proveth what order that Divine and separate Essence is, and by this means, he is able by assisting the Essence to bring about all Magical purposes which may be divided into two parts.

4

One is from God which he bestoweth on the Creatures of Light, such as Love, Justice and Mercy. The second is to such as belong to Creatures of Darkness and delight in Base and Wicked Practices. Yet either of them are brought about by various means pointed out in the following Divisions.

First. Magical purposes are brought about by visible Instruments, by which it affects the Invisible Spirit of Visible things, and acts on Simple or Compound Bodies, so as to produce wonderful effects.

Secondly. Magical purposes are brought to pass by Invocation to God alone. This is partly Prophetical and Philosophical, and partly as it were Theophrastical, other things there are which by reason of the True God are done with the Princes of Spirits that his desires may be fulfilled, such is the work of the Mercurialists.

The Third Method of Exercising Magic, is by means of the Good Angels instead of God, by which means a communication is received from the Most High. Such was the Magic of Balaam, But some make use of an opposite Magic by which actions are produced by the chief of the Evil Spirits, such were they who wrought by the minor Gods of the *Heathen.*

The Fourth Method of Exercising Magic is performed with Spirits openly face to face which is given but to few! Others do work by Dreams, and other signs, which the ancient took from their Auguries and Sacrifices.

The Fifth Method, method of working, is by Immortal Creatures, others by Mortal Creatures, as Nymphs, Satyrs, and such like Inhabitants of other Elements as Pigmies &c.

The Sixth Method, of Magic is performed by such Magicians whom the Spirits serve of their own accord without Art, but, scarcely will attend, being called by those who are not ordained by Nature for that <u>Great Work</u>.

But among the various Species of Magic, we find various Degrees. *The First* and best is that Magic which dependeth on God alone.

The Second, those who perform Magic by the aid of those Spirits who serve them faithfully of their own accord. The Third is the peculiar property and privilege of Christians who work by the power of Christ which he hath both in Heaven and Earth.

It is therefore necessary that every one who practises the Magic Art, attend to the Observations following.

First that they Meditate Day and Night how to attain to the true knowledge of God, not only by his word revealed from the foundation of the World, but also the Seal of the Creation and Creatures, and the wonderful effects produced by such Visible and Invisible agency. It is also necessary that a Man descends down into himself, and study the Art of Spiritual Attraction and Repulsion, with the Virtue, Measure, Order, and Degree of His own Soul. That he is a passionate Lover of Truth, and has strong faith and Taciturnity, especially that he discloses no secret which the Spirit hath forbidden him as He commanded Daniel to seal some things, that is, not to declare them in public; So it was not lawful for Paul to speak openly of all things which he saw in a Vision. Scarce any Man will believe how much is contained in this one precept.

We are also to take care that we understand when the Spirits are assisting us in this Great Work, or Business, for He that understands this shall be made a Magician of the Ordination of God, that is such a person who useth the Ministry of the Spirits to bring excellent things to pass.

But in these matters, it is necessary that a Magician undertakes nothing that is Ungodly, Wicked, or Unjust, for whoever sins through Negligence, Ignorance, or Contempt of God, they will by practising this Art, draw upon themselves Swift Destruction.

But if on the contrary, he is willing to do Justice, Love Mercy, and walks humbly with his God, he shall be divinely defended from all evil and by joining his Understanding to any Good Spirit may produce what he will, for all things are possible to them that Believe.

E. Sibley.

Clavis or Key
To Unlock the Mysteries of
Magic

= What Disposition those ought to possess who are willing to participate in the Secrets = of the Cabalistic Art.

Whoever wishes to make a progress in this Study must take care that no part of it is neglected, in all the circumstances that relate to the Mysteries and Operations of this Great Art. It is useless to ask the question, what affinity there is between the Planets and a piece of fair parchment, or a plate of metal whereon several figures are engraved, or some Characters produce Effects as admirable as those are which are described in what follows. It is also useless to enquire whether there is any implicit, or explicit part in this art, since there is none gone to ask, what Great Men have gone before us in this Science, or the wonderful and prodigious things which they have done, whereas it belongs only to you happily to experience it with content.

Chap. 1. Second Part

You must be laborious and apply yourself with the utmost attention to this _Art_, and be sober, detached from the pleasures of a debauched Life, that you may not be either Dissipated, or Distracted, for there is no error that you can commit, but will involve in it some serious consequences. You must be learned, or at least Directed by one who is proficient in Astronomy and Elementary Philosophy. You must not be sparing of a little pains, or trouble to make successful progress in this Art. You must pay a proper respect to the recital of Orations, Conjurations, Invocations, and other requisite Ceremonies, and above all be firm and intrepid in in the time of Apparitions and Genii, they desire your Boldness.

You must be accompanied by some discreet person, who will encourage you, and animate you, for a weak Imagination is apt to be alarmed and to portray unto the mind wonderful Phantoms, which never had an existence. Finally, you must have great confidence and a firm hope of succeeding, observing exactly all that is written in this _Precious Book_, which contains the Mysteries of the Society.

Chap. 2.

What is the proper place, also Time for the Exercise of this Great Art.

The attention which is extremely necessary to Study without Distraction requires a retired place, and which is remote from the Hurry of Business in order to be adapted to the Nature of Heavenly Genii, Intelligences which from their Spirituality possess a Divine Nature, are seen and communi-cated more freely in silence and tranquil solitude. You must have then a small Chamber, or Closet, to which none have access but Women or Girls, who go there to discharge their menstrual infirmities. It must be a place where there are no sumptuous ornaments to divide or distract the Attention. It will suffice to have a Table placed therein, some Chairs, and a Chest of Drawers to shut in under lock and key, which is necessary for carrying on this Art. It is also requisite that all this Furniture should be new, at least very neat, and purged by odoriferous perfumes, afterwards sprinkled with water of which I shall speak afterwards, and great care must be taken to keep a proper Utensil for the exigencies of _Nature_, for this place must be kept with the greatest cleanliness and decency. As to the time adapted to this purpose, the rising of the Sun is the most suitable, because the mind being then undisturbed is less liable to interruption, and not occupied by external objects. If nevertheless, the circumstance, and the situation of the Planet require that it should be in the middle, or the close of the Day, you must remain from the morning until the Hour of Labour in a state of watchfulness, endeavouring to prepare yourself of everything necessary, that it may be conducted with the precision requisite without losing the time so important to the managing of it well during the Influence of the Star that appears at the operation and the least moment that the Constellation shall endure.

Chap. 3

Of Matters relating to the Operations and the manner of preparing them Cabalistically. The Talismans, Pentacles, Mysterious Magic Characters, and other Figures, which are the Principal Matters of the Science, and may be formed different ways.

You may make them on clean Parchment, or Plate Metal, or Jasper, Agate or other precious Stones. You must observe that this parchment must be prepared in a manner as shall be afterwards described and may serve the whole indifferently, but it is not so commonly used as Metals, which have a greater affinity to Planets, besides parchment soon gets dirty, and the least spot is capable of diminishing the virtue of the Talisman or the Mysterious Image. The other matters are also essential, they ought to have a relation and bear an analogy to the Planet under the Constellation of which the Cabalistical Figures under the rays of the Sun will be useless, and so likewise will other planets. Lastly, that we should not be deceived by this means we will mention what Metals are under the Seven Planets, viz, **Gold** to the **Sun**, **Silver** to the **Moon**, **Iron** to **Mars**, **Quick-Silver** to **Mercury**, **Tin** to **Jupiter**, **Copper** to **Venus**, **Lead** to **Saturn**. It is evident that by these, we are to understand that **Gold**, suits the operation of **Sunday**, **Silver**, the operation of **Monday**, **Iron**, the operation of **Tuesday**, **QuickSilver**, the operation of **Wednesday**. **Tin**, the operation of **Thursday**, **Copper** or **Brass**, the operation of **Friday**, **Lead**, the operation of **Saturday**. The manner in which you should raise a Cabalistical Figure, or a Talisman on the Hour and Day of one of the Seven Planets, it must be done on a small Metal Plate suitable to the Planet. It is indifferent whether the Plate be round, or otherwise, provided that it be a regular Geometrical Figure, for you will make all sorts of characters on it. But if you prefer the making use of fair parchment than Metal Plates, you must for a greater certainty of success, take care not to purchase it of certain cheats, who mix improper Materials in it, but take the trouble to make it yourself. This then, is the manner in which it must be prepared. It must be of Virgin Parchment. You must be ready on the Vigil of St John the Baptist's Day with a little <u>White Lamb, or Kid</u> of six weeks old. You must lead it to a Fountain, the water of which is clear and flowing, and after having plunged it seven times to clear it of all sorts of filth, you must cut its throat with a new Knife, which should be devoted to the operation of this <u>Art</u>. And which has never been applied to any other purpose. Then you must let all the Blood run out with the water of the Fountain, and having cut it it you must fix the Hide in the running Water, while you are employed in burying the Body deep enough to prevent its being devoured by Beasts.

Afterwards, you shall draw the Hide from out of the Water, and prepare it in the same manner as the Manufacturers usually prepare parchment, with the Circumstance that everything made use of on this occasion shall never be applied to a profane use. You will find in the sequel of this Book the Orations of the seven Planets for the Seven Days in the week, which must be recited during this Operation. There is a little Trouble, and subjection to Labour, but we must consider that a Hide prepared with exactness in this manner, is a provision which will last a long time, and if one knows that it will serve according to the rules of this Art, he shall derive great advantage from it, for the Composition of the Talismans and other Figures will reward the pains we have taken. When you have finished the preparation of the Skin of parchment, you must cut it in pieces about three inches square, and put them in a new Box, after having wrapped them up properly in a bit of Taffeta, or white Cloth. If you are unable to work by yourself in making this parchment, you may without hesitation, employ therein, a wise discreet Workman, but be always present that nothing may be omitted. We have taken notice that this preparation must be begun on the Eve of St John the Baptist's Day, because, in the original Hebrew, it is said, it should take place while the Sun is in his Apogee and his greatest Elevation above our Hemisphere, which happens on the twenty third of June. The Metal Plates which must be made use of as well as the Virgin Parchment, you make the Talismans, Pentacles, Characters &c on, are joined after the usual manner, except that they must be dipt quite hot in the water in pronouncing the Speeches and Conjurations which belong to the Planets to which these Metal Plates are subject, Afterwards they must be made even and polished in the best manner possible, and they must be used like the Virgin Parchment, until you have occasion to employ them. The Animals, Birds, Insects, Plants, and other things which you must make use of in the Secret Mysteries of the Cabala ought to be prepared likewise under a favourable Constellation at a good Hour if it happens on the Eve of St John the Baptist, for it will have a wonderful efficacy in accomplishing all the ends proposed. But take Notice of the manner of making Talismans &c.

You must remember there will be Instruments and Utensils which you will stand in need of for these Mysterious Operations which will be the subject of the following chapter. _____

Chap. 4.
Concerning the Necessary Instruments

It will be necessary to have a little Box provided, that should be new doubled with a white Towel, and furnished with a little lock, and fill it with the following Materials. A Long White Robe, or Linen Garment, a Cap and Stockings of the same Materials. Light Shoes, White Gloves, also a Girdle of parchment or Leather quite new on which are written the Names of the Planetary Angels and the seven presiding Spirits over the seven days of the Week. All this little Equipage will serve in operations of importance. You must also have some consecrated Ink (viz. made from the Smoke of a Consecrated Wax Candle) also Ink of various Colours, suitable to the Seven Planets for the purpose of drawing the Mysterious Characters &c on parchment. these Inks together with several Crow quill pens, or very fine Steel pens proper to write with, a penknife with a white handle, a well tempered Bodkin pointed in the form of a graving tool, and a pair of Scissors to be kept in a small square Box. Also another little Box to contain the small instruments, such as a pair of Compasses to draw the Circles on the Metal plates, an Engraver a burnishing tool, a mould of about three inches in diameter in which to cast the different Metals for the Talismans. You should also have a Box or Drawer to keep the other following Materials in, viz a Flint and Steel proper to light a fire, a Roll of Virgin Wax. You should have in the same Box or Drawer a Phial full of Holy Water, that is to say, such as is used at the sacred Ceremonies of Easter moreover you must keep in the Box three Knives, one pointed with a white handle and engraven as seen in the frontispiece, one, in the point of which shall be the figure and shape of a Sickle, with a Black Handle, moreover you must have a Hazel Stick of the

7

of the length of the Box and about one inch thick, and a little green stick of the same wood of a year's growth, about the same length as the former. You must likewise have another small Box containing little Packets of Perfumery suitable to the Seven Planets, and according to their several Destinations, also a little Chafing Dish made of Earth, or some other matter, with new coals to make a fire on necessary occasions, and for the incense and fumigations, also a Ladle in which to melt the different Metals.

It is necessary to have a pair of Compasses of sufficient Radius to Draw the Circle according to the Model in frontispiece, of at least seven feet in Diameter, also a piece of new Twine attached to a piece of Consecrated Chalk or Charcoal to trace with accuracy the Grand Figures that it will be necessary to make on the floor which must be perfectly clean and even for the purpose. For these things are important and necessary for Conducting the **Grand Cabalistic Art.**

Chap. 5.

Concerning the Influences, and Secret Virtues, which the Different Situations of the Moon Produce, requisite to be known and understood in this Art. ———

Wise men have called the Sun and Moon the Eyes of Heaven, being willing to express by their appellation what the Creator of the Universe hath given to those two Planets a principal inspection, and above all that which they make in the Works of Nature. It is for this reason they have judged it important to take notice in conducting the Operations, that these two Heavenly Luminaries have some benign Influence by their favourable Conjunction, and are not contrary by the opposition, or aspect of bad auguries. The Moon is the first and principal receptacle of the Influences of the Sun, she passes every month through her Heavenly Orb, and is often found in Conjunction with the Sun and

9

other planets. In order to succeed then in an exact View of her motions and to know that they are benign, as I have before said, we must make use of an Ephemeris, or of the advice of a skilful *Astrologer*.

The most exact observers remark that the Moon commences her gradations by the Head or Sign of the Ram, and at the time her Influence indicates prosperity in Voyages or Business Talismans and Characters that are formed at the point of this Constellation are preserved from Danger, when the Moon is in the middle of this Constellation, she has an Influence over Riches and Discovery of Treasures and this point is favourable to make Talismans and Characters but chiefly if in a benign aspect with Jupiter who is the sovereign disposer of fortunate events. When she is arrived at the Head of the Bull. Her Influence on the Talismans and Characters, tends to the Ruin of Buildings Fountains, to the breach of Friendship, and of Marriage Contracts, Twenty five minutes after she has passed the sign of the Bull she produces perfect Health and a Disposition to acquire Science, to obtain the favour of persons of Distinction, and if in this state, she is in Conjunction with Venus, the Talismans and Characters will be so much the more favourable. It is an excellent sign to cause love by the assistance of Secrets to be given hereafter. When the MOON makes a Conjunction with Castor and Pollux, this sends a favourable Influx, it makes them Successful, and renders those Invulnerable who bear the Talisman Mysterious figures or Characters formed under the auspices of that Constellation.   The MOON continuing her course and finishing the first part of her Revolution, is productive of good Influx, afterwards entering the sign Cancer, which the Ancients have called Alnaza, which is to say a Dark House, she diffuseth some influence, to cause Conquerors to succeed, and other such dangerous attempts if never- -theless she is in a benefiting or benign Aspect of Jupiter or Venus, or Mercury. the Talisman shall be favourable to Love, Gaming, and the Discovery of Treasures.   When she enters in the sign Leo, if she is in aspect to Saturn.

she has an Influx on all fatal Undertakings, tho' seldom to avert their evils, but on the contrary being advanced in this sign, and ready to depart from thence. She is liberal in all kinds of prosperity, and continues so even into the sign of the **Virgin**, at least if she does not find herself in aspect to the mournful and Melancholy Planet Saturn. In the manner in which the Talismans and Characters direct their course under this Constellation are advantageous to Gamesters, Travellers, Lovers, and all who aspire after Great Honours. Her entering in the Sign **Libra**, which the Cabalists have called **Algar- -pha** favours much the search after all kinds of Treasures, Metals and Fountains, and when she is passed to **Scorpio**, she is Invincible to Travellers, and to those who are married, and enter into social Intercourse. When she arrives at the Sign **Capricorn**, favoured with the Auspicies of **Jupiter** or **Venus**, she Influences Health, and Love of the Fair Sex, in the manner in which Talismans and Characters raised under this Constellation, have a tenden- -cy to unravel difficult points, and to hinder the evil occurrences to which Marriage is liable, and to keep up a friendly Correspondence between Married People. Finally the Moon being arrived at the last sign, which the Cabalists call **Albotham Alchatha**, which signifies Heavenly Poison, there is only the evil Aspect of Saturn to fear, for those who will raise Talismans &c under this Constellation. for provided it be favourably guarded by **Jupiter**, **Venus** or **Mercury**, she Infallibly governs Health, Honour, and good Suc- cess in Gaming. This is what every one must study who wishes to succeed in the Use of this Occult Art. Happy is _He_ who is able to profit from discovery made by the Ancients Sages by Laudable Experience of those properties which are peculiar to the Stars. They will have very little trouble in discovering these Mysteries, and by means of these _Figures_, will effect surprising things. —————————

Chap. 6.

Of the manner of working the Figures of Talismans, Characters &c according to the Rules of Art.

They who have not yet practised the Mysterious Figures of the Occult Science, ought to begin by the Eight Pentacles, the Figures of which they shall see in the Sequel of this Work. To know where are the twelve great names of God, and the Seven other Names which are at the Head of every Day of the Week, and done in Honour of the Genii, who preside over the seven Planets to whom they have appropriated every day of the week, they may do it as beforesaid on Virgin Parchment, or on Metal, or whether he may choose to commence his operations on a happy Constellation of the Stars. let them be in a benign aspect, to proceed therein with success. The Operator must retire into a secret place destined to the Mysteries, sequestered from the Intrusion of a busy World, there he must be Invested with a white Garment and the other ornaments before mentioned. Afterwards, he shall Sprinkle the Secret Chamber, and the Table on which he shall work, with Holy Water in reciting the Orations, Invocations, and Conjurations proper to the Day of Operation, and which agree with the Genii who ought to preside there. The Holy Water must be used on the Instruments and Materials employed in the operation afterwards. as soon as you begin to draw upon the Metal or Virgin parchment. the proper Charac- -ters that you intend to make in order to facilitate the undertaking. You will find a great number of Models with various Engravings and with an Explanation of their Virtues and Properties. Observe, if you work on this Virgin parchment you must have a Raven's or crow quill pen or at least employ a very fine Steel pen. (and prepared in the manner aforesaid) some new Ink in your Box, and if you work upon Metals you must have punches and Engraving Tools in the same Box. You must write or engrave the proper Characters very distinctly in the Circles, which You have formed with the Compasses belonging to the Art.

Grand Pentacle of Solomon

The Pentacles are commonly chased with a Double Circle of the Mysterious Names of God, or of a passage of Holy Scripture, signifying what you desire to obtain by the Pentacle. For Example, if you be engaged in the Pursuit of Riches or Honours, You must put in the Double Circle of the Pentacle these words (*Gloria et Divitiæ in domo ejus*) and in the Centre of the round, you must Engrave with Symetry and proportion the Characters of the Planets, under which you form the Pentacles, the Models of which will be given in their place, and will explain it more fully. In order to proceed Methodically, and without confusion in this Book of Instruction, You may begin by making the Eight Pentacles, and you must place one of the said Pentacles at the Head of the Day which it governs, and that of Solomon commonly called the Great Pentacle at the Head of all. It ought to be made with much exactness, because it must be present at all the Operations of the Great Art. You must choose the Happiest Constellation of the whole year to work wherein, and particularly the Spring Season, when all Nature seems to wear a new Form. You may work any Day of the Week except Saturday, because this Day is not in common being under the Mournful Influence of Saturn. In the foregoing Page, You have the Model of this Mysterious Pentacle. When you have perfectly finished it, you must wrap it up very properly in a bit of Silk, Stuff, or new White Linen Cloth and shut in a Box to be ready when you have occasion for it. Its particular virtue is to defend you from the Terror of Apparitions when they are Invoked to appear during the Operations. The Virtue of this Wonderful and Mysterious Pentacle, is so efficacious, that the most Evil Genii which are Saturnine cannot hurt you while it is present.

13

Chap. 7.

Concerning the Hours of the Day and Night for the Seven Days of the Week and their respective Planets which Govern them.

It is not sufficient to observe here the Hours of the Day and Night through the whole Week with the planets that govern them, it is not enough that you know that the First Hour of every Day begins at Sun rising, but that you be warned that the Sun rises sooner, and later at different places according to the different Degrees of the Climate. From which you may see, that it is not without Reason that after the most Skilful Master of the Great Art, you may know that it is very necessary for those who will be exercised in the Practice of this Wonderful Science, that he or they ought to understand Astrology, and also Arithmetic. You will find in the Sequel of this Work, Cabalistic Tables which contain the Mysterious Names of the Angels who preside over every Hour of the Day and Night, and likewise the Names of the Hours of the Seven Planets. It is again necessary to caution you against waiting for a favourable Hour before you prepare for the Operation, for everything must be ready that you may begin to work immediately to gain time, and have leisure to observe properly the different Characters which you must make use of in your Operations.

Observation on Talismans

There is yet something very singular to be remarked on the Subject of Talismans, Pentacles, Characters and Mysterious figures, both in respect to their matter and manner of working in the Circumstances that are essential to the principles of this Art, as will appear in what follows.

14

Chap. 8.

Concerning the Perfumes that are proper for the Seven Planets for every Day of the Week and the manner of composing them.

We have before observed that you must have among the utensils belonging to the Art, a little New Chafing Dish, either of Earth, or Iron with new Charcoal, and that for the use of the Perfumes, the Fire, must be lighted by means of a small Steel and a Bougie belonging to the Art, and if you make use of them when the Talismans &c. are finished, it must be in the following manner. After having Sprinkled them with Holy Water, of which it has before been spoken, you must throw on the Fire a Pinch of Perfume or Incense which belongs to the planet, the name of which is above the Work when you recite the Invocations &c. and you must observe this afterwards on Speaking of the Days, beside that you may not imagine it to be a Chimerical Ceremony, for it is too certain that the Airy Spirits which are destined by the Creator to the Service of Men, may be drawn by Perfumes, and on the Contrary, Evil Spirits may be kept from you by the Vapours of these perfumes, and this may be seen in the History of Tobit in the Sacred pages, where the Angel who guides him orders that when he shall be in the Chamber with his Wife, he shall not fail to make a Perfume on the Burning Coals, with a persuasion that he shall draw up a Fish by the secret Virtue of these Perfumes, the Evil Spirit, who injured his Wife, can no longer hurt her, and shall be driven from the Nuptial Chamber.

Chap. 9.

Concerning the Orations, Invocations and Conjurations for every Day in the Week.

The true followers of the Grand Art, and Lovers of the Secret Science, ought not to be content with Reciting Orations &c. only during the time of the Operations, but they ought to repeat them exactly every Day, whether

13

they are engaged or not in the Operation. This hath been the practice of all who have been successful in this Art. upon which we must observe that these Orations ought to be recited with the faces turned towards the East, and with great attention. You will find them with the Days of the Week. ____

____ Chap. 10 ____

= Concerning Orations in the form of Exorcisms to Consecrate all things which belong to the Operation of this Grand Work. ____

These sort of Operations in the form of Exorcisms are only performed but once; that is to say, on the first of the Cabalistic Operations. and when it hath not been consecrated either by ourselves or any other.

You must on a little Table. covered with a white Linen cloth, have some very clear Spring Water in a Delf Dish. and some New Charcoal in another which is proof against the Fire, and this Fire must be kindled by striking the flint to make a fresh fire. and when it shall be lighted. You must repeat over the Fire and Water the following Oration in making the sign of the Cross. which is marked thus ✠.

O Theos Omnipotens qui de nihilo mundum Condidis tua oratum Cuncta erastiper virtutem tuorum ineffabilium nominum Jehovah. Grigion. Adonay Elohim da his Creaturis ✠✠ quas ad nostrum usum condidisti talem efficaciam ultabica ennria possint pivoi ficape et sanctificare per aspersinem et adustioneri sic te precor et oro Tantos Tautapon Bararhedi Gedita Imator Igeon. Amen.

This being finished you must Sprinkle the Consecrated Water on the Fire and having put a little Storax or Benzoin into the Fire you shall perfume the Water with it afterwards you shall begin to Purify the Closet or Secret Chamber appropriated to these operations, and you must Sprinkle this place with scented water, saying. ____

16

Agathos misericors **Agathos** potens **Agathos** terribilis qui per tuum cherub **Sachiel** Au tuum **Romphed** protoplastum peccatorum expulisti exparadiso deliciarum Pariter expelle exhoc loco cureto miseiva et hunc sanctifica munda et pristo ut sit idoreus meis operationibus et delectabilis bones spiritibus quos invocabo ad mea ujuranum sic te precor **Tautos Tautayon Barachedi Gedita Igeon.** Amen. ————————

————————

After this, you must put on a little Table everything that is necessary for the operation, which has been described in the beginning of this Work, sprink- ling them with Holy Water and Perfumery three different times, saying the oration as follows. ————————

Athanatos sapientissime artisex qui servo tuo dedestint justins febricar Omnia que ad- sum tabernaculi debebant inservi et a sanctificaret impende his Omnibus Instrumentis et aliis rebus hic precentibus talem virtutem et efficaciam ut nitei operanti seliciter ensor- vant ⚔⚔ sicti precor **Tautos Tautayon Barachedi Gedita Igeon.** Amen.

————————

When it shall be necessary to consecrate anything afresh according to the Cabalistic custom You must use the ceremonies before mentioned. ————————

The following mentioned Tables must be attended to, the first contains the Hours of the Day and Night for the whole Week and the Good Genii who preside at every Hour   (see the plate)
The Hours of the Day and Night of Sunday (see the plate)
The Mysterious Characters of the Sun in three Columns or Lines. (see plate)
Sunday being the first day of the Week and governed by the Sun You may begin by making the Pentacle of the Sun in the Hour of the Sun on a plate of pure Gold, or on Virgin parchment. taking great care that the Lines of the Circle and the Characters and Names therein be plainly drawn engraved or written. ————————

————————

Part 2. Pentacles

Pentacle for Sunday under the Sun

This Pentacle of the Sun represents in its first Interior Circle the Names of the Four Heavenly Genii who prevail according to the Influence of the Stars on Sunday which must be invoked during the Operations that are performed on this Day. **Arcan Rex** is the most Noble of the four, and he whom you must Invoke the first in Turning towards the East, and the other three, in turning towards the other three quarters of the world in pronouncing respectively the Invocations &c. that belong to Sunday and which are hereafter described. The second Circle of the Pentacle represents the Names of several Heavenly Angels and Genii who have influence over different Hours. You will also see in this Second Circle, the Seal of the Angel who directs the Planet which you may also Engrave or Write if you choose on the Talismans or Cabalistic Figures which you make use of. You will see in the third Circle the Venerable Names of God which you must pronounce during the Operation, and what is said of this Pentacle for Sunday will serve as an Explanation for all the Pentacles of the Week.

The Perfume to be perfect ought to be composed of Saffron, the Wood of Aloes, the Wood of Balsam of Myrrh of Caurier, and the sixth part of an ounce of these Drugs, add to it, a grain of Musk and Ambergris, the whole pulverized and mixed together, After this Confectionary is made in small Seeds which you shall use on Sunday under the Auspicies of the Sun. The Oration, Invocation, and Conjuration for the Sun on Sunday will be given in their proper place.

The Operator must remember that no attention is to be paid to the Ornaments or Embellishments which may be placed around, or in the Figures, but simply to form the Figures plain and correctly.

18

Oration for Sunday under the Sun.

Lord **Adonai** who hast originally formed an unworthy sinner after thine own Image and likeness to elevate him to the knowledge of profound Mysteries. deign by thy Holy Name which thou hast made known by thy Servant Moses in the Mysterious Tables to Bless and Sanctify all my Operations and Undertakings **Otari bonus Yerablem Yudadoe Tophiel Elop. Abrax.**

Invocation

Come Heavenly Spirits who hast the Effulgent Rays of the Sun. Luminous Spirits who are ready to obey the Powerful voice of the Great and Supreme **Tetragrammaton** come and assist me in the Operation that I am going to undertake under the Auspicies of the Grand Light of Day which our Creator hath formed for the use of Universal Nature I Invoke You for these purposes be favourable and Auspicious to what I shall do in the Name of Him who would bear the Glorious Names of **Amioram Adonai Sabaoth.**

Conjuration

Happy Spirits who have been Created to behold the face of Him who is seated on the Cherubims I Conjure you Genii full of thought in the Name of Saday **Cados Phao Saraye Elohim** and by the name of the first Light which is the Sun that you will come and Contribute to the success of the Operation I am undertaking. I beseech you will employ your Power and Virtue in keeping off the Evil Spirits that might overturn the Benign Influence Influence of my work I repeat my supplication by the Virtue of the Divine Names of **Abaye. Radiel Caracaza. Amadai.**

19

If you intend to make a Pentacle which is to raise you to Honour Dignity and Riches, you must use it on a Sunday under the Auspicies of the Sun, or on Thursday in the Hour of Jupiter, after having observed the time when the Constellation be favourable, which happens often enough in the Spring and in the beginning of Autumn; and you must take verses out of the Sacred Writings according as shown hereafter in the Models. ———

In respect of the admirable Talisman about to be given, to Command the obedience of Spirits, in the first face of this Sacred Talisman, you will see in the middle of the square four Holy Names in the small squares, and four others which are in the Double Circle. In the second face or reverse side, is placed in the Middle a Mysterious Name with 7 Letters, the interpretation of which is in the Double Circle drawn a small Hebrew Verse on the wonderful subject of the Creation, or the World in the form of a Mystery of which arose, marks frequently in the Prodigies he wrought. This Sacred Pentacle is taken from the Mysterious Book of Rabbi Hama, which is entitled the Cabalistical Speculation. It is of great efficacy when it is made with everything suitable for the operation for Sunday. Its Material is a Plate of pure Gold, or of Virgin Parchment which is unadulterated from which you may rest assured of all kinds of Prosperity when you are furnished with this Pentacle. It is chiefly good for Honours, Riches and Amorous Intrigues. Rabbi Castor Ben Luca says, that it may be made on Thursday under Jupiter.

The Talisman has two faces (fig   ) on the first you must engrave the Seal or Character proper to the Familiar Spirit which is ⊕℧ who Directs the Influence of the Planet, and upon the Second, is to be engraven the Mysterious Numbers in small Squares, placed so that whatever you read the number, either above or below, or on one Angle, or another or on the same line to the right, or to the left you will find the same number which is 111. These two Pentacles tend to Conciliate the Spirits of the Sun. ———

——— Precious Stones affected by the Sun. ———

The Egal Stone, the Crysolite, the Stone of the Rainbow, the Jacinth, the Ruby, a Stone which the power of attracting other Stones as the Magnet draws Iron or Steel.

——— Trees affected by the Sun. ———

——— The Laurel, the Palmer Tree, the Ash, the Ivy. ———

21

PLATE. III.

The Hours of the Day and Night on Sunday.

1	☉	Michael	1	♃	Zachiel
2	♀	Anael	2	♂	Samael
3	☿	Raphael	3	☉	Michael
4	☾	Gabriel	4	♀	Anael
5	♄	Cassiel	5	☿	Raphael
6	♃	Zachiel	6	☾	Gabriel
7	♂	Samael	7	♄	Cassiel
8	☉	Michael	8	♃	Zachel
9	♀	Anael	9	♂	Samael
10	☿	Raphael	10	☉	Michael
11	☾	Gabriel	11	♀	Anael
12	♄	Cassiel	12	☿	Raphael

The Mystical Characters of the Sun for Sunday ☉

Fortuna Majore.	First Characters.	Fortuna Minore.

Second.

Third.

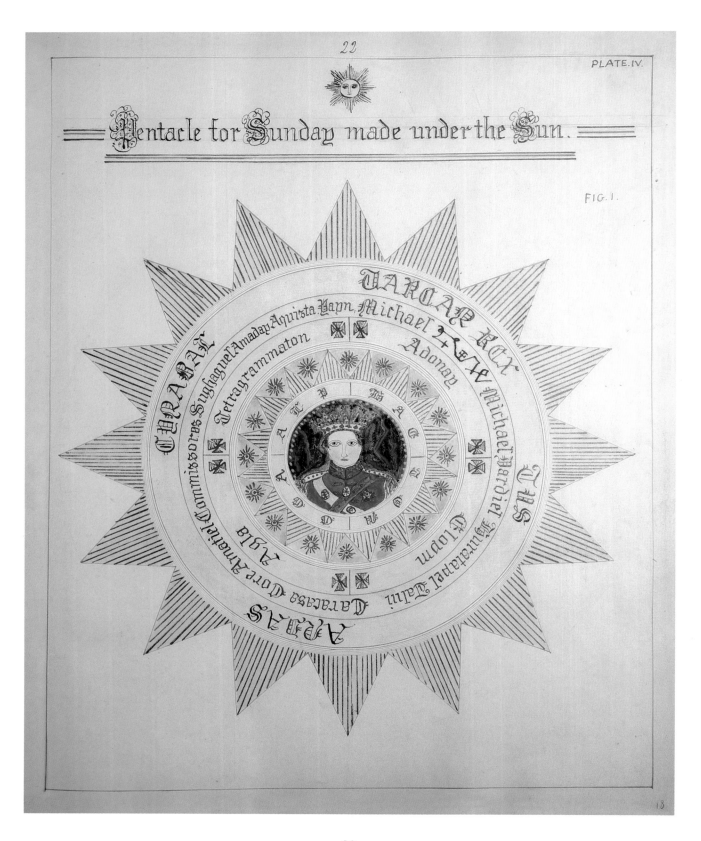

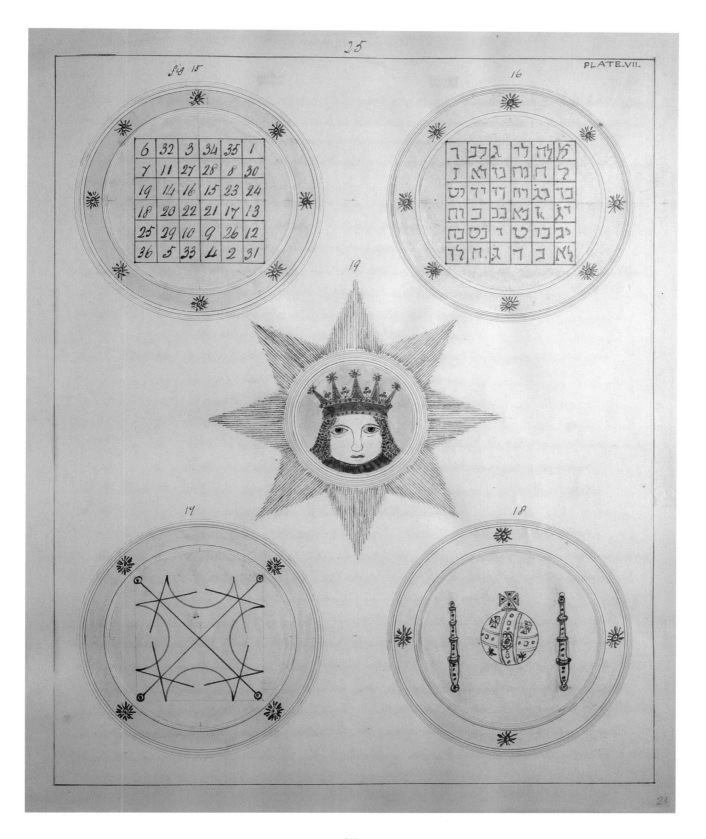

Description and Use of the foregoing Mysterious Figures or Talismans to be made on Sunday in the Hour of the Sun, with Observation thereon.

Fig. Plate. IV. The Pentacle for the Sun on Sunday which must be present during the Operation on Sunday.

Fig 1. Plate. V. A Pentacle for Honour and Riches.

" 2 " Second Model for the same purpose.

" 3 " " A Pentacle for Honour and Dignities.

" 4 " " A Pentacle against the Dread and Fear of the Darkness of the Night.

" 5 " " A Pentacle against Unclean Beasts and Fishes.

" 6 " " The Character of the Benevolent Planet Jupiter.

" 7 " " The Character of the Fair Planet Venus.

Fig 8 Plate. VI. A Pentacle at the view of which all Spirits are Obedient.

" 9 " " A Pentacle the reverse of the above.

" 10 " " Another Pentacle for a similar purpose.

" 11 " " A Pentacle to Preserve Health.

" 13 " " A Form similar to which the Spirit of Jupiter sometimes appears

" 14 " " A Form similar to which the Spirit of Venus often appears

Fig 15 Plate. VII. The Mysterious Number of the Sun which is 111.

" 16 " " The same in Hebrew Characters.

" 17 " " The Seal or Character of the Intelligencies of the Sun.

" 19 " " A Form of Regal Dignity in which the Spirit of the Sun often Appears.

" 18 " " Another Form which sometimes presents itself when Invoked.

General Observation

Notwithstanding all that has been said Concerning the various Pentacles or Talismans mentioned in this Mysterious Work, the Operator must be reminded that the more exact as to the time, the Composition and the true formation of the various Lines Characters of the Talismans and Mysterious Figures, he is, the greater will be the certainty of Success, not only that, the more earnest he is in repeating the Orations, Invocations, and

Conjurations having great Confidence, that what he earnestly entreats will be granted besides the power, virtue, and efficacy given to these Mysterious Images will greatly depend upon the firmness sincerity and faith of the Operator or possessor of these Invaluable Figures. for they will lose none of their virtue and Efficacy by being transferred from one person to another, providing the party accepting them adhere to, and believe in their Influence. for depend upon it, that if a person who may possess one or more of these Talismans and has not that firm Confidence required, he cannot expect any good result issuing therefrom. He must be temperate live a good Moral Life if not not a true religious Life, or he cannot expect prosperity by the Guardian -ship and Assistance of those Blessed Spirits the bright Messengers of Heaven Therefore it is evidently true that the more Holy he leads his Life, the more he will be assured of Success. It must not be objected for the Operator or possessor of these Talismans to be cautioned against making them public or by telling persons about your possession for as the Agency by which they operate is Invisible, So is the knowledge thereof with held from all but the Wise and prudent which means not to be made public.

———————

The Operator must also be reminded that the foregoing Talismans under the Sun must be formed of Virgin Gold or Virgin parchment duly consecrated but if parchment be employed you must either use liquid Gold or Ink of a Yellow Colour to write the Characters &c. the Inks of different Colours suitable to the seven planets are as follows; Yellow or Gold for the Sun, pale red or Silver for the Moon, Red for Mars, Mixed Colours for Mercury, Blue for Jupiter, Green for Venus, Black for Saturn each of these Should be kept in small Vials properly prepared and consecrated and not used for any other purpose but that for which they are designed. Great care must be taken of these Talismans when not in use, they should not be exposed to the eye of the Vulgar ——————

—————— The following prayer is recommended to be repeated every day during you are wearing a Talisman —————— O my Good Angel whom God by his Divine Appointment have appointed to be my Guardian Enlighten, Protect, and Direct me. ——————

28

Pentacle for Monday under the Moon

This Pentacle of the Moon represents to you in the first Interior Circle the Names of the four Heavenly Genii who prevail this Day which must be Invoked for the Operation of Monday. Arcan is the principal Heavenly Genii that prevails this day, and which, must be Invoked, and is contained in this Pentacle. when therefore you Invoke him, turn yourself towards the East, afterwards the other Genii by turning to the other quarters, this Apparition is without terror because he appears in an Agreeable Figure. You must Dismiss him and his attendants respectfully when you have obtained what you wish.   It is favourable to Riches and Amours.

Composition of Perfumes for Monday

This Perfume in order to be perfect, must be composed of the following Ingredients Viz. The Head of a Frog, the Eyes of a Bull, a Grain of White Poppy, Storax, a Loadstone, Benjamin, a little Camphor, the whole well pulverized, and made into Paste or Dough, made with the Head of Young Barley, which You must make use of in your Operation for Monday, under the Auspices of the Moon.

Oration for Monday under the Moon

All Powerful Anarbone who hast formed out of Eternal Nature the Great Lumi-
-nary which presides by Night, I pray you by the Intercession of your favour-
-ed Genii Gabriel Madyet Abroy Janiel that you will direct the benign Influence
of the Celestial Bodies in such manner that the Operation I Undertake this
Day may have the desired Effect and Success, and that I may give Glory and
Honour to the Great Curaniel Hanum Baliel.

Invocation

Run ye Sublime and Sublunary Genii who are obedient to the Sovereign
Arcan come and assist me in the Operation that I undertake under the
Auspicies of the Grand Luminary of the Night I invoke you to the purpose
be favourable and hear my Intreaties in the Name of Him who commands
the Supreme Spirits which are Superior in the Regions that you inhabit
Mizzabu Aburaha.

Conjuration

I Conjure you Analgii Ophaniel Abym and all you Heavenly Quoristers
in the Name of the Great Luminary of the Firmament which is the Moon
that you will Contribute to the success of the Operation that I am going to
Undertake under her Auspicies. Employ your power and Influence in
keeping off the Evil Spirits that might hurt me in my undertaking
come in haste and defer not your assistance long Arhym Cados Yea.

30

Pentacles and Talisman for Monday

As it often happens that we undertake a journey on Monday, because on that day we have more leisure, for this reason the Ancient Magi and Learned in the Cabalistic Art have thought that a Talisman, made on a Monday before such a Journey would be propitious to Travellers both by Sea and Land.

You must work them according to the following Model, and whosoever shall be sufficiently experienced in the Mysterious Science to work with exactness may assure himself, that by the Virtue of This Talisman he can command the Spirits to carry him in a little time from one place to another a great distance off without the least injury to his Person.

The Materials of this Talisman must be of True Virgin Parchment or of a silver Plate highly polished.

You may make the Talisman (fig 3) on a Monday for the purpose of serving in Amorous Intrigues under the Auspices of Venus, for although Friday seems under Venus to be destined for that purpose, You may nevertheless be assured if you find the Moon in a favourable situation on Monday, the Talisman You shall then make will be of equal efficacy, as if you had worked on a Friday.

The last two Pentacles or Talismans, make but one, having two faces, One on which you must Engrave the Seal or Character of the Familiar Spirit of the Moon and the Director of her Influence. The Second on which you must Engrave or write, the Mysterious Number of the Moon in several small squares, so that whatsoever side you read, whether above or below, on one side or the other, being in the same line to the right or to the left, or from one Angle to another, the number will always be found the same which is

369.

===== Precious Stones affected by the Moon =====

The Beryl. The Diamond

===== Trees affected by the Moon =====

The Poplar, The Female Palm Tree and the Rosemary.

32

PLATE VIII.

The Hours of the Day and Night on Monday

1	☽	Gabriel	Arcan	1	♀	Anael	Sarabotes
2	♄	Cassiel	Maymon	2	☿	Raphael	Modiath
3	♃	Zachiel	Zebul	3	☽	Gabriel	Arcan
4	♂	Samael	Samax	4	♄	Cassiel	Maymon
5	☉	Michael	Varcan	5	♃	Zachiel	Zebul
6	♀	Anael	Sarabotes	6	♂	Samael	Samax
7	☿	Raphael	Modiat	7	☉	Michael	Varcan
8	☽	Gabriel	Arcan	8	♀	Anael	Sarabotes
9	♄	Cassiel	Maymon	9	☿	Raphael	Modiat
10	♃	Zachiel	Zebul	10	☽	Gabriel	Maymon
11	♂	Samael	Samax	11	♄	Cassiel	Maymon
12	☉	Michael	Varcan	12	♃	Zachiel	Zebul

The Mysterious Characters for Monday under the Moon

First Characters

Ab Via ———— Apopulo

Second

Third

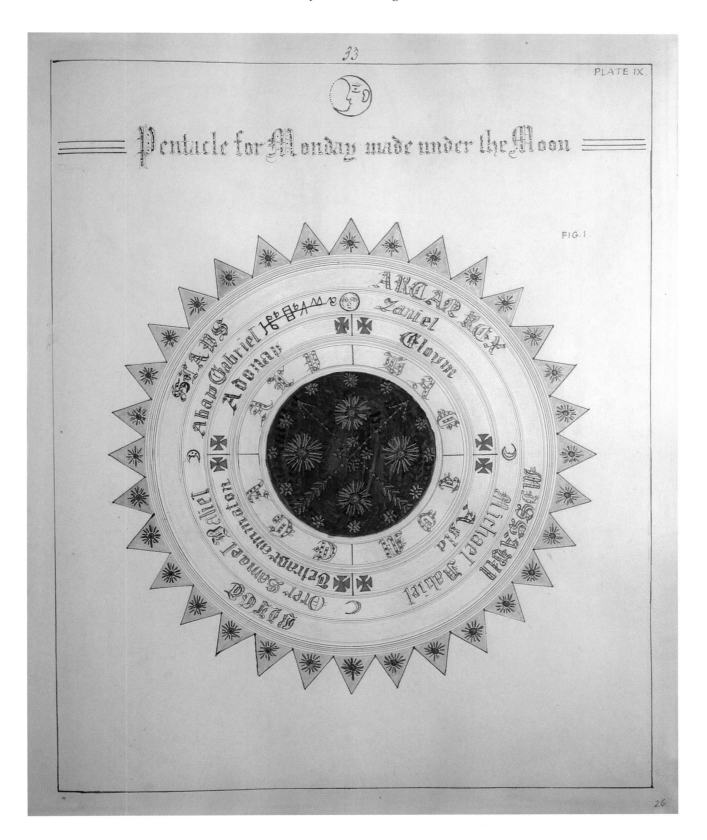

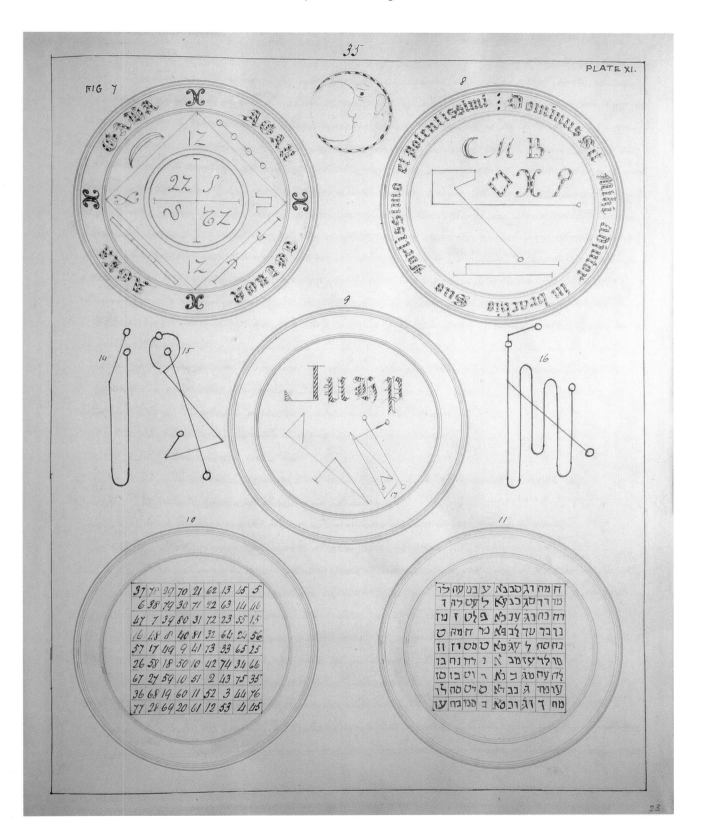

The foregoing Pentacles or Talismans must be made of pure Silver highly polished and Engraven distinctly as before directed, or they may be made of Pure Virgin Parchment and Characters &c written thereon with much exactness. These Talismans under the Moon must be made on Monday at the first Hour after sun rising. Should you not have sufficient time to complete your work during the first Planetary Hour, you must wait with patience till the next Hour of the Moon arrives, which is always at the end of every seven planetary Hours counting from Sunrise on a Monday. and so of the rest, as each planet governing each day of the week, his reign or rule commences at Sunrise. A Table will be given in a subsequent part of this work shewing the Length of the Planetary Hour During the Day and Night for all seasons of the Year and in any Climate.

The following Talismans to be made on Monday under the Moon according to the foregoing Models

Plate IX. Fig 1. Pentacle for Monday under the Moon.
 " X. " 2. Talisman for Travelling by Sea or Land.
 " " 3. Talisman for Love.
 " " 4. Talisman against Earthquakes, and to Enchant Treasures.
 " " 5. Talisman to Enchant Treasures.
 " " 6. Talisman to have Familiar Spirits at Command.
 " XI. 7. Talisman to have Familiar Spirits at Command.
 " " 8. Talisman against Dangers, Travellers are exposed to by Sea or Land.
 " " 9. Seal of the Familiar Spirit of the Moon and Director of Her Influence.
 " " 10. The Mysterious Number of the Moon.
 " " 11. The Mysterious Number of the Moon in Hebrew Characters.
Plate X. 12. Seal and Character of Luna (Dæmonii)
 " 13. Seal and Character of Luna
Plate XI. 14.15. Two Characters of Luna (Dæmonii Dæmoniorum
 " 16.17. Intelligentiæ & Intelligentiarum of Luna ———

Pentacle for Tuesday under Mars

This Pentacle of Tuesday under Mars represents to us in its first Interior Circle the names of the Four Heavenly Genii contained in this Pentacle which governs the Influence of this Star on Tuesday, which must be Invoked and conjured in the operation of this Day. Samael is the principal Governor or Genii contained in this Pentacle, You must Invoke him by turning to the East. You must not be terrified at his appearing any more than the Spirits which accompany though they appear under Strange figures. You must Dismiss them with respect, when you have obtained what you want of them. It is favourable to everything belonging to Arms.

Composition of Perfumes for Tuesday

In order to have this Perfume made in perfection it must be composed of the following Drugs, Euphorbium, Bdellium, Sal Ammoniac, Roots of Hellebore, the powder of Loadstone, and a little Sulpher, make of the whole, a paste of the Blood of a Black Cat, and the Brains of a Raven, and afterwards, make small Grains which you shall use in the Operation of Tuesday.

Oration for Tuesday

Satael Divine Virtue who causes thy Power to shine in thy enterprizes and Combats which take place both by Sea and Land. I pray you by the Interposition of your well beloved Caimax Ismoli Paffran that you will deign to Direct the benign Influence of the Planet which governs this Day in such a manner that the Operation I undertake may prove successful and that I may give Glory and Honour to the Great Celestial Genii Calzas Mama Yrel Ozael.

Invocation

Come Military and Warlike Genii who have executed the order of the Sovereign Master of the Universe upon the armies of the Rash Sennacherib. come and serve me in the Operation that I undertake undertake under the Auspicies of this third and Brilliant Luminary of the Firmament be favourable to my Intreaties in the Name of Him who commands the formidable Spirits **Boncas. Taxel Zaliel Ouael.**

Conjuration

I Conjure you **Elibra Eloym** all your Cohort in the Name of the third Luminary of the Firmament that you will contribute to the Success of the Operation which I undertake this day use all your power to keep the Evil Spirits at a Distance that they may not Counteract the Assistance necessary for my undertaking. I Conjure you in the formidable names of the Governors **Damael Lobquin Saraphiel**

The following Pentacle and Talisman to render a Military Life or Employment Happy also one to make one Invulnerable must be made with much exactness. and observe that the Constellation of Mars must govern the Operation in Conjunction of Mercury, in a favourable Aspect to Venus on a Tuesday and during the Spring Season. ——

The Last two Pentacles or Talismans (fig 10-11) make but one, having two faces. on one. You must Engrave the Seal or Character proper to the Familiar Spirit who directs the Influx of the Planet Mars, on the other side or face You must Engrave the Mysterious Number of the Same Planet in several small squares, So that whatsoever side you read whether above or below, on one Angle or another. it being in the same line to the right or the left The Number will always be found the Same. which is 65. ——

39

Precious Stones affected by Mars

The Diamond. The Amethyst. The Carbuncle.
The Jasper marked with Red

Trees affected by Mars

The Box Tree. The Maple Tree.

Pentacle of Tuesday under Mars

41

PLATE XIII.

Hours of the Day and Night on Tuesday

1	♂	Samael		1	♄	Cassiel
2	☉	Michael		2	♃	Zachiel
3	♀	Anael		3	♂	Samael
4	☿	Raphael		4	☉	Michael
5	☽	Gabriel		5	♀	Anael
6	♄	Cassiel		6	☿	Raphael
7	♃	Zachiel		7	☽	Gabriel
8	♂	Samael		8	♄	Cassiel
9	☉	Michael		9	♃	Zachiel
10	♀	Anael		10	♂	Samael
11	☿	Raphael		11	☉	Michael
12	☽	Gabriel		13	♀	Anael

The Mysterious Characters for Tuesday under Mars.

Rubeo ——— First Characters. ——— Puero

second

Third

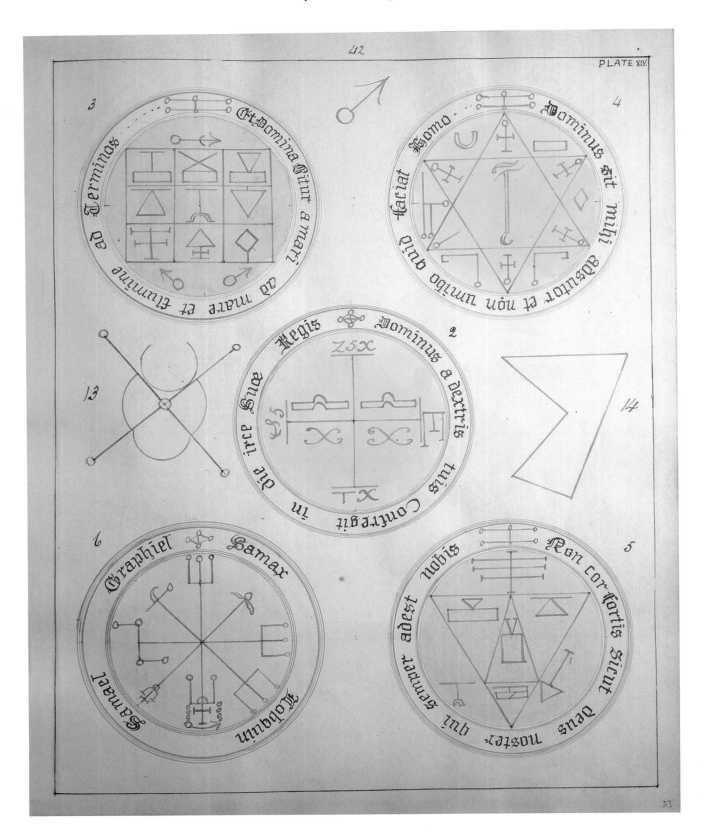

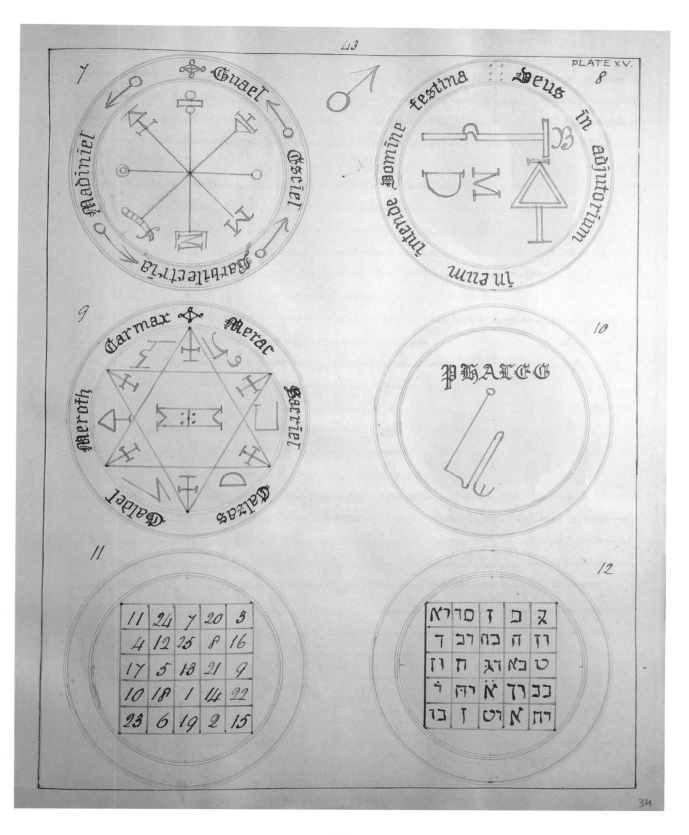

The Talismans under Mars to be made on Tuesday according to the foregoing Models. They must be formed of Iron. highly polished. and Engraven with much exactness. or on fair Virgin Parchment, and the Names and Characters written with Ink peculiar to the Planet.

Plate XIV. Fig III. Talisman to render a Military Life Happy.

" " 2. Talisman for Military Expeditions Bad Rencontres.

" " 4. Talisman to make one Invulnerable.

" " 5. Talisman to avoid evil Vexation Country Divisions & Insurrection

" " 6. Talisman to make one Invulnerable and inspire Arms.

Plate XV. " 7. Talisman against Assaults of Traitors.

" " 8. Talisman against Fire Arms and other offensive Weapons.

" " 9. Talisman to defend oneself against Ambushes and Traitors.

" " 10. Pentacle containing the Name and Seal of the Familiar Spirit of Mars

" " 11. Pentacle containing the Mysterious Number of Mars. 65.

" " 12. " " " " " in Hebrew Ch.

Plate XIV. " 13 - 14. Seal and Characters of the Intelligences &c.

Plate XII. " I. Pentacle for Tuesday under Mars.

The Wearer of these Talismans must again be reminded that the Virtue possessed by these plates of Metals or Parchment is owing to the exactness with which they are formed, also the divine Influences governing at the time of Operation, therefore the more confidence he places in their Influence and the more secrecy he employs, the greater will be the certainty of success.

405

Pentacle for Wednesday under Mercury.

This Pentacle under Mercury represents in the first Interior Circle the Names of the four Heavenly Genii who govern the Influence of the Stars on Wednesday, and which you must Invoke in the Operations that are made on that day. **Modiat**, is the principal Heavenly Genie contained in this Pentacle You must Invoke him in turning towards the East. This Apparition is no more than the Spirits of those which accompany him, and therefore cannot affright those who have the least firmness. You will dismiss them respectfully, when you have obtained their Assistance. They are disposed towards them who are Lovers of Science, and Games of Hazard.

Composition of Perfumes for Wednesday.

In order to have the perfume in a perfect state, it must be composed of the following Drugs. Mastic of the East, Chosen Incense, Cloves, Flowers, or Powder of Agate. Beat it all into powder and make thereof a paste with a Foxes Blood, and the Brains of a Magpie, and afterwards make thereof Beads, which you shall use in the operation of Wednesday under Mercury.

Oration for Wednesday

Great and Swift **Parabozath** we pray you to hear our humble Supplication that we make by the Intercession of your favourites the Heavenly Genii **Mathlai, Tarmiel Jerescue Mitraton** that you will be pleased to favour the Operation that I engage in this Day, and that the whole may be performed to your Honour.

Invocation

Run to me with speed, come ye Spirits who preside over the Operation of this Day, hear favourably the present Invocation that I make to you under the Divine Names of Venahel, Viernuel, Kael, Abuiori, be kind and ready to second my undertakings in a manner that shall render them efficacious.

Conjuration

I Conjure you by the Heavenly Name Elohim O ye Heavenly Genii who have power over the wonders that are wrought on this Sacred Day of the Fourth Luminary of the Firmament. I Conjure you by all that can Incline you to serve me that you will not Delay coming Saday, Asaraie, Varathaiel, Chie, to remove the Evil and Rebellious Spirits, and cause me by your Influence to succeed in my undertakings.

The following Pentacle and Talisman (fig 2) for Wednesday is useful to preserve you from being taken prisoner either by Sea or Land, and its virtue extends ever from Prison those who are confined, and rescuing from Slavery even if reduced to it. You must work under Mercury in a favourable Conjunction of Jupiter or Venus, and on a fine day in the Spring.

It is not only common that Men have now thought, Mercury presided over Games of Hazard, but many famous Cabalists have been of the same opinion, here, in the pages following (fig 3) You have a Talisman composed on this subject.

The last two Pentacles or Talismans (fig 9.10) make but one, having two faces. On one, you must Engrave the Seal or character of the Familiar Spirit who Directs the Influence of the Planet Mercury, and on the Second you must Engrave the Mysterious Number of the same planet, which number you must place in several small Squares, so that on whatsoever side you read the number, whether above or below, on one side or the other, or on the same line to the right, or to the left, you will always find the same Number.

Precious Stones under Mercury

The Emerald. The Topaz. The Porphyry.

Trees affected by Mercury

The Cornal Tree. The Medlar Tree.

PLATE XVI.

Hours of the Day and Night on Wednesday

1	☿	Raphael		1	☉	Michael
2	☽	Gabriel		2	♀	Anael
3	♄	Cassiel		3	☿	Raphael
4	♃	Zachiel		4	☽	Gabriel
5	♂	Samael		5	♄	Cassiel
6	☉	Michael		6	♃	Zachiel
7	♀	Anael		7	♂	Samael
8	☿	Raphael		8	☉	Michael
9	☽	Gabriel		9	♀	Anael
10	♄	Cassiel		10	☿	Raphael
11	♃	Zachiel		11	☽	Gabriel
12	♂	Samael		12	♄	Cassiel

The Mysterious Characters for Wednesday under Mercury.

Conjunctione. ——— First Characters. ——— Ab albo.

Second

Third

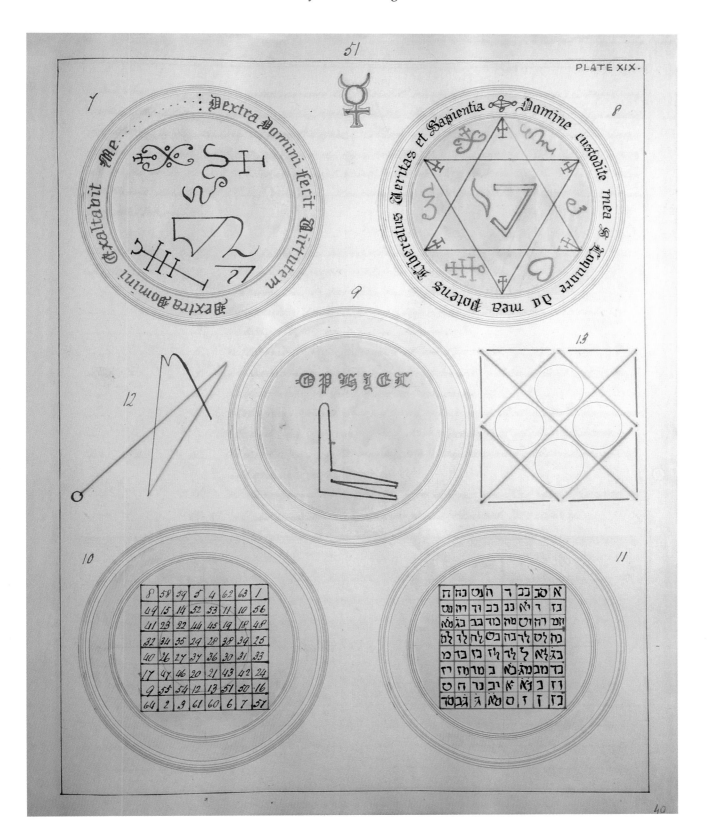

The Foregoing Talismans must be formed on Wednesday under Mercury while he is in a favourable Aspect with Jupiter or Venus and if possible in the spring season as said before. They must be made of Fixed Quicksilver which is best prepared by Melting a small portion of Tin with it so as to prevent breaking, not omitting to use a small portion of the Perfume suitable to the planet Mercury in the operation of casting or forming the Talisman.

Plate XVII	fig 1.	Pentacle for Wednesday under Mercury.
Plate XVIII	fig 2.	Talisman against Slavery.
"	"	3.	Talisman to favour Games of Hazard.
"	"	4.	Talisman for success of Merchants. Travellers, Students &c.
"	"	5.	Talisman to render one Invincible.
"	"	6.	Talisman to be successful in Games of Hazard.
Plate XIX	"	7.	Talisman to be fortune in Games of Chance Traffic &c.
"	"	8.	Talisman to acquire Eloquence.
"	"	9.	Talisman containing the Name and Seal of the Familiar Spirit of Mercury, and the Director of His Influence.
"	"	10.	Talisman containing the Mysterious Number of Mercury which is 260.
"	"	11.	Talisman containing the Same in Hebrew Characters.
		12-13.	Seals and Intelligences of the Planet Mercury.

53.

Pentacle for Thursday under

JUPITER

This Pentacle of Thursday represents to you in its Interior Circle the Names of the Four Heavenly Genii who prevail over the Star of Thursday and which you must Invoke and Conjure in the operation of that Day. Zebul is the principal of the Heavenly Genii contained in this Pentacle. You must Invoke Him in turning towards the East, as we have said on speaking of Sunday. You must fear no Evil from this Apparition, because it usually appears in a Magnificent manner its Equipage being like that of a King when crowned, and you must Dismiss it very respectfully, after having obtained what is mentioned.

Composition of Perfumes for Thursday

In order to have this Perfume in a state of Perfection, it must be composed of the following Drugs. The seed of the Ash Tree, The Wood or Shoot of an Aloe, Storax, Loadstone, Benjamin, Powder of Blue, and the end of a Quill, the whole mixed in powder together, in such proportions as will make the Odour Agreeable; then of this Confectionary, you must make some small seeds, which you must use in the Cabalistical Operation on Thursday under the Auspicies of Jupiter, and the Spirits who direct his Influence.

Oration for Thursday

O Kind and Beneficent **Castiel** who art loaded with Honours and disposeth Riches with a liberal Hand reject not the Prayer that I make unto thee through the Intercession of your wellbeloved favourites **Maguth Gutriz Gachiel Soheith** and give to my under-takings such success that I may give you the Glory of it.

Invocation

Come Speedily ye Blessed Spirits who preside over the Operation of this Day Come In-comparable **Zebul** and all your Legions run to my Assistance and be propitious to my under-takings be kind and refuse me not your powerful Aid.

Conjuration

I Conjure you by the Holy Name **Emanuel** all ye Heavenly Genii who second by your Aid the Grand Distributor of Honours Riches and Health. I Conjure you by the Singular Inclination that you try to please those who rely on your wonderful Power **O Rael, Miel, Retrapha, Calbat.** be ready here to put to flight all those Spirits which might impede my undertakings.

Observation on the Talismans

Jupiter being one of the most fortunate Planets, you may draw Mysterious Figures under his Auspicies, as well for Gaming at Hazard as under Mercury, because Jupiter governs Kingly Riches. The Model of this Talisman (fig 2) which is given hereafter will be very efficacious to render you fortunate chiefly at play, if you work under the Constellation of Jupiter, or if Jupiter is not in opposition to Mercury, but is favoured with a Bene-volent Aspect with Venus. It must be made in the Spring (on Thursday) or some Season when the weather is Serene.

You will have another Talisman for the same purpose, and under the same Constellation. If you travel with exactness success will Infallibly follow, it will be very convenient, and I can even say necessary before you Engage in this Game, to recite Orations, Invocations and Conjurations on the Talisman, and to perform some action in Honour to the Genii who directs the Influence of the Planet, as for Example to Distribute Alms in consideration of this Genii. As to the rest, the Talisman may be made on Wednesday under Mercury, in changing only the Orations, Colours, Characters &c

The Two Pentacles, or Talismans (fig 9–10) make but one, having two faces, On one, You must Engrave the Seal of the Familiar Spirit who directs the Influence of the Planet Jupiter, and on the Second You must Engrave the Mysterious Number of the same Planet, which number you must place in several small Squares, so that on whatever side this number whether from above or below, on one side, or angle, or on one side to the left or the right, being in the same line, it will always be the same which is 34.

Precious Stones affected by Jupiter

The Beryl, The Sapphire, The Green Emerald.

Trees affected by Jupiter

The Oak, The Poplar, The Ash Tree, The Fig Tree, The Pear Tree, The Plum Tree, and above all the Filberd Tree.

56

PLATE XX.

Hours of the Day and Night on Thursday.

1	♃	Zachiel	1	☽	Gabriel
2	♂	Samael	2	♄	Cassiel
3	☀	Michael	3	♃	Zachiel
4	♀	Anael	4	♂	Samael
5	☿	Raphael	5	☀	Michael
6	☽	Gabriel	6	♀	Anael
7	♄	Cassiel	7	☿	Raphael
8	♃	Zachiel	8	☽	Gabriel
9	♂	Samael	9	♄	Cassiel
10	☀	Michael	10	♃	Zachiel
11	♀	Anael	11	♂	Samael
12	☿	Raphael	12	☀	Michael

The Mysterious Characters for Thursday under Jupiter

Ab Acquisitione. ———— First Characters —— A letitia.

Second

Third

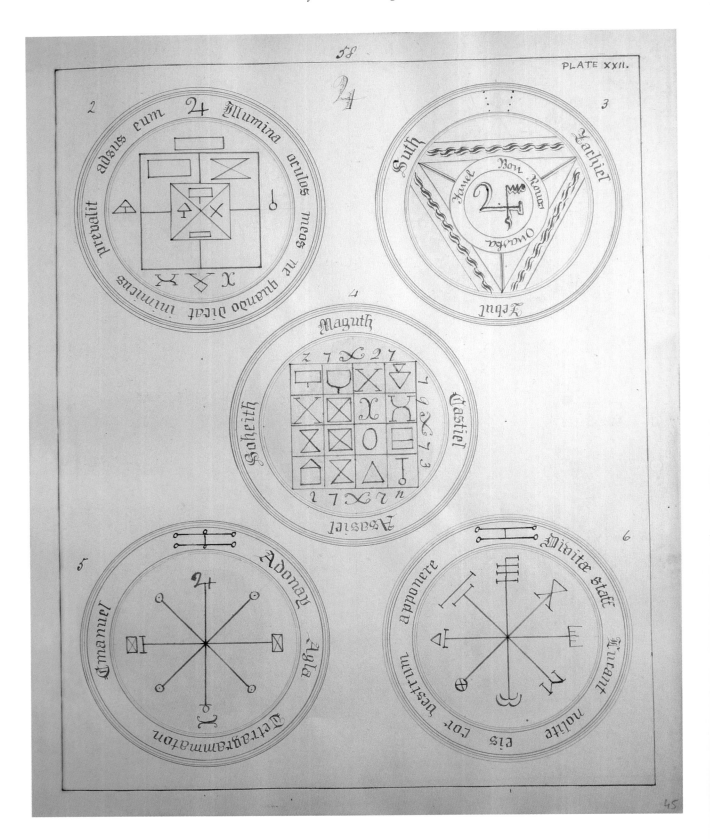

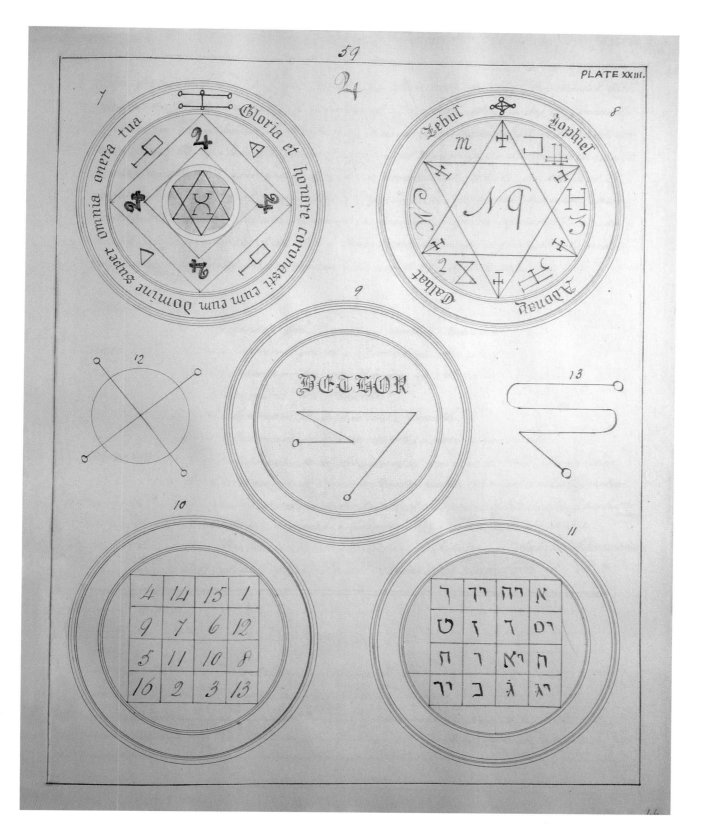

60

The foregoing Talismans with the Pentacle for the Day must be made on Thursday in the Hour of Jupiter they may be formed of Virgin Parchment observing the proper Ink for the Characters &c. or on a plate of Tin or Pewter. If Tin is employed it would be as well to mix with it a portion of Brass to harden it, while in the act of melting, do not omit using the Perfume, as before mentioned likewise repeat the oration in an earnest manner, for as aforesaid, On an exact performance of all that is here required with a firm trust and Confidence, depend the accomplishment of your desires.

Plate XXI   Fig I.

               Pentacle for Thursday under Jupiter.

Plate XXII   " 2. Talisman for the Game of Hazard.

"   "   " 3. Talisman for the Game of Hazard.

"   "   " 4. Talisman for Health.

"   "   " 5. Talisman to preserve Health.

"   "   " 6. Talisman to Discover Hidden Treasures.

Plate XXIII   " 7. Talisman to be successful in Trade and Finances.

"   "   " 8. Talisman to Obtain Honourable Charges and Dignities.

"   "   " 9. Seal of the Familiar Spirit of Jupiter, and Director of his Influence.

"   "   " 10. The Mysterious Number of Jupiter which is 34.

"   "   " 11. The Mysterious Number of Jupiter in Hebrew Characters.

"   "   " 12-13. Seals of the Intelligences of Jupiter.

61

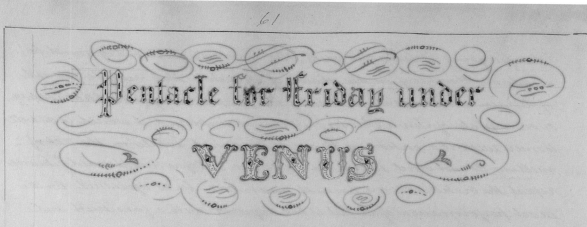

Pentacle for Friday under VENUS

This Pentacle for Friday represents to us in its first Interior Circle the Names of the four Heavenly Genii who govern the Stars on Friday, and which you must Invoke and Conjure on this Day. **Sarabotes** is the principal Heavenly Genii contained in this Pentacle. You must Invoke him in turning to the East, as we have already said in speaking of that of Sunday. So far from his Apparition being frightful, it is commonly very agreeable, its suit is composed of Small Genii, and is often accompanied by delightful and melodious sounds of Music &c which, inspire Youth with Joy. You must Dismiss him with Honour, after having received favours required. _____

Composition for Perfumes of Friday

For this Perfume to be in a state of perfection, it must be composed of the following Drugs, Musk, Ambergris, Wood of Aloes, Dried Red Roses, Red Coral. the whole pulverized and made into paste with the Blood of a Pigeon or Turtle Dove, and the brains of two or three Sparrows in such proportions that you can make an agreeable odour, and after this Confectionary is finished. You must make Small seeds or pills of it, which you must use in the Cabalistical Operations for Friday, under the Auspicies of Venus, and the Spirits which Direct her Influence. _____

62

Oration for Friday.

Lord Abalidoth, who lovest thy Servants and will be loved by them, I pray you by the Interposition of those among the Heavenly Genii whom you cherish most which are Raniel Corat. Kadie Penat I intreat you to diffuse on my Operations the Treasures of your kindness. so that my undertakings on this Day may be successful, conformable to my Intention and redound to your Glory with all suitable acknowledgement.

Invocation

Come on the wings of the Zephyrs ye happy Genii who preside over the workings of the Heart, Come Heavenly Sarabotes, Husaltiel Doremiel Setchiel, hear favourably the Invocation that I make this Day destined to the wonders of Love. be ready to lend me your Assistance to succeed in what I have undertaken under the Hope You will be favourable to me.

Conjuration

I Conjure you by the Veneration you have for the Mysterious Name Setchiel O Beneficent Genii who preside over the Operations that are done on this Day I Conjure you Talarath, Miveg, Cuphaniel, Clearos, that you will come with all your power to scatter and put to flight the Evil Spirits which are inimical to good Operations cause me by thy Powerful Virtue to succeed in what I have undertaking this Day which is Consecrated to Venus.

It is so Natural for Men to Love and be loved, that there is nothing in all nature which we are more strongly disposed to, or that we wish for with more ardour. but as there are often obstacles to overcome, which are not within the Limits of Mediocrity, the two following Pentacles or Talismans (fig 2.3) will be of great Assistance, if you are happy enough to make them according to the circumstances prescribed by the principle of the Art. You must begin on Friday during the Spring Season at Sun-rise, in calm serene Weather, it will be right also to prepare at the same time the Ingredients which serve for the Composition of Amorous Love Potions, and above all the Herb called *Enrula Campana*. You must gather it the same day that you make the Talisman, and Consecrate it with the same Sprinkling and Perfume agreeable and proper to the Planet Venus and preserve it in a Box proper to be made use of on these occasions as we have more fully explained.

The last two Talismans (fig 9-10) make but one, having two faces, On one You must Engrave the Name, and Seal or Character of the Familiar Spirit who directs the Influence of the Planet Venus, and on the Second You must Engrave the Mysterious Number of the same Planet, which number you must place in several small Squares, so that whatever side you read whether from above or below, from one angle to another or on the same side to the right hand or the left, being in the same line. You will always find the same Number which is 175.

Precious Stones Affected by Venus

The Cornelian. The Beryl. The Coral

Trees Affected by Venus.

The Myrtle, The White Laurel, The Orange, and other Odoriferous Trees.

64

PLATE XXIV.

Hours of the Day and Night on Friday

1	♀	Anael	1	♂	Samael
2	☿	Raphael	2	☉	Michael
3	☽	Gabriel	3	♀	Anael
4	♄	Cassiel	4	☿	Raphael
5	♃	Zachiel	5	☽	Gabriel
6	♂	Samael	6	♄	Cassiel
7	☉	Michael	7	♃	Zachiel
8	♀	Anael	8	♂	Samael
9	☿	Raphael	9	☉	Michael
10	☽	Gabriel	10	♀	Anael
11	♄	Cassiel	11	☿	Raphael
12	♃	Zachiel	12	☽	Gabriel

The Mysterious Characters for Friday under Venus.

Ab Amissione ——— First Characters. — A Duello.

Second

Third

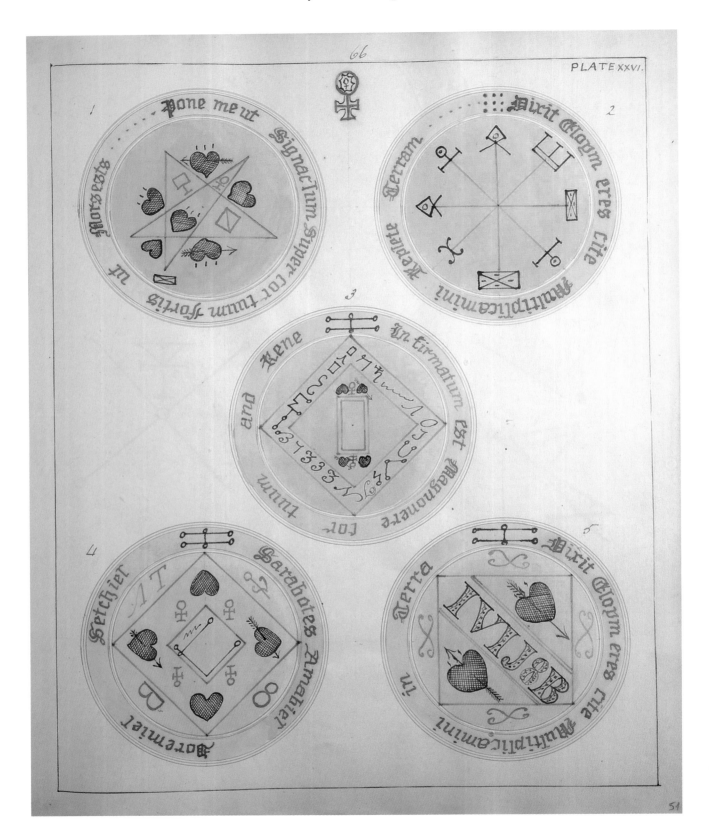

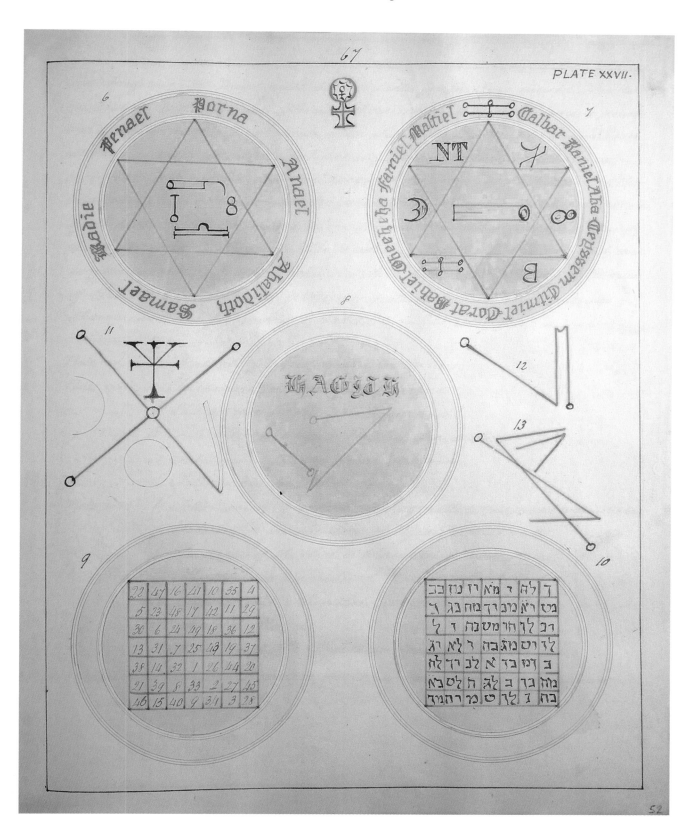

68

The foregoing Talismans, with the Pentacle for the Day, must be made on Friday under Venus. Should there not be sufficient time to finish one of them in the first hour after Sunrise, the Operator must wait with patience till the next hour of Venus arrives, then he may complete his work. but on no account let him neglect reciting the Orations, Invocations, and Conjurations, for upon a strict observance of all these Rules, Forms, and Ceremonies given, depends the certainty of his success.   They may be formed of Fair Virgin Parchment, and written with Ink of a Green or silver colour, or they may be made of Brass or Copper Plates properly polished and Engraven as shown in the foregoing Models. ————

	Figs.	
Plate XXV.	1.	Pentacle for Friday under Venus.
Plate XXVI.	1.	Talisman for Amorous Intrigues.
"	" 2.	Talisman for the same purpose.
"	" 3.	Talisman to Engage the Fair Sex to Love.
"	" 4.	Talisman for the same purpose.
"	" 5.	Talisman for Secret Love.
Plate XXVII.	6.	Talisman to make ourselves agreeable to those we are willing to please.
"	" 7.	Talisman for the Love of Aged Persons.
"	" 8.	Pentacle of the Seal or Character of Venus.
"	" 9.	Mysterious Number of Venus, which is 175.
"	" 10.	Mysterious Number in Hebrew.
"	" 11.	Seal of Venus
"	" 12-13.	Seals of the Intelligences of Venus.

53

69

Pentacle for Saturday under Saturn.

This Pentacle of Saturn represents to you in the first Interior Circle the Names of the Heavenly Genii who prevail over the Influence of the Stars on Saturday and which you must Invoke and Conjure in the Operation of this Day. **Maymon** is the Principal Heavenly Genii contained in this Pentacle. You must Invoke him in turning towards the East. Although his Apparition is not terrible, nevertheless you will behold them under such Melancholy Figures, that you will feel a kind of trembling, but it will be attended without Danger, and if the Constellation is Happy, they will become favourable and propitious. I have before warned you, that you will very seldom find Saturn in a happy situation for receiving favourable Influences, and likewise Saturday, which is affected by this Planet is usually attended with unlucky apparitions, on which account a true follower of this Art, ought never to be then employed, our principal Motive is, in the exercise of this Science, that we ought only to have a desire of procuring good to ourselves, and rendering Service to others and not Evil. You may nevertheless, with some application and attention, find some Saturday in the course of the year, and chiefly during Spring, when Saturn is in a Happy Conjunction with Jupiter or Venus, or in a favourable Aspect with Mercury, and then You will obtain advantageous Operations. —————

70

Compositions of Perfumes for Saturday

These Perfumes must be in a state of perfection, and composed of the following Drugs. Grains of Black Pepper. Grains of Hogsbane. Roots of Mandrake. Powder of Loadstone. Myrrh of the East, the whole pulverized, and made into a paste with the blood of a Bat, and the Brains of a Black Cat in necessary proportion. After the Confectionary is finished. You shall make thereof small Pills of which you must use in the Cabalistic Operation on Saturday under the Auspicies of Saturn and the Spirits which direct his Influence.

Oration for Saturday

Heavenly Machatan who disdainest not to listen to those who prayeth with confidence to you and in the power of your Arm. I intreat you with affection through the interposition of the Genii who are subject unto you, and who are principally Uriel Balidet Assaibi Abumalith, that you will conduct the Heavenly Influences with so much dexterity in the Operation. I am going to make, that the whole may succeed according to my desire, and to your Glory.

Invocation

Come out of your Gloomy Solitude ye Saturnine Spirits and thou powerful Maymon, come with your Cohort come with Diligence to the place where I am going to begin an Operation under your Auspicies, be attentive to my labours and Contribute your Assistance to what may redound to the Honour and Glory of Him to whom you are subject, and in whose Name I Invoke you.

Conjuration

I Conjure you by the Great Name Arpheta, which causeth the rebellious Spirits to to tremble I Conjure you benign Spirits who are destined to favour the Undertaking of this Day constituted to the Seventh Luminary of the Firmament to be kind to your

71

Heavenly **Balidet, Machaton, Archaziel Talidomer.** Put to flight by your power the Genii who oppose my Labours so that I may finish them according to my own wishes as I would begin them with Confidence to you. ————————

————————

Though the Planet Saturn prevails over Saturday, it is not commonly happy in its Influence, as has been already remarked, yet nevertheless if you can find it in a favourable situation, which sometimes happens during the Spring Season. You may profit by this event, in working the two following Talismans, in order to have favourable seasons for the fruits of the Earth, to produce Rain, or fertilizing Dews, during a Drought, and to avert Hail, Tempest, or other Natural effects. The Talismans will be wonderfully useful. It will be likewise efficacious to Dig with success in places where there are Mines, Precious Stones, Hidden Treasures &c. They who have tried the virtue of this last Talisman, affirm they have Dreams in which are sensibly represented to the Imagination, the places, you may be assured to find Moneys, or Precious Metals, by the Ministry of Saturnine Spirits.

You must put the Talisman under the Bolster, in lying down after having perfumed it with Incense suitable to the Planet Saturn. This Talisman not only preserves men from a number of Maladies, but even cures them; when they proceed from an over heated Bile, and this what Experience will prove, better than any discourse thereon. If you make it Virgin parchment you must observe the proper Colours.

The Pentacle or Talisman fig 8-9 make but one, having two faces, on one, You must Engrave the Seal or Mysterious Character of the Familiar Spirit who directs the Influence of the Planet Saturn; On the second, You must Engrave the Mysterious Number of the same planet which you must place in several small Squares, so that on whatever Side you read this number whether from above or below, or on one Angle, or the other, or on the same line to the right or to the left, you will find the same Number, which is 15.

72

PLATE XXVIII.

===== Precious Stones affected by Saturn =====

The Sapphire, The Chalcedony, The Dark Jasper, The Loadstone

===== Trees affected by Saturn. =====

The Cypress, The Pyne.

Hours of the Day and Night on Saturday

#		Angel	Name	#		Angel	Name
1	♄	Cassiel	Machatan	1	☿	Raphael	Suquinos
2	♃	Zachiel	Asasiel	2	☽	Gabriel	Madiel
3	♂	Samael	Amabiel	3	♄	Cassiel	Balidet
4	☀	Michael	Cynabal	4	♃	Zachiel	Castiel
5	♀	Anael	Abalidoth	5	♂	Samael	Calzas
6	☿	Raphael	Mitraton	6	☀	Michael	Anael
7	☽	Gabriel	Missabu	7	♀	Anael	Sarabotes
8	♄	Cassiel	Assaibi	8	☿♄	Cassiel Raphael	
9	♃	Zachiel	Maguth	9	♃☽	Zachiel Gabriel	
10	♂	Samael	Carmax	10	♄	Cassiel	Maymon
11	☀	Michael	Baciel	11	♃	Zachiel	Gutriz
12	♀	Anael	Corat	12	♂	Samael	Arragon

===== The Mysterious Characters for Saturday under Saturn. =====

A Carcere ——— First ——— Characters.— a Tristitia

Second

Third.

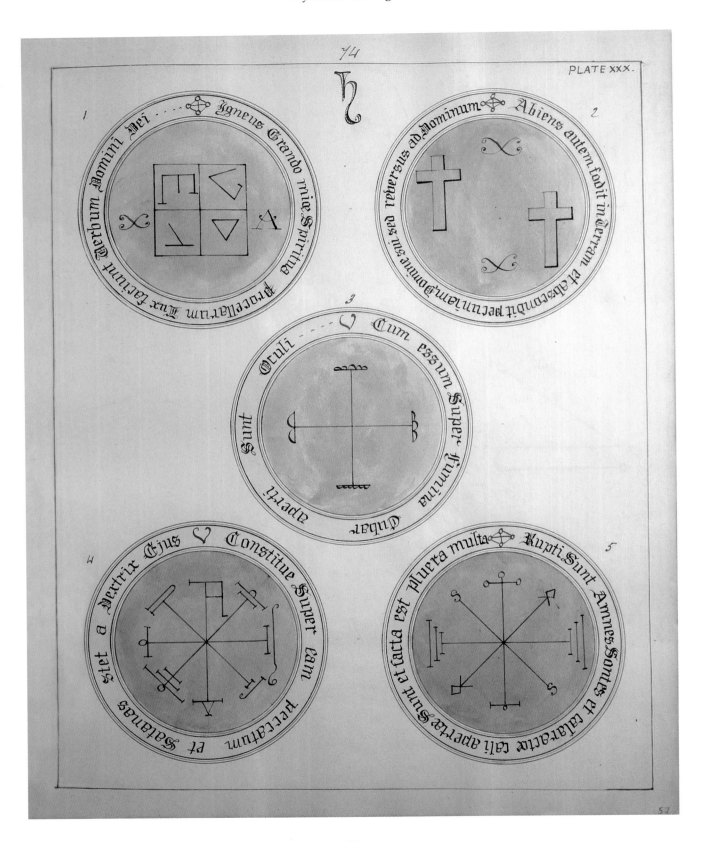

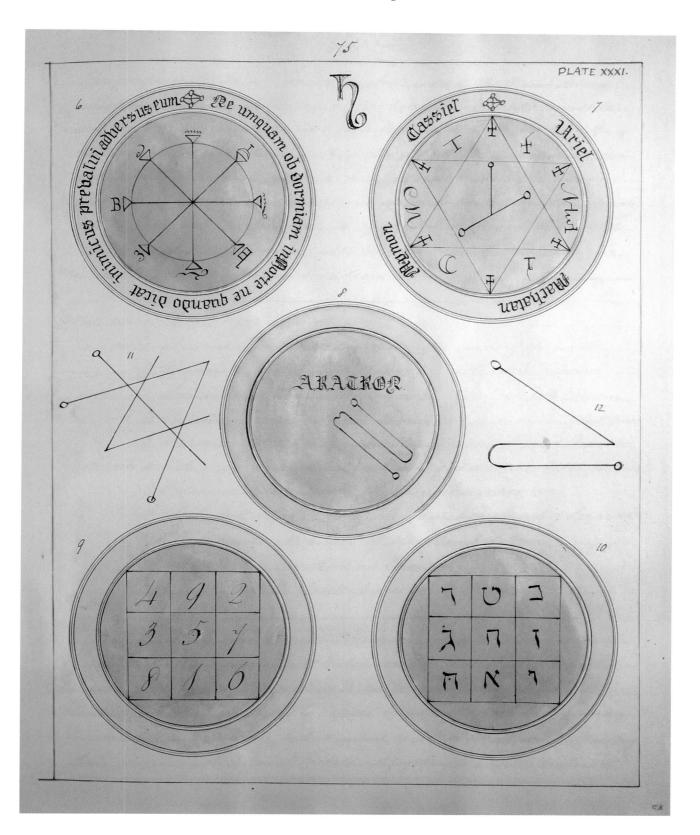

"The foregoing Talismans under the Influence of the Planet Saturn must be made on Saturday in his hour; the Operator must be very particular about waiting for a favourable Configuration of the Planet he works under, with either or both the Luminaries, also with Venus or Jupiter, because his Influence naturally, unless assisted by fortunate Configurations of the Fortunes, tends to promote evil and discord, particularly so, if opposed, or Squared by Herschel or Mars. But the Talismans will be productive of much benefit, if raised according to the Conditions aforesaid. —————

Plate XXIX 1. Pentacle for Saturday under Saturn.
  "   XXX. 1. Talisman for success in raising the Fruits of the Earth.
  "   " 2. Talisman to discover Mines and Hidden Treasures.
  "   " 3. Talisman to have a Revelation in the Night by a Dream.
  "   " 4 Talisman against Sounds, Charms, and the possession of Evil Spirits.
  "   " 5 Talisman against Tempests, Thunder, Hail, Inundations &c.
Plate XXXI 6. Talisman against sudden Deaths, and accidents, that cause them
  "   " 7. Talisman to discover Hidden Treasures &c.
  "   " 8 Seal and Character of the Familiar Spirit of Saturn.
  "   " 9 Mysterious Number of the Planet Saturn.
  "   " 10 The same in Hebrew Characters.
  "   " 11–12 Seals of the Intelligences &c of Saturn.

The above mentioned Talismans may be formed or made of True Virgin Parchment or of Metal composed of Lead, properly cleaned and Engraven according to the foregoing Models. Should any of the Metal Plates be defaced by wear, or accident, they may be repolished and Engraven, but all must be done in their respective planetary Hour governing the different Metals, not forgetting to recite the Orations &c.

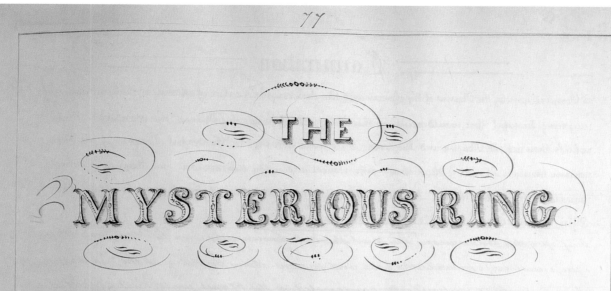

THE MYSTERIOUS RING

The Mysterious Ring, which several Doctors of the Cabala have used with wonderful success. It is not in order to impose on the credulity of the curi--ous Followers of the Occult Science, that I say, that it is more than Two Thousand years since the Ring which I have mentioned has been in use. This is in general the manner of making the Ring. After having made a Ring of suitable Metal, according to the Planet whose Influx we wish to obtain, (according to the Cabalistic Art,) and having set in it a stone, suited to the Nature of the Planet, You must Engrave within the Ring the Name of the Familiar Spirit who governs the planet, the foregoing of which we have seen. You must then form a Circle of about seven feet in diameter, of the following Model, and being in the middle of the Circle, You must burn in a small vessel, some fresh Perfume, the scent of which is suitable to the Planet, which governs the Ring. Gravely pronouncing the Name which is Engraved in the Ring, and holding your hand a lighted Wax Candle, or Torch, You must repeat the Conjuration under the Name of the Spirit which is Engraved in the Ring.

78

Conjuration

I Conjure you by the Name of the Spirit and the Sovereign Creator of all things, that without noise or anything frightful You would print on this Ring which bears thy Name, the wonderful Virtue of which thou art the Master and Disposer. I Conjure you by the Wonderful Names of the Deity to whom thou art subject. Hear these with respect and ready submission, the Names of which are terrible to all Created things. Adonay, Agla, Tetragrammaton, Gaha, Agari, Thetron, Hie, Elhi, Ygaha, Emanuel, Henry, Eloym, Goth, Genü.

Or if after this Conjuration, the Spirit should be known either in a Visible or Invisible form You must turn towards the East and present Him the Ring, at the end of a small Ring, which is particularly consecrated to the Planet, under the Auspicies of which you work. The said Ring, that it may be impressed with those qualities we wish for.   Immediately after, you must Dismiss him saying.

— Faithful Minister go in peace in the Name of Your Great Master who hath sent to be favourable to me. —

Before You go out of the Circle, You must put the Ring on that Finger where Rings are usually worn, and burn the Perfume a second time, effacing the Circle properly, and returning with the profoundest silence.

These sort of Rings ought be preserved with the utmost care, in a New Box or a small new Purse, made with silk of a colour that is suitable to the planet. If you are happy enough to make them under a good Constellation, with the preparations and Ceremonies, similar to those of the Talismans and Pentacles, they will not lose their Efficacy in Changing their Master, provided that he who receives them consents to all that is done in the Operation of which we have spoken, and that he burn the Perfumes in the Name, and to the Honour of the Spirit who governs the Aforesaid

Ring.

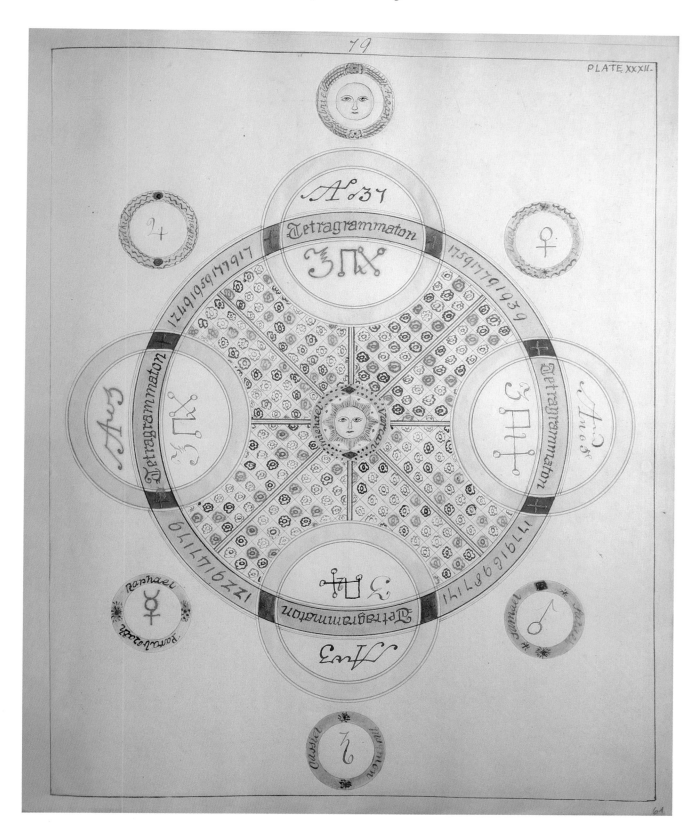

An

Experiment of the

SPIRIT

BIRTO

As hath often been proved at the Instant Request of

Edward the Fourth

KING OF ENGLAND

81

Experiment of Invocating the Spirit Birto and holding Converse with him.

The Operator must be reminded that Ceremonies in the Magic Art must be performed earnestly, and faithfully, with a determination to succeed in his Operations by faithfully adhering to all the cautions and Rules given so that no part be omitted. He must be bold and courageous in the time of Operations, for Aeriel Spirits are much more powerful and obstinate than the planetary Angels, and require all the skill and firmness of the Operator, they are often very subtle and require severe Conjurations &c to compel them to Appear, but when once they have been invocated to Appear, they will afterwards almost at the Will of the Operator appear without difficulty, but the Operator must always be on his guardes at the time of Operation, not suffering himself to be Overcome with fear or trembling, He must be chaste leading a Religious Life. As the manner and form of the Circle hereafter described must be Drawn Let him be careful to guard it with Seals and Holy Names round about. So shall he be safe. but on no account Leave the Circle till the Spirit is finally departed As all the necessary Instruments and Apparatus have been described in a former part of this Mysterious Book, it is unnecessary to advert to it any farther, for they will answer the same purpose in Ceremonial Magic as in Cabalistical.

The Invocant may now make preparation for Invocating the Spirit _Birto_, as an Experiment.

On the Second, Fourth, Sixth, Tenth and Twelfth Days of the Moons increase, go to the place appointed for this and the like purpose, And in the Evening when the Air is Serene, lay down the Circles and their Characters in the order hereafter explained in the Copies thereof. then Invocate as follows.

Invocation

I Exorcise Call upon and Conjure thee Spirit which art called **Birto** by the Dignity of the Prince **Ornothocos** and **Booth** and in the Name of the Father, and of the Son, and of the Holy Ghost, and by the Power of Potent, Inestimable, Divine and Commanding Names of the Almighty and Everlasting God **Jehovah El Elohim Sabaoth Adonay Tetragrammaton Alpha et Omega**, and by the Name of Jesus of Nazareth, born of a Virgin the only begotten Son of God, the Father Almighty Maker of Heaven and Earth, our only Saviour and Redeemer Advocate and Mediator, whose Name all the Celestial Host of Angels Honour and Obey, and whereat all knees on Earth bow and all Aeriel, Terrestrial and Infernal Spirits do fear and tremble. by all the aforesaid, I do yet again powerfully Exorcise Conjure and Command thee Spirit which art called **Birto**, that thou do immediately forthwith and at this present appear Visibly before me in that Circle appointed for thee in fair and human form and shape of a man, and no ways terrible or hurtful to me or any other person whatsoever, and I Constrain thee to tell me the truth without Fraud Guile Deceit &c in his Name to whom be all Honour Power Glory Majesty and Dominion for Ever and Ever **Amen.**

Let the Conjuration be often repeated and said over with ample courage confidence and resolution, and when he appears, receive him courteously and gently. Bind him with the Bond of Spirits, and then he will freely and faithfully declare and make answer to whatever

shall be demanded and will serve, obey, fulfill all commands &c. Then

License him to depart in peace.

Let the Circle for the Invocant which is that wherein the Name

MAGISTER is written, be made as here described viz not less than nine

feet in diameter and as before said, well fortified with Divine Names

Seals &c. Let the Effigy, Character, or Wivern be fairly Drawn ⁓⁓

or Painted upon an Abortive as above.

As for the Circle wherein the Spirit Appeareth, it may be made

two or three several ways, according to the place made choice of

to act in, and the Ground or floor. If the Ground be nought or

rugged, as in Woods, or Coppices they generally are, Then must the

Ground be paved, and made very even, so that an impression

may be made visible and plain thereon, or else let it be made on large

Calfskin Parchment, but it is better on the Ground, and if upon

64

Parchment or a floor, then let the Circle be made or drawn thereon with Consecrated Chalk or marking Stone and place them three feet asunder and herein take a serious and deliberate Consideration, let reason and prudence be thy principal Guide, without which principles a Magician is but a shadow to a substance, and shall as miss as hit of his Expectation. ————————————

————————————

Note. —— The Invocant must not be impatient nor discouraged at the Prolixity or Delay of the Appearance of the Spirit, for it is the property of all Aeriel Spirits to be slow in their first Appearance but after they have once appeared, they will afterwards with less trouble. their Departure is very slow sometimes, therefore it behoveth the Operator to very particular in repeating the License to Depart. and not be in too much hurry to quit the Circle.

The forms of a Bond of Spirits and Licence to Depart will be given in the Sequel of this Work. ————————————

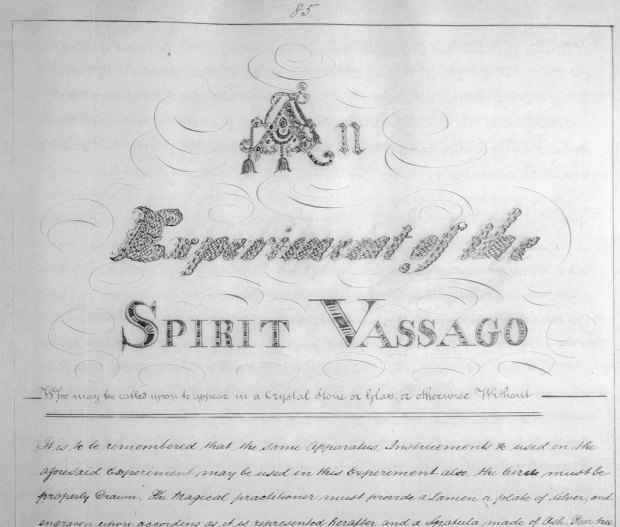

An Experiment of the SPIRIT VASSAGO

Who may be called upon to appear in a Crystal Stone or Glass, or otherwise Without

It is to be remembered that the same Apparatus, Instruments &c used in the aforesaid Experiment, may be used in this Experiment also, the Circle must be properly Drawn. The Magical practitioner must provide a Lamen or plate of Silver, and engraven upon according as it is represented hereafter, and a Spatula made of Ash, Pear tree or any other solid wood the thickness of a third part of an inch, and the square top thereof to be three inches Square, and the stem or handle to be nine inches long, and gilded all over with Gold, and the Character written thereon, as is shewn forth in the Example following. Having all things in readiness, repair to the Chamber or place appointed for practice, which ought to be clean, and a Table placed therein, covered with a clean Linen Cloth, and a Taper on each Side of the Crystal Stone or Glass, and being seated therein, Invocate as follows.

I Exorcise, Call upon, and Command the Spirit Tassago by and in the Name of the immense and Everlasting God, Jehovah, Adonay, Elohim, Agla, El, On, Tetragrammaton, and by and in the Name of Our Lord Jesus Christ the only Son of the Eternal and true God, Creator of Heaven and Earth and all that is in them Mipius, Sother, Emanuel, Primogenitus, Homonzion, Romex, Via, Veritas, Sapientia, Virtus, Leof, Mediator, Agnus, Rex, Pastor, Prophetas, Sacerdos, Athanatos Paraclotus Alpha and Omega, by all these High, Great, Glorious, Royal, and Ineffable Names of the Omnipotent God, and of His only Son our Lord and Saviour Jesus Christ the second Essence of the Glorious Trinity. I Exorcise, Command, Call upon, and Conjure thee Spirit Tassago wheresoever thou art (East, West, North or South, or being bound to any one under the Compass of the Heavens) that you come immediately from the place of your private abode or residence and appear to me visibly in Fair and Decent Form in this Crystal Stone or Glass ✶ I do again Exorcise and powerfully Command thee Spirit Tassago to come and appear visibly to me in this Crystal Stone or Glass, or otherwise as above in a fair, solid, and decent Form. I do again strongly bind and Command thee Spirit Tassago to appear visibly to me in that Crystal Stone or Glass as aforesaid. By the Virtue and Power of these Names by which I can bind all Rebellious Obstinate and Refractory Spirits Alla, Carital, Marihat, Carion, Urion, Spyton, Korean, Stabea, Corian, Marmox, Agaion, Cador, Son, Catator, Yron, Astron, Gardeong, Caldabrie, Bear, Tetragrammaton, Strallay, Spignox, Sother, Yah, On, El, Elohim, by all aforesaid I charge and Command thee Spirit Tassago to make haste and come away, and appear visibly to me as aforesaid without any farther tarrying or Delay in the Name of Him who shall come to Judge the Quick and Dead and the and the World by Fire. Amen. ————————————————

This Conjuration after being repeated, and the Invocant being patient and constant in his perseverance and not Disheartened nor Dismayed by reason of any tedious Prolixity or Delay, the Spirit will at last appear, Bind him with the Bond of Spirits, then you may talk with him.

✶ Here note, that the Invocant mentioneth a Stone or Glass if he have one; or else he saith "to Me visibly in fair and Decent Form and human shape before this Circle."

87

That this is a true Experiment, and that the Spirit hath been obliged to the fellowship and Service of a Magic Artist heretofore is very certain, as may appear by this following Bond or Obligation, which the Invocant may if he please, have fairly written on an Abortive, and laid before him, and discourse with the Spirit concerning it.

Bond or Obligation of the Spirit Vassago

I **Vassago** under **Varo** the King of the West not compelled by command nor fear, but of my own accord and free will especially oblige myself by these presents firmly and faithfully and without ✳ Deceit to **T.W.** to obey at any time and at any place whensoever and wheresoever he shall call upon me per- -sonally to appear whether in a Stone or in the Middle without a Stone and to fulfil his Commands truly in all things wherein I can by the Virtue of all the Names of God especially by these the most Powerful in the Magical Art **Laye, Abrpta, Mura Syron Walgaba Kyshin Layagamum Arasin Laysai** and by the Virtue wherewith the Sun and Moon were Darkened and my Planet and by the Celestial Characters thereof and by this Seal binding most Solidly ⸻

In Witness of which Guilty Person he commanding, I have signed this Present Obli- -gation with mine own Seal to which I always stick close. ⸻

That this a true Experiment is apparent, and that the Spirit hath been by the great Diligence, and constant Perseverance of Learned and Intelligent Magicians ⸻ brought to Obedience and fellowship is manifestly true by this recited precedent, besides what myself hath Seen, and as for the calling upon, and the other Spirits either in the Crystal Stone, or Glass, shall be shewn at the end of the next Experiment, because they are both of one Nature.

✳ The Name of the person who wishes to obtain the Spirit in the Crystal or otherwise.

66

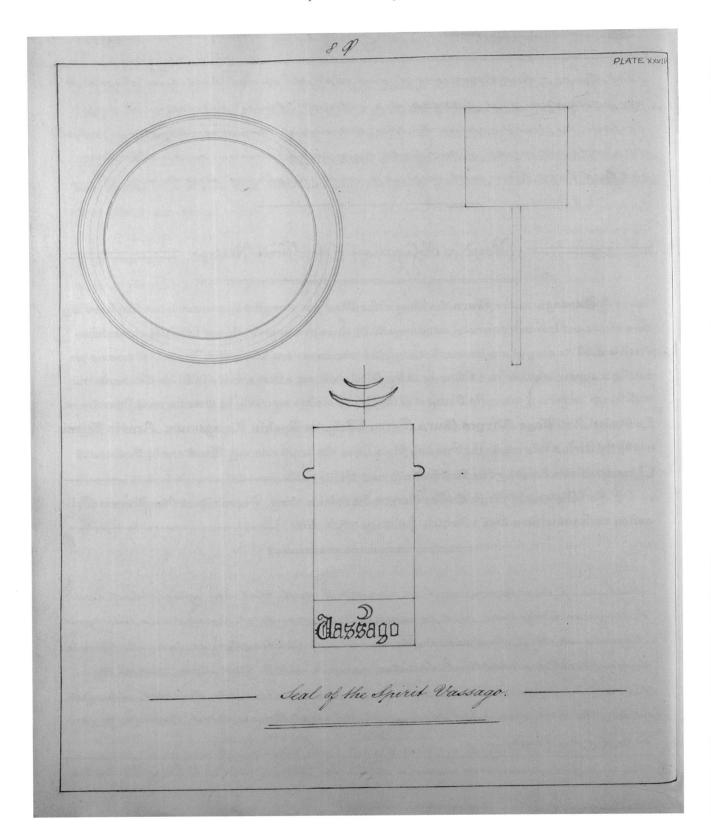

Seal of the Spirit Vassago.

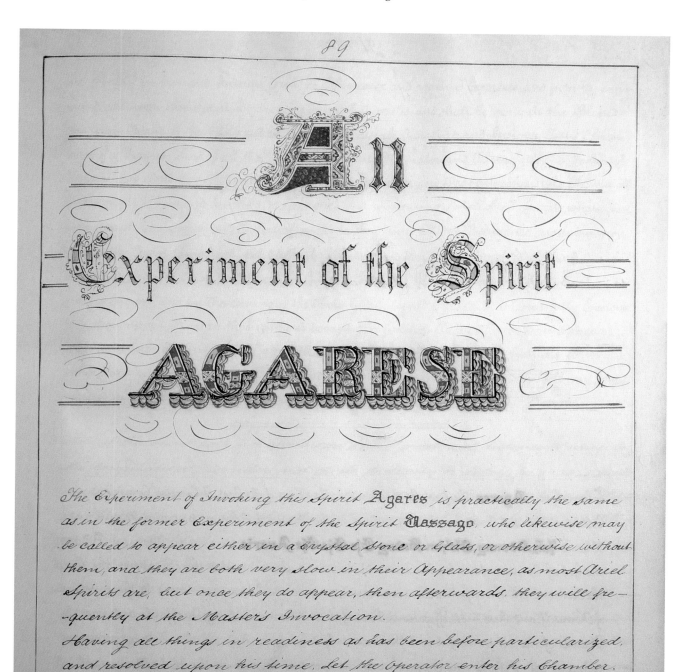

89

An Experiment of the Spirit AGARES

The Experiment of Invoking this Spirit *Agares* is practically the same as in the former Experiment of the Spirit *Tassago*, who likewise may be called to appear either in a Crystal Stone or Glass, or otherwise without them, and they are both very slow in their Appearance, as most Ariel Spirits are, but once they do appear, then afterwards, they will frequently at the Master's Invocation.

Having all things in readiness as has been before particularized, and resolved upon his time, Let the Operator enter his Chamber, or place, appointed for Action, and Invocate as follows.

[page number skipped in the manuscript – no content is missing]

91

Thou Spirit Agares the first Captain under the King of the East, I Exorcise, Command and Call upon thee and Constrain thee, by calling in the Name of the most powerful Fearful and Blessed Jah, Adonay, Elohim Saday Eje Eje Eje Asarie and in the Name of Adonay the God of Israel whose by his immediate word alone created the Heavens, the Earth, the Sea, and all things therein contained, and made Man according to the similitude of Himself, and these most efficacious, Powerful, and Commanding, Ineffable, and Sacred Names of the all powerful and Immense God Jehovah Agla El On Tetragrammaton, wherein all Visions and Apparitions are wont to be, and by the Holy Name which was written on the Brow of Aaron the Priest of the Most High and Everlasting God, I powerfully Exorcise and Command thee Spirit Agares that wheresoever thou art in any part of the Air, Earth, East, West, North or South or being bound to any one, that immediately without tarrying or Delay you presently appear to

me Visibly in fair and human form ✳ Moreover and again I Exorcise, and potently com-
-mand, call upon thee Spirit Agares by Him that was, is, and shall be even in the Blessed
and Great Name of the Holy and Heavenly Messiah Our Lord and Saviour Jesus Christ
born of a Virgin, Lord of all the World, and its only Mediator and Advocate to the Father of
Mercies, God of all Consolation, at whose Great, Glorious, and Incomprehensible Names, all
knees ought to bow, and humbly do reverence, and at naming whereof all Spirits whatsoever,
both Aeriel Terrestrial and Infernal ought to obey with all due Reverence and Submission
who is the Great Emanuel, the faithful Witness and Primogeniture, Alpha and Omega
who lived, and was Dead, and liveth for Ever, and by His Glorious Passion, Resurrection
and Ascension, and by the coming of the Holy Ghost, by all Aforesaid, I Powerfully Exorcise
thee thou Spirit Agares that without tarrying, or further Delay, You do now appear
Visibly to me, I now calling upon thee † in a fair, solid, decent and human form,
wherefore make haste, come away and shew thyself immediately to fulfill my my
request in the Name of the Father, and of the Son, and of the Holy Ghost. Amen.

Now if this Spirit doth not appear in some material distance of time to
the Conjuration, wonder not at its prolixity or delay, for as it is said
elsewhere before it is the Nature of the Aeriel Spirits to be very slow
in their appearance, therefore, the Invocant must be patient, Dili-
-gent and Watchful, and on no account must he leave the Circle, till
the Spirit be finally Dismissed.
Therefore let the Magician be constant in his perseverance herein, that this
Experiment is all needful, and that this Spirit Agares hath been called
upon, and been brought to Obedience and Familiar Association is manifest
-ly true and apparent by this following Obligation made by him to some learned
——— Master. ———

✳ Here you are to observe, that if you call him into a Stone, or Glass, then you are to say "In this
Stone or Glass". If you have none, you need specify but say "to Me", or, "to me before this Circle &c", and so
the like elsewhere in other places of this Conjuration observe the same where you shall meet with
the like Occasion † Here mentioning as before; as whether without or within a receptacle.

93.

I Agares the first Captain under the King of the East not compelled by command or Dread, but willingly and of my own accord, do especially bind myself by these presents firmly to obey at all times, and in every place I.M. ✳ to do his commands in all things appertaining to my Duty and especially by these words the most powerful in this Magical Art, Zay, Mara Sydon, Walgabe, Rythin, Tapaganum, Tapanarim, Tasia and by that virtue wherewith the Sun and Moon were darkened before that terrible Day of the Lord (as in the Gospel) and shall be turned into Blood, and by the Head of my Prince, and by His Circle and Characters, and chiefly by this Seal firmly binding. ————

In Witness of which Guilty Person, I have signed this Obligation with mine own Seal He commanding Me, to which I always stick close. ————

This Bond or Obligation must be written on Virgin Parchment and laid before the Spirit Agares, then the Invocant may discourse with him thereon. He must take care that he asks or inquires nothing through Carelessness nor Curiosity, of the Spirit, but act as become a person who is cautious, prudent, and has a firmer reliance on the Dispenser of all good. by so doing, he will obtain his desires.

The Operator must be reminded once again, that every preparation connected with the Magic Art, should be made during the Increase of the Moon, About two or three days before the full, is said to be the best time, and should the Significator a Planet under which the Operata is born be in a fortunate Aspect with this Luminary, so much the better for him.

94

An Experiment of the Spirit BEALPHAROS

To Invocate Call upon and have converse with this Spirit Bealpharos these Rules must be observed

On Thursday and Friday in the Increase of the Moon repair to the place appointed for action and write on a piece of Virgin Parchment as hereafter followeth in the Copy, and write also on a Girdle or Thong of a Lion's, Harts, or Bucks skin as also hereafter followeth with directions thereunto annexed, and before you Enter the Circle to Invocate write ✠ Agla on the right hand, and on the left these Characters ♊ ℞ ☊ ℞, and when you enter the Circle, make the sign of the Cross thereon and say, *Per crucis hoc Signum Salvatur quodnes benignum,* then Invocate as followeth, being courageous and not at all dismayed. Before reciting the Invocating part of the Ceremony, the Invocate must rehearse with great earnestness the following words written on the Breast Plate viz *Homo Sacarus Muselomea Cherubosea.*

95

I Exorcise Conjure and Command thee Spirit **Bealpharos** by and in the great Name of the Omni-potent and Everlasting God **Jehovah Tetragrammaton Agla El On Adonay Saday** and by His Mighty Holy and inspeakable Majesty and Goodness, and by and in the Great Powerful and Ines-timable Names of the Only Begotten Son Jesus Christ our Lord, the Redeemer of the World, the second Essence in the Holy Trinity, sitting at the Right Hand of God the Father Maker of Heaven and Earth; Messiah Saviour and Emanuel, Alpha and Omega, and by the truest and most Especial Names of your Master, I do hereby Powerfully Exorcise, Command, and Constrain thee Spirit **Bealpharos** to Come and appear Visibly here before this Circle in fair and Human shape of Man or Womankind, and not terrible in any manner of ways, neither to us, nor any other person whatsoever this Circle being our Tuition, Fortress and Defence through the Merciful Goodness of our Heavenly God and loving Father, I Command thee to make haste and come away and show thyself Visibly, apparently, and peaceably to us here before this Circle immediately without tarrying or Delay, and with all humility and obedience, doing whatsoever I command and request and desire of you without any Illusion, Guile, or Deceit whatsoever, but faithfully, truly and certainly, to answer, fulfill, and perform such things as I shall require of you in the Name of Him who said and it was done, even the Most Great and Incomprehensible God the Creator of Heaven and Earth who shall come to Judge the Quick and the Dead ————————— and the World by Fire ———————————

————————— Amen —————————

PLATE. XXXV.

This Spirit, is somewhat Obstinate and pernicious by Nature, and is therefore as usually more slow and prolix in his appearance, wherefore it is requisite that the Ignorant should persevere herein with Constancy Fervency and Patience and not to despair at all, though the Experiment may prove more tedious than expected, for it will appear in a form similar as above with a fierce and angry Countenance, his coming is very swift on motion and sudden, therefore let the Exorcist be on his guard and rehearse the Invocation as often as he may well do according to his reason and prudence, shall direct him as at every half quarter of an Hour, whilst he is upon action and be very diligent to discover his apperance and motion that he

70

may immediately receive him, he will then assume a more mild natural appearance and become more tractable in a proper human form Bind him with the Bond of Spirits ⁜ to stay and abide so long peaceably and obediently with him in such form and shape as he shall appoint and approve until his demands and desires be fulfilled, which when done, License him to Depart, and on no account whatever neglect it, for any omission of this kind through Carlesness or neglect is attended with Danger, but if the Invocant comply with all the Forms, Ceremonies. &c he may have his Desires gratified in perfect Security and peace.

⁜ The Same form of the Bond of Spirits used in the Former Experiments may be used in this, only change the name of the Spirit.

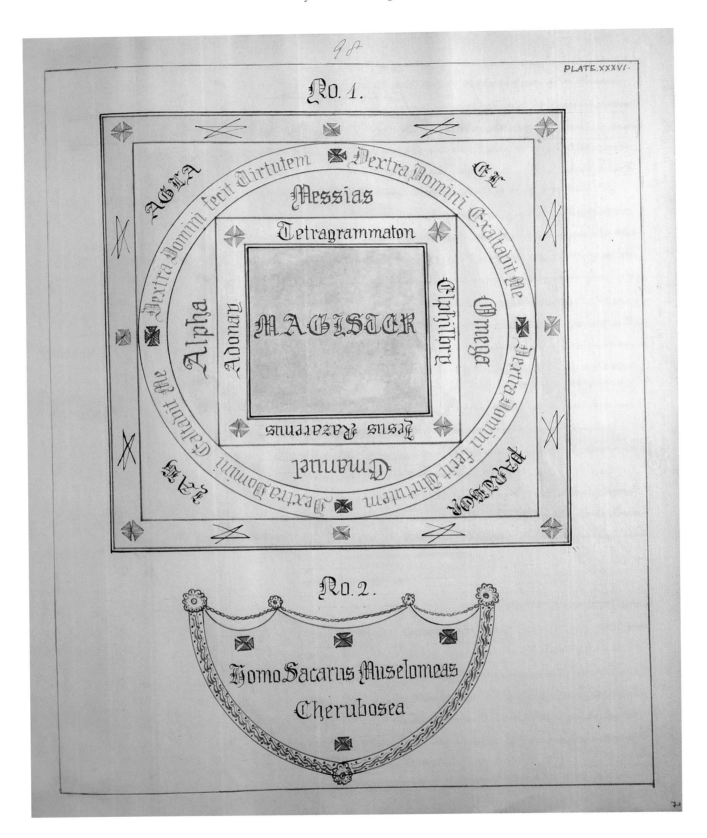

The Exorcist must observe, in this and all other Experiments of Aerial Spirits, that as soon as a Spirit is bound, and is perceived to become obedient and familiar as by Degrees he will, that the Questions and Demands be first concluded and resolved on and fairly written on Paper or Parchment, that you may have them ready to propose as occasion shall require. The Spirit resolveth many Dubious Questions and Enquiries, and is also a Carrier &c.

This that followeth, must be written on a Girdle made of Leather, or Parchment of the Skin of a Dragon, or Lion, or of a Hart and put on by the Invocant before he entereth the Circle, and so by him to be worn, so long as he is upon Action. ————

Elion Escherie Deus Eterney Elop Clemeris Deus Sanctus Sabaoth Deus Exercitum Adonay Deus Mirabilis Jao Hirax Anephepeton Deus Ineffabilis Saday Dominetos orfortissimus Aglaon Tetragrammaton Alpha et Omega. ————

The Circle, No 1. Wherein the Invocant standeth when he Invoketh or calleth upon the Spirit *Bealpharos* must be made according to the foregoing Model and in the maner as before taught in the former Experiments. It would not be amiss, if the Master Exorcist had a white Vestment or surplice on him, and white shoes, and one or two wise and discreet persons with him in the Circle, only shod with white shoes also.

The Figure, No 2. must be written on Virgin Parchment and then fixed fastened on a New piece of Linen Cloth, and worn on the Breast of the Invocant during the whole time he is upon Action, in the Circle. ————

———— Licence to Depart ❋ ————

I Conjure thee Spirit Bealpharos by all the Most Holy Names of God that as thou hast appeared at my Call or Invocation and hast assumed a quiet and peaceable form and answered unto my petition, fulfilled my desires, for which I give humble and hearty thanks unto Almighty God, that thou now Depart in peace unto thine order without any noise and terror whatsoever, and return unto me I Charge thee whensoever I shall thee call by thy Name, Order or Office without Delay or tract of time not molesting me, nor any other Creature God has made to his Glory now or hereafter. by the virtue of Our Lord Jesus Christ, the Father and the Holy Ghost go thy way in peace be between thee and Me In Nomine Patris + et Filii + et Spiritus Sancti + Amen.

❋ This License may be used in the former Experiments, changing the name of the Spirit.

72

Part 4. The Wheel of Wisdom

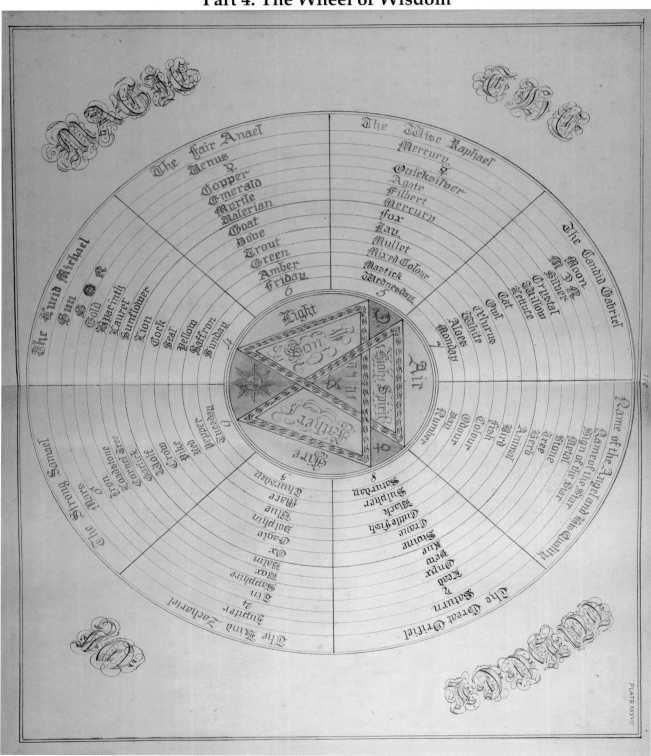

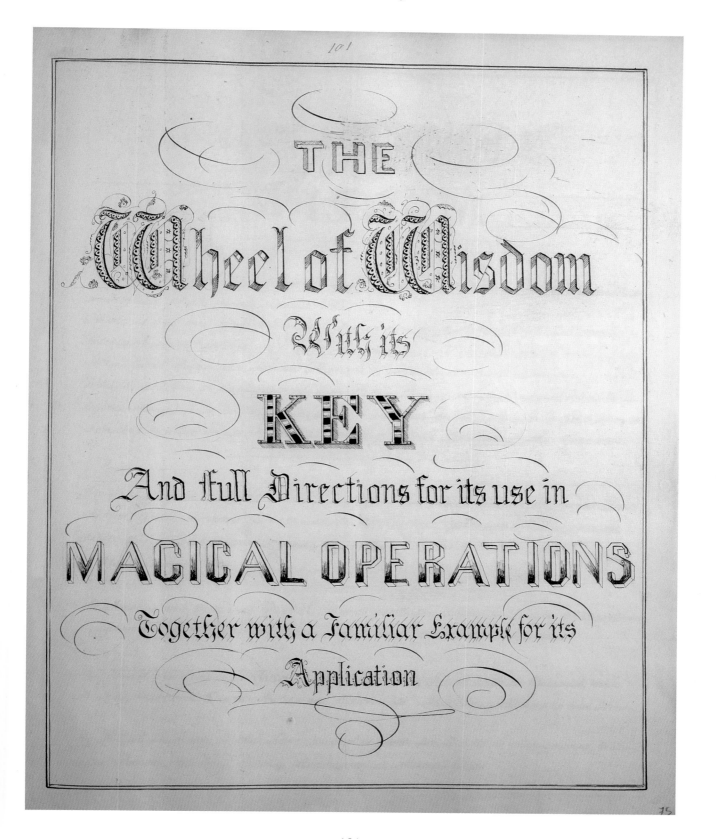

THE

Wheel of Wisdom

With its

KEY

And full Directions for its use in

MAGICAL OPERATIONS

Together with a Familiar Example for its

Application

102

The Key to the Wheel of

WISDOM

He that knoweth God, loves Him fervently, and believes in Him with an unfeigned faith, may peruse this.

There is but one God, a Trinity, Father Son and Holy Ghost, whosoever believeth it not, shall not have the Key, much less a right to peruse this.

After God, there are Seven Planets, or Intelligences, or Secondary causes which act in a proper order by themselves over all known and Intelligible things, and as far as they are conjured by the Name of God, they do wonders by His Consent, and according to the Design of the Operator.

The first Planet is **Saturn**, this is evil for it acts Destruction, Sickness, Death, Hatred, Grief, Sorrow, Melancholy, Afflictions, Gaols, Misfortunes, and Subtle things, but it proves good in Agriculture and Metallurgy, and tends to Edification.

The Second in Order is **Jupiter**, this is good, for it acts to Health, Riches, Honours, Judgement, Love of Princes, Greatness of Soul, Happiness and Rest.

The Third in Order is **Mars**, which is evil, for it acts to Discord, War, Snares, Violent Death, Boldness, Rashness, Military Honours and Terrors.

The Fourth in order is the **Sun**, and it is good, for it acts to Kingdoms, Empires, Power, Victory, Glory, Riches and Happiness.

The Fifth in order is *Venus*, and she acts Love between Men and Women, and all the Animal Friendships, Graces, Lucre, Music, Joy and Beauty.

The Sixth in Order is *Mercury*, this is good and evil mixed, for it produces Docility, Memory, Science, Eloquence, Wit Craftiness, and getting Riches by Fraud and Dexterity.

The Seventh, and the last in Order is the *Moon*, this good, for acts to Good, Journeys, True Dreams, Divinations, Invisibility, Theft, Illusions, Rain, Hail and Waters.

In the order of the Worlds all these Stars have a peculiar Spirit or Angel, a Name, a Sign, a Metal, a Precious Stone, a Tree, a Plant, a Beast, a Bird, a Fish, a Colour, an Odour, a Number, or a Measure, and there are like Degrees that one may ascend from the lowest to the Highest order as appears in the Wheel. From this Wheel are Drawn all the Operation of Secrets by the Wise and Faithful Yet here we have subjoined some particulars, which could not be so easily placed in it for the Unskilful to use that they may be wise.

There are many Secrets done from Similitude, from Sympathy, and from Antipathy, and which happen by an ordained Series of Nature agreeable to the Superior Wheel, for every thing has in itself something peculiar to itself, as for instance, the Dog may boast of his faithfulness, the Cock of his Crowing &c. for by that we know that these Animals naturally prevail by that which is their own property.

The same, is to be understood of the other Animals, whose nature I should here explain was it not necessary to Elucidate things, which in themselves are as clear as the Sun.

104

Full Directions for Magical Operations

The First Receipt is that at the Beginning of thine Operations in Magic, thou must call upon God with all thine Heart.

The Second is, that the operator should be continent and chaste three Days at least before he begins his Operation.

Thirdly, All operations must be done in a secret place, without Fear, Contempt, or Derision.

Fourthly. The Operator must be pure and cleansed, and must have made a proper Expiation having washed himself with the water of a pure fountain as many times as answer to the Number of the Star which ruleth at the Operation.

Fifthly. The Operator must be silent, for if he knoweth not how to keep his tongue, all his labour will be in vain, and the effect will not answer.

Sixthly. The Operator must have some Vessels for each Star, signed with the sign of the star, and likewise of colours and odours belonging to all the Stars, which must be kept in readiness in a pure clean place.

Seventhly. All things that are to be used in Magical Operations must be virginal, that is to say quite new, having never been employed before to any use whatever, such as Paper, or Parchment, the Pen and Ink, the colours, the Needles, Thread, Cloth, and all other things necessary; and those things must be of the Nature of the Star which ruleth the Operation, they must not be touched nor seen by a Woman that is out of order, for they would immediately lose their Virtue.

Eighthly. All things must be written on Virgin Parchment in an Angular figure, and the Angles of the Figure must answer to the

Number of the Star.

Ninthly. The Angular figure, the forms, the days, the Mixture, and all such like things must answer perfectly well in proportion to the Number, Weight and Measure of the Star.

Tenthly. If any part of an Animal is to be used, you must take that part from the Animal, while it is yet living or breathing.

Eleventhly. If fire is to be employed, you must light it with such wood as will suit your Operation, and the ashes thereof must be buried.

Twelfthly. All Operations must be done in their proper day and Hour, as for Example, if you work in Venerial, or belonging to Venus, it must be done in the first Astronomical Hour of the Sun Rising on a Friday and so of the rest. If the Hour is not sufficient for you to do the whole work in, You must take another, such Hour of Venus as Astronomy teaches. For many reasons we will not relate the Evils caused by Saturn or Mars, but shall pass to the Secrets of Venus, which are soft and harmless, we will give an Example therefrom for all Operations, for instance we will take LOVE, wishing to make a person love me, this may be done by Rings, Images, Touching, Writings, Words, Dreams, Philters, which and many other ways, may be easily wrought by the help of our Wheel.

Of all these Methods, let us use the Philter, and we will make a Powder, which if any one Drink to another, shall be loved by them to the End of their Lives.

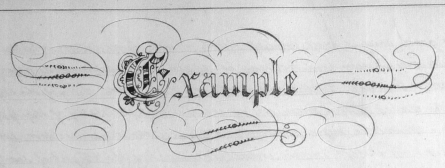

Go to the Wheel and see what flying Animal belongs to Venus. You will find the Dove take therefore, if for a Man a Pigeon, if for a Woman a Dove, saying this Prayer.

In the Name of God the Father. God the Son. and God the Holy Ghost whom I most efficaciously call to my help that through his consent I may bring my Operations to a happy Issue to the Glory of His Name. Amen.

Be favourable to us O thou fair Angel of God **Anael** Prince of Love, be propitious to my Vows that through thy Mediation I may hopefully fulfill my Desires by Christ Jesus Our Lord **Amen.**

Go afterwards into a Secret place, and with a Copper or Brass Knife open the Breast of the Pigeon or Dove take out the heart, and while yet panting, burn it and reduce it to a powder, but gather the running blood in a proper Vessel. then gather some Valerian with the root, draw the Juice out of the Leaves, burn the root into Ashes, mix these Ashes with the Juice. adding to it a little of the Powder of Amber, moisten it with the Juice of Myrtle, and put all in a Vessel to dry. Afterwards reduce again the whole to Powder, take a Copper or Brass Needle, and with it prick your Right Hand to Draw some drops of Blood, at the Mount of Venus, saying six times the Name of Anael, with these drops of Blood moisten your powder, adding also a little of your Flesh, or if you choose not to use that, the Hippomanes ※

※ Hippomanes, is a piece of Flesh on the head of a Colt newly foaled, which the Mare bites off.

will be as good, and it will Operate with more Sacredness; make a Lump and dry it up, and reduce it again to Powder take afterwards a little Yellow Amber, and a few of the feathers of the Belly of the Pigeon or Dove, of the leaves of the Valerian of the Hairs of the Belly of the Goat, put all in a Vessel to mix with the Blood of the Pigeon or Dove, which has been kept by itself, make small Lozenges, of the Weight of six grains make afterwards a fire with Myrtle, and put over the fire one of these Lozenges, make a Fumigation with the Powder, which you will have put into a Cylinder of a Green colour, and which is always to be preferred, a Copper or Brass Vessel, whilst making the Fumigation you must say, Hail **Anael** thou who rejoicest at these smells come to receive them, be favourable and kind unto me Vouchsafe to Bless this Powder and to Consecrate it so that it may have Power to Bind all Women and to make them to Love Me by Christ Jesus Our Lord. **Amen**. Afterwards burn up the Body of the Pigeon, and all that remains. Gather all the Ashes in a Vessel and bury it Six feet deep in the Earth. Then this Powder is called the Universal matter, but still, it has no power whilst it wants the form and the Spirit, but now I am going to teach you the way of Animation and formation of the World. Although indeed, it is with some reluctancy in my mind to reveal so Sublime a Secret, Yet I have let my good-will towards Mankind be the Conqueror.

Take Virginal Parchment of a Goat and Draw on it Geometrically in Green Colours with the Pen of a Pigeon, an Hexagon Figure. in which write with your own Blood your Name and that of your Beloved. Join them together by the Name Anael between them as shown in the Figure.

108

PLATE. XXXVIII.

Example

Edwin Anael Emma

Burn afterwards the Figure, reduce it to Ashes, mix them with an equal quantity of the Universal Powder, so that they may make up the weight of Six Grains, and Drink that to your Beloved. This is Great Secret, for by it many have gained not only the Affections of Human Creatures, but also of Wild Beasts.

The Operator must be reminded, that the more earnest and faithful he is in his Operations (particular in his Invocation of the Spirit who will assuredly render the Assistance required) the more will be the certainty of his success. This Fair and Beautiful Angel, is said to be more easily Invocated either Visibly or Invisibly than any of the other Planetary Angels.   With this only, Be thou Content O Reader, for if thou art wise in this alone, thou mayest understand all the Rest. Carefully keep this from Vulgar Eyes.   Farewell.

Finis

Part 5. A Secret and Complete Book of Magic Science

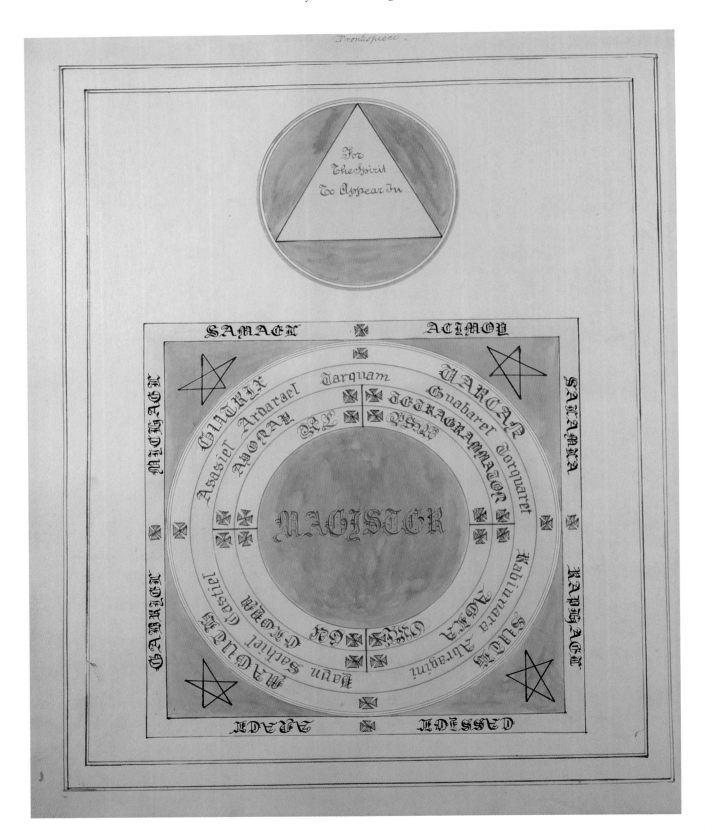

Secret And

COMPLETE BOOK

OF

MAGIC SCIENCE

Containing the Method of Constraining Spirits
To Visible Appearance. The Consecrations of
Lamens, Pentacles and the Seals and Characters of the

PLANETARY ANGELS

With a Form of a Bond of Spirits

1573.

81

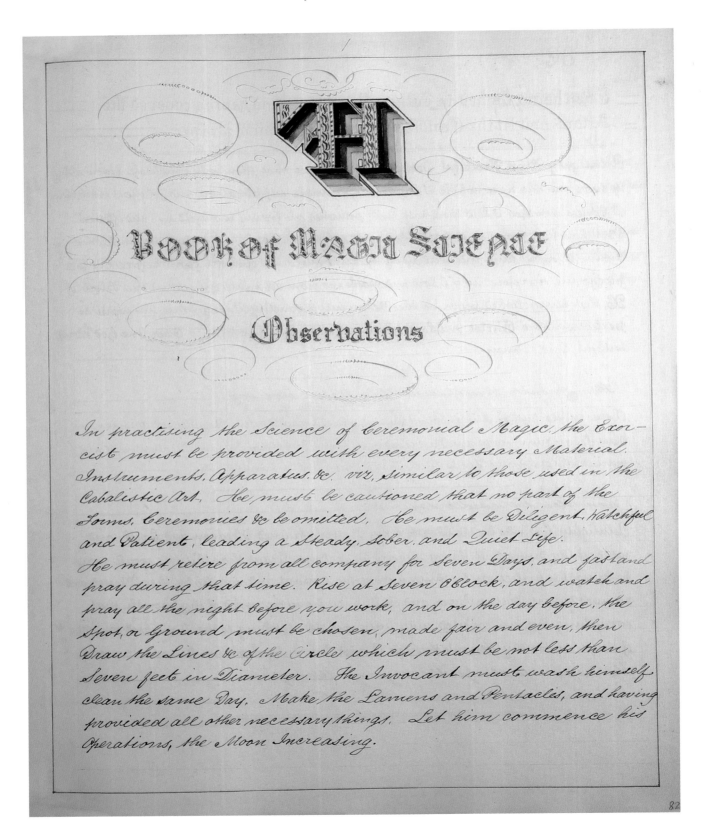

Book of Magic Science

Observations

In practising the Science of Ceremonial Magic, the Exorcist must be provided with every necessary Material. Instruments. Apparatus. &c. viz, similar to those used in the Cabalistic Art. He must be cautioned, that no part of the Forms. Ceremonies &c be omitted, He must be Diligent. Watchful and Patient, leading a Steady, Sober, and Quiet Life.

He must retire from all company for Seven Days, and fast and pray during that time. Rise at Seven O'Clock, and watch and pray all the night before you work, and on the day before. the Spot, or Ground must be chosen, made fair and even, then Draw the Lines &c of the Circle which must be not less than Seven feet in Diameter. The Invocant must wash himself clean the same Day. Make the Lamens and Pentacles, and having provided all other necessary things. Let him commence his Operations, the Moon Increasing.

2

== Then being clothed in White Vestments, and having covered the ==
= Altars and lit the Candles. Say the following Prayer. =

Almighty Most Merciful Father I Beseech thee that thou wilt vouchsafe favourably
to hear me this time while I make my humble supplication and prayers unto thee.
I Confess unto thee O Lord thou hast justly punished me for my manifold sins and offences.
But thou hast promised at what time soever a sinner repent him of his sins and wickedness
thou wilt forgive him and turn away the remembrance of them from before thy face,
purge me therefore now O Lord and wash me from all mine offences in the Blood of
X, that being clothed pure in the Vestments of Sanctity I may bring this work to
perfection thro' Christ Our Lord who livest and reignest with thee Ever One God World
without End. Amen. _____

_____

Then sprinkle thyself with Holy Water and say. _____

Asperges me hysopo et mandabor Lavabis me et supra Nivens Decalbabor Miscam me
Deus Secundum magnum Misercordinm tuam Te C*na Inuam Decalbabor Gloria
patri et Filii et Spiritus Sancto Sicet Erat in primapo et Eximus. _____

_____

Then Bless the Girdle saying, _____

Almighty God who by the breath of thy Nostrils framed Heaven and Earth, and
wonderfully disposed all things therein in six Days: Grant that this my work may
be brought to perfection by thine unworthy servant and may be by thee Blessed and
received divine Virtue, Power, and Influence from the word of thy mouth, that
everything therein counted may fully operate according to the hope and confidence
of thine unworthy servant through Christ Our Only Saviour. Amen. _____
Then Sprinkle the Girdle saying. Asperges &c. _____

_____

PLATE.1.

Blessing of the Lights

I Bless thee in the name of the Father and of the Son and of the Holy Ghost. O Holy, Holy, Holy, Lord God, Heaven and Earth are full of thy Glory, before whose face there is a bright shining light for ever. Bless now O Lord I beseech thee, these creatures of Light which thou hast given for the kindly use of Man, that by thee they being sanctified, may not be put out or Extinguished by the Malice, Power, or Filthy Darkness of Satan, but may shine forth brightly and lend their Assistance to this Holy Work thro' Christ Our Lord, Amen. *(Then say,)* I Bless thee in the Name of the Father and of the Son and of the Holy Ghost.

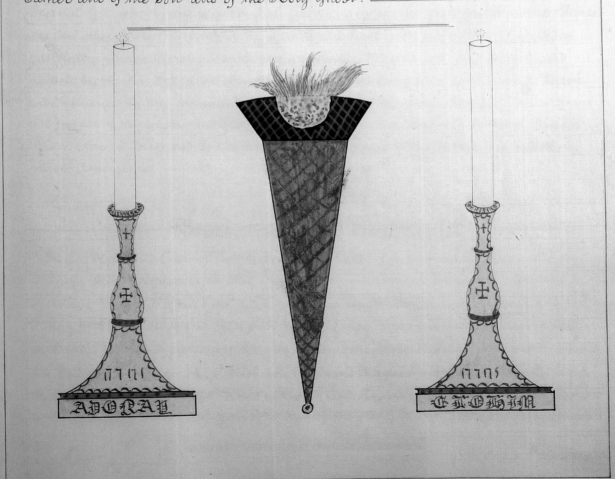

4

Benediction of the Lamen.

O thou God of my Salvation I call upon thee by the Mysteries of all thy most Holy and Glorious Names I Worship Adore and Beseech thee by thy Mighty Names Tetragrammaton Saday that thou wilt be seen in the Power and force of these thy Holy Names so written filling them with Divine Virtue and Influence through X Our Lord. Amen.

5

Consecration of the Girdle

O Great God of Strength who art greatly to be feared. Bless O Lord this Instrument. that it may be a terror unto the Enemy and therewith I may overcome all Phantasms and Oppositions of the Devil through thy Influence and help of thy Holy and Mighty Names On El Agla Tetragrammaton and in the Cross of Christ Our only Lord.
Amen.

Benediction of the Pentacles

Eternal God who by thy wisdom hast given and appointed great power in the Characters and other Holy Writings of thy Spirits and hast given unto that useth them faithfully. power thereby to work many things. Bless these O Lord framed and written by the hand of thine unworthy Servant. that being filled with divine Virtue and Influence by thy command O Most Holy God. they may show forth their Virtue and power to thy praise and Glory through Christ Our Lord and Saviour. Amen. Then Say, I Bless and Consecrate thee in the Name of the Father Son and Holy Ghost. Asperges &c.

Benediction of the Vestments

O Blessed Holy and Eternal Lord God who art the God of purity and delighteth that thy Servants should appear before thee in clear pure and undefiled Vestments. Grant O Lord that these Vestments of this Outer Order may be cleansed. Blessed and Consecrated by thee I may put them on, being therewith clothed. I may appear whiter than snow, both in Soul and Body in thy presence this Day in an through the Merits. Death and Passion of Our Only Lord and Saviour Christ who liveth and Reigneth with thee in the Unity of the Holy Spirit Ever one God World without End Amen. Bless thee. Purge thee in the Name of the Father. and of the Son and of the Holy Ghost.

6

The Benediction of the Ground

Per hoc crucis signum fugiat procul Omne Maligna Et per Idem Signum Salvator quoque benignum Emicat Deus et dispectum inimicus Ejus Omnes Spiritus laudet Dominum Molans habent et prophetas. ———————

Depart from me all ye workers of Iniquity. ————————————

Then say the prayer of Solomon (I Kings Chap VIII – 22.) ——— Then say. —

Bless O Lord. I beseech thee this Ground and drive away all evil and wickedness far from this place. Sanctify and make it become meet and convenient for thy Servant to finish and bring to pass therein all my Desires through Our Lord and Saviour. Amen. Be thou Blessed, Purified, and Consecrated, in the Name of the Father, and of the Son, and of the Holy Ghost. Asperges &c.

Benediction of the Perfumes

The God of Abraham, The God of Isaac, The God of Jacob, Bless here the Creatures of these kinds that they may fill up the power of their Odours so that neither Enemy nor any false Imagination may be able to enter into them through Our Lord God to whom be honour and Glory both now and henceforth Amen. ————————————

————————— (Sprinkle them saying Asperges &c.) —————————

Exorcism of the Fire &c.

I Exorcise thee O thou Creature of Fire by Him by whom all things are made that forthwith thou cast away every Phantasm from thee that it shall not be able to do any hurt in anything. Bless O Lord this Creature of Fire Sanctify it that it may be Blessed to set forth the praise of thy Holy Name through the virtue and Defence of our Lord **Christ. Amen.**

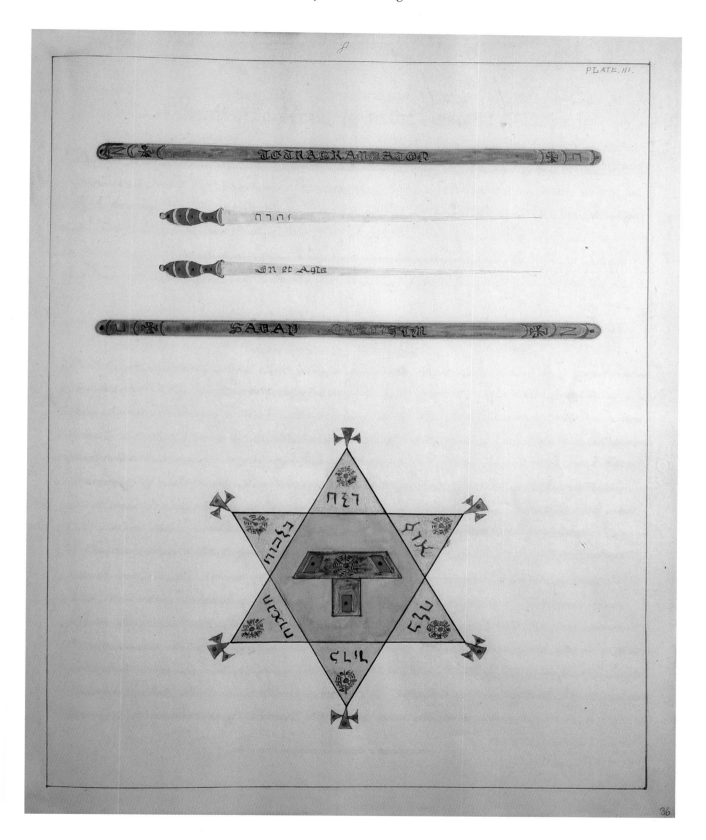

9

Oration on putting on the Uesture

Ancor, Amacor, Anides, Theadanias Anitor by the Merits of thy Angels O Lord I will put on the Garment of Salvation that this which I desire I may bring to effect through the Merits Death and Passion of our Lord **Christ** who liveth and reigneth Ever One God World without End Amen.

Then commence your Work by saying, kneeling, the following

Prayer

O Holy, Holy, Holy, Lord God from whom all Holy desires and good works do proceed I beg thou wilt be merciful unto me at this time, Granting, that I may become a true Magician and Contemplator of thy wondrous works in the Name of the Father, Son, and Holy Ghost, and being inspired and assisted with thy Holy Spirit I may set forth his praise and Glory Knowing of a Certain, I can perform or do nothing but what is given unto me from above, therefore, in all my Acts, and at all times, I will call upon thy most Holy Name for thine help and assistance.

I Beseech thee O Lord God that thou wilt purge me and wash me and clean me in the Blood of our Saviour from all my sins and frailties. And that thou wilt henceforward Vouchsafe to keep and defend me from Pride, Lust, Lying, Swearing, Blasphemy, Drunkeness, Sloth, Covetousness, Evil Communications, and all deadly sins and offences, profaneness and Spiritual wickedness, But that I may lead a Godly, Sober, Constant, Holy, Pure, and Undefiled Life, walking uprightly in thy sight through the Merits of Christ our Lord and Saviour, Amen.

87

Omnipotent and Eternal Lord God, who sittest in Heaven and dost from thence behold all the Dwellers upon Earth, Most mercifully I beseech thee to hear and answer the petitions of thine Unworthy servant, which I shall make unto thee through Christ our Lord who liveth and reigneth with thee in the Unity of the Holy Spirit Ever one God World without end, Amen.

Send down O Lord the Spirit of thy Grace upon us, Enabling us to bring to pass what I now desire. Give me strength and courage to call thy Spirits from their several coasts that they may Commune with me, and truly fulfill my Desires in all things. O Lord put fear far from me, Give me an abundance of thy Grace and faith whereby all things are made possible unto man, put Envy and wicked Phantasms far from my mind and grant me true Zeal, Favour, and an Intentive Spirit of Prayer, that I may offer up a wellpleasing Sacrifice unto thee.

I Beseech thee O Holy Father, that thou wilt purge me from all uncleanness, both of Flesh and Spirit, that neither the Deceiver, nor any of his Spirits may have power to hurt me in Soul or Body, or any way hinder the Accomplishment of my Desires, or hurt, or terrify, or affright me in any manner of way, but let me use thy Ministering Spirits and Angels O Lord so as I may thereby have wisdom and knowledge. Grant O Most Merciful God that this which I desire may come to Effect, and that whichsoever of thine Angels I shall call, may speedily attend to the words and Conjura-tions of my mouth, and come unto me in the peace of the Lord Christ, Amen.

Lord, I believe help my unbelief, in thee alone is fulness of all things &c. from thee proceedeth Every good Gift, for thou art Alpha and Omega, to to thee therefore be ascribed, as is rightly due, all Honour and Glory.

O Blessed and Most Merciful God, who art full of Pity and Compassion,

11

thou hast promised at what time soever a sinner doth repent him of his sins, from the bottom of his heart, thou wilt turn away the remembrance of them from before thy face. I confess unto thee O Father, most humbly and sorrowfully, that I was born, and hath lived in iniquity and transgression, ever since I came forth from my mother's womb. I have most justly merited thine indignation. But do thou O Lord forgive me in the Blood of our Lord Christ, and grant that for the future I may walk in Newness of Life, and Holiness of Conversation, in and through Our only Lord and Saviour Jesus Christ. Amen.

O Lord, I beseech thou wilt hear and answer in the Wounds of Our Blessed Saviour as He Himself hath taught us, saying, Our Father, which art in Heaven &c, &c.

In the Name of Our Lord Jesus Christ, the Father and the Holy Ghost, the Holy Trinity, and Unspeakable Unity, I Call upon thee that thou mayest be my Salvation and Defence, and the Protector of my Body and Soul, and of all my Goods, through the Virtue of thy Holy Cross, and through the Virtue of thy Passion, I Beseech thee O Lord, Jesus Christ that thou wilt Bless and Sanctify these Consecrations and Benedictions which I shall utter with my mouth, and offer up and make in thy Most Holy Name, and that thou wilt give me thy Divine Virtue and Strength, that which of thy Angels or Ministering Spirits I shall Invoke, or Conjure, may readily appear unto, and attend to the words and Conjurations of my mouth. Grant this O Lord, for the Merits of this thy Holy Name, Amen.

Holy, Holy, Lord God of Sabaoth, who shall come to Judge the Quick and the Dead, thou art Alpha and Omega, First and Last, King of Kings and Lord of Lords, Ith Aglanbroth, El Abiel Anathiel Kel Messias Escherie Athanatos Imas. By these thy Holy Names, by all others,

88

12.

I do call upon thee and beseech thee O Lord Christ. By thy Nativity and Baptism, By thy Cross and Passion, By thy Precious Death and Burial. By thy Glorious Resurrection and Ascension, By the coming of the Holy Ghost, By the Bitterness of thy Soul when it departed from the Body, By thine Angels, Archangels Prophets and Patriarchs, and by all Sacraments which are made in thine honour. I do worship and beseech thee to accept these prayers, conjurations and words of my mouth which I shall utter and use, and that being strengthened, Sanctified and Blessed by the power of thy Holy Spirit, they may by thy Holy Command be Efficacious. And that such of thy Spirits, or Angels, as I shall Invoke may thereunto attend [and readily appear forthwith unto me from their several Coasts] according to the words by one to be pronounced, and then truly fulfill and satisfy all my re- quests in the Name of the Father, and of the Son, and of the Holy Ghost, Amen.

I Beseech thee by thy Humility and Grace. I Implore thee O Holy Adonay Vegadona, and by all thy Holy Names, and by all thine Angels, Archangels, Powers, Dominations and Virtues, and by thy Names with which Solomon did Bind the Devils and shut them up Elbrack Elion Egla Goth Joth Nabrock, and by all thy Holy Names which are written in this Book, and by the Virtue of them all, that thou Enable me to Congregate all thy Spirits that they may give me true Answers to all my Demands, and that I receive satisfaction in all my requests without hurt in Body Soul or Goods, through Our Lord Jesus Christ who liveth and reigneth with thee in the Unity of the Holy Spirit Ever one God World without End, Amen.

O Father Omnipotent, O Wise Son, O Holy Ghost the Comforter, and Searcher of all hearts, O Ye three persons in one Godhead in Substance, who didst spare Adam and Eve in their sins, And O thou Lord who died for their sins a most filthy, and ignominious Death, testifying it upon the Cross. O thou Most Merciful God, when I fly unto thee and beseech thee by all the means I can, By these the Holy Names of thy Holy Son, Alpha et Omega, and all other his Names. Grant me thy Virtue and Power, that what I now desire, I may be able to bring to pass through thy assistance of thy Holy Angels that which of thy Spirits soever I do call upon in the Name of the Father, and of the Son, and of the Holy Ghost, may forthwith come unto me, talk and converse, so that I may plainly understand and audibly hear them speak unto me, and that I may plainly understand the words which they shall utter, through the Virtue and Merits of Our Lord Jesus Christ thy Son who liveth and reigneth with thee in the Unity of the Holy Ghost Ever one God World without end, Amen.

O Great and Eternal Virtue of the Highest which through disposition these being called to Judgment Vaichron Tetragrammaton Kioram Aoym Messias Sother Emanuel Adonay. I worship thee, I invocate thee, I implore thee with all the strength of my mind that by thee my present prayers and conjurations may be Hallowed, and that all the Angels and Spirits which I call from their several Regions and Places, by and in the Virtue of thy several Glorious, Mysterious, Incomprehensible Unspeakable Names may come unto me forthwith and fulfill my will and requests in all things, In the Name of the Father, and of the Son, and of the Holy Ghost.
Fiat. Fiat. Fiat. Amen. Amen. Amen.

In the Name of the Most Glorious God of Paradise of Heaven, and of Earth, of the Seas, and of the Infernals by thine Omnipotent help, May I perform this work who liveth and reigneth, Ever One God World without End, Amen. O Most Strong and Almighty God, without beginning or ending by thy Clemency and knowledge, I desire that my Questions, Work, and Labour may be fulfilled and truly accomplished through thy worthiness Good Lord, Amen.
O Holy, Patient and Merciful God the Lord of all Wisdom, Clear and Just I most heartily desire thy Clemency and Mercy, Holiness and Justness to fulfill and perform this my Will and Work, through thy worthiness

14

and blessed Power who livest and reignest Ever one God World without end, Amen.

O Most Merciful Father, have mercy upon me and defend me from all Wicked, Evil, and Deceitful Spirits, restrain their power Good Lord from touching, hurting, terrifying, or affrighting me in Body and Soul for thy great Mercy's sake. I beg, implore, and beseech thee O my God and rock of my Salvation, my stay and my Guide. But that I beg thy Divine Nature will please and assist that I may become a Contemplator of thy Glorious Works, and may be illustrated with all Divine Wisdom and Knowledge, that thereby, I may bring Honour and Glory to thy Most Blessed Name. Amen.

In Nomine **Orphaniel** Angelo Magno precioso et honorato, Vene in pace.

In Nomine **Zebul** Angelo Majori atque forti et potento, Vene in pace.

In Nomine **Dagiel** Angelo magno principe forte atque potenti, Vene in pace.

In Nomine **Salamia** Angelo potentissima magni et honorato, Vene in pace.

In Nomine **Arimoy** Angelo Magniforti potentis et honorato, Vene in pace.

In Nomine Pastoris Angelis Sancti et Magni, Vene in pace.

In Nomine Popellus Angeli Magni et potentis et principis, Vene in pace.

Samae Salamana Belmai Geragam Raamansin Eschoire Mirel Egnephas Iosamm Sabach Harm-Robe Iroha Sother Ramar Seirol Lemare Pherain Ariaphin Gesegon Amen Amen Amen.

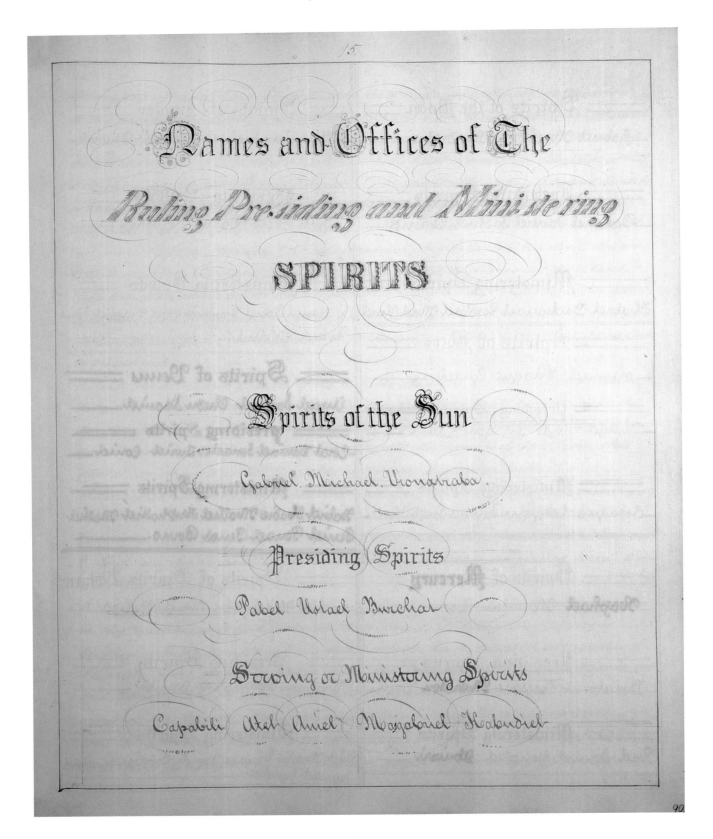

Names and Offices of The
Ruling, Presiding and Ministering
SPIRITS

Spirits of the Sun

Gabriel. Michael. Vionatraba.

Presiding Spirits

Pabel Ustael Burchat

Serving or Ministering Spirits

Capabili Atel Aniel Magabriel Kabudiel

16

Spirits of the Moon

— Gabriel Michael Madiel —

Presiding Spirits

— Deanuel Tamael Sachiel Zaniel —

Ministering Spirits

Habiel Bachanael Corabiel Mael Moael

Spirits of Mars

— Samael Friague Gmael —

Presiding Spirits

— Damael Calzas Arragon Lama —

Ministering Spirits

— Astagna Lobquin Soucas Sayel Israel —

Spirits of Mercury

— Raphael Makhlar Tarmiel —

Presiding Spirits

— Baraborat Teresene Mistraton Thiel —

Ministering Spirits

Rael Serabel Venabel Abuiori

Spirits of Jupiter

— Zadkiel Sachiel Cassiel Asasiel —

Presiding Spirits

— Iuih Rex Maguth Guriz —

Ministering Spirits

Curaniel Pabiel Hamun Osael Vianiel Iamel
Jenbiel Milliel

Spirits of Venus

Anael Sachiel Cheow Suaniel

Presiding Spirits

— Corat Camael Senacier Iuriel Coriel —

Ministering Spirits

Babiel Kadie Maltiel Huphaltiel Malhel
Perriel Penael Penat Porro

Spirits of Spirits Saturn

— Cassiel Machatan Uriel Baliser —

Presiding Spirits

— Maymon Abumalith Assaibr —

Ministering Spirits

Bilet Misolas Caimay Ismoli Potron Suajmus
Kunabel Cynabal

127

17

Omnipotent and Eternal God who hast ordained the whole Creation
for thy praise and Glory, and for the Salvation of Man, I earnestly Beseech
that thou wouldst send one of thy Spirits of the order of Jupiter, one of
the Messengers of Zadkiel whom thou hast appointed governor of thy
Firmament at this present time most faithfully, willingly and readily
to shew me these things which I shall ask, Command, or require of Him,
and truly Execute my desires, nevertheless, O Most Holy God, thy will, and
not mine be done, through Christ thine only begotten Son our Lord, Amen.
O Lord we place our hope is in thee. Doubt not the Righteousness of our heart,
Thou lovest the dust, hatest the wicked, be our protector, Thou art our Strength
and thou alone can help us, strengthen us with thy Divine Power, we have
nothing to fear from Evil Spirits, be in the midst of our hearts and we cannot
be frightened.
O Lord, the Almighty Creator of the Air, the Heaven, the Earth and the Water,
deign to be with me in this Circle, we are here with humility by the
Inspiration of an Eternal Goodness, of a Divine prosperity and abun-
-dant charity, may the adverse Spirits be removed far from this
place, and may the Angels of peace succour us.
O Lord, Condescend to Extend over us thy Infinite Mercy, and may
these thy Holy Names be ever blessed, and protect our operations, this
Celestial and Mysterious Circle incloses thy Hallowed Names.
O Lord our hope and sustainer, have mercy upon us and En-
-able us to bring our Operations to perfection, Amen.
O Lord hearken unto us, let our Exclammations reach even unto thy Greatness O God, who hast reigned throughout all ages, who
by thine Infinite Mercy and Wisdom, hast created every-thing
Visible and Invisible, we praise thee, we blesst thee, we adore thee,
and Glorify thee for ever. Deign to be propitious unto us, we are the
work of thy hands, deliver us from the night of Ignorance,
which conceals thee from the Unjust who deserve not thy
blessing, Enlighten our hearts, with a portion of wisdom,

18

take away from our sense all wicked and criminal desires, be favour-
-able unto us by thy power and Greatness, and by thy Terrible and
Ineffable Name which is Saday at which all tremble in the Heavens,
in the Air, in the Earth, in the Abyss of waters. Cause that the
Spirits of whom we have need may come and shew themselves to us
with mildness, that they may be obedient and shew unto us that which
we desire. Amen.

INVOCATION

Spirits whose Assistance I require. behold the Sign and the very Hallowed
Names of God, full of power who with a breath is able to bow everything.
Tremble and Obey the power of this our Pentacle, Go out of your hidden Caves
and dark places Cease your hurtful Occupations to the unhappy Mortals
whom without ceasing you torment. Come into this peace where the
Divine Goodness has assembled us, be attentive to our Orders and known
to our just Demands. believe not that your Resistance will cause us to
abandon our Operations, nothing can dispense with your obeying us,
We Command you by the Mysterious Names. Elohe Agla Elohim
Adonay Gibor. Amen.
I call upon thee Zadkiel in the Name of the Father, and of the Son,
and of the Holy Ghost, Blessed Trinity. Unspeakable Unity.
I Invoke and Intreat thee Zadkiel in this hour to attend to the words
and Conjurations which I shall use this Day by the Holy Names of God
Elohe El Elohim Elion Zebaoth Escherie Iah Adonay Tetragrammaton.
I Conjure. thee, I Exorcise thee thou Spirit Zadkiel by these Holy Names
Hagios O Theos Iscyros Athanatos Paracletus Agla On Alpha et Omega Ioth Aglanbroth

19

Abiel Anakiel Tetragrammaton ————————————

הוהי ————————————

and by all other Great and Glorious, Holy and Unspeakable Names, the Mysterious
Mighty, Powerful, Incomprehensible Names of God that you attend unto the words
of my mouth, and send unto me Pabiel, or other of your Ministering
serving Spirits who may shew me such things as I shall demand of him
in the Name of the Father, and of the Son, and of the Holy Ghost, Amen.
I Intreat the Pabiel by the whole Spirit of Heaven, Seraphim Cherubim,
Thrones, Dominations, Witness, Powers, Principalities Archangels, Angels, by the
Holy Great and Glorious Angels Ophaniel, Tetra, Dagiel, Salimia, Acimoy,
pastor poti, that thou come forthwith readily shew thyself, that we may
see you, and audibly hear you speak unto us, and fulfill our Desires, and
by your Star which is Jupiter, and by all the Constellations of Heaven,
and by whatsoever thou obeyest, and by thy Character which thou has given,
proposed, and confirmed, that you attend unto me according to the Prayers
and Petitions which I have made unto Almighty God. And that, thou
forthwith sendest unto me one of thy Ministering Spirits, who may
willingly, truly and faithfully fulfill all my Desires, and that thou
commandest him to appear unto me in the form of a Beautiful
Angel, Gently Courteously, Affable and Meekly, entering into Communica-
-tion with me, and that he neither permitting any Evil Spirit to approach
in any sort of way to hurt terrify or affright me, nor deceiving me in any
wise. Through the Virtue of our Lord and Saviour Jesus Christ in
whose Name I attend, wait for, and expect thy Appearance. ————

———————————— Fiat Fiat Fiat ————————————
———————————— Amen, Amen, Amen, ————————————

After repeating this powerful Invocation earnestly and with great faith and Devotion
the Spirit will be compelled to appear receive him courteously, Bind him with
the Bond of Spirits then the Invocant need not fear, but he must take care that he asks nothing but
what is lawful and right. His Appearance is generally attended with great
Splendour.

20.

Interrogatories

Comest thou in peace, in the Name of the Father, Son, and Holy Ghost?

Yes

Thou art Welcome Noble Spirit, what is thy Name?

Yes

I have called thee in the Name of Jesus of Nazareth at whose Name Every knee doth bow both, in Heaven, Earth, and Hell, and every tongue shall confess there is no Name like unto the Name of Jesus who hath given power unto Man to bind and to loose all things in his most Holy Name, Yea even unto those that trust in his Salvation. Art thou the Messenger of Zadkiel?

Yes.

Wilt thou Confirm thyself unto me at this time and henceforth reveal all things unto me that I shall desire to know, and teach me how I may, Increase in Wisdom and Knowledge and shew unto me all the Secrets of the Magic Art, and of all Liberal Sciences, that I may thereby set forth the Glory of Almighty God.?

Yes

Then I pray thee give and Confirm thy Character unto me whereby I may call at all times, and also swear unto me this Oath, and I will Religiously keep my Vow and Covenant unto Almighty God and will courteously receive thee at all times where thou dost appear unto me.

22

Form of a Bond of Spirits

I Pabiel, Ministering Spirit and Messenger of the Presiding and Ruling Spirit of Jupiter, appointed thereunto by the Creator of all, Visibly and Invisible do swear, promise, and plight my faith, and unto thee in the presence, and before the Great יהוה and the whole Company and Host of Heaven, and by all the Holy Names of God do swear and bind myself unto thee by all the contents of God's sacred Writ, by the Incarnation, Sufferings, Passion and Death, By the Resurrection and Glorious Ascension of Our Lord and Saviour Jesus Christ, By all the Holy Sacraments, By the Mercy of God, By the Glory and Joys of Heaven, By the Forgiveness of Sin, and hope of Eternal Salvation, By the Great Day of Doom, By all Angels, Archangels, Seraphim, Cherubim, Dominations, Thrones, Principalities, Powers and Virtues, and all other be blessed and Glorious Company of Heaven, By all the Constellations of Heaven, and by all the Several Powers and Virtues above rehearsed and by whatsoever Else is Holy or binding through, Do I swear and promise and Vow unto thee that I will Come, appear, and haste unto thee, and at all times and places, and in all Hours, Minutes and Days, from this time forward unto thy life's end, Wheresoever thou shalt Call me by my Name, or by my Office, and I will come unto thee in what form thou shalt Desire, either Visibly or Invisibly, and will answer all thy Desires, and give testimony thereof, and let all the powers of Heaven witness it. I have hereunto Subscribed my Hand and Confirm my Seal and Character unto thee. Amen.

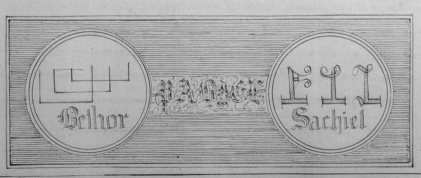

Bethor   Sachiel

94

23

The aforesaid Bond of Spirits, together with the Seal and Character of the Planetary Angel must be written on Virgin Parchment and laid before the Spirit when he appears; at that time The Invocant must not lose confidence but be patient, firm bold and persevering and as aforesaid take care that he requires nothing of the Spirit but with a view to the Glory of God, and the well being of his fellow creatures. Having obtained his Desires of the Spirit, The Invocant may License him to Depart in the following manner. ————————

Licence to Depart

Forasmuch as thou comest in peace and quietness, and hast answered unto my Petition, I give humble and hearty thanks unto Almighty God in whose name I called thee and thou camest, and now thou mayest Depart in peace unto thine Orders, and return unto me again at what time soever I shall call thee by thine Oath, or by thy Name, or by thine Order, or by thine Office which is granted thee from the Creator, and the power of God be with me and thee, and upon the whole Issue of God Amen.

Glory be to the Father, and to the Son, and to the Holy Ghost. ————————

It would be advisable for the Invocant to remain in the Circle for a few minutes after reciting the Licence, and if the place of Operation be in the open air, let him destroy all traces of the Circle &c and return quietly to his home — But should the Operation be performed in a retired part of a House, the Circle may remain as it might serve in a like future Operation, but the Room or Building must be locked to avoid the intrusion of the Vulgar. ————————

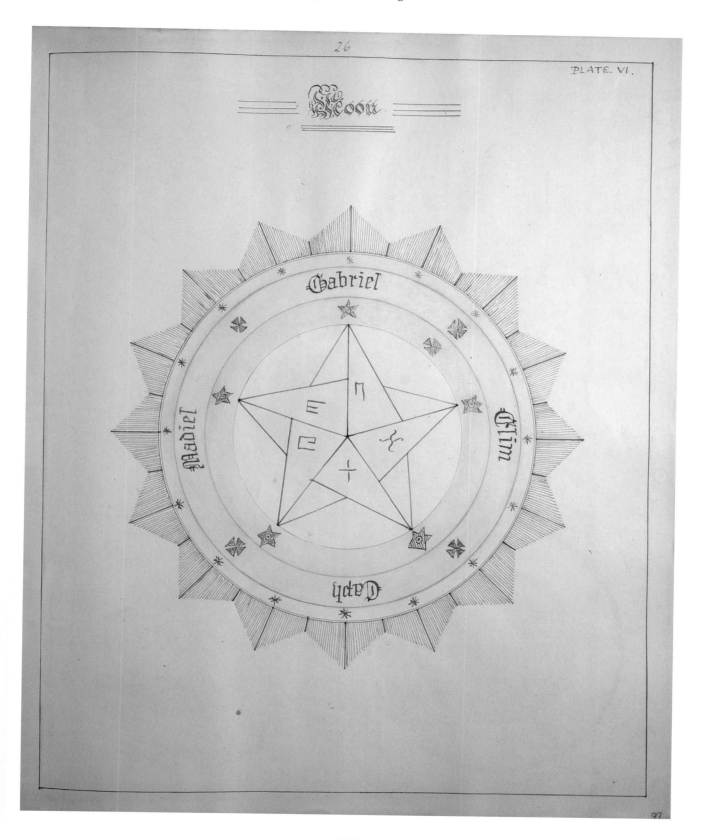

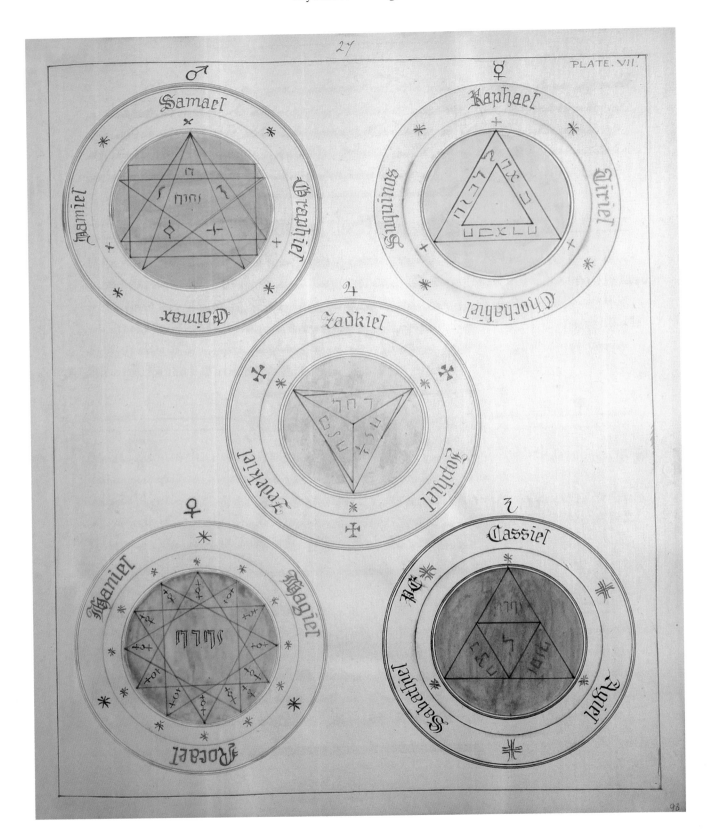

28

The following Invocations of the Seven Planetary Spirits, or Angels must be earnestly recited before the Appearance of the Spirit whom the Invocant wishes to Invoke using one of the Invocations proper for the Spirit, and so of the rest in addition to the forms of prayer and Invocations before rehearsed.

Invocation of the Spirits of the Sun.

O Ye Heavenly Spirits who have been created to behold the face of Him who is seated on the Cherubims, I Conjure you in the Name **Saday, Cados, Phaa,** and by the name of the first Light which is the Sun, that you come and Contribute to the Success of my Operations. I beseech you to Employ your power and virtue in keeping off the Evil Spirits that might overturn the benign Influence of my work by virtue of **Abiaye Kapdiet Caravazad Amadiel.** ff.

Invocation of the Moon

Haste ye Sublime and Sublunary Genii who are obedient to the Sovereign Grace Come and Assist in the Operation that I undertake under the Auspicies of the Grand Luminary of the Night, I Invoke you to this purpose be favourable and hear my Entreaties in the Name of Him who Commands the Spirits in the Regions you inhabit **Bileth, Missabu Abuzaha.** ff.

Invocation of Mars

Come Military Warlike Genii who execute the Commands of the Sovereign Ruler of the Universe, Come and assist me in the operation that I undertake, Come I conjure you by the Name **Gihra, Elohim Saday,** Keep from me all Evil Spirits that my Labours of this Day may not be frustrated. I Conjure you by the Mighty name of your Rulers **Damael Lobquin** ff

29

Invocation of Mercury.

Great and Swift Spirits of Mercury, we pray you to hear our humble petiti on and Supplication, Come to us Ye Spirits who preside over the operation of this day, hear favourably the Invocation I now make unto you O Ye Heavenly Genii who have power over the wonders that are wrought on this Day, Come and remove the Rebel Spirits, and cause me to succeed in my Operation. ff

Invocation of Jupiter

I Conjure you by the Holy Name **Emanuel** all your Heavenly Genii, who second by your Aid the Great Distributor of Health Honour and Riches, Come to my Assistance, reject not the prayer that I make unto you through the Intercession of thy Spirits **Maynth Gutrix** be kind and refuse me not thy powerful Aid. ff.

Invocation of Venus

Come on the wings of the wind ye happy Spirits, who preside over the workings of the Heart, I Conjure you by the Veneration you have for the Mysterious Name **Setchiel**; hear favourably the Invocation that I make this Day destined to the wonders of the Lord. Be ready to lend me your Assistance to Succeed in what I have now undertaken. ff

Invocation of Saturn

I Conjure you by the Name of the Spirit, and the Sovereign Creator of all things by the wonderful Names of the Deity to whom thou art Subject **Adonay, Agla, Tetragrammaton Vaha**, hear me I Adjure you O Mighty Spirit, and grant me your Assistance that I may succeed in my Operations of this Day. ff

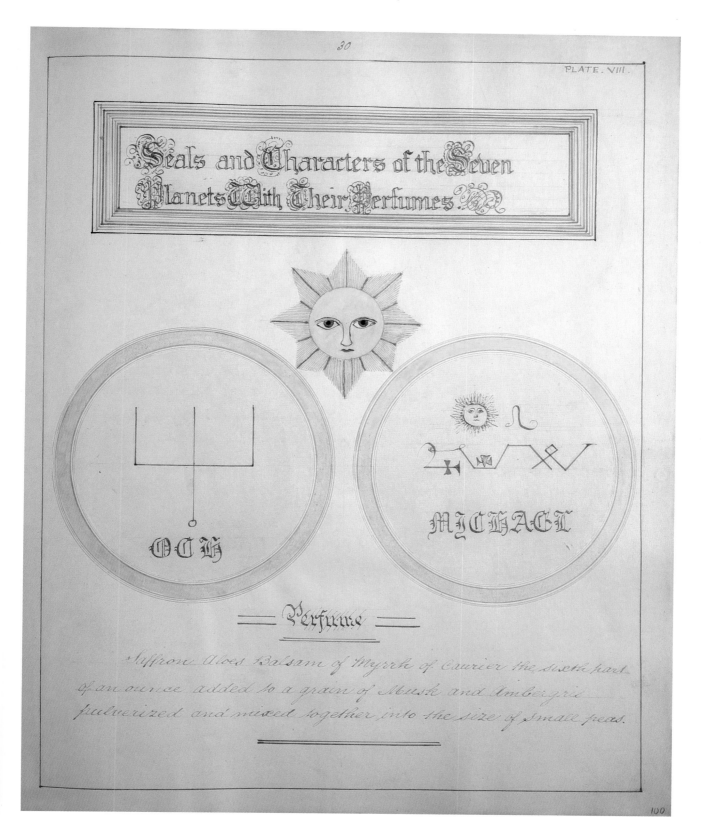

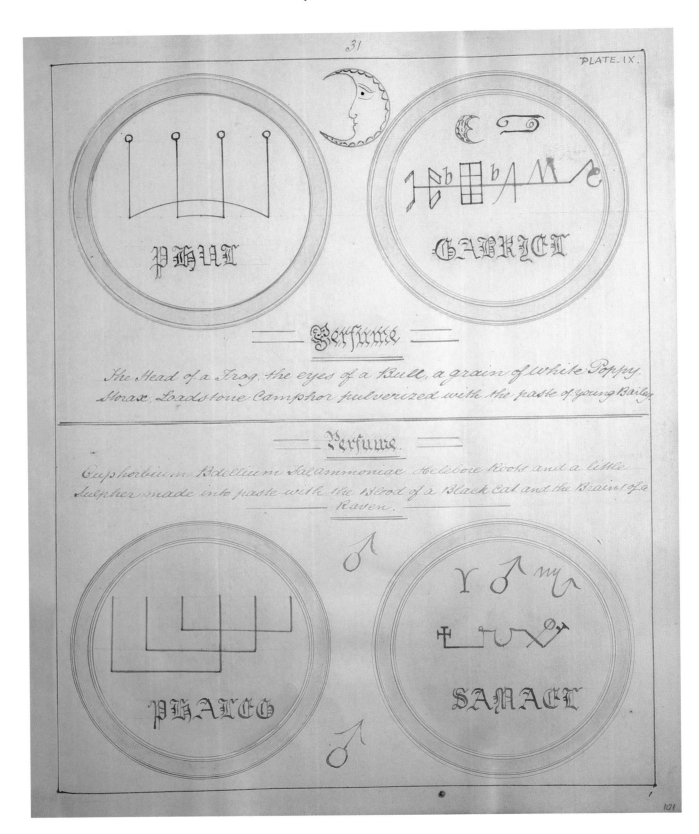

31

PLATE. IX.

PHUL

GABRICL

Perfume

The Head of a Frog, the eyes of a Bull, a grain of White Poppy, Storax, Loadstone Camphor pulverized with the paste of young Bailey.

Perfume

Euphorbium Bdellium Salammoniac Helebore Roots and a little Sulpher made into paste with the Blood of a Black Cat and the Brains of a Raven.

PHALEG

SAMAEL

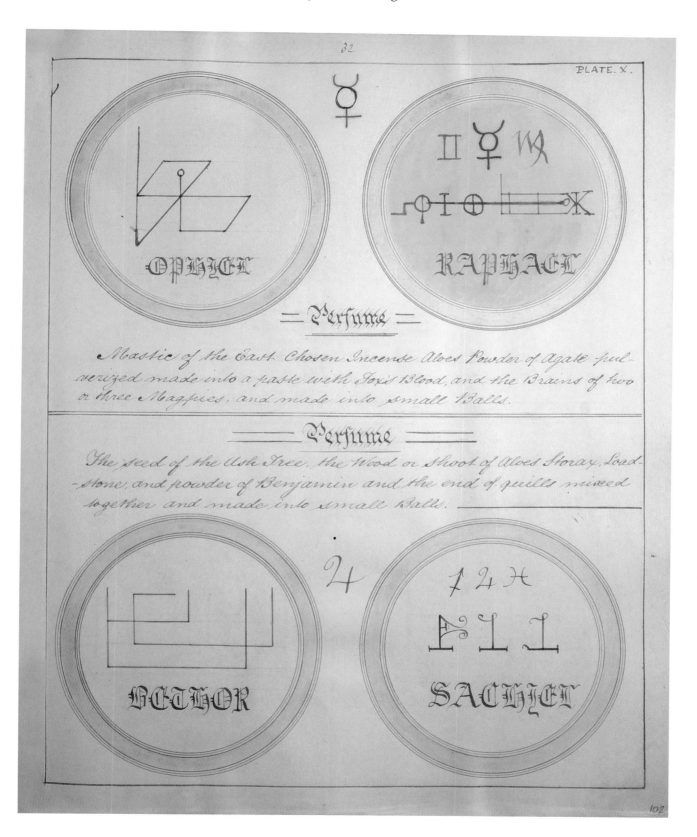

= Perfume =

Mastic of the East Chosen Incense Aloes Powder of Agate pulverized made into a paste with Fox's Blood, and the Brains of two or three Magpies, and made into small Balls.

Perfume

The seed of the Ash Tree, the Wood or Shoot of Aloes Storax, Loadstone, and powder of Benjamin and the end of quills mixed together and made into small Balls.

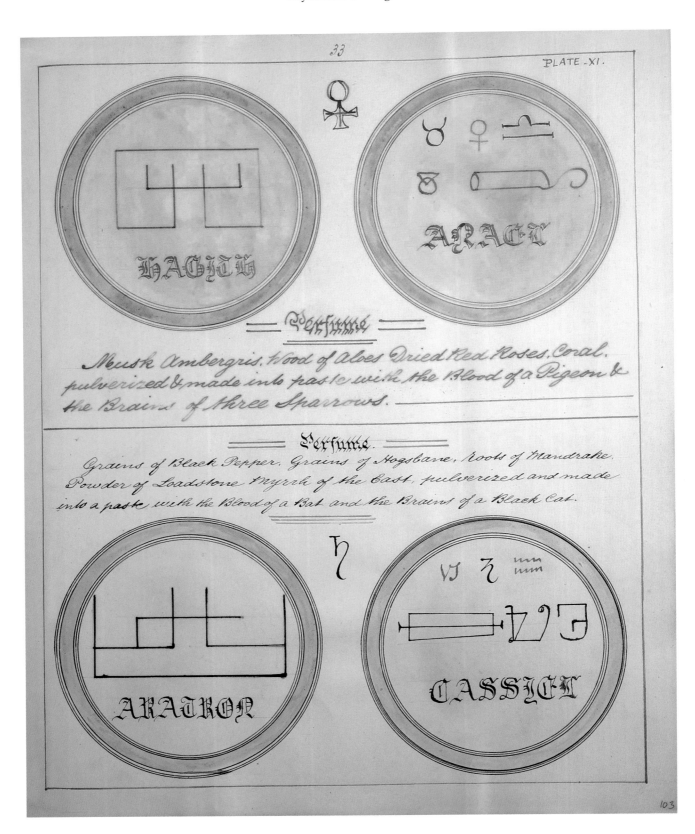

33

PLATE · XI.

HAGITH

ANAEL

=== Perfume ===

Musk Ambergris. Wood of Aloes Dried Red Roses. Coral. pulverized & made into paste with the Blood of a Pigeon & the Brains of three Sparrows. ———

=== Perfume ===

Grains of Black Pepper. Grains of Hogsbane. Roots of Mandrake. Powder of Loadstone Myrrh of the East, pulverized and made into a paste with the Blood of a Bat and the Brains of a Black Cat.

ARATRON

CASSIEL

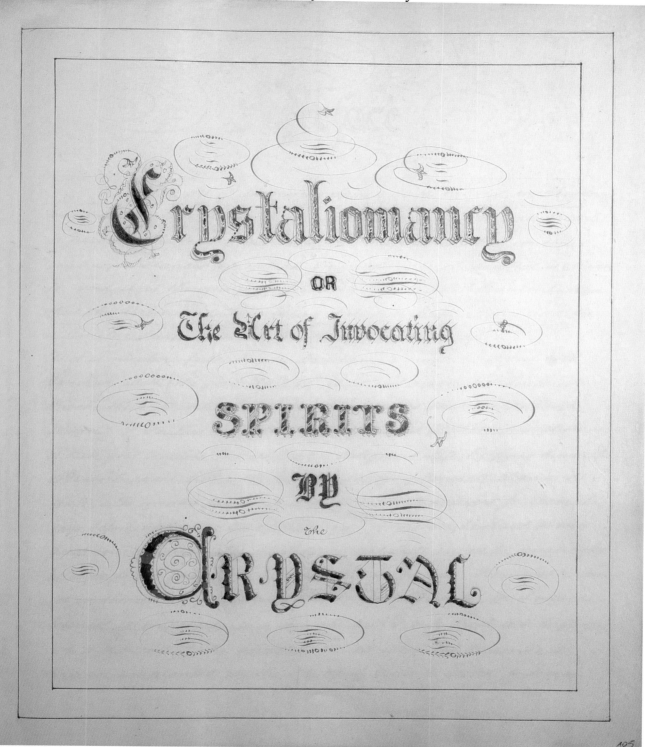

Preface

The art of Invocating Spirits by the Crystal was known and practised by the Ancients, which all those who read Sacred or profane History, may discover. The Sacred Text contains many instances in which Invocation by the Crystal is alluded to, and it is the opinion of many Learned and Eminent Men, that the Urim and Thummim of the Holy Scripture was used for a Similar purpose as the Crystal is in our day.

As it is nowhere forbidden in Scripture to enquire of, and hold Converse with the good Spirits, it is not accounted Sinful to Invoke their Spiritual Aid in all matters that are just and lawful. For this purpose whoever wishes to obtain the assistance of these good Spirits, must lead a Religious Life, keeping himself as it were apart from the World, making himself clean and pure, also make frequent Ablutions and prayers for several days before he begins his Operations. Moreover, he must possess great courage, firmness, Confidence and Skill in all he undertakes relative to the Operation he is about to perform. He must be earn-est in the recital of the Benedictions, Invocations, &c for if only care-lessness is employed, he or they who do this, only trifle to be trifled with to their cost. For doubtless The All wise and Benevolent Creator implanted in the Heart of Man a desire to search

106

into the future to a certain extent as far as this life is concerned. at the same time He allowed him lawful and just means to gratify it such as that Transcendant Science of pure Astrology teaches But Crystaliomancy being of a higher order still, Man is capable by the assistance of and holding Converse with the Celestial Messengers, of arriving at that knowledge and perfection that will be of the utmost benefit to him in this Life, also assist in fitting him for another and better World.

It will be vain for any one who thinks of gaining any of this World's riches &c, by calling upon these bright Spirits for their assistance, for such would be most assuredly denied them. for it is only to the Wise and prudent that these secrets are revealed. Therefore any one wishing to Experimentalize with unlawful wishes Unchaste or Unholy desires would meet with nothing but Shame, Confusion and Disappointment.

3

<u>Concerning the Rules, Forms, Ceremonies, &c to be necessarily observed in the Practice of this Art.</u>

The Invocant may if he choose at the commencement of his operations, have one or two wise, discreet persons as companions to assist him, but he, or they must conform to all the rules and forms necessary likewise consent to all that is required to carry this Operation in effect. Every preparation made for this purpose (during the Increase of the Moon) must be done. The Invocant may perform these Operations at any Season of the Year providing he finds the Luminaries in fortunate aspect with each other also with the Benefic Planets Jupiter and Venus. When the Sun has reached his greatest Northern Declination is said to be the best time. All the Instruments Apparatus &c. required in the Operation must be entirely new, having never before been devoted to any other purpose, they must be made or provided by the Operator himself or under his immediate supervision and at the proper time as he shall direct. He must be careful to leave no part of the Operation un-performed, for upon the exactness with which its performed depends the certainty of his success. The Operator must take notice every thing employed in this Art must be duly consecrated before being used After which he should allow no person to touch or handle any Instrument &c particularly the Crystal. except himself or his companions in the Operation The more Sacred they are kept the more fit for that which they are designed. The forms of Consecration may be found in the sequel of this Work.

4

Concerning the Room Containing the
CIRCLE

The Invocant must in order to carry on his work have a small Room in a retired part of the House such as an Attic, or a low kitchen might be preferred, made clean and neat, having no sumptuous ornaments to divide or distract his attention, also free from the Hurry of Business and from the prying and curious intruder. the floor must be perfectly clean and even so as to receive the lines of the Circle and Characters to be traced thereon.

The Circle may then be drawn seven feet in diameter and the Holy Names and Characters written therein according to the following Model, with Consecrated Chalk or Charcoal. Should not the Invocant have a pair of Compasses of sufficient radius to trace the lines of the Circle. He may use a piece of Twine attached to a pin as a centre, and the other end fastened to the Chalk or Charcoal. He may if he choose, in the absence of the above mentioned articles, sprinkle the floor with fine sand and then draw the Circle, Characters &c with the Magic Sword; but the first method mentioned is by far the best, and being the most durable, may by being used carefully, so preserved as to serve in several of the like Operations. The Room when not in use must be kept locked up.

The Invocant must be reminded that this preparation also must be made during the Increase of the Moon.

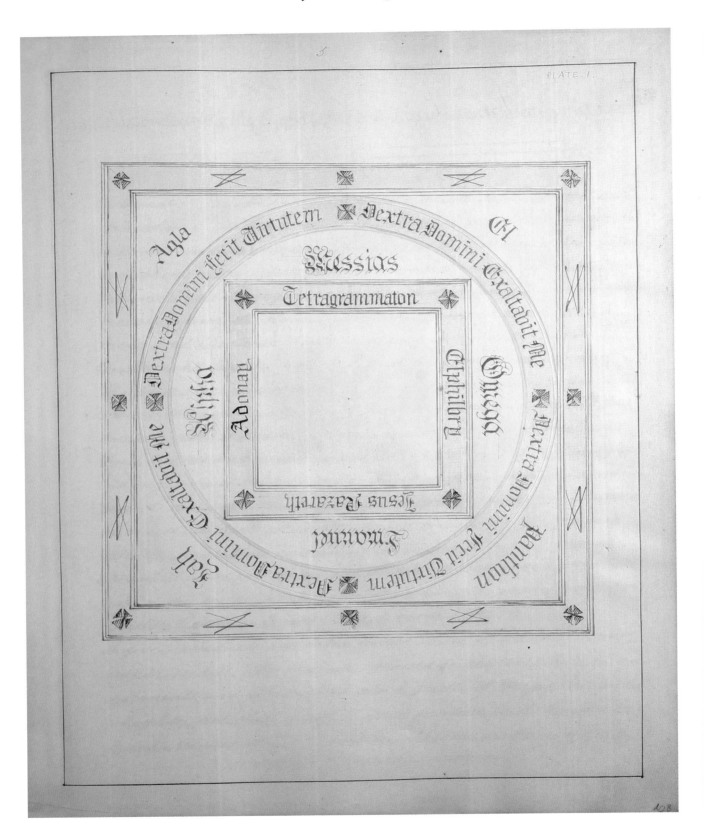

6

Concerning the Apparatus and Instruments used in this Art

The Operator must be provided with a small Table covered with a fair white Linen Cloth, also a Chair which should be placed in the Room ready for the Operation. Also the necessary Apparatus for making a fire when required in order to burn the perfumes and making a fumigation proper to the Planet governing the Operation and the Hour in which he would work. Also a Torch, and Two wax Candles placed in Gilded or Brass Candlesticks highly polished and Engraven as shown. The Operator must have a pair of Compasses wherewith to Draw the Circle, also some Twine or Thread, a Knife, a pen-knife, a pair of Scissors. A Magic Sword of pure steel and about two feet and a half in length, and about one inch in width and engraven as shown; Also a Wand of Hazel Wood of a year's growth and a yard in length and Engraven as shown. The Opera-tor must also have a Small New Box containing the following Articles, small Vials containing the perfume for each planet, also small bottles containing ink suitable to each planet, (see former part of this work) Some Paper, Parchment, with proper pens of either Raven or Crow's Quill, to write thereon.

To give sacredness, also extra power to the Operation in an Experiment, The operator should be Clad in white Linen Garments and white shoes also a girdle of Virgin Parchment or highly polished Leather, and fortified with the Twelve Great Names of God written thereon in letters of Gold.

Description of the Crystal

The Invocant must be provided with a Crystal of about four inches in Diameter or at least the size of a large orange, properly ground and polished (on a Friday when the Sun gets into his own sign Leo) so as to be free from Specs or Spots. it must be enclosed in a Frame of Ivory, Ebony, or Boxwood. highly polished and around which must written in raised Letters of Gold the Mighty Names of Supreme Majesty Tetragrammaton. Adonay, Emanuel. Agla. Round this Frame are fixed five small Crystals to represent the Animal, Vegetable, Mineral, and Astral kingdoms, and the one at the top to represent the △ of the Lord. The pillar and Pedestal to which the frame containing the Crystal is fixed may be formed of any suitable wood and design as shewn to be gilded, or highly polished, the Name written thereon as aforesaid.   N.B.   If the Operator cannot do all this himself he must employ therein some discreet and skilful Artist, to do it but he must be present in order to see that no part of the work is neglected or done improperly, and to employ the proper days and hours for such Work. When completed it must be duly Conse-crated as aforesaid, and then placed in a New Box, or Drawer properly fastened with lock and key to keep it free from Dust, also from the touch and sight of the Vulgar or common people.

The Crystal may be used in a Common plain frame, and without the five additional Crystals; but it has not so much virtue & power, for by their Addition & the manner in which the whole is Executed is said to be more efficacious in the Operations.

9

Consecration of the Ground

Bless O Lord I beseech thee this Ground and place and drive away all evil and wickedness from this Circle. Sanctify and make it become meet and convenient for me thy servant to finish and bring to pass therein all my Desires through Our Lord and Saviour, Amen. Be thou Blessed, Purified and Consecrated in the Name of the Father and of the Son and of the Holy Ghost.

Blessing of the Lights

I Bless thee in the Name of the Father, and of the Son, and of the Holy Ghost. O Holy Holy Holy Lord God, Heaven and Earth are full of thy Glory, before whose face there is a bright Shining Light for ever. Bless now O Lord these creatures of light which thou hast given for the kindly use of Man, that they by thee being Sanctified, may not be put out or extinguished by the Malice, power, or filthy darkness of Satan. But may shine forth brightly and lend their assistance to this Holy Work through Christ Our Lord. Amen.

Consecration of the Instruments

O Great God, who art the God of strength and greatly to be feared, Bless O Lord these Instruments that they may be a terror unto the Enemy and therewith I may overcome phantasms and oppositions of the Devil through thy Influence and help of thy Holy and Mighty Names, On El Agla Tetragrammaton. and in the Cross of Christ our Lord, Amen.

10

Consecration of the Crystal

Eternal God who by thy wisdom hast given and appointed great power in the characters and other Holy Writings of thy Spirits. and hast given unto them that useth them faithfully power thereby to work many things. Bless now O Lord this Crystal formed, framed and written by the hand of thine unworthy servant that being filled with Divine Virtue, Power and Influence by thy Command O Most Holy God it may shew forth its virtue and power to thy praise and Glory Through Christ Our Lord and Saviour. Amen.

———————— Then say ————————

I Bless and Consecrate this Crystal in the Name of the Father. and of the Son, and of the Holy Ghost. ————

The Invocant must have the Seal of the Spirit he would Invoke, also the Pentacle and Character of the Planet governing the Day and hour of Operation. and above all, the Grand Pentacle of Solomon※ the Model of which is given in the former part of this Book. these must be written on Virgin Parchment with proper ink and duly Consecrated in the Aforesaid manner. In consecrating all the Instruments &c necessary in this Art. The Invocant must recite the Forms &c while placing his hands upon the different Articles with his Face turned towards the East.

※ This All powerful Pentacle should be present at all Magical Operations where the good Angels or Spirits are Invoked to appear.

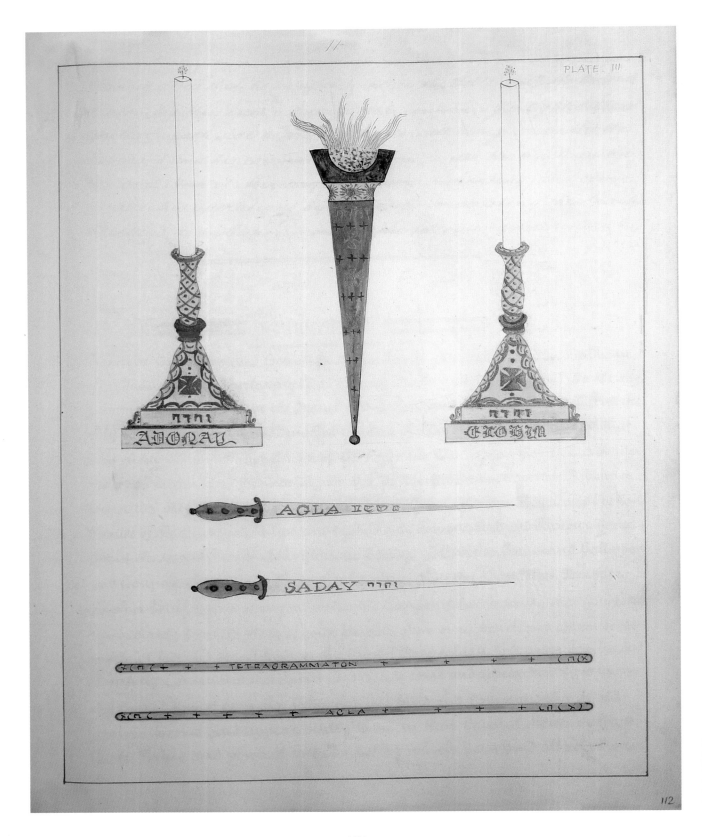

12

Having done that he may then place the Table with the Crystal thereon together with a candlestick containing a lighted wax candle on each side before the Circle. All being ready. Let the Invocant and his companions (if any) enter the Circle in the Day and Hour of Mercury (the Moon increasing) and commence his Operations by earnestly Invocating the Spirit Vassago, as an Experiment in the following manner.

Invocation

I Exorcise Call upon and Command thee Spirit Vassago by and in the Name of the Immense and Everlasting God Jehovah Adonay Elohim Agla El On Tetra-grammaton and by and in the Name of Our Lord and Saviour Jesus Christ the only Son of the Eternal and true God Creator of Heaven and Earth, and all that is in them Alipius Sother Emanuel Primogenitus Homonzion Bomes Dia Veritas Sapientia Virtus Leof Mediator Agnus Rex Pastor Prophetas Sacerdos Athanetos Paracletus Alpha et Omega, by all these High Great Glorious Royal and Ineffable Names of the Omnipotent God, and by His only Son our Lord and Saviour Jesus Christ the second essence of the Glorious Trinity. I Exorcise Command, Call upon and Conjure thee Spirit Vassago wheresoever thou Art (East, West, North or South or being bound to any one under the Compass of the Heavens.) that you come immediately from the place of your private abode or residence, and appear to me visibly in fair and decent form in this Crystal Stone or Glass. I do again Exorcise and Powerfully Command thee Spirit Vassago to come and appear Visibly to me in this Crystal Stone or Glass. I do again strongly bind and Command thee Spirit Vassago to come and appear visibly to me in that Crystal Stone or Glass, by the Virtue and power of these Names by which I can bind all rebellious

13

Obstinate and Refractory Spirits Alla Carital Marihal Carion Urian Spyton Korean Marmos Agaion Cados Pron Astron Gardeong Tetragrammaton Strallay Spignos Jah On El Elohim, by all aforesaid, I Charge and Command thee Spirit Tlazzago to make haste and come away and appear visibly to me as aforesaid without any further tarrying or Delay in the Name of Him who shall come to Judge the Quick and Dead and

——————————— the World by Fire ———————————

——————————— Amen. ———————————

This Conjuration after repeated and the Invocant being patient and constant in his perseverance, and not disheartened no dismayed by reason of tedious Prolixity or Delay. The Spirit will at last appear, Bind him with the Bond of Spirits. and then you may talk with him &c. ———————————

That this is a true Experiment. and that the Spirit hath been obliged to the fellowship and service of a Magic Artist heretofore is very certain as may appear by this following Obligation the which, the Invocant may if he pleaseth have fairly written an an Abortive and laid before him and discourse with the Spirit concerning it. ———————————

14

Bond of Spirits

I **Vassago** under **Baro** the King of the West not compelled by command or fear but of my own accord and free will, especially oblige myself by these presents firmly and faithfully and without deceit to T.W. ✳ to obey at any time and at any place whensoever and wheresoever he shall call upon me personally to appear in this Crystal Stone or Glass and to fulfill his Commands truly in all things wherein I can by the virtue of all the Names of God, especially by those words the most powerful in the Magical Art **Lay Abryca Mura Spron Walgaba Ryshin Layagamum Arasin Layson** and by virtue wherewith the Sun and Moon were darkened and my Planet and by the Celestial Characters thereof and principally by this Seal binding most solidly. In Witness of which Guilty Person he commanding I have signed this Present Obligation with mine own Seal to which I always stick close. ⸺

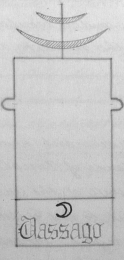

Seal of the Spirit Vassago.

114

15

After the Invocant has obtained the assistance and the desired Information of the Spirit he may courteously License him to Depart in the following manner.

Licence to Depart

Forasmuch as thou comest in peace and quietness without noise, terror, or hurt to me (or my fellows) and hast answered unto my petition, I give humble and hearty thanks unto Almighty God, in whose Name I called thee and thou camest and now thou Tassago mayest Depart in Peace unto thine Orders and return unto me again at what time soever I shall call thee by thine Oath, or by Name, or by thine Order, or by thine Office which is Granted from the Creator, and the power of God be with me and thee and upon the whole Issue of God. Amen.
Glory be to the Father, and to the Son, and to the Holy Ghost.

As all Aerial Spirits are very Powerful, and slow in their appearance so also is their Departure, and it would be as well for the Invocant not to leave the limits of the Circle for a few minutes after the Licence is recited.

The above powerful Experiment proves the possibility and truth and reality of the existence of Aerial Spirits who may be com-pelled to appear at the will of the Operator, and be so bound as to become Subservient to his Desires provided he asks nothing but what is just and right. which will assuredly be granted if he retains the firm Confidence and strict secresy.

16.

Invocation by the Crystal may be used for the purpose of Conversing with, and obtaining the assistance of the Planetary Angels, And as they are not so Obstinate and Refractory as the Aerial Spirits they are more easily invoked to appearance, and being gentle and mild generally in their Demeanour, there is no danger in the Opera-tion of calling them to appear, which they will readily do afterwards at the will of the Operator, particularly the Angel or Spirit governing the Planet under whose Influence the person desirous of Assistance is born. The Invocant must take care that in Invocating any one of these Beautiful Spirits, he must first be earnest in his request and that it is according to the Nature and Office of the Spirit he invokes, for instance if he wish for Honour, Dignity, or Riches, he must perform his Operations in the Hour of the Sun on Sunday, and so of the rest which the first part of this Book teaches. The Operator may use the same forms & Ceremonies as for the Aerial Spirits, taking great care that no part of them be neglected, then he may expect success infalli-bly to follow.   To Conclude, The Invocant must observe the greatest peculiarities in the Science of Magic, are the particular Ingredients required, Tools Apparatus &c, Times & Seasons of Conducting the Operation, And Secresy, for every portion or part must be performed stictly according to the rules given and every Detail with the minutest exactness & Care.

115

Part 7. Miscellaneous Examples and Experiments

Miscellaneous

Examples and Experiments

In

Natural, Cabalistic, and Ceremonial

MAGIC

With the Experiment in all its Details of Raising the
Powerful Spirit Oberion

Also the

Measure, Proportion and Harmony of the Human Body

Magic Tables &c.

The whole Enriched with Illuminated and Coloured

Figures, Circles &c.

Concluding With the Art of Fascination &c.

1520

116

2

NATURAL MAGIC
CHARMS&c
To Fascinate Birds.

Mix together the juice of rue and vinegar and steep corn there-in, this corn thrown to birds, shall so fascinate them upon eat-ing thereof that they may be easily caught with the hand. In like manner poppy seeds steeped in brandy for twenty-four hours will have the same effect. —————

= To make a Room appear in Flames, or to be filled with Serpents &c. Take half an ounce of Sal-ammoniac, one ounce of Camphor, and two ounces of Aqua Vitæ (or requisite, rectified Spirits of Wine) put them in an earthen pot narrowing towards the top, and set fire to it. The effect will be so immediately alarming, that the persons in the room will even fancy their own garments are on fire. But the Illusory flames will, nevertheless do no harm.

117

3

To make a Room appear full of Serpents. Take the skin of a Snake or Serpent, and in it place a wick of the like skin dried and twisted fill up the skin with the fat of the Snake or Serpent with which you must mix some aqua vita, and light it when the sign Scorpio is ascending with the Moon therein, and the room will instantly appear full of Serpents Snakes &c, hissing and writhing about in every direction to the horror and astonishment of the spectators, so perfect will the allusion be that they would believe it a reality. _____

= To make the Faces of a party appear Ghastly and Death Like. =

In order to perform this strange feat take half a pint of Spirits of wine or strong Brandy, and having warmed it put a handful of salt with it into a Basin, then set it on fire with a lighted piece of paper, and will have the effect of making every one present look, "As if they were newly Risen from their cold Graves." N.B. This can only be done in a close room. _____

===== Properties of Herbs &c. =====

"Anoint thee with the juice of Canabus and Archangel; and before a mirror of steel, call Spirits, and thou shalt see them, and have power to bind and to loose them." "The fume of Heniculis chaseth away Spirits" "Take the herb Avisam, and join it to camphire, and thou shalt see spirits, that shall dread thee. It helpeth much to the achieving of secret things." "Petersilion chaseth away all the Spirits of Wicked".

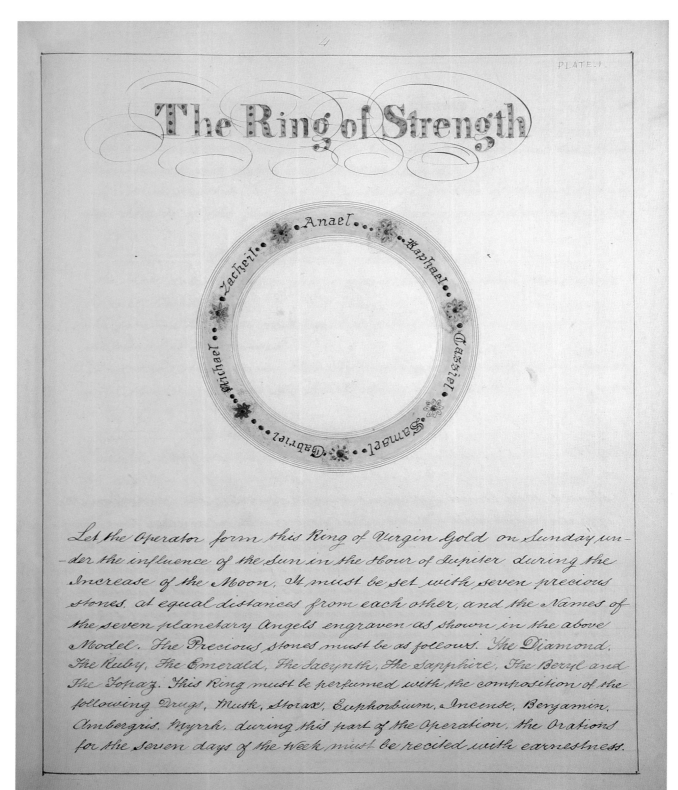

PLATE. I.

The Ring of Strength

Let the Operator form this Ring of Virgin Gold on Sunday, under the influence of the Sun in the Hour of Jupiter during the Increase of the Moon. It must be set with seven precious stones, at equal distances from each other, and the Names of the seven planetary Angels engraven as shown in the above Model. The Precious stones must be as follows. The Diamond, The Ruby, The Emerald, The Jacynth, The Sapphire, The Beryl and The Topaz. This Ring must be perfumed with the composition of the following Drugs, Musk, Storax, Euphorbium, Incense, Benjamin, Ambergris, Myrrh, during this part of the Operation, the Orations for the Seven days of the Week must be recited with earnestness.

Should there be not sufficient time to complete the Operation, the Operator must wait till the next favourable planetary hour arrives on the next day of the Sun, Also should he not be able to form this Ring himself, he may employ therein some wise and discreet Artist to assist him, but he must be present in order to see that no part of the Operation be omitted. This Ring may be of any convenient size and worn any were about the person, or may be made small enough to be worn on the finger where rings are usually worn. The Composition of this Ring is attended with much Labour and expense, but the Virtue and power it possesses repays for all, being invaluable, and renders the wearer thereof Invincible as Achilles; fearing no man.

6

Charm against Furious Beasts

Repeat earnestly and with sincere faith these words:—

"At destruction and famine, thou shalt laugh, neither shalt thou be afraid of the beasts of the earth."

"For thou shalt be in league with the stones of the field, and the beasts of the field shall be at peace with thee. Job. V – 22. 23.

Charm against Troubles in General

" He shall deliver thee in six troubles, yea in seven there shall no evil touch thee".

"In famine he shall redeem thee from death, and in war from the power of the sword."

" And thou shalt know that thy tabernacle shall be in peace, and thou shalt visit thy habitation and shalt not err. Job. V – 19. 20. 24.

Charm against Enemies

"Behold, God is my salvation; I will trust, and not be afraid for the Lord Jehovah is my strength and my song; he is also become my Salvation.

"For the stars of Heaven, and the constellations thereof, shall not give their light; the Sun shall be darkened in his going forth, and the moon shall not cause her light to shine.

" And behold at eventide, trouble; and before the morning he is not: this is the portion of them that spoil us, and the lot of them that rob us. Isaiah XII – XVII.

This also, when we would avoid peril by fire or water, we make use of this passage:— "When thou passest through the waters, I will be with thee and through the rivers they shall not overflow thee: when thou walkest through the fire, thou shalt not be burnt, neither shall the flame kindle upon me. Isaiah XLIII – 2

119

Charm to bind or Compel a Thief.

To bind a thief so that he shall have neither rest nor peace till he return thee thy lost goods; go to the place from whence they were stolen away, and write the name of the person or persons thou suspectest upon fair Virgin Parchment, and put the same underneath the threshold of the door they went out of. Then make four crosses on the four corners or posts of the doorway, and go your ways saying; Thou thief who hast stolen and taken away (here name the Article or goods) from this place, Abraham by his virtue and the power God gave him call thee back again. Isaac by his power stop thee in the way. Jacob make thee go no farther, but Bring them back again. And Joseph by his power and virtue, and also by the grace and might of the Holy Ghost force thee to come again into this place, and that neither Solomon let thee nor David bid thee but that thou or the same through Christ Our Lord do cause thee presently and without stay to come again into this place and bring them with thee. Fiat, fiat, fiat. Cito, Cito, Cito. In the Name of the Father, and of the Son, and of the Holy Ghost.

Repeat these words three times, and the thief shall not rest nor delay till he return thee thy lost goods.

A Ring of Power to overcome Enemies.

Let the character of Saturn (♄) be engraven upon a Magnet or piece of Loadstone in the time of the moon's increase, and being worn on the right hand no enemy shall overcome the wearer.

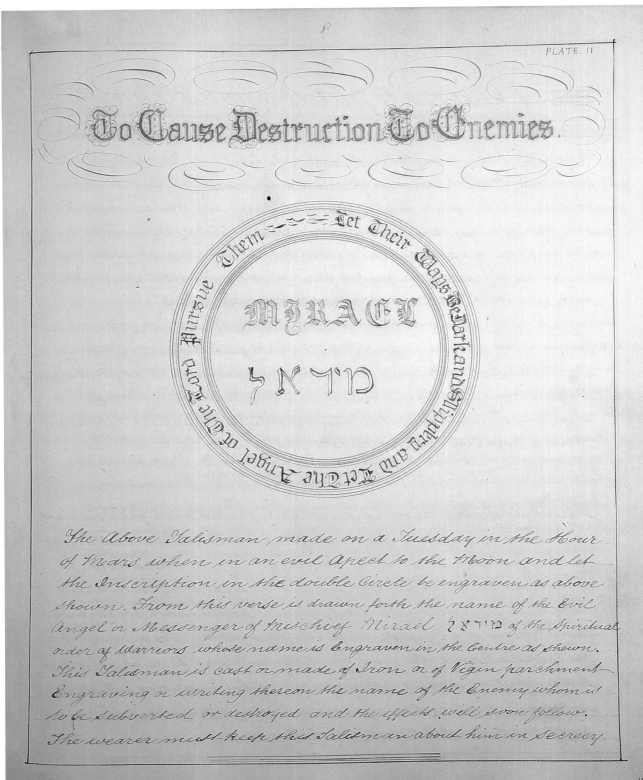

9

A Charm to protect against Thieves.

Deus autem transiens per medium illorum ibat + Ihus xpus + benedictus Deus quotidie prosperus iter facit Deus salutaris noster + Ihus obstinenter occuli eorum ne videant, et dorsum eorum, ne curva + Ihus + effundis supra eas iris tua, et furor ire tue comprehendat eos + Irnat + supra inimicos meos formido et pavo in magnitudine brachii fiant eniobiles quasi Lapis, donec per transeat famulus tuus + quem redemisti + dextera tua magnificata est, in Virtute Domini per crusist inimicus in multitudine virtutis tue deposuisti omnes adversarious meos + Ihesu + eripe me et ab in surgentibusque in me libera me + Ihesu + custodi me, et demanu peccatoris et ab hominibusque iniquis eripe me + Ihesu + eripe me de opera tibis que iniquitate et a viris sanguine salva me + Gloria Patri + Awthos + Anostro + Moxio × Bay + Eloy + Apen + Agias + Yskiros. _____

_____

The words of these Charms must be repeated with great earnest-ness and confidence for according to the Vehement Desire of the Operator, so will be the result of the Operation: it is not the mere repeating the words that will ensure suc-cess, but a firm trust and sincere faith must accompany them; then the Charm will be efficacious. For according to the learned and the wise in these matters, there is not a Verse, Line, Word, or even a letter in the Holy Scriptures which has not some particular meaning, either offensive or defensive, being read in the original Hebrew.

Method of Raising and Invocating Spirits.

The various manuscripts relative to the fact of spiritual intercourse all agree in declaring, that those who would invocate spirits must, for some days previously, prepare themselves to these high and mysterious ceremonies by living in a manner secluded from the rest of the world, being religiously disposed, and at least for three days must live free from sensual gratifications.

The place chosen, must be secluded, solitary, and isolated from the resort of men, where no business is carried on, where no unhallowed eye must enter, and where the pryings of curiosity remain ungratified. For this reason, dilapidated buildings, free from the tread of human footsteps, or in the midst of forests, lonely caves, or rocks by the sea shore, or where the general appearances indicate desolation and darkness. It must be remembered that all and every order of these unearthly Agents are averse to visible appearance, that when they do appear, they make use of the most horrid forms, accompanied by the loudest thunders, and most furious lightnings to affrighten the Invocator, and swerve him from his purpose.

The Invocator must accustom himself to see and hear all this, without the least appearance of agitation; for this purpose, he must be a man of undaunted courage, quick foresight, of great firmness and resolution, also possessing great confidence. He must also have two associates with him, who must be well acquainted with Magic Rites, and particularly in dismissing Spirits; for it is far easier to raise than to dismiss or lay a Spirit through the unaccountable antipathy existing by these Invisible

11

agents towards the human race. The place being chosen secure and free from interruption, the Invocant must choose the proper day and hour for working, according to the nature, order, and office of the Spirit he would invoke, not forgetting to raise the good Spirits in the increase of the Moon. He must also be provided with the Seals of the Earth, the Seals of the Spirit, and the Sacred Lamen or Pentacle, above all the Pentacle of Solomon, the Magic Sword, Vestments. and other Instruments necessary for the operation the description of which have already been given in the first part of this Mysterious Book. the whole of which must be completed in the hour of Mercury. Also he must have the perfume agreeable and proper to the Spirit. Also he must Exor- -cise or Consecrate the place he would Invocate in after the accus- -tomed manner. He may then proceed to draw the Circle nine feet in diameter; within the outer circle, two contren- -tric circles of a hand's breadth must be made, and the four quarters of the world marked therein by a correct compass. In the midst for divine protection, must be described the great and powerful Names of God Jehovah, Tetragrammaton, Adonai Sadai. and appropriate inscriptions; taking care that the circles be correctly formed, and duly joined and fortified with sacred crosses with- -in and without; the chalk or charcoal being first properly consecrated. The Lights used upon the occasion must be of wax, and each candle- -stick inclosed in a magic pentacle. The sword must be of purely steel, made expressly for the occasion, and, indeed so must all the Instruments and properly Consecrated, and never be devoted to any other purpose. All things being ready, the Invocant with his associates, must enter the Circle in the proper planetary hour, and having entered, must with the sword proceed to consecrate and close the circle in the accustomed manner, after which he must proceed as he thinks fit to adjure, contrain and force the spirits to visible appearance. In doing which he must be patient not despairing, but determined to bring his will and purpose to the desired effect. After earnestly repeating the Invocation, let the Invocant book round, to see if any spirit does appear, which if he delays, then let him repeat the Invocation three times, and if the Spirit be obstinate, and will not appear, then let the Invocant adjure it with Divine power according to the nature and office of the Spirit; Thus shall he effect his purpose. When the Spirit appears, let the Invocant turn himself towards it, courteously receiving it, and demanding answers to his questions; but if the Spirit shall be obstinate ambiguous, lying, or else refractory, let the Invocant bind it with the Bond of Spirits if necessary, and if you doubt any thing, make without the circle with the consecrated sword, the figure of a triangle or pentagon, and compel the spirit to enter it; then having obtained of the Spirit that which you desire, License it to depart with courteous words, giving it command that it do no hurt whatever. And when it is departed, make a short stay in the circle, and use some prayer giving thanks to God and the good angels; then you may depart. The Invocant must take notice that when he begins his work the air must be clear and serene, if it be in the day see that the sun shines; if it be in the night, let the Moon be unobscured, or the sky full of Stars, for in foul or close weather the spirit will not be visible, because it cannot receive bodily form or shape from the Elements. After having completed the Ceremonies &c The Invocant may destroy all traces of the circle &c and depart in peace to his own home.

13

Incantation

To Bind the Ground, whereby neither Mortal nor Spiritual Beings can have Power to Approach within a Limited Distance. —————

Having made your necessary suffumigations and mystic preparations, describe a circle of a hundred feet or more in diameter, or as much more or less as you may think fit; and if you wish to keep all living creatures from within a quarter of a mile or more of your Experiment, make, at the four parts of the same, East, West, North and South, proper crosses, and devoutly pronounce thrice the following Incantation. —————

In the Name of the Father and of the Son and of the **Holy Ghost** Amen. I bind all mortal and immortal, celestial and Terrestrial, visible and invisible beings excepts those spirits whom I have occasion to call, to avoid and quit this space of ground, which I now mark, and wherein I now stand, and that with all possible speed and despatch. I bind you to avoid and no longer to tarry, by the unspeakable power of Almighty **God**, by the most high and Mighty name of **+ Tetragrammaton +** by the all-powerful names **+ Agla + Saday + Jesu + Messias + Alpha + et Omega +**. By all these most high and powerful names, I charge, adjure, bind and constrain both mortal and immortal, terrestrial, Celestial, visible and invisible beings to avoid, quit, and depart this ground, and do request that none of you, except those I have occasion to call at this time, be suffered to come within these sacred limits. These things I request in the Name of the **Father** and of the Son and of the **Holy Ghost**, Amen. —————

Then dig a certain depth at the four parts of the compass, and bury the seal of the earth in each part, and now no power either visible or invisible, shall have power to come near thee, or to interrupt thy proceedings.

The Invocant who would raise or Invocate this powerful Spirit Oberion must in the first place, draw out his seal and Character, and the different offices subservient to him, in the first Monday after the full moon, and in the hour of the Moon, Mars, Mercury, or Saturn; and when these are made, he must repeat the following ceremonial words: —

O ye Angels of the **Sun** and **Moon** I Conjure and pray you, and Exorcise you, that by the virtue and power of the Most High God **Alpha** and **Omega**, and by the name that is marvellous ✠ **El** ✠ and by Him that made and formed you, and by these signs that be here, so drawn forth in these resemblances, and now in the might and virtue of your Creator and in the name of him the most shining **God**, and by the virtue of the **Holy — Ghost**, that now, or whensoever that I shall call on **Oberion**, whose image is here pictured, made, or fashioned, and his name that is here written, and his signs here all drawn and graven, written or made, that **Oberion** be compelled now to obey me, and here to appear openly before me, and fulfil my request.

The next day, write or make the name of his first counsellor, **Taberyon**, and on the right side, that of Oberion's character, saying,

I Exorcise thee **Taberyon** by the power of God, and by the virtue of Heavenly Kings, earthly kings, and infernal kings, and by king Solomon, who bound thee, and made thee subject unto him, and by all his signs and seals, and by the four elements, by which the world is sustained and nourished, and by the serpent that was exalted in the wilderness. — that thou Taberyon now help to give true council to thy Lord **Oberion**, that he do show himself instantly unto me and fulfil my request.

This must be said three times each day, and three times each night, over the writings. The third day, in the third hour, write and make the name of his other counsellor Teveyron, with his signs and characters, and do and say as before rehearsed.

16

This done, suffumigate your seals and writings with a suffumigation of saffron, aloes, mastic, olibanum, and orpient; and note the fire used for this purpose must be of elder-wood, or thorns.

Then choose such a secret and retired place, as has been described & where no human footsteps may interrupt thee make thy Circle of the following form. Note; the ground or floor must be perfectly clear and even in order to trace the lines of the Circle, Characters &c with much exactness according to the foregoing Model, which being made, and consecrated according to the rules of Ceremonial Magic; Let the Invocant & his associates enter the Circle in the Hour of Mercury, closing it properly and guarding it with Crosses &c as before said, then begin his Invocations in the following manner on bended knees and with great devotion. ———

I Conjure Invocate, and Call upon the Oberion by the Father, the Son and the Holy Ghost, and by Him who said, and it was done; who commanded and it stood fast: who willed, and it was created: and by his Son Jesus Christ, in whose name all Heavenly, Earthly, and Infernal do bend and obey; and by the unutterable name of Ineffable Majesty + Tetragrammaton + O thou Spirit Oberion. I Command thee wheresoever thou now art, whether in sea, fire, air or flood, whether in the air above or in the region beneath, to appear instantly unto me and my fellows, without hurting me or them, or any living creature which God has made. This I thrice command thee in the name of the Ineffable Adonai. Amen.

If at the third repetition of this Invocation, the Spirit gives no visible token of his appearance (which generally is accompanied with tre- mendous noises frightful hissings tumultuous yellings and fearful shrieks) then begin to rehearse the following great bond or incantation and if the spirit were bound in chains of darkness, in the lowest pit of the infernal regions, he must appear, when this great Sentence is rehearsed. ———

Form in which the Spirit Oberion Usually Appears

18

The Great and Powerful Incantation ※

O thou rebellious and fearful spirits prince amongst the fallen angels, Oberion, I conjure and bind thee to visible appearance by the following most high, most terrible, and mighty Invocation.—

Hear O ye Heavens, and I will speak, saith the Lord, and let the sea, the earth—yea, hell, and all that is within them contained, mark the words of my mouth: Did not I, saith the Lord, fashion you, and make you? Did not I, as an eagle, who stirreth her nest, fluttereth over her young ones with her wings, and carrieth them on her shoulders? have I not so nourished you, that you were fat, and loaden with plenty? Why have you, then so spurned with your heels against me, your Maker? Why have you seemed to coequal yourselves with me? What thereby have you reaped? Have you not purchased, instead of that heavenly felicity, hellish perplexity? How have you that fire kindled which doth and shall for ever, at my pleasure, burn you in the bottomless pit of perdition? Why are you so unfaithful and disobedient to my most Holy names and words? Know you not that I am God alone, and that there is none but me? Am not I the only יהוה. Is it not in my power to kill and make alive—to wound and to heal—to oppress and to deliver? If I whet the edge of my sword, and my hand take hold of it to do justice against them who disobey my holy name who are able to abide the same? To have their sword, eat their flesh, and my sharp arrows of hell fire to be drunk in their blood? Which of you that are disobedient to my name (saith the Lord) is able to withstand mine anger? Am not I Lord of Lords, and Omnipotent, and none but I? Who can command the Heavens to smoke, the Earth to fear, the waters to flow, and hell to tremble? Are not the corners of them all in my hands O thou obstinate and stubborn Spirit, why hast thou dealt so froward with me (saith the Lord) to urge me to command my faithful servant

※ This great Call or Invocation is said to be equally powerful in raising any other Spirit.

126

Michael, my valiant champion, to expel and put thee out of the place where thou wast filled wisdom and understanding, continually beholding my wondrous works? Diost not thou see my glory with thine eyes and did not thy ears hear the Majesty of my voice? Why art thou gone out of the way? Why art thou become an open sepulchre? With thy tongue dost thou deceive my servants, for poison is under thy lips, thy mouth is full of cursing and bitterness, and thy feet are swift to shed innocent blood. Is this the obedience thou owest unto me, and the service thou offerest? Verily, for this thy obstinacy, disobedience, pride and rebellion, thou shalt be bound, and most cruelly tormented with intolerable pains and endless and eternal perdition. ⸻

Then, if the Spirit be still rebellious or refractory, make a fire of brimstone and stinking substances. thorns briars &c. Then write the Name of the Spirit in Virgin Parchment, and burn it thrice, repeating the following adjuration:—

I Conjure thee, creature of God, Fire, by him who commanded and all things were done, and by the living God, and by the true God, and by the Holy God, and by Him who made thee and all the elements by his word, by Him who appeared to Moses in fiery bush, and by Him who led the children in a fiery pillar, through the wilderness and by Him who shall come to judge the World by fire and brimstone, that thou perform my will upon this refractory and disobedient spirit: till he come unto me, and show himself in all things as I shall command him. O Heavenly God, Father and author of all virtues, and the Invisible king of Glory, most strong and mighty Captain of the strong and triumphant arm of Angels, God of Gods, Lord of hosts, which on thy hands the corners of the earth which with the breath of thy mouth makest all things to shake and tremble, which makest thy Angels lightnings, and thy Spirits

20

flames of fire. vouchsafe. I beseech thee O Lord, to send thy Holy Angels into this place of fire, to torment, vex, and persecute this disobedient Spirit. **Oberion**. and overcome him. as Michael the Archangel overcame Lucifer the prince of darkness, till he come to me, and fulfil all my will and desire. **Fiat, fiat, fiat. Amen.** _____

O thou most puissant prince **Radamanthus**, which dost punish in thy prison of perpetual perplexity, the disobedient Spirits, and also the grisly ghosts of men dying in dreadful despair, I conjure. Bind and charge thee, by **Lucifer, Beelzebub, Satan, Tamanill**, and by their power. and by the homage thou owest unto them; and also I charge thee, by the triple crown of **Cerberus** by **Styx** and **Phlegethon**. by the Spirit **Daran-tos** and by his ministers, that you torment and punish this disobe-dient Spirit **Oberion**, until you make him come corporally to my sight, and obey my will and commandment in whatsoever I shall charge or command him to do. **Fiat, fiat, fiat. Amen.**

_____

These things being rightly performed, the Spirit will be constrained to visible appearance; but it will be in a horrible and ghastly form. at first, and attended by terrible convulsions of the elements. This mighty Spirit is chiefly under the dominion of the Sun and Moon, he will then assume the appearance in great pomp and terror, that of a scaly monster, with the face of a woman, and a royal crown upon his head. attended by innumerable and countless legions. which will astound and frighten the Invocant if he be not on his guard, also he will be in great danger and peril if the Magic circle be not well made and fortified. But if all the before mentioned rules be followed, he need not fear any harm from this rebellious and Powerful Spirit who _must_ become obedient when thus exorcised. His office is to give Prosperity in Journeys and Voyages, also Riches. Dignity and Honour!

_____

127

21.

after the Spirit has appeared, and performed thy will and request, the Invocant must use the utmost caution in quitting the limits of the Magic Circle, for this end, he must devoutly rehearse the following license to Depart.

I Conjure thee **Oberion** by the visible and holy temple of Solomon, which he did prepare to the most holy God, by all the elements, and by that most Holy Name that was graven on Solomon's Sceptre, that for this time, thou do depart quickly, quietly and peaceably without lightnings, thunder, rain, wind, storm, or tempest, or any noise terror whatsoever; and whensoever I shall call thee, I charge thee that thou do come to me and my fellows without delay or tract of time, not molesting me or any other creature that God hath made to his glory and praise, and the use of man, or without disordering any thing, putting up or casting down anything, or doing any hurt any other way whatsoever, either in thy coming or going, not hurting, troubling, or molesting me or any other creature, neither by thyself, nor any spirit or spirits for thee or at thy procurement, at any times or times, now or hereafter; by the virtue of our **Lord Jesus Christ**, the **Father**, and the **Holy Ghost**, go thy way in peace to the place God hath appointed for thee, and peace be between thee and me   **In nomine Patris + et Filii + et Spiritus Sancti. + Amen**

The Invocant must repeat Licence three times, and afterwards repeating the Lords Prayer must leave the circle walking backwards. He, must then destroy all traces of the circle and remove all Instruments used for the purpose, and return home by a different path from that by which he came. So shall no spirit have power to harm him, but let him on no account neglect any of the foregoing rules for they are essential to his safety.

Such were the mystic rights, ceremonies &c used by the ancient and learned in the Art a study to the sublimity of which modern times afford no parallel as the experiment already evinces, which is here given; not to be put in practice being too powerful for most of the present sceptical generation to attempt, were they to do so, they would experience the stern realities of these Mighty Spirits who can be invocated to appear with such tremendous powers, and such awful attributes, as to cause many persons to shrink back and tremble.

22.

Concerning the Proportion, Measure, & Harmony of the Human Body.

Homo quoniam pulcherrimum absolutissimum que Dei opus, and imago, and minor mundus, ideoque perfectiore compositione, ac suaviori harmonia, sublimiorique dignitate omnes numeros, mensuras, pondera, motus and elementa, cæteras; omnium illum componétia in se continet ac sustinet, om- niaque in eo velut in supremo artificio, supremam quandam sortem ultra communem consonantiam quam habent in aliis cópositis, consequuntur: hinc antiqui omnes, digitis olim numerabant, and digitis numeros indi- -cabant, ex ipsisque humani corporis articulus, omnes numeros mensuras, proportiones, ac harmonias inventas fuisse, probare visi sunt. Unde ad hanc corporis commensurationem, templa, ædes, domos, theatra, insuper and navigia, and machinas and quodcunque artificii genus, and artificio- -rum ædificiorumque quæcunque sunt partes, and membra, puta columnas, epistilia, bases, antes, stilobates and hujusmodi cæteramomnia partiuntur, atque ex humano corpore deducunt. Quin and ipse Deus docuit Noe fabricare area ad humani corporis mensuram, ut qui ipse totam mundi machinam humano corpori symmetra fabricavit: unde ille magnus, hic vero minor mundus nuncupatur. Hinc microcosmologi nonnulli, humanum corpus per sex pedes, pedem vero per X grades, and gradum quemque per minutias V metiun- -tur: unde numerantur IX grades, qui faciunt minutias CCC. quibus æquiparan- -tur totidem cubiti geometrici quibus descripta est arca à Mose: sicut enim cor- -pus humanum est in longitudine trecentum minutorum, in latitudine quinquaginta in altitudine triginta: sic and longitudo arcæ facit cubitorum trecentorum, latitudo quinquaginta altitudo triginta, ut sit utrobiq; lon- -gitudinis ad latitudinis ad altitudine seseulpa proportio, ad altitudinem deculpa, latitudinis ad altitudinem super partiens duas tertias: pariq; modo omnium membrorum comensurationes sunt proportionatæ and

123

consonantes, and cum mundi membris atq. archetypi mensuris sic conve

-nientes, ut nullum sit in homine membrum, quod non respondeat alicui

signo, alicui stellae, alicui intelligentiae, alicui divino nomini in ipso arche-

-typo Deo tota autem corporis mensura tornatilis est et à rotunditate prove-

-niens ad ipsam tendere dignoscitur.

Est etiam quadrata mensura corpus proportionalissimum quippe statu-

-atur expassis brachiis in coniunctos pedes erectus homo, quadratum constituet aequi

-laterum, cuis centrum est in imo pectinis.

Quòd si super eodem centro circulus fabricetur per summum caput, demissis

brachiis, quousque extremi digiti circuli illius circumferentiam contingant,

passique pedes in eadem circumferentia quantum extrema manuum à

summo vertice distat, tunc circulum illum super imi pectinis cetro

ductum in quinque aequas partes dividunt, perfectum que pentagonum

constituunt, ipsique pedum extremi tali ad umbilicum relati, trian-

-gulum faciunt aequilaterum.

Quòd si immotis talis pedes dextrorsum sinistrorsum que in utrumque latus

protendantur, & manus ad capitis lineam eleventer, ipsi tunc extremi

pedum manuumque digiti aequilaterum quadratum dabunt, cuius centrum

supra umbilicum in cinctura corporis.

Quòd si manibus sic elevatis, taliter pedes, crura pandantur quo homo

decimaquarta parte erectae staturae suae brevior sit; tunc pedum

distantia ad imum pecten relata, aequilaterum triangulum faciet, and

centro in umbilico posito, circumductus circulus manuum pedumque

extrema continget.

Quòd si manus supra caput quam altissimè extendantur cubitus

aequabunt verticem: et si tunc iunctis pedibus ita stans homo in

quadratum aequilaterum locetur, per extrema manuum et pedum

conductum centrum illius quadrati in umbilico erit: qui idem

medium est inter summum verticem et genua.

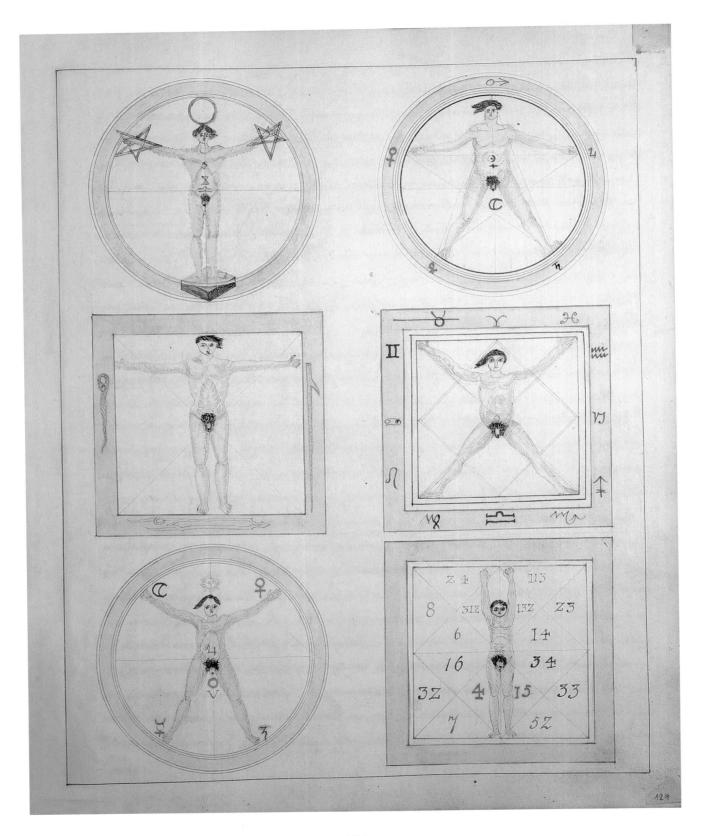

Sed iam ad particulares mensuras perveniamus Circuitus hominis sub alis, medietatem continet suæ longitudinis, cuis medium est in imo pectore: abinde verò sursum ad medium pectus inter utrasque mamillas, et à medio pectore in summum verticem utrobique pars quarta: similiter ab imo pectine usque sub genua, et inde ad extremos talos pars hominis quarta. Eadem est latitudo spatularum ab uno extremo in alterum: eadem est longitudo à cubito in extremum longioris digiti, ideoque hic cubitus dicitur: hinc quatuor cubiti constituunt longitudinem hominis: latitudinem verò quæ in spatulis est cubitus unus que verò in cinctura est, pes un cubitum autem constituunt palmi sex pedem verò quatuor: et quatuor digiti palmum: totaque hominis longitudo palmarum viginti quatuor, pedum sex, digitorum sex et nonaginta. Ab imo pectinis ad summum pectoris, pars longitudinis sexta: à summo pectore ad supremam frontem, et radices imas capillorum, pars longitudinis septima: corporis robusti et bene quadrati pes, est pars longitudinis sexta: procerioris autem septima: nec potest Varrone et Gellio testibus humanum corpus proceritatem septem pedem excedere. Denique cincturæ diameter et quod à restricta manus usque in interiorem plicaturam cubiti spatium est: et quod à pectore usque ad utrasque mamillas, sursum ad suprema labra, sive deorum usque ad umbilicum est, quodque est inter extrema offium, supremi pectoris gulam cingentium, et quod ad planta pedis ad finem lacerti: et exinde in mediam genu rotulam. omnes hæ mensuræ, sibi cœquales sunt, et septimam totius altitudinis costituunt. Caput hominis ab imo mento in summum verticem, pars longitudinis octava: totidem à cubito in finem spatularum: tantus etiam reperitur procerioris hominis cincturæ diameter. Circulus capitis per supremam frontem et imas radices occipitis ductus, facit totius longitudinis partem quintam: tantundem

26

etiam prestat latitudo pectoris. Hominem quadratum et compactum constituunt facies novem, procerum vero decem. In novem itaque portiones hominis longitudine partita, facies à suprema fronte usque in extremu mentum, una est: deinde ab imo gutturis five supremo pectoris ad summu stomachu altera: abinde ad umbilicu, tertia: ab hoc ad imum femur, quarta: ab illo coxendices ad poplitem constituunt duas. abinde usque ad nodum pedis. crura continent duas alias: quæ omnes partes sunt octo. Porro arcus a summa fronte ad summum verticem et quodã est à mento ad summum pectoris guttur, atque quod à nodo pedis ad imam plantam. hæc tria spacia coniuncta constituunt nonam. In latum quoque pectus habet partes duas et utraque brachia septem. Quod vero corpus decem facies constituunt ipsum est proportionatissimum. Hujus itaque primo portio est à summo vertice ad imas nares: abinde ad supremum pectus secunda et consequenter ad supremum stomachum, tertia. ab eo ad umbilicum, quarta. et inde ad imum pecten quinta, ubi est medium humanæ longitudinis. à quo usque in extremas plantas, sunt quinque aliæ partes, quæ prioribus juncta, faciut decem integras, quibus proinde corpus omne mensura proportionatissima commensuratur. nam facies hominis ab imo mento ad summam frontem et radices imas capilli est, quãta pars una decima. Manus hominis à restricta usque ad extremum longioris digiti, etia pars una: similiter inter utraque mammillarum puncta, pars una: et ab utrisque ad imam gulam, triangulus æquilaterus. Frontis inferioris ab una aure ad alteram, latitudo est partis unius: totius autem pectoris latitudo videlicet à supremo pectore ad juncturas spatularum, utrobique partis unius: quæ faciunt duas. Circulus capitis transversus ab interstitio superciliorum per supremam frontem

27

usque in finem occipitis ubi terminatur capallitium, etiam partium duorum: ab humeris extrinsecus ad juncturas articulorum manus et intrinsecus ab axellis ad confinia palmæ digitorum, partes tres: circulus capitis per mediam frontem, partium trium. Circulus cincturæ tenet partes quatuor, in robusto homine: in delicatiore corpore, pars tres cum dimidia, seu quantum est a summo pectore in imum pecten. Circulus pectoris per alas ad tergum partes quinque, videlicet quantum longitudinis totius medium. A summo vertice ad nodum gulæ, sunt totius altitudinis quæ decimatertiæ: elevatis in altum brachiis cubitus accedit Summo vertici. Cæterum nunc quæ adhuc reliquæ commensurationes sibi æquales sunt: spectemus. Quantum est à mento ad summum pectus, tanta est latitudo colli: quantum à summo pectore ad umbilicum, tota est colli circulatio: quantum à mento in supremum verticem, tanta est latitudo cincturæ: quantum est ab interciliis ad summ...tanta mas hares, tantum à jugulo distat productio nicti, quantum que à summis naribus ad mentum tantum ad mentum, tantum à jugulo ad imam gulam. Item oculorum ab interciliis ad interiores angulos concavitas, ac summarum narium prominentia and quod ab imis naribus ad extremum supremi labri interstitium est, hæc tria sunt interse aqualia. _____

28

The following Talisman must be formed as follows,
Take a piece of Virgin parchment about three inches square and on
it Engrave according to the model. it has two faces therefore
the words and Characters are to be written on each respective side, as
shewn, or a plate of Iron highly polished, and of a circular
form (the size immaterial) may be employed instead of parchment.
this plate must be engraven on both sides as shewn, the formation
and preparation belonging to this Talisman must be made in
the day and hour of Mars which is the first hour and the Eighth
hour after sunrise on Tuesday when the Moon is in sextile
or Trine to Mars and if possible when both the Luminaries are
in fortune aspects with Jupiter, Venus, or Mercury, which every
Astrologer knows, and which the Ephemeris will teach; all must be
done in the Increase of the Moon. If Parchment is to be em-
-ployed the ink must be consecrated and of the proper colour
suitable to Mars and the lines & Characters must be drawn and written
distinctly. if Metal is employed it must be engraven in the same
manner. When completed the person for whom it is made must
retire to a secret place and fumigating it with the Magical suffumigation
of the Spirits of Mars which consists of Red Saunders, Frankincense & pepper
repeating the orations &c for Tuesday, as given in a former part of this Work
likewise he, may recite one or two passages from the Psalms where
David prayed that he might overcome his enemies, also there are numerous
passages in the scriptures that might be repeated for the same purpose
but firm trust and sincere faith must be employed in repeating these
orations & passages, or but little benefit will be derived. After the Talisman
be completed it must kept clean & suspended from some part of the Body
of the wearer and in great Secrecy, or it may be worn on the finger in the
form of a ring, the Characters &c engraven on the inside. It is said to give
Victory over every earthly Enemy when rightly formed.

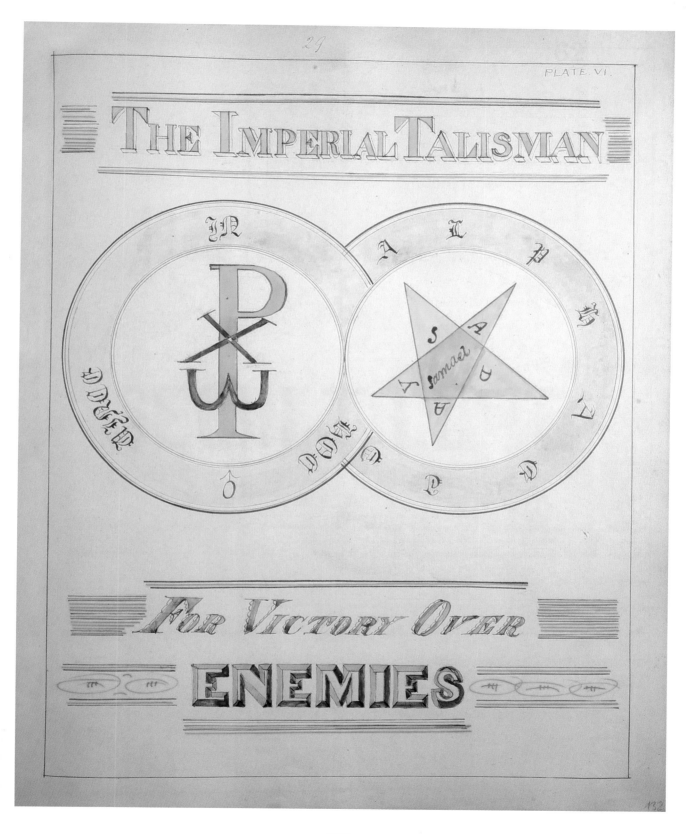

30

Powerful Talisman

FOR

SECRET LOVE

This Invaluable and Admirable Talisman is copied, and the manner in which it is composed is translated from an ancient Manuscript. Its Virtue and Power have been often proved and verified by the most learned and skilful in the Occult Sciences. This Mysterious Image when formed according to the Rules of Art, has the means of producing that Secret and pure Love in the heart of either Male or Female on whom it acts, that neither Time Distance nor Circum-stance can dissolve, and nothing but Death separate.

133

31

The manner of composing the Talisman is as follows, Get a plate of
Silver of about three inches in diameter put it in the fire for a few
minutes till it is hot enough to receive the essence of the perfumes proper
the Planet Venus, which are Valerian, Enrula Campana, Red Coral, Dried
Red Roses, Musk and Ambergris, these must all be properly dried and
pulverized and the powder sprinkled on the silver plate while it is hot
after which the plate must be polished and engraved according
to the following Model. All this Operation must be perform in
the hour of Venus on Friday or Monday, the size of the Talisman
or is of no consequence. In constructing this Talisman if Silver
be not employed, Virgin Copper managed in the same way will serve
All these little materials & Ingredients must be consecrated before being used

33

The Artist is fully aware, that without the assistance of an Invisible power subject to an All Wise Creator, a senseless plate of Metal engraven with Mysterious Names and Characters is useless - notwithstanding whatever secret or hidden property it may possess. Now as has been said in the former part of this Book that every kind of plant, Mineral, or Metal is appropriated to one or other of the seven planets and each of these Planets governed by a Celestial Angel or Intelligency under whom are many Heavenly Genii who are permitted to Execute the earnest and lawful demands, of the operator according to the Sovereign Will of an Omnipotent God Such a power governing the Day and Hour of Operation, to give Life and virtue thereto, must be invoked visibly or invisibly present at the operation to render the desired aid. The Invocant must have firmness, Courage, patience, and great Faith & Confidence in the success of his operation. And not in any way quake, or tremble, or be dismayed at the presence of these Glorious and Celestial Beings with their Mighty Attributes, for they are harmless. There must be mutual Sympathy existing between the Operator and the wearer of the of the Talisman, also a small part conducive to success must be taken and submitted to as a cooperation in the Work by the latter. Having begun his Operation at the time stated, let the Operator repeat his Invocation earnestly as follows. After which, the Spirit will appear, if the Invocant be patient and watchful If he appears not at the first call, or Invocation, it must be repeated, even the third time, but if the operator be confident he rarely has to repeat this All powerful Conjuration but once, for this Glorious and Celestial being is neither obstinate nor refractory, but become subservient to the Will of the Invocant and he will come either in a Visible or Invisible form.

135

34

Invocation

O Thou Mighty Prince of Love **Lord Ahalioth** who lovest thy servants and will be loved by them I pray you to make this Operation successfull by granting my desires and give Virtue and Power to this Talisman so that it may not fail in being Efficacious in winning and for Ever sacred Pure and Genuine Love of M.L.K towards me by the Inter-position of those among the Heavenly Genii whom you cherish most which are **Raniel Corat Madie Penat** I intreat you to diffuse on my Operation such success as shall be conformable to my intention and redound to your Glory with all suitable acknowledgement O thou fair Angel of God **Anael** Prince of Love be propitious to my Vows that through thy mediation I may hopefully fulfil my Desires by Jesus Christ our Lord Amen. Come on the wings of the Zephyrs fair **Anael** and all ye Happy Genii who preside over the workings of the Heart Come Heavenly **Sarahotes Husaltiel Doremiel Setchiel** hear favourably the Invocation that I make this Day devoted to the Wonders of Love. Be ready to lend thy Assistance to succeed in gaining the pure sincere undivided and unchangeable Love of M.L.K that he or she may feel its powerful influence and be both able and willing to exercise its benign power and Virtue to its fullest extent. I Conjure you by the Veneration you have for the Mysterious Name **Setchiel** O beneficent Genii who preside over the Operation of this Day I conjure you fair **Anael** who rejoicest at these fumigations and smells come to receive them be favourable and kind unto me vouchsafe to Bless this Talisman and to Consecrate it so that it may have Power to bind M.L.K and make him or her to Love me with a secret and undying love. I again Conjure **Talaroth, Niveg Cuphaniel Clesros** that you will come with all your power to scatter and put to flight the Evil Spirits which are hurtful and inimical to good operations cause me to succeed by the Powerful Virtue in what I have undertaken this Day in the Name of the Father and of the Son and of the

Holy Ghost

The sign of the coming of this fair and beautiful Angel, is a furious west wind mingled with gentle Zephyrs accompanied with invisible and Heavenly music delightful to the ear and thrilling the heart and Soul with enchanting strains of harmony, then follow sweet sounds of the most melodious voices in concert, to which the most accomplished earthly singer with the richest voice affords no parallel or comparison. After these sweet Sounds have ceased, there will be bright and shining light in the midst of which will appear innumerable forms of handsome maidens in the most enticing forms mingling with their presence, Music, Joy, and Beauty. These disappearing, will be succeeded to the astonishment of the Invocant, sweeter sounds even than before, heralding the approach of this Mighty and Glorious Spirit who appears with a fair body, mean stature with an amiable pleasant and handsome countenance and of a pure white, and golden coloured hair, his motion is like a clear Star, and when properly and earnestly invoked he will appear willingly in the above form in all the plenitude of Majestic Glory and surrounded by a brilliant light of resplendent beauty which will ravish the senses and fill the soul of the Operator with Delight and wondrous amazement. When this Glorious Angel is summoned to appear visibly, the Invocant must receive him affably and courteously, present unto him his petition written on Virginal parchment, which after he has granted by his presence, License him to Depart in the usual and respectful manner. This will be accompanied with similar sounds to those heard on the approach of this beautiful Spirit. After the Invocant has succeeded so far let Him complete the Talisman ∴ according to the Rules of Art omitting nothing, after which let him return thanks unto Allmighty God for his permission in allowing these Heavenly beings to assist in the Operation. This Matchless Charm when completed must be worn in Secret in some part of the Dress nearest the heart, its power and virtue is to make the wearer become so lovely charming & fascinating in the eyes of him or her whose heart, is stirred up with an unconquerable and Secret Love that he cannot be happy only in the presence of his or her adorned one. All this powerful Operation must be done in secret & at the proper times.

∴ The figures on the outside of the Talismanic circles are not to be engraved thereon, being only an embellishment.

After the Artist has Invoked to visible appearance this Beautiful and Mighty Spirit who from his gentle mild and amicable nature is ever ready to lend his assistance according to true and earnest desires of the Invocant therefore it would afford an excellent opportunity to have all ready in the operation by the Wheel of Magic (as per example) to further solicit the aid of this powerful Spirit during his presence and so to blend the two operations together which would act with a two fold power on the object acted upon and cause this potent Charm to act with certainty and success but the wearer of this infallible Talisman must not lose sight of the fact that all the power which is given in Heaven and on Earth is derived from God alone, who maketh his Angels Ministers for the purpose of executing his Holy Will. therefore he or they who would solicit and Invoke their aid must bear in mind that it is only by Divine permission according to the strength of our faith and vehemence of our desires that these Glorious and Celestial Intelligences are allowed to leave their bright abods thus breaking the bonds of natural order and to hold converse with us finite mortals. Therefore it behoves all who desire to the aid of these Heavenly beings must pray for Protection and Help of God, to whom we must appeal in every time of need, not forgetting to return thanks for every favour and success granted to us.

Whoever wears the Talisman &c must be reminded that he or she must conform to all the details of the Operation and be willing & ready to comply with whatever request the he has the power to grant for the for the furtherance and success of the Operations which when combined in the manner aforesaid will have the effect of producing that secret, genuine and imperishable Love in the heart of the Object on whom the Operator or wearer has fixed his or her choice. also it will gain the Universal Love and respect of all mankind. and in a great degree ameliorate the feelings of the most Malicious and Inveterate foes of him or her who trusts in it.

38

The Letters which compose this Charm, must be written in a pyramidal form as shewn, on Virgin Parchment, with the Quill of a Raven and with Ink formed out of the smoke of a consecrated Wax candle, in a plain and distinct manner without any regard to ornament, colouring &c of any kind, this Figure may be surrounded with a double circle and the sentences therein written in a common plain hand with the ink aforesaid, it is said to give more force to the Charm.   Let the party who is afflicted of the disease, which he would have cured, wear the Charm hung round his neck during the time that the Moon performs one circuit through the twelve signs of the Zodiac, and let it be performed on the day of the full Moon, and if possible while the Moon is in the Magical signs Sagittarius or Pisces and in a fortunate Aspect with Jupiter, Venus, or Mercury.   It is necessary that the wearer have a firm and confident faith in the Power of Divine Omnipotence; and the following Oration must be said upon first beginning to wear this Holy Charm with great earnestness and devotion; and in very difficult cases the Patient should repeat the Oration daily in the same manner. ————————————————————

Oration

O sweet Lord Jesus Christ ✕ the true God, who didst descend from the kingdom of thy Almighty Father, being sent to wash away our sins, to release those who were in prison and afflicted, to console the sorrowful and the needy, to absolve and to liberate me, thy servant, from my affliction and tribulation in which I am placed. So, O Omnipotent Father, thou that didst receive us again by his expiation, into that Paradise by thy blood, O Jesu ✕ obtained, and didst make us equal among Angels and men. Thou, O Lord Jesus Christ ✕ wert worthy to stand between me and mine enemies, and to establish my peace and to show thy grace upon me, and to pour out thy mercy. And thou, O Lord didst extinguish the anger of mine enemies, which they contained against me, as thou didst take away the wrath of Esau, which he had against Jacob his brother O Lord Jesus ✕ extend thine arm towards me, and deliver me, and deliver me from my affliction, even as thou didst deliver Abraham from the hands of the Chaldean, and his son, Isaac from the sacrifice, and Jacob from the hand of his brethren, Noah, from the deluge; and even as thou deliveredst thy servant Lot; thy servants Moses and Aaron, and thy people Israel, from the hands of Pharaoh, and out of the land of Egypt, David from

138

39

the hands of Saul, and the giant Goliath; or as thou didst deliver Susannah from her accusers; Judith from the hands of Holofernes; Daniel from the den of lions; the three youths from the fiery furnace, Jonah from the whale's belly; or as thou deliveredst the son of Canannea who was tormented by the devil; even as thou deliveredst Adam from hell, by thy most precious blood; and Peter and Paul from chains. So, O, most sweet Lord Jesus × Son of the living God, preserve me, thy servant, from my affliction, and mine enemies; and be my assistant, and my blessing. By thy Holy Incarnation, By thy fasting and thirst, By thy labours and affliction, By thy stripes, By thy thorny Crown, By thy drink of gall and vinegar, By thy most cruel Death, By the words which thou spakest upon the Cross, By thy descent into hell, By thy consolation of thy Disciples, By thy Wonderful Ascension, By the Appearance of the Holy Spirit, By the Day of Judgment, By thy great Gifts, and by thy Holy Names Adonay× Gloym × Aelaym× Pary× Zazael× Paliel× Saday × Pxoe × Paras× Caelphi× Saday × and by thy Ineffable Name יהוה Jehovah.× By all these Holy, Omnipotent, and All-powerful names of singular effica-cy and extraordinary power, which the elements obey, and at which the devils tremble: O most gra-cious Jesu × grant, I beseech thee that this Holy Charm which I now wear about my person, may be the means of healing my lamentable sickness; so shall the praise thereof be ascribed, O Lord, to thee alone, and thou alone shalt have all the Glory. Amen. —————————

————————— Fiat ——— Fiat ——— Fiat ——————————

By making use of the above occult and sacred remedy the most miraculous cures have been heretofore performed; and as there is nothing therein which is in any way derogatory to the power of the Supreme being, or inimical to our fellow-creatures, there certainly can be no harm in making continual use thereof upon every occasion

This admirable Charm is translated from a curious Manuscript of the Twelfth Century. —————————

410

Another Way

If it were required to perform a cure upon one at a distance, or without the afflicted party's knowledge thereof, let the Charm be written on Virgin Parchment, and then you may perform the cure without their knowledge, by scraping out one line of the Charm every day with a new knife, kept for the express purpose; and at scraping out each line, say as follows :—

So as I destroy the letters of this Charm, **Abracadabra**, so, by the virtue of this sacred Name, may all grief and dolor depart from **A.B.** In the Name of the Father, and of the Son, and of the Holy Ghost. In the Name of the Father, I destroy this disease. In the Name of the Son I destroy this disease; and in the Name of the Holy Spirit, I destroy this disease. Amen.

By performing the Operation with strict Confidence and earnestness, many have healed divers diseases this way; the disease wearing by little and little, away. Therefore keep it a secret, and fear God. (Ancient Manuscript.)

139

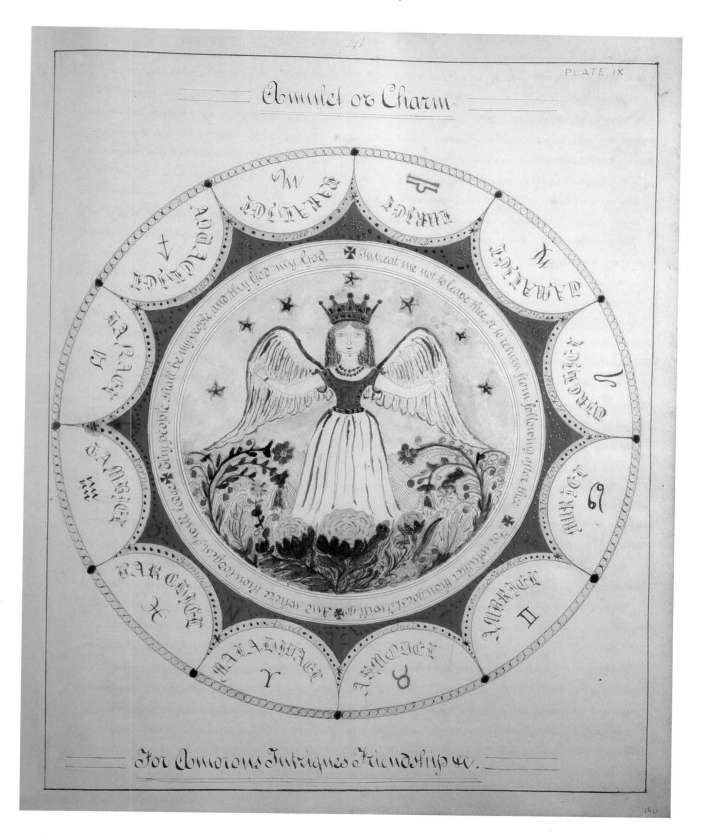

To compose this Amulet or Charm according to the Rules of Art, the following in-grediences are necessary. A piece of fair Virgin parchment about three inches square, or a plate of Copper highly polished, of the same size, on which must be engraven in the circles, or written in green Ink properly consecrated; the perfumes composed as mentioned in the last Experiment, to which must be added a small lock of hair from the nape of the neck, et pubes pubendam of the person who is to wear the charm, also a little menstruous sanguis, and a small quantity of blood drawn from the right hand by piercing gently with a small penknife or needle at the mount of Venus, a portion of the blood must be mixed with the hair cut very fine and used with the perfumes in suffumigating the Pentacle, if metal be employed. The perfume is to be used as mentioned elsewhere. The Figure in the interior circle of the foregoing Model is a rude representation of the form in which the spirit usually appears when invoked to aid in the operation. This figure is not to be drawn on the pentacle but in the place thereof, the Names of the parties consenting to the operation, to be written in their own blood and joined by the name Anael between them thus, James+Anael+Jane The Pentacle of Solomon, or the character of the Spirit governing the operation may be engraven or written on the reverse side of this Amulet, according to the models already given. This Operation being under the influence of the Planet Venus, must be performed at Sun-rise on Friday, the Moon increasing, and in fortunate aspect to Venus, Jupiter or Mercury.

Now as has been remarked in the preceding Experiments that these plates of Metal &c with their mysterious characters have no power nor force in themselves though there may be a latent virtue. It is therefore necessary to Invoke one of those Glorious and powerful Angels who governs such operation to give vivifying power, force, and virtue to succeed in the Operation. For which purpose the Operator must be of a religious frame of mind, intrepid in Spirit, persevering in pursuit, fearless in danger, faithful and patient in waiting, earnest in his desires and confident of success. He may then earnestly commence invoking the Spirit to visible appearance. If he does not appear at the first call, let the Operator after waiting a short time, repeat the Invocation, even the third time if he does not appear. The Spirit generally appears in a visible form at the first call if the Air is calm and bright and a cloudless sky, but if the sky is overcast by clouds rain or tempest or the elements otherwise disturbed the Spirit may appear but not in a visible form not being able to take form or shape at that time, therefore clear sky serene weather by day or night is requisite for intercourse with those Glorious inhabitants of the Spheres.

43

Invocation

Happy Spirits and Genii who preside over the softest emotions of the heart I pray you to hear favourably the Invocation that I make this Day destined to the wonders of pure Love and Sincere Friendship, be ready with the power and virtue you possess through the Sovereign command, will and permission of the Omnipotent and Eternal God whose All-seeing eye searcheth the secret recesses of the heart and reins of his people; lend me your assistance to succeed in what I have undertaken.

I Invoke, and Call upon, and Command thee Fair Amabel prince of Love by the Mighty, Incomprehensible, and Ineffable Names of the great יהוה. Saday, El &c Adonay Elohim Tetragrammaton that thou will send unto me Amabiel or other of your Ministering Spirits who shall appear visibly to me in the fair and beautiful form of an Angel to give virtue and power and success to this Operation and impress upon this mysterious Image that virtue to accomplish the desired effect.

I Invoke again thou powerful Spirit Amabiel to appear before me visibly in fair and perfect Form without delay and render unto me thy powerful aid in the Operation of this day.

I again Conjure thee Spirit Amabiel by the Names of the heavenly Genii Abalidoth Sitchiel Susaltiel Doremiel that thou immediately appear to me as aforesaid with all your power to scatter and put to flight the Evil Spirits which are inimical to good Operations, cause me by thy powerful Virtue to succeed in what I have undertaken this Day which is consecrated to Venus.

Therefore, through the Virtue of our Lord and Saviour Jesus Christ in whose Name I attend, wait for, and expect thy appearance.

The Invocant need be under no apprehension or fear of harm or danger in Invocating this Celestial Intelligence who is Humane, Affable, and kind, and perfectly harmless, and may be invoked to appear in less time & with less trouble than the other Planetary Angels.

44

After reciting the Invocation, the Invocant must wait with patience the appearance of the Spirit, who generally appears at the first call if the Atmosphere be clear and serene, the signs of his coming are similar to those mentioned in the foregoing Experiment, viz a furious west wind which lasts but a few minutes when all becomes calm and quiet, then are heard the most enchanting strains of Heavenly music, accompanied by melodious voices, so powerful rich and sweet as to charm the ear and feelings with exstacy, these sounds die away in sweet distant murmurings, which are followed by the appearance of innumerable handsome maidens, lovely to behold, being full of Music Joy & Beauty, their stay is short, and again the elements seem in commotion for a few seconds, when all again becomes quiet. Suddenly a Glorious and shining light, appears in the midst of which a clear Star is seen quick in motion, which suddenly resolves itself into the form of a beautiful Angel, surrounded by resplendent beams of Angelic Glory and brightness, which so enchant the feelings of the Invocant as to cause him to fall down and adore the Creator who has given him by his sovereign will, permission to hold converse with those Glorious Inhabitants of the Celestial Spheres.   This beautiful Spirit thus appearing, ✷ the Invocant must receive him courteously fearing no harm from him, for his presence, is to promote Love between Married persons, Amorous intrigues, and friendship with all. The Operator must lay the prepared Amulet or charm before this Immortal being, signi- fying his intention and wish, which will be notified & answered by his presence, duly impressing the Mysterious Image with Power and virtue requisite for the accom- -plishment and success of the Operation.

After the Invocant has obtained his desires &c of the Spirit, he may License him to Depart in the same courteous manner as he received him, his departure will be attended with sounds, appearances &c similar to those which heralded his coming. All being completed, the person who is to wear the charm must sew it up in a new piece of Silk or Cloth of a green colour, and fasten it in the lining of the dress so as not to be seen, & worn day and night next the heart. This being kept a profound secret & having faith, the wearer may secure the Love of his most dearest friends, and the good will and friendship of most of those persons with whom he may come in contact. The Operator should return hearty thanks to God, for his success in the Operation.

✷ This Glorious Being sometimes appears in the form of a beauteous female with Angel's wings, and a regal Crown upon her head, her countenance of surpassing loveliness.

142

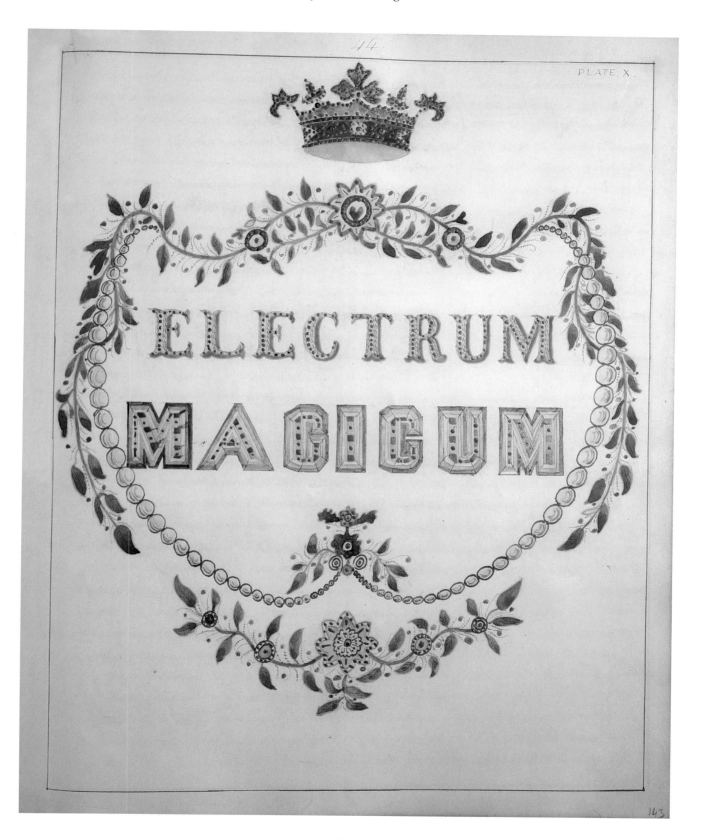

45

The Electrum Magicum is a compound of all the Seven Metals in a due order and fit time melted together into one Mass of Metal in which all the Virtues of the Seven Planets are joined together, under their influences. In this Electrum, the Operations of the Heavens, and Influences of the Seven Planets are combined and stored up. Therefore the Ancient Persian Magi; and the Chaldæans found out and performed many wonderful things by its means. The manner in which this Electrum is composed is as follows. Take four half ounces of pure Gold which must be poured through the Antimony, melt it on Sunday in the hour of the ☉ which, is the first hour after Sun rise, when it is well fused, throw purified saltpetre into it, until it emits sparks of all kinds of colours, when it is well purified, pour it into a new vessel, afterwards, melt in it, on a Monday in the hour of the Moon ☽ four half ounces of refined silver; purify it with salt of tartar, which has no culinary salt in it, and do not continue the operations beyond their respective planetary hours. On a Tuesday, in the hour of ♂, melt clean pure Iron with potashes, and cleanse it further with pitch or tar. On a Wednesday, in the hour of ☿, melt four half ounces of Quicksilver, which purify with pitch. On Thursday, in the hour of ♃, melt three half ounces of Tin; purify it with the fat of a ram. On a Friday in the hour of ♀, take four half ounces of Virgin Copper, purify it with vinegar and Saltpetre carefully; then strain it through a piece of leather. On the Saturday, in the hour of ♄, melt pure Lead, throw a good deal of pitch or tar upon it, and put it by, and take, in the hour of the Sun, Jupiter, Venus, or Mercury, the Moon increasing in Light and in a favourable aspect to one or more of the fortunate planets to melt in the same hour all the Metals together. Put therefore, your purified Lead first into the crucible, afterwards the Tin before it is too hot, then pour the quicksilver into it and stir it about with a hazel stick, then put the Copper into it, and give it a strong heat, afterwards the Silver; next the Gold. While all this fusing, throw into it the eighth part of an ounce of mineral steel, also a small portion of perfume peculiar to each planet, viz. Musk, Ambergris, Storax, Benjamin, Euphorbium, bdellium, Mastic, Incense, Loadstone, Red Roses, Red Coral, Myrrh of the East and grains Black pepper, these perfumes must be pulverized and cast into the Crucible while the mass is fusing & properly incorporated with it. After this compound is thoroughly mixed and incorporated & become as one Metal. It must be taken & placed in the crucible & put over the fire which must be fierce till it is all melted, this must be done in

144

46

the first hour after sunrise on Sunday or Thursday. In order to cast this melted metal in plates, the operator must be provided with a mould of about three inches in diameter the thickness of the plate is immaterial but of a substance so as not liable to be broken, while pouring the metal into the mould, the operator must repeat the following prayer three times.

Prayer.

⊙ ✕ Tetragrammaton ✕ thou powerful God and Father! we praise, love, and pray to thee, we also here are collected laying before thee like poor earth, and ashes. We honour thy Holy and Majestic Name, we pray thee thou will permit thy Glorious Inhabitants of the Spheres to assist and bring to pass the lawful, just, and earnest desires of thy humble servants and that thou wilt impress this Image and Characters thereon, with Divine Power and Virtue, through Our Lord and Saviour Jesus Christ. Amen.

Then sing a song of praise to God such as the Psalm Te Deum Laudamus &c. The Latent properties of these Metals when compounded as above described have power and Secret virtue to drive away Evil Spirits and to assist in promoting Health, Honour, Riches, Eloquence, Trade Business, Love and Friendship, Secret Dreams, discovery of Hidden Treasures. Victory over Enemies also to Defend against and moderate chief of the Troubles & inconveniences of Life.

It must not be supposed a person possessing a Mysteries Image composed of this invaluable metal will enjoy any of the above gifts without Divine Aid added to an earnest faith of the possessor, for which purpose a plate of this precious compound must have seven circles engraved upon it in each must be engraven or written a short sentence descriptive of the Wish or desire of the Operator peculiar to the Seven planets, according to the following model. The Seals of the Seven Planetary Angels & their Characters must be engraven in the respective circles during which time (at Sunrise) on Sunday the prayer should be repeated with great earnestness, such will be the power & virtue of this admirable Talisman that success generally will attend the operator if the manner of composing it be Strictly observed. It will not lose its virtue by a change of Masters providing the New Master Agrees & believes with faith & confidence in its efficacy.

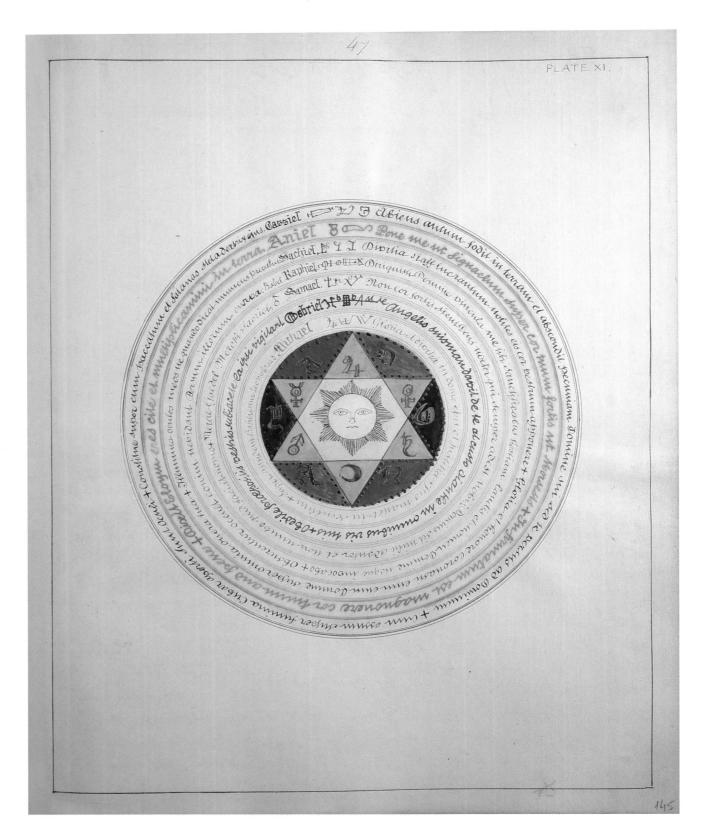

48

PLATE. XII.

Magia Campanum

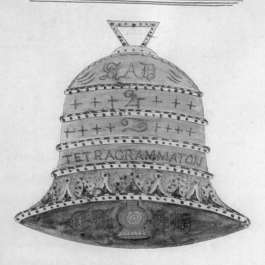

This bell must be formed of electrum magicum, and fashioned as above shown, and according to the rules as before mentioned, round it the words + Tetragrammaton + and + Sadai + must be engraven in relief, and also the sign and planet under which the operator is born. Also inside thereof the word + Elohim ÷ and the clapper Adonai. It must be kept in a clean chamber, and not touched or handled but by the operator. When the Celestial Spirits or agents are to be Invoked, make a fire with incense and proper perfumes agreeable to the good Angel to be invoked, then rehearse devoutly an appropri- ate incantation such as the one already written, naming the Spirit, and ring the bell thrice, when the Spirit will instantly appear before thee, and thou wilt have thy wishes performed. This must be kept a great secret. This Bell may be of any size & weight. Its virtue & power is when rung, to draw many Spirits and Spectres of various kinds. Also to drive away all evil Spirits. By an earnest desire for any new undertaking, and express- ing the same on the inner surface of the Bell in words & characters, the Bell being rung as before, the Spirit governing such and undertaking would appear in any form the Operator wished, by renewing the words & characters Evil Spirit, wild beasts & even men

146

49

would be driven away at the sound of this instrument, for being made of the Electrum, it is of more importance than words, although the latter must be expressed, earnestly desiring our wish to be gratified. The Operator must take care that he expresses, nor desires any thing that is not agreeable, or in accordance with the nature of the Good Spirits he wishes to Invoke, for by doing so, he might be annoyed by the appearance of Evil Spirits & instead of the good, in that case, he must dismiss by powerful adjurations, ringing the bell three times. Therefore when any of the Celestial Messengers or Glorious Spirits are invoked to appear, the Operator must wait with patience, and be firm, courageous, possessing great Confidence trusting in God. When the Spirit appears, he must be received courteously, and without fear, terror or dismay; after the Operator has had his desire granted, and his wishes gratified, Let him dismiss the Spirit in the same courteous manner as he received him by ringing the Bell and repeat the Licence to Depart, which he will do imperceptibly, vanishing as into thin air. It has been said, that if a constellated Peale, made of the Electrum, after the manner as before described, and placed under a person's pillow at night, will give him extraor-dinary and beautiful Dreams, and make him hear heavenly Music.

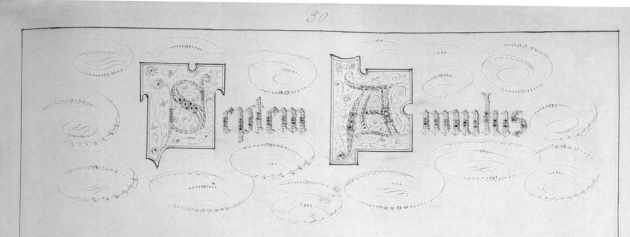

Septem Annulus

Compositio Septem Annulorum is formed as follows: The operator must be provided with the Seven virgin Metals, which are governed by the seven Planets as have been mentioned in the former part of this Book, they must be pure and unadulterated. On Sunday at Sunrise, having everything ready for the operation as before described, take a sufficient portion of pure Gold and put in a ladle of Iron over a fierce fire till it is thoroughly melted, during this process cast a small portion of perfume proper to the Sun, and when thoroughly melted & mixed, take the ladle containing the melted metal and cast therefrom a ring (the size of the fourth finger) into a mould formed for the purpose, which being done, the ring must be polished and engraven with the Name, Seal, Character and Number of the Planetary Angel who governs the Operation on Sunday. While performing the Operation, the Operator must devoutly, and with confidence, repeat the Oration, Invocation & Conjuration proper to the Sun. (See Talismans.) Should there not be sufficient time during the Planetary hour to complete the Operation, the Operator must wait patiently till the next hour of the Sun arrives, and so on till the ring is completed, which, when done must be carefully wrapped up in a piece of silk of a Yellow or gold colour, and kept by itself secretly till it is to be worn on the finger. The same process must be gone through in respect to the other rings on their respective days and in their respective planetary hours, which is always the first hour after sunrise and so on The Operator must take care that he omits not the reciting of the Orations &c. proper the planets on their respective days, but carry out the details with much exactness & punctuality in each operation. The Operator must remember that the remaining six rings are composed of the following Metals, viz, Silver for Monday under the Moon, Iron for Tuesday under Mars, Quicksilver for Wednesday under

51

Mercury. Tin for Thursday under Jupiter. Copper for Friday under Venus. Lead for Saturn on Saturday. Every operation must be performed during the Increase of the Moon. Each of these rings when made, polished and engraven with the Seals, characters, &c. (on the inside) of the respective planets governing the operations, must be kept like the one for sunday, wrapped up separately, and in secresy till the wearer thinks proper to wear them. They are intended to be worn as follows, only one on each day. viz. the Gold one on Sunday, for Health, Honour, and Riches. the Silver on Monday, for safety in Travelling by Sea or Land, the Iron for Tuesday, against Enemies Troubles &c. The Quicksilver for Wednesday, for acquiring Eloquence, Liberty &c. Tin for Thursday, for prosperity in Trade & dealings. Copper for Friday, for Secret Love and Amorous Intrigues, friendship &c. Lead for Saturday, for Discovery of Treasures, remarkable Dreams &c. The secret properties of the Septem Annulorum when properly formed according to the rules of Art, will considerably aid their possessor in the common affairs of life, providing he consents to all that is done in their formation and posses an earnest belief in their efficacy. It has been proved that a ring of Virgin Silver, made on Monday in the hour of the Moon when in fortunate Aspect with Jupiter has a singular effect in curing fits of Epilepsy by constantly wearing the ring night and Day. The manner of forming this powerful Ring is as follows: If a married person is afflicted; there must Collected a silver coin such as a shilling or sixpence of each of the opposite sex who are married also, till a sufficient number is collected to purchase a sufficient weight of Virgin silver ring to form the ring which must be formed in the same manner as before described. If the unmarried be afflicted, then the silver coins, must be collected of the opposite sex of the same condition, each contributing to the success of the Operation by repeating a short earnest prayer for the recovery of the patient. This ring is efficacious in driving away Fits of Melancholy &c. The engraving must be inside.

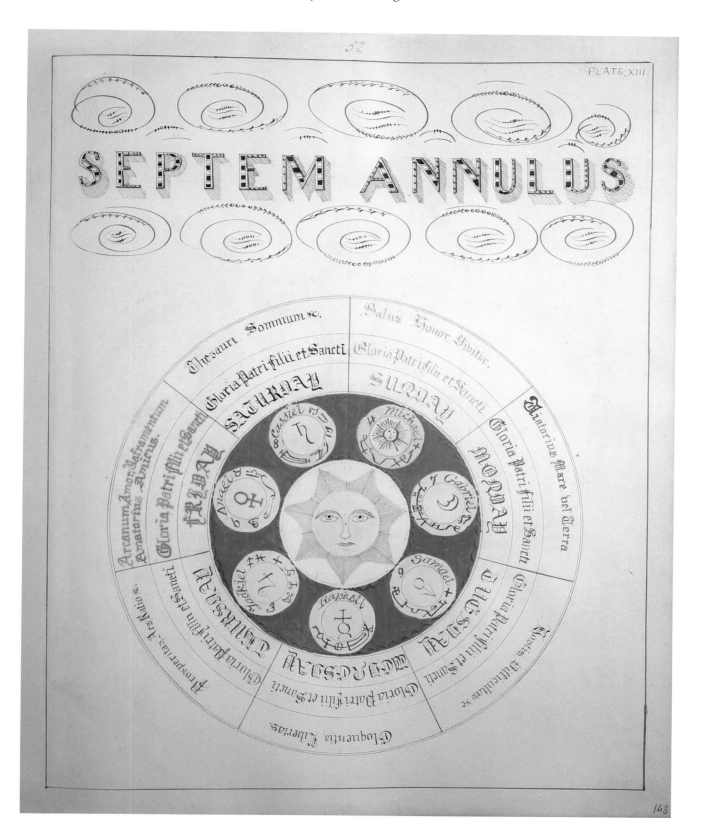

54

De Fascinatione atque eius Artificio.

Fascinatio est ligatio quæ ex spiritu fascinatis per oculos fascinati ad cor ipsius ingressa pervenit. Fasci-nationis autem instrumentum spiritus est scil vapor quidam purus, lucidus subtilis, à cordis calore ex puriori sanguine generatus, hic similes sibi radios per oculos semper emittit radii isti emissi vaporem spiritualem secum ferunt: vapor ille sanguinem, sicut apparet in lippis ac rubentib oculis, cuius radius usque ad obvios spectantis oculos emissus, vaporem una secum corrupti sanguinis trahit, cuius côtagione cogit spectatis oculos morbo simili laborare sic patefactus et in aliquem intentus oculus cum forti imaginatione pro suorum radiorum aculeis, qui spiritus vehicula sunt, ipsos in adversos oculos jaculatur: qui quidem lentus spiritus fascinati deverberans oculos, cũ à percutientis corde micatur, percussi præcordia, tanquam regionem propriam feritus, cur vulnerat et spiritum inficit peregrinus his spiritus. Unde Apuleius: Isti, inquit, oculi tui per meos oculos ad intima delapsi præcordia acerrimum meis medulis commovent incendium. Scias itaque homines tum maxime fascinari quando frequentissimo intuitu aciem visus ad aciem dirigentes, oculi oculis reciproce intuant radii radiis copulantur et lumina luminibus junguntur, tunc spiritus spiritui jungitur et scintillas designi sic fortissimæ ligationes, sic amores acerrimi solis oculorum radiis accenduntur etiam vel repentino quodam intuitu, veluti jaculo seu ictu totum corpus penetrante: unde tunc spiritus et sanguis amatorius sic vulnerati, non aliter in amantem et fascinantem feruntur, quâ sanguis et spiritus vindictæ alicuius cæsi prolabuntur in cædentem unde Lucret. de his amatoriis fascinationis cecinit:

Idq. petit corpus mens unde est saucia amore.
Namq omnes plerung cadunt in vulnus, et illam
Emicat in partem sanguis quaq. lædimur, ictu.
Et si comminus est, hostem ruber occupat humor.

Tanta est fascinationis potentia, præsertim quando affectu vapores oculorum subserviunt. Ideirco utuntur fascinantes collyriis, unctionibus, alligationibus et huiusmodi, ad spiritum tali vel tali modo afficiendum et corroborandum. Ut ad inducendum amorem collyriis utuntur venereis, ex hippomane sanguine columbarum vel passerum et ex similibus: Ad inducendum timorem, collyriis utuntur Martialibus, ut ex oculis luporum hiænæ et similibus. Ad calamitatem vel ægritudinem utuntur Saturnalibus. similis de singulis ratio est habenda.

150

217

55

= A few remarks on Invocation of the Planetary Angels by the Crystal. =

As a full and clear explanation has already been given of the method of Invoca-ting Spirits by the Crystal, accompanied by an experiment, it is quite unneces-sary to say any more on that head. Therefore those who desire a view of those glorious inhabitants of the planetary world, or to gain any information from them, that is according to their nature to grant, must have a humble faith and trust in God; under such a feeling of earnestness and confidence, it never can be offensive to Him. Because as has been before remarked, a method similar to this was doubtless employed by the ancients when they wished to inquire of the Lord for any special object, or of the Heavenly Messengers for any lawful information of which the scripture affords many proofs. Also the evidence that this practice is not lawful is not to be found in the word of God, on the contrary it is an undeniable fact that the Blessed Jesus did not forbid the practice of making such enquiries. David asked the Lord, "Shall I go up into any of the cities of Judah"? The Lord answered, עלה, olah, "go up". This and many other answers to the good seers of old. No doubt that then as now, great purity was required, or no answer would be given. Good seers in the crystal can always read plainly all that is written, or revealed therein; but indifferent seers only perceive a degree of splendour or brightness in the crystal, when any truth was alleged; and a certain darkness of the stone when falsehood was stated. In this way they decided on the credibility of witness Among the many visions and revelations that have appeared in the crystal in our day to good seers of both sexes, leading pure lives and undoubted veracity, many of the miracles of our Lord, and other scriptural events. Also among other questions and answers have been the following:— "Should we make our supplications in the name of our Lord"?— Answer—"Why, He is our Mediator". "Are the Catholics right to pray to the Virgin Mary"? In reply, there instantly appeared a vision of the cross, as represented in Plate in one of the quadrants with the words as in the double circle annexed. By this Vision it was understood, that not to the Virgin Mary, but to Him who suffered on the cross, and in his Name should Christians supplicate. It appears that 'twas Michal an Angel of the Sun, from whom these revelations came, but who does not often appear except by powerful invocations such as are made by good and faithful persons, such as Daniel and the seers of old who all enquired of the Lord in a similar manner. The Spirits of Jupiter when called to appear in the crystal, or make any revelation; the vision is generally accompanied with majestic splendour and such astounding brightness, as to compel the seer or seeress to withdraw his or her eyes therefrom. Such was the manner in which the Prophets, Priests & Seers of the Holy Scriptures obtained their answers, when a question was seriously & faithfully asked. For God by various means reveals his will to mankind. ——

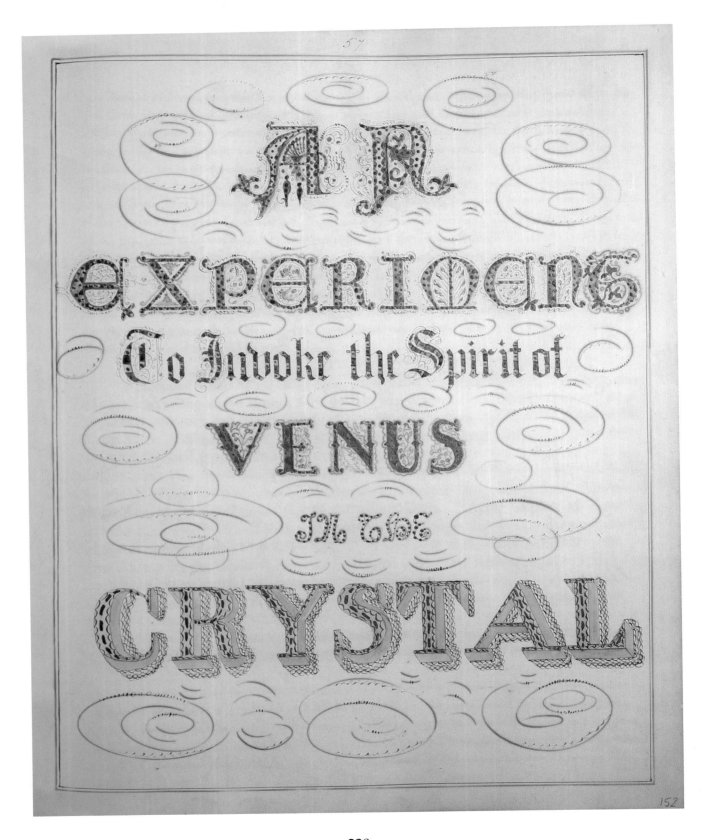

An experiment To Invoke the Spirit of VENUS In The CRYSTAL

The Method of Invocating this Beautiful Spirit in the Crystal differs somewhat from those Experiments performed in Invocating the Aerial Spirits and with less trouble and no danger. When this Operation is performed in all its details with much exactness this Glorious Being will appear in the Crystal Globe in the form of a clear star at first, immediately afterwards it will assume the form of a beauteous female most fascinating to behold, and surrounded with green and silver coloured rays so brilliant and glistening as almost to dazzle the eye of the beholder. The signs of the coming of this Glorious Angel are similar to those described in the foregoing experiments. The Operator must be pure in mind and body, expressing his desires earnestly and faithfully, asking nothing but what is lawful and right and not offensive to God nor contrary to the nature and office of the Spirit who is so mild and gentle as to become almost subservient to the human will after being once invocated to appear, particularly by those born under the resplendent Orb governed by this Beautiful Angel. It is presumed that every preparation connected with Experiment is made in the manner as aforementioned described, which after being completed, the Moon increasing. Let the Operator and the company (if any) surround the Crystal, and commence earnestly Invocating the Spirit as follows. ─────────

I call upon thee Setchiel in the name of the Father, and of the Son, and of the Holy Ghost Blessed Trinity Unspeakable Unity. I Invoke and intreat thee Setchiel in this hour to leave your bright abode, and come and appear visibly to us in thy glorious form of a Beautiful Angel in this Crystal Stone or Glass and and attend to the words and conjurations which I shall use this Day by the Holy Names of God Elohe El Elohim Elion Jah Adonay Tetragrammaton, that you attend to my requests and grant my desires according to the Sovereign Will of Him who is Alpha et Omega, and by all other Great, Glorious, Holy, Unspeakable, Mysterious, Mighty, Powerful, Incomprehensible Names of the Most High. I again conjure, call upon thee Fair Angel of God Setchiel, Prince of Love and Friendship, that thou wilt come without delay and appear to me in this Crystal in all the plenitude of thy Virtue and Power and reveal to me by thy wisdom and counsel such knowledge, and answers to my requests that they may redound to thy Honour, and to the Glory of God, and the welfare of mankind. Again I invoke and intreat thee Setchiel that you will come with all your power and scatter and put to flight the Evil Spirits which are inimical to this Operation, Anael Sarabotes Abalidoth, Amabiel. Waiting patiently in the Name of the Father, Son, and Holy Ghost, for thy appearance and aid which, I hope thou wilt give to succeed in this Operation.

─────────

The Operator after reciting with great earnestness and devotion the above Invocation, must remain silent for the appearance of of the Spirit, which will be in the manner as aforesaid, but must diligently watch for the Spirit as it assumes the human form, and instantly make known his requests in a courteous and becoming manner, the answer will be given in a clear and intelligent manner which there is no mistaking although not given in an Audible Voice. Should the Operator fail in obtaining satisfactory answers to his

59

earnest appeals through any failing mishap or negligence of his own, he must repeat the Invocation as before, till he gets his desires granted. The office of this Mild and Gentle Spirit is to unfold the secrets of human nature and to promote Love and Friendship. After having obtained his desires of the Spirit of Venus, the Invocant may rehearse a short sentence as a dismissal as follows. —————————

Blessed and fair Setchiel who by the sovereign command, will, and permission of the Omnipotent Creator of the Universe hast appeared in this Crystal and hast answered my requests and petitions for which I return sincere thanks and now thou mayest Depart in peace unto thy abode where peace and contentment reign, and return unto me again and appear in this whensoever I shall call thee by thy Name or by thy Office. and the peace of God be with me and thee and with all mankind. Amen.

Glory be to the Father and to the Son and to the Holy Ghost. —————————

The truth of this Experiment has been proved by eminent professors of the Occult Science and of undoubted veracity. and who all agree in declaring that the Glorious Spirit of Venus, from its mild, gentle and friendly nature, is more easily invoked than any of the other Planetary Spirits either in the crystal or out of it, still it is said, that any one wishing to invoke the Spirit governing the Planet under the influence of which he was born can do so with more certainty & less trouble, even if it were the Spirit of Saturn or Mars.

A certain amount of caution is required in Invocating these Beautiful Spirits in the crystal lest the Evil Spirits by their craftiness and subtlety may so transform themselves and gain admittance into the crystal, and thus deceive the Operator into a belief that he is dealing with the Good Spirits if he is not well on his guard. It is not always requisite that the Spirit should always appear in human form in the crystal, but at all times his presence is manifested by a brilliant display of light and scenery, far surpassing any thing produced by any of the powers of darkness. not only that. the manifest tokens of the presence of the Good Spirits produce in the mind pure thoughts and feelings, while the other, whatever are the forms assumed, are only so many allurements and temptations. to deceive and betray the unwary. After all, if the Operator be firm, sincere, faithful, confident & persevering with patience, he will obtain that knowledge and assistance of those Bright Celestial Messengers that will render him Wiser, Happier & Better in this World, and in that to come.

Part 8. Geomancy

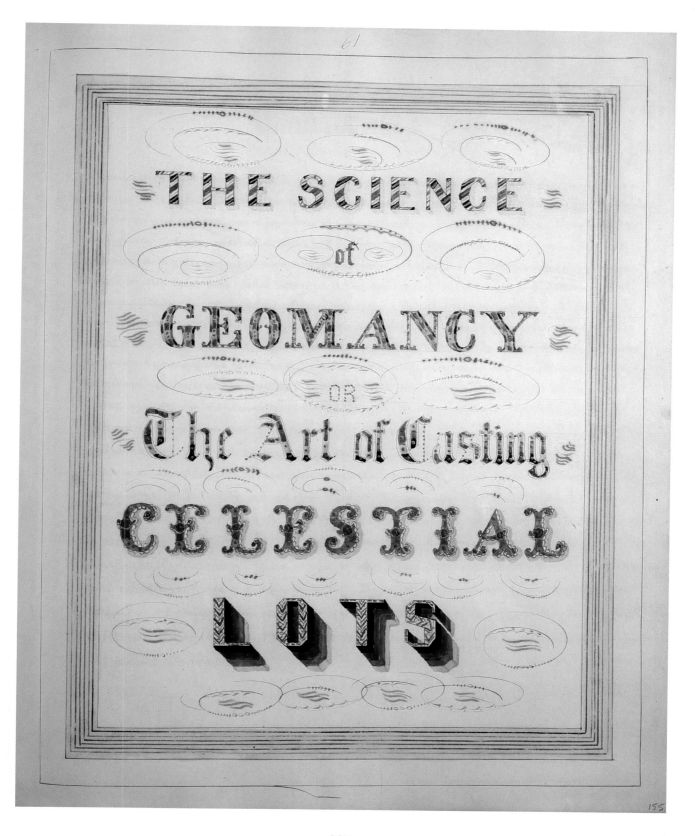

Geomancy

Geomantica ipsa est ars quae per sortem tradit nobis judicium ad omnem quaestionem de qua—eunque &. Consistit autem sors hujusmodi in punctis, ex quibus deducuntur certae quaedam figurae secundum rationem paritatis et imparitatis: quae figurae tandem reducuntur ad figuras coelestes, earum naturas et proprietates assumentes, juxta signorum and planetarum rationes. Hoc ante imprimis nobis considerandum est, quoniam sors hujus—modi in quantum talis, nihil veritatis portendere potest, nisi radicata fuerit in virtute aliqua sublimiori: et hanc duplicem posuerunt hujus scientiae autores: unam quae in Religion et ceremoniis consistit: et ideo voluerunt projectiones punctorum hujus sortis fieri in terra cum digito indice quare hic sors huic elemento appropriata est, sicut hydromantia igni: et hydromantia aqua: tum, quia arbitrantur manum projicientis potissime per terrestres spiritus dirigi atq; moveri: et ideo praemittebantur sacra quaedam incantamenta et deprecationes cu aliis quibusdam ritibus et magicis observationibus hujusmodi spiritus ad hoc allicientes. Alia potestas hanc sortem diri—gens et regens, ipsa est anima proficientis, quando fertur in aliquam magnum egressum sui desiderii. Tunc enim omnis sors habet naturalem obedientiam ad ipsam animam: et de necessitate habet efficaciam, et movetur ad id quod anima ipsa desiderat. Et haec via est longe verior et purior, nec refert, ubi, vel quomodo pun—ta projiciantur. Habet itaq; hoc artificium tandem radicem cum artificio quaes—onum astrologicarum: quae et ipsae non aliter verificari possunt, nisi constan—ti et recessivo affatu ipsius quaerentis. Nunc ad praxim stanti hujus artificii pro—cedamus: et primo sciendum est, quod omnes figurae super quibus totum hoc artificium fundatur, duntaxat sedecim sunt: ut hic infra cum suis nomini—bus annotata vides.

This curious science termed Geomancy is of high antiquity, and was in great repute amongst the ancient Chaldeans, Babylonians, Hebrews, Arabians, and other orientalists. It was a favourite study amongst the Druids, and constitutes a singular feature at the present day in freemasonry, it being the chief study of the Rosie Crucians, and was much practised by that singular race of beings whose secrets are now in the care of that society. In the Holy Scriptures we have frequent mention made of "Casting Lots", which was, no doubt, a species of geomantic divination, and was allowed as a final decision amongst the early Christians. In remote ages, the answers given by the seers as recorded in holy writ, was no doubt given by this species of curious knowledge. And in later years, we have had many professors thereof, although not since the seventeenth century: yet few have given the subject the consideration it merited; for there is little doubt but it might in proper hands be brought to such perfection, as to become almost an universal knowledge; and as it does not require so much attention to arithmetical data, as astrology, it becomes far more facile and pleasing on that account.

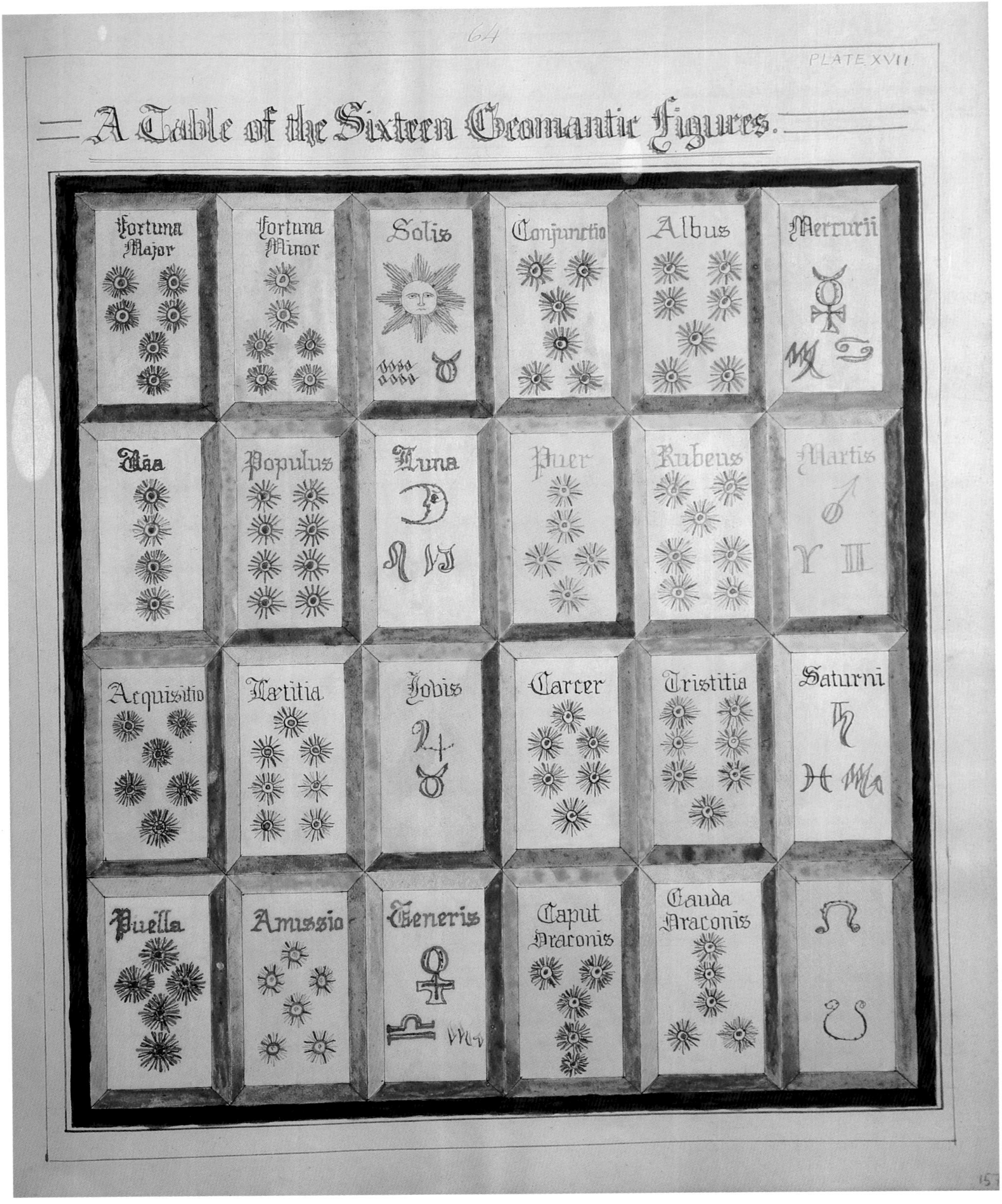
64
PLATE XVII.
A Table of the Sixteen Geomantic Figures.
Fortuna Major
Fortuna Minor
Solis
Conjunctio
Albus
Mercurii
Via
Populus
Luna
Puer
Rubeus
Martis
Acquisitio
Lætitia
Jovis
Carcer
Tristitia
Saturni
Puella
Amissio
Veneris
Caput Draconis
Cauda Draconis

65

Quibus vero planetis figuræ istæ distribuuntur, dicamus, ex hoc enim omnis figurarum proprietas atq; natura, totiusq; artificii indicium dependet. Sunt itaq; Fortuna Major atque minor solem referentes: sed prima solem diurnum and in dignitatibus suis constitutum: altera autem noctur-num, vel in minoribus dignitatibus constitutum. Via autem atq; populus Lunam referunt: prima ab initio semper crescentem: secunda plenam lumine and decrescentem. Acquisitio vero and Letitia Jovis sunt; sed prior Jovem magis fortunatu habet: secunda minus, sed extra detrimentum. Puella and Amissio Veneris sunt: prior fortunata, altera tanquã retrograda, vel combusta. Conjunctio and Albus, utræq; Mercu-rii figuræ sunt, and utræq; bene: sed prima fortunatior. Puer atq; Rubeus Martem referut: quarum prior Martem habet benevolum, secunda autem maleficum. Carcer atq; Tristitia utræq; figuræ Saturni sunt, and malæ: sed prima majoris detrimenti. Caput vero and Cauda suas naturas sequuntur. Hæc itaq; cũ sint infallibiles figurarũ comparationes. facile ex his signorum æquiparantiam dignoscemus. Habent itaq; Fortuna Major and Minor signum Leonis, quod est domi Solis. Via autem atq; Populus signum Cancri, quod est Lunæ. Acquisitio signum Piscium. Letitia vero Sagittarum quæ sunt domicilia Jovis. Puella Taurum, Amissio Libram, quæ sunt domus Veneris. Conjunctio Virginem, Albus Geminos domus Mercurii. Puer autem and Rubeus Scorpionem, domum Martis. Carcer Capricorum. and Tristitia Aquarium domicilia Saturni. Caput vero and Cauda ita distribuuntur, ut Caput adhæreat Capricorno, Cauda vero Scorpioni. Hinc facile triplicitates signorum elicere potes secundum rationẽ triplicitatum signorum Zodiaci. Constituunt itaque triplici-tatem igneam, Puer, utraque Fortuna, ac Lætitia: Terram vero

Puella, Conjunctio, Carcer, atque Caput. Aëream Albus, Amissio atque Tristitia : Aqueam Via, Populus, Rubeus, Cauda atq: Acquisitio. Et hic ordo secundùm rationem signorum sumptus est. Qui verò secundum naturas Planetarum atq; ipsarum figurarum triplicitates constituere velit, hic hāc observet regulam, ut triplicitatem igneam constituant : Fortuna Major, Rubeus, Puer and Amissio. Aëream Fortuna Minor, Lætitia, Puella and Conjunctio. Aqueam Acquisitio, Cauda, Via and Populus. Terream Carcer, Tristitia, Albus atque Caput. Et hæc via magis observatur, quàm prima, quam secundum signorum rationem constituere docuimus. Hic ordo longè verior est atque rationabilior, quàm ille qui vulgò celebratur hujusmodi descriptus. Triplicitatis ignæ sunt Cauda, Fortuna Minor, Amissio and Rubeus : Aeræ, Acquisitio, Lætitia, Puer and Conjunctio : Aquæ Populus, Via, Albus and Puella : Terræ, Caput, Fortuna Major, Carcer and Tristitia : Distribuunt enim istas figuras duodecim signis Zodiaci in hunc modum : Arieti datur Acquisitio : Tauro Fortuna Major cum minori : Gemellis Lætitia : Cancro Puella atq; Rubeus Leoni Albus : Virgini Via : Libræ Caput atq; Conjunctio : Scorpioni puer : Sagittario Tristitia atq; Amissio : Capricorno Cauda : Aquario populus : Piscibus Carcer.

67

Triplicities of the Sixteen Geomantic Figures.

Figura	Nomen	Elementum	Planeta	Signum
	Via / Iter	Aqua	☽ (Moon)	♌
	Populus / Congregatio	Aqua	☽	♍
	Conjunctio / Coadunatio	Aer	☿	♍
	Carcer / Constrictus	Terra	♄	♓
	Fortuna Major / Auxilium majus / Tutela intrans	Terra	☉	♒
	Fortuna Minor / Auxilium minor / Tutela exiens	Ignis	☉	♉
	Acquisitio / Comprehensum intus	Aer	♃	♈
	Amissio / Comprehensum extra	Ignis	♀	♎
	Lætitia / Ridens sanus / Barbatus	Aer	♃	♉
	Tristitia / Damnatus / Transversus	Terra	♄	♏
	Puella / Mundus / facie	Aqua	♀	♎
	Puer / Flavus / Imberbis	Ignis or aer	♂	♈
	Albus / Candidus	Aqua	☿	♋
	Rubens / Ruffus	Ignis	♂	♊
	Caput / Limen intrans / Limen superius	Terra	☊	♍
	Cauda / Limens exiens / Limen inferius	Ignis	☋	♐

231

68

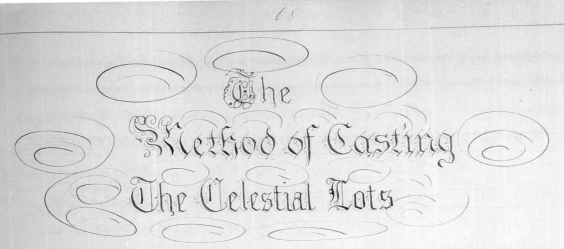

The Method of Casting The Celestial Lots

"And they gave forth their Lots, and the Lot fell upon Matthias, and he was numbered with the eleven Apostles." — Acts 2. 26.

According to the system of the ancients, as the manuscript which has been consulted exemplifies, the diviner, or seer, who wishes to predict by these lots, should procure a quanti- ty of clean earth or clean sand, either of which should be mixed with water, for seven days, in equal portions; which should be done either under the arising of the fortu- nate constellations, or in the hours of the seven planets; and when this is done, the earth so formed into portions should be mixed together, in a fortunate day and hour, whereby they affirm that "the universal effect may be more plainly and easily known and declared." Others made their figure in wax tables, but they all declare that the pro- jection on earth, is the surest and most conducive to the dis- covery of truth; and that the figure should not be made or

160

cast at any time, but that divination should only be made, "when the weather is bright and clear, and neither dark nor windy, for distemperance in the elements, may cause changes in the passions of the soul". They also affirm, that when a figure is made, or judged, "the moon should be from all impediment, for if the Moon apply to Saturn or Mars, the soul thereby is inclined to lie. and also, that the figure should be made with the most sincere desire to ascertain the truth thereof.

MODERN METHOD

The modern method of casting these celestial lots, is by making the points either upon paper or a slate, with any convenient instrument, either pen, crayon, chalk, pencil, or pointer, whichever may be nearest at hand; and the modern Geomancers affirm that great verity may be found in the art, when thus practised. Although they allow that the ancient method is the more exact. This being seriously thought of, and the mode thereof selected, the diviner must proceed to make sixteen lines of points, which points must be made from right to left, contrary to the usual mode of writing; and in so doing he must not count the number of points he makes, but leave that entirely to chance, or the sympathetic impulse which will guide the hand, so as to produce a figure corresponding to the true answer of the event sought after. _____

The following example will suffice to set this doctrine in easy light. _____

Example of forming the Points.

The points being made as directed, let them be joined together two and two, leaving the last points unjoined, as in the example, where the first line being even, two points are left; the second line being odd, one point is left; and so of the rest.

This being done, arrange the four figures thus found, in order, from right to left, calling the first No. 1, the second No. 2, and so of the others thus:—

Then proceed to take the points of each figure is they stand in a line, and form thereof another figure; thus in the first line of the figure, No. 1, are 2 points; in No. 2, 2 points; in No. 3, 1 point; and in No. 4, 2 points; which collected together, form this symbol:—

Do the same with the lines of the other three figures, which will give the second row of figures, thus—

Which are termed No. 5, 6, 7, and 8.

72

These being found, place the whole eight in a line thus :—

| 8 | 7 | 6 | 5 | | 4 | 3 | 2 | 1 |

(rows of geomantic dots)

And then join each figure to its companion; that is to say—take the number of points in the first and second, third and fourth, and so of the rest, calling two or four points _even_, and one or three points _odd_, by which means you find out four other figures, which are placed thus :—

| 8 | 7 | 6 | 5 | | 4 | 3 | 2 | 1 |

(rows of geomantic dots)

| 12 | | 11 | | 10 | | 9 |

(rows of geomantic dots)

And which correspond to Nos. 9, 10, 11, and 12.

This being done, you have the whole of the figures, which the twelve Geomantic houses, and which constitute the chief part of the scheme. But there yet remain four other accidental figures, namely, the two _witnesses_, the _judge_, and the _sixteenth figure_.

73

The witnesses are formed from the 9th and 10th, and the two adjoining figures in the second row, and are these:—

And the judge is formed from out of these too, in like manner and is— The formation of the sixteenth figure, has been hitherto unknown, but it is of the utmost consequence in the formation of the judgement, especially where the answer seems ambiguous, and we will therefore give the secret of finding it, which is done by joining together the 1st and 15th figures (the judge) and out of these extracting the figure in question. The sixteenth figure is:—

We will now place the figure in its proper order, as it will give a clear idea of the process.—

8th House. 7th House. 6th House. 5th House. 4th House. 3rd House. 2nd House. 1st House.

12th House. 11th House. 10th House. 9th House.

Left Witness. Right Witness.

Judge.

16th Figure or Final Result

16th Fig.

74

The Method of Divining by a figure of Geomancy.

In order to be perfect in the use of Geomancy, it is absolutely necessary that the student should be well acquainted with the science of Astrology, as it regards the houses and quality of the seven planets; which are made use of in Geomancy, in the same manner, except as far as the symbolical nature of the figures themselves are concerned. _____

The Nature of The Sixteen Figures of Geomancy

Acquisitio Is the best of the whole sixteen figures, and is a sign of riches, joy, gain, acquisition, profit, and a good end of all enterprizes; it is the symbol of good fortune, of honour, renown, and happiness; it denotes long life, fortunate marriages, and success in every undertaking. It is a figure of Jupiter, and under the sign Aries, it is exalted in the first house, and has its fall in the seventh, which is to be judged the same as in Astrology. _____

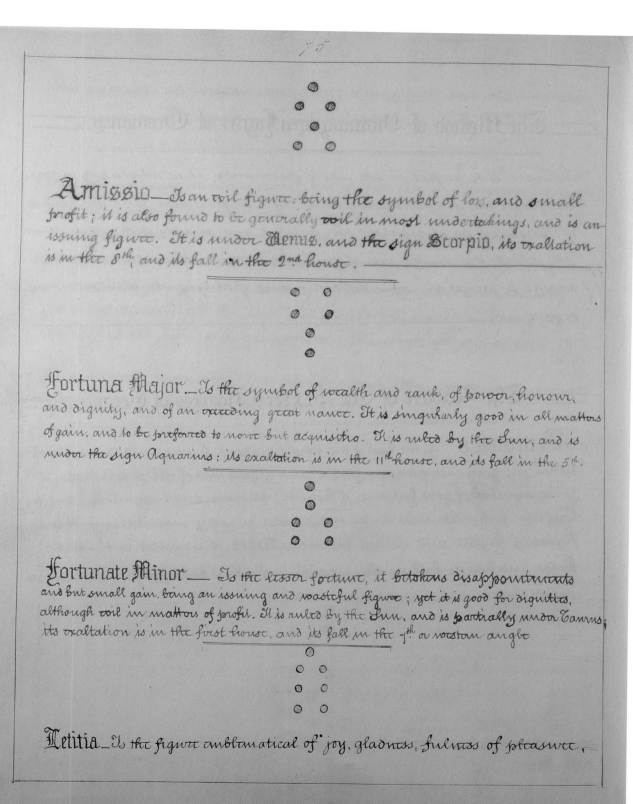

Amissio—Is an evil figure, being the symbol of loss, and small profit; it is also found to be generally evil in most undertakings, and is an issuing figure. It is under Venus, and the sign Scorpio, its exaltation is in the 8th, and its fall in the 2nd house. _____

Fortuna Major.—Is the symbol of wealth and rank, of power, honour, and dignity, and of an exceeding great name. It is singularly good in all matters of gain, and to be preferred to none but acquisitio. It is ruled by the Sun, and is under the sign Aquarius; its exaltation is in the 11th house, and its fall in the 5th.

Fortunate Minor—Is the lesser fortune, it betokens disappointments and but small gain, being an issuing and wasteful figure; yet it is good for dignities, although evil in matters of profit. It is ruled by the Sun, and is partially under Taurus; its exaltation is in the first house, and its fall in the 7th or western angle

Letitia—Is the figure emblematical of joy, gladness, fulness of pleasure,

76

and gay delights; endearments, profit, gain, and all favourable things, which it signifies similar to acquisitio. It is a very fortunate symbol wherever found, and productive of success. It is under Jupiter, and the sign Taurus; it is exalted in the second house, and its fall is in the 8th opposite. _____

Tristitia __ Is the origin or source of sorrow, melancholy, heaviness of heart, lowness of spirits, dolor, grief, malice, and mischief and is extremely unfortunate in all the affairs she may signify. She is also the cause of loss, disgrace, and trouble. It is under the evil planet Saturn, and in the sign Scorpio, and has its exaltation in the 8th and its fall in the 2nd house.

Rubeus __ Is another no less violent and wicked figure, it is the source of war and bloodshed, signifying guile, deceit, and perversion of truth; and intestine quarrels, animosities, and discord. It is highly unfortunate in every undertaking; when it is found in the ascendant, Geomancers frequently destroy the figure. It is under Mars, in the sign Gemini; it is exalted in the 3rd house, and has its fall in the 9th.

Albus __ Is a figure termed meanly good and oftentimes conducts to gain; especially in affairs of science and learning. It is under Mercury, and the sign Cancer. It is exalted in the 6th house, and its fall in the 12th house, which is opposite thereto. _____

77

Conjunctio —— Is a figure of gathering or conjoining; it is a controvertible figure, good with good, and evil with evil; it is a symbol of a funeral, "for it representeth the bier on which dead men are borne." The points being 4 before, 2 behind, and 2 in the centre; it is under **Mercury**, retrograde in **Virgo**. It is a Bicorporeal figure, exalted in the 6th house, and has its fall in the 12th house.

Carcer. —— Is the emblem of a prison, imprisonment, close shut-up places, close vessels, and is amazingly evil, as its name imports. It gives loss in all things, poverty and wretchedness, it is also unlucky in every undertaking; it is under **Saturn**, and the sign **Pisces**; it is exalted in the 12th house, and has its fall in the 6th house, or house of evil fortune.

Populus —— Is the symbol of a multitude, a congregation, an assembly, a confused retinue. It is generally accounted evil and unpropitious: and generally signifies moving or journeys. It is under the full moon in the sign Capricorn, and is exalted in the 2nd house, having the fall in the 8th

78

Via —— Is the figure of quickness and facility; of travelling, removals, journeys, and voyages. It is a wasting and dissipating figure, and unlucky in all matters of gain or profit. It denotes hasty news and short visits, when found in the salient. It is under the new Moon in Leo, and is exalted in the 5th house, having its fall in the 11th.

Caput —— Is the symbol of the Dragon's head and is generally accounted as fortunate and propitious in the undertakings. It is good for matters of gain, and in money-affairs is well. It signifies something quickly coming on being an entering figure. It is the Dragon's head in Virgo and is a commixture of Jupiter and Venus conjoined.

Cauda —— Is the symbol of evil and misfortune, disgrace, scandal, slander, poverty and ruin. It wastes the substance, annoys the asker, and hinders the undertaking. It is always and at all times evil. This is the Dragon's Tail in Sagittarius, formed out of a mixture of Saturn and Mars.

Puella ———— Is a pleasant and favourable symbol: it signifies fulfilment of wishes, joy and contentment, success in love, and may be equally propitious wards; it is favourable also in money affairs; it is the sacred emblem of the cross; and is also found to be a sign of equality, justice, and section. It is under the planet Venus and the sign Libra. It is exalted in the seventh house, and has its fall in the ascendant.

In order to judge from the figures, as before observed, the student must learn to be well acquainted with the essential and accidental dignities, stations, aspects, and positions of the geomantic emblems, and be ready in his reference to the twelve celestial houses, by which means, if he be sincere in his wishes, the most astonishing answers may be obtained.

Puer ———— Is the emblem of a drawn sword, and of war, battles, hostility, quarrels, contentions, and discord. It conduces but poorly to gain or profit, being naturally evil and malignant: consequently no success can attend the question where it is a significator. It is under Mars and the warlike sign Aries, the ascendant of England. It is exalted in the first house, and has its fall in the angle opposite.

Part 9. Magical Experiments

THE
EXPERIMENT

As an Experiment for Secret Love is given and performed by the Wheel of Magic, and one of a powerful nature it is intended to be employed in the following Operation thus blending the two Experiments together, the combined influence of which acts with ten-fold power, particularly when aided by a Sympathetic feeling in the parties concerned. The manner of performing this Grand Experiment in its united form, which must be strictly carried out according to the rules of Art in every detail with much exactness, as follows. The Operator must have a plate of pure Silver highly polished of about three inches in diameter, of a hexagonal form (thickness immaterial) He must next make a suffumigation of the following ingredients, Lavender, Valerian, Red Roses, Red Coral, Musk, Ambergris, these must be mixed with small portions of Hair from the nape of the neck or pudendum of the wearer of the Amulet, the whole must be thoroughly dried and reduced to a powder, then mix with the blood of a pigeon or dove while quite warm, also a small quantity of sanguis mensis into a paste of which, form lozenges of the weight of ten grains, dry them thoroughly, then heat the silver plate quite hot and while in this state grate thereon on both sides a portion of the lozenges so as to produce an agreeable odour, after which, repolish the plate, and engrave it according to the foregoing Model with much care and distinctness, omitting the ornaments or embellishments, which are not required. Should the Operator prefer to make use of a fair Virginal parchment to the Silver plate, he must dissolve five of the Lozenges in pure water with which he must sprinkle the parchment on both sides, and dry it well before a fire composed of Sweet Brier, Sweet Marjoram, or other scented Woods. Then draw the requisite lines and figures with consecrated Ink of a green colour, not omitting to recite the Orations &c. for Friday which are contained former part of this Book, with great earnestness. at this stage of the Operation, the Operator must now use the Philter which has been prepared as aforesaid, by drinking a portion of this powerful potion to his beloved pronouncing his or her Name three times also the Name Aniel, this potion should be taken every time you recite any sentence for spiritual aid. The two Christian Names of the Lover and Beloved must be written in the Bloody joined together by the Name Aniel, also the two hearts joined together as in the Model. All this operation must be done in the day and hour of Venus (which the Cabalistic Art teaches,) the Moon increasing, and in fortunate aspect to Jupiter, Venus, or Mercury from the sign Taurus. It really seems vain to endeavour to explain anything more than what has been already said in former Experiments, that a plate of Metal or a piece of parchment with certain figures, or Mysterious Characters, engraven or written thereon, can have any power or life giving principle in them, whatever other latent properties they may possess. But at the expense of repetition, we will once more explain, that the Vivifying power and vital principle so necessary in Experiments of this kind, cannot be given to a senseles plate of Metal &c (they being but visible and earthly agents) but by Invoking the aid of the good Spirits to impress their divine virtue and power upon them and make them efficacious   For this purpose, let the Operator choose a retired spot in which to perform his Operations, and thereon draw a Circle not less than seven feet in diameter in which he and his associates (if any) may enter; it being their fortress and defence against all evil and Malignant Spirits who might assail the Operator and thwart him in his undertaking. Having great courage, confidence, perseverance and patience. All being ready, let him commence by earnestly invocating the Fair and beautiful Angel Aniel as follows

Invocation

O Thou fair Angel of God Aniel who by Divine Permission and Sovereign Grace of Almighty God hast condescended to leave thy bright abode, and appeared in a beautiful form visibly to mortals sinful as they are, I pray you by the interposition of your favourites Sarabotes, Susastiel, Doremiel Setchiel to hear favourably my petition, that you will once more leave your celestial sphere, or send one of your Ministering Spirits to aid me in this operation, impress this Talisman with a double portion of thy mighty power and virtue so that I may secure the pure unchange-able and eternal Love of A.B. I again beseech and entreat thee Aniel who preside over the workings of the heart to come on the wings of the Zephyrs thou fair and beautiful Angel, Prince of Love, Gentleness and Peace and appear unto me before this circle in all the plenitude of thy Power and Glory, and hearken to my request which I now make unto thee in the Name of Him who, and by His Almighty Power commanded and it was done. Be propitious to my undertaking impress this mysterious image with Divine virtue and make it efficacious in producing that sincere Love and Affection towards me thy unwor-thy servant from the heart of the object of my adoration, which no earthly power can vanquish and nothing but death can separate or dissolve. I pray that thou wilt extend thy mighty power fair Aniel and cause sincere friend-ship and good-will towards me by all mankind. Come powerful and mighty Spirit Sarabotes with all your cohort and scatter and put to flight all

169

evil Spirits that may be inimical to my operations of this day. Cause me to succeed by thy mighty power in what I have undertaken this day destined to the
wonders of Love. I invoke intreat and call upon thee Haniel once again.
to come from thy blest abode or residene and appear unto me in the form of a Glorious
and beautiful Angel without delay or hindrance. notify by thy presence thy
power and willingness to hear favourably the prayers and appeals for aid
in my operations of this day under the influence of that beauteous orb of Venus
the sixth Luminary in the firmament. Be favourable unto me blessed Spirit
which will redound to thy glory with all suitable acknowledgement, while I hope
for, wait for and expect thy appearance in the Name of the Father, and of the
Son and of the Holy Ghost Abahooth, Amalnel Aba Sartanael.

After this powerful Invocation has been once recited, and the Spirit does not appear in a reasonable
distance of time, viz, from three to five minutes, repeat the Invocation, even the third time if required, but the
Spirit generally appears at the first call, the sign of his coming is similar to those in the former experi-
-ments. the appearance is attended with even more splendour, beaming forth with such Angelic
glory as to dazzle the eye of the Operator and entrance his soul with ravishing delight. He must be received cour-
-teously and with humility, his nature is so mild gentle and pacific that no danger is to be apprehend
-ed from this Brilliant inhabitant of the spheres the prince of Love and Friendship. nor from those Spirits
which accompany him. When all has been done and his presence duly acknowledged, let him be bound with
the Bond of Spirits. The Operator must then present unto him his request written on Virginal parchment
together with the prepared Talisman sprinkled with the Philter or Love potion which will be immediately
impressed with divine power and virtue according to the wish and design of the Operator. For the
more ardent, earnest, and chaste he is in his desires. the stronger will be the golden cord
of sympathy and Friendship. and the tighter will be the silken bands of Love and affection which
bind two such loving hearts together. After the operator has obtained his desires of the Spirit
he may request him to depart in the same courteous manner as he received him, which
will be instantly followed by signs of departure similar to those of his coming. The operator
must efface all traces of the Circle &c. after giving humble and hearty thanks unto God for per-
-mitting this Glorious Angel to come at his call and to his Operation. giving the required aid to
render it successful. This admirable Talisman thus prepared, will render the wearer thereof
so enchanting in the sight & feelings of his or her adored object as to render a rival impossible.
provided he or she consents and complies with all that is requisite in every detail of the Operation.
It must be worn constantly Night & Day near the heart with the strictest secresy & confidence of its efficacy.

A Safe Way to Secure a House.

Whoso wishes to protect himself against thieves by night or by day, also to secure his House from the same, must proceed as follows: The Charm in Latin against Theft given in a former page of this work must be translated and written on Virgin Parchment, and worn about him constantly, and repeat the words every morning, so shall no theft happen to annoy him personally. Then to bind or secure his house or any particular room containing money or other valuable property; Let him draw a circle of any convenient size on the floor of the room with consecrated chalk or charcoal, and write therein any sentence expressive of his desires to retain the thief (should he enter) similar to the foregoing model, also the Seals and Crosses must not be omitted. Then the operator must write on Virginal parchment of an Octagonal form these characters ♌ ♈ ♑. then add the Name Zariel or other of the Spirits of Saturn together with his planetary character, also these numbers 1. 3. 5, 4, 4/7 in black ink; after this is done he must make a fire of thorns elder wood. producing smoke in which the parchment must be held till perfumed, then sprinkle it over with Nightshade three times. deposit it in the earth under the floor so as to conceal it, and retire to rest. This powerful operation must be performed in the night on Saturday in the Hour of Saturn when

he is in evil aspect with the Moon and in her decrease.
and if the thieves enter the House they will not be able to
leave it till sunrise. unless spoken to by Name.

═══ For Outhouses ═══

The Operator must prepare for the operation at the same time
and in the same manner as the foregoing Operation with the
Exception of the Circle (which is not here required) He must
write on parchment these Characters ♈ ♉ ♍ Add the
Name of the Spirit this Character as before also these figures
4, 8, 5, 3, 6, 7. Perfume as before, then sprinkle the parchment
with the juice of hemlock, and place it under the threshold of
the entrance, or in some secret corner of the Outhouse under the
floor or earth, there the thieves must remain till sunrise
if they enter. the Operator must not omit repeating the words of the
charms he wears about him, as before. for upon the exactness.
earnestness & Confidence with which any Magical Experiment
is performed, much depends the certainty of success. Instances
are recorded in which such operations as the above, have been
performed according to the Rules of Art by which Depradators
have been defeated in their attempts to approach within
a limited Distance of a House or premises.

There are several powerful Experiments relating to the secret
Influences of Saturn and Mars, which in the hands of evil disposed
or ignorant persons, ~~sometimes~~ much mischief is produced, therefore we will forbear to mention them at present, as it is only to
the wise and prudent, such Occult secrets are intended to be revealed.

But as prevention is at all times better than a cure, or punishment for crime, we have let our good will reign triumphant, thinking & feeling that we are justified, if we can by any lawful or secret means, which are only to be discovered in the great store house of Nature, perform an Experiment which has the power to defend us or any of our friends from any unlawful act wherein which any evil disposed persons may attempt, by keeping them at a distance from us and our premises. As we shall Invoke Divine and Powerful Aid to assist in the Operation, we see nothing sinful nor unlawful in performing such Experiment which has for its object the welfare of our fellowmen.

= To bind the Ground & Premises, whereby neither Mortals nor Spiritual Beings can = approach within a limited distance.

This all-powerful Experiment must be performed in the day and hour of Jupiter, by describing a circle of a hundred feet or more in diameter whereby the Dwelling, Garden & orchard, is inclosed if possible, fortify it with Divine Names, Crosses each of which must be written on Virgin parchment and deposited within the circle in the Earth opposite the four Cardinal points. After suffumigating them with the perfumes proper to the Sun, Jupiter, & Mercury, viz Saffron, Myrrh, Benjamin, Storax, Mace, Incense &c. in the Day, & hour of Mercury. The Moon increasing, and in fortunate Aspect to Jupiter or Venus The Operator having the Grand Pentacle of Solomon and the pentacles of the Sun & Jupiter before him, may commence reciting in the centres of the circle the following great Bond or Incantion, which must be earnestly repeated in the Day & Hour of Mercury.

173

Incantation

In the Name of the Father, and of the Son, and of the Holy Ghost, Amen. I bind all mortal and immortal, celestial and terrestrial, visible and invisible beings, except those who are my real friends and are well disposed towards me, to avoid and quit this space of ground, which I now mark, and wherein I now stand, and that with all possible speed and despatch. I bind you to avoid and no longer tarry, by the unspeakable power of Almighty God, by the most high and Mighty Name of +Tetragrammaton+ by the all-powerful names. +Agla + Saday + Jesu + Messias + Alpha + and Omega +.

By all these most High and powerful Names, I charge, adjure, bind, constrain both mortal and immortal, terrestrial, celestial, visible, and invisible beings to avoid, quit, and depart this ground, and do request that none of you, except those who are my real friends &c. as afore-said, be suffered to come within these sacred limits. These things I request in the Name of the Father, and of the Son, and of the Holy Ghost, Amen.

This powerful Incantation must be recited three times with great earnestness & faith. Then let the operator dig a depth just outside the circle, of three feet, at the four parts of the Compass, and bury the seal of the Earth in each part, and no power, either visible, or invisible will have power to enter this boundary having a dishonest intention or purpose. The operator will be still far-ther defended personally from Fraud or Theft, if he wear the Latin Charm, also the Pentacle of Solomon & repeat the Charm as (in former Experiment.

To Find out, Bind, and Compel a Thief to return Lost Goods when stolen.

To bind a Thief so that he shall have neither rest nor peace till he return thee thy lost goods; go to the place from whence they were stolen away and write down the day, hour and minute if you can when the Goods were stolen, and the name of the planet ruling the day, also the name of the suspected thief on virgin parchment, and place the same under the threshold of the door he or they went out of. Then make four crosses on the four corners or posts of the doorway. After this is done so far, write down on virgin parchment the following charac-ters ☽ ☉ ♃ ✳ △ ☌ together with the name Samael, then turn round three times and repeat the charm each time, written in page 7. viz. Thou thief who hast stolen &c. If you hear no news of Thief in 48 Hours, as it is most certain you will; then prick the parchment full of holes and hang it up in chimney where the heat of the fire may scorch it, and thief or thieves will be so restless and ill at ease, being discovered, and having no peace, till he or they bring home your goods, throw them privately into your house, or some place belonging to you.

It must be remembered, that unless the goods are actually stolen the above charm will have no effect, for if they are only mislaid, or taken away in jest, or lost through carelessness or neglect, a theft is not committed. To ascertain whether the goods are stolen or not, apply to a skilful Astrologer who will give the required information. This is a grand secret and must be strictly guarded and inviolably kept or little or no success will attend the Operation. —————

Hominem Rebus Fascinum Liberare.

For this purpose a small private Room must be chosen, and a fire made of charcoal thorns and briars, and a little sulphur must be thrown in, taking care to have a ventilator that the carbon may escape, Then fasten the door and window of the room so that no person can enter or look in, for the person or persons performing the Operation must be calm, quiet and undisturbed, not a word must be spoken during the Operation by the parties concerned. The Operation may now be commenced by cutting some of the afflicted person's hair from the nape of the neck, also the parings of the finger and toenails, clip them small, and burn them to powder, put the powder in Sal-Amoniac, write the suspected parties name back — —wards on parchment which must be dipped in aqua-vitae (water of life) or Spirits of wine place the Sal-Ammoniac with the powder, together with the written parchment in some convenient vessel over a slow fire, (composed as aforesaid) then let the afflicted person sit by it and watch it that it catcheth not fire, speak no word, and if there is a noise, write down how often it is heard, and affix the sign of the ☽ before each writing. the person offending will then be compelled to come to the house, being so restless, and knock at the door or shutter under some excuse, such as wanting to borrow something or give some information about some person or other, but on no consideration make any reply in any way, but keep your seat, when after a short time the person will appear before you.

This important and powerful Experiment is best performed in the night at the hour of twelve, in the decrease of the Moon she being in Scorpio, and is good aspect to Mercury, but if possibly in evil position to Saturn. Many instances in which this Experiment has proved successful, where the patient has recovered, and ended in the disgrace and punishment of the offender. Keep this a Secret.

To conceal or hide Money or Treasures so that they may never be stolen or discovered.

Take Coriandrum of the second kind, which maketh one to sleep; and join thereto Croco, insgreno, and apio, and grind them together with the juice of hemlock: then make a suffumigation therewith, and suffume the place where thou wilt hide any treasure in, when the ☽ is joined to the ☀, in the angle of the earth; and that treasure, so hidden, shall never be found. particularly if hidden in the earth, the ☽ being in an earthy sign, and the planet Saturn ruling the hour of concealment

A Talisman against Enemies

The Operator must observe that every preparation connected with this Admirable Talisman must be made as before mentioned in this Book, and according to the ancients being under the dominion of the Sun and Jupiter. It must be cast of the purest grain Tin, in the day and hour of Jupiter when in good aspects to the Sun from the signs ♈ ♌ or ♐ and to the Moon in her increase. The characters &c must be engraven as in the above model in the day and hour of Mercury and if possible in fortunate aspect to Saturn or Mars. When finished it may be suspended about the neck or any part of the body of the wearer, keeping it a secret from all but him or herself. Its effects are, to give decisive victory over enemies, to defend against their machinations, and to inspire the wearer with the most remarkable confidence. The Orations &c must be said

Part 10. Magical Tables

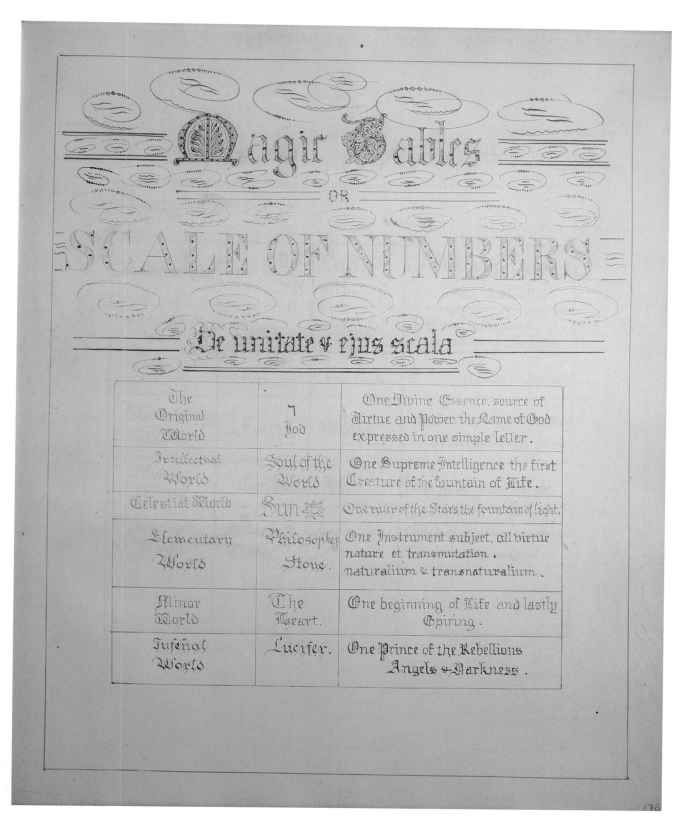

Magic Tables

OR

SCALE OF NUMBERS

De unitate & ejus scala

The Original World	ᛃ Jod	One Divine Essence, source of Virtue and Power, the Name of God expressed in one simple letter.
Intellectual World	Soul of the World	One Supreme Intelligence the first Creature of the fountain of Life.
Celestial World	Sun ✶	One ruler of the Stars the fountain of light.
Elementary World	Philosopher Stone.	One Instrument subject, all virtue nature et transmutation. naturalium & transnaturalium.
Minor World	The Heart.	One beginning of Life and lastly Expiring.
Infernal World	Lucifer.	One Prince of the Rebellious Angels & Darkness.

176

SCALA BINARII

In Archetype	חו אל	JAH. EL.	Name of God in Two Letters
Intellectual World.	Angel	Soul	Two intelligent substances of Choler.
Celestial World.	SOL	LUNA	Two Great Luminaries
Elementary World.	Earth	Water	Two Elements producing Animal Life.
Minor World	Cor. Heart	Brain	Two principles of Life
Infernal World	Behemoth Fletus	Leviathā Stridor dentium	Duo quæ comminatur Christus damnatis.

17

Scala Trenarii

In Archetypo	Pater	שדי Sadai Filius	Holy Spirit	Name of God in three Letters. Three persons in the Divine Essence
In The Intelligible World	Above Innocents	Middle Martyrs	Low or Beneath Confessors	Three Hierachies of Angels. Three Degrees of The Blessed.
In The Celestial World	Motion Cardinal Diurnal	Fixed Succedent Nocturnal	Common Cadent Between	Three Quaternions of Signs. Three Quaternions of Houses. Three Lords of The Triplicities
Elementary World.	Simple.	Composite	Decomposite	Three Degrees of The Elements.
The Minor World	The Head in which groweth the intellects answering to the intellertual World	The Breast wherein the Heart the seat of life is, answers to the Celestial World	The Belly wherein engendereth strength in genital members answering the Elementary World.	Three Births answering to the Triple World
In Mundo Infernali	Alecto Minos Malefici	Magera Aacus Apostatæ	Tesiphone Radamanth Infideles	Tres Furiæ Infernales Tres indices Infernales Tres Gradus Damnatorum.

Scala Quaternarii ad Quatuor.

Elementorum Correspondentiam.

Name of God Quadriliterum	יהוה				In mundo Archetypo unde lex providentia
Four Triplicities of the Hierarchies of the Intelligencies	Seraphim Cherubim Thrones	Dominatio Powers Virtues	Principalities Archangels Angels.	Innocents Martyrs Confessors	In mundo intellectuali unde fatalis
Four Principal Angels presiding in Celestial World	מיכאל Michael	רפאל Raphael	גבריאל Gabriel	אוריאל Uriel	
Four Rulers of the Elements	שרפ Seraph	כרוב Cherub	שיש-וח Tharsis	אריאל Ariel	
Four Devoted Animals	Lion	Eagle	Man	Calf	
Four Triplicities of The Tribes of Israel.	Dan Asa Nephtha lim	Judah Issachar Zabulon	Manasses Benjamin Ephraim	Reuben Simeon Gad.	
Four Triplicates of the Apostles	Matthias Peter James the Gr.	Simon Bartholomew Matthew	John Philip James the Less	Thaddæus Andrew Thomas	
Four Evangelists	Mark	John	Matthew	Luke	
Four Triplicities of the Signs.	Aries Leo Sagittarius	Gemini Libra Aquarius	Cancer Scorpio Pisces	Taurus Virgo Capricornus	In the Celestial World which is from the Law of Nature

Stella and Planets relating to the Elements	Mars and Sol	Jupiter and Venus	Saturn and Mercury	Fixed Stars and the Moon	
Four Qualities of the Celestial Elements	Lume	Diaphanum	Agilitas	Sodalitas	
Four Elements	אש Ignis	רוח Air	מים Aqua	עפר Terra	The elementary World, subi ley generationis & corruptionis
Four Qualities	Heat	Moisture	Cold	Dry	
Four Seasons	Summer	Spring	Winter	Autumn	
Four Cardinal points of the World	East	West	North	South	
Four perfect created ingredients &c.	Animals	Plants	Metals	Stones	
Four qualities of Animals	Walking	Flying	Swimming	Creeping	
Plantes answering to the four Elements	Seeds	Flowers	Leaves	Roots.	
Quæ in Metallis	Gold and Iorum	Copper and Tin	Quick-Silver	Lead and Silver	
Four Qualities in Stones	Clear and Hard	Light & Transparent	Bright and Congealed	Heavy & Opaque	
Four Elementas homi-nus	Mind	Spirit	Life or Soul	Body	Minor World

Four Powers of The Soul	Understand-ing-	Reason	Imagination	Sense	
Four indiciariæ Potestates.	Faith	Knowledge	Judgment	Experience	
Four Moral Virtues	Quietness	Temperance	Prudence	Fortitude	
Senses answering to the Four Elements	Seeing	Hearing	Tasting & Smelling	Touching	
Four Elements of The Human Body.	Spirit	Flesh	Humours	Bones	
Fourfold qualities of the Spirit	Animal Spirit	Life	Creation or Birth	Nature	
Four Humours.	Choler	Blood	Phlegm	Melancholy	
Four degrees comprising manner	Force	Nimbleness	Rest	Slowness	
Four princes of the evil Demons in the Elementary World.	טמאל Samael	עזריאל Azazel	עזיאל Azael	מהזראל Maharael	In mundo infernali ubi lex iræ
Quatuor flumina Inferna	Phlegeton	Cocytus	Styx	Acheron	and punitionis
Quatuor principes dæmonorum super Angulos mundi	Oriens	Paymon	Egyn	Amayon.	

Scala Quinarii

Name of God in five Letters Name of Christ in five Letters	אלֵהֵיֹ אֱלֹהִים יֵהֹשׁוּה	Eleon Elohim Ihesuh				In Archtypo
Five properties of the Understand-ing	Spirits of of the first Hierarchy vocati dii sive filii Dei.	Spirits of the Second Order dicti Intelligentia.	Spirits of the third Order vocati angeli qui mittutur.	Celestium Animal. Body	Heroes or Souls of the bless-ed.	In the Intellectual World.
Five erratic Stars ruling	Saturn	Jupiter	Mars	Venus	Mercury	In the Celestial World
Five genera corruptibilu	Aqua	Aer	Ignis	Terra.	Mixtis	In the Elementary
Five species of Mixture	Animals	Plants	Metals	Stones	Zophytes.	
Five Sensus	Tasting	Hearing	Seeing	Feeling	Smelling	In the Minor World.
Quinque Tormenta Corporalia	Amaritudo Mortificans	Ululatus Horrisoni	Tenebræ Terribiles	Ardour Inextingui-bilis	Fætor Penetrans	In Mundo Infernali.

SCALA SENARII

In Archetypo	םל	חו	לא֫	יך	גב	אל	Name of Six Letters
The Intelligible World	Seraphim	Cherubim	Thrones	Dominion	Powers	Virtues	Six Order of Angels who are not of the former order
The Celestial World	Saturn	Jupiter	Mars	Venus	Mercury	Luna	Six Planets zodiacal per Latitudes from the ecliptic.
The Elementary World.	Quietness	Thinness	Sharpness	Bluntness	Thickness	Motion	Six substantial qualities of the Elements
The Minor World	Intellect	Memory	Sense	Motion	Life	Essence	Six degrees of Man.
In Mundo Infernali	Actus	Megalesius	Ormenus	Lycus	Nicon	Minor	Six Demons calamitatum omnium autores

Scala Septenarii

In Archetypo	Ararita	אראריד הא			Assor Ehiel	אהיה	אשר	Name of God in Seven Letters.
Intelligible World	צדקיאל אל Zaphkiel	צדקיאל אל Zadkiel	סמאל Samael	רפאל Raphael	אניאל Aniel	מיכאל Michael	גבריאל Gabriel	Seven Angels who stand before the face of God.
Celestial World	שבתאי Saturn	צדק Jupiter	מאדים Mars	שמש Sol	נוגה Venus	כוכב Mercury	לבנה Luna	Seven Planets
Elementary World	Lapwing Cuttle fish Mole Lead Onichinus	Eagle Dolphin Whale Tin Sapphire	Vulture Pike Wolf Iron Diamond	Swan Sea Calf Lion Gold Carbuncle	Pigeon Thymallus Tiger Copper Emerald	Stork Mullet Ape Quicksilver Agate	Owl Arulus Cat Silver Chrystal	Seven birds, Planets Seven Fishes, Planets Seven Animals, Planets Seven Metals, Planets Seven Metals, Stones of the Planets.
Minor World	Right Foot Right Ear	Head Left Ear	Right Hand Right Nostril	Heart Right Eye	Pudendum Left Nostril	Left Hand Bone	Left Foot Left Eye	Seven perfect members distributed Seven foramina capitis planetis distributa
In Mundo Infernali	Gahenna גיהנום	Gate of Death שערי מות	Shadow of Death צלמות	Puteus interitus באר שחת	Lutum Fœcis טיט היון	Perditio אבדון	Fovea שאול	Septem habitacula inferorum, quæ discribit Rabbi Joseph Castiliensis, Cabalista in tractu mucis.

SCALA OCTONARII

	Eloha	Aedaath		Tetragrammaton	Aedaath			In archetype
Name of God in eight Letters	אלוה ודעת			יהוה ודעת				
Octo beatorum Praemia	Haereditas	Incorruptio	Potestas	Victoria	Visio Dei	Gratia	Regnum	Gaudium	Intelligent World
Octo coeli visibiles	Coelum stellatum	Coelum Saturni	Coelum Jovis	Coelum Martis	Coelum Solis	Coelum Veneris	Coelum Mercurii	Coelum Lunae	Celestial World
Octo qualitates particulares	Siccitas terrae	Frigiditas aquae	Humidatus aeris	Caliditas ignis	Caliditas aeris	Humiditas aquae	siccitas ignis	Frigitas Terrae	Element ary World
Octo beatirum rogandae	Pacifici	Quaerentes sitientes justitiam	Mites	Persecuti onster vissia	Mundi Corde	Misericordes	Pauperes Spiritu	Lugentes	In Minore Mundo
Octo damnatorum praemia	Carcer	Mors	Indicium	Ira Dei	Tenebra	Indignatio	Tribulatio	Angus tia	Mundo Infernali

Introduction

Background to Magic

For those readers new to magic it is necessary to give a bit of background. Before the 19th century, with its materialistic outlook on the universe, it was universally thought that magic was done by magicians who had the ability to control spirits, demons, etc. It was only in the late 19th and 20th century that magic began to be explained in terms of psychology, by people like Dion Fortune who wished to be seen to be in the vanguard of science with this explanation of the subject.

As anthropology became a science, it was also roped in to assist in re-defining magic. Later in the 20th century, with the advent of 'New Age' thinking writers attempted to explain magic in terms of 'sympathy' or later 'vibrations,' and finally it became identified with the wish fulfilment techniques of popular 'success gurus' and techniques like NLP, a psychotherapeutic method that even arrogated the term 'magic' to itself.

The result of these 'advances' was that nobody, not even academics, understood what magic really was. By throwing out any reference to spirits or demons, it became impossible to define magic, and academics attempted to even replace the word with other words like 'esotericism.' Magic became undefinable because its roots had been removed.

In order to understand what magic really is, and how it works, it is necessary to re-introduce the ideas of spirits and demons, for without them it is impossible to explain or understand either the methods of magic, or what it truly is. It has been understood from ancient times that only gods, angels, spirits, daemons or other 'spiritual creatures' were able to perform those things traditionally thought of as 'magic.' Man alone, no matter how much he visualised or sweated or strained or prayed, could not do those things that made up the repertoire of the traditional magician.

Let us draw a parallel: man cannot run at 40 kph (25 mph) unaided, or traverse 20 miles in a day on foot. But with the taming of horses this feat became possible, even easy. Likewise many of the feats of magic are not viable without the aid of spirits. The art of magic consists in knowing how to 'tame' these spiritual creatures, and then to utilise their help in doing things which are considered as impossible as running at 40 kph.

The methods used in taming wild horses are not known to the average man. Indeed few city dwellers actually interact with wild horses, and would not know what to do if they had to. The methods used for calling spirits and constraining them are just as specialised as the methods used in taming horses. Indeed spirits are just as wary, and unwilling to come and be bidden, as are wild horses. But just as mankind learned how to tame horses thousands of years ago, so he also learned how to tame spirits.

The methods used were and are complex and technical, but have been around virtually unchanged for thousands of years. One of the strangest things about magic is that its methods have hardly changed over the last 2000 years: the words have changed, but the *methods* and materials used by a first century Graeco-Egyptian magician have close parallels with the methods and materials used in the 18th century or even today. These involve protective circles inscribed on the ground, specific incantations, the selection of specific times on the correct day, the use of the correct incenses and other tools. Just as a horse tamer know what he has to whisper to tame a wild horse, or how to slip a bridle on without startling the horse, so a magician must know what form of words to use, and how to successfully bind the spirit when it does arrive.

The details of the formulae, procedures, timing and equipment used in the magic which sprung up around the Mediterranean littoral, were to be found in the magical papyri of the Graeco-Egyptian magicians, and later in the Mediaeval grimoires, or 'grammars' of sorcery. These methods have been passed hand to hand from one magician to another in manuscript form (predominantly in Greek and later in Latin) from the ancient Egyptians (the *PGM*) through to the grimoires of the Middle Ages right up to the 19th century. Increasingly, especially in the last 20 years these grimoires have been passing into print or online, and have become more accessible, a process that both of the present editors have had a hand in.

For those who have not been lucky enough to be apprenticed to someone who has already successfully worked these methods and knows what is essential and what is not, it is necessary to observe what appear to be many trivial restrictions, like fasting for 3-9 days, using parchment rather than paper, observing the exact day and times, using the correct natural incense, and repeating the invocations a specific number of times in a particular manner. Magic is not easy to learn from books, as it has always been an essentially a master/apprentice type of craft. Some grimoires are more complete than others, and the present grimoire (which was written predominantly in English) goes into more detail than most. Having said that, not all the procedures here recorded are equally efficacious.

The Present Manuscript

The method of invoking and binding spirits using the methods outlined in the grimoires is often referred to as Solomonic magic. The present manuscript is a Solomonic grimoire assembled in 1789, but made up of parts dating as far back as 1520, plus later additions added during the 19th century (probably between 1836 and 1848).

At first glance this manuscript looks like a triumph of design over content, but on closer inspection it can be seen that it contains a lot of useful information. Parts 1 and 2 are a very clear organisation of the style of Solomonic magic found primarily in a late 18th century French *Key of Solomon*. The *Key of Solomon* comes, as it were, in various flavours, or text families. The first two Parts of this manuscript belong to the family that is specifically associated with Rabbi Solomon (not King Solomon) and the translator Professor Pierre Morrisoneau. These were then translated from French into English by (or at the behest of) Ebenezer Sibley in 1789.

Part 3 comes from a group of manuscripts dating back to the 16th and 17th centuries and features evocations of just four specific spirits associated with a forerunner of the *Goetia*.

Part 4 includes a range of correspondences, necessary for practising magic. The rationale being that the environment used for the invocation should have as many thing as possible compatible with that spirit, and these compatibilities or 'chains of correspondence' are arranged and grouped under the seven Planets.

After the manuscript passed from Sibley's hands, a number of other magical essays and formulae were added. Frederick Hockley was prominent amongst the 19th century magicians that added additional magical texts and Part 5 is one such Hockley addition, but the *source* of the material in this Part dates back to 1573, according to the copyist. [2]

One of Hockley's main interests was crystal skrying where he would consult with a spirit seen in a crystal rather than attempting its full evocation. Part 6 is concerned with crystallomancy, the Art of invoking the image of a spirit into a crystal or skrying stone so it can be communicated with.

Following this Part 7 and Part 9 deal with a number of simple charms, bindings and the construction of talismans which work in conjunction with spirits to bring about magical results. These are interestingly described as 'Experiments,' which is a term that was used in grimoires long before it because a commonplace in scientific studies. It was traditional for even classical grimoires to accumulate a range of such experiments in the blank pages at their end.[3] These experiments are dated from 1520 and 1573 and probably come from manuscripts which may have been in Sibley's library, but were more than likely

---

[2] Part 5 is identified by Hockley's monogram, a backwards 'F' linked to an 'H.'
[3] An example of this can be seen in Skinner & Rankine, *A Collections of Magical Secrets and A Treatise of Mixed Cabalah*, London: Avalonia, 2009.

copied from manuscripts which formed part of the stock of John Denley's Covent Garden bookshop, some of which came from Sibley's library anyway. Rather than being of one date, the experiments in Parts 7 and 9 probably represent experiments recorded over many decades.

Part 8 embarks on a simplified description of divination by geomancy, derived predominantly from *Theomagia, or the Temple of Wisdom* by John Heydon (1629-1667). Robert Cross Smith, one of the scribes who we will meet later in this introduction, also helped popularise geomancy.[4]

Part 10 gives a number of correspondence tables which have been derived directly from Agrippa's *Three Books of Occult Philosophy* (1533).[5]

Why another Edition of the Clavis?

It could be argued that this present publication is pointless because Joseph Peterson has already produced a version of the *Clavis*.[6] But of the many manuscript copies of this work (see Appendix 1 and later in this Introduction for details of each one), the present manuscript is by far the most elaborate and aesthetically interesting. In terms of showiness, it forms without doubt, the high point of Victorian grimoire production.

The second reason for publishing this text is that it is far more complete and considerably longer than any other extant version (published or unpublished) as it contains all the supplements and additions mentioned above, many of which (Parts 6-10 specifically) are not present in any other printed versions. In terms of content, Joseph Peterson's edition corresponds to roughly about 55% of the present text.

In a strange way it is appropriate that this manuscript,[7] finished up residing in the National Library of Israel, as it claims to be a translation originally from a Hebrew source. This would have been most appropriate if it really was the translation of a Hebrew source magical text. But is this really so? It is a form of the grimoire the *Key of Solomon*, and it is now well known that the *Key of Solomon, Clavicula Salomonis* or *Clavis* was in fact derived from the Greek *Hygromanteia*.[8] There is however considerable doubt that an original Hebrew version ever existed for either the *Key of Solomon* or the *Hygromanteia*, and this attribution might simply have been promoted to boost its pseudepigraphic Solomonic appeal.

---

[4] For more information on the history and practice of geomancy consult Skinner, *Geomancy in Theory & Practice*, Singapore: Golden Hoard, 2011.

[5] Book II, Chapters iv-xiv.

[6] Joseph Peterson, *The Clavis or Key to the Magic of Solomon*, Lake Worth: Ibis, 2012, pp. 327-400.

[7] National Library of Israel MS Yar. Var. 18.

[8] See Stephen Skinner, *Techniques of Solomonic Magic*, Singapore, Golden Hoard, 2015, pp. 36-45.

Analysis of the Magic in *Clavis*

Frontispiece

The figures in the Frontispiece (page xviii) are derived primarily from Reginald Scot's *Discoverie of Witchcraft* dating from 1584.[9] Scot in turn allegedly derived his material from the works of two Cunning-men 'T.R' (who might have been Thomas Rudd) and John Cokars.[10] This illustration was re-engraved for Sibley and used in his *Complete Illustration of the Astrological and Occult Sciences*, 1784, Part 4, opposite page 1102 (see Figure 03). It was then reorganised and used as a Frontispiece in the present manuscript.

The two top left 'Seals of the Earth' are said to facilitate the arrival of spirits, but in fact the triangular 'seal' is the external triangle used to constrain the spirit after it has arrived, and the cylindrical shaped 'seal' is meant to be used as a protective lamen to be worn on the magician's chest.

On page xviii, Fig. (1), a triangle in a circle, is a *locus spirituum*, the triangle which is to be drawn on the floor to mark the point where the spirit should manifest or be bound. The second seal (2) is a lamen and calls upon the great God, in Greek (*O Theos Pon Mala*) and in Latin (*Alpha et Omega*) to protect the magician. The hexagram (4) and folded pentagram (5) are for the protection of the magician or to act as placeholders for the candles. The two pentacles at the bottom are designed to ensure the spirits do homage to the magician (9), and to preserve the magician from any foe, spiritual or otherwise (10). This Plate also illustrates some of the magical equipment required including four knives (7, 8), with Solomonic inscriptions,[11] one poignard and two wands (3). The figure in the centre (6) is of key importance as it is a simplified drawing of the protective floor circle. The descriptions are more apparent on the original Scot illustration from which they were taken (see Figure 02).

An interesting application of this plate arose in 1830 when the Mormon prophet Joseph Smith used some of its constituents in one of his three manuscripts (see Figure 04), later owned by his brother, which he referred to as his 'magic parchments.' Three of the sigils on the parchment are obviously from the frontispiece of Sibley's *Clavis* or possibly, but less likely, from Reginald Scot's illustrations. Joseph Smith has now been convincingly demonstrated to have had interests in ritual magic, skrying and digging for spirit-protected treasure. He possessed several skrying stones which he referred to (as does Sibley in his Preface) as the Urim and Thummin of the Bible.[12]

The parchments likely belonged to Joseph Smith Sr. and Joseph Smith Jr., but were

---

[9] Scot, *Discoverie of Witchcraft*. London, 1584 rpt. 1651 & 1665, Book 15, chapter 7, pages 400-401.
[10] Sloane MS 3847 also shows these seals on ff. 126-127.
[11] "One pointed with a white handle and engraven as seen in the frontispiece, one, in the point of which shall be the figure and shape of a sickle, [and one] with a Black Handle" (see page 6).
[12] *Exodus* 28:30.

inherited by Hyrum Smith's family after Joseph's and Hyrum's death in 1844.[13] These parchments were designed to be carried in a bag hung round the neck, performing the same function as a magician's lamen. The ownership of these three parchments confirms that the Smith family had more than a passing interest in Solomonic magic. Of the symbols from Smith's parchment reproduced in Figure 04, all have been copied from magical texts or grimoires. The most obvious figures obviously come from Sibley's *Clavis*, or less likely *The Discoverie of Witchcraft* by Reginald Scot (1665 edition).

The characters of the angels of the seaven daies, with their names: of figures, seales and periapts.

{ These figures are called the seales of the earth, without the }
{ which no spirit will appeere, except thou have them with thee. } //

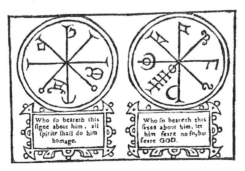

Figure 02: Reginal Scot's source illustration which was copied and redesigned by Sibley for several of his books, and then for the Frontispiece of the *Clavis*.[14]

---

[13] Hyrum's name is suspiciously Masonic sounding.
[14] Scot, *Discoverie of Witchcraft*, 1665, Book 15, Chapter VII, p. 400-401 (*aka* 284-285).

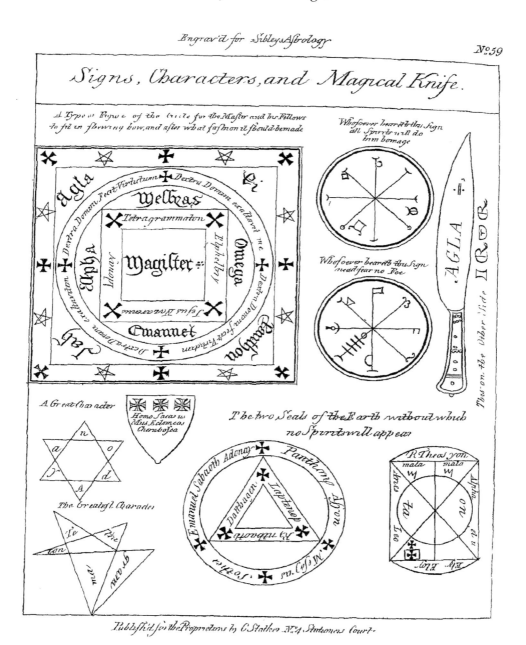

Figure 03: The page from Sibley's *A New and Complete Illustration of the Celestial Science of Astrology* first published in 1784. This engraving was assembled from Reginald Scot's *Discoverie of Witchcraft* (1665). It eventually was re-engraved to form the frontispiece of Sibley's *Clavis*. The re-use of illustrations from one publication to another was not unknown in this period when the production of engraved copper plates was slow and expensive. It can be seen that the illustration of the circle marked 'Magister' was also re-used in the present manuscript on pages 98 and 150, whilst the other images were used in the present Frontispiece.

A PHOTO OF A MAGIC PARCHMENT OWNED BY JOSEPH SMITH'S BROTHER, HYRUM.

Figure 04: One of the three manuscripts owned by Joseph Smith's brother Hyrum Smith, as reproduced in a newspaper, captioned "Holiness to the Lord," which were meant to be used as a lamen. As you can see the images have degenerated, but are nevertheless derived from Scot or more likely Sibley.

Preface

The Preface was not translated from a French source but was probably originally written by Sibley, incorporating as it does references to, and quotes from, Jacob Behmen (Boehme) who was one of his favourite authors, and incidentally also a shoemaker, Sibley's initial profession.[15] The Preface is concerned with Jacob Behman's theories about earthbound human spirits (ghosts), necromancy and theology. Apart from references to heavenly spirits, Sibley is not afraid to make the point that both ghosts and spirits/demons respond to offerings of blood.

> ...therefore Demons appear not but after Sacrifices used, &c. which must be the Effusion of Human, or some Blood of Black Cattle, for they are allured by the Vital Spirits of living Creatures.[16]

Sibley then outlines six methods of magic, divided up according to the type of 'spiritual creature' employed. Magic, according to this text, is done by:

1. the application of 'visible instruments', i.e. wands, circles, etc.;
2. by direct appeal to God alone, achieved through the mediation of the Princes of Spirits;
3. via the good Angels, or their opposites the Chief of the Evil Spirits, or the "minor Gods of the Heathen;"
4. via direct interaction with spirits;
5. via Elementals;
6. by natural magicians.

In every case magic is performed via a 'spiritual creature,' or a magician that "useth the ministry of the Spirits to bring excellent things to pass" and not by the mind of the magician, or 'vibrations' or by 'sympathy,' or any other modern New Age procedure.

The manuscript then breaks down into ten well defined Parts, which are marked in bold in the Contents list. Of these, the Peterson edition only covers the first five Parts, or about 55% measured in terms of the page numbers of the present manuscript.

Part 1. Clavis or Key

The first Part consists of 10 chapters outlining the rules of evocation, with the Grand Pentacle imbedded in between chapter 6 and chapter 7. The Grand Pentacle is in fact a floor circle but has been made almost unrecognisable by the scribe's irksome habit of writing the godnames in solid gothic capitals.[17] The plain hexagram in the centre is mistakenly replaced by an 8-pointed star, although the 'AGLA' is still recognisable.

---

[15] Behmen (or Böhme) also wrote a work entitled *Clavis* in 1623 which may have influenced Sibley in his choice of title, apart from the obvious *Clavicula Salomonis* connection.
[16] Page xx.
[17] In normal gothic usage only the first letter of any word would be capitalised.

The 10 chapters summarise the basic rules that the magician needs to know before engaging in evocation: how to find the proper place; decide on the proper time; what instruments are needed; how to work with pentacles/talismans; the planetary rulership of the hours of the day and night; what incenses or 'perfumes' are required, and how to make the necessary orations, invocations and conjurations.

Chapter 1

This chapter recommends care in following the instructions in this book, leaving nothing out. Proficiency in astrology is predictably considered necessary. It also recommends avoiding a dissolute life whilst practising magic with "great confidence."[18]

Chapter 2 – Planetary hours and days

A tranquil environment far from the bustling crowd is recommended, in a room clean, neat and perfumed. Sibley recommends with what equipment the room of practice is to be furnished. It is necessary to work in the correct planetary hour on the correct planetary day. This is the first hour of the day beginning at sunrise, but it can also be the 8th, 15th or 22nd hour after sunrise, however the first hour is best. For example the first hour of the day of the Moon (Monday) is also the hour of the Moon, as each day begins with its own hour.

Chapter 3 - Pentacles

This chapter recommends that pentacles should be made on virgin parchment, on a semi-precious stone, or engraved on a metal plate corresponding to the planet (i.e. tin for Jupiter/Thursday, iron for Mars/Tuesday, etc). A pure metal plate is preferred over parchment, according to Sibley as parchment can be damaged or dirtied, thereby reducing its powers. If parchment is used then it should be prepared by the magician himself, preferably on the summer solstice (the day of St. John the Baptist).

Chapter 4 - Equipment

This chapter outlines the other pieces of equipment required, the robe, the cap, the gloves, the shoes and the quills and ink. Such detailed pre-rite preparation of equipment is a hallmark of Solomonic magic.

Chapter 5 - Timing

This chapter stresses the importance of Moon phases and aspects made between the Moon and other planets. As the Moon completes its cycle in 28 days, it makes many more aspects than the slower moving planets. The chapter also advises avoiding a time

---

[18] Another, and possibly better introduction to the basic rules, is to be found in the 'Full Directions for Magical Operations' on pages 104-108.

when it (or any other planets) is 'combust,' that is to say close to conjunction with the Sun. This is usually specified as within an 8 degree orb of the Sun. These times are to be avoided both for ritual magic and even for the simpler consecration of talismans or pentacles.

This chapter considers in detail the effects of the Moon as it passes through each of the zodiacal signs. These effects range from "prosperity in voyages or Business" and "the Discovery of Treasures" to "the Ruin of Buildings, Fountains" to "the breach of Friendships" just in the short space of 30 degrees. These portents by themselves mean little, unless they are concentrated or 'congealed' in a pentacle or talisman created and consecrated at the appropriate moment. The section goes past generalised zodiacal signs to consider the effect of a momentary alignment of the Moon with specific constellations or planets, and the effect of creating talismans at that precise moment. The planetary days and hours need to also take into consideration the aspects made between that planet and the Moon. For example, it is clear that the creation of a talisman "for luck in gambling" needs to be made when the Moon is favourably aspected, but also during the hour and day of Mercury.

Chapter 6

This chapter shows how to combine much of the previous knowledge such as astrological time selection with the correct invocations, materials and the words to be written on the pentacles.

The Grand Pentacle

As already remarked, Part 1 and Part 2 of the *Clavis* has been translated from the version of the *Key of Solomon* found in Wellcome MS 4670 (or a close copy) which in turn has been assembled from various sources. In doing so the French scribe, F. Fyot, has confused the protective floor circles with the pentacles. Hence the 'Grand Pentacle,' shown here is not actually a pentacle, but is really a protective floor circle (although it does not say so in either manuscript) which in turn was derived from Peter de Abano's *Heptameron*, where it is correctly identified as such.

This circle has also suffered significant corruption. Although the names are mostly intact, the inner ring has been inexpertly rendered back into Hebrew. Reading clockwise from the top in the original French text, the names should be Agla, Eloym [Elohim], Adonai and Jessemon. The central figure should be a hexagram, not an eight-pointed star as shown. Refer to Figure 05 for the original French circle design.

Chapter 7 - Tools

This chapter offers a very practical piece of advice, that all the tools, incenses, quills, ink, etc. should be prepared well in advance, so that you don't waste any of the precious hour in which you should actually make the talisman or pentacle, or do the invocation.

In that way you will not be rushed, but can draw or engrave with complete attention to what you are doing. It is no use starting to assemble things in that hour, it is much better to use all of that hour for the drawing, painting or engraving of the pentacle or talisman so that you are not forced to go beyond the end of the hour in order to finish. Furthermore if you choose to use the first hour of the day, which is the hour immediately after sunrise, you had better complete all preparations whilst it is still dark, or on previous days.

Figure 05: The Grand Pentacle as it appears in the original French text, Wellcome MS 4670, p. 30. The basic design of this floor circle was originally derived from the *Heptameron*. [19]

Chapter 8 - Perfumes

This concerns the incenses and perfumes to be used. Remember that spirits are sensitive to appropriate smells, particularly those attributed to the planet they work under, "for it

---

[19] See Skinner & Rankine (2008), p. 92.

is certain that the Airy Spirits which are destined by the Creator to the Service of Men may be drawn by Perfumes" (page 14). The author reminds the reader of the history of Tobit where the reverse of this takes place and the burning of "stinking fish entrails" is designed to effectively drive away an unwelcome demon.

Chapter 9 - Invocations

The invocations are divided into Orations, Invocation and Conjuration for each planet. It is strongly suggested in Chapter 9 that these are not just performed at the time of the ceremony, but are practiced on a daily basis, selecting the correct set of invocations for each particular day of the week. Such a regular practice will ensure that when the time of ceremony arrives that they will be fluently declaimed (ideally from memory), and more importantly that they will accustom the spirits to expect such a set of invocations. These should not be done casually but with full attention to each word, and preferably at the same time each day.

Chapter 10 - Exorcisms

The 'Orations in the form of Exorcisms' on the other hand must only be used for specific magical operations, such as for consecrating things like the fire or sword. In this case 'exorcism' does not mean the driving out of a spirit, but the driving out of any residual influences left in the item, plus the attraction of a good indwelling spirit or blessing.

Part 2. Pentacles

This section is repeated seven times, one time for each of the planets/days from Sunday through to Saturday, or the Sun through to Saturn. Using the Sun as an example, each section contains:

> Description of the Pentacle for Sunday under the Sun, with its incense & perfume;
> Oration, Invocation and Conjuration for Sunday, with the precious stones and trees sympathetic to the Sun;
> Names of the Hours of the Day and Night on Sunday, with their angel of the hour;
> The Mysterious Characters for Sunday under the Sun;[20]
> Pentacle for Sunday made under the Sun (i.e. the floor circle to be used);
> Between one and three pages of Sun Pentacles (or Talismans);[21]
> Description and Use of the foregoing Pentacles (or Talismans) and general observations, including a list of the benefits of each Pentacle or Talisman.

---

[20] These are in fact characters based on stylised geomantic figures attributed to this planet.

[21] Five to a page, including the seal of the Olympic spirit and the kamea of the planet. There is a very real difference between Pentacles and Talismans, but in this manuscript the terms are used interchangeably. Talismans are made to be worn for general protection from ills and accidents. Pentacles are made to achieve specific magical objectives, and are not often worn.

The text has inherited several minor defects from its source, the Fyot French manuscript of Professor Pierre Morissoneau. The large 'pentacle' at the beginning of each planetary section (e.g. page 22, 33, 40, 49, etc.) is in fact not a pentacle but the floor circle to be used for that day and planet. This is a strange error, and one might wonder if it was intentional as the instructions clearly state that:

> It is necessary to have a pair of Compasses of sufficient Radius to Draw the Circle according to the Model in [the] frontispiece, of at least seven feet in Diameter,[22] also a piece of new Twine attached to a piece of consecrated chalk or charcoal to trace with accuracy the Grand Figures that it will be necessary to make on the floor which must be perfectly clean and even for the purpose. For these things are important and necessary for conducting the Grand Cabalistic Art.[23]

It is obvious that this refers to the procedure of drawing a floor circle, not to drawing a pocket-sized pentacle. In practice, the string and chalk is much more useful than the large pair of compasses which are seldom seen these days.[24] This is a key passage and it refers to both the main 'pentacle' in each planetary group, and to the fairly modest central illustration Fig. 6 on the Frontispiece. What the *Clavis* does not explain is that for each planetary operation there is a different circle, for example the circle for the Sun is shown on page 22, and the circle for the Moon is shown on page 33. Both however are incorrectly labelled as pentacles. In each case they contain god and angelic names as prescribed by the *Heptameron* for floor circles of that specific planet and day.

Throughout all versions there is also a constant confusion between the terms 'pentacle' and 'talisman.' A pentacle is used by the magician to bring about a *specific* magical objective – it is not usually worn. A talisman on the other hand is made by the magician (sometimes for a client) to be worn or kept in the pocket every day as a preventative or preservative against various non-specific ills or accidents, not for a specific magical objective. In the 7 planetary sections marked 'Pentacles' the scribe fluctuates between the two terms, sometimes mixing them up in the same section. In the latter half of the manuscript (for example on pages 189 or 201) there were some items which are obviously really talismans, meant to be carried with the owner for daily for protection.

For each planet, the last couple of 'pentacles' are actually the kamea (number square) of the planet from which the sigils of the spirit and the intelligence (angel) are generated. The kamea of the Sun is shown on page 25 in the numeric form (Fig. 15) and the Hebrew equivalent (Fig. 16). The Seal of the Intelligence of the Sun derived from the kamea, is shown on the same page in Fig. 17.

---

[22] Older sources speak of 7 (or even 9) feet in *radius*, thereby allowing adequate room for several assistants inside the circle.

[23] Chapter 4, page 7.

[24] The largest pair of compasses that I remember ever seeing was used in school by the geometry master to inscribe circles on the chalk board, and even they would not have been able to manage a seven foot diameter circle.

At the end of the pentacles proper for each planet is a figure (Fig. 12, page 24 in the case of the Sun) which is supposed to be the 'Familiar Spirit' of the planet. Unfortunately the illustration purporting to be the seal of Och in the *Clavis* on page 24 is in fact wrong. It shows the seals of two other solar spirits, Nakhiel and Sorath instead.

This confusion is constant throughout all the Planetary 'Familiar Spirits.'[25] A clear explanation of how the Intelligence and Spirit seals are generated can be found in *Techniques of High Magic* along with the correct Olympic spirit seals.[26] Strangely, the seals of the Olympic Spirits are shown correctly on pages 141-144 of the present manuscript.

There has been much discussion about the Olympic spirits with suggestions such as they come from Mount Olympus, or that they must be associated with the Greek gods. The answer is much simpler – it simply meant they were spirits of Greek origin, from a Greek grimoire source. Their original names in Greek are as shown in Figure 06. The tag 'Olympic' simply means 'Greek' rather than directly referring to the gods of Olympus.

Planet	'Olympic' Spirit	Spirit's Name in Greek	Isopsephy of the Spirit's Name
♄	Araithron	Αραιθρον	341 = 11 x 31
♃	Bethor	βεθορ	186 = 6 x 31
♂	Phaleg	φαλεκγ	558 = 18 x 31
☿	Och	ευξ	465 = 15 x 31
♀	Hagith	ηαγιθ	31 = 1 x 31
☿	Ophiel	οφιιλ	620 = 20 x 31
☾	Phul	φυλ	930 = 30 x 31
	Total =		3131 = 101 x 31

Figure 06: Table of the original names of the 'Olympic' or Greek spirits. The fact that the isopsephy[27] totals are all multiples of 31 indicates that this family of spirit names was deliberately constructed in Greek, rather than randomly generated, or gathered from assorted mythical or historical sources.

---

[25] Moon: page 35, Fig. 9; Mars: page 43, Fig. 10; Mercury: page 51, Fig. 9; Jupiter: page 59, Fig. 9; Venus: page 67, Fig. 8; Saturn: page 75, Fig. 8.

[26] Francis King & Stephen Skinner, *Techniques of High Magic*, Singapore: GHP, 2016, pp. 102-109, 114.

[27] 'Isopsephy' was the Greek practice, like Hebrew Gematria, of assigning a numeric value to the letters of a word. The result of totalling all the values of the letters in a word, or a name, gives a number which was thought to indicate the essence of the word or name so summed.

As proof of the age of these spirit names and seals, a stone ball was discovered near the Dionysus Odeon at the foot of the Acropolis in Athens, and it now resides in the New Acropolis Museum nearby. I suspect this is one of seven such planetary balls, this one being the ball of the Sun. It features an impressive image of Helios on one side, with images of the lion and what appears to be the serpent constellation Ophiuchus on the other sides. On the reverse it has a talismanic formula in Greek made from the names of related solar spirits. Most significantly it also has the sigil of Och the solar Olympic Spirit, demonstrating that the spirit Och dates back at least to the 2nd-3rd century CE.

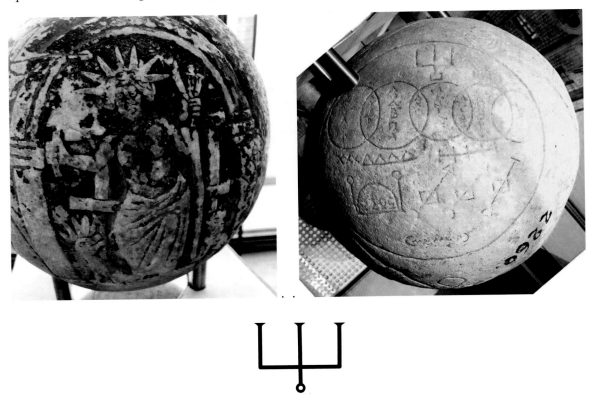

Figure 07: Two sides of the 2nd-3rd century stone talismanic ball of the Sun found near the Acropolis in Athens, showing Helios (god of the Sun) on one side (left) and the Seal of the spirit Och (spirit of the Sun) at the top on the other side, with a very detailed and clear Greek magical formula.[28] Below is the seal of Och, the spirit of the Sun, as it appeared in the *Arbatel* in the 16th century. The point of showing this is to demonstrate that the same spirits are invoked today, as they were in the *Clavis* in the 18th century, in the *Arbatel* in the 16th century, and as they were almost 2000 years ago in Athens.[29]

---

[28] This formula will be explained in a forthcoming book.
[29] Photos copyright Navaneeta Das.

This spirit along with all seven Olympic Spirits, has endured down to the present day, appearing in the *Arbatel* in 1554,[30] as well as being mentioned in Sibley's *Clavis*. This same pattern is followed for all the pentacles of the other six planets.

The Mysterious Ring

This section comes from a different *Key of Solomon* text-group,[31] but also appears in Wellcome MS 4670 where there is more background information on magical rings in general, referencing the ring of Gyges (for invisibility) and historical references in the works of Josephus. This is in fact a procedure for making any of the seven planetary finger rings. This particular circle is garbled in other versions of the *Clavis*, where the characters linking the sub-circles are usually wrongly interpreted as corrupt Hebrew. Here (on page 79) you can clearly see that these are in fact number strings separated by the repetition of the word 'Tetragrammaton.'

The present manuscript and MS 40 have the clearest numbers. These seem to fall into groups of four digits resembling dates. Reading from the top of the Ring we have:

1759	1779	1939
1779	1398	7171
1229	1471	[17]79 [32]
1249	1959	1779

One oddity is that 1779 appears in each group, four times in all. Apart from the fact that Sibley moved to Portsmouth in that year there seems to be no special significance to those four digits, or to that date.

This short but interesting free-standing operation is designed to link a ring made of the correct planetary metal and set with the correct stone to a specific 'Familiar spirit.' A diagram of the Ring is given (page 79 – Plate XXXII), which is a combination of a floor circle of protection surrounded by seven sketches of the planetary finger rings, each with an angel name and planetary symbol. The name and sigil of the spirit must be engraved on the ring, and after the spirit is evoked, the magician must gingerly extend the ring beyond the limits of the circle on the end of a specially consecrated rod, so that the spirit (who is of course outside the circle) can imprint it, to create a link between the ring and himself without endangering the magician. The magician is enjoined to then put the ring on and perfume it, before leaving the circle.

---

[30] ארבעתאל. *Arbatel of Magick: of the Magic of the Ancients* in Skinner (Ed.), *Fourth Book of Occult Philosophy*, Latin edition Marburg 1554; English edition Maine: Ibis, 2005, Aphorism 16-17.
[31] Text-group Zk. Manuscript published in Mora (1914), pp. 69-79.
[32] The '17' is taken from the two excess numbers at 11 o'clock position on the circle to fill the gap at the 8 o'clock position.

Part 3. Four Experiments with Specific Spirits

This Part includes specific invocations of the spirits Birto, Vassago, Agares and Bealpharos. These first three spirits appear in a number of 16th-19th century manuscripts. Vassago and Agares both appear in the *Goetia* (part of the *Lemegeton*). Bealpharos is not so well represented in other manuscripts, but is probably related to Baal, the first spirit listed in the *Goetia*. The material concerning the evocation of these four spirits is probably derived from Welcome MS 2842 written by Frederick Hockley in 1829, which is derived in turn from Elias Ashmole's 1649 Sloane MS 3824, both of which include evocations for these spirits.[33]

In each case the spirit may either be conjured into a triangle outside the circle, or its image may be seen in a "crystal stone or glass" on the Table of Practice inside the circle. The text reminds the practitioner that Aerial spirits (of which these four are examples) are slow to arrive. The invocations must be repeated a number of times before they arrive. They are also slow to leave so the magician is advised not leave the circle till some time after the completion of several repetitions of the License to Depart.

Two of the spirits specifically chosen in this section are the 2nd and 3rd spirits of the *Goetia,* suggesting strongly that the magician who wrote this section did so after experimenting with an early recension of that grimoire, starting at the beginning, but not advancing much further. The 'Experiments' of these spirits are claimed to have been authored by, or even carried out by one 'T.W.' (or J.W.) in one manuscript.

The Spirit Birto

Although the 'Four Experiments of the Spirits Birto, Agares, Bealpharos and Vassago' appear in nearly every example of the Sibley *Clavis* it is the procedure of Birto, and indeed the spirit himself that still retains the greatest aura of mystery.

The invocation of the spirit Birto extends in the present manuscript from page 81 to 85. This particular spirit appears in a number of other grimoires, and two distinct Birto operations seem to have developed roughly coexistent with each other. Some of the earlier know examples of the Birto Experiment can be found in:

- Bodleian Rawlinson MS D. 253 - 'The Secret of Secrets,' a 17th century grimoire used by at least three known Cunning-men, but with its roots in the early 16th

---

[33] Wellcome MS 2842 written by Frederick Hockley in 1829, and Wellcome MS 3203 copied by his friend Henry Dawson Lea both contain these four experiments "of the Spirits Birto, Agares, Bealpharos and Vassago. Comprising the Forms of Conjuration, Circles, Lamens and Obligations, or Bonds of Spirits." Wellcome MS 3203, a manuscript entitled *An Experiment of the Spirit Birto* was listed by Denley (in his 1818 catalogues) as being bound with the *Clavis*. The source for these spirits may have been Sloane MS 3824 written by Elias Ashmole (1617-1692) in 1649, and containing the additional spirit Brett, which in turn may have been derived from the papers of Dr. Richard Napier (1559-1634).

century.[34]

- FSL (Folger Shakespeare Library) MS V.b.26 - 'Book of Magic, with instructions for invoking spirits, etc.' written c. 1577-1583.[35]
- British Library Sloane MS 3824 – 'Magical Treatise,' 1649, f. 107-107v.

The Folger manuscript, more commonly known as *The Book of Oberon* in its published form, is unique in that it gives the details of the type of operation in which, even though the wyvern is illustrated, its portrait or effigy is not actually used in the procedure itself, this is something which sets this experiment apart from the other examples which would go on to feature in the *Clavis*. The Folger experiment also features the use of the 'white-handled knife' to scribe the circles on the ground, a very Solomonic reference.

The second variety of the Birto ritual appears in:

- The Sibley *Clavis* (the present manuscript and all its copies), pp. 80-84.
- Wellcome Library MS 2842 'Four Experiments of the Spirits' (penned by Hockley).
- Wellcome Library MS 3203 – 'Five Treatises upon Magic' (copied by Henry Dawson Lea with introductory notes by Hockley).[36]

These all follow the same format. There are two noteworthy inclusions in this operation. The first is the assertion that the invocation of Birto was successfully performed before Edward IV King of England, which suggests it originally dates from the late 15th century (if you believe this attribution).

There is no certainty that King Edward IV (1442-1483) actually watched the evocation of Birto, but it seems quite possible as his wife Elizabeth Woodville (1437-1492) had a reputation for being a witch, who may have had dealings with spirits. She also had a family connection with the half-human half-serpent Mélusine whose legends featured a wyvern (see Appendix 2). We will see later how this information may help to explain the function of the wyvern image.

The reference to King Edward IV in association with the spirit Birto is additionally interesting as it is illustrated in this and other manuscripts with the image of a wyvern,[37]

---

[34] Edited by Stephen Skinner & David Rankine, *A Cunning Man's Grimoire,* Singapore: Golden Hoard, 2018. See page 71-74.

[35] Published as *The Book of Oberon: A Sourcebook of Elizabethan Magic* by Daniel Harms, James Clark and Joseph H. Peterson, Llewellyn, 2015, pp. 25, 399-400.

[36] Hockley states that MS 3203 was "Transcribed by my friend Henry Dawson Lea from MSS I lent to him in the year 1843."

[37] It is a wyvern not a dragon as suggested by some authors, as it stands on two legs, not four. Also because its tail clearly ends in an arrow point.

drawn between two magic circles (see page 84, Plate XXXIII).[38] The circles are obviously protective floor circles used during the evocation, as one is marked 'Magister', the Master, and the other one for the spirit, simply marked 'Birto.' In the Weiser MS the wyvern is missing, however all other versions show two equal sized circles separated by a wyvern. We may have become used to the magician standing in a circle, whilst the spirit is forced into a triangle, but here both occupy a circle. This arrangement is quite unusual as normally the magician would occupy a much larger circle than the circle or triangle designed to hold the spirit. This is not the only occurrence of a spirit being given his own circle, but it is not common to see both circles of equal size.

The image of Birto used as the frontispiece (page iv) to this book is not from the present manuscript but from Sloane MS 3824, which was a probable source of most of the material found in Part 3 of the *Clavis*. The words above the wyvern suggest that this image was meant to be consecrated:

> Tros Habos Biffouns so / With Harts, Toungs & Eyes / Tuos Salvo so / The father, The sone and The / Holy Goast, &c. / dinon / Housn Forsuth / Charrity *

Which reads as:

> [By] Tros Habos Biffouns, so with hearts, tongues & eyes for your salvation [through] the Father, Son, and Holy Ghost, now shelter us in truth and charity.

The words under the wyvern are:

> Omecron & Omega / First & Last.[39]

The instructions for calling this spirit also make interesting remarks about the creation of the protective circles:

> As for the Circle wherein the Spirit Appeareth it may be made [in] two or three several ways, according to the place made choice of to act in, and the Ground or floor. If the Ground be nought or rugged, as in Woods, or Coppices [as] they generally are, then must the Ground be paved, and made very even, so that an impression may be made visible and plain thereon, or else let it be made on large Calfskin Parchment, but it is better [directly] on the Ground, and if upon Parchment or a floor, then let the Circle be made or drawn thereon with Consecrated Chalk or marking stone and place them three feet asunder and herein lies a serious and deliberate consideration, let reason and prudence be thy principal Guide, without which principles a Magician is but a shadow to a substance, and shall miss as hit of his Expectations.[40]

The magician is warned not to be impatient or discouraged by delay. A Bond of Spirits and Licence to Depart are later given, both an essential part of the Solomonic method.

---

[38] See also Harms, Clark, Peterson (2015), p. 399-400; and Rankine (2009), p. 132.
[39] This should of course read "Alpha & Omega / First & Last."
[40] Page 84.

Birto is said to report to two Princes: Ornothocos and the unlikely sounding 'Booth.' The singularly most distinct and recognisable trait of this spirit is its association with the appearance of the green wyvern.[41] This in itself has resulted in confusion, as it is never clearly stated if this is the spirit's preferred form of manifestation.

It has been suggested that the wyvern is the form in which this Spirit will present itself, however this is unlikely as the evocation commands Birto to:

"Appear Visibly before me in the Circle appointed for thee in fair and human form and shape of a man, and no ways terrible or hurtful."

Figure 08: The Wyvern drawn by Frederick Hockley. Wellcome MS 2842.

Anyway, it would also seem unlikely that if the wyvern was his desired form, that it would be drawn outside of his summoning circle.

A second suggestion is that the wyvern is actually there as a type of barrier or protection for the magician's benefit. The positioning of the image adds weight to the idea that the wyvern is perhaps used as a form of protection against molestation by a belligerent spirit, as the magician is required to place the drawn image of the wyvern upon the ground between the two circles. This procedure seems very curious, and one wonders what good a simple illustration of a wyvern would be in the overall outcome of the experiment? It would seem to be much more effective if rendered as a wearable layman.

There is a third possibility. C. J. S. Thompson in his 1927 publication *Mysteries and Secrets of Magic* writes of a procedure from an unnamed sixteenth century manuscript, that:

> ...to obtain the presence of Birto, it was necessary that the circle of the invocant should have the effigy or character of a dragon fairly drawn or painted, and the circle in which the spirit is to appear should be made on a calve's skin parchment.

Here we have an interesting clue. Instead of protection, the object of the wyvern is actually "to obtain the presence of Birto," so the actual purpose was to aid the evocation. It should also be noted that the wyvern was to be drawn on an 'abortive' or thin vellum procured from the skin of a still-born animal, so that it could be consecrated like any other ritual

---

[41] Wyvern or wivern is a sub-class of dragon, depicted as having a dragon's head & wings, a reptilian or serpentine body ending in a triangular barbed tipped tail, and two talloned bird-like legs. Its image is most familiar from its associated use within heraldry. – Ed.

tool, and then placed in the invocant's circle. Indeed, the wyvern could be fashioned as an effigy rather than just a painted scrap of parchment, and it therefore could have been seen as a tool. Perhaps the scenario was more an assertion of the authority of the magician? After all, if the magician was perceived to have command over such a beast then this would be a very effective "ace up the sleeve" when commanding a powerful spirit.

There is yet a fourth possible reason for the wyvern which relates directly to the association with King Edward IV. Was the image meant as a reminder of the Mélusine story? Was the point of the image of the wyvern to identify the magician with Mélusine's family and hence with their magical power? This would give the magician even greater authority, and claiming association with a powerful magician (or in this case a half human) is definitely a part of the Solomonic method. More details of this legend and its relevance are to be found in Appendix 2.

Detachable parchments

The experiment of Birto is unique within the world of ceremonial magic, and something rather interesting presents itself to us when we look at its incorporation in the pages of the Sibley *Clavis*. Joseph Peterson first mentions in his edition of this work, that the Utah manuscript has an image of the Birto wyvern *glued* in. After having the opportunity to examine this manuscript for ourselves it can clearly be seen where this has happened. Our initial thought was that the image had been perhaps sourced from an different manuscript at a later date. However after viewing the other known copies it was soon discovered, and rather surprisingly so, that every single manuscript we examined, but one, had the illustration of the circles and wyvern effigy pasted in on a separate piece of parchment.

It soon became apparent that this practice was a consistent part of the creation and copying of this work. As far as the purpose behind using a glued in plate as opposed to physically drawing the illustrations directly onto the manuscripts page itself one can only speculate. Very little instruction for its use is given in the main body of the text however it is a possibility that the wyvern plate was intended to be a completely removable item from the manuscript? Something that could be used practically, especially if it was already drawn on a ritually prepared 'abortive' parchment and particularly if the would-be magician was not adept in his artistic ability to draw the image effectively. In this manner the illustration could then be replaced back into the work without the need to damage or cut out the page in question and ruin the manuscript. This method suggests that many owners wished to use the image practically. It would seem that this practice of pasting in the Birto plate only occurs with the *Clavis* copies. Examples of manuscripts outside of this group, although almost identical in description and method, are penned directly onto the page itself. One can only wonder if this innovative and practical addition was created by Sibley himself when compiling his original work and subsequently carried over into the many copies made thereafter, or was it an idea or method sourced from an earlier as yet unknown manuscript once in Sibley's possession?

	Manuscript Identifier	Description of Illustration	Separate Paste-in
1	Weiser MS	Two circles unshaded in purple and red inks. No wyvern present. Simple red border.	Yes
2	University of Utah MS	Green coloured wyvern standing on ground between two circles shaded in yellow.	Yes
4	University of Manchester (Rylands) MS 40	Beautiful green coloured and shaded wyvern between two uncoloured and undecorated circles. Simple red & black border.	Yes
4a	National Library of Scotland Acc. 9769	Access not available.	N/A
5	S. E. E. MS	Two uncoloured circles plain and undecorated. The word "Effigy" written between (no wyvern present).	No
6	London University Senate House Library MS HPF 1/10	Large green coloured wyvern in right corner surrounded by three coloured circles.[42] Simple red & blue border.	Yes
8	National Library of Israel MS Yah. Var. 18	Green coloured wyvern on ground between two circles of pink & yellow. Multicoloured border.	Yes
9	Library and Museum of Freemasonry MS SRIA 2083	Manuscript incomplete. Experiment of Birto not included.	N/A
10	Bibliotheca Philosophica Hermetica MS PH 304	Page torn/cut from manuscript. Dark ink remaining near spine indicating that the illustration may have been elaborate.	Unknown

Figure 09: Table of the variations in the Birto seal across all known *Clavis* manuscripts. It is instructive to see exactly what proportion of the manuscripts had this user facility.

---

[42] The Senate House *Clavis* is unique because of its addition of a 3rd Circle reminiscent of "The Great Pentacle of Solomon" featured much earlier in the work.

Figure 10: Circles and wyvern from Wellcome MS 3203 – 'Five Treatises upon Magic.'

The operation of Birto also impinged on other occultists of the 19th century particularly the astrologer Robert Cross Smith, better known as the first Raphael (1795-1832) who wrote *Tales of the Horrible, or the Book of Spirits*,[43] a work of fiction attributed to "an Astronomer *(sic)* of the nineteenth century." In it Birto is depicted as a "a knight with black armour" an imaginative idea but nothing more than that, at least as far as the present grimoire is concerned.

But to return to the four spirits in Part 3, the second spirit is Vassago.

The Spirit Vassago[44]

This spirit is the 3rd of those listed in the *Goetia*. Vassago is a Prince, traditionally under the rulership of Lucifer, although our text states that he falls under "Baro the king of the West." He is considered a good-natured spirit, who "declares things Past & Future; Discovers the Hidden & Lost." Strangely, Vassago is one of the few *Goetia* spirits that do not also appear in Weyer's *Pseudomonarchia Daemonum.*

The instructions for calling this spirit are quite interesting as they bear upon the practical use of the Demon Kings. It is usually recommended that magicians do not attempt to evoke the Demon Kings directly, but use their names to command and motivate the lesser spirits, and that is done here where the magician is instructed to hold a sceptre that identifies him with the Demon King, or gives him the power to speak for that King.

> The Magical practitioner must provide a Lamen or plate of silver, and engraven upon [it] according as it is represented hereafter, and a Spatula made of Ash, Pear tree, or any other solid wood the thickness of a third part of an inch, and the square top thereof to be three inches square, and the stem or handle to be nine inches long and gilded all over with Gold, and the Character written thereon, as is shown forth in the Example following.[45]

---

[43] Published by C. Wright, 1837.

[44] The Weiser MS initially erroneously identifies this spirit as 'Wassago."

[45] Page 85.

The magical 'spatula' is not shown, except in outline, but another manuscript written by Elias Ashmole in Sloane MS 3824 makes up the deficiency as shown in Figure 11. The 'spatula' is actually meant to be used as a sort of sceptre to confirm the kingly power and majesty of the magician. The sceptre is used in both the Vassago and the Agares rite.

On the sceptre is written "Mathon Egyn ♄ II," confirming that this spirit is a Saturnine spirit under the rulership of Egyn, Demon King of the North.[46] The prestige and power of Egyn is conferred upon the magician by virtue of holding this sceptre.

Figure 11: An illustration of the magical 'spatula' or magician's sceptre is shown top left, with the lamen bottom left. The seal of Agares is shown top right. The text is more detailed but otherwise very close to that of the *Clavis* and was probably its source.[47]

The silver Lamen with the spirit's sigil worn on his breast completes the magician's personal protection.[48] This manuscript further confirms that the Bond or obligation of the spirit should be written out in full and laid on the altar next to the skrying crystal or glass if that is how the spirit is to be contacted.

The list of written requests/demands should be also accompanied by the seal of the spirit and written on an "abortive" by which the text means a piece of virgin parchment made from an unborn (i.e. aborted) lamb or calf.

Where 'N' would usually appear in other grimoires, meaning the name of the magician

---

[46] This is a bit odd as Vassago was mentioned as being under the King of the West, and Agares under the King of the East. Directional confusion is also rife amongst the spirits of the *Goetia*.
[47] Sloane MS 3824, f. 112v.
[48] See bottom left of Figure 11.

performing the conjuration, here either 'J. M.' or 'J. W.' appears as before mentioned. These initials also appear in the relevant Bond of the Spirit. These were obviously the initials of the magician who copied out the manuscript and maybe used it. See page 89 for the Bond of this spirit.

Figure 12: The *Goetia* describes one spirit as "an old Man riding on a Crocodile, carrying a Goshawk on his fist." The above illustration is a modern vision of Vassago.[49] But note this description is more correctly referred to the spirit Agares.

The Spirit Agares

This spirit is the 2nd of those listed in the *Goetia*. Agares is a Duke under the rulership of Lucifer, with command of 31 legions. In the *Clavis* he is called "the first Captain under the King of the East." Weyer in *Pseudomonarchia Daemonum* says of Agares that:

> He appears willingly in the form of an older man, riding a crocodile, and carrying a hawk in his hand. He teaches all types of languages well. He causes fugitives to return, and causes those who remain to flee. He gets rid of privileges and dignities, and makes spirits of the earth dance.[50]

Sloane MS 3824 mentions that Agares aids in invocations to summon spirits that guard

---

[49] Painting copyright of Michael Sugianto, Jakarta, www.artstation.com/michaelsugianto.
[50] Causes earthquakes, literally *tripudiare facit spiritus terrae*.

treasure. The use of the sceptre and lamen is also recommended when evoking Agares, as with Vassago.

The Spirit Bealpharos

Although there is a Conjuration of Bealpharos in Scot's *Discoverie of Witchcraft,*[51] Sibley was conscious that this is quite different from the text he followed in *Clavis.* The spirit Bealpharos has an interesting name, which may be a combination of 'baal' and 'pharos.' The spelling 'Bealpharos' is probably a slight corruption of how it is mentioned in one

ILLUSTRATION, No. XV.

CIRCLE III.—SECT. I.

Figure 13: The Spirit Bealpharos as he appears in the *Straggling Astrologer,* 1824. See page 96 of the present manuscript. Illustration re-purposed to represent necromancy.

manuscript with the spelling 'Baalpharos.' This spelling may give some clues to its meaning and derivation. Baal is the first spirit listed in the *Goetia,* so at some point his name may have become truncated. If so that would mean that the first three spirits of the *Goetia* are all included here.

That spelling also immediately suggests an interpretation of his name. Baal, a well know spirit and Syrian/Palestinian god, has the meaning 'Lord.' Pharos, in Greek φάρος, refers to the famous lighthouse of Alexandria. Taken together, a not unlikely interpretation of this spirit's name as 'Lord of the Pharos' or even 'Lord of the Light.' As such his portrayal with an angelic figure in Plate XXXV seems appropriate.

The description of this spirit suggests that the magician should wear a "Girdle or Thong of a Lion's, Hart's or Buck's skin."[52] This is important for two reasons, first it shows the origin of the requirement in the *Goetia,* for the magician to wear a lion skin belt. Secondarily it widens the equipment options to allow the magician to substitute a hart or buck skin, a widening of options that will gladden the heart of many a would-be magician unable to easily secure a lion's skin.

---

[51] 1651 edition, Book XV, p. 296.
[52] Page 94.

Circle and Lamen

The section on Bealpharos is immediately followed by a diagram of the floor circle to be used and a form of lamen to be made in silver, applicable to all four spirits.[53] For all four of these spirits, Fig. No. 1 on page 98 is the design of the circle in which the magician must stand. Fig. No. 2 on the same page is the design of the lamen which the magician must wear. The wording on these varies considerable from manuscript to manuscript.

The words on the lamen are "Homo Sacarus Muselomea Cherubosea," or more accurately "Homo Sacarus, museo lomeas, cherubozea."[54] Sacarus means 'consecrated.'[55] Therefore this lamen indicates to the evoked spirit that the 'consecrated person' wearing it is protected by an angel. The circle is also taken from Scot.[56]

Each of these spirits is supplied with a Licence to Depart which must be used without exception after each conjuration. This step should not be ignored even if the conjuration appears to have failed.

Part 4. Wheel of Wisdom

This Part is illustrated with the 'Wheel of Magic' as a frontispiece. This diagram is effectively a table of planetary correspondences arranged in a circular fashion and divided according to the 7 planets. The eighth sector (at the '4 o'clock' position) serves to identify the categories of correspondence, e.g. metal, stone, tree, herb, animal, bird, etc. The Key to the Wheel summarises the qualities of the planets. Such chains of correspondences have long been a staple of magical thinking, especially for the creation of talismans and pentacles.[57]

'Full Directions for Magical Operations' is a good list of basic requirements for magical operations. An example operation of Venus with the angel Anael follows, with detailed instructions how to join two people together in love.[58]

Here ends the continuous pagination of the first four Parts, and a new 'book' begins. It is probable that this also ends the four Parts of the original Sibley material. Although the manuscript begins a new numbering sequence at this point, we will continue to refer to it by the continuing printed page number sequence at the foot of the page.

---

[53] Page 98.

[54] See Scot (1665), p. 296 (416 in first edition).

[55] The sacring bell is the bell rung at the time the host is consecrated and elevated.

[56] See Scot (1665), p. 295 (414 in first edition).

[57] A much fuller set of correspondences will be found in Skinner, *Complete Magician's Tables*, Singapore: Golden Hoard, 2017. The 5th expanded edition.

[58] In this case Edwin and Emma.

Part 5. A Secret and Complete Book of Magic Science.

The addition of a monogram 'FH' (with a reversed 'F') on page 112 suggests that this separate work was probably generated from a Frederick Hockley copy. This text appears to be substantially the same as the text claimed by Hockley as his own assembly, although he also claims to have copied it from a 1573 text, which date appears at the foot of the title page. The script however is not in Hockley's hand.

This Part has recently been published as *A Complete Book of Magic Science* by Teitan Press, 2008, from a copy transcribed by Frederick Hockley and edited with an introduction by Dietrich Bergman.[59] Bergman compares and contrasts this text with the *Grimoire of Turiel* by 'Marius Malchus' which parallels this text. Bergman concludes that *A Complete Book of Magic Science* is the longer and more authoritative text. Although both grimoires have a questionable beginning, it is clear that both stem from a common source which both texts dated as 1518/1519.

No original Latin document has yet surfaced, but Bergman points out that the Latin passages in the *Secret Grimoire of Turiel* are more distorted, and therefore it is probably the less reliable text.[60] Bergman notes that *The Secret Grimoire of Turiel* also includes two appended sections: 'The Powers and Offices of the Seven Olympic Spirits' and 'The Times' which are not included in *A Complete Book of Magic Science* but are to be found elsewhere. He points out that the list of 'The Powers and Offices of the Olympic Spirits' appears to have been taken from A. E. Waite's section on *The Arbatel of Magic* in his *Book of Black Magic and Pacts*, published in 1898 suggesting a late 19th century composition. The author Marius Malchus claimed to have bought the Latin manuscript and an English translation in Palma in 1927, and adds a romantic story about its purchase, claiming that he subsequently conveniently destroyed the Latin version.

Turiel is one of the Presiding Spirits of Venus listed on page 127 of the present manuscript, but is hardly of sufficient prominence to have an entire grimoire named after him. In *The Secret Grimoire of Turiel*, Turiel is listed as messenger for the angel Sachiel, but Sachiel is attributed to both Jupiter and Venus (also on page 127) but just Jupiter (on page 142).

This Part begins with six pages of prayers and benedictions (pages 113-119) designed to consecrate the equipment to be used in the ritual, an important part of all ceremonial magic, and something that should be done well before the day of the actual operation.

The illustration on page 118 is incomplete as the contents of the outer ring are totally missing. The restored words of that ring, from MS HPF 1/10, are as follows:

---

[59] Hockley & Bergman, *A Complete Book of Magic Science.* York Beach: Teitan, 2008, published from a different manuscript to the one here reproduced, and so has a number of differences.
[60] Hockley & Bergman (2008), p. xiv.

Facit. Behold God is my Salvation. I will trust and not be afraid for the Lord Jehovah is my strength and my song; he is also become my Salvation.[61]

י. ט ד .אתגיטור כאכו .אחח גכרו לעולם ארני

For the Stars of Heaven and the Constellations thereof shall not give their light; the Sun shall be darkened in his going forth and the Moon shall not cause her light to shine.[62]

Further prayers follow for 'putting on the Vesture,' and form part of the *Invocatio* of the Solomonic method. On page 126 the Register of spirits is laid out for each planet, divided into three categories: Spirits, Presiding Spirits and Ministering Spirits.

A 'Register of Spirits' is a necessary part of all Solomonic magic, the most commonly known example of which is the *Goetia*.[63] The first category includes the names of the planetary angels, and the last category contains the names of the spirits which the magician will typically constrain to do specific tasks. This list of the ruling, presiding and ministering spirits is followed by their conjurations, interrogatories,[64] and bonds, in other words the verbal parts of the ritual.

An example invocation of the Jupiterian spirit messenger Pabiel is given.[65] By looking at the list of spirits you can see that Pabiel is ruled by Zadkiel, the angel of Jupiter.

The next section marked 'Interrogatories' is particularly interesting as it shows a typical format for testing the spirit to ensure that he is who he claims to be. It also acts as a form of binding:

> ...confirm thy Character unto me whereby I may call at all times, and also swear unto me this Oath, and I will Religiously keep my vow...and will courteously receive thee at all times where thou dost appear unto me.[66]

This is an important section that is seldom to be found in most grimoires, as it would usually have been verbally explained by the Master to his pupil.

The layout of both spirit and magician's circles with the ruling angel Zadkiel, appears on page 132. The central image is, according to other versions of this manuscript, "the form in which the Spirit Pabiel sometimes appears." The Bond for the spirit Pabiel appears on the next page, along with the seals of Bethor (the Olympic spirit of Jupiter) and Sachiel

---

[61] *Isaiah* 12:2.

[62] *Isaiah* 13:20.

[63] Spirit Registers are not confined to Solomonic magic and are known across the whole range of magic. In Taoist magic, Spirit Registers are jealously guarded secrets, which are passed from master to pupil, but only when the student has demonstrated sufficient practical ability.

[64] The sequence of testing questions that must be asked of the spirit to ensure it is the correct one.

[65] In the illustration of the two circles of conjuration (one for the Master and one for the spirit) the name is misspelled as Pabel.

[66] Page 131.

(the angel of Jupiter). Following this is the all-important License to Depart.

A full set of planetary pentacles for use with this ritual follows. The emphasis of these pentacles is upon the use of appropriate geometric forms. The associated short form invocations are given on pages 139-140.

The Seals and Characters of the seven planets consist of the character of the corresponding Olympic spirit plus the Seal of the relevant angel. The traditional 'perfume' or incense of the 7 planets are also to be found in this section. Here the seals of the Olympic spirits are shown correctly.

This is the last section appearing in most other versions of the *Clavis* (except for some fragmentary crystal skrying material in manuscript number 3). Certainly the rest of this manuscript (about 45% of the whole book) has never appeared before in published form.

Part 6. Crystallomancy[67] or the Art of Invoking Spirits by the Crystal.

This is the art of evoking an image of the spirit to appear in a crystal rather than outside the circle in a triangle. This was a subject that held a lot of fascination for Frederick Hockley. Peterson claims that Sibley was also quite interested in conjuring spirits into the crystal,[68] whilst Susan Sommers[69] is of the opposite opinion that Sibley had no interest in skrying, and did not even possess a crystal. Be that as it may, this Part is an important division of invocation.

The question has often been put as to where the crystal is located, and if in the circle how is this possible, if the spirit is prevented from entering the circle. The answer is simply that what appears in the crystal is an image of the spirit, a reflection if you like, which is quite different in nature from the manifestation of the spirit outside the circle in the Triangle of Art.

Hockley is keen to confirm that "it is nowhere forbidden in Scripture to enquire of, and hold converse with the good Spirits, it is not accounted sinful to Invoke their Spiritual Aid in all matters," an understandable concern in Victorian England, but not so controversial nowadays. However the discipline of prayer over a number of days prior to the invocation is still useful. The conditions of the room for practice and basic timing rules are laid out. The circle for the operation is shown on page 150, and the equipment for drawing it. Hockley recommends a crystal about 4 inches across. It must be real rock crystal not simply glass, and mounted in a frame. An over-elaborate frame, surrounded by appropriate godnames, is illustrated on page 153. The crystal is to be consecrated before use, and other equipment is shown on page 156. The Bond of Spirits for Vassago is shown on pages 159-161, rather than the more appropriate position after page 89.

---

[67] Spelled 'Crystaliomancy' by Sibley.
[68] Peterson (2012).
[69] Sommers (2018), 237, 260-261.

Part 7. Miscellaneous Examples and Experiments.

The first part on 'Natural Magic' is typical of the end of grimoire material where assorted procedures that the magician found useful are often recorded. Examples include 'fascination' procedures, which sound a bit like party tricks, but are not really part of the procedures of evocation/invocation. 'Fascination' (in the original sense of the word) was a magical staple dating back to first century Graeco-Egyptian magical papyri.

Examples of these 'tricks' include making a room appear to be on fire, or to be crawling with serpents, or to make the occupants look as if they were "newly risen from their cold graves." Other snippits include the properties of herbs and how to fascinate birds. This is followed by various talismans (e.g. for strength, to keep thieves out of the house, to cause destruction of enemies) and 'charms' against troubles in general, or to overcome enemies.

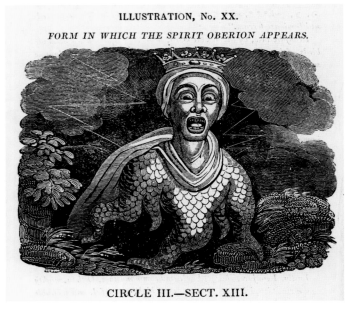

Figure 14: The Spirit Oberion as illustrated in the *Straggling Astrologer*, 1824.

Page 172 reverts to 'Methods of Raising and Invocating Spirits' which is more properly the stuff of grimoires. The main Experiment is the "Raising of the Powerful Spirit Oberion."[70] This is illustrated by a pictire of how Oberion "usually appears" as a rather effeminate king (page 179). This section also includes "The Great and Powerful Incantation" that is to be used if Oberion proves refractory (page 180).

Oberion was a very popular spirit, and has recently had a whole grimoire named after him.[71] This grimoire also had sections on the spirits Birto, Vassago and Beallphares (*sic*), but strangely not Agares. Oberion and his invocation appeared later in various 19th century occult magazines such as *The Straggling Astrologer,* which was edited by Robert Cross who was responsible for at least

---

[70] Page 176.

[71] Harms, Clark and Peterson, *The Book of Oberon,* Woodbury: Llewellyn, 2015. The name change from 'Oberion' to 'Oberon' was a bit of artistic licence by the publishers in an effort to make a Shakespearean connection.

one manuscript copy of the *Clavis*.[72] The *Straggling Astrologer* also featured a woodland version of the circle used to invoke him (see Figure 15).

Oberion is also mentioned in *The Book of the Offices of Spirits* dated 1583, in which he is described as:[73]

> Obeyryon, rex,[74] he appeareth like a king with a crown on his head, and he is under the government of the sun and moon, and he teacheth a man knowledge in physic [medicine], and he showeth the nature of stones, herbs and trees and all metals, and is a great and mighty king, and he is king of the fairies, he causeth a man to be invisible, and he showeth where hidden treasure is, and how to obtain the same, he telleth of things past, present and to come, and if he be bound to a man, he will carry or bring treasure out of the same, his burden is £100,000, he holdeth the waters and low parts of the earth, ≈ ℋ.

ILLUSTRATION, No. XXI.
THE CIRCLE FOR RAISING Oberion.

Figure 15: The circle used to evoke Oberion, as it appears in *The Straggling Astrologer*, 1824. This is a simplified copy of the circle seen in the present manuscript (on page 176), but without the woodland.

Still part of the same Part 7 is a strange addition which consists of a rather bad reproduction of the Vitruvian man drawings of Leonardo da Vinci, with gratuitously prominent pubic hair, and a five page Latin commentary which has no obvious magical connection (page 184-189).

More relevant are a set of talismans for Secret Love; for Healing Diseases; and for Amorous Intrigues & Friendship (page 203), interspersed with appended orations and invocations. Another talisman entitled 'The Imperial Talisman, for Victory over Enemies uses a variation on Christ's monogram.

Electrum Magicum is a chapter on creating a disk shaped pentacle made of all the planetary metals, which is supposed to draw in all seven angels of the planets (page 210).

---

[72] *Clavis* Manuscript number 5 published by S. E. E. See Figure 25.

[73] Porter, John, Colin Campbell (ed.), *A Book of the Offices of Spirits,* York Beach: Teitan, 2011, p 26.

[74] In the 16th century 'i' and 'y' were interchangeable. Rex = king.

Immediately following the description of the mixture of the seven planetary metals comes an unusual passage on the magical bell (Magia Campanum) because this bell is also made out of exactly the same mixture of metals. It was better known as the famous bell of Girardius, used by him for calling demons.

An 18th century manuscript belonging to Cardinal de Rohan,[75] in Latin and French describes how the bell was originally composed of seven metals, and was used in magical evocation and necromancy.[76]

At the bottom of the bell is the name Tetragrammaton, and above it the symbols of the seven planets and the word Adonai, and finally, Jesus, around the circle, and the names of the seven Olympic spirits of the planets by which the operation is done.

Sometimes the bell is cast on the birth day of the person who intends to use it. This birthdate is sometimes also written on the bell itself. The bell must then be wrapped in a piece of green silk and kept until the person undertaking the operation has time to leave (or bury) that bell in a cemetery for seven days where the bell will supposedly make the necessary connections with the chthonic spirits of the graveyard.

To use the bell, ring it to the four cardinal directions and invoke with four Paternosters:

> By the vertue of these names, the voyce of the bell shall enter into their hearts, to cause them to feare and obay, and that donne, let them prosecute there worke, that they may fullfill it, that they may renew the circle and fumigations and soe proceede in there worke.[77]

Septum Annulus

The central seven rings in Plate XIII (page 213) are reminiscent of the Table of Practice seen in the 'Art Pauline' book of the *Lemegeton*.[78]

Plate XIV is followed by its instructions for fascination and binding of spirits in Latin. A talisman for Vision in the Crystal (page 219), which might have been better placed in Part 6, preceeds a specific example, to invoke the spirit of Venus, Anael, into the crystal. Interestingly, Anneal was a spirit of of prime importance for Dr John Dee, and his *Tuba Venerus*, or 'Trumpet of Venus' was also concerned with that operation. Plate XVI shows Anael in the crystal.

---

[75] 'The Secret of Secrets, the Grimoire of Tosgraec,' Bibliothèque de l'Arsenal MS 2350.
[76] It is also mentioned in *Girardius parvi lucii libellus de mirabilibus naturae arcanis, anno domini*, 1730.
[77] See Sloane MS 3847. There is also a similar bell in an anonymous German grimoire (1505).
[78] See Skinner & Rankine, *Goetia of Dr Rudd*, Singapore: Golden Hoard, 2007, p. 310.

Part 8. Geomancy

This Part is a fairly straightforward description of geomancy, and has almost certainly been tacked on after the main material at a much later date, possibly even after the Hockley content. The basis of this method was probably taken from John Heydon's *Theomagia*. A more detailed and cogent description of the history and evolution of geomancy can be found in my book on geomancy.[79] That work also contains a more detailed description of the method, than is afforded by Part 8. The key interpretive table is to be found on page 231. Despite the use of 'lots' in the description, divination by lots is a quite different process from geomancy. Interestingly, the zodiacal attributions of the 16 geomantic figures look as if they have been derived from Gerard of Cremona's geomancy rather than either Agrippa or the sources of the Golden Dawn attributions.

Part 9. Experiments

This is really a contination of Part 7, before it was split by the introduction of the chapter on geomancy, in fact the operation of Anael begun on page 220 is here continued on page 251. The first pages of this Part (pages 245-251) are concerned with operations of love. Subsequent experiments are concerned with the setting of magical boundaries to secure a house (even including a separate operation to secure its outhouses).[80] A third operation is not just concerned with keeping thieves away, but is also concerned with magical protection designed to keep any 'spritual beings' at bay. However if a thief does manage to steal something then there is also an operation to bind that thief and compel him to return the lost goods.[81] To further hamper theft, there is an operation "to conceal or hide Money or Treasure so that they may never be stolen." This Part concludes with a general talisman against enemies.

Part 10. Magical Tables

Part of every magician's armory is a set of correspondence tables designed to let him know what colours or metals or divine and angelic names he should use for a particular operation or talisman. Typically in many 16th and 17th century grimoires there will also be a section devoted to correspondences between animals, fish, birds, trees, stones, and many other categories of natural products that can be used in planetary operations. Typically these often contain 15 items in each group.

More logically, the correspondences will be divided into sets of four (the Elements) or sets of 7 (the Planets) or sets of 12 (the Zodiac). When Agrippa devised an even more complete set of correspondences he used these basic building blocks, but added other sets of all the other numbers up to 12. Agrippa's tables form the basis of the tables to be

---

[79] Skinner, *Geomancy in Theory & Practice,* Singapore: Golden Hoard, 2011, p. 180-233.
[80] I have seen similar operations carried out in modern day Malaysia. – SS.
[81] I have had first-hand experience of the benefits of this particular piece of magic. – SS.

found in Part 10 but sadly the tables are incomplete and only cover numbers one (*De unitate*) to nine (*Scala Novenarii*).[82]

MacGregor Mathers adopted these tables for the knowledge lectures of the Hermetic Order of the Golden Dawn, but decided to use the 32 Paths of the Tree of Life as the basis of categorisation. This resulted in rather forced association of mixed correspondences, with Elemental, Planetary and Zodiacal correspondences inter-cut in the same table. Aleister Crowley, following his policy of plagiarising Mather's scholarly work, added a few more columns and published the work as his own under the title *777*. This slim volume was revised and fleshed out by Gerald Yorke in 1956 under the title *Liber 777 Revised*.[83]

Reverting to Agrippa's arrangement by Zodiac, Element, and Planet (or 'ZEP' arrangement), the present author added much addirional material such as the names of angels, spirits and gods from many of the grimoires, plus groupings of gods from polytheistic sources and published it at *The Complete Magician's Tables*.[84]

---

[82] Agrippa, *Three Books of Occult Philosophy*, 1993, Book II, Chapter xxii, pp. 318-328.

[83] Crowley did the exact same thing when he published Mather's manuscript of the *Goetia*, which he had 'borrowed' from the Golden Dawn Order's premises at 33 Blythe Road, Hammersmith, London W6. Crowley added an introduction that referred to Mathers as a "dead hand," and added a curse against him, an action that can only be seen in the light of a guilty conscience. One clear indication that Crowley did not understand what he was copying, and had not bothered to check the original grimoire in the British Museum, is that he copied Mathers notes, sketches and doodles on a completely different subject that appear on subsequent pages of Mathers' notebook, and published these as if they were part of the *Goetia*.

[84] The 5th and final edition of *The Complete Magician's Tables* was enlarged by an additional 64 pages and published in 2017 by Golden Hoard.

The French Source

The first part of the *Clavis* (Part 1 and Part 2) is a translation from a French original. The translation from the French was done (or caused to be done) by Ebenezer Sibley on or before 7th August, 1789, whilst he was living or working at No. 18 Bartlett's Buildings, Holborn, London (see Figure 32) because this is the date and place found on the title page of another manuscript version of this text (see below for details of MS 40).

As MS 40 contains these additional details of place and date it is tempting to see it as the original Sibley manuscript. However it does not match known samples of his handwriting and is therefore a later copy of the original. For a sample of Sibley's handwriting see Figure 18. The present manuscript is also not in Sibley's handwriting either, and has been done by another scribe. For some reason Frederick Hockley stated that he transcribed his copy "from the holograph by Eb[enezer] Sibly in 1793."[85] This suggests that Sibley may have made two copies in his own hand, one in 1789 and another four years later in 1793, but that theory needs further research to verify it. We have looked in detail at the handwriting of the various manuscript versions listed later in this Introduction in an effort to locate Sibley's original text, but without luck.

It is certain that Sibley (or someone working for him) translated the first two Parts of the present text from one of the French Morissoneau texts of the *Key of Solomon*, quite possibly from one of those that ended up in the Wellcome Library in London. These manuscripts belong to the Rabbi Solomon Text-Group (RS) of manuscripts as identified by Robert Mathiesen, and later documented by myself and David Rankine.[86]

In the course of searching for this ancestor manuscript grimoire we came across an article in the September 18, 1880 issue of *The Freemason* magazine which concerned an enquiry about the status of the *Clavis*. It confirms that there were other recensions of this French text circulating much earlier:

> Can you give me any information through your magazine as to a book on Magic or Astrology, having for its title or titles (for in works I have consulted I have been referred to it under various names) "The Clavis of Rabbi Solomon," "Solomon's Clavis," "Les Clavicules de Rabbi Solomon," "Traduites exactement du texte Hebreu par M. Pierre Morrisoneau Proffesseurs *(sic)* des Langues Orientales et Sectateur de la Philosophie des Sages Cabalistes?"
>
> I do not know if it has been printed, or whether it exists only in MS.; I have not been able to find it in the Bodleian Library. Can you solve the mystery for me?
>
> Oxford.   G. O. De Carfex.
>
> [This book is probably the same as "La Clavicule Magique et Cabalistique du Sage Roy Solomon, traduite du texte Hebraique, par C. Agrippa, et mise en Francais, par Rabis

---

[85] As quoted in John Hamill, *The Rosicrucian Seer, Teitan*, 2009, pp. 9.
[86] Mathiesen (2007); and Skinner & Rankine (2008), p. 28.

Nagar." French MS. of 235 pages, with emblematic drawings. Vellum, 4to., 1632. This MS. Is to be found in Bernard Quaritch's most curious list of alchemical works in his catalogue 47... – Ed. F.M.]"[87]

Clearly, relying upon the Quaritch catalogue, a French manuscript of a similar text existed in 1632. The closest French original (of the RS text-group) that we have been able to identify is Wellcome MS 4670. Although Joseph Peterson correctly points out that this is not the *direct* ancestor of Sibley's *Clavis*,[88] it is very close in both arrangement and content. It is therefore probably a 'brother' manuscript rather than an ancestor, and was written about the same time.[89] It follows the same structure and contains the same talismans, circles and pentacles, in the same order. The first 10 chapters also bear the same headings and content, down to details like the Grand Pentacle of Solomon ('La Grande Pentacule de Salomon') falling precisely between Chapters 6 and 7.

A useful table tracking the exact correspondences of the pentacles between the Sibley's *Clavis* and Wellcome MS 4670 can be found in the Appendix of Joseph Peterson's edition of the *Clavis*.[90] This confirms that the planets attributed to each pentacle also completely agree, which is not always the case with the other manuscripts he lists. Wellcome MS 4670 includes some pentacles that were not included by Sibley. It also included additional trivial and irrelevant insect illustrations which were, perhaps fortunately, not carried across into Sibley's English edition. [91]

Wellcome MS 4670 has a noteworthy provenance as it is mentioned in Chapter 4 of Edward Bulwer-Lytton's classic novel of the magical path, *Zanoni*.

> "Les Intelligences Célestes se front voir, et se communiquent plus volontiers, dans le silence, et dans la tranquillité de la solitude. On aura donc une petite chamber ou un cabinet secret, &c. – *Les Clavicules de Rabbi Salomon, chap. 3; traduites exactement du texte Hebreu par M. Pierre Morissoneau, Professeur des Langues Orientales, et Sectateur de la Philosophie des Sages Cabalistes.*"[92]

The wording of this reference to Pierre Morissoneau is taken verbatim from the beginning of manuscript Wellcome MS 4670, and this is the *only one* of the Morissoneau manuscripts with such a detailed reference. So it is almost certain that this manuscript (or a very exact copy of this manuscript) was what Bulwer-Lytton was referring to. He came across it in a certain Covent Garden second-hand bookshop which was mentioned

---

[87] The comment in brackets is from the editor of the *Freemason*, and not a comment by the present editors. The Quaritch *Key of Solomon* however belongs to the *Key of Solomon* CMC text-group.

[88] Peterson (2012), p. x.

[89] The French manuscript Wellcome MS 4670 was written by the scribe F. Fyot in 1796, whilst Sibley's translation was made slightly earlier in 1789, from a close copy of Wellcome MS 4670.

[90] Peterson (2012), Appendix 1, pp. 406-408.

[91] A complete English translation of Wellcome 4670 made by Paul Harry Barron appears in Skinner & Rankine, *The Veritable Key of Solomon*, Volume 4 SWCM, 2008, pp. 69-368.

[92] Bulwer-Lytton, *Zanoni*, 1842, London: Routledge, 1856, Book 2, Chapter IV, page 53.

in the introduction of *Zanoni*. In that book he refers to the owner of the shop as 'old D—,' who can be confidently identified with the real-life bookseller John Denley (1764-1842) who had a Covent Garden bookshop with a large collection of books and manuscripts on magic, and who worked with Sibley on the copying, sale and propagation of grimoires in manuscript form. In the late 18th and early 19th century, Denley also employed Frederick Hockley to copy out grimoires, and lent a number of books and manuscripts to Francis Barrett, who was at that time compiling his classic book, *The Magus*.[93]

Both the *Magus* and the *Clavis* (generated within a decade of each other) were very influential throughout the 19th and much of the 20th century. We have summarised the lives of the people associated with the later development of the *Clavis* and its redaction later in this Introduction.

It is not unlikely that Bulwer-Lytton, a man of some means, actually bought this manuscript from Denley, as he quoted its contents so precisely. In the fullness of time after his death in 1873, some of Lytton's collection of books and manuscripts came up for

sale. Whether that included this manuscript we don't know, but Wellcome MS 4670 was later bought by the Wellcome Collection in 1932.

Sibley simply repeats Morissoneau's assertion that the manuscript was translated from Hebrew without adding any further information, in fact he does not even mention Morissoneau, the putative translator from Hebrew. Certainly some of the Hebrew letter forms are much better formed in Wellcome MS 4670 than in Sibley' English translation, the most noticeable being the Hebrew for Tetragrammaton which on occasion looks more like והדה (VHDH) in Sibley than the correct יהוה (IHVH) in the French manuscript.[94]

Figure 16: Edward Bulwer-Lytton.

Elsewhere we have demonstrated that the French manuscripts could not have been derived from any *known* Hebrew manuscript of the *Key of Solomon*. However there is always an outside chance that its origins were in a yet undiscovered Hebrew manuscript. However this seems even less likely when you analyse the text and see that many of the ingredients come from other predominantly

---

[93] Barrett is often accused of having plagiarised Agrippa's *Three Books of Occult Philosophy,* and of not adding anything to the world's knowledge of magic. This may be true, but he made magic accessible, so people did not have to wade through Agrippa in Latin, or search for information about the lives of the great magicians or magical authors of the past. As such the *Magus* became a firm favourite with not just ritual magicians but also the Cunning-men of the 19th century and later.
[94] See for example pages 130 and 132.

French, Italian and Latin sources.

For example, the design of the large 'pentacles' which are actually floor circles and not pentacles, definitely come from the *Heptameron,* whilst other ingredients obviously come from Agrippa and other European grimoires.

The chapters which have been carried over from French into English are:

1. Which skills you must Possess to involve yourselves in Cabalistic Secrets.
2. What are the most fitting Times and Places for the Operations.
3. Concerning the Materials which are used for the Operations.
4. What Instruments and Utensils are Important for the Operations.
5. What are the Lunar Influences and Secret Qualities affected by the Moon.
6. Concerning the Manner of Working with the Figures and Characters.
7. Concerning the Hours of the Day and the Night for the seven days.
8. Concerning Perfumes appropriate to the Seven Planets for each day.
9. Concerning Prayers, Invocations and Conjurations for each day.
10. Concerning the Prayers in the form of Exorcisms.
11. Concerning the Colours Corresponding to the Seven Planets.
12. Names of the Seasons and the Angels which preside over each.
 Pentacles, Seals, Characters, Spirits, Intelligences of the Seven Days.
15. Concerning the Mystical Rings.
16. Concerning the Names of the Angels of the hours of the Day & Night.

The specific descriptive chapters missing from Sibley's *Clavis* (although some of this information appears in another form) are:[95]

13. In which we Explain the Process for making the Pentacles.
14. Concerning Items which are specifically affected by the Seven Planets.
17. Concerning Mystical Dreams and the manner of preparing to have them.
18. How to set Quicksilver Plates and make Talismans out of them.
19. Designs for the Pentacles for each day of the week for each Season.
20. In which the Secrets of great Curiosity are revealed.

About 20 Pentacles from Wellcome MS 4670 are absent from even the most complete version of Sibley's *Clavis.*

Another French manuscript with similar content claims to be from the hand of Gregorius Niger. It contains in French exactly the same 10 initial chapter headings, followed by 30 pentacles arranged by planet, together with Chapter 13 the Mysterious Ring. Gregorius Niger was the 24th abbot of the Cloister of Michaelstein, a Cistercian monastery located in Blankenburg in the Hartz mountains, founded in 1146 by Beatrix of Büren-Hohenstaufen. [96]

---

[95] These chapters can however be read in full in Skinner & Rankine, *The Veritable Key of Solomon,* Singapore: Golden Hoard, 2015, pp. 224-272.
[96] Skinner & Rankine, *The Veritable Key of Solomon,* Singapore: GHP, 2015, p. 422-423 for its contents.

English Sources

Reginald Scot (c.1538 – 1599) was another one of Sibley's main sources. Sibley even used graphical material from Scot's works in the frontispiece to the *Clavis*. Scot was a down to earth English country gentleman and Member of Parliament for New Romney.[97] He was the grandson of Sir John Scott and described himself as an armiger (someone who was entitled to a family coat of arms). Scot wished to curb what he considered unwarranted prosecutions for witchcraft by demonstrating that it did not exist, and he maintained that those who were prosecuted for witchcraft were often locally ostracised or disliked old women. His main work, written with this in mind was *The Discoverie of Witchcraft*,[98] which was first published in 1584. Scot intended to expose how (apparently miraculous) feats of magic or of legerdemain, were done with no attendant element of the supernatural involved. His skepticism, which extended beyond legerdemain to witchcraft, stemmed from his Protestant Calvinist religious affiliations. Scot was nothing if not thorough, and he enumerated no less than 212 Latin authors, and 23 authors who wrote in English, to support his contention. His most heavy criticisms were directed against Jean Bodin and Sprenger's *Malleus Maleficarum* (Nuremberg, 1494),[99] which was used as an Inquisitor's manual and guide.

His aim was to prevent the persecution of poor, aged, and simple persons, who were popularly credited with being witches and consequently unjustly prosecuted. He maintained that manifestations of witchcraft were either willful impostures or illusions caused by mental disturbance. Scot studied superstitions and accounts of witchcraft in the records of courts of law in country districts, where the prosecution of witches was ongoing, as well as directly investigating local village life.

Scot believed that the persecution of witches was un-Christian and an unpleasant carry over from Roman Catholicism. Fortunately for Scot he was no longer alive when James I ascended the throne in 1603. James was a great believer in witchcraft and set about burning every copy of Scot's book that he could find, and no doubt would have burned Scot too if he had been alive.

However history, or his printers, played tricks on Scot, for when his book was reprinted long after his death in 1665, new sections were added which included practical grimoire and Cunning-man material that directly contradicted his contentions. Instead of showing the supposed fatuousness of magic, it supplied a compendium of its methods.

---

[97] Ironically, Romney Marsh and its surroundings have seen something of a renaissance of interest in modern wicca in recent years.

[98] This work on witchcraft was entitled in full *The Discoverie of Witchcraft, wherein the Lewde dealing of Witches and Witchmongers is notablie detected, in sixteen books … whereunto is added a Treatise upon the Nature and Substance of Spirits and Devils*, 1584.

[99] Literally translated 'The Hammer of the Evil-doers' but usually rendered 'The Hammer of the Witches.'

The publisher probably decided that as the first part of the book was so resolutely rational and anti-supernatural that clerics or censors may look no further, and so felt able to bind in a new Book XV, which contained (amongst other things) a lot of practical magic including:[100]

> 2-4. A complete copy of Wierus' *Pseudomonarchia Daemonum* (Basle, 1566), which contains a register of spirits (some of which were included in the *Clavis*). This Register of Spirits (or its like) later formed the basis of the *Goetia*.
>
> 5. "A confutation of the manifold vanities conteined in the precedent chapters, speciallie of commanding of divels." This chapter trots out the old argument that if the spirits can hand the magician wealth, the love of a beautiful woman, and happiness, why do so many witches "lead their lives in all obloquie, miserie, and beggarie."[101]
>
> 6. "The names of the planets, their characters, togither with the twelve signs of the zodiake, their dispositions, aspects..." This deals with planetary hours and the astrological background to evocation which is to be found in numerous places in the present text.[102]
>
> 7. "The characters of the angels of the seaven days, with their names: of figures, seales and periapts...[103] figues called the seales of the earth, without the which no spirit will appear, except thou have them with thee."[104]
>
> 8-9. An experiment of the dead. Apart from the necromantic reference, this chapter primarily deals with the invocation of the virgin fairy the 'faire Sibylia.' This is interesting because it links back to the evocation of Sibylla in the *Magical Treatise of Solomon* or *Hygromanteia*, the forerunner of the *Key of Solomon*.[105] This chapter also deals with conjuration into the crystal, a topic covered in Part 6 Crystallomancy of the present text.

Scot would have been appalled. The result is one of the earliest grimoires in print in English. The material is grimoire magic with a dash of Cunning-man magic rather than witchcraft *per se,* treated as 'icing on the cake' of a book which disputed the very existence of magic or witchcraft.

---

[100] The numbers below represent the Chapters inside of Book XV.

[101] The answer to this question can only be properly provided by those magicians who have done their apprenticeship and learned how to converse with and bind spirits, and who live in ample comfort.

[102] This is treated in much greater detail in *The Cunning-Man's Grimoire,* Vol 9 SWCM, Singapore: Golden Hoard, 2018.

[103] A *periapt* is a amulet that should be worn. Greek *periapton,* from *peri* 'around' + *haptein* 'fasten.'

[104] The accompanying illustration from Scot (Figure 02) is incorporated in the frontispiece of the *Clavis*.

[105] See Marathakis (2011), p. 112.

Other printed sources available to Sibley in English included the *Three Books of Occult Philosophy* by Henry Cornelius Agrippa originally printed in Latin in 1533, and translated into English in 1651 by 'J. F.'[106] This work is the foundation stone of much of the knowledge of magic in Europe and the UK in subsequent centuries, and is the source of the planetary kameas and sigils in Part 2 of the *Clavis*.[107] It in turn, owes its contents to the amazing collection of manuscripts on magic accumulated by Trithemius, the Abbot of Sponheim.

The Part 8 on Geomancy is obviously drawn from the *Theomagia* of John Heydon.

One of the few names mentioned in the present text was a certain 'J. W.,' mentioned in conjunction with the bond of Vassago (page 88) with a date of 1573. This may have been John Weston, as suggested in the *Book of Oberon*.[108] This might even have been the same John Weston who married Joane Cowper in 1579 and died in May 6, 1582. After John Weston's death his widow married Edward Kelley in April 1582, thereby staying within the same 'family' of grimoire magicians, but this cannot be asserted with certainty.[109]

Robert Cross Smith, who at some stage annotated the *Book of Oberon* wrote that John Porter = John Weston, and next to Weston's name he wrote "142." On page 142, in the same handwriting, someone has marked the part of the text that says "I Iohn Weston gent." It would be an interesting connection if it could be proven.

---

[106] 'J. F.' is often interpreted as James Freake, as in the edition edited by Donald Tyson in 1993. However the actual translator was John French, MD, who authorship was clearly indicated as such by Elias Ashmole.

[107] See Book II, Chapter xxii.

[108] Harms, Daniel and Joseph Peterson, *The Book of Oberon*, Woodbury: Llewellyn, 2015, p. 11.

[109] There is also a 'J. M.' mentioned in the Bond of Agares (page 93). This may be the same individual as capital 'M' and capital 'W' are often confused particularly in faux gothic script.

Versions of the Clavis Manuscript

Upon starting this project, we were faced with three great challenges. Firstly, like most grimoires of this nature, many copies have been made, and passed from one owner to another, from private collections to auctions, and onwards to major libraries and institutions around the globe. As such a wide distribution of this work has occurred it makes trying to track down all copies, and work out the family relationship between them, rather difficult. This difficulty can also be magnified by manuscripts being incorrectly named or identified within a holding establishment's catalogue by the cataloguing librarian. The third problem, and probably the most vexing issue of all, is that nearly every known example of the *Clavis* that has been unearthed and made available to date appears to be written in a different hand: no doubt a testimony to the efficient manuscript production line of John Denley's Covent Garden bookshop.

Let us look in detail at the various copies of the text of the *Clavis* to see how they fit together, and what they contain. For a detailed analysis of the exact contents of each, and to be able to see at a glance which is most complete, and what is missing from some exemplars, see Figure 25 and Appendix 1. Joseph Peterson identified 7 exemplars, which does not include the present manuscript.[110] We have retained his numbering system, so that comparisons can be easily made, but added to it another seven manuscripts, making 14 manuscripts in all. We have numbered the current manuscript as '8.' We have also split the fourth manuscript he lists into '4' and '4a,' as we have discovered that there were in fact two different manuscripts: one previously owned by the Crawford family in the John Rylands Collection, and one still in the Crawford family archives in the National Library of Scotland.

1. Weiser MS, edited by Joseph Peterson

The Clavis or Key to Unlock the Mysteries of Magic of Rabbi Solomon translated...By Ebenezer Sibley. M.D. This manuscript has been brought out in a beautifully printed edition edited by Joseph Peterson and published by Ibis Press in 2009/2012 (hereafter referred to as the Weiser MS). It contains a complete facsimile of one manuscript of Sibley's *Clavis*, previously owned by the noted antiquarian bookseller and publisher Donald Weiser[111]

---

[110] See Peterson (2009), pp. xiv-xvii.

[111] Don was of course much more than a publisher and bookseller. He was a warm human being with an extensive knowledge of both Western and Eastern esoteric subjects, although he sometimes modestly claimed that he didn't read the books he stocked and published. I knew Don from 1974 when we first did business together. With my first wife Helene Hodge we ran Askin Publishers, and Don as our US distributor often came to London, frequently staying with us in Chiswick. Askin published books by Agrippa, Paracelsus, Crowley, A O Spare (long before he became popular) and Dr John Dee (the first reprint of his *True and Faithful...*). The three of us also went on book buying expeditions to Wales, where we bought many of the books that later stocked his bookshop shelves in Broadway. – SS.

(1928 – 2017) and before that by John Watkins (Cecil Court, London) and the Libraries des Sciences Occultes (Amsterdam). As Joseph Peterson has covered most aspects of this particular manuscript there is no need for us to do so here, other than to say that it is written in a very distinctive cursive hand, but the scribe has yet to be correctly identified, despite it being falsely attributed to Hockley.[112]

This manuscript has been excellently transcribed and annotated by Joseph Peterson, but as can be seen in Appendix 1, the material covered is somewhat less in extent than the present manuscript..

2. University of Utah MS

The University of Utah in Salt Lake City holds a copy of the Sibley *Clavis* under the catalogue number MS. BF1601-C53-1700z, in their Marriott Library Special Collections, entitled *The Clavis or Key to Unlock the Mysteries of Magic* (hereafter referred to as the Utah MS). This manuscript was transferred from the Salt Lake City public library to the University of Utah in roughly 2006 when the new city library was built. The decision was made by the City Public Library not to retain the small collection of old and "more unique" books that they had classified as rare to preserve them, and as such passed them on to the University for safe keeping. The inside front cover contains a label stating, "This Book is the Gift of Mary J. Springer, Salt Lake City, March 1936." Regrettably that is the only information available for this manuscript, and its earlier provenance remains unknown.

Although the Utah *Clavis* is less ornate and elaborate than MS 18 and MS 1/10 it is still beautifully written in a clear flowing hand with virtually no errors, indicating that some time was spent preparing it by an expert calligrapher, with the illustrations also being precisely rendered.

Peterson's description of the interior of this *Clavis* manuscript at the University of Utah,[113] surprisingly does not match the digital copy supplied to us by that library, especially in the number of pages (241 instead of 268 in our copy), colouring, or in the identification of specific missing pages. An even more pointed difference is Peterson's location of the Birto wyvern image on folio 143v, whilst our copy has it at page 207.[114] Either Peterson's description was prepared from an erroneous epitome made by someone else, or there are two manuscript copies of the *Clavis* in the University of Utah's library.

---

[112] A clue to the identity of the scribe may possibly be found in the initials which appear on the binding, 'G. O. F.' (unless those initials have some other meaning).

[113] Peterson (2012), xiv.

[114] It is certainly true that many page numbers have been cut off during rebinding, but even after these have been logically restored, these differences are too large to be accounted for.

3. Private MS of 168 folios

This manuscript was identified by Adam McLean. It was also listed as 'Sibley Private Collection MS 4' in Appendix F of *The Veritable Key of Solomon,* where you will find a breakdown and chapter list. [115] Its full title is:

> The Clavis or Key to Unlock the Mysteries of Magic of Rabbi Solomon. Translated from the Hebrew into French and from French into English with additions by Ebenezer Sibley M.D. Fellow of the Harmoniac Philosophical Society at Paris, Author of the Complete Illustration of Astrology, Editor of Culpepper's Complete Herbal, Placidus De Titus *On Elementary Philosophy,* etc. The whole enriched with Coloured Figures, Talismans, Pentacles, Circles, Characters, etc." – Late 18th Cent. 168 Folios.[116]

4. University of Manchester Library John Rylands GB 0133 Eng MS 40

The Clavis or Key to Unlock the Mysteries of Magic of Rabby (sic) Solomon (hereafter MS 40) resides in the University of Manchester where it is part of the John Rylands collection. The catalogue listing states that it was "Purchased by Mrs. Enriqueta Rylands, on behalf of the John Rylands Library, in 1901 from James Ludovic Lindsay, 26th Earl of Crawford."

James Lindsay, 26th Earl of Crawford and 9th Earl of Balcarres, was born on the 28th of July 1847 in St Germaine, France. The son of Alexander (the 25th Earl of Crawford and 8th Earl of Balcarres) and his wife Margaret, he suffered terribly from asthma and therefore spent much time on the open ocean (away from land-based pollens) which afforded him respite and considerable periods to read over and study books from the family library which he would often take with him.

From an early age he had a keen interest in astronomy and was instrumental, along with his father, in building the Dunecht estate observatory in Aberdeenshire, at which pioneering work was carried out in the fields of astrophotography and the mapping of the constellations.

The Bibliotheca Lindesiana was an idea envisioned by the 25th Earl, and with the aid of his son it soon became one of the largest private collections of rare and unique items in Britain at that period. The library was expanded in 1864 with the bulk of it being housed at Haigh Hall, Wigan, Lancashire and the remaining volumes at Balcarres.

An extensive catalogue was drawn up in 1910 under the title *Catalogue of the Printed Books Preserved at Haigh Hall, Wigan,* 4 vols. Maintaining this catalogue and the vast library was a full-time job for a sizeable team of librarians.

---

[115] Skinner & Rankine (2017), pp. 420-421.

[116] Adam McLean's Alchemy website http://www.alchemywebsite.com/clav_eng.html. See the present Appendix 1 for a breakdown of its contents. Its date is probably 19th century rather than late 18th century.

Figure 17: The bookplate of Bibliotheca Lindesiana, the library of the Earls of Crawford.

The collection of manuscripts that the library held was eventually sold to Enriqueta Augustina Rylands for the John Rylands Library, with the remaining parts of the library eventually being distributed amongst various institutions which included the National Library of Scotland. They were further distributed by the decisions made by later Earls, and in 1946, the collections were shared between the John Rylands Library,[117] the British Library (or British Museum as it was then known), and Cambridge University Library.

Mrs Rylands originally opened the John Rylands Library on the 1st of January 1900. It was dedicated to the memory of her late husband and contained around 40,000 books, many of which were rarities that had been collected by George Spencer, the 2nd Earl Spencer, and purchased from him by Mrs. Rylands earlier in 1892. In 1972 The John Rylands Library merged with the University of Manchester to become the John Rylands University Library of Manchester, or more simply The University of Manchester Library, and this is the current resting place of MS 40.

This manuscript has 243 pages, and is a much more visually reserved copy of the Sibley *Clavis*, written in a beautiful cursive hand with subtle coloured inks for its illustrations. The initial impression when first looking at this manuscript relates to the title page. Its use of a specific style of letter form and layout for the title page, frontispiece and chapter headings is almost identical to those used in known Ebenezer Sibley holographs. The frontispiece, 'The Signs, Seals and Magical Knife' are drawn in fine line detail and are very neat, close to the page created by Sibley in his 1787 *Complete Illustration of the Astrological and Occult Sciences*.[118] The title page also has the inclusion of Sibley's address and date at "London. No 18 Bartletts Buildings, Holborn - 7th August. 1789."

This is the only version which shows the date and Sibley's address, suggesting it may have actually been written by Sibley at that address. The question then arises "could this in fact be the long lost Sibley original?" So many aspects of this manuscript match up

---

[117] The Crawford family muniments were removed from the John Rylands Library in 1988.
[118] Volume 4, opposite page 1102.

with his other identified works. For example the initial capital 'P' and 'T' are very similar with another example of Sibley' handwriting (see Figure 18). [119]

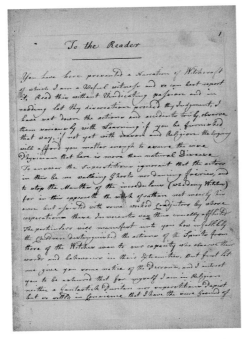

Figure 18: An example of Sibley's handwriting in his 1793 transcript of *A Treatise on Witchcraft Demonstrated by facts in the Family of Edward Fairfax..1621... Transcribed from an old Manuscript by Ebenezer Sibly. MD.*

In addition this version has a much larger number of carefully drawn full page pentacles. Does this imply that it is the only manuscript with a full range of pentacles, and therefore is again more likely to be the original? Or do we assume they were added later by other copyists from other *Key of Solomon* manuscripts?

On the other hand, one strange inconsistency is that the title page shows his name as 'Sibley' but the signature at the end of the Preface clearly shows 'Sibly.' What are we to make of that? It is a mistake unlikely to have been made by Sibley himself.

Also problems start when closely examining the script. Although it is very cursive, just like Sibley's hand, not all the letter forms quite match up; they are close but definitely different. For example lower case 'd' is backward looping in Sibley's hand, but not in MS 40. Therefore to date the whereabouts of the Sibley original remains a mystery, although MS 40 is visually the closest candidate.

Susan Sommers says this is one of two Hockley copies, but that is very unlikely. [120] A more likely candidate is John Denley, because the frontispiece has a very tiny credit in the bottom right of its frame: 'J.D.' Denley had in his possession at one point Sibley's original manuscript. It is possible that Denley might have been forced to copy works for himself when he was unable to pay someone to do the copying for him? Or maybe he simply wanted to identify that it had passed through his hands.

Of note, MS 40 also includes two chapters that are in two completely different hands from the main body of the work, and definitely added at a different date. One small chapter at the start of the manuscript discusses 'Creatures Governed by the Planets' and another separate incomplete chapter in a very different hand at the end of the manuscript with the heading of 'Form of a Bond of Spirits.'

---

[119] UCLA William Andrews Clark Memorial Library MS 2004.002, f. 1.
[120] Sommers (2018), p. 240.

4a. National Library of Scotland Acc. 9769 Personal Papers

One specific issue we had when looking into the Rylands *Clavis,* was a result of confusion evident in the conflict between already existing library catalogue information, and previously published scholarly material. As stated above the Rylands manuscript was purchased as part of the manuscript collection from the Bibliotheca Lindesiana, however the family muniments of the Earls of Crawford & Balcarres, and other parts of the Crawford collection, were transferred to the National Library of Scotland (NLS) in 1988 where they still reside. If that was so, how could there still be a listing for the Sibley *Clavis* at the Library of Manchester?

After investigation it turns out that the Bibliotheca Lindesiana did in fact hold *two* separate Sibley manuscripts, with the second now housed at the National Library of Scotland. This second manuscript has remained hidden under the unremarkable catalogue identification of "Acc. 9769, Personal Papers, 84/1/12," and had apparently been bundled together with a large quantity of other un-related papers of the Earls of Crawford dating from the 14th century to 20th century. An old printed handlist of the Personal Papers from the muniments of the Earls of Crawford & Balcarres deposited in the John Rylands Library (and subsequently transferred to the NLS in 1988) lists the NLS manuscript as:

> Alchemy: *The Clavis or Key [to] Unlock the Mysteries of Magic of Rabbi Solomon. Translated… with Additions by Ebenezer Sibley; A Complete Book of Magic Science... 1525."* 19th cent. Copy, 1 vol.[121]

Access to the collection in which Acc. 9769 resides is extremely restricted. One of the conditions laid down is that written permission must be obtained from the current Earl of Crawford, something which is very rarely given, and on the unique times it is granted, it is always on a limited basis. Very luckily we were given permission by the Earl to view a small handful of pages only. Manuscript Acc. 9769 is yet again another stunning work of art with extremely precise and breath-taking calligraphy that is one of the best visual examples of handwriting of all the known Sibley *Clavis.* It contains exquisitely executed coloured renderings but the hand of the scribe remains unidentified.

It is possible that the manuscript previously referred to as 'Crawford MS 158' may be a *third* Crawford manuscript, especially as Adam noted that it only has 152 folios.[122] The Catalogue entry for MS 40 also claims 152 folios, but the actual manuscript has 243 pages, while the manuscript Acc. 9769 has 290 pages. This suggests that there may be a third.

---

[121] Information courtesy of Kenneth Dunn, Head of Archives & Manuscript Collections, National Library of Scotland. The 1525 only refers to the original of the *Complete Book of Magic Science.*

[122] Rylands MS 40 has been referenced as Crawford MS 158 by Adam McLean on: www.alchemywebsite.com as: "National Library of Scotland MS. Crawford 158. Paper. 152 folios. 18th Century. E. Sibley. *The Clavis or Key to unlock the mysteries of Magick of Rabby Salomon. Translated from the Hebrew into French and from French rendered into English with additions by Ebenezer Sibley, M.D.... and enriched with Figures, Talismans, Pentacles, Circles, Characters, etc.* London, No 18 Bartlett's Buildings, Holborn, 7th August, 1789."

5. Society of Esoteric Endeavour/Caduceus

This manuscript was published in book form by the Society of Esoteric Endeavour (Caduceus Books) in 2008 (hereafter referred to as the S.E.E. MS).[123] The facsimile is entitled *Solomon's Clavis or Key to unlock the Mysteries of Magic...by E. Sibley.* It is far more modest in appearance than those mentioned above. It was purchased at auction in Chichester, and was listed with no recent provenance at that time; and was sold alongside other works by Frederick Hockley and Herbert Irwin. The manuscript also bears the bookplate of Major F. G. Irwin, having once resided in his collection.

Figure 19: Major F G Irwin's Bookplate found in the front of the S. E. E. *Clavis* manuscript.

After close examination and comparison with the hands of known scribes that frequented Denley's establishment we believe the creator of this manuscript to be Robert Cross *aka* the astrologer 'Raphael.' The last page also confirms that it was written in 1868 by him, as it bears the inscription "R. C. 1868." On this we are in agreement with Ben Fernee of The Society of Esoteric Endeavour who also believes this manuscript was more than likely commissioned by Denley, to produce several copies for varying clients, ranging in quality and detail. We believe this copy could have possibly been made by Cross hastily for a client, or that it was destined for his personal collection.

The Irwin *Clavis* has been confused in recent times with an original Hockley transcript, a mistake that could easily be made at first glance as it does resemble Hockley's script style. Joseph Peterson states in his excellent edition of the Weiser *Clavis* that "the handwriting is identical to the handwriting to Wellcome MS 2842, which has been identified as Hockley's."[124]

However on close examination of Wellcome MS 2842, and indeed other known Hockley manuscripts, the letter forms are seen to not be the same as those of the Irwin *Clavis*, having subtle yet definite differences. Furthermore, Hockley never used an abbreviated ampersand '&' in the body of any of his acknowledged manuscripts, instead preferring to write the word 'and' in full. Having identified the scribe as Robert Cross the ascription to Hockley can now be safely laid to rest.

---

[123] *Solomon's Clavis, or Key to Unlock the Mysteries of Magic,* Society of Esoteric Endeavour, 2008, limited edition of 144 copies.
[124] Peterson (2012), p. xvii.

6. Senate House Library HPF 1/10

Interestingly the closest example to MS 18 visually is London University's Senate House Library manuscript HPF 1/10, but strangely it has a slightly different title, *Clavis resero arcana mysteria Rabbi Solomonis* (hereafter MS 1/10).

MS 1/10 was donated to London University's Senate House Library by the late writer and psychical researcher Harry Price (1881 - 1948). The Price collection consisted of nearly 13,000 manuscripts, books, periodicals and pamphlets. These were deposited by Harry Price in 1936 and finally bequeathed in 1948, with an endowment to purchase additional material for the collection. His collection was housed on the 8th floor of the Senate House and requires special permission to visit. [125]

Some of the treasures kept there included some of the original colour artwork used in Crowley's early Volume 1 of the *Equinox*. Another photo in their archives showed Price walking with a goat on a leash on the Brocken, carrying a copy of a German grimoire, during a Goethe celebration in 1932. There Price read the appropriate conjuration from the grimoire to commemorate the Walpurgis Eve scene in Goethe's *Faust*. [126]

Price was a very guarded individual who liked to build up an air of mystery around himself. He was born in 1888 and deliberately fabricated the details of his upbringing claiming that he was from a wealthy family who hailed from Shropshire in the West Midlands, England. Reality however was far less glamorous with the truth being that he was actually from a middle-class working family in the much poorer suburb of New Cross in south east London, where his father was a traveling paper salesman.

Price spent most of his life in the pursuit of psychical research and made a point of exposing frauds and tricksters, going out of his way to devise experiments to show how mediums and their associates could go about creating false 'spirit photographs,' hypnotic states, and conversations with and messages from the dead. He was most famous for his investigation of Borley Rectory, near Sudbury, reputedly "the most haunted house in England."

Initially he joined the Society of Psychical Research, but it wasn't long before they went their separate ways, probably due to Price's habit of alienating those around him with a rather narcissistic and less than humble personality. Price would go on to form his own

---

[125] In 2008, rumours circulated that the Harry Price Library might be broken up in a cost-cutting exercise as a result of the University of London losing some of its external funding. The University sought to sell the Harry Price collection, presumably because they did not consider its contents a subject suitable for academic enquiry. One might guess that several American university libraries would have been very interested. Fortunately, due to lobbying by friends of the Library, it was proved that the University was not able to legally do so under the terms of the original bequest.

[126] The Brocken or Bloksburg is the highest peak in northern Germany, and famous for reputedly being a regular gathering place for witches, especially each year on April 30th (Walpurgisnacht). The actual experiment in conjuration however took place on June 18th, 1932.

organization known as he 'National Library of Psychical Research' or NLPR.

It was during that period of his life that Harry Price built up a particularly well-established collection of works on parapsychology and associated topics. He died at his home in West Sussex in 1948. Unfortunately, no further information is available as to where he obtained his copy of the Sibley *Clavis,* all records of it have long been lost.

Who is the Scribe?

MS 1/10 is written in a very legible hand and is beautifully illustrated and ornate with some plates rivalling MS 18 in their detail and artistic flair. This manuscript is particularly interesting for several reasons. It is written in several different styles of script but by the same person, with some of the text being done in a block gothic style with decorative headings, while other sections revert to a more natural hand that almost matches MS 18's hand. Another feature common to both is the 'floating spirals' decoration,[127] which is not seen in any other exemplar. Another thing common to both manuscripts is the ugly habit of writing 'e' with a bar over it, which makes the writing much harder to read. Because of these similarities there quite a chance that MS 1/10 could be from the same pen as MS 18. Both scribes have the same style, and the layout is close to MS 18 visually.

There is one further clue on page 36, at the bottom amongst the 'Mystical Characters' generated from the geomantic figure Via. The fifth character has the letters Raph… inside circles. This is a most unusual format for a geomantic seal and is obviously deliberate. Could this be the scribe indicating his name? Maybe this manuscript was written by Raphael, probably Robert Cross Smith because of the date.

One thing that makes MS 1/10 different from all the other Sibley *Clavis* manuscripts is the inclusion at the end of a chapter entitled *Experimentum potens magna in occult philosophy arcanorum,* a work that has been attributed to Frederick Hockley. It does not appear grouped in this way in any of the other known copies of the *Clavis,* except for MS 18. This particular section was first published separately by Caduceus Books many years ago as a limited run and has since been long out of print.[128]

7. Private MS No. 2

This manuscript has been described by Joseph Peterson, but we have no further details:

> Private 2. Manuscript in private collection. 227 pages (4 unnumbered, i-xvi, 1-207). Watermark: A. Annandal and Sons (active 1832-1879). Contents same as U[tah MS], i.e. all the texts in W[eiser MS] except the *Complete Book of Magic Science.* Handwriting is identical to that in U[tah MS], so maybe this was another copyist hired by Denley.[129]

---

[127] For example page 6 in MS 1/10, and page 215 in MS 18.

[128] *Experimentum, Potens Magna in Occult Philosophy,* Society of Esoteric Endeavour, 2012, numbered limited edition of 100 copies. Introduction by Dan Harms.

[129] Peterson (2012), p. xvii.

8. National Library of Israel Yah. Var. MS 18 (the present manuscript)

The present manuscript National Library of Israel Yah. Var. 18 – *The Clavis or Key To Unlock The Mysteries of Magic of Rabbi Solomon...By Ebenezer Sibley, MD* (hereafter MS 18), is not listed by Peterson. It found its way to Israel around June of 1967 shortly after the end of the Six Day War. After having been donated by the estate of the late Prof. Abraham Shalom Yahuda, who passed away in 1951, it was transferred to the JNUL (today known as The National Library of Israel) where it now resides.

Figure 20: An 1897 photo of Abraham Shalom Yahuda (1877 - 1951), the previous owner of the present manuscript.

Born in Jerusalem and growing up in a Jewish family, as a tenacious youth, Abraham Shalom Yahuda wrote his first book in Hebrew at the age of fifteen in 1895 entitled *Arab Antiquities* and in 1897 (just two years later) he was present at the first Zionist Congress held in Basel, Switzerland.[130] He would then later on begin a career in teaching, starting in Berlin around 1905, that would eventually see him reside in New York at the New School for Social Research.

An avid collector of manuscripts and books the Yahuda collection contains around 1,400 manuscripts of which a considerable number are in Arabic, 250 in Hebrew and 50 in Latin or English. The collection also holds a surprising archive of the unpublished writings of Sir Isaac Newton, which Prof. Yahuda purchased at auction in London in 1935. It is unknown when or how he came to own MS 18, but it was more than likely obtained during one of his visits to England, or perhaps (more intriguingly) may have even been part of the Isaac Newton auction. We can only speculate at this time, but Newton's manuscripts did contain texts on alchemy, so why not one on magic? One 19th century member of the Sibley family bore the given names 'Isaac Newton,' although that may have been a coincidence, rather than an indication of any family connection.

---

[130] Zionism was thought to have been conceived by Theodor Herzl around 1896, however it was evident as early as 1870 amongst the Jewish settlers in Palestine. The theme of return to the Jewish homeland, in its broadest sense, dates back to the 'Babylonian captivity' of 597 BCE.

Figure 21: Yahuda dressed for an audience with King Alfonso the 13th of Spain in 1916.

MS 18's script is a very legible hand with very few or almost no mistakes. Great time and effort was obviously taken in the production of this manuscript, and it is the most complete version of this work, containing all the additions (by Hockley and others), like the section on crystal skrying. It is without a doubt the most ornate and beautiful example of the *Clavis*. Its closest rival is MS 1/10, the Senate House Library *Clavis*, which is very similar in style and layout, and is possibly from the same scribe.

MS 18 was more than likely commissioned by John Denley for a wealthy client as it goes above and beyond all others in terms of ornateness, and one can only begin to imagine the amount of time needed for its completion, as it is a veritable magnum opus of Victorian transcription and grimoire art. Although too florid for some tastes, it would have been the centre piece of any private collection. The question then remains, who was its creator? There are some reasons to suspect that 1836 was its creation date, although the last sections may have been added as late as 1848.

Frederick Hockley was without a doubt the most famous person known to be employed by Denley, the Covent Garden bookseller. In his employ Hockley produced a great number of transcript copies from the various manuscripts in Denley's care to fulfil requests from his customers and clients. However MS 18 is not written in his hand. Some Parts of MS 18 were clearly copied from a Hockley original as they bare his distinctive personalized FH monogram, for example on the page 111 chapter heading, but we cannot say definitively who its creator was at this point.

Figure 22: The three hieroglyphs written on the last page of MS 18.

Within the pages of the work itself there is very little indication or any tell-tale signs, however the final page does present a rather unique curiosity in the form of three markings of a hieroglyphic nature. These could be just some random nonsensical addition scribbled at the very end, or perhaps they are the initials of a previous owner? Or do these encoded initials belong to the creator of this spectacular grimoire? One possible transliteration might be 'K. D. B.' The mystery remains unsolved.

9. Library and Museum of Freemasonry S.R.I.A. MS

To date the only known copy of the *Clavis* safely identified as a Hockley original currently resides in the Library and Museum of Freemasonry, in Queen Street, London, where it is on loan from the Societas Rosicruciana in Anglia High Council Library. We believe that other examples reside in institutions or private collections, waiting to be identified or discovered. This particular copy was written by Frederick Hockley, and runs to 168 pages. It is listed in their catalogue as:

> *A Book of the Offices of Spirits* [manuscript]: *the occult virtue of plants and some are magical charms & spells / transcribed from folio manuscript on magic & necromancy by John Porter AD. 1583;* [bound with] *The Keys of Rabbi Solomon* [manuscript] / *transcribed from a manuscript translation from the original Hebrew into French and thence rendered into English by Dr. Eb[eneze]r Sibley. –* 1832.

This particular copy was owned by Frederick Hockley and was his personal transcription rather than one made for sale. It appears in the *List of Books Chiefly from the Library of the late Frederick Hockley, Esq.* published by George Redway, York Street, Covent Garden, London, 1887.

However regrettably, upon finally being given permission from the S.R.I.A to view this manuscript, it proved to be rather disappointing, as almost all its talismans and pentacles are incomplete, often being no more than the lines of the initial annulus. In fact only three pentacles have been completed, and even Sibley's Preface is completely missing. It is one of the most incomplete copies, and even the text has only been erratically filled in. Surprisingly, this copy seems to have been done with less care and attention that any of the foregoing manuscripts. Although actually in Hockley's hand, it was clearly one of his many unfinished projects with virtually all the illustrations having yet to be inked in.

The Masonic library holds a tremendous amount of important material originally relating to the Rosicrucians (an Order Hockley and Irwin were both involved with) so many of the manuscripts in this collection may be his original transcripts. Hopefully in the future this material may become more accessible.

The Masonic library also contains various other works by Hockley related to the contents of the *Clavis*, of which two are entitled:

> *The Wheel of Wisdom* [manuscript]: *with a key and directions for use in magical operations;* [and], *An experiment of one T.W. with the spirits Birto, Agares, Baalpharos, and Vassago* [manuscript] / *transcribed from an autograph & manuscript of Dr Sibley's by Fredk: Hockley. -* 1834; [and], *A treatise concerning divine magic or cabalistic mysteries* [manuscript]; [and], *Introduction to the theory and practice of the Cabala /* Dr. Pistor.

> *The Wheel of Wisdom with its key and full directions for its use in all magical operations: transcribed from the autograph MS. of Dr. E. Sibly /* by Frederick Hicklby [Hockley], Dec. 19th. 1836.

These may well have been the immediate source of the material in Parts 3 and 4 of the *Clavis*, even though they are in turn copies of earlier manuscripts.

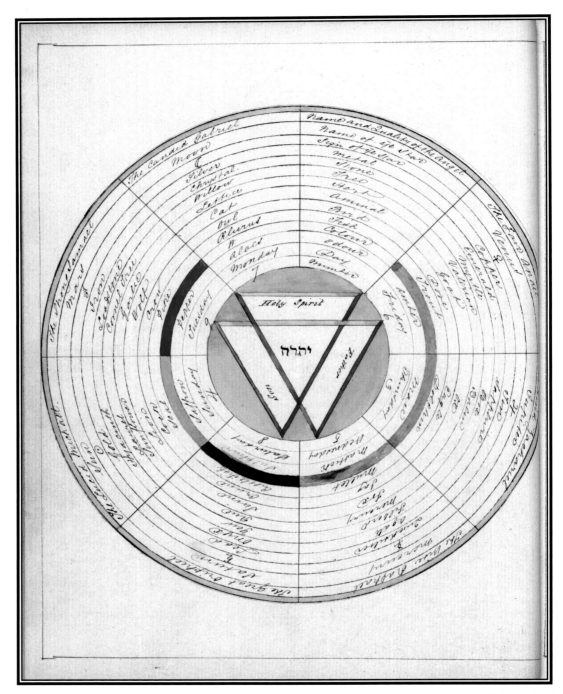

Figure 23: A page from Wellcome MS 3203 – 'Five Treatises upon Magic' showing 'The Wheel of Wisdom, with a Key for its use in Magical Operations.' It is likely that Wellcome MS 3203 may have been the immediate source of Part 4. Courtesy of the Wellcome Library.

10. Ritman Library MS PH304 / M183

Within the core collection of the Bibliotheca Philosophica Hermetica in Amsterdam there is the manuscript *PH304 / M183* entitled [*Clavicula Salomonis*] *The clavis or key. (vert. uit het frans door Ebenezer Sibley)*, (hereafter MS M183). This manuscript is now part of the State-owned collection of the Ritman Library, which is located in the Royal Library in The Hague.

The Embassy of the Free Mind[131] has been responsible for bringing the collection of the Ritman Library *aka* the Bibliotheca Philosophica Hermetica into the 21st century by digitising its core collection, thanks to the very generous donation by well-known author Dan Brown.

One interesting paste down inside the front cover identifies the scribe as "Professor..." but here the paste down has been torn away leaving the scribe's name still a mystery. Another interesting sticker inside the front cover shows a bookseller's price as 'RM500', a clear indication that the manuscript had once been for sale in a Malaysian bookshop, as no other country uses the ringgit as currency. An intriguing speculation is that it may well have been the property of Gerald Gardner (1884-1964), the 'father of modern witchcraft,' as he spent much of his life as a rubber planter and customs inspector in Johor Bahru, Malaysia.

11. The Dreweatts Auction manuscript

It is unknown just how many copies of the Sibley *Clavis* reside in private collections. On the rare occasions that they do come up for sale at auction they are soon brought and removed again from the public eye. Such manuscripts from private collections tend to be unique, and can often add great insight into the evolutionary path from the original text to copies of more recent times. An example of this is a manuscript which was sold by the Dreweatts Auction house in St. James's, London on July of 2015. It was listed as:

> Sibley (Ebenezer, translator) *The Clavis or Key to Unlock the Mysteries of Magic of Rabbi Solomon*, manuscript fair copy, 300pp., hand-coloured frontispiece ('The Grand Pentacle of Solomon'), title and numerous drawings in the text, slightly browned, original half calf, rubbed, joints splitting but holding, lacks part of spine, sm. 4to, n.d. [c. 1880]; and 2 others [on] Hermeticism, including a modern printed copy of the first, 4to (3). 300pp.

As the 300 pages may include all three items, we have no clear understanding of the *Clavis* pagination, but it might have been the largest of all the known copies. This particular *Clavis* contained a rather unique and colourful variant of the 'Great' or as it was referred to in this text 'Grand Pentacle of Solomon' (see Figure 24) which was used as a frontispiece. The particular rendition of this image does not appear in any other Sibley *Clavis* that we have seen so far and as such begs the question of its origin.

---

[131] http://embassyofthefreemind.com/en/.

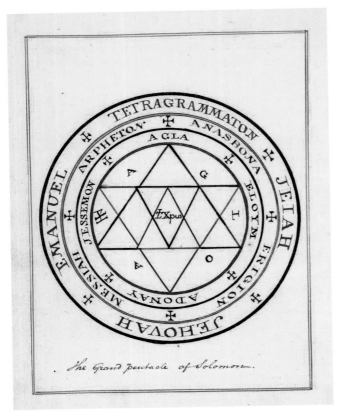

Figure 24: The Grand Pentacle of Solomon from the Dreweatts Auction *Clavis* manuscript that sold to an unidentified private buyer in 2015.

12. *Hell Fire Club edition*

Another more recently published manuscript is from Hell Fire Club Books. This very short manuscript was listed as 'Edward Hunter Private Collection MS 3' in *The Veritable Key of Solomon*.[132] It is entitled *The Keys of Rabbi Solomon, Translated accurately from the Hebrew into English by Edward Hunter*. This particular work was also mentioned by Adam McLean who described it as a "MS. in Private Collection. 58 folios. Late 18th or nineteenth centuries."

Sadly, the Hell Fire *Clavis*, by comparison with its description, is very incomplete, with all the later sections missing or left out entirely, and running to just 60 pages (30 folios). It simply stops part way through the pentacle section with a flourish that suggests the scribe just could not be bothered to complete it, rather than the MS having actually lost any pages. The style of script that is used throughout suggests a fairly modern 20th century hand, despite its claim to a 19th century origin.[133] The publication itself has no supporting information about its provenance beyond what was published in its advertising flyer, which is rather disingenuous for the following reasons.

The work claims possible authorship by the "Mormon Bishop" Edward Hunter, although it was earlier described by the publisher as being by Edward Hunter, a merchant of Bristol, but a gentleman who reputedly had ties to Mormon groups in the United States. Recent comparisons made by Daniel Harms between the handwriting of a known letter written by the Bishop Edward Hunter to Joseph Smith dated October 27, 1841 and that of the Hell Fire *Clavis* definitely do not match, and show clearly that they

---

[132] Skinner & Rankine (2017), p. 419.
[133] Its use of abbreviations such as "pp." rather than 'pages' suggests the scribe was more familiar with 20th century academic monographs rather than the manuscripts of the 19th century.

are by a completely different hand, dismissing this claimed authorship altogether.[134] Also questionable is the use of the Hebrew on the title page which indicates very clearly that the author was not at all competent in that language, and as such is unlikely to have had the ability to translate it, as claimed on the title page.

13. *Ancient Manuscript of Talismanic Art*

Robert T Cross (*aka* Raphael), like Sibley was also an astrologer, who produced a manuscript which was later printed (in several editions) called *Raphael's Ancient Manuscript of Talismanic Magic,* 1880. Its subtitle *Selections from the Works of Rabbi Solomon, Agrippa, F. Barrett, etc.* helps to confirm where the bulk of its material came from. The handwriting is also identical with Cross's other version of the *Clavis* (S.E.E. MS), so it is effectively yet another manuscript copy of the *Clavis.*

This brings the total number of manuscripts of the *Clavis* examined to 14 (remembering that exemplar 4 has now been ascertained to be two separate manuscripts, 4 and 4a).

Other Manuscripts

There are also traces and records of yet other manuscripts of the *Clavis* which were noted but whose present whereabouts is not known. Other copies of the Sibley *Clavis* have also appeared in sales catalogues and book advertisements throughout the centuries, just as it was listed in the original John Denley (Figures 34 and 35), George Redway, [135] and Puttick & Simpson (Figure 45) catalogues.

Denley's Catalogue of 1827 had the following interesting entry:

> 2734. The Clavis, or Key to Unlock the Mysteries of Magick of Rabby Soloman, translated from the Hebrew into French, and from French rendered into English, with additions, by E. Sibly, M. D.; An Experiment of the Spirit Birto, as hath been often proved at the instant Request of Edward the Fourth, King of England; *and,* The Wheel of Wisdom, with its Key, and Full Directions for its Use in Magical Operations, *a Manuscript, with a great number of coloured drawings of figures, talismans, pentacles, circles, characters, &c. neat in calf,* £20.

This is the standard four Part version of the *Clavis.* Without a date and pagination it is not possible to know if this maps onto one of those manuscripts detailed above or if it is yet another copy. A further two manuscripts of the *Clavis* were listed in the 1895 catalogue of Major Irwin's manuscripts (items 489 and 491). One is almost certainly the manuscript published by S. E. E. (number 5) with his bookplate, dated 1868. The identity of the second one, dated 1836 is not so clear, but it could possibly be the present manuscript. The following tabulation (Figure 25) summarises much of the above.

---

[134] https://danharms.wordpress.com/.

[135] Also *List of books chiefly from the library of the late Frederick Hockley, Esq., consisting of important works relating to the occult sciences, both in print and manuscript / now on sale at the prices affixed;* by George Redway. Published London, 1887.

	MSS Date		No. of Parts	Pages	FH monogram	Name in Example	Scribe/Script	Pentacle distribution
1	Weiser MS.	1878	4.5	281		Edwin - Emma	Not by Hockley. Maybe scribe 'G.O.F.'	Single page pentacles
2	Utah University MS	19th century	4	268		James - Jane	Same hand as No. 7. May have had Mormon connections because Utah location	Single page pentacles
3	Private MS 1	Not "late 18th century"	4.5	168			No access	-
4	University of Manchester Rylands MS 40	c. 1825-1835 (but dated 1789)	4	243		James - Elizabeth	'J.D.' on frontispiece frame. John Denley?	Single page pentacles
4a	National Library of Scotland Acc. 9769 [MS Crawford 158?]		?	13 +204 + 73 =290			No access	Single page pentacles
5	Society of Esoteric Endeavour S.E.E. MS [with Irwin's bookplate]	1868 Date on last page.	4	150		James - Mary	Robert T Cross because 'R.C.' on last page. Handwriting matches *Raphael's Art of Talismanic Magic*.	Single page pentacles
6	London University Senate House MS HPF 1/10.	Written after 1822 [Peterson].	9 *(missing Part 8)*	186 [246 incl. blanks]	FH on p. 116	James - Elizabeth	Raphael? Same hand as No. 8.	Plates with 4/5 pentacles per page
7	Private MS 2.	1832-1879	?	4+16+ 207=227			Same hand as Utah MS 2 [Peterson].	-
8	National Library of Israel MS Yar. Var. 18. *(the present manuscript)*	1836	10	265	FH on p. 111	Edwin - Emma	Raphael? Same hand as No. 6. [Egyptian letters on last page – scribe initials?]	Plates with 4/5 pentacles per page
9	Freemasons Library SRIA MS 2083.	1832	2	172			Frederick Hockley very incomplete.	Single page pentacles
10	Ritman Library MS PH 304/M183	1874	7	166 (270 pages originally)	FH on p. 132	James - Elizabeth		Two per page, mostly
11	Dreweatts Auction MS	c. 1880		300?			No access	Single page pentacles
12	Hell Fire Club Publishers MS	20th century?	1.5	60			Edward Hunter? (not the Mormon Bishop)	No pentacles
13	*Ancient Manuscript*	1880	2	104			Robert T. Cross	4 per page

Figure 25: Identification of scribes, dates, pagination and number of Parts for each of the 14 known *Clavis* manuscripts. Other hints which may help identify connected manuscripts or scribes include: the occurrence of Frederick Hockley's monogram; the disposition of the pentacles; and the example names used on the love talisman on page 108.

Several conclusions can be drawn from this comparative table:

1. It is likely that the original form of the manuscript of the *Clavis* consisted of just 4 Parts (as illustrated by manuscript numbers 1, 2, 3, 4, and 5).

2. Later additions boosted the number of Parts to 7-10 (as illustrated by manuscript numbers 6, 8 and 10).

3. Production of these copies occurred in two distinct periods: 1822-1836 (manuscript numbers 4, 6, 8, 9) and 1868-1880 (manuscript numbers 1, 5, 10, 11), assuming that the dating is reliable. Manuscripts 2, 3, 7 could fall in either period. We conjecture that the first period of copying activity was probably due to Denley, but the second period was probably due to Hockley, the Irwins and Robert T Cross ('Raphael').

4. The male name shown in the Example of a love talisman on page 108 varies over the different versions. 'James' occurs in numbers 2, 4, 5, 6, and 10, while 'Edwin' occurs in numbers 1 and 8 (the present manuscript). This name might possibly indicate the name of the scribe or the owner. For example, the fact that 'Edwin' is paired with 'Emma' might be significant as Emma Louisa Leigh was Hockley's scryer.

Because of the differences in content between the various versions of Sibley's *Clavis*, it is probable that its generation occurred in a series of accretive steps after the initial production of Parts 1 and 2 by Sibley. He may have added Parts 3 and 4. But it is more likely that other Parts were added to after his death by copyists such as Frederick Hockley, or others hired by Denley. It is certain that some sections that are not directly related to evocation, like the summary of the practice of geomancy (Part 8) or crystal skrying (Part 6), were added by later copyists.

Short Biographies of the Main Players

Ebenezer Sibley (1751 – 1799)

Ebenezer Sibley, or Sibly, advertised himself as an "Astro-Philo" [lover of astrology], Fellow of the Harmoniac Philosophical Society in Paris,[136] MD of the King's College in Aberdeen, FRHS, and Fellow of the Royal College of Physicians, Aberdeen. Although he is often said to have graduated as a Doctor of Medicine from King's College, Aberdeen in 1792, his biographer throws considerable doubt upon this, suggesting he bought the degree, naming a college as far away from London as possible.

Only one biography of Sibley exists,[137] and that is by Susan Sommers, the Professor of History at Saint Vincent College in Latrobe, Pennsylvania, an expert on Freemasonry who has been working on Sibley, the esoteric fringes of Georgian England, and the connections between Freemasonry, magic, and politics for the last 30 years.[138]

Figure 26: Ebenezer Sibley.

---

[136] This was the English version of the 'Société de l'Harmonie Universelle,' a society organised in 1783 to support the teachings and practice of Franz Mesmer. The initiation fees collected by this society allegedly supplied Mesmer with 343,764 livres in exchange for teachings on mesmerism and animal magnetism. Antoine Court de Gébelin (c. 1719-1784) was amongst these subscribers. Court de Gébelin is remembered for his enthusiastic support of the tarot as a route into the ancient mysteries which distorted the real history of the tarot for the next two centuries. Cagliostro was also involved.

[137] Susan Sommers, *The Siblys of London*, Oxford University Press, 2018.

[138] Private communication from Susan Sommers. An interesting coincidence is that this author has the same surname as Baron Sommers of Evesham (1651-1716), the Lord Chancellor of England in the 17th century who was a collector of manuscripts on magic and probably a practising angel magician of note.

Ebenezer Sibley was born in the morning of January the 30th, 1751 at 11.23 am in the city of Bristol. Growing up in a relatively large extended family Ebenezer and his sister Kezia were the two eldest children of Edmund Sibley, a shoe-maker of rather humble means,[139] and his then wife Mary Larkholm. After remarrying in 1754 to Charity Standard, Ebenezer would gain two more half-brothers with Manoah[140] and Job Sibley. Edmund world marry one final time after the death of his wife Charity in 1768 to Elizabeth Reed in 1769, and in 1772 the Sibley's would gain yet another member of the family with the birth of a daughter, Charity Sibley.

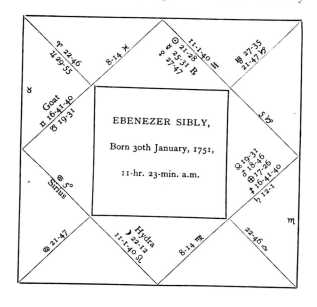

As a child Ebenezer was brought up in a strong Calvinist Baptist environment and after the death of his father's wife, Charity, he was removed from schooling at the age of seventeen, and along with his brothers, was forced to continue his academic studies under his own discipline.

Little is recorded of his childhood and early life, however records show that in May of 1770 he was married to Sarah Wainwright, three years younger than him. A few years later the marriage dissolved and they parted ways by mutual understanding.

Figure 27: Personal horoscope drawn up originally by Sibley himself and included in *The Astrologers Magazine,* Vol II (1891-1892).

With absolutely no interest in the family's shoe business and with a desire to start afresh, Ebenezer moved to Hampshire where he would once again take a bride, Anne Hollaway, with whom in 1782 he had a daughter named Urania.[141]

Sibley then settled down in Portsmouth Common (Portsea Island) with his new family. It was here that he commenced his new profession as a bookseller, a trade also enjoyed by his brother Manoah. During this endeavour Sibley began to support his very modest income by casting horoscopes. His growing interest in this later profession of astrology

---

[139] Eliphas Levi was another occult writer whose father was a shoemaker.

[140] Manoah Sibley (1757-1840) was a recognized linguist and taught Hebrew, Greek, Latin and Syriac, a skill no doubt useful to his older brother. Manoah would go on to open his own bookshop where he would sell both his and his brother's books on religion, astrology, astronomy and other esoteric and medicinal topics.

[141] From the ancient Greek Οὐρανία, Ourania, meaning "heavenly" or "of heaven." More to the point, in Greek mythology Urania was the muse of astronomy and astrology.

would slowly result in him building up a clientele that in turn fuelled his progression in the newly emerging esoteric circles of that period. Sibley, along with his brother Manoah, would write multiple works of an astrological nature from 1780 onwards, with Ebenezer's first publication, and probably his most famous work, going into print in 1784. It was adorned with a somewhat gargantuan title:

A New and Complete Illustration of the Occult Sciences: or, the Art of foretelling future Events and Contingencies, by the Aspects, Positions, and Influences, of the Heavenly Bodies. Founded on Natural Philosophy, Scripture, Reason, and the Mathematics. In Four Parts. Part I. An enquiry into, and Defence of Astrology…; Part II. Examples for acquiring a Practical Knowledge of Astrology, with Rules for calculating, rectifying, and judging Nativities…; Part III. Meteorological Astrology defined and explained… To which is added, a Collection of improved Tables, contrived to answer all the Purposes of Astronomical Calculations. Part IV. The Distinction between Astrology and the Diabolical Practice of Exorcism; in which the Methods used for raising up and consulting Spirits are laid open, with various instances of their Compacts with wicked Men. Account of Apparitions and Spirits, including a general Display of the Mysteries of Witchcraft, Divination, Charms, and Necromancy. Compiled from a Series of intense Study and Application, and founded on real Examples and Experience.

By Ebenezer Sibly, Fellow of the Harmonic *(sic)* Philosophical Society at Paris. Embellished with Curious Copper-Plates.

A veritable tome, the work ran to over a thousand pages and was embellished with 185 tables, charts and varying types of illustration. Many of the different published editions are now available online, with the Wellcome Library holding a substantial collection of print exemplars. Both the Sibley brothers' books would have been greatly influenced by the numerous esoteric works that passed through their hands and over the counters of their respective businesses.

Equally as important to Sibley during this period of his life was his admission to the Masonic brotherhood. In June of 1784 Sibley was initiated into Freemasonry as a member of the Portsmouth Lodge No 79. This was the start of a long and active relationship with the brotherhood in which he would rise through the degrees and with time become a member of the Knights Templar Order, initiated in Bristol in 1785.

The year of 1784 would once again see Sibley return to his hometown of Bristol where he would continue to deal in the sale, trade and loan of books. It was also around this period that Bristol became a hub of leading edge medical practice, something by which Sibley would be greatly influenced, particularly by his good friend Till Adams, MD. This exposure would turn his interests towards medicine and in particular its astrological applications. Doctor Adams become a mentor figure for Sibley, possibly teaching him many of his techniques and allowing him access to his personal library. After Doctor Adams' death in February of 1786, as a result of fever, Sibley would write memorials devoted to his departed friend, one of which appeared in his *A Key to Physic.*

Figure 28: A plate by J. Roberts used by Sibley as a frontispiece for *A New and Complete Illustration of the Occult Sciences,* 1784.

Once more deciding to leave his home town of Bristol to seek his fortune elsewhere in London, we find Sibley with a third wife Charlotte Henrietta Carolina Thomas, daughter of a well to do Bristol family. What is known of the fate of Sibley's previous wife Anne is only speculation, although it is possible that she may have passed away during a second childbirth in 1786. Sibley would also during this period father a bastard son named James on Elizabeth Pidding, with whom he had no ongoing relationship.

Upon Sibley's arrival in London he would soon, through his interests in astrology and related sciences, become acquainted with John Bell, a man claiming to be one of England's finest mesmerists who had gained his proficiency in Paris. Bell also claimed among many other things to be a confidante of Count Alessandro di Cagliostro (*aka* Giuseppe Balsamo) who personally invited him to join his 'Egyptian Rite' and in turn taught him other occult matters. Bell began advertising his many 'talents' in the local newspapers in January of 1785 in the form of twelve lectures advertised at the fee of three guineas. Not surprisingly the endeavour failed to gather little interest with only one lecture ever being held.

Bell would decide to try his hand again, several years later, this time joined by two of his fellow Freemasons, including Stephen Freeman, a man of standing and respect within the Masonic world. Bell re-organized the material into his newly established 'College for Instructing Pupils in Mesmer's Philosophy' which also offered various medicinal treatments using 'electrical machines.' It was at the end of June that Sibley would join this group using the title "E. Sibley Astro-Philo."

The College was once again a failure and Sibley moved on, however for a time after 1784 he continued to use the title 'Astro-Philo' as can be seen in the frontispiece of his *Uranoscopia*.[142] Like his previous partners Sibley by this time had also become a 'Fellow of the Harmoniac Philosophical Society of Paris,' a title which hereafter would appear in both Sibley's manuscripts and printed works. Over the next few years Sibley would work increasingly hard at publishing works of a medical nature with the hopes of making his name in that field.

For a brief period he was called to Ipswich in February 1790 where he adroitly and profitably used his knowledge of Masonic affairs to further the career of a local politician. He returned to London by the end of 1791 and returned to furthering his hoped for medical career.[143]

On the 20th of April, 1792 Sibley's long running ambition finally came to fruition when

---

[142] *Uranoscopia, or the pure Language of the Stars, Unfolded by the motion of the Seven Erratics, etc.,* 1790. A very short unpaginated booklet. Erratics = planets.

[143] The Sibley name continued to be associated with Freemasonry, with a W. G. Sibley publishing *The Story of Freemasonry* in 1913. This book went through at least 3 editions and sold at least 31,000 copies. He is not unlikely to be connected with Ebenezer Sibley, because of both their common name and common interests.

he was granted an MD from King's College, Aberdeen.[144] Sibley would thereafter use 'MD' on the title page of his works along with a reference to his membership of the 'Royal College of Physicians in Aberdeen.'

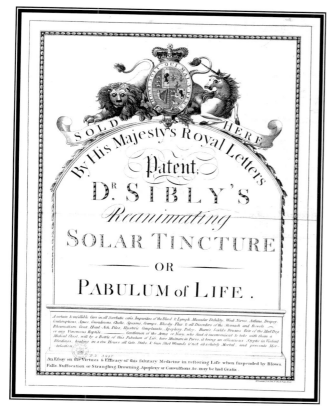

Figure 29: One of the trade cards for Dr Sibly's Solar Tincture, 1760-1818 which was not only medicinal, but also offered the hope of reanimation of the recently dead.

The Medical Society of Aberdeen was founded by a small group of medical students of Marischal College in late 1789, and it is speculated that Sibley was invited to join them. This is unlikely, according to Sommers, because Sibley was not physically present in Aberdeen, and that medical society was never granted the title of a Royal College. Nevertheless it gave Sibley a very official sounding title, albeit rather less grand in reality.

After the publication of some works of a medical nature, Sibley began advertising the sale of his cure-all remedy 'Dr Sibly's Reanimating Solar Tincture' complete in a bottle adorned with a blazing Sun and the adopted Sibley crest and motto *Triumpho morte tam vita* ("I triumph in death as in life").

In the year 1796 Sibley moved to No. 40 New Bridge Street in Ludgate Hill. It was here that he would reside until his death in December 1799. No. 40 was a substantial home having twelve rooms beautifully furnished, a laboratory and even a shop front, in fact everything that Sibley required to help run his struggling business.

Sibley was indeed a man of many facets, and many interests, and as such his life can be viewed from several distinct perspectives.

On one hand, as portrayed in Susan Sommers' detailed biography of him and his family members, he was a man of questionable academic and medical qualifications, often turning to rather desperate means to avoid looming bankruptcy.

---

[144] At this period in history a medical degree could be purchased from the University of Aberdeen for varying undisclosed sums regardless of an applicant's actual medical history and training.

Another perspective of more relevance to this book, is the persona of an intelligent man at the forefront of thought creating a new hybrid subject by combining occult methodology with the newly emerging techniques of Victorian science and medicine against the background of a Baptist upbringing, to form (at least in his mind) a workable and well balanced system.

Of perhaps equal merit, and something which unfortunately Sibley would never witness in his life, was the impact and importance of the books and manuscripts on astrology and magic which

he had collected over many years. These and his library would go on to play a profound role in the revival of magic in Victorian England.

Figure 30: The 'adopted' crest used by Sibley featuring a griffin and often appearing on his remedies.

Sibley's primary interests were magic, astrology, and various types of alternative healing. He was responsible for bringing some rigor to astrology after its image had declined as a result of the Enlightenment. He published numerous works on both astrology and medicine, including *Uranoscopia, or the pure Language of the Stars* (1780), *A New and Complete Illustration of the Celestial Science of Astrology* (1784-8), *Key to Physic and the Occult Science of Astrology* (1794), and *The Medical Mirror, or a treatise on the impregnation of the human female* (c. 1796).

Sibley was not just interested in the occult sciences, but he was also interested in the latest scientific advancements. As Allen Debus explains:

> Sibley also felt comfortable with the most recent scientific journals and he sought to accommodate this research to his own world view. Heberden, Newton, Priestley, and Lavoisier were no less important to him than Aristotle, Hermes Trismegistus, Khunrath, and Paracelsus. Even more important, the recent work of Mesmer seemed to offer the most powerful proof of his own cosmic interpretation of man and nature.[145]

Co-workers and Associates

Sibley had a rather contorted marital life, and it is thought that he often failed to finalise a divorce before contracting his next marriage. A contemporary, John Parkins who knew Sibley, had this to say:

> ...the late Dr Sibley, had both Saturn and Mars located in the seventh house in his nativity, and the consequence was this; he had two or three wives, but could not live with any of them. No person could have imagined or thought this to be the case, neither from his common conversation, address, accomplishments, or his company; yet that unfortunate

---

[145] Alan Debus (1982), p. 278.

gentleman during the time that I was at his house in Upper Titchfield Street, London, in the year 1796, he was then living in a state of separation from his wife, whom I never saw all the while I was in town...[146]

John Parkins (1771 – 1830) appears to have been a student of magic and astrology with both Sibley and Francis Barrett. There is an interesting set of connections between Parkins, Sibley and Barrett, the author of *The Magus* which was published just two years after Sibley's death (1801). Francis King relates their relationship probably extended beyond studentship, and this also can be seen in the context of the local geography of London.

> ...Parkins, subsequently a pupil of Francis Barrett, definitely knew Sibley and may have for some time resided with him in Upper Titchfield Street. I feel that this fact provides some evidence in favour of an occult tradition, with which I first became acquainted in the 1950s, that Barrett learned his magical crystal gazing techniques from Sibley.

> A further point of interest is that Sibley's address in 1796, Upper Titchfield Street, now the northern part of Great Titchfield Street, was the next road to Norton Street, now Bolsover Street, and the gardens of the houses on the western side of Upper Titchfield Street met the gardens of the houses on the eastern side of Norton Street. In other words, 99 Norton Street, where Francis Barrett established his magical school in 1801, was in remarkably close proximity to the house in which Ebenezer Sibley was living in 1796...

> John Parkins was an associate of both Sibly and Barrett and it was from them that he learned many of the occult techniques he employed for the benefit of those who sought his help at the 'Temple of Wisdom' he established at some time before 1810 at Little Gonerby, near Grantham.[147]

Besides the confirmation of geography, Barrett's landlady, Catherine Collier, was either a pupil or associate of Sibley's, so it would seem that Barrett's 'School of Magic' was more real than just an advertisement in *The Magus*. It is also noteworthy that Dr. Sigismund Bacstrom, who claimed Rosicrucian initiation on the island of Mauritius, also lived in Marylebone in 1798, and was "doing Alchemical work with a considerable circle of adepts and aspirants. The simplest (and kindest) interpretation of the initials placed after Francis Barrett's name 'F.R.C.'[148] is that he was initiated in due form by his Marylebone neighbour."[149]

The connections between Rosicrucianism and magic were amplified by Frederick Hockley, the founding of the SRIA in 1867, and later by MacGregor Mathers who wrote the rituals of the 'Rosicrucian grades' of the Hermetic Order of the Golden Dawn.

---

[146] Parkins, *Book of Miracles,* London, 1817, p. 17.
[147] King, *The Flying Sorcerer,* Oxford: Mandrake, 1992, p. 40.
[148] Frater Rosae Crucis. A title adopted by Barrett.
[149] Godwin (1994), p. 120.

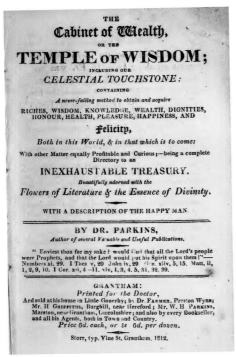

THE
Cabinet of Wealth,
OR THE
TEMPLE OF WISDOM;
INCLUDING OUR
CELESTIAL TOUCHSTONE:
CONTAINING
A never-failing method to obtain and acquire
RICHES, WISDOM, KNOWLEDGE, WEALTH, DIGNITIES,
HONOUR, HEALTH, PLEASURE, HAPPINESS, AND
Felicity,
Both in this World, & in that which is to come:
With other Matter equally Profitable and Curious;—being a complete
Directory to an
INEXHAUSTABLE TREASURY.
Beautifully adorned with the
Flowers of Literature & the Essence of Divinity.
— ◆ —
WITH A DESCRIPTION OF THE HAPPY MAN.
—————————
BY DR. PARKINS,
Author of several Valuable and Useful Publications.
—————————
" Enviest thou for my sake? would God that all the Lord's people
were Prophets, and that the Lord would put his Spirit upon them !"—
Numbers xi. 29. I Thes v, 20 John iv, 29 Gen xiv, 5, 15. Matt, ii,
1, 2, 9, 10. I Cor. xii, 4 –11. xiv, 1, 3, 4. 5, 31, 32, 39.
—————————
GRANTHAM:
Printed for the Doctor,
And sold at his house in Little Gonerby; by Dr. Farmer, Preston Wynn;
Mr. H Griffiths, Burghill, near Hereford ; Mr. W. H Parkins,
Marston, near Grantham, Lincolnshire ; and also by every Bookseller,
and all his Agents, both in Town and Country.
Price 6d. each, or 4s 6d. per dozen.
—————————
Storr, typ. Vine St, Grantham. 1812.

Figure 31: The book of talismans produced by John Parkins at his 'Temple of Wisdom' in Little Gonerby near Grantham in Lincolnshire in 1812.

Parkins produced a publication to be sold at his office/home (which he referred grandly as the 'Temple of Wisdom') which contained a number of talismans (which he erroneously referred to as 'lamens'). Parkins also produced a slim volume called *The Book of Miracles* which derived a lot of its contents from both Sibley and Barrett. His *Universal Fortune-Teller* (1810) included some geomancy along the same lines as Part 8 of the present manuscript, as well as liberal servings of physiognomy, palmistry and fortune telling by cards. There are many examples of geomantic divinations in Parkin's casebooks or commonplace books. Like Sibley, Parkins also claimed the title of 'Doctor' but his medical practice probably did not extend much beyond herbalism and urine diagnosis.

Barrett was very interested in crystal skrying, or summoning the image of a spirit into a crystal. His essay on this procedure was very influential on subsequent magicians, right up to the present day. In the present century this work has been used by Frater Ashen Chassan to produce a body of magical knowledge that is well worth reading.[150] The crystal gazing essay written by Barrett and later used to such good effect by Ashen Chassan was, according to Francis King, written specifically for Parkins.[151] Barrett almost certainly practiced the magic he wrote about, and he once claimed in print (in *The Magus*) that he could use magic to produce thunderstorms.[152]

Both Sibley and Parkins published revised versions of Culpeper's *Herbal*,[153] an area of common interest. Parkins also adopted yet another one of Sibley's money-making ploys: manuscript production

> For sums varying between twenty and thirty guineas he sold copies of a manuscript on the subject of ceremonial magic...and he also manufactured and sold talismans, which he termed 'holy consecrated lamens.'[154]

---

[150] Frater Ashen Chassan *aka* Bryan Garner (2013 & 2016).

[151] See Wellcome MS 3770 for confirmation of this.

[152] An ability also claimed in the 20th century by the Austrian magician Franz Bardon.

[153] Parkin's edition of Culpepper was later resurrected by David Thomas Jones who published it in a Welsh edition in 1862.

[154] Francis King (1992), p. 45-46.

This manuscript on ceremonial magic is quite likely to have been another copy of the *Clavis*. It therefore seems highly likely that at least one copy of the present manuscript may have been written by Parkins.

Some of Parkins' practice reflected the typical life of a Cunning-man, but in his case with a more sophisticated knowledge of formal ritual magic. He even devised a 'talismanic ready reckoner' which enabled him to calculate the exact time of any planetary hour, at any time of the year (for his latitude). This enabled him to conscientiously consecrate a talisman in the correct planetary hour and day, as indeed is recommended in the *Clavis*.

Figure 32: Bartlett's Buildings circa 1850. Print by Thomas Shepherd.

Sibley's and Barrett's interest in crystal skrying later passed to Frederick Hockley in the 19th century, and it may be Hockley who is to thank for the addition of Part 6 of this manuscript.

In addition to his published works, Sibley acquired, copied and created grimoires, many of which were later copied and expanded by Frederick Hockley and Robert Cross Smith some 30+ years later. The present book is perhaps the most elaborate of all these copies.

Some of Sibley's addresses in London are known. Tax records for 1789 state it as No 18 Bartlett's Building, Holborn, and this very address appears on the title page of the MS 40 of the *Clavis*. Sibley would also use the address of No 1 Upper (Greater) Titchfield Street where he would advertise himself as a "Student of Physic and the Occult Sciences," using this address repeatedly on numerous advertisements. His other addresses included New Bridge Street in Blackfriars, and No 12 Grafton Street, Tottenham Court Road, both of which were listed in British Directories of the period.

On his death Sibley's papers and manuscripts found their way to the shop of bookseller John Denley. There of two views on how this happened, one via a feckless nephew who promptly sold them to Denley, according to Hockley.[155] The alternative story quotes Sibley's Will which states, "it is my will that Mr John Richard Saffell shall have the whole of my Library." John Saffell (1747-1816) was not Sibley's nephew but the son of his last business partner in the Solar Tincture, Charles Saffell. It is possible that the bequest of his library to Saffell's son might have been to pay off his debt to the father who had invested heavily in Sibley's business.[156]

---

[155] As noted in John Hamill, *The Rosicrucian Seer*, Teitan, 2009, p. 39.
[156] Sommers (2018), p. 240.

John Denley (1764-1842)

Many of the occult and esoteric works that are available to us today may have never even surfaced, or simply passed into obscurity, had it not been for the efforts of John Denley and his famous little book store. Located originally at Gate Street (Lincoln's Inn Fields), then 13 Catherine Street, Strand, and finally at 24 Brydges Place (both in Covent Garden) London, the establishment housed not only one of the greatest collections of original manuscripts and rare books dealing with magic, astrology in Victorian England at that time, but was also a centre of manuscript production and information interchange.

Denley's resources were indeed the focus of the voracious reading appetite of many learned individuals of the period, many striving to carve their names into the annuals of magic or astrology. One such notable individual was Francis Barrett.

Barrett, most famous for his publication of *The Magus,*[157] reportedly used a great deal of the resources provided to him via Denley's shop when compiling this work. Something from which Denley apparently would receive no recognition or reparation.

Denley was also responsible for the publication in 1822 of *The Philosophical Merlin* by Robert Cross Smith a work based on a manuscript claiming to having once been used by Napoleon himself. Although this is very unlikely, as it was derived from much later sources including the *Magus.* Denley would go on to publish Smith's *Urania; or, The Astrologer's Chronicle, and Mystical Magazine.* Unfortunately both were commercial failures.

Without any doubt, The Covent Garden bookshop's greatest wonder was its ability to provide customers with hand written transcripts and compilations from its large collection of material. The individual most noted for this service and employed by Denley from a young age was Frederick Hockley. Hockley himself would, with time, and thanks to Denley's resources, accumulate a truly extraordinary library of his very own, a result of his paid position and diligent work at transcription and coping. Denley also possibly paid other talented and meticulous individuals like Hockley to engage in the transcription and copying of manuscripts, although no other names have been recorded as such. Indeed towards the end when money and business was at its leanest it is feasible to surmise that perhaps Denley himself had taken over the mantle of this very task?

One of the largest assets for Denley's business arrived in the form of the stock made available by the death of Ebenezer Sibley in 1799. Sibley had dreamed that his prized collection would be kept intact for future generations to reap the benefits from the

---

[157] *The Magus, or Celestial Intelligencer* published by Lackington 1801. According to Owen Davis's in his *Grimoires: A History of Magic Books,* the *Magus* was reportedly "the first major English discourse on Spirit conjuration since the seventeenth century" A description which did not ingratiate Barrett very well with his peers.

knowledge that it contained. Unfortunately for him, and despite his best wishes, in less than two months of taking ownership of it, his nephew (or the son of his partner, Saffell) sold it all to one of the biggest book dealers and publishers in London at that time, George Lackington. From there Denley was able to purchase the majority, if not all of the manuscripts from the collection for his shop.[158] Lackington, Allen & Co., of Finsbury Square, London was a much larger and more fashionable operation than Denley's shop (see Figure 33). Probably coincidently, George Lackington issued his first catalogue in 1799, the year of Sibley's death. It reputedly listed an amazing 200,000 books. Three years later in 1803 Lackington issued his second catalogue with no less than 800,000 books, an almost unbelievable number by today's standards. His bookshop called itself the 'Temple of the Muses' and it was said to be large enough to drive a mail-coach and four horses round it.

Many of the newly obtained works would be listed for sale in the future and in the 1826 Denley catalogue the *Clavis, or Key to Unlock the Mysteries of the Magick of Rabby Solomon* was advertised for sale at the considerable sum of 20 pounds.

In recent times a statement began to circulate that Denley had in fact sold his original Sibley manuscript of the *Clavis* "for an extraordinary sum to the Duke of Wentworth" however Sommers states that this is incorrect, as no one of that title existed in Denley's lifetime.

Figure 33: Denley's competitor Lackington, Allen & Co. at the 'Temple of the Muses,' Finsbury Square, London.

With the proclamation of his retirement and the sale of most of his stock John Denley closed the doors of his shop at 13 Catherine Street in 1829. This was not to remain the case for long however because in 1831 Denley had once again gone back into business. This time at his newly acquired location of 24 Brydges Street.[159]

It was during the final years of Denley's business that things declined to a much less grand scale with the acquisition of far less stock, something that certainly didn't go unnoticed by Hockley himself, who commented on the matter in passing. It was also during this period that Denley had organized many copies of his

---

[158] Susan Sommers, *The Siblys of London: A Family on the Esoteric Fringes of Georgian England,* Oxford: OUP, 2018, pp. 237-244. Very strangely there is no mention of the library when the estate was valued, so maybe Saffell had removed the books rapidly before probate was granted.

[159] 24 Brydges Street was a continuation of the same thoroughfare as Catherine Street and close to the Theatre Royal entrance, Drury Lane.

personal collection to be made by Hockley and others for sale and for commissions from customers and clients, a further attempt at supporting himself despite the lack of newly acquired stock.

Regrettably what is known of John Denley himself is only recounted in the memoires of those who frequented his shop. Of Denley's personal life all that is written was that he was born in 1764 and passed away in 1842.

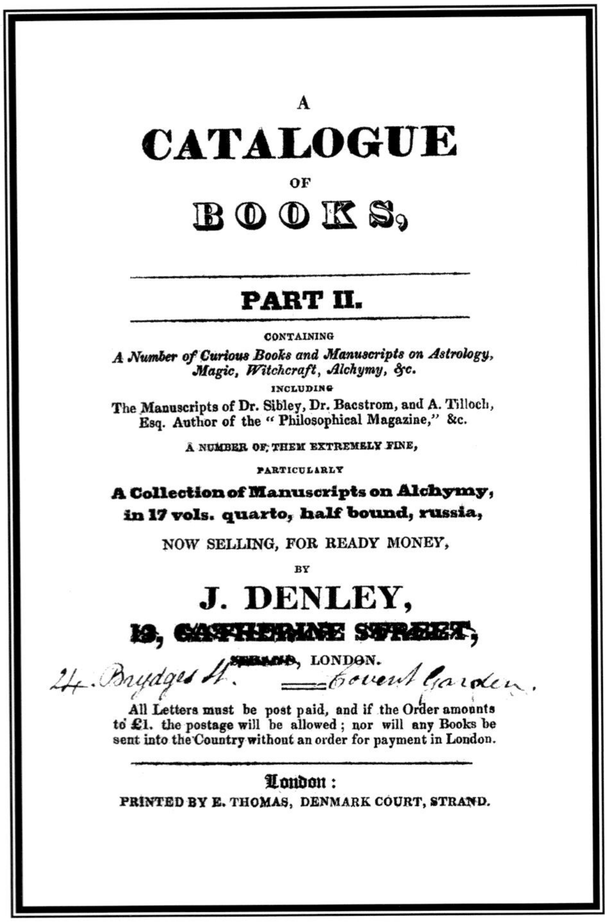

A

CATALOGUE

OF

BOOKS,

PART II.

CONTAINING

A Number of Curious Books and Manuscripts on Astrology, Magic, Witchcraft, Alchymy, &c.

INCLUDING

The Manuscripts of Dr. Sibley, Dr. Bacstrom, and A. Tilloch, Esq. Author of the " Philosophical Magazine," &c.

A NUMBER OF THEM EXTREMELY FINE,

PARTICULARLY

A Collection of Manuscripts on Alchymy, in 17 vols. quarto, half bound, russia,

NOW SELLING, FOR READY MONEY,

BY

J. DENLEY,

19, CATHERINE STREET,

STRAND, LONDON.

24. Brydges St. Covent Garden.

All Letters must be post paid, and if the Order amounts to £1. the postage will be allowed ; nor will any Books be sent into the Country without an order for payment in London.

London :

PRINTED BY E. THOMAS, DENMARK COURT, STRAND.

Figure 34: Cover of the 1826 issue of Denley's catalogue. His new address in Brydges Street has been written in by hand.

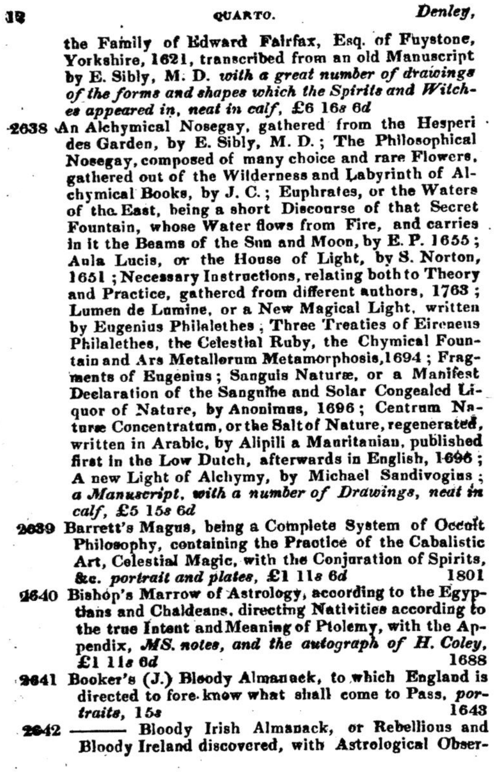

the Family of Edward Fairfax, Esq. of Fuystone, Yorkshire, 1621, transcribed from an old Manuscript by E. Sibly, M. D. *with a great number of drawings of the forms and shapes which the Spirits and Witches appeared in, neat in calf,* £6 16s 6d

2638 An Alchymical Nosegay, gathered from the Hesperides Garden, by E. Sibly, M. D.; The Philosophical Nosegay, composed of many choice and rare Flowers, gathered out of the Wilderness and Labyrinth of Alchymical Books, by J. C.; Euphrates, or the Waters of the East, being a short Discourse of that Secret Fountain, whose Water flows from Fire, and carries in it the Beams of the Sun and Moon, by E. P. 1655; Aula Lucis, or the House of Light, by S. Norton, 1651; Necessary Instructions, relating both to Theory and Practice, gathered from different authors, 1763; Lumen de Lumine, or a New Magical Light, written by Eugenius Philalethes; Three Treaties of Eireneus Philalethes, the Celestial Ruby, the Chymical Fountain and Ars Metallorum Metamorphosis, 1694; Fragments of Eugenius; Sanguis Naturæ, or a Manifest Declaration of the Sanguine and Solar Congealed Liquor of Nature, by Anonimus, 1696; Centrum Naturæ Concentratum, or the Salt of Nature, regenerated, written in Arabic, by Alipili a Mauritanian, published first in the Low Dutch, afterwards in English, 1696; A new Light of Alchymy, by Michael Sandivogius; *a Manuscript, with a number of Drawings, neat in calf,* £5 15s 6d

2639 Barrett's Magus, being a Complete System of Occult Philosophy, containing the Practice of the Cabalistic Art, Celestial Magic, with the Conjuration of Spirits, &c. *portrait and plates,* £1 11s 6d   1801

2640 Bishop's Marrow of Astrology, according to the Egyptians and Chaldeans, directing Nativities according to the true Intent and Meaning of Ptolemy, with the Appendix, *MS. notes, and the autograph of H. Coley,* £1 11s 6d   1688

2641 Booker's (J.) Bloody Almanack, to which England is directed to fore-know what shall come to Pass, *portraits,* 15s   1643

2642 ——— Bloody Irish Almanack, or Rebellious and Bloody Ireland discovered, with Astrological Obser-

Figure 35: A page from John Denley's *Catalogue of Books* (1826) showing one of Sibley's alchemical 'Collections' plus Francis Barrett's *Magus*. The partial item at the top is the source of the sample of Sibley's script in Figure 20.

Robert Cross Smith aka 'Raphael' (1795-1832)

Robert Cross Smith (1795-1832) was an English astrologer who was the first, in a long line of others to follow, who would write and publish under the pseudonym of 'Raphael.'[160] He was author of The *Astrologer of the Nineteenth Century* (1825), *Royal Book of Fate* (1829), *Royal Book of Dreams* (1830), *Raphael's Witch* (1831), *The Familiar Astrologer* (1831), and *The Straggling Astrologer* (1824).

Robert Cross Smith is included because he took sections from the *Clavis* and published them, along with engravings of the associated spirits, in *The Straggling Astrologer* a short running astrology magazine which only lasted for one year (1824-1825). Mixed in with the astrology were short pieces on geomancy and the evocation of spirits (rather romantically treated). He must not be confused with Robert Thomas Cross (1850-1923) who would become the 7th and last 'Raphael' in line, and was much more important to the history of the *Clavis* manuscripts.

Smith was born in Abbots Leigh just outside Bristol in 1795. A carpenter by trade, he married Sarah Lucas in 1820 and moved to London beginning a new life as a clerk in Upper Thames Street. During this period Smith developed his interest in astrology, eventually leaving his job to pursue a career in that field professionally. After moving once again to a house located off Oxford Street, Smith together with G. W. Graham, the balloonist and friend who helped Smith financially, published a book together on geomancy in 1822 entitled *The Philosophical Merlin*.[161]

Figure 36: A romantic illustration of an evocation from The *Straggling Astrologer* published in 1824.

Smith began to edit the periodical entitled *The Straggling Astrologer* in 1824, but failed to acquire enough subscribers and the periodical was discontinued after a few issues. He collected the issues of the failed periodical in a volume entitled *The Astrologer of The Nineteenth Century* in the same year. The volume claimed to be the 'sixth edition,' but there is no certainty that editions one to five ever existed. A substantially enlarged edition appeared in 1825 with additional material attributed to 'Merlinus Anglicus

---

[160] The seven astrologers taking the pseudonym of 'Raphael' during the nineteenth century were: 1. Robert Cross Smith; 2. John Palmer; 3. Dixon; 4. Medhurst; 5. Wakely; 6. Sparkes (who was also 'Zadkiel' for a very brief period); 7. Robert Thomas Cross.
[161] Translation of a script supposed to have once been in the possession of Napoleon Bonaparte. It was dedicated to the French cartomancer Marie Anne Adelaide Lenormand (1772–1843).

Junior' another pseudonym.[162]

Figure 37: Title page of *The Astrologer of the Nineteenth Century* published in 1825.

Although Robert Cross Smith was known for his work on astrology, he also had a keen interest in magic and alchemy, a fact which would open him to much criticism. In 1825 Smith reportedly joined a magical group founded by Francis Barrett. This may or may not have been the 'Society of Mercurii,' with whom he claimed association.

The initials 'RSC' can be found in the Folger Shakespeare manuscript (aka *The Book of Oberon*). This manuscript once belonged to Richard Cosway who was probably a member of Mecurii. Upon his death Cosway's large library of occult books found their way into Smith's hands, and portions of that work where later published in his *Astrologer of the Nineteenth Century*.

There was an anonymous gentleman who went by the pseudonym of "Philadelphus" was also a noted member of Mercurii and it is this very pseudonym that appears written at the foot of a page towards the end of Senate House Library MS 1/10 leaving one to speculate if he could in fact be the yet unidentified scribe?

From 1827 until his death Smith edited an astrological almanac, entitled *The Prophetic Messenger*. In 1828 he produced *The Familiar Astrologer* and *A Manual of Astrology*.

After Smith died in 1832 his almanac continued to be edited as *Raphael's Ephemeris* and it became a standard work for both British and American astrologers. Like Sibley, *Raphael's Ephemeris* popularized the Placidian system of astrological house division which became a feature of modern Western astrology. He left behind a widow, six children and the sum of £1000.

FORM IN WHICH THE SPIRIT USUALLY APPEARS.

Figure 38: Romanticised image of the spirit Egin (Demon King of the North) from *The Astrologer of the Nineteenth Century*.

---

162 Derived from *Merlinus Anglicus Junior: The English Merlin Revived* which was the title of a 1644 book by William Lilly. This 564 page volume has been republished in Delhi by Isha Books, 2013.

Frederick Hockley (1808-1885)

Figure 39: Frederick Hockley (1808-1885).

One name frequently mentioned in passing (in relation to the Golden Dawn) but written about more often in recent years, is that of Frederick Hockley. Hockley was still largely unknown 30 years ago, before the publication of John Hamill's *Rosicrucian Seer*.[163] Even so, most of his writing remained in manuscript till his work began to get published in 2008.[164] He was a man whose dedication and calligraphic skills contributed more to the revival of magic in Victorian England than is often given credit.

The early years of Frederick Hockley's life are poorly documented. He was born in Lambeth which was then at that time part of Surry but since has become a Borough of London. It was Hockley himself who gave his exact birthday for luckily it was written down in his copy of *Uranoscopia*,[165] which he received from his friend John Denley in 1833. Recorded in a nativity chart are the details "Nat[ivity]: Oct. 13th 2h.20 am 1808 Lat 51 32N," or in other words the 13 October 1808 in London. The book also contains the Hockley family crest drawn by Hockley himself (see Figure 42).

Of Hockley's parents little is known. His father was John Hockley (1771-1838). His mother was Ann Hockley who died in 1822 in London and his grandmother was Jane Hockley (1740-1819).

Hockley's early education occurred at Captain Webb's School for the sons of sailors at Hoxton, which he attended up to the age of eight, as attested by himself in a letter to his friend Herbert Irwin. It was at a very early age that Hockley began to develop his interests in the occult and his earliest experiments with magic mirrors and crystals took place in 1824. He was sixteen at the time.[166]

Hockley's early career remains somewhat elusive, except for the fact that he was employed by John Denley (a man for whom Hockley had much admiration) for a period of time in the copying and producing of manuscripts from the large collection that Denley had managed to procure (much of it from Sibley's estate).

---

[163] First published in 1986, but then re-issued in an expanded edition in 2009 by Teitan.

[164] Many titles recently published by Teitan. See Bibliography for details.

[165] *Uranoscopia, or the pure language of the Stars, Unfolded by the motion of the Seven Erratics, etc"* by E. Sibly, 1790. Frederick Hockley's personal copy now resides in the Wellcome Library.

[166] Hockley gave evidence to the London Dialectical Society in a special Committee of Spiritualism, Tuesday the 8th June 1869 saying "I have been a spiritualist for 45 years, and have considerable experience." – John Hamill, *The Rosicrucian Seer*, Teitan, 2009, page 75.

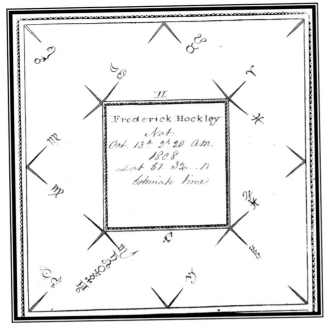

Figure 40: Frederick Hockley's birth details as recorded by himself in his copy of Sibley's *Uranoscopia*.

Hockley would go on to marry Sarah Lee Hockley (born 1812) in Kensington in 1838. Sarah Hockley passed away on the 8th December 1850 in Croydon aged 38 and was buried at Beckenham in Saint George's churchyard.[167] Suicide was suspected.

The death certificate is said to indicate that her husband held the profession of accountant. Mrs. Hockley was reported to have also been a keen acquirer of occult secrets, with one tale recounting her discovery in her husband's collection of one particular spell which gave the user the ability to "summon anyone to your presence."[168] This item she reputedly used frequently to help counter her husband's rather unfortunate habit of abiding long hours at the horserace tracks.

Hockley's connection to and reverence for his wife would remain strong long after her death. He would spend much time engaged in spiritualist experiments with the hope of contacting her from beyond the grave. Although spiritualism and magic do not share much of the same following today, in the mid-1800s many occultists were also spiritualists, including Hockley.

In September 1846 Hockley would take on the position of public accountant in partnership with two other individuals and a beginning salary of around 140 pounds a year. In April of 1873 the business was known as Begbie, Robinson and Hockley, located at 3 Raymond Buildings, Gray's Inn. It was here that he would remain faithfully employed as a senior audit clerk until his eventual death.

The period of 1850 onwards would mark a time when Hockley became more serious in his studies of spiritualism and skrying with crystals and mirrors. Although Hockley (like John Dee) was unable to see anything in the crystals himself he documented that some of his greatest successes occurred with the use of young girls as mediums, in particular one Emma Louisa Leigh whom he first met in Croydon in the 1850s. Interestingly Hockley would go on to be later known as "the Crystal Seer of Croydon."[169]

---

[167] https://www.kentarchaeology.org.uk/Research/Libr/MIs/MIsBeckenhamStGeo/01.htm#Index

[168] John Hamill, *The Rosicrucian Seer*, Teitan Press, 2009, page x.

[169] *Yorkshire Spiritual Telegraph* - April 1855.

Emma was 13 when they met, but died at the young age of 20 in 1858. During those seven years during which they worked together Emma received a lot of material from the spirits and angels, but none of the revelations were more cherished by Hockley than the revelations from an entity he identified as the Crowned Angel. Hockley recorded these revelations in a magnum opus he later called *The Metaphysical and Spiritual Philosophy*.[170]

Hockley's private journals and notes from these experiments are exhaustingly extensive and extremely detailed, and yet despite his generosity in sharing of much esoteric knowledge, these particular documents would remain hidden from all eyes but his own during his lifetime.

Socialising in circles of like-minded individuals Hockley would prove a great mentor figure to the likes of Kenneth Mackenzie and Reverend C. M. Davis. Hockley was renowned for his generosity in lending out and sharing works from his own personal library, with Henry Dawson Lea and F. G Irwin gaining much from this friendship.

It wasn't until Hockley's more senior years that he became involved with fraternal organizations, and in 1864 at the age of 56 he was initiated into the Freemason's British Lodge No.8. It was here that Hockley began a long running friendship with the Irwins.

Hockley soon developed devotion to the lodge's ritual and it wasn't long before he was moving up through the ranks. Within 15 months of his initial joining he later become Junior Warden and Master in 1867. Hockley's involvement with other branches of the Masonic Order were also dually noted with his regular attendance at Emulation Lodge of Improvement (1866-1868), a member of Alnwick Lodge No. 1167 which he joined on 27 September 1870, and after becoming a Grand Steward was involved with the Grand Stewards' Lodge in 1867, also becoming its Junior Warden in 1875 and then its secretary in 1877, a title he would hold for the remainder of his life. According to John Hamill, Hockley was above reproach when it came to his activities within the Lodge commenting that,

> He was so assiduous in the performance of his duties as Secretary that the members in 1885 voted unanimously to present him with a special jewel, as Masonic medals are called, as a token of their esteem. He died, unfortunately, before the jewel was finished, but as a mark of their sincerity and a lasting memorial to him the jewel was completed, accepted by the lodge and ordered to be worn by successive Secretaries, which it still is today.[171]

As part of his work within British Chapter No. 8, Hockley was elevated to the British Chapter of Royal Arch Masonry on the 1st of December 1865, but filling more humble offices. John Hamill notes in his book that it is surprising that Hockley did not pursue a more prominent position within this Order, as its focus was inclined to the mystical.

---

[170] Listed by George Redway in a catalogue of the library of Walter Moseley circa 1899. See *The Metaphysical and Spiritual Philosophy of the Spirit Eltesmo*. York Beach: Teitan, forthcoming.
[171] John Hamill, *The Rosicrucian Seer*, Teitan, 2009, page xvi.

Indeed this does seem counterproductive in view of Hockley's inquisitive disposition.

In 1867, thanks to the help of Robert Wentworth Little, the Societas Rosicruciana in Anglia (SRIA) was revived. This was not, as claimed by W. Wynn Westcott in his history of the Order, with the help of Frederick Hockley and Kenneth R. H. Mackenzie, as Hockley himself would not join the Order until 1872, five years after its reformation due in part to his contact with Irwin. Hockley was already considered a Rosicrucian Adept, as far as Irwin was concerned, for he did not even have to attend Irwin's Bristol College to be initiated into the grade of Zelator. It was also Irwin who bestowed on Hockley the VII Degree of *Adeptus Exemptus,* the highest grade he could confer after he was accepted, and all without Hockley having ever set foot in the Bristol College of the SRIA.

Figure 41: Kenneth R. H. Mackenzie, Freemason, linguist, orientalist and dedicated Rosicrucian. He made a point of not only visiting Eliphas Levi in Paris, but also the American Rosicrucian Paschal Beverley Randolph in 1854.

In 1875, and three years after, Hockley would apply and be accepted into the Metropolitan College of the SRIA (London). Although not a regular attendee Hockley did present at one meeting the Rosicrucian certificate and diary of Sigismund Bacstrom,[172] two documents that Hockley made several copies of, the original of which would later be in the possession of the Theosophical Society, but destroyed by fire in the late nineteenth century, luckily not before copies were made by Hockley in 1839.[173]

Hockley possibly remained distant from more involvement within this particular college as a result of a brief period of distain he felt towards Kenneth Mackenzie, a man he thought harboured grand personal desires to seize control of SRIA in the hopes of transforming it into a more 'magical' Order. This coupled with the fact that Hockley's knowledge and abilities far outweighed many of the other members, which would have left him feeling perhaps rather unsatisfied and indifferent.

He would remain distant from the many of the Orders, fraternities and mystical societies that began to flourish during Hockley's time, having no dealings with them, with the exception of one, the Fratres Lucis, also known as 'The Brotherhood of the Cross of Light' or the 'Order of the Swastika.'

---

[172] Sigismund Bacstrom (c.1750-1805) a doctor, surgeon, and a notable artist of the early Maritime Fur Trade. He was also a prominent author and translator of alchemy and Rosicrucian texts.

[173] Harvard University bMS 677, 'Admission of Sigismund Bacstrom into the Fraternity of the Rosicrucians.'

The Fratres Lucis originated in 1873. Between the 31st of October to the 9th of November of that year, F G Irwin, through the use of his son Herbert and the crystal, recorded the history and rituals of the Order,[174] as supposedly dictated to them by the shade of the late Count Cagliostro himself.[175] According to the Count, the Order was first established in 14th century Florence and spread to Rome, Paris and Vienna. It also enjoyed the membership of such notable individuals as Vaughan, Fludd, Comte de St. Germain and many more including Cagliostro. The 19th century Order was set up to study the many faceted aspects of magic and mysticism, however it was never established how often the few members would actually meet, and it was very possible that it only existed on paper rather than as an actual working fraternity. The known members of the Fratres Lucis included F G Irwin, Kenneth Mackenzie, Benjamin Cox and Frederick Hockley.

Figure 42: Hockley's family crest drawn by himself and appearing on several of his manuscript flyleaves such as Sibley's *Uranoscopia* in the Wellcome.

Although this Order has been claimed to have been the prototype on which the Hermetic Order of the Golden Dawn was based, W. Wynn Westcott was rejected for membership due to the "dislike & mistrust" the other members had for Westcott's motto of *Sapere Aude* ('Dare to Know'), as recorded by Capt. E. J. Langford Garstin (a later member of the Golden Dawn) in a letter to Gerald Yorke in 1950. Hamill suggests that "perhaps this refusal was the spur to Westcott concocting the Golden Dawn."[176]

Hockley himself is never recorded in any of his known correspondence or personal letters making any reference to his involvement in the Order, and the only proof of his membership as such is derived from a letter to Irwin from Benjamin Cox in which is written "I was very sorry to hear of the death of Bro. Hockley. There is now one member less of the Order of [a Swastika]."[177]

As previously mentioned, although Hockley had no direct involvement with most other

---

[174] Anon (Herbert Irwin), *Book of Magic*, Society of Esoteric Endeavour 2014, 1st Edition.

[175] Count Alessandro di Cagliostro (1743 –1795) an Italian adventurer and self-styled magician and Freemason. Sibley was briefly in touch with Cagliostro through their mutual interest in Mesmer.

[176] John Hamill, *The Rosicrucian Seer*, Teitan Press, 2009, page xxii.

[177] Ibid. The swastika is left facing and should not be confused with the emblem used in Nazi Germany which was inverted and faced right.

fraternities or Orders, the ones that were to follow after Hockley's demises were indeed touched by him, albeit indirectly. Hockley added to many people's lives with either his personal knowledge, or through access to his manuscript copies or his library. These individuals and friends would go on to become prominent members in such magical groups such as the Hermetic Order of the Golden Dawn in which Westcott himself would refer to Hockley as a "major influence" in the creation of the Order.

As far as Hockley's source of inspiration goes, a pivotal influence would have been Ebenezer Sibley. Certainly many of the works copied by Hockley either for himself, or for a commission from Denley, were drawn from Sibley's old library. Francis King in his work *Ritual Magic in England* suggests a direct line of transmission from Sibley passing to Francis Barrett and from there through one of Barrett's pupils to Hockley.[178] This does seem rather questionable. Indeed Hockley knew of Barrett but appears to have had a rather poor opinion of him and his magnum opus *The Magus,* stating in one of his papers that:[179]

> The above which is an abridgment of the title sufficiently gives the scope of the work which consists of an unacknowledged compilation from other Authors. In fact, all that is of real value is taken from C[ornelius] Agrippa & the Clavis or Key to unlock the Mysteries of Rabbi Solomon, and an ancient Work on Telesmata of great rarity which only exists in MS of which, however, there are a large number of copies extant. For compiling this book my late friend John Denley, the Occult Bookseller of Catherine Street, lent Barrett the whole of the materials, and my friend complained that B[arrett] never recompensed him even with a copy. At the sale of Lackington's stock in 18[18] Mr Denley brought the MS blocks, plates and copyright, which were for several years in my possession. Barrett, notwithstanding his professorship of Magic, lived and died in poverty.[180]

The later years of Hockley's life were increasingly busy with his involvement in various groups and activates taking up a considerable amount of his free time, something which in turn seemed to afford him little opportunity to rest at home. Indeed his home life itself was particularly unstable due to the curious fact that he would frequently move from residence to residence, without any recorded provocation or reason. Suffering from severe migraines and insomnia, his health started to deteriorate in his final years, and on the 10th of November 1885 at the age of 77, Frederick Hockley passed away at 1 Vernon Chambers, Southampton Row, London.

Hockley's cousin, present at the time, stated that his death was a result of "natural decay and exhaustion."[181] Hockley's Will was concise and to the point: it was proved at £2,033. His remaining assets are sometimes quoted at a little more than £3,500 in monies,

---

178 King, *Ritual Magic in England: 1887 to the Present Day,* NEL, 1973.
179 The late Gerald Yorke's notes copied from the collected papers of Frederick Hockley in the possession of the late John Watkins.
180 John Hamill, *The Rosicrucian Seer,* Teitan, 2009, p. x.
181 John Hamill (2009), page xiii.

household goods, library (books and manuscripts), crystals and mirrors. This was to be distributed amongst his remaining (distant) relatives after his library was sold.

James Burns & Co. were recorded as having purchased Hockley's crystals and mirrors, but sold them onwards shortly thereafter.

As for Hockley's truly spectacular library, which he himself claimed to exceed 1000 items at one period, the majority of it was purchased by George Redway,[182] who prepared a 40 page catalogue entitled *A List of Books Chiefly from the Library of the Late Frederick Hockley, Esq. Consisting of Important Works Relating to the Occult Sciences, both in Print and Manuscript,* 1887. Parts of Hockley's library are also listed in a second 44 page catalogue prepared by Redway in 1889 entitled *A Catalogue of a Portion of the Valuable Library of the late Walter Moseley Esq.* Likewise on 6th of April 1887 an auction held by Sotheby, Wilkinson & Hodge was also reported to have sold selected works from Hockley's library. Indeed Sotheby's would go on to sell more of Hockley's works at auctions occurring in more recent times such as a sale of several manuscripts on the 13 December 2007.

Today Hockley's library, one of his most treasured possessions has been scattered to the winds, having been split up through auctions or private sales or donated to libraries and universities around the globe. Many of his manuscripts have been accounted for and even published in recent times but more still remain hidden or simply forgotten, indeed even his copious volumes of personal notes and journals containing the results of his lifelong experiments with crystals and mirrors have vanished, with the exception of several volumes in the Harry Houdini collection at the Library of Congress. Other volumes are held in Freemason's Hall, courtesy of the SRIA. Perhaps other examples were destroyed by someone ignorant of their value and worth. The one thing that is without question, and cannot ever be forgotten, is the profound contribution Frederick Hockley made to the revival and dissemination of magic during the period in which he lived, an effect that is still felt today by collectors, scholars and magicians alike.

The obituary written by Thomas Shorter on November 28, 1885 said this of Hockley:

> Mr. Frederick Hockley, after some years of illness and pain, passed away November 10th, in his seventy-seventh year, at his residence in Vernon Chambers, Bloomsbury. He maintained throughout his life and an uninterrupted and active interest in Occult science, commencing more than half a century ago with astrology. Then the study of the phenomena of animal magnetism prepared him for the intelligent comprehension of the subject of Spiritualism... The communications which he received through the mirror - one of his mediums being a most remarkable seeress - were carefully recorded by him and bound up in volumes to form part of his extensive library, which included works in every department in Occult science, including rare works on astrology. It is hoped that his library may be kept intact.

---

[182] George William Redway (1859–1934) was a bookseller who also began publishing in 1884, and later joined with the publisher Kegan Paul in 1889.

Francis George Irwin (1828-1892)

Figure 43: Major F. G. Irwin (1882-1892) with medals and Masonic apron.

Francis George Irwin was born in Armagh, Northern Ireland on the 19th June 1882, the son of Robert Irwin (a sapper in the Royal Sappers and Miners,[183] and his wife Ellen McAuliffe.

More commonly referred to as Major Irwin, his life remains somewhat enigmatic. At the very early age of fourteen, Irwin enlisted in his father's regiment of the Royal Sappers and Miners in Kent in 1842. From the time served here he would obtain the rank of Lance-Corporal.

In 1851 Irwin married his wife Catherine by which he would eventually have one son, Herbert F. Irwin. In that same year he participated in the Great Exhibition,[184] held at the Crystal Palace (Hyde Park) in May, for which he won a bronze medal certificate signed by Prince Albert.

It was not, however, until sometime much later that Major Irwin's involvement in Freemasonry and like-minded fraternities, would really establish his name, particularly in matters of the occult, which was his true passion.

In 1856 Irwin was sent to the Crimea with his company and from there eventually transferred to Gibraltar with the position of Sergeant in the Royal Engineers.

It was here that Irwin would obtain the rank of Major and remain until a brief posting in Malta, before finally returning to England in 1865. In 1866 after serving in the military for close to twenty-four years, Irwin was given the post of Adjutant to the 1st Gloucestershire Engineer Volunteer Corps located at Bristol where he had moved to that year.

---

[183] 'Sappers and Miners' are terms used for combatant soldiers who perform military engineering tasks such as demolition, breaching fortifications, bridge-building, tunnelling etc.
[184] The Great Exhibition of the Works of Industry of All Nations was the first in a string of World Fairs in the UK exhibiting works of culture and industry.

Major Irwin became a Freemason on the 3rd of June 1857 when he was initiated into the Rock Lodge, No. 325, Gibraltar. As a devoted attendee Irwin would go on to join many of the Masonic Orders available in England at that time, and would become Chief Adept of the Bristol College of the Societas Rosicruciana in Anglia.

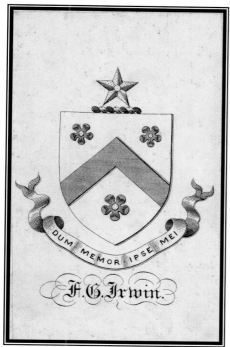

Figure 44: Major Irwin's book plate as used before the death of his son in 1879, after which a book plate with a memorial inscription to his son was used instead.

Considered by many to be students of Frederick Hockley, the Irwins both enjoyed a strong and fruitful relationship with their friend and mentor. Major Irwin, just like Hockley, also indulged in the habit (or perhaps addiction) of collecting and copying manuscripts concerning the esoteric, a habit which helped to fuel his insatiable thirst for knowledge, particularly on matters concerning spiritualism. It was from this interest and the instruction and teaching received from Hockley that, in 1873, with the help of his son Herbert as seer, the Irwins were able to form the Fratres Lucis, a secret Order as directed by the spirit of Count Cagliostro through the medium of the crystal.

Tragically Major Irwin's son Herbert passed away at an early age in 1879 due to an overdose of laudanum,[185] which was then an over the counter treatment, which he was self-administering with the hope of calming his nerves, a result of having recently failed his medical student examinations amplified by his highly strung constitution. Completely devastated and broken by his son's demise Major Irwin withdrew from much of his social life and Masonic fraternal activities, instead concentrating more on matters of spiritualism and séances with the hope of contacting his son.

After the death of Frederick Hockley some of his manuscripts ended up in the hands of W. B. Mosley. Upon his death in 1888 the manuscripts were procured by Irwin. Together with some transcripts already made by Irwin from Hockley's working library (whilst Hockley was alive), the new additions of Hockley's works, would have made Major Irwin's collection one of the most noteworthy of his time, containing as it did the remnants of Hockley's once great collection. Of particular importance was the fact that Irwin had managed to make transcripts from Hockley's crystal gazing records.

---

[185] Laudanum was notoriously bitter in taste and contained practically all of the opium alkaloids which included morphine & codeine. Historically it was used to treat a variety of conditions but was most famous for its use as a pain & cough suppressant.

Many of these are currently located in the Library of the United Grand Lodge of England. Although some of these manuscripts would later reportedly help establish the structure of the Hermetic Order of the Golden Dawn, Major Irwin would had no involvement in its foundation, and despite popular belief, was never a member. Major Francis George Irwin died in Bristol on 26 July 1893.

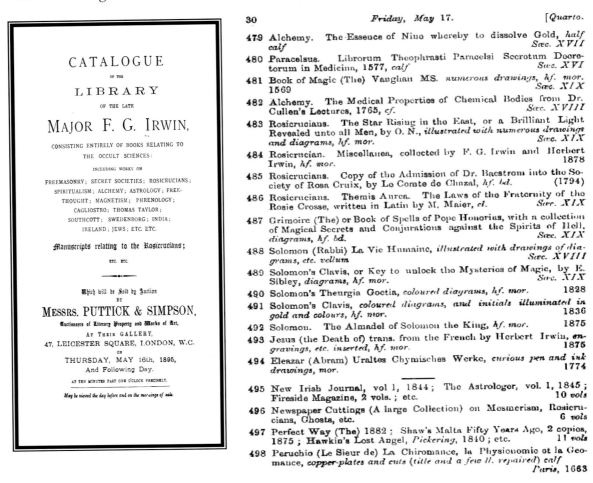

Figure 45: Catalogue of the sale of Major F G Irwin's library on May 16, 1895. Note that Irwin's library contained two manuscript copies of Sibley's *Clavis* (items 489 and 491). One is dated 1836 and illuminated in gold. The other is simply dated as 19th century.

Robert Thomas Cross aka 'Raphael' (1850-1923)

Robert Thomas Cross was born on 15th May 1850 at 2.35am at Brockley Farm, Worstead, East Anglia, England. Originally named Frederick Robert Cross he would later drop the Frederick settling instead for the name Robert Thomas Cross before later in life adopting the pseudonym 'Raphael.'[186]

Married with two sons by the age of twenty-five and living in Westwick, Cross had already developed a strong passion for astrology resulting very early on in life. This in time would lead him into teaching astrology before eventfully becoming the editor of *The Prophetic Messenger*.[187] By the 1870s he had obtained the copyright of *Raphael's Ephemeris*, which the Cross family held until 1985, whereupon it was sold to the publisher W. Foulsham & Co.

Figure 46: The monogram of Robert Cross (Raphael) from the title page of the 1905 edition of his *Guide to Astrology*.

Cross's *Guide to Astrology* which was published in two volumes over a period from 1877 to 1879, was in great demand despite his rather controversial policy of presenting the study of astrology to all walks of society and not just the elite or well-to-do. Cross remained humble in his endeavours, and would shy away from claims of mathematical or scientific prowess often claimed by his peers. By 1893 his printed almanac had reportedly sold in excess of 200,000 copies.

Returning to Worstead in 1885, Cross purchased Lyngate Cottage for the sum of £440 where he set up eight greenhouses to indulge in another passion, the growing of exotic plants, as well as a variety of fruits and vegetables, with many of his orchids being sent for sale in London, and his produce even further afield.

Cross would also remain very active in his community, from serving as church warden for several years, to working on the local coal board, distributing coal during the cold winter months. He was even renowned for owning some of the very first motor vehicles in the country, from steam driven models to the eventual arrival of early petrol powered vehicles.

Cross's most recognized achievements would be his work in astrology, and other esoteric matters. After becoming the seventh person in line to take up the title of 'Raphael,' Cross

---

[186] Not to be confused with Robert Cross Smith (1795-1832) who was the first in a long line of astrologers to use the pseudonym of "*Raphael*."
[187] later renamed *Raphael's Ephemeris*.

became a prolific writer, and at one stage even advertised 'The Society of the Most Ancient Magi - Institute for the especial purpose of advocating Astrology in its purity and for the spreading of occult knowledge,' a group which he hoped would help further his ideals. Sadly this was not a lucrative venture as it resulted in little participation.

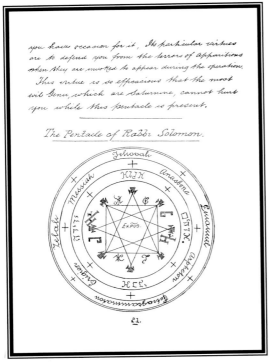

Figure 47: A page from *The Art of Talismanic Magic* by Raphael first published in 1880. This is clearly taken from the *Clavis*. See page 11.

The year 1889 would also see Cross advocate the formation of another group in his *Raphael's Almanac*, this time an Astrological Society, a suggestion which would take shape on the 14th of January 1896 with the Society being founded by Alan Leo[188] as president and Cross as vice-president.

Cross, or Raphael as he was better known, was a man known to be very vocal within the circles of astrology. He was not afraid to present his opinion and his name appeared repeatedly in the periodicals of the time. He was however probably less known for his contribution to magic. His best known work in that area was:

Raphael's Ancient Manuscript of Talismanic Magic, Containing Nearly One Hundred Rare Talismanic Diagrams, Seals of Spirits, Charms, Magical Squares, and Pentacles for the Orations and Invocation of Elementary Spirits, and the Magical Ritual of Their Conjuration. Recondite Wisdom by Raphael [Being Selections from the Works of Rabbi Solomon, Agrippa, F. Barrett etc.], 1879.[189]

His contribution in these areas may be less obvious but no less important. Robert Cross (the seventh *Raphael*) passed away in 1923. He was 72 at the time.

---

[188] William Frederick Allan *aka* Alan Leo (1860-1917) A prominent British astrologer, author and publisher. Often referred to as "the father of modern astrology."
[189] Later reprinted (pirated) by De Laurence in Chicago in 1916.

Full Transcription of the *Clavis*

Editorial Conventions observed in the Transcription

We have kept the transcription as close as possible to the original text, including the spelling, punctuation and capitalisation. We have used bold to represent the faux black letter which has mostly been reserved for angelic and god names. Square brackets have been used to introduce clarifications, as are all footnotes marked with '- Ed.' All other footnotes are part of the original text. We have not attempted to represent the position of illustrations but have marked the page numbers in square brackets so location of the corresponding illustration should not pose too much of a problem.

For reading clarity we have indented all passages meant to be spoken, and enclosed then in quote marks, features that are not part of the original manuscript. Because of the sheer size of this grimoire, narrower margins and more compressed type have been used.

Frontispiece

1, 2. The two Seals of the Earth, without which no Spirit will appear.

3. Magic Wands & Sword.

4. A Great Character. 5. The Greatest Character. 6. Magic Circle.

7. Magic Knife reversed. 8. Engraving tools.

9. Seal. Whosoever beareth this sign, all Spirits will do him Homage.

10. Seal, Whosoever beareth this sign need fear no foe.[190]

---

[190] A clearer interpretation of these captions might have been:

1. Triangle in which spirit should appear. 2. Lamen to be worn on breast of magician. 3 Magic Wands & Sword.

4. Hexagram. 5. Folded Pentagram. 6. Protective Circle. 7. Magic Knife, and reverse. 8. Burin and engraver.

9. Pentacle to force the spirits to do homage to the magician. 10. Pentacle to remove fear of foes.

The

Clavis or Key

To Unlock the Mysteries

OF

MAGIC

OF

RABBI SOLOMON

*Translated from The Hebrew into French and from the
French Rendered into English with Additions.*

By Ebenezer Sibley, MD.

*Fellow of the Harmoniac Philosophical Society at Paris
Author of the Complete Illustration of Astrology.
Editor of Culpepper's Complete Herbal,
Placidus De Titus, on Elementary Philosophye.
The whole Enriched with Coloured Figures,
Talismans, Pentacles, Circles, Characters &c.*

The Doctrine of Spirits was universally believed in throughout all ages, both by Philosophers, Patriarchs, Apostles, and Prophets, and approved of by the greatest men the World ever produced. The Testimony of Jacob Behmen, the Teutonic Philosopher, is not the least in Vindication of the truth thereof, viz. in his *Book of the Forty Questions on the Soul,* where he saith when speaking on the spontaneous appearing of the Spirits departed,

"That those Souls which have not attained Heaven, and so stick in the source, in the principle, in the Birth, those have yet the human form and Essence with the works in them; they diligently search out the cause of their Retention, and therefore many of them come again with the Astral Spirits, and wander up and down in their Houses and places of abode, appear in human shape, and desire this and that, and oftimes take care about their Wills and Testaments, and also think to procure the blessing of the Saints, that they may rest, and if their Earthly Affairs do stick in them, they take care many times about their Children and Friends. This condition of theirs continueth so long, till they fall into their Rest, till their Astral Spirits be consumed, then all such doings, care, and perplexities are at an End, and they have then no more knowledge thereof, but see them only in the Wonders of the Magic Art."

He saith also when speaking of the possibility of raising the Spirits of Deceased persons,

"that a living Man hath such power, that he is also able with his Spirit [xx, *2*] to go into Heaven to the separated or departed Souls, and stir them up about some question by a hearty Desire, but it must be earnest, it must be faith that can break open a principle, and this we see in Samuel the Prophet, whom the King of Israel raised up."

But he that would accomplish any of these great things, must take away as much as possible Corpority from things, or else he add Spirit to the Body, or awaken the Sleepy Spirit, or join his Imagination to the Imagination of the Soul of the World, he will never do any great things. Behmen in his *Clavis* (page 21) saith,

"The Spirit of the World is hidden in the four Elements, as the Soul is in the Body, and is nothing else but an Effluence and Working power proceeding from the Sun and Stars, its dwelling from whence it worketh is spiritually encompassed with the four Elements, therefore, he that knoweth how to infuse the propitious Influx of the Stars into things, or the mixture of things may perform wonders, for as the Stars do tie the Vital Spirits to the Bodies, by Light and Heat, so by the same means do they infuse it into the Body"

It is therefore necessary, He that would wish to work in any Magical Operations, that he knows, that neither Soul, Spirit, nor Intelligence can be worked with, but by the means of some living Spirit, for two extremes cannot be joined together without a mean, therefore Demons appear not but after Sacrifices used &c., which must be the Effusion of Human, or some blood of Black Cattle, for they are allured by the Vital Spirits of living Creatures. - So they are put to flight, where sharp and venomous things are used, thus wonderful things in Nature are performed by a due Application of Actives to passives, thereunto disposed, and Jacob Behmen saith in his *Threefold Life* (page 192). After he has finished speaking of External things, "That Heaven, Earth, and <u>Everything Lie in Man</u>." This is clear, if we consider the Materials of which we are composed, as first, our Body is of the [xxi, *3*] earth, Dead, inert and heavy and has no feeling. Second, but Life which is Light, quickeneth, moveth and giveth sense to it, and the Heavens are the sole spring of this Light. Third. The Soul is the Spirit of God being the free Will or understanding, in this is Power, and from which three considerations, we find the Reason of this joining or connection found in a living man whereby he receives such great Power, for the Body void of itself is joined to Light, and through Light or Heat to the Heavens, and by the Heavens to a thin Spiritual substance which is the first mover, and put in motion the Heavens, by which we see in what order things are Created and knit together. Body and Soul being very far substances, very far distant one from another, and have need of a mean or Bond to join such distant substances together and for this purpose, is that thin and Spiritual mean which the Philosophers call Spirit. This Copulating Spirit is more excellent than the Elements, and even answers to Heaven. <u>Aristotle</u> speaks of the proportion thus,

> Like as the virtue of the Heavens is conveyed to the Earth by the Vehicle of Light, so all the faculties of the Soul, viz. Light, Motion, and Sense, are by the help of this bright Spirit conveyed and transferred to the 'Terrene Body,' for the passage from a common Life unto a Magical is no other but a sleep from this Life, and awaking to that.

For those things which happen to the willing and knowing Magician, is the same which happen to the Ignorant and Unwise Men in their falling to sleep, only the Magician by his knowledge doth know when his mind doth meditate of himself, therefore it is he [that] deliberateth, reasoneth, and determineth what is to be done. He observeth when his Cogitations proceed from a Divine and separate Essence, and proveth what order that Divine and separate Essence is, and by this means, he is able by assisting the Essence to bring about all Magical purposes which may be divided into two parts.

[xxii, *4*] One is from God which he bestoweth on the Creatures of Light, such as Love, Justice and Mercy. The second is to such as belong to Creatures of Darkness and delight in Base and Wicked practices. Yet either of them are brought about by various means pointed out in the following Divisions.

First, Magical purposes are brought about by visible Instruments, by which it affects the Invisible Spirit of Visible things, and acts on Simple or Compound Bodies, so as to produce wonderful effects.

Secondly. Magical purposes are brought to pass by Invocation to God alone. This is partly Prophetical and Philosophical, and partly as it were Theophrastical, other things there are, which by reason of the True God are done with the Princes of Spirits that his desires may be fulfilled, such is the work of the Mercurialists.

The Third Method of Exercising Magic, is by means of the Good Angels instead of God, by which means a communication is received from the Most High. Such was the Magic of Balaam. But some make use of an opposite Magic by which actions are produced by the chief of the Evil Spirits, such were they who wrought by the minor Gods of the Heathen.

The Fourth Method of Exercising Magic is performed with Spirits openly face to face which is given but to few! Others do work by Dreams, and other signs, which the ancient[s] took from their Auguries and Sacrifices.

The Fifth Method, method of working, is by Immortal Creatures. Others by Mortal Creatures, as Nymphs, Satyrs, and such like Inhabitants of other Elements as Pigmies, &c.

The Sixth Method, of Magic is performed by such Magicians whom the Spirits serve of their own accord without Art, but, scarcely will attend, being called by those who are not ordained by Nature for that <u>Great Work</u>.

But among the various Species of Magic, we find various Degrees. The First and best is that Magic which dependeth on God alone.

[xxiii, 5] The Second, those who perform Magic by the aid of those Spirits who serve them faithfully of their own accord. The Third is the peculiar property and privilege of Christians who work by the power of Christ which he hath both in Heaven and Earth.

It is therefore necessary, that everyone who practices the Magic Art, attend to the Observations following.

First, that he or they Meditate Day and Night how to attain to the true knowledge of God, not only by his word revealed from the foundation of the World, but also by the Seal of the Creation and Creatures, and the wonderful effects produced by such Visible and Invisible agency. It is also necessary that a Man descends down into himself, and study the Art of Spiritual Attraction and Repulsion, with the Virtue, Measure, Order and Degree of His own Soul. That he is a passionate Lover of Truth, and has strong Faith and Taciturnity, especially that he discloses no secret which the Spirit hath forbidden him as He commanded Daniel to Seal some things, that is, not to declare them in public; So it was not lawful for Paul to speak openly of all things which he saw in a Vision. Scarce any Man will believe how much is contained in this one precept.

We are also to take care that we understand when the Spirits are assisting us in this Great Work, or Business, for He that understandeth this shall be made a Magician of the Ordination of God, that is, such a person who useth the Ministry of the Spirits to bring excellent things to pass.

But in these matters, it is necessary that a Magician undertakes nothing that is Ungodly, Wicked, or Unjust, for whoever sins through Negligence, Ignorance, or Contempt of God, they will by practising this Art, draw upon themselves Swift Destruction.

But if on the Contrary, he is willing to do Justice, Love, Mercy, and walks humbly with his God, he shall be divinely defended from all evil and by joining his Understanding to any Good Spirit may produce what he will, for all things are possible to them that Believe.

E. Sibley

[Part 1. The Clavis]

[1] Clavis or Key
To Unlock the Mysteries of
Magic

[Chap. 1.] What Dispositions those ought to possess who are willing to participate in the Secrets of the Cabalistic Art.

Whoever wishes to make a progress in the Study must take care that no part of it is neglected in all the circumstances that relate to the Mysteries and Operations of this <u>Great</u> <u>Art</u>. It is useless to ask the question, what affinity there is between the <u>Planets</u> and a piece of fair parchment, or a plate of metal whereon several figures are engraved or some Characters produce <u>Effects</u> as admirable as those are which are described in what follows. It is also useless to enquire whether there is any implicit or explicit part in this art, since there is none gone to ask, what Great Men have gone before us in this Science or the wonderful and prodigious things which they <u>have done,</u> whereas it belongs only to you happily to experience it with content.

[2] Chap. 1. Second part.

You must be laborious, and apply yourself with the utmost attention to this <u>Art</u>, and be sober, detached from the pleasures of a debauched Life, that you may not be either Dissipated, or Distracted, for there is no error that you can commit, but will involve in it some serious consequences. You must be learned, or at least Directed by one who is proficient in Astronomy and Elementary Philosophy. You must not be sparing of a little pains, or trouble to make successful progress in this Art. You must pay a proper respect to the recital of Orations, Conjurations, Invocations, and other requisite Ceremonies, and above all be firm and intrepid in the time of Apparitions and Genii, they desire your boldness.

You must be accompanied by some discreet person, who will encourage you, and animate you, for a weak Imagination is apt to be alarmed and to portray unto the mind wonderful Phantoms, which never had an existence. Finally, you must have great Confidence, and a firm hope of succeeding, observing exactly all that is written in this <u>Precious</u> <u>Book</u>, which contains the Mystery of the Society.[191]

Chap. 2.
What is the proper place, also Time for the Exercise of this Great Art.

The attention which is extremely necessary to study without Distraction requires a retired place, and which is remote from the Hurry of Business in order to be adapted to the Nature of Heavenly Genii, and Intelligences[192] which from their Spirituality possess a Divine Nature, are seen and communicated more freely in silence and tranquil solitude. You must have then a small Chamber, or Closet, to which none have access [3] but, [especially not] Women or Girls, who go there to discharge their menstrual infirmities. It must be a place where there are no sumptuous ornaments to divide or distract the attention. It will suffice to have a Table

---

[191] This suggests that Sibley hoped, as did Francis Barrett, to found a Society dedicated to the practice of magic. – Ed.

[192] Spirits and angels. – Ed.

placed, therein, some chairs, and a Chest of Drawers to shut in under lock and key, which is necessary for carrying on this Art. It is also requisite that all this Furniture should be new, at least very neat, and purged by odoriferous perfumes, afterwards sprinkled with water of which I shall speak afterwards, and great care must be taken to keep a proper Utensil for the exigencies of Nature,[193] for this place must be kept with the greatest cleanliness and decency. As to the time adapted to this purpose, the rising of the Sun is the most suitable, because the mind being then undisturbed is less liable to interruption, and not occupied by external objects. If nevertheless, the circumstance, and the situation of the Planet require that it should be [done] in the middle, or the close of the Day, you must remain from the morning, until the Hour of Labour in a state of watchfulness, endeavouring to prepare yourself of everything necessary, that it[194] may be conducted with the precision requisite without losing the time so important to the managing of it well during the Influence of the Star that appears at the operation and the least moment that the Constellation shall endure.[195]

Chap. 3.

Of Matters relating to the Operations and the manner of preparing them Cabalistically. The Talismans, Pentacles, Mysterious Magic Characters, and other Figures, which are the Principal Matters of the Science and may be formed [in] different ways.

You may make them on clean Parchment, or Plate Metal, or Jasper, Agate, or other precious Stones. You must observe that this parchment must be prepared m a manner as shall be afterwards described [4] and may serve the whole indifferently, but it is not so commonly used as Metals, which have a greater affinity to Planets, besides parchment soon gets dirty, and the least spot is capable of diminishing the virtue of the Talisman or the Mysterious Image. The other matters are also essential, they ought to have a relation and bear an analogy to the Planet under the Constellation of which the Cabalistical Figures under the rays of the Sun will be useless, and so likewise will other planets. Lastly, that we should not be deceived by this means we will mention what Metals are under the Seven Planets, viz. **Gold** to the **Sun**. Silver to the Moon. Iron to Mars. Quicksilver to Mercury. Tin to Jupiter. Copper to Venus, Lead to Saturn. It is evident that by these, we are to understand that Gold, suits the operation of Sunday. Silver, the operation of Monday. Iron, the operation of Tuesday. [Fixed] Quicksilver, the operation of Wednesday. Tin, the operation of Thursday. Copper or Brass, the operation of Friday. Lead, the operation of Saturday. The manner in which you should raise a Cabalistical Figure, or a Talisman on the Hour and Day of one of the Seven Planets, it must be done on a small Metal Plate suitable to the Planet. It is indifferent whether the Plate be round or otherwise, provided that it be a regular Geometrical Figure, for you will make all sorts of characters on it. But if you prefer the making use of fair parchment than Metal Plates, you must for a greater certainty of success, take care not to purchase it of certain cheats who mix improper Materials in it, but take the trouble to make it yourself. This then, is the manner in which it must be prepared. It must be of Virgin Parchment. You must be ready on the vigil of St. John the Baptist's Day with a little White Lamb, or Kid of six weeks old. You must lead it to a Fountain, the water of which is clear and

---

[193] A urinal. A better arrangement would be not to use this room at all for toiletry functions. – Ed.

[194] The ritual. – Ed.

[195] You should attempt to complete the operation within the limits of the Planetary hour. – Ed.

flowing, and after having plunged it 7 times to clear it of all sorts of filth, you must cut its throat, with a new Knife, which should be devoted to the operation of this <u>Art.</u> And which has never been applied to any other purpose. Then you must let all the Blood run out with the water of the Fountain, and having cut it you must fix the Hide in the running Water, while you are employed in burying the Body deep enough to prevent its being devoured by Beasts. [5] Afterwards you shall draw the Hide from out of the Water, and prepare it in the same manner as the Manufacturers usually prepare parchment, with the circumstance that everything made use of on this occasion shall never be applied to a profane use. You will find in the sequel of this Book the Orations of the Seven Planets for the Seven Days in the week, which must be recited during this Operation. There is a little Trouble, and subjection to Labour, but we must consider that a Hide prepared with exactness in this manner, is a provision which will last a long time, and if one knows that it will serve according to the rules of this Art, he shall derive great advantage from it, for the Composition of the Talismans and other figures will reward the pains we have taken. When you have finished the preparation of the Skin of parchment, you must cut it in pieces about three inches square, and put them in a new Box, after having wrapped them up properly, in a bit of Taffeta, or white cloth. If you are unable to work by yourself in making this parchment, you may without hesitation employ therein, a wise discreet Workman, but be always present that nothing may be omitted. We have taken notice that this preparation must be begun on the Eve of St. John the Baptist Day, because in the original Hebrew, it is said, it should take place while the Sun is in his Apogee and his greatest Elevation above our Hemisphere, which happens on the twenty third of June. The Metal Plates which must be made use of as well as the Virgin Parchment, you make the Talismans, Pentacles, Characters &c. on are joined after the usual manner, except that they must be dipt quite hot in the water in pronouncing the Speeches and Conjurations which belong to the Planets to which these Metal Plates are subject. Afterwards they must be made even and polished in the best manner possible, and they must be used like the Virgin Parchment, until you have occasion to employ them. The Animals, Birds, Insects, Plants, and other things which you must make use of in the Secret Mysteries of the Cabala ought to be prepared likewise under a favourable Constellation at a good Hour if it happens on the Eve of St. John the Baptist [Day], for it will have a wonderful efficacy in accomplishing all the ends proposed. But take notice of the manner of making Talismans &c. [6] You must remember there will be, Instruments and Utensils which you will stand in need of for these Mysterious Operations which will be the subject of the following chapter.

Chap. 4.
Concerning the Necessary Instruments.

It will be necessary to have a little Box provided, that should be new doubled, with a white Towel, and furnished with a little lock, and fill it with the following Materials. A Long White Robe, or Linen Garment, a cap and stockings of the same Materials. Light Shoes, White Gloves, also a Girdle of parchment or Leather quite new, on which are written the Names of the Planetary Angels and the seven presiding Spirits over the seven days of the Week. All this little Equipage will serve in operations of importance. You must also have some consecrated Ink, (viz. made from the smoke of a Consecrated Wax Candle) also Ink of various Colours suitable to the Seven planets for the purpose of drawing the Mysterious Characters &c. on parchment, these Inks together with several Crow quill pens, or very fine Steel pens proper to write with, a penknife with a white handle, a well tempered Bodkin pointed in the form of a graving tool, a pair of Scissors to be kept in a small square Box. Also another little Box to contain the small instruments, such as a pair of Compasses to draw the circles on the Metal Plates, an Engraver, a burnishing tool, a mould of about three inches in diameter in which to cast the different Metals for the Talismans. You should also have a Box or Drawer to keep the following Materials in, viz. a Flint and Steel proper to light a fire, a Roll of Virgin Wax. You should have in the same Box or Drawer a Phial full of Holy Water, that is to say, such as is used at the Sacred Ceremonies of Easter moreover you must keep in the Box three Knives, one pointed with a white handle and engraven as seen in the frontispiece, one, in the point of which shall be the figure and shape of a sickle, with a Black Handle, moreover you must have a Hazel stick of the [7] length of the Box and about one inch thick, and a little green stick of the same wood of a year's growth, about the same length as the former. You must likewise have another small Box containing little packets of Perfumery suitable to the Seven Planets, and according to their several Destinations, also a little Chafing Dish made of Earth, or some other matter, with new coals to make a fire on necessary occasions, and for the incense and fumigations, also a Ladle in which to melt the different Metals. It is necessary to have a pair of Compasses of sufficient Radius to Draw the Circle according to the Model in the frontispiece, of at least seven feet in Diameter, also a piece of new Twine attached to a piece of Consecrated Chalk or Charcoal to trace with accuracy the Grand Figures that it will be necessary to make on the floor, which must be perfectly clean and even for the purpose. For these things are important and necessary for conducting the <u>Grand</u> <u>Cabalistic</u> <u>Art</u>.

Chap. 5.
Concerning the Influences, and Secret Virtues, which the Different Situations of the Moon Produce, requisite to be known and understood in this Art.

Wise men have called the Sun and Moon the Eyes of Heaven, being willing to express by their appellation what the Creator of the Universe hath given to those two Planets a principal inspection, and above all that which they make in the Works of Nature. It is for this reason they have judged it important to take notice in conducting the operations, that these two Heavenly Luminaries have some benign Influence by their favourable Conjunction, and are not contrary by the opposition, or aspect of bad auguries. The Moon is the first and principal receptacle of the Influences of the Sun, she passes every month through her Heavenly Orb, and is often found in Conjunction with the Sun and [8] other planets. In order to suc[c]eed then in an exact view of her motions, and to know that they are benign, as I have before said, we must make use of an *Ephemeris*, or of the advice of a skilful *(sic)* <u>Astrologer</u>.

The most exact observers remark that the Moon commences her gradations by the Head or Sign of the **Ram**, and at the time of her Influence indicates prosperity in Voyages or Business Talismans and Characters that are formed at the <u>point</u> of this Constellation are preserved from Danger, when the Moon is in the middle of this Constellation, she has an Influence over Riches and Discovery of Treasures and this point is favourable to make Talismans and Characters but chiefly if in a benign aspect, with **Jupiter** who is the sovereign disposer of fortunate events. When she is arrived at the head of the **Bull**, her Influence on the Talismans and Characters, tends to the Ruin of Buildings, Fountains, to the Breach of Friendship, and of Marriage Contracts. Twenty-five minutes after she has passed the sign of the **Bull**, she produces perfect Health and a Disposition to acquire science to obtain the favour of persons of Distinction, and if in this state, she is in Conjunction with **Venus**, the Talismans and Characters will be so much the more favourable. It is an excellent sign to cause love by the assistance of Secrets to be given hereafter. When the **Moon** makes a Conjunction with **Castor** and **Pollux**, this sends a favourable Influx, it makes them successful, and renders those Invulnerable who bear the Talisman Mysterious figures or Characters formed under the auspicies of that Constellation. The Moon continuing her course and finishing the first part of her Revolution, is productive of good Influx, afterwards entering the sign **Cancer,** which the Ancients have called **Alnaza**, which is to say a Dark House, she diffuseth some influences, to cause Conquerors to succeed, and other such dangerous attempts if nevertheless she is in a benefiting or benign aspect of **Jupiter**, or **Venus**, or **Mercury**, the Talisman shall be favourable to Love, Gaming, and the Discovery of Treasures. When she enters the sign **Leo**, if she be in aspect to Saturn, [9] she has an Influx on all fatal undertakings, tho[ugh] seldom to avert their evils, but on the contrary being advanced in this sign, and ready to depart from thence, she is liberal in all kinds of prosperity, and continues so even into the sign of the **Virgin**, at least if she does not find herself in aspect of the mournful and Melancholy Planet Saturn. In the manner in which Talismans and Characters direct their course under this Constellation are advantageous to Gamesters, Travellers, Lovers, and all who aspire after Great Honours.

Her entering in the sign **Libra**, which the Cabalists have called **Algarpha**, favours much the search after all kinds of Treasures, Metals, and Fountains, and when she is passed to **Scorpio**, she is Invincible to Travellers, and to those who are married [on her way through **Sagittarius** her Influence is fortunate to those who are married][196] and enter into social Intercourse. When she arrives at the sign **Capricorn**, favoured with the Auspicies of **Jupiter** or **Venus** she Influences Health, and the Love of the Fair Sex [and as she passes through **Aquarius**][9] in the manner in which Talismans and Characters raised under this Constellation, have a tendency to unravel difficult points, and to hinder the evil occurrences to which Marriage is liable and to keep up a friendly Correspondence between Married People. Finally the Moon being arrived at the last sign which the Cabalists call **Albotham Alchalha** which signifies Heavenly Poison[197] [**Pisces**] there is only the evil Aspect of Saturn to fear for those who will raise Talismans &c. under this Constellation, for provided it be favourably guarded by **Jupiter, Venus,** or **Mercury** she Infallibly governs Health, Honour, and good success in Gaming. This is what every one must study who wishes to succeed in the use of this Occult Art. Happy is He who is able to profit from discovery made by the Ancient Sages, by a Laudable Experience of those properties which are peculiar to the Stars. They will have very little trouble in discovering these Mysteries, and by means of these <u>Figures</u> will effect surprising things.

[10] Chap. 6.

Of the manner of working the Figures of Talismans and Characters &c., according to the Rules of Art.

They who have not yet practised the Mysterious Figures of the Occult Science, ought to begin by the Eight Pentacles, the figures of which they shall see in the Sequel of the Work.[198] To know where are the twelve great

---

[196] Restored by reference to Weiser MS. – Ed.

[197] 'Fishes' not 'poison' would have been the correct translation of 'poisson.' In other words Pisces. – Ed.

[198] This refers to Part 2. – Ed.

names of God, and the Seven other Names which are at the head of every Day of the Week, and done in Honour of the Genii,[199] who preside over the Seven Planets to whom they have appropriated every day of the week, they may do it as before said on Virgin Parchment, or on Metal, or whether he [the operator] may choose to commence his operations on a happy Constellation of the Stars let them be in a benign aspect to proceed therein with success. The Operator must retire into a secret place destined to the Mysteries, sequestered from the Intrusion of a busy World, there he must be Invested with a white Garment and the other ornaments before mentioned. Afterwards he shall sprinkle the Secret Chamber, and the Table on which he shall work, with Holy Water in reciting the Orations, Invocations, and Conjurations proper to the Day of Operation, and which agree with the Genii who ought to preside there. The Holy Water must be used on the Instruments and Materials employed in the operation afterwards, as soon as you begin to draw upon the Metal or Virgin parchment, the proper Characters that you intend to make in order to facilitate the undertaking.

You will find a great number of Models with various Engravings and with an Explanation of their Virtues and Properties. Observe, if you work on this Virgin parchment you must have a Raven's or Crow Quill pen or at least employ a very fine Steel pen, (and prepared in the manner aforesaid) some new Ink in your Box, and if you work upon Metal you must have punches, or Engraving Tools in the same Box. You must write or engrave the proper Characters very distinctly in the Circles, which you have formed with the Compasses belonging to the Art.

[11] Plate I - Grand Pentacle of Solomon

[12] The Pentacles are commonly chased with a Double Circle of the Mysterious Names of God, or of a passage of Holy Scripture, signifying what you desire to obtain by the Pentacle. For Example, if you be engaged in the Pursuit of Riches, or Honours, you must put in the Double Circle of the Pentacle, these words (*Gloria et Divitiae in domo ejus*)[200] and in the Centre of the round, you must Engrave with Sym[m]etry and proportion the Characters of the Planets, under which you form the Pentacles, the Models of which will be given in their place, and will explain it more fully. In order to proceed Methodically, and without confusion in this Book of Instruction, you may begin by making the Eight Pentacles, and you must place one of the said Pentacles at the Head of the Day which it governs, and that of Solomon commonly called the Great Pentacle at the Head of all. It ought to be made with much exactness, because it must be present at all the Operations of the Great Art. You must choose the Happiest Constellation of the whole year to work wherein, and particularly the Spring Season, when all Nature seems to wear a new Form. You may work any Day of the Week except Saturday, because this Day is not in common being under the Mournful Influence of Saturn. In the foregoing page [page 11], you have the Model of this Mysterious Pentacle. When you have perfectly finished it, you must wrap it up very properly, in a bit of Silk, Stuff, or new White Linen Cloth and shut it in a Box to be ready when you have occasion for it. Its particular virtue is to defend you from the Terror of Apparitions, when they are Invoked to appear during the Operations. The Virtue of this Wonderful and Mysterious Pentacle is so efficacious, that the most Evil Genii, which are Saturnine cannot hurt you while it is present.

---

[199] Spirits. – Ed.

[200] Glory and wealth will be in his house.

[13] Chap. 7.
Concerning the Hours of the Day and Night for the Seven Days of the Week and their respective Planets which Govern them.

It is not sufficient to observe here the Hours of the Day and Night through the whole Week with the planets that govern them, it is not enough that you know that the First Hour of every Day begins at Sun rising, but that you be warned that the Sun rises sooner, and Later at different [times of the Year, and at different] places according to the different Degrees of the Climate.[201] From which you may see, that it is not without Reason that [it has been said] after the most skillful Master of the <u>Great Art</u>, you may know that it is very necessary for those who will be exercised in the Practice of this Wonderful Science, that he or they ought to understand Astrology and also Arithmetic. You will find in the Sequel of this work,[202] Cabalistic Tables, which contain the Mysterious Names of the Angels who preside over every Hour of the Day and Night, and likewise the Names of the Hours of the Seven Planets. It is again necessary to caution you against waiting for a favourable Hour before you prepare for the Operation, for everything must be ready that you may begin to work immediately to gain time, and have leisure to observe properly the different Characters which you must make use of in your Operations.

Observation on Talismans

There is yet something very singular to be remarked on the Subject of Talismans, Pentacles, Characters and Mysterious figures, both in respect to their matter and manner of working in the Circumstances that are essential to the principles of this Art, as will appear in what follows.

[14] Chap. 8.
Concerning the Perfumes that are proper for the Seven Planets for every Day of the Week and the manner of composing them.

We have before observed that you must have among the utensils of the Art, a little New Chafing Dish, either of Earth, or Iron with new Charcoal, and that for the use of the Perfumes, the Fire must be lighted by means of a small Steel and a Bougie belonging to the Art, and if you make use of them when the Talismans &c., are finished, it must be in the following manner. After having sprinkled them with Holy Water, of which it has before been spoken, you must throw on the Fire a Pinch of Perfume or Incense which belongs to the planet, the name of which is above the Work, when you recite the Invocations &c., and you must observe this afterwards on Speaking of the Days, beside that you may not imagine it to be a Chimerical Ceremony, for it is too certain that the Airy Spirits which are destined by the Creator to the Service of Men may be drawn by Perfumes, and on the contrary, Evil Spirits may be kept from you by the Vapours of these [noxious] Perfumes, and this may be seen in the *History of Tobit* in the sacred pages, where the Angel who guides him orders that when he shall be in the Chamber with his Wife, he shall not fail to make a perfume on the Burning Coals, with a persuasion that he shall draw up a Fish by the Secret Virtue of these perfumes, the Evil Spirit who injured his Wife, can

---

[201] i.e. at different latitudes. – Ed.

[202] Part 2. – Ed.

no longer hurt her, and shall be driven from the Nuptial Chamber.

Chap. 9.
Concerning the Orations, Invocations, and Conjurations for every Day in the Week.

The true followers of the Grand Art, and the Lovers of the Secret Science, ought not to content themselves with Reciting Orations &c., only during the time of the Operations, but they ought to repeat them exactly every Day, whether [15] they are engaged or not in the Operation. This hath been the practice of all who have been successful in this Art, upon which we must observe, that these Orations ought to be recited with the face turned towards the East, and with great attention. You will find them with the Days of the Week.

Chap. 10.
Concerning Orations in the form of Exorcisms to Consecrate all the things which belong to the Operation of this Grand Work.

These sorts of Operations in the form of Exorcisms, are only performed but once; that is to say, on the first of the Cabalistic Operations, and when it hath not been Consecrated either by ourselves or any other.

You must on a little Table, covered with a white Linen cloth, have some very clear Spring Water in a Delf[t] Dish, and some new Charcoal in another which is proof against the Fire, and this Fire must be kindled by striking the flint to make a fresh fire, and when it shall be lighted, you must repeat over the Fire, and Water the following Oration in making the sign of the Cross which is marked thus ✝

"**O Theos** Omnipotens qui de nihilo mundum Condidis tua erratum [creatum] Cuncla [cimcta] erastiper [creasti per] virtutem tuorum ineffabilium nominum **Jehovah, Erigion, Adonay, Elohim** da his Creatur is ✝ ✝ quas ad nostrum usum condidisti talem efficaciam ultabica eumia [utalia omnia] possint pirid ficape [purificare] et sanctificare per aspersinem et adustioneri sic te precor et oro **Tantos, Tautayon, Barachedi, Gedita, Imator, Igeon**, Amen."

This being finished, you must sprinkle the Consecrated Water on the Fire and having put a little Storax or Benzoin into the fire you shall perfume the water with it afterwards you shall begin to Purity the Closet or Secret Chamber appropriated to these operations, and you must Sprinkle this place with scented water, saying,

[16] "**Agathos** misericors **Agathos** potens **Agathos** terribilis qui per tuum cherub **Sachiel,** Autuum **Romphed** proteplastum peccatorem expulisti exparadiso deliciarum Paniter expelle ex hoc loco cureto useiva et hunc sanctifica munda et pristo ut sit idorens meis operationibus et delectabilis bones spiritibus quos invocabe ad mea ujuranem sic te precor **Tautos, Taytayon, Barachedi, Gedita, Igeon.** Amen."

After this you must put on a little Table everything that is necessary for the operation, which has been described in the beginning of this Work, sprinkling them with Holy Water and Perfumery three different times, saying the Oration as follows:

"**Athanatos** sapientissime artisex qui servo tuo dedestint justins febricar omnia que adsum tabenaculi debebant inservi et a sanctificaret impende his Omnibus Instrumentis et alius rebus hic precentibus talem virtutem et efficaciam ad mitei operanti selicter enservant ✝ ✝ sicti precor **Tautos, Tautayon, Barachedi, Gedita, Igeon.** Amen."

When it shall be necessary to consecrate anything afresh according to the Cabalistic Custom you must use the Ceremonies before mentioned.

The following mentioned Tables must be attended to, the first contains the Hours of the Day and Night for the whole Week and the good Genii who preside at every Hour (see the plate [II]).
The Hours of the Day and Night of Sunday (see the plate [III]).
The Mysterious Characters of the Sun in three Columns or Lines (see [the] plate [III]).
Sunday being the first day of the Week and Governed by the Sun you may begin by making the Pentacle of the Sun in the Hour of the Sun on a plate of pure Gold, or on Virgin Parchment, taking great care that the Lines of the Circle and the Characters and Names therein be plainly drawn engraved or written.

[Part 2. The Pentacles]

[17] Pentacle for Sunday under the Sun

This Pentacle of the Sun represents in its first Interior Circle the Names of the Four Heavenly Genii who prevail according to the Influence of the Stars on Sunday, which must be invoked during the Operations that are performed on this Day. **Arcan Rex** [Varcan Rex] is the most Noble of the four, and he whom you must Invoke the first in Turning towards the East, and the other three, in turning towards the other three quarters of the World in pronouncing respectively the Invocations &c., that belong to Sunday and which are hereafter described. The second Circle of the Pentacle represents the Names of several Heavenly Angels and Genii who have influence over different Hours. You will also see in this Second Circle, the Seal of the Angel who directs the Planet which you may also Engrave or Write if you choose on the Talismans, or Cabalistic Figures which you make use of. You will see in the third Circle the Venerable Names of <u>God</u>, which you must pronounce during the Operation, and what is said of this Pentacle for Sunday will serve as an Explanation for all the other Pentacles of the Week.

[Composition of Perfumes for Sunday]

The Perfume to be perfect ought to be composed of Saffron, of the Wood of Aloes, the Wood of Balsam of Myrrh of Caurier [Laurier], and the sixth part of an ounce of these Drugs,[203] add to it a grain of Musk and Ambergris, the whole pulverized and mixed together. After this Confectionary is made in small Seeds which you shall use on Sunday under the Auspicies of the Sun. The Oration, Invocation, and Conjuration for the Sun on Sunday will be given in their proper place.

The Operator must remember that no attention is to be paid to the Ornaments or Embellishments which may be placed around, or in the Figures, but simply to form the Figures plain and correctly.

[18] Oration for Sunday under the Sun.

"Lord **Adonai** who hast originally formed an unworthy sinner after thine Image and likeness to elevate him to the knowledge of profound Mysteries, deign by thy Holy Name which thou hast made known by thy Servant Moses in the Mysterious Tables to Bless and Sanctify all my Operations and Undertakings **Otari bonus Jerablem Judadoe Iophiel Eloy Abrax[as].**"

Invocation

"Come Heavenly Spirits who have the Effulgent Rays of the Sun, Luminous Spirits who are ready to obey the Powerful voice of the Great and Supreme **Tetragrammaton** come and assist me in the Operation that I am going to undertake under the Auspicies of the Grand Light of Day which our Creator hath formed for the use of Universal Nature I Invoke You for these purposes, be favourable and Auspicious to what I shall do in the Name of Him who would bear the Glorious Names of **Amioram Adonai Sabaoth.**"

---

[203] At a time when many medicines were herbal, herbs and drugs were used synonymously in this grimoire. – Ed.

Conjuration

"Happy Spirits who have been Created to behold the face of Him who is seated on the Cherubims I conjure you Genii full of thought in the Name of **Saday Cados Phao Elohim** and by the name of the first Light which is the Sun that you will come and Contribute to the success of the Operation I am undertaking. I beseech you will employ your Power and Virtue in keeping off the Evil Spirits that might overturn the Benign Influence/Influence[s] of my work I repeat my supplication by the Virtue of the Divine Names of **Abaye Radiel Caracaza Amadai**."

[19] If you intend to make a Pentacle which is to raise you to Honour Dignity and Riches, you must use it on a Sunday under the Auspicies of the Sun, or on a Thursday in the Hour of Jupiter, after having observed the time when the Constellation be favourable, which happens often enough in the Spring, and in the beginning of Autumn, and you must take Verses out of the Sacred Writings, according as shown hereafter in the Models.

In respect of the Admirable Talisman about to be given, to Command the obedience of Spirits, in the first face of this Sacred Talisman, you will see in the middle of the square four Holy Names in the small squares, and four others which are in the Double Circle. In the second face or reverse side, is placed in the Middle a Mysterious Name with 7 Letters, the interpretation of which is in the Double Circle drawn a small Hebrew verse on the wonderful subject of the Creation, or the World in the form of a Mystery of which arose marks frequently in the Prodigies that he wrought.

This Sacred Pentacle is taken from the Mysterious Book of Rabbi Hama, which is entitled the *Cabalistical Speculation*. It is of great efficacy when it is made with everything suitable for the operation for Sunday. Its Material is a plate of pure Gold, or of Virgin Parchment which is unadulterated from which you may rest assured of all kinds of prosperity when you are furnished with this Pentacle. It is chiefly good for Honours, Riches and Amorous Intrigues. Rabbi Castor Ben Luca, says that it may be made on Thursday under Jupiter.

The Talisman has two faces (fig [12, Plate VI]) on the first you must engrave the Seal or Character proper to the Familiar Spirit[204] which is **Och** who Directs the Influence of the Planet, and upon the Second [face], is to be engraven the Mysterious Number in small squares, placed so that whatever you read the number, either above or below, or on one Angle, or another, or on the same line to the right, or to the left you will find the same number which is 111. These two Pentacles tend to Conciliate the Spirits of the Sun.

Precious Stones affected by the Sun.

The Egal [Eagle] Stone, the Crysolite, the Stone of the Rainbow, the Jacinth, the Ruby, a stone which [has] the power of attracting other stones as the Magnet draws Iron or Steel.

Trees affected by the Sun.

The Laurel, The Palmer Tree, The Ash, The Ivy.

[20] **Plate II - The Mysterious Cabalistic Names of the Hours of the Day and Night for the whole Week and the good Genii who preside [over] every Hour.**

---

[204] The Olympic spirit. Not a familiar spirit in the normal sense of the phrase. – Ed.

[Day Hours]		[Night Hours]	
1	Yayn	1	Beron
2	Janor	2	Barol
3	Nasnia	3	Thami
4	Salla	4	Athir
5	Sadedali	5	Mathon
6	Thamur	6	Rana
7	Ourer	7	Netos
8	Thamie	8	Tafrac
9	Neron	9	Sassur
10	Jayon	10	Aglo
11	Abay	11	Calerna
12	Natalon	12	Salam

[21] **Plate III - The Hours of the Day and Night on Sunday.**

[Day Hours]			[Night Hours]		
1	☉	Michael	1	♃	Zachiel
2	♀	Anael	2	♂	Samael
3	☿	Raphael	3	☉	Michael
4	☽	Gabriel	4	♀	Anael
5	♄	Cassiel	5	☿	Raphael
6	♃	Zachiel	6	☽	Gabriel
7	♂	Samael	7	♄	Cassiel
8	☉	Michael	8	♃	Zachiel
9	♀	Anael	9	♂	Samael
10	☿	Raphael	10	☉	Michael
11	☽	Gabriel	11	♀	Anael
12	♄	Cassiel	12	☿	Raphael

The Mystical Characters of the Sun for Sunday[205]

Fortuna Major -   - First Characters -   - Fortuna Minore

- Second -

- Third -

[22] **Plate IV. Pentacle for Sunday made under the Sun.**[206] Fig. 1.

[23] **Plate V.**

---

[205] These are the characters generated from the geomantic figures of the planet (in this case the Sun). – Ed.

[206] Actually the floor circle made for Sunday, not a pentacle. – Ed.

[24] **Plate VI.**

[25] **Plate VII**.

[26] **Description and Use of the foregoing Mysterious Figures or Talismans to be made on Sunday in the Hour of the Sun, with observation thereon.**

[Fig.]	[Plate]	[Description/Function]
Fig. [1]	Plate IV	The Pentacle [Circle] of the Sun which must be present during the Operation on Sunday.
Fig. 1	Plate V	Pentacle for Honour and Riches.
Fig. 2	Plate V	Second Model for the same purpose.
Fig. 3	Plate V	A Pentacle for Honours and Dignities.
Fig. 4	Plate V	A Pentacle against Dread and Fear of the Darkness of the Night.
Fig. 5	Plate V	A Pentacle against unclean Beasts and Fishes.
Fig. 6	Plate V	The Character of the Benevolent Planet Jupiter.
Fig. 7	Plate V	The Character of the Fair Planet Venus.
Fig. 8	Plate VI	A Pentacle at the view of which all Spirits are Obedient.
Fig. 9	Plate VI	A Pentacle the reverse of the above.
Fig. 10	Plate VI	Another Pentacle for a similar purpose.
Fig. 11	Plate VI	A Pentacle to Preserve Health.
[Fig. 12]	Plate VI	[The Seal of Och, Olympic Spirit of the Sun]
Fig. 13	Plate VI	A Form similar to which the Spirit of Jupiter sometimes appears.
Fig. 14	Plate VI	A Form similar to which the Spirit of Venus often appears.
Fig. 15	Plate VII	The Mysterious Number of the Sun which is 111. [Kamea of the Sun]
Fig. 16	Plate VII	The same in Hebrew Characters.
Fig. 17	Plate VII	The Seal or Character of the Intelligencies (sic) of the Sun.
Fig. 18	Plate VII	A Form of Regal Dignity in which the Spirit of the Sun often Appears.
Fig. 19	Plate VII	Another Form which sometimes presents itself when Invoked.

General Observation

Notwithstanding all that has been said Concerning the Various Pentacles or Talismans mentioned in this Mysterious Work, the Operator must be reminded that the more exact as to the time, the Composition and the true formation of the Various Lines Characters of the Talismans and Mysterious Figures, he is, the greater will be the certainty of Success, not only that, the more earnest he is in repeating the Orations, Invocations, and [27] Conjurations having great Confidence, that what he earnestly entreats will be granted besides the power, virtue, and efficacy given to these Mysterious Images will greatly depend upon the firmness sincerity and faith of the Operator or possessor of these Invaluable Figures for they will lose none of their virtue and efficacy by being transferred from one person to another, providing the party accepting them adhere to, and believe in their Influence, for depend upon it, that if a person who may possess one or more of these Talismans and has not that firm Confidence required, he cannot expect any good result issuing therefrom. He must be temperate live a good Moral Life if not ~~not~~ a true Religious Life, or he cannot expect prosperity by the Guardianship and Assistance of those Blessed Spirits the bright Messengers of Heaven. Therefore it is evidently true that the more Holy he leads his Life, the more he will be assured of success. It must not be objected for the Operator or possessor of these Talismans to be cautioned against making them public or by telling persons about your possession for as the Agency by which they operate is Invisible, so is the knowledge thereof withheld from all but the Wise and prudent which means not to be made public.

The Operator must also be reminded that the foregoing Talismans under the Sun must be formed of Virgin Gold or Virgin Parchment duly consecrated but if parchment be employed you must either use liquid Gold or Ink of a Yellow Colour to write the Characters &c. the Inks of different Colours suitable to the seven planets are as follows; Yellow or Gold for the Sun, pale red or Silver for the Moon, Red for Mars, Mixed Colours for Mercury, Blue for Jupiter, Green for Venus, Black for Saturn, each of these should be kept in small Vials properly prepared and consecrated and not used for any other purpose but that for which they are designed. Great care must be taken of these Talismans when not in use, they should not be exposed to the eye of the Vulgar.

The following prayer is recommended to be repeated every day during [the time] you are wearing a Talisman –

"O my Good Angel whom God by his Divine Appointment have appointed to be my Guardian Enlighten, Protect, and Direct me."

[28] Pentacle for Monday under the Moon

This Pentacle of the Moon represents to you in the first Interior Circle the Names of the four Heavenly Genii who prevail [on] this Day which must be Invoked for the Operation of Monday. **Arcan** is the principal Heavenly Genii that prevails [on] this day, and which must be Invoked, and is contained in this Pentacle, when therefore you Invoke him, turn yourself towards the East, afterwards, the other Genii by turning to the other quarters. This Apparition is without terror because he appears in an Agreeable Figure. You must Dismiss him and his attendants respectfully when you have obtained what you wish. It is favourable to Riches and Amours.

Composition of Perfumes for Monday

This Perfume, in order to be perfect, must be composed of the following Ingredients, viz. the Head of a Frog, the eyes of a Bull, a Grain of White Poppy, Storax, a Loadstone, Benjamin, a little Camphor, the whole well pulverized, and made into Paste or Dough, made with the Head of young Barley, which you must make use of in your operation for Monday, under the Auspicies of the Moon.

[29] Oration for Monday under the Moon

"All powerful **Anasbone** who hast formed out of Eternal Nature the great Luminary which presides by Night, I pray you by the Intercession of your favoured Genii **Gabriel Madyet Abroy Janiel** that you will direct the benign Influence of the Celestial Bodies in such manner that the Operation I undertake this Day may have the desired Effect and Success, and that I may give Glory and Honour to the Great **Curaniel Hanum Baliel.**"

Invocation.

"Run ye Sublime and Sublunary Genii who are obedient to the Sovereign **Arcan** come and assist me in the Operation that I undertake under the Auspicies of the Grand Luminary of the Night. I invoke you to the purpose, be favourable and hear my Intreaties (*sic*) in the Name of Him who commands the Supreme Spirits which are Superior in the Regions that you inhabit **Missabu Abuzaha.**"

Conjuration.

"I conjure you **Analgui Ophaniel Abym** and all ye Heavenly Quoristers [Choristers] in the Name of the Great Luminary of the Firmament which is the Moon that you will Contribute to the success of the Operation that I am going to Undertake under her Auspicies. Employ your power and Influence in keeping off the Evil Spirits that might hurt me in my undertaking come in haste and defer not your assistance long **Achym Cados Iea.**"

[30] Pentacles and Talisman for Monday

As it often happens that we undertake a journey on Monday, because on that day we have more leisure, for this reason the Ancient Magi and Learned in the Cabalistic Art have thought that a Talisman made on a Monday before such a journey would be propitious to Travellers both by Sea and Land.

You must work them according to, the following Model, and whosoever shall be sufficiently experienced in the Mysterious Science to work with exactness may assure himself, that by the Virtue of This Talisman, he can command the Spirits to carry him in a little time from one place to another a great distance off without the least injury to his Person.

The Materials of this Talisman must be of True Virgin Parchment or a Silver Plate highly polished.

You may make the Talisman (fig 3) on a Monday for the purpose of serving in Amorous Intrigues under the Auspicies of Venus, for although Friday seems under Venus to be destined to that purpose, you may nevertheless be assured if you find the Moon in a favourable situation on Monday, the Talisman you shall then make will be of equal efficacy as if you had worked on a Friday.

The last two Pentacles or Talismans make but one, having two faces, one on which you must Engrave the Seal or Character of the Familiar Spirit of the Moon,[207] and the Director of her Influence. The second [face] on which you must Engrave or write the Mysterious Number of the Moon in several small squares, so that whatsoever side you read, whether from above or below, on one side or the other, being in the same line to the right or to the left or from one Angle to another, the number will always be found the same which is 369.

[31] Precious Stones affected by the Moon

The Beryl, The Diamond.

Trees affected by the Moon

The Poplar, The Female Palm Tree, and the Rosemary.

---

[207] The Olympic Spirit of the Moon. – Ed.

[32] Plate VIII. The Hours of the Day and Right on Monday.

1	☽	Gabriel Arcan	1	♀	Anael Sarabotes
2	♄	Cassiel Maymon	2	☿	Raphael Modiath
3	♃	Zachiel Zebul	3	☽	Gabriel Arcan
4	♂	Samael Samax	4	♄	Cassiel Maymon
5	☉	Michael Varcan	5	♃	Zachiel Zebul
6	♀	Anael Sarabotes	6	♂	Samael Samax
7	☿	Raphael Modiath	7	☉	Michael Varcan
8	☽	Gabriel Arcan	8	♀	Anael Sarabotes
9	♄	Cassiel Maymon	9	☿	Raphael Modiath
10	♃	Zachiel Zebul	10	☽	Gabriel Maymon[208]
11	♂	Samael Samax	11	♄	Cassiel Maymon
12	☉	Michael Varcan	12	♃	Zachiel Zebul

The Mysterious Characters for Monday under the Moon.

- First Characters –

Ab Via – A[b] populo [Populus]

- Second -

- Third -

[33] Plate IX. Pentacle for Monday made under the Moon.

[34] Plate X.

[35] Plate XI.

[36] The Foregoing Pentacles or Talismans must be made of pure Silver highly polished and Engraven distinctly as before directed, or they may be made of Pure Virgin Parchment and Characters &c. written, thereon with much exactness. These Talismans under the Moon must be made on Monday at the first Hour after Sun rising. Should you not have sufficient time to complete your work during the first Planetary Hour. you must wait with patience till the next Hour of the Moon arrives, which is always at the end of every seven planetary Hours counting from Sunrise on a Monday, and so of the rest as each planet governing each day of the week his reign or rule commences at sunrise. A Table will be given in a subsequent part of this work shewing the Length of the Planetary Hour During the Day and Night for all seasons of the Year and in any Climate.

The following Talismans to be made on Monday under the Moon according to the foregoing Models.

---

[208] This should be Arcan. – Ed.

[Plate]	[Fig.]	[Description/Function]
Plate IX	Fig. 1.	Pentacle [Circle] for Monday under the Moon.
Plate X	Fig. 2.	Talisman for Travelling by Sea and Land.
Plate X	Fig. 3.	Talisman for Love.
Plate X	Fig. 4.	Talisman against Earthquake, and to Enchant Treasures.
Plate X	Fig. 5.	Talisman to Enchant Treasures.
Plate X	Fig. 6.	Talisman to have Familiar Spirits at Command.
Plate XI	Fig. 7.	Talisman to have Familiar Spirits at Command.
Plate XI	Fig. 8.	Talisman against Dangers, Travellers are exposed to by Sea or Land.
Plate XI	Fig. 9.	Seal of the Familiar Spirit of the Moon and Director of Her Influence.
Plate XI	Fig. 10.	The Mysterious Number of the Moon.
Plate XI	Fig. 11.	The Mysterious Number of the Moon, in Hebrew Characters.
Plate X	Fig. 12.	Seal and Character of Luna (*Daemonii*)
Plate X	Fig. 13.	Seal and Character of Luna
Plate XI	Fig. 14,15.	Two Characters of Luna (*Daeomonii* [*Daemonii*] *Daemoniorum*)
Plate XI	Fig. 16,17.	Intelligentiae & Intelligentiarum of Luna

[37] Pentacle for Tuesday under Mars

The Pentacle for Tuesday under Mars represents to us in his first Interior Circle the names of the Four Heavenly Genii contained in this Pentacle which governs the Influx of this Star [planet] on Tuesday, which must be Invoked and conjured in the operation of this Day. **Samael** is the principal Governor or Genii contained in this Pentacle. You must Invoke him by turning to the East. You must not be terrified at his appearing any more than the Spirits which accompany [him] though they appear under strange figures. You must Dismiss them with respect, when you have obtained what you want of them. It is favourable to everything belonging to Arms.

Composition of Perfumes for Tuesday

In order to have this Perfume made in perfection it must be composed of the following Drugs, Euphorbium, Bdellium, Sal Ammoniac, Roots of Hellebore, the powder of Loadstone, and a little Sulphur, make of the whole a paste, of the Blood of a Black Cat, and the Brains of a Raven, and afterwards make small Grains which you shall use in the Operation of Tuesday.

Oration for Tuesday

"**Satael** Divine Virtue who causes thy Power to shine in thy enterprises and Combats which take place both by Sea and Land. I pray you by the Interposition of your well beloved **Caimax Ismoli Paffran** that you will deign to Direct the benign Influences of the Planet which governs this Day in such a manner that the Operation I undertake may prove successful and that I may give Glory and Honour to the Great Celestial Genii **Calzas Lama Irel Osael.**"

[38] Invocation

"Come Military and Warlike Genii who have executed the order of the Sovereign Master of the Universe upon the armies of the Rash Sennacherib, come and serve me in the Operation that I undertake under the Auspices of this third and Brilliant Luminary of the Firmament, be favourable to my Intreaties in the Name of Him who commands the formidable Spirits, **Soncas Jaxel Zaliel Guael.**"

Conjuration

"I Conjure you **Elibra Eloym** all your Cohort in the Name of the third Luminary of the Firmament that you will contribute to the Success of the Operation which I undertake this day use all your power to keep the Evil Spirits at a Distance that they may not Counteract the Assistance necessary for any undertaking. I Conjure you in the formidable names of the Governors **Damael Lobquin Saraphiel.**"

The following Pentacle and Talisman to render a Military Life or Employment Happy also one to make one Invulnerable must be made with much exactness, and observe that the Constellation [planet] of Mars must govern the Operation in Conjunction of Mercury, in a favourable Aspect to Venus on a Tuesday and during the Spring Season.

The Last two Pentacles or Talismans (Fig. 10-11 [Plate XI]) make but one, having two faces, on one. You must Engrave the Seal or Character proper to the Familiar Spirit [Olympic Spirit] who Directs the Influx of the Planet Mars, on the other side or face You must Engrave the Mysterious Number of the same Planet in several small squares, so that whatsoever side you read whether above or below, on one Angle or another, it being in the same line to the right or the left, The Number will always be found the same, which is 65.

[39] Precious Stones affected by Mars

The Diamond, The Amethyst, The Carbuncle, The Jasper marked with Red.

Trees affected by Mars

The Box Tree, The Maple Tree.

[40] Plate XII. Pentacle of Tuesday under Mars.

[41] Plate XIII. Hours of the Day and Night on Tuesday.

1	♂	Samael	1	♄	Cassiel
2	☉	Michael	2	♃	Zachiel
3	♀	Anael	3	♂	Samael
4	☿	Raphael	4	☉	Michael
5	☾	Gabriel	5	♀	Anael
6	♄	Cassiel	6	☿	Raphael
7	♃	Zachiel	7	☾	Gabriel
8	♂	Samael	8	♄	Cassiel
9	☉	Michael	9	♃	Zachiel
10	♀	Anael	10	♂	Samael
11	☿	Raphael	11	☉	Michael
12	☾	Gabriel	12	♀	Anael

The Mysterious Characters for Tuesday under Mars.

- Rubeo - - First Characters - - Puero -

- Second -

- Third -

[42] **Plate XIV.**

[43] **Plate XV.**

[44] The Talismans under Mars to be made on Tuesday according to the foregoing Models, they must be formed of Iron, highly polished, and Engraven with much exactness or on fair Virgin Parchment, and the Names and Characters written with Ink peculiar to the Planet.

[Plate]	[Fig.]	[Description/Function]
Plate XIV	Fig. III	Talisman to render a Military Life Happy.
Plate XIV	Fig. 2.[209]	Talisman for Military Expeditions Bad Rencontres [Encounters].
Plate XIV	Fig. 4.	Talisman to make one Invulnerable.
Plate IV	Fig. 5.	Talisman to avoid evil Vexation Country Divisions & Insurrections.
Plate XIV	Fig. 6.	Talisman to make one Invulnerable and inspire Arms.
Plate XV	Fig. 7.	Talisman against Assaults of Traitors.
Plate XV	Fig. 8.	Talisman against Fire Arms and other offensive Weapons.
Plate XV	Fig. 9.	Talisman to defend oneself against Ambushes and Traitors.
Plate XV	Fig. 10.	Pentacle containing the Name and Seal of the Familiar Spirit of Mars.
Plate XV	Fig. 11.	Pentacle containing the Mysterious Number of Mars. 65.
Plate XV	Fig. 12.	Pentacle containing the Mysterious Number in Hebrew Ch[aracters]
Plate XIV	Fig. 13-14.	Seal and Characters of the Intelligencies (sic) &c.
Plate XII	[Fig.] 1.	Pentacle [Circle] for Tuesday under Mars.

The Wearer of these Talismans must again be reminded that the Virtue possessed by these plates of Metals or Parchment is owing to the exactness with which they are formed, also the divine Influences governing at the time of Operation, therefore the more confidence he places in their Influence and the more Secrecy he employs, the greater will be the certainty of success.

[45] Pentacle for Wednesday under Mercury.

The Pentacle under Mercury represents in the first Interior circle, the Names of the four Heavenly Genii who govern the Influence of the Stars on Wednesday, and which you must Invoke in the Operations that are made on that day. **Modiat**, is the principal Heavenly Genii contained in this Pentacle. You must Invoke him in turning towards the East. This Apparition is no more than the Spirits of those which accompany him, and therefore cannot affright those who have the least firmness. You will dismiss them respectfully, when you have obtained their Assistance. They are disposed towards them who are Lovers of Science, and Games of Hazard.[210]

---

[209] Figures 3 (III) and 2 are listed in reverse order. – Ed.

[210] Gambling. – Ed.

Composition of Perfumes for Wednesday.

In order to have the perfume made in a perfect state, it must be composed of the following Drugs, Mastic of the East, Chosen Incense, Cloves, Flowers, or Powder of Agate. Beat it all into powder and make thereof a paste with a Foxe's Blood, and the Brains of a Magpie, and afterwards make thereof Beads, which you shall use in the operation of Wednesday under Mercury.

Oration for Wednesday

"Great and Swift **Parabozath** we pray you to hear our humble Supplication that we make by the Intercession of your favourites the Heavenly Genii **Mathlai, Tarmiel Jerescue Mitraton** that you will be pleased to favour the Operation that I engage in this Day, and that the whole may be performed to your Honour."

[46] Invocation

"Run to me with speed, come ye Spirits who preside over the Operation of this Day, hear favourably the present Invocation that I make to you under the Divine Names of **Venahel, Viemuel, Rael, Abuiori,** be kind and ready to second my undertakings in a manner that shall render them efficacious."

Conjuration

"I Conjure you by the Heavenly name **Elohim**, O ye Heavenly Genii who have power over the wonders that are wrought in this Sacred Day of the fourth Luminary of the Firmament. I Conjure you by all that can Incline you to serve me that you will not Delay coming **Saday, Asaraie, Varathaiel, Ehie,** to remove the Evil and Rebellious Spirits, and cause me by your Influence to succeed in my undertakings."

The following Pentacle and Talisman (Fig. 2) for Wednesday is useful to preserve you from being taken prisoner either by Sea or Land, and its virtue extends ever from Prison those who are confined, and rescuing from Slavery even if reduced to it. You must work under Mercury in a favourable Conjunction of Jupiter or Venus, and on a fine day in the Spring.

It is not only common that Men that have now thought Mercury, presided over Games of Hazard, but many famous Cabalists have been of the same opinion, here in the pages following (Fig. 3) You have a Talisman composed on this subject.

The last two Pentacles or Talismans (Fig. 9, 10) make but one, having two faces, on one, you must Engrave the Seal or Character of the Familiar Spirit who Directs the Influence of the Planet Mercury, and on the Second you must Engrave the Mysterious Number of the same planet, which number you must place in several small squares, so that on whatsoever side you read the number, whether above or below, on one side or the other, or on the same line to the right, or to the left, you will always find the same Number.

[47] Precious Stones under Mercury The Emerald, The Topaz, The Porphyry.

Trees affected by Mercury

The Cornal Tree, the Medlar Tree.

[48] Plate XVI. Hours of the Day and Night on Wednesday.

1	☿	Raphael	1	☉	Michael
2	☽	Gabriel	2	♀	Anael
3	♄	Cassiel	3	☿	Raphael
4	♃	Zachiel	4	☽	Gabriel
5	♂	Samael	5	♄	Cassiel
6	☉	Michael	6	♃	Zachiel
7	♀	Anael	7	♂	Samael
8	☿	Raphael	8	☉	Michael
9	☽	Gabriel	9	♀	Anael
10	♄	Cassiel	10	☿	Raphael
11	♃	Zachiel	11	☽	Gabriel
12	♂	Samael	12	♃	Cassiel

Mysterious Characters for Wednesday under Mercury.

- Conjuctione.-   - First Characters. -   - Ab albo [Albus]. -

- Second -

- Third -

[49] Plate XVII. Pentacle for Wednesday under Mercury.

[50] Plate XVIII.

[51] Plate XIX.

[52] The Foregoing Talismans must be formed on Wednesday under Mercury while he is in a favourable aspect with Jupiter or Venus and if possible in the Spring Season as said before. They must be made of Fixed Quicksilver which is best prepared by Melting a small portion of Tin with it so as to prevent breaking; not omitting to use a small portion of the Perfume suitable to the planet Mercury in the operation of casting or forming the Talisman.

[Plate]	[Fig.]	[Description/Function]
Plate XVII	Fig. 1.	Pentacle [Circle] for Wednesday under Mercury.
Plate XVIII	Fig. 2.	Talisman against Slavery.
Plate XVIII	Fig. 3.	Talisman to favour Games of Hazard.
Plate XVIII	Fig. 4.	Talisman for success of Merchants, Travellers, Students &c.
Plate XVIII	Fig. 5.	Talisman to render one Invincible.
Plate XVIII	Fig. 6.	Talisman to be successful in Games of Hazard.
Plate XIX	Fig. 7.	Talisman to be fortune (sic) in Games of Chance Traffic &c.
Plate XIX	Fig. 8.	Talisman to acquire Eloquence.
Plate XIX	Fig. 9.	Talisman containing the Name and Seal of the Familiar Spirit of Mercury, and the Director of His Influence.
Plate XIX	Fig. 10	Talisman containing the Mysterious Number of Mercury which is 260.
Plate XIX	Fig. 11	Talisman containing the same in Hebrew Characters.
Plate XIX	Fig. 12-13.	Seals and Intelligences of the Planet Mercury.

[53] Pentacle for Thursday under JUPITER

This Pentacle of Thursday represents to you in its Interior Circle the Names of the Four Heavenly Genii who prevail over the Star of Thursday and which you must Invoke and Conjure in the Operation of that Day. **Zebul** is the principal of the Heavenly Genii contained in this Pentacle. You must Invoke Him in turning towards the East, as we have said on speaking of Sunday. You must fear no Evil from this Apparition, because it usually appears in a Magnificent manner its Equipage being like that of a King when crowned, and you must Dismiss it very respectfully, after having obtained what is mentioned.

Composition of Perfume for Thursday

In order to have this Perfume in a state of Perfection, it must be composed of the following Drugs. The seed of the Ashe Tree, The Wood or Shoot of an Aloe, Storax, Loadstone, Benjamin, Powder of Blue, and the end of a Quill, the whole mixed in powder together, in such proportion, as will make the Odour Agreeable; then of this Confectionary, you must make some small seeds, which you must use in the Cabalistical Operation on Thursday under the Auspicies of Jupiter and the Spirits who direct his Influence.

[54] Oration for Thursday

"O Kind and Beneficent **Castiel** who art loaded with Honours and disposeth Riches with a liberal Hand reject not the Prayer that I make unto thee through the Intercession of your well beloved favourites **Maguth, Gutriz, Cachiel, Soheith,** and give to my undertakings such success that I may give you the Glory of it."

Invocation

"Come Speedily ye Blessed Spirits who preside over the Operation of this Day, Come Incomparable **Zebul** and all your Legions run to my Assistance and be propitious to my undertakings be kind and refuse me not your powerful Aid."

Conjuration

"I Conjure you by the Holy Name **Emanuel** all ye Heavenly Genii who second by your Aid the Grand Distributor of Honours Riches and Health. I Conjure you by the Singular Inclination that you try to please those who rely on your Wonderful Power, **O Rael, Miel, Netrapha, Calbat,** be ready here to put to flight all those Spirits which might impede my undertakings."

Observation on the Talismans

Jupiter being one of the most fortunate Planets, you may draw Mysterious Figures under his Auspicies, as well for Gaming at Hazard as under Mercury, because Jupiter governs Kingly Riches. The Model of this Talisman (Fig. 2) which is given hereafter will be very efficacious to render you fortunate chiefly at play, if you work under the Constellation [planet] of Jupiter, or if Jupiter is not in opposition to Mercury, but is favoured with a Benevolent Aspect with Venus. It must be made in the Spring (on Thursday) or some Season when the weather is Serene.

[55] You will have another Talisman for the same purpose, and under the same Constellation, if you travel

[travail] with exactness success will Infallibly follow, it will be very convenient, and I can even say necessary before you Engage in this Game, so recite Orations, Invocations and Conjurations on the Talisman, and to perform some action in Honour to the Genii who directs the Influence of the Planet, as for Example to Distribute Alms in consideration of this, Genii. As to the rest, the Talisman may be made on Wednesday under Mercury, in changing only the Orations, Colours, Characters &c.

The Two Pentacles, or Talismans (Fig. 9-10) make but one, having two faces, on one, You must Engrave the Seal of the Familiar Spirit who directs the Influence of the Planet Jupiter, and on the Second You must Engrave the Mysterious Number of the same Planet, which number you must place in several small squares, so that on whatever side this number whether from above or below, on one side, or angle, or on one side to the left or the right, being in the same line, it will always be the same which is 34.

Precious Stones affected by Jupiter

The Beryl, The Sapphire, The Green Emerald.

Trees affected by Jupiter

The Oak, The Poplar, The Ash Tree, The Fig Tree, The Pear Tree, The Plum Tree, and above all the Filberd Tree.

[56] Plate XX. Hours of the Day and the Night on Thursday.

1	♃	Zachiel	1	☽	Gabriel
2	♂	Samael	2	♄	Cassiel
3	☉	Michael	3	♃	Zachiel
4	♀	Anael	4	♂	Samael
5	☿	Raphael	5	☉	Michael
6	☽	Gabriel	6	♀	Anael
7	♄	Cassiel	7	☿	Raphael
8	♃	Zachiel	8	☽	Gabriel
9	♂	Samael	9	♄	Cassiel
10	☉	Michael	10	♃	Zachiel
11	♀	Anael	11	♂	Samael
12	☿	Raphael	12	☉	Michael

The Mysterious Characters for Thursday under Jupiter

- Ab Acquisitione. -   - First Characters -   - Ab Letititia -

- Second -

- Third -

[57] Plate XXI. Pentacle for Jupiter on the day of Thursday.

[58] Plate XXII.

[59] Plate XXIII.

[60] The foregoing Talismans with the Pentacle for the Day must be made on Thursday in the Hour of Jupiter they may be formed of Virgin Parchment observing the proper Ink for the Characters &c. or on a plate of Tin or Pewter. If Tin is employed it would be as well to mix with it a portion of Brass to harden it, while in the act of melting, do not omit using the Perfume, as before mentioned, likewise repeat the Oration in an earnest manner, for as aforesaid, on an exact performance of all that is here required with a firm trust and Confidence, depend the accomplishment of your desires.

[Plate]	[Fig.]	[Description/Function]
Plate XXI	Fig. 1.	Pentacle [Circle] for Thursday under Jupiter.
Plate XXII	Fig. 2.	Talisman for the Game of Hazard.
Plate XXII	Fig. 3.	Talisman for the Game of Hazard.
Plate XXII	Fig. 4.	Talisman for Health.
Plate XXII	Fig. 5.	Talisman to preserve Health.
Plate XXII	Fig. 6.	Talisman to discover Hidden Treasures.
Plate XXIII	Fig. 7.	Talisman to be successful in Trade and Finances.
Plate XXIII	Fig. 8.	Talisman to Obtain Honourable Charges & Dignities.
Plate XXIII	Fig. 9.	Seal of the Familiar Spirit of Jupiter, and Director of his Influence.
Plate XXIII	Fig. 10.	The Mysterious Number of Jupiter which is 34.
Plate XXIII	Fig. 11.	The Mysterious Number of Jupiter in Hebrew Characters
Plate XXIII	Fig. 12-13.	Seals of the Intelligences of Jupiter

[61] Pentacle for Friday under VENUS

This Pentacle of Friday represents to us in its first Interior Circle the Names of the four Heavenly Genii who govern the Stars on Friday, and which you must Invoke and Conjure on this Day. **Sarabotes** is the principal Heavenly Genii contained in this Pentacle. You must Invoke him in turning to the East, as we have already said in speaking of that of Sunday. So far from his Apparition being frightful, it is commonly very agreeable, its suit[e] is composed of small Genii, and of often accompanied by delightful and melodious sounds of Music &c. which inspire Youth with Joy. You must Dismiss him with Honour, after having received favours required.

Composition of Perfumes for Friday

For this Perfume to be in a state of perfection, it must be composed of the following Drugs, Musk, Ambergris, Wood of Aloes, Dried Red Roses, Red Coral, the whole pulverized and made into paste, with the Blood of a Pigeon, or Turtle Dove, and the brains of two or three Sparrows, in such proportions that you can make an agreeable odour, and after this Confectionary is finished, You must make small seeds, or pills of it, which you must use in the Cabalistical Operations for Friday, under the Auspicies of Venus, and the Spirits which Direct her Influence.

[62] Oration for Friday.

"Lord **Abalidoth** who lovest thy Servants, and will be loved by them, I pray you by the Interposition of those among the Heavenly Genii whom you cherish most which are **Raniel Corat, Kadie Penat** I intreat you to diffuse on my Operations the Treasures of your kindness, so that my undertakings on this Day may be successful, conformable to my Intentions, and redound to your Glory with all suitable acknowledgement."

Invocation

"Come on the wings of the Zephyrs ye happy Genii who preside over the workings of the Heart. Come Heavenly **Sarabotes, Husaltiel Doremiel Setchiel**, hear favourably the Invocation that I make this Day destined to the wonders of Love, be ready to lend me your Assistance to succeed in what I have undertaken under the Hope You will be favourable to me."

Conjuration

"I conjure you by the Veneration you have for the Mysterious Name **Setchiel** O Beneficent Genii who preside over the Operations that are done on this Day, I conjure you **Talarath, Miveg, Cuphaniel, Clearos,** that you will come with all your power to scatter and put to flight the Evil Spirits which are inimical to good Operations cause me by thy Powerful Virtue to succeed in what I have undertaking this Day which is consecrated to Venus."

It is so Natural for Men to Love and be loved, that there is nothing in all nature to which we are more strongly disposed to, or that we wish for with more ardour, but as there are often obstacles to overcome, which are not within the Limits of Mediocrity, the two following Pentacles or Talismans (Fig. 2. 3) will be of great Assistance, if you are happy [63] enough to make them according to the circumstances prescribed by the principles of the Art. You must begin on Friday, during the Spring Season at Sun-rise, in Calm Serene Weather, it will be right also to prepare at the same time the Ingredients which serve for the composition of Amorous Love Potions, and above all the Herb called Enrula Campana. You must gather it the same day that you make the Talisman, and Consecrate it with the same Sprinkling and Perfume agreeable and proper to the Planet Venus and preserve it in a Box proper to be made use of on these occasions as we have more fully explained.

The last two Talismans (Fig. 9-10) make but one, having two faces, on one You must Engrave the Name, and Seal or Character of the Familiar Spirit who directs the Influence of the Planet Venus, and on the Second you must Engrave the Mysterious Number of the same Planet, which number you must place in several small squares, so that on whatever side you read whether from above or below, from one angle to another or on the same side to the right hand or the left, being in the same line, You will always find the same Number which is 175.

Precious Stones Affected by Venus

The Cornelian, The Beryl, The Coral.

Trees affected by Venus.

The Myrtle, The White Laurel, The Orange, and other Odoriferous Trees.

[64] **Plate XXIV. Hours of the Day and Night on Friday.**

1	♀	Anael	1	♂	Samael
2	☿	Raphael	2	☉	Michael
3	☾	Gabriel	3	♀	Anael
4	♄	Cassiel	4	☿	Raphael
5	♃	Zachiel	5	☾	Gabriel
6	♂	Samael	6	♄	Cassiel
7	☉	Michael	7	♃	Zachiel
8	♀	Anael	8	♂	Samael
9	☿	Raphael	9	☉	Michael
10	☾	Gabriel	10	♀	Anael
11	♄	Cassiel	11	☿	Raphael
12	♃	Zachiel	12	☾	Gabriel

Mysterious Characters for Friday under Venus.

- Ab Amissione -   - First Characters. -   - A[b] Puello. -

- Second -

- Third.-

[65] **Plate XXV. Pentacle for Thursday [Friday] under Venus.**

[66] **Plate XXVI.**

[67] **Plate XXVII.**

[68] The Foregoing Talismans with the Pentacle for the Day must be made on Friday under Venus. Should there not be sufficient time to finish one of them in the first hour after Sunrise, the Operator must wait with patience till the next hour of Venus arrives, then he may complete his work, but on no account let him neglect reciting the Orations, Invocations, and Conjurations, for upon a strict observance of all these Rules, Forms, and Ceremonies given, depends the certainty of his success. They may be formed of Fair Virgin Parchment, and written with Ink of a Green or Silver Colour, or they may be made of Brass or Copper Plates properly polished and Engraven as shown in the foregoing Models.

[Plate]	[Fig.]	[Description/Function]
Plate XXV	Fig. 1.	Pentacle [Circle] for Friday under Venus.
Plate XXVI	Fig. 1.	Talisman for Amorous Intrigues.
Plate XXVI	Fig. 2.	Talisman for the same purpose.
Plate XXVI	Fig. 3.	Talisman to Engage the Fair Sex to Love.
Plate XXVI	Fig. 4.	Talisman for the same purpose.
Plate XXVI	Fig. 5.	Talisman for Secret Love.
Plate XXVII	Fig. 6.	Talisman to make Ourselves agreeable to those we are willing to please.
Plate XXVII	Fig. 7.	Talisman for the Love of Aged Persons.
Plate XXVII	Fig. 8.	Pentacle of the Seal or Character of Venus.

Plate XXVII	Fig. 9.	Mysterious Number of Venus, which is 175.
Plate XXVII	Fig. 10.	Mysterious Number in Hebrew.
Plate XXVII	Fig. 11.	Seal of Venus.
Plate XXVII	Fig. 12-13.	Seals of the Intelligences of Venus.

[69] Pentacle for Saturday under Saturn.

This Pentacle of Saturn represents to you in the first Interior Circle the Names of the Heavenly Genii who prevail over the Influence of the Stars on Saturday and which you must Invoke and Conjure in the Operation of this Day. **Maymon** is the Principal Heavenly Genii contained in this Pentacle, you must Invoke him in turning towards the East. Although his Apparition is not terrible, nevertheless you will behold them under such Melancholy Figures, that you will feel a kind of trembling, but it will be attended without Danger, and if the Constellation is Happy,[211] they will become favourable and propitious. I have before warned you, that you will very seldom find Saturn in a happy situation for receiving favourable Influences, and likewise Saturday, which is affected by this Planet is usually attended with unlucky apparitions, on which account a true follower of this Art, ought never to be then employed, our principal Motive in the exercise of this Science, that we ought only to have a desire of procuring good to ourselves, and rendering service to others and not Evil. You may nevertheless, with some application and attention find some Saturday in the course of the year, and chiefly during Spring, when Saturn is in a Happy Conjunction with Jupiter, or Venus, or in a favourable Aspect with Mercury, and then you will obtain advantageous Operations.

[70] Composition of Perfumes for Saturday

These Perfumes must be in a state of perfection, and composed of the following Drugs, Grains of Black Pepper, Grains of Hogsbane, Roots of Mandrake, Powder of Loadstone, Myrrh of the East, the whole pulverized, and made into a paste with the blood of a Bat, and the Brains of a Black Cat in necessary proportion. After the Confectionary is finished, you shall make thereof small Pills of which you must use in the Cabalistic Operation on Saturday under the Auspicies of Saturn and the Spirits which direct his Influence.

Oration for Saturday

"Heavenly **Machatan** who disdainest not to listen to those who prayeth with confidence to you and in the power of your Arm, I intreat you with affection through the interposition of the Genii who are subject unto you and who are principally **Uriel Balidet Assaibi Abumalith,** that you will conduct the Heavenly Influences with so much dexterity in the Operation, I am going to make, that the whole may succeed according to my desire, and your glory."

Invocation

"Come out of your Gloomy Solitude ye Saturnine Spirits and thou powerful **Maymon,** come with your Cohort come with Diligence to the place where I am going to begin an Operation under your Auspices be attentive to my labours and Contribute your Assistance to what may redound to the Honour and Glory of Him to whom you are subject, and in whose Name I Invoke you."

---

[211] If the planet is well aspected. – Ed.

Conjuration

"I Conjure you by the Great Name **Arpheta,** which causeth the rebellious Spirits to tremble, I Conjure you benign Spirits who are destined to favour the Undertaking of this Day constituted to the Seventh Luminary of the Firmament to be kind to your [71] Heavenly **Balidet, Machaton, Archaziel, Talidomer.** Put to flight by your power the Genii who oppose my Labours so that I may finish them according to my own wishes as I would begin them with Confidence to you."

Though the Planet Saturn prevails over Saturday, it is not commonly happy in its Influence, as has been already remarked, yet, nevertheless, if you can find it in a favourable situation, which sometimes happens during the Spring Season. You may profit by this event, in working the two following Talismans, in order to have favourable seasons for the fruits of the Earth, to produce Rain, or fertilizing Dews, during Drought, and to avert Hail, Tempest, or other Natural effects. The Talismans will be wonderfully useful. It will be likewise efficacious to Dig with success in places where there are Mines, Precious Stones, Hidden Treasures, &c. They who have tried the virtue of this last Talisman, affirm they have Dreams in which are sensibly represented to the Imagination, the places, you may be assured to find Moneys, or Precious Metals by the Ministry of Saturnine Spirits. You must put the Talisman under the Bolster, in lying down after having perfumed it with Incense suitable to the Planet Saturn. This Talisman not only preserves men from a number of Maladies, but even cures them, when they proceed from an over heated Bile, and this [is] what Experience will prove, better than any discourse thereon If you make it on Virgin Parchment you must observe the proper Colours.

The Pentacle or Talisman Fig. 8-9 make but one, having two faces, on one, you must Engrave the Seal or Mysterious Character of the Familiar Spirit who directs the Influence of the Planet Saturn, on the second, you must Engrave the Mysterious Number of the same planet which you must place in several small squares, so that on whatever side you read this number whether from above or below, or on one angle, or the other, or on the same line to the right or to the left, you will find the same Number which is 15.

[72] Plate XXVIII. Precious Stones affected by Saturn.

The Sapphire, The Chalcedony, The Dark Jasper, The Loadstone.

Trees affected by Saturn.

The Cypress, The Pyne [Pine].

Hours of the Day and Night on Saturday

1	♄	Cassiel Machatan	1	☿	Raphael Suquinos
2	♃	Zachiel Asasiel	2	☾	Gabriel Madiel
3	♂	Samael Amabiel	3	♄	Cassiel Balidet
4	☉	Michael Cynabal	4	♃	Zachiel Castiel
5	♀	♀ Anael Abalidoth	5	♂	Samael Calzas
6	☿	Raphael Mitraton	6	☉	Michael Anael
7	☾	Gabriel Missabu	7	♀	Anael Sarabotes
8	♄	Cassiel Assaibi	8	♄ ☿	Cassiel Raphael

9	♃	Zachiel Maguth	9	♃ ☽	Zachiel Gabriel [212]
10	♂	Samael Carmax	10	♄	Cassiel Maymon
11	☉	Michael Baciel	11	♃	Zachiel Gutriz
12	♀	Anael Corat	12	♂	Samael Arragon

The Mysterious Characters for Saturday under Saturn.

- A[b] Carcere -   - First Characters.-   - A[b] Tristitia -

- Second -

- Third -

[73] **Plate XXIX. Pentacle for Saturday under SATURN.**

[74] **Plate XXX.**

[75] **Plate XXXI.**

[76] The foregoing Talismans under the Influence of the Planet Saturn must be made on Saturday in his hour; the Operator must be very particular about waiting for a favourable Configuration of the Planet he works under, with either or both the Luminaries, also with Venus or Jupiter, because his Influence naturally, unless assisted by fortunate Configurations of the Fortunes [fortunate planets], tends to promote evil and discord, particularly so, if opposed, or Squared by Herschel [Uranus] or Mars. But the Talismans will be productive of much benefit, if raised according to the Conditions aforesaid.

[Plate]	[Fig.]	[Description/Function]
Plate XXIX	1.	Pentacle [Circle] for Saturday under Saturn.
Plate XXX	1.	Talisman for success in raising the Fruits of the Earth.
Plate XXX	2.	Talisman to discover Mines and Hidden Treasures.
Plate XXX	3.	Talisman to have a Revelation in the Night by a Dream.
Plate XXX	4.	Talisman against Sounds, Charms, and the possession of Evil Spirits.
Plate XXX	5.	Talisman against Tempests, Thunder, Hail, Inundations &c.
Plate XXXI	6	Talisman against sudden Deaths, and accidents that cause them.
Plate XXXI	7.	Talisman to discover Hidden Treasures &c.
Plate XXXI	8.	Seal and Character of the Familiar Spirit of Saturn.
Plate XXXI	9.	Mysterious Number of the Planet Saturn.
Plate XXXI	10.	The same in Hebrew Characters.
Plate XXXI	11-12.	Seals of the Intelligences &c. of Saturn.

The above mentioned Talismans may be formed or made of True Virgin Parchment or of Metal composed of Lead, properly cleaned and Engraven according to the foregoing Models.

Should any of the Metal Plates be defaced by wear, or accident, they may be repolished and Engraven, but all must be done in their respective Planetary Hour governing the Different Metals, not forgetting to recite the Orations &c.

---

[212] Error printed in smaller type. – Ed.

[77] THE MYSTERIOUS RING

The Mysterious Ring, which several Doctors of the Cabala have used with wonderful success. It is not in order to impose on the Credulity of the curious Followers of the Occult Science, that I say that it is more than Two Thousand years since the Ring which I have mentioned has been in use. This is in general the manner of making the Ring. After having made a Ring of suitable Metal, according to the Planet whose Influx we wish to obtain, (according to the Cabalistic Art) and having set in it a stone, suited to the Nature of the Planet, you must Engrave within the Ring the Name of the Familiar Spirit who governs the Planet, the foregoing of which we have seen. Then you must form a Circle of about seven feet in diameter, of the following Model, and being in the middle of the Circle, you must burn in a small vessel some fresh perfume, the scent of which is suitable to the Planet which governs the Ring. Gravely pronouncing the Name which is Engraved in the Ring, and holding [in] your hand a lighted Wax Candle, or Torch, you must repeat the Conjuration under the Name of the Spirit which is Engraved in the Ring.

[78] Conjuration

"I Conjure you by the Name of the Spirit and the Sovereign Creator of all things, that without noise or anything frightful you would [im]print on this Ring which bears thy Name, the wonderful Virtue of which thou art the Master and Disposer. I Conjure you by the Wonderful Names of the Deity to whom thou art subject. Hear these with respect, and ready submission, the Names of which are terrible to all Created things. **Adonay, Agla, Tetragrammaton Gaha Agari Thetron He Elhi Ygaha Emanuel Venry Eloym Goth Genii.**"

Or if after this Conjuration, the Spirit should be known, either in a Visible or Invisible form you must turn towards the East, and present Him the Ring, at the end of a small Ring [rod], which is particularly consecrated to the Planet, under the Auspicies of which you work. The said Ring, that it may be impressed with those qualities we wish for. Immediately after, you must Dismiss him saying: "Faithful Minister go in peace in the Name of your Great Master who hath sent you to be favourable to me."

Before you go out of the Circle, you must put the Ring on that Finger where Rings are usually worn, and burn the Perfume a Second time, effacing the Circle properly, and returning with the profoundest silence.

These sort of Rings ought to be preserved with the utmost care, in a New Box or a small new Purse, made with silk of a colour that is suitable to the Planet. If you are happy enough to make them under a good Constellation, with the preparations and Ceremonies, similar to those of the Talismans and Pentacles, they will not lose their efficacy in Changing their Master, provided that he who receives them consents to all that is done in the Operation of which we have spoken, and that he burn the perfumes in the Name, and to the Honour of the Spirit who governs the Aforesaid Ring.

[79] Plate XXXII.

[Part 3 – Four Experiments with Specific Spirits]

An Experiment of the

Spirit

BIRTO

As hath often been proved at the Instant Request of

Edward the Fourth

KING OF ENGLAND

[81] **Experiment of Invocating the Spirit Birto and holding Converse with Him**

The Operator must be reminded that Ceremonies in the Magic Art must be performed earnestly, and faithfully, with a determination to succeed in his Operations by faithfully adhering to all the cautions and Rules given so that no part be omitted. He must be bold and courageous in the time of Operations, for Aeriel Spirits are much more powerful and obstinate than the Planetary Angels, and require all the skill and firmness of the Operator, they are often very subtle and require severe Conjurations &c. to compel them to Appear, but where once they have been invocated to Appear, they will afterwards almost at the Will of the Operator appear without difficulty, but the Operator must always be on his guarde at the time of Operation, not suffering himself to be overcome with fear or trembling. He must be chaste leading a Religious Life. As the manner and form of the Circle hereafter described must be Drawn. Let him be careful to guard it with Seals and Holy Names round about. So shall he be safe, but on no account Leave the Circle till the Spirit is finally departed. As all the necessary Instruments and Apparatus have been described in a former part of this Mysterious Book, it is unnecessary to advert to it any farther, for they will answer the same purpose in Ceremonial Magic as in Cabalistical.

The Invocant may now make preparation for Invocating the Spirit **Birto,** as an Experiment.

[82] On the Second, Fourth, Sixth, Tenth, and Twelfth Days of the Moons increase, go to the place appointed for this and the like purpose, and in the Evening when the Air is Serene, lay down the Circles and their Characters in the order hereafter explained in the Copies thereof, then Invocate as follows.

Invocation

"I Exorcise Call upon and Conjure thee Spirit which art called **Birto** by the Dignity of the Prince **Ornothocos** and **Booth** and in the Name of the Father, and of the Son, and of the Holy Ghost and by the Power of [the] Potent, Inestimable, Divine, and Commanding Names of the Almighty and Everlasting God **Jehovah El Elohim Sabaoth Adonay Tetragrammaton Alpha et Omega,** and by the Name of Jesus of Nazareth, born of a Virgin the only begotten Son of God, the Father Almighty Maker of Heaven and Earth, our only Saviour and Redeemer Advocate and Mediator, whose Name all the Celestial Host of Angels Honour and Obey and whereat all knees on Earth bow and all Aerial Terrestrial and Infernal Spirits do fear and tremble, by all the aforesaid, I do yet again powerfully Exorcise, Conjure and Command thee Spirit which art called **Birto,** that thou do immediately forthwith and at this present appear Visibly before me in that Circle appointed for thee in fair and human form and shape of a man, and no ways terrible or hurtful to me, or any other person whatsoever, and I Constrain thee to tell me the truth without Fraud Guile Deceit &c. in His Name to whom be all Honour Power Glory Majesty and Dominion for Ever and Ever **Amen.**"

Let the Conjuration be often repeated and said over with ample courage confidence and resolution, and when he appears, receive him courteously and gently. Bind him with the Bond of Spirits, and then he will freely and faithfully declare and make answer to whatever

[83] **Plate XXXIII.**

shall be demanded and will serve, obey, fulfill all commands &c. Then License him to depart in peace.

Let the Circle for the Invocant which is that wherein the Name Magister is written, be made as here described viz. not less than nine feet diameter and as before said, well fortified with Divine Names Seals &c. Let the Effigy, Character, or Wivern [wyvern] be fairly Drawn or Painted upon an Abortive as above.

As for the Circle wherein the Spirit appeareth, it may be made two or three several ways, according to the place made choice of to act in, and the Ground or floor. If the Ground be nought or rugged, as in Woods, or Coppices they generally are, then must the Ground be paved, and made very even, so that an impression may be made visible and plain thereon, or else let it be made on large Calfskin Parchment, but it is better on the Ground, and if upon [84] Parchment or floor, then let the Circle be made or drawn thereon with Consecrated Chalk or marking Stone and place them three feet asunder and herein take a serious and deliberate consideration, let reason and prudence be thy principal Guide, without which principles a Magician is but a shadow to a substance, and shall as miss as hit of his Expectation.

Note. - The Invocant must not be impatient nor discouraged at the Prolixity or Delay of the Appearance of the Spirit, for it is the property of All Aeriel Spirits to be slow in their first Appearance but after they have once appeared, they will afterwards with less trouble, their Departure is [also] very slow sometimes, therefore it behoveth the Operator to [be] very particular in repeating the License to Depart, and not to be in too much hurry to quit the Circle.

The forms of a Bond of Spirits and Licence to Depart will be given in the Sequel of this Work.

[85] **An**

Experiment of the

SPIRIT VASSAGO

Who may be called upon to appear in a Crystal Stone or Glass or otherwise Without [outside the Circle]

It is to be remembered that the same Apparatus, Instruments &c. used in the aforesaid Experiment may be used in this Experiment also, the Circle must be properly Drawn. The Magical practitioner must provide a Lamen or plate of silver, and engraven upon according as it is represented hereafter and a Spatula made of Ash, Pear tree or any other solid wood the thickness of a third part of an inch, and the square top thereof to be three inches square, and the stem or handle to be nine inches long, and gilded all over with Gold, and the Character written thereon, as shewn forth in the Example following. Having all things in readiness, repair to the Chamber or place appointed for practice, which ought to be clean, and a Table placed therein, covered with a Clean Linen Cloth, and a Taper on each side of the Crystal Stone or Glass, and being seated therein. Invocate as follows. —

[86] "I Exorcise Call upon, and Command the Spirit **Vassago** by and in the Name of the immense and Everlasting God **Jehovah, Adonay, Elohim, Agla, El, On, Tetragrammaton** and by and in the Name of our Lord Jesus Christ the only Son of the Eternal and true God, Creator of Heaven and Earth and all that is in them **Wipius, Sother, Emanuel, Primogenitus, Homonsion, Bomes, Via, Veritas, Sapientia, Virtus, Leof, Mediator, Agnus, Rex, Pastor, Prophetas, Sacerdos, Athanatos, Paracletus, Alpha and Omega,** by all these High, Great, Glorious, Royal, and Ineffable Names of the Omnipotent God, and of His only Son our Lord and Saviour Jesus Christ, the second Essence of the Glorious Trinity. I Exorcise, Command, Call upon, and Conjure thee Spirit **Vassago** wheresoever thou art (East, West, North, or South, or being bound to any one under the Compass of the Heavens) that you come immediately from the place of your private abode or residence and appear to me Visibly in Fair and Decent Form in this Crystal Stone or Glass.[213]

I do again Exorcise and powerfully Command thee Spirit **Vassago** to come and appear Visibly to me in this Crystal Stone or Glass, or otherwise as above in a fair, Solid, and decent Form.

I do again strongly bind and Command thee Spirit **Vassago** to appear visibly to me in that Crystal Stone or Glass, as aforesaid. By the Virtue and Power of these Names by which I can bind all Rebellious Obstinate and Refractory Spirits **Alla, Carital, Marihal, Carion, Urion, Spyton, Lorean, Stabea, Corian, Marmos, Agaion, Cados, Son, Catator, Yron, Astron, Gardeong, Caldabrie, Bear, Tetragrammaton, Strallay, Spignos, Sother, Yah, On, El, Elohim,** by all aforesaid I charge and Command thee Spirit **Vassago** to make haste and come away, and appear visibly to me as aforesaid, without any further tarrying or Delay in the Name of Him who shall come to Judge the Quick and Dead and the World by Fire. **Amen.**"

This Conjuration after being repeated, and the Invocant being patient and constant in his perseverance, and not Disheartened nor Dismayed by reason of any tedious Prolixity or Delay, the Spirit will at last appear. Bind him with the Bond of Spirits, and then you may talk with him &c.

[87] That this is a true Experiment, and that the Spirit hath been obliged to the fellowship and Service of a Magic Artist heretofore is very certain, as may appear by this following Bond or Obligation, which the Invocant may if he please, have fairly written on an Abortive, and laid before him, and discourse with the Spirit concerning it.

Bond or Obligation of the Spirit Vassago

"I **Vassago** under **Baro** the king of the West not compelled by command nor fear, but of my own accord and free will especially oblige myself by these presents firmly and faithfully and without Deceit to **J.**

---

[213] Here note, that the Invocant mentioneth a Stone or Glass if he have one, or else he saith "to <u>Me</u> visibly in fair and decent Form and human shape before this Circle." – Sibley.

W.[214] to obey at any time and at any place whensoever and wheresoever he shall call upon me personally to appear whether in a Stone or in the Middle without a Stone and to fulfill his Commands truly in all things wherein I can by the Virtue of all the Names of God especially by these most Powerful in the Magic Art **Laye, Abryca, Mura Syron Walgava, Ryshin Layagamum Arasin Laysai** and by the Virtue wherewith the Sun and Moon were Darkened and my Planet and by the Celestial Characters thereof and by this Seal binding most Solidly.

In Witness of which Guilty Person[215] he commanding, I have signed this Present Obligation with mine own Seal to which I always stick close."

That this a true Experiment is apparent, and that the Spirit hath been [bound] by the great Diligence, and constant Perseverance of Learned and Intelligent Magicians, brought to Obedience and fellowship is manifestly true by this recited precedent, besides what myself hath seen, and as for the calling upon, and the other Spirits either in the Crystal Stone, or Glass, shall be shown at the end of the next Experiment, because they are both of one Nature.

[88] **Plate XXVIV.**
Seal of the Spirit Vassago**.**

[89] An

Experiment of the Spirit

AGARES [216]

The Experiment of Invoking this Spirit **Agares** is practically the same as in the former Experiment of the Spirit **Vassago** who likewise may be called to appear either in a Crystal Stone or Glass, or otherwise without them, and they are both slow in their Appearance, as most Ariel Spirits are, but once they do appear, then afterwards, they will frequently at the Master's Invocation.

Having all things in readiness as has been before particularized, and resolved upon his time. Let the Operator enter his Chamber, or place, appointed for Action, and Invocate as follows.

[90] [blank]

[91] "Thou Spirit **Agares** the first Captain under the King of the East, I Exorcise Command and Call upon thee and Constrain thee, by calling in the Name of the most powerful Fearful and Blessed **Jah, Adonay, Elohim Saday Eje Eje Eje Asarie** and in the Name of **Adonay** the God of Israel whose by his immediate word alone created the Heavens, the Earth, the Sea, and all things therein contained, and made Man according to the similitude of Himself and these most efficacious, Powerful, and Commanding, Ineffable, and Sacred Names of the all powerful and Immense God **Jehovah Agla El On**

---

[214] The Name of the person who wishes to obtain the Spirit in the Crystal, or otherwise. – Sibley.

[215] This phrase is probably present because this bond was originally modelled on a legal Bond involving the binding over of a person found guilty by a court of law. – Ed.

[216] Misspelled as 'Agarese.' – Ed.

Tetragrammaton wherein all Visions and Apparitions are wont to be, and by the Holy Name which was written on the Brow of Aaron the Priest of the Most High and Everlasting God, I powerfully Exorcise and Command thee Spirit **Agares** that wheresoever thou art in any part of the Air, Earth, East, West, North, or South or being bound to any one, that immediately without tarrying or Delay you presently appear to [92] me Visibly in fair and human form.[217] Moreover and again I Exorcise, and potently command, call upon the Spirit **Agares** by Him that was, is, and shall be even in the Blessed and Great Name of the Holy and Heavenly Messiah Our Lord and Saviour Jesus Christ born of a Virgin, Lord of all the World, and its only Mediator and Advocate to the Father of Mercies, God of all Consolation, at whose Great, Glorious and Incomprehensible Names, all knees ought to bow, and humbly do reverence, and at naming whereof all Spirits whatsoever, both Aeriel Terrestrial and Infernal ought to obey with all due Reverence & Submission who is the Great **Emanuel,** the faithful Witness and Primogeniture **Alpha and Omega** who lived, and was Dead, and liveth for Ever, and by His Glorious Passion, Resurrection and Ascension, and by the coming of the Holy Ghost, by all Aforesaid, I Powerfully Exorcise thee thou Spirit **Agares** that without tarrying, or further Delay. You do now appear Visibly to me. I now calling upon thee † [218] in a fair, solid, decent, and human form, wherefore make haste, come away and shew thyself immediately to fulfill my ~~my~~ request in the Name of the Father, and of the Son, and of the Holy Ghost. **Amen.**"

Now if this Spirit doth not appear in some material distance of time to the Conjuration, wonder not at its prolixity or delay, for as it is said elsewhere before it is the Nature of the Aeriel Spirits to be very slow in their appearance, therefore, the Invocant must be patient, Diligent and Watchful, and on no account must he leave the Circle, till the Spirit be finally Dismissed.

Therefore let the Magician be constant in his perseverance herein, that this Experiment is all needful, and that this Spirit **Agares** hath been called upon, been brought to Obedience and Familiar Association is manifestly true and apparent by this following Obligation made by him to some learned Master.

[93] **Bond [of Agares]**

"I **Agares** the first Captain under the King of the East not compelled by command or Dread, but willingly and of my own accord, do especially bind myself by these presents firmly to obey at all times, and in every place **J.M.**[219] to do his commands in all things appertaining to my Duty and especially by these words the most powerful in this Magical Art, **Zay, Mara, Sydon, Walgave, Rythin, Layaganum, Layanarim, Lasia** and by that virtue wherewith the Sun and Moon were darkened before that terrible Day of the Lord (as in the Gospel) and shall be turned into Blood, and by the Head of my Prince, and by His Circle and Characters, and chiefly by this Seal firmly binding.

---

[217] Here you are to observe, that if you call him into a Stone, or Glass, then you are to say "In this Stone or Glass." If you have none you need specify but say "to Me," or, "to me before this Circle &c." and so the like elsewhere in other places of this Conjuration observe the same where you shall meet with the like Occasion. – Sibley.

[218] † Here mentioning as before; as whether without or within a receptacle. – Sibley.

[219] The initials of a previous Invocant, possibly James Morrison. – Ed.

In Witness of which Guilty Person, I have signed this present Obligation with mine own Seal He commanding Me, to which I always stick close."

This Bond or Obligation must be written on Virgin Parchment and laid before the Spirit **Agares,** then the Invocant may discourse with him thereon. He must take care that he ask or inquires nothing through Carelessness nor curiosity, of the Spirit, but act as become a person, who is cautious, prudent, and has a firm reliance on the Dispenser of all good by so doing, he will obtain his desires.

The Operator must be reminded once again, that every preparation connected with the Magic Art, should be made during the Increase of the Moon, about two or three days before the full, is said to be the best time, and should the Significator or Planet under which the Operator is born be in a fortunate Aspect with this Luminary, so much the better for him.

[94] **An**

Experiment of the Spirit

BEALPHAROS

To Invocate Call upon and have converse with this Spirit **Bealpharos** these Rules must be observed.

On Thursday and Friday in the Increase of the Moon repair to the place appointed for action and write on a piece of Virgin Parchment as hereafter followeth in the Copy, and write also on a Girdle or Thong of a Lion's, Hart's, or Buck's skin as also hereafter followeth with directions thereunto annexed, and before you Enter the Circle to Invocate write ☩ **Agla** on the right hand, and on the left these Characters, and when you enter the Circle, make the sign of the Cross thereon and say: "*Per Crucis hoc Signum Salvatur quodnes [quodque] benignum.*"[220] Then Invocate as followeth, being courageous and not at all dismayed. Before reciting the Invocating part of the Ceremony the Invocate [Invocant] must rehearse with great earnestness the following words written on the Breast plate viz. "Homo Sacarus Muselomea Cherubosea."

[**Invocation**]

[95] "I Exorcise Conjure and Command thee Spirit **Bealpharos** by and in the great Name of the Omnipotent and Everlasting God **Jehovah, Tetragrammaton, Agla El On Adonay Saday** and by His Mighty Holy and unspeakable Majesty and Goodness, and by and in the Great Powerful and Inestimable Names of the Only Begotten Son Jesus Christ our Lord, the Redeemer of the World, the second Essence in the Holy Trinity sitting at the Right Hand of God the Father the Maker of Heaven and Earth: Messiah Saviour and Emanuel Alpha and Omega, and by the truest and most Especial Names of your Master.

I do hereby Powerfully Exorcise, Command, and Constrain thee Spirit **Bealpharos** to Come and appear Visibly here before this Circle in fair and Human shape of Man or Womankind, and not terrible in any manner of ways, neither to us, nor any other person whatsoever this Circle being our Tuition, Fortress and Defence, through the Merciful Goodness of our Heavenly God and Loving Father. I Command thee to make haste and come away and show thyself Visibly, apparently and peaceably to us here before this Circle immediately without tarrying or Delay and with all humility and obedience, doing whatsoever I

---

[220] "By the sign of the Cross may all benevolent [persons] be saved." – Ed.

command and request, and desire of you without any Illusion, Guile, or Deceit whatsoever, but faithfully truly and Certainly to answer, fulfill and perform such things as I shall require of you in the Name of Him who said and it was done, even the Most Great and Incomprehensible God, the Creator of Heaven and Earth who shall come to Judge the Quick and the Dead and the World by Fire. Amen."

[96] **Plate XXXV.**

This Spirit is somewhat Obstinate and pern[i]cious by Nature, and is therefore as usually more slow and prolix in his appearance, wherefore it is requisite that the Ignorant should persevere herein with Constancy, Fervency and Patience and not to despair at all, though the Experiment may prove more tedious than expected, for it will appear in a form similar as above with a fierce and angry Countenance, his coming is very swift in motion and sudden, therefore let the Exorcist be on his guard and rehearse the Invocation as often as he may well do according to his reason and prudence shall direct him as at every half quarter of an Hour, whilst he is upon action and be very diligent to discover his appearance and motion that he [97] may immediately receive him, he will then assume a more mild natural appearance and become more tractable in a proper human form. Bind him with the Bond of Spirits[221] to stay and abide so long peaceably and obediently with him in such form and shape as he shall appoint and approve until his demands and desires be fulfilled, which when done, License him to Depart, and on no account whatever neglect it, for any omission of this kind through Carelessness or neglect is attended with Danger, but if the Invocant comply with all the Forms, Ceremonies, &c. he may have his Desires gratified in perfect Security and peace.

[98] **Plate XXXVI.**

[99] The Exorcist must observe in this and all other Experiments of Aeriel Spirits, that as soon as a Spirit is bound, and is perceived to become obedient and familiar as by Degrees he will, that the Questions and Demands be first concluded and resolved on and fairly written on Paper or Parchment that you may have them ready to propose as occasion shall require. The Spirit resolveth many Dubious Questions and Enquiries, and is also a Carrier &c.

This that followeth must be written on a Girdle made of Leather, or Parchment of the Skin of a Dragon, or Lion, or of a Hart and put on by the Invocant before he entereth the Circle, and so by him to be worn so long as he is upon Action.

Elion Escherie Deus Eterney Eloy Elemeris Deus Sanctus Sabaoth Deus Exercitum Adonay Deus Mirabilis Iao Virax Anephepeton Deus Ineffabilis Saday Dominetos on fortissimus Agla On Tetragrammaton Alpha et Omega.

The Circle, No.1.[222] Wherein the Invocant standeth when he Invoketh or Calleth upon the Spirit **Bealpharos** must be made according to the foregoing Model and in the man[n]er as before taught in the former Experiments. It would not be amiss, if the Master Exorcist had a white vestment or surplice on him, and white shoes, and one or two wise and discreet persons with him in the Circle, only shod with white shoes also.

---

[221] The same form of the Bond of Spirits used in the Former Experiments may be used in this, only change the name of the Spirit.

[222] This is the protective floor Circle. See page 98, top illustration. – Ed.

The Figure, No. 2.[223] must be written on Virgin Parchment and then fixed or fastened on a New piece of Linen Cloth, and worn on the Breast of the Invocant during the whole time he is upon Action in the Circle.

Licence to Depart[224]

"I Conjure thee Spirit **Bealpharos** by all the Most Holy Names of God that as thou hast appeared at my Call or Invocation and hast assumed a quiet and peaceable form and answered unto my petition, fulfilled my desires, for which I give humble and hearty thanks unto Almighty God, that thou now Depart in peace unto thine order without any noise and terror whatsoever and return unto me I Charge thee whensoever I shall thee call by thy Name, Order, or Office without Delay or tract of time not molesting me, nor any other Creature God has made to his Glory now or hereafter, by the Virtue of Our Lord Jesus Christ, the Father and the Holy Ghost, go thy way in peace be between thee and Me, In Nomine Patris + et Filii + Spiritus Sancti + Amen."

---

[223] This is the Lamen. See page 98, lower illustration. – Ed.

[224] This License may be used in the former Experiments, changing the name of the Spirit. – Sibley.

[Part 4. The Wheel of Wisdom]

[100] Plate XXXVII. The Wheel Of Magic.

[101] The Wheel of Wisdom
With its KEY
and full Directions for its use in
MAGICAL OPERATIONS
Together with a Familiar Example for its Application

[102] The key to the Wheel of
WISDOM

He that knoweth God, loves Him fervently, and believes in Him with an unfeigned faith may peruse this.

There is but one God, a Trinity, Father, Son and Holy Ghost, whosoever believeth it not, shall not have the Key, much less a right to peruse this. After God, there are Seven Planets, or Intelligences, or Secondary causes which act in a proper order by themselves over all known and Intelligible things, and as far as they are Conjured by the Name of God they do wonders by His Consent, and according to the Design of the Operator.

The First Planet is **Saturn**, this is evil for it acts [to] Destruction, Sickness, Death, Hatred, Grief, Sorrow, Melancholy, Afflictions, Gaols *(sic)*, Misfortunes, and Subtle things, but it proves good in Agriculture and Metallurgy, and tends to Edification.

The Second in Order is **Jupiter,** this is good for it acts to Health, Riches, Honours, Judgement, Love of Princes, Greatness of Soul, Happiness and Rest.

The Third in Order is **Mars,** which is evil, for it acts to Discord, War, Snares, Violent Death, Boldness, Rashness, Military Honours and Terrors.

The Fourth in order is the **Sun**, and it is good, for it acts to Kingdoms, Empires, Power, Victory, Glory, Riches and Happiness.

[103] The Fifth in order is **Venus,** and she acts [to] Love between Men and Women, and all the Animal Friendships, Graces, Lucre, Music, Joy and Beauty.

The Sixth in order is **Mercury,** this is good and evil mixed, for it produces Docility, Memory, Science, Eloquence, Wit, Craftiness, and getting Riches by Fraud and Dexterity.

The Seventh, and the last in Order is the **Moon,** this [is] good, for acts to Good, Journeys, true Dreams, Divinations, Invisibility, Theft, Illusions, Rain, Hail and Waters.

In the order of the Worlds all those Stars have a peculiar Spirit or Angel, a Name, a Sign, a Metal, a Precious Stone, a Tree, a Plant, a Beast, a Bird, a Fish, a Colour, an Odour, a Number, or a Measure, and those are like Degrees that may ascend from the lowest to the Highest order as appears in the Wheel. From this Wheel are Drawn all the Operations of Secrets by the Wise and Faithful. Yet here we have subjoined some particulars which could not be so easily placed in it for the Unskilful to use that they may be wise.

There are many Secrets done from Similitude, from Sympathy, and from Antipathy, and which happen by an ordained Series of Nature agreeable to the Superior Wheel, for every thing has in itself something peculiar to itself, as for instance, the Dog may boast of his faithfulness, the Cock of his Crowing &c. for by that we know that these Animals naturally prevail by that which is their own property.

The same is to be understood of the other Animals, whose nature I should here explain was it not necessary to Elucidate things, which in themselves are as clear as the Sun.

[104] Full Directions for Magical Operations

The **First** Receipt is that at the Beginning of thine Operations in Magic, thou must call upon God with all thine Heart.

The **Second** is, that the operator should be continent and chaste three Days at least before he begins his Operation.

Thirdly, all operations must be done in a Secret place, without Fear, Contempt, or Derision.

Fourthly. The Operator must be pure and cleansed, and must have made a proper Expiation having washed himself with the water of a pure fountain as many times as answer to the Number of the Star [planet] which ruleth at the Operation.

Fifthly. The Operator must be silent, for if he knoweth not how to keep his tongue, all his labour will be in Vain, and the effect will not answer.

Sixthly. The Operator must have some Vessels for each Star signed with the sign of the star, and likewise of Colours and Odours belonging to all the Stars, which must be kept in readiness in a pure clean place.

Seventhly. All things that are to be used in Magical Operations must be virginal, that is to say quite new, having never been employed before to any use whatever, such as Paper, or Parchment, the Pen and Ink, the Colours, the Needles, Thread, Cloth, and all other things necessary; and those things must be of the Nature of the Star which ruleth the Operation, they must not be touched nor seen by a Woman that is out of order, for they would immediately lose their virtue.

Eighthly. All things must be written on Virgin Parchment in an Angular figure, and the Angels of the Figure must answer to the [105] Number of the Star.

Ninthly. The Angular figure, the forms, the Days, the Mixture, and all such like things must answer perfectly well in proportion to the Number, Weight and Measure of the Star.

Tenthly. If any part of an Animal is to be used, you must take that part from the Animal, while it is yet living or breathing.

Eleventhly. If fire is to be employed, you must light it with such Wood as will suit your Operation, and the Ashes thereof must be buried.

Twelfthly. All operations must be done in their proper Day and Hour. As for Example, if you work in Venerial, or belonging to Venus, it must be done in the first Astronomical Hour of the Sun Rising on a Friday and so of the rest. If the Hour is not sufficient for you to do the whole work in, You must take another such Hour of Venus as Astronomy teaches. For many reasons we will not relate the Evils caused by Saturn or Mars, but shall pass to the Secrets of Venus, which are soft and harmless. We will give an Example therefrom for all Operations, for instance we will take Love, wishing to make a person love me, this may be done by Rings, Images, Touching, Writings, Words, Dreams, Philters, which and many other ways, may be easily wrought by the help of our Wheel.

Of all these Methods, let us use the Philter, and we will make a Powder, which if any one Drink to another shall be loved by them to the End of their Lives.

[106] Example

Go to the Wheel and see what flying Animal belongs to Venus. You will find the Dove, take therefore, if for a Man a Pigeon, if for a Woman a Dove, saying this Prayer.

> "In the Name of God the Father, God the Son, and God the Holy Ghost whom I most efficaciously call to my help that through his consent I may bring my Operations to a happy Issue to the Glory of His Name. Amen.
>
> Be favourable to us O thou fair Angel of God **Anael** Prince of Love, be propitious to my Vows, that through thy Mediation I may hopefully fulfill my Desires by Christ Jesus Our Lord. Amen."

Go afterwards into a Secret place, and with a Copper or Brass Knife open the Breast of the Pigeon or Dove take out the heart, and while yet panting, burn it and reduce it to a powder, but gather the running blood in a proper Vessel, then gather some Valerian with the root, draw the Juice out of the Leaves, burn the root into Ashes, mix these Ashes with the Juice, adding to it a little of the Powder of Amber, moisten it with the Juice of Myrtle, and put all in a Vessel to dry. Afterwards reduce again the whole to Powder, take a Copper or Brass Needle and with it prick your Right Hand to Draw some drops of Blood, at the Mount of Venus, saying six times the Name of **Anael**, with these drops of Blood moisten your powder, adding also a little of your Flesh, or if you choose not to use that, the Hippomanes[225] [107] will be as good, and it will operate with more Sacredness; make a Lump and dry it up, and reduce it again to Powder take afterwards a little Yellow Amber, and a few of the feathers of the Belly of the Pigeon or Dove, of the leaves of the Valerian, of the Hairs of the Belly of the Goat, put all in a Vessel to mix with the Blood of a Pigeon or Dove, which has been kept by itself, make small Lozenges, of the Weight of 6 Grains, make afterwards a fire with Myrtle, and put over the Fire one of these Lozenges, make a Fumigation with the Powder, which you will have put in a Cylinder of a Green Colour, and which is always to be preferred, a Copper or Brass Vessel, whilst making the Fumigation you must say,

> "Fair **Anael** thou who rejoicest at these smells come to receive them, be favourable and kind unto me. Vouchsafe to Bless this Powder, and to Consecrate it so that it may have Power to Bind all Women and to make them to Love Me, by Christ Jesus Our Lord. Amen."

---

225 Hippomanes is a piece of Flesh on the Head of a Colt, newly foaled, which the Mare bites off.

Afterwards burn up the Body of the Pigeon, and all that remains. Gather all the Ashes, in a Vessel and bury it six feet deep in the Earth. Then this Powder is called the Universal matter, but still, it has no power whilst it wants the form and the Spirit, but now I am going to teach you the way of Animation and formation of the World. Although indeed it is with some reluctancy in my mind to reveal so Sublime a Secret. Yet I have let my good-will towards Mankind be the Conqueror.

Take Virginal Parchment of a Goat and draw on it Geometrically in Green Colours with the Pen of a Pigeon, an Hexagon Figure, in which write with your own Blood your Name and that of your Beloved. Join them together by the Name **Anael** between them as shown in the Figure.

[108] **Plate XXXVIII. Example.**

Burn afterwards, the Figure, reduce it to Ashes, mix them with an equal quantity of the Universal Powder, so that they may make up the weight of Six Grains, and Drink that to your Beloved. This is Great Secret, for by it many have gained not only the Affections of Human Creatures, but also of Wild Beasts.

The Operator must be reminded, that the more earnest and faithful he is in his Operations (particular in his Invocation of the Spirit who will assuredly render the Assistance required), the more will be the certainty of his success. This Fair and Beautiful Angel, is said to be more easily Invocated either Visibly or Invisibly than any of the other Planetary Angels. With this only, Be thou Content O Reader, for if thou art wise in this alone, thou mayest understand all the Rest.

Carefully keep this from Vulgar Eyes. Farewell.

Finis.

[109] [Part 5. A Secret & Complete Book of Magic Science]

[110] Frontispiece.

[111] **A Secret And**

COMPLETE BOOK OF

MAGIC SCIENCE

Containing the Method of Constraining Spirits

To Visible Appearance. The Consecration of

Lamens, Pentacles, and the Seals and Characters of the

PLANETARY ANGELS

With a Form of a Bond of Spirits.

1573.

[112] **FH**

BOOK OF MAGIC SCIENCE

Observations

In practising the Science of Ceremonial Magic, the Exorcist must be provided with every necessary Material, Instruments, Apparatus, &c. viz. Similar to those used in the Cabalistic Art. He must be cautioned that no part of the Forms, Ceremonies &c. be omitted. He must be Diligent, Watchful and Patient, leading a Steady, Sober, and Quiet Life.

He must retire from all company for Seven Days, and fast and pray during that time. Rise at Seven o'Clock, and watch and pray all the night before you work, and on the day before, the Spot, or Ground must be chosen, made fair and even, then Draw the Lines &c. of the Circle which must be not less than Seven feet in Diameter. The Invocant must wash himself clean the same Day. Make the Lamens and Pentacles, and having provided all other necessary things. Let him commence his Operations, the Moon Increasing.

[113] Then being clothed in White Vestments, and having covered the Altars and lit the Candles. Say the following Prayer.

> "Almighty Most Merciful Father I Beseech thee that thou wilt vouchsafe favourably to hear me this time while I make my humble supplication and prayers unto thee. I confess unto thee O Lord thou hast justly punished me for my manifold sins and offences. But thou hast promised at what time soever a sinner repent him of his sins and wickedness, thou wilt forgive him and turn away the remembrance of them from before thy face, purge me therefore now O Lord and wash me from all mine offences in the blood of **JC**, [226] that being clothed pure in the Vestments of Sanctity I may bring this work to perfection thro[ugh] **Christ** Our Lord who livest and reignest with thee Ever one God World without End. Amen."

Then sprinkle thyself with Holy Water and say,

---

[226] Jesus Christ. – Ed.

"Asperges me hysopo et mandabor Lavabis me et supra Mivens Decalbabor Miseam me Deus Secundum magnum Misercordium tuam Te Eppua Invam Decalbabor Gloria patri it Filii et Spiritus Sancto Lucet Erat in primapo et Extimus."[227]

Then Bless the Girdle saying,

"Almighty God who by the breath of thy Nostrils framed Heaven and Earth, and wonderfully disposed all things therein in six Days: Grant that this my work may be brought to perfection by thine unworthy servant and may he by thee Blessed and received divine Virtue, Power, and Influence from the word of thy mouth that everything therein counted may fully operate according to the hope and confidence of thine unworthy servant, through **Christ** Our Only Saviour. Amen."

Then sprinkle the Girdle saying. "Asperges &c."

[114] **Plate I. Blessing of the Lights**

"I Bless thee in the name of the Father and of the Son and of the Holy Ghost.

O Holy, Holy, Holy, Lord God, Heaven and Earth are full of thy Glory, before whose face there is a bright shining light for ever. Bless now O Lord I beseech thee, these creatures of Light which thou hast given for the kindly use of Man, that by thee they being sanctified, may not be put out or Extinguished by the Malice, Power, or Filthy Darkness of Satan, but may shine forth brightly and lend their Assistance to this Holy Work thro[ugh] **Christ** Our Lord. Amen."

(Then say,) "I Bless thee in the Name of the Father and of the Son and of the Holy Ghost."

[115] **Benediction of the Lamen.**

"O thou God of my Salvation I call upon thee by the Mysteries of all thy most Holy and Glorious Names. I Worship Adore and Beseech thee by thy Mighty Names **Tetragrammaton Saday** that thou wilt be seen in the Power and force of these thy Holy Names so written filling them with Divine Virtue and Influence through **JC**[228] Our Lord. Amen."

[116] **Consecration of the Girdle**

"O Great God of Strength who art greatly to be feared. Bless O Lord this Instrument that it may be a terror unto the Enemy and therewith I may overcome all Phantasms and Oppositions of the Devil through thy Influence and help of thy Holy and Mighty Names **On El Agla Tetragrammaton** and in the Cross of **Christ** Our only Lord. Amen."

---

[227] "Asperges me Domine hyssopo, & mundabor, lavabis me, & supra nivem dealbabor. Miserere mei Deus, secundum magnam misericordiam tuam, & supra nivem dealbabor. Gloria atri, & filio, & spiritui sancto: sicut erat in principio, & nunc, & semper, & in saecula saeculorum, Amen." This is often recommended as a prayer to be read during the full ablutions of the Invocant. See also See Scot (1665), p. 304.- Ed.

[228] Jesus Christ. – Ed.

Benediction of the Pentacles

"Eternal God who by thy wisdom hast given and appointed great power in the Characters and other Holy Writings of thy Spirits and hast given unto [them] that useth them faithfully, power thereby to work many things. Bless these O Lord framed and written by the hand of thine unworthy Servant, that being filled with divine Virtue and Influence by thy command O Most Holy God, they may show forth their Virtue and power to thy praise and Glory through **Christ** Our Lord and Saviour. Amen."

Then Say, "I Bless and Consecrate thee in the Name of the Father Son and Holy Ghost, Asperges &c."

Benediction of the Vestments

"O Blessed Holy and Eternal Lord God who art the God of Purity and delighteth that thy Servants should appear before thee in clear pure and undefiled Vestments. Grant O Lord that these Vestments of this Outer Order may be cleansed, Blessed and Consecrated by thee. I may put them on, being therewith clothed, I may appear whiter than snow, both in Soul and Body in thy presence this Day in and through the Merits, Death and Passion of Our Only Lord and Saviour Christ who liveth and Reigneth with thee in the Unity of the Holy Spirit, Ever one God, World without End, Amen. Bless thee. Purge thee in the Name of the Father and of the Son, and of the Holy Ghost."

[117] The Benediction of the Ground

"Per hoc crucis signum fugiat proseul Omne Maligna Et per Idem Signum Salvator quidque benignum Emicat Deus et disjectum inimicus Ejus Omnes Spiritus laudet Dominium Motans habent et prophetas. Depart from me all you workers of Iniquity."

Then say the prayer of Solomon, (I *Kings* Chap VIII-22.) – Then say

"Bless O Lord, I beseech thee this ground and drive away all evil and wickedness far from this place. Sanctify and make it become meet and convenient for thy Servant to finish and bring to pass therein all my Desires through Our Lord and Saviour. Amen. Be thou Blessed, Purified, and Consecrated, in the Name of the Father, and of the Son, and of the Holy Ghost. Asperges &c."

Benediction of the Perfumes

"The God of Abraham, the God of Isaac, the God of Jacob, Bless here the Creatures of these kinds that they may fill up the power of their Odours so that neither Enemy nor any false Imagination may be able to enter into them through Our Lord God to whom be honour and Glory both now and henceforth Amen.

Sprinkle them saying "Asperges &c."

Exorcism of the Fire &c.

"I Exorcise thee O thou Creature of Fire by Him, by whom all things are made that forthwith thou cast away every Phantasm from thee that it shall not be able to do any hurt in anything. Bless O Lord this Creature of Fire Sanctify it that it may be Blessed to set forth the praise of thy Holy Name through the virtue and Defence of our Lord **Christ.** Amen."

[118] **Plate II.**

[119] **Plate III.**

[120] **Oration on putting on the Vesture**[229]

"**Ancor Amacor Anides Theodonias Anitor** by the Merits of thy Angels O Lord I will put on the Garment of Salvation that this which I desire, I may bring to effect through the Merits Death and Passion of our Lord **Christ** who liveth and reigneth Ever One God World without End. Amen."

Then Commence your Work by Saying, kneeling, the following

Prayer

"O Holy, Holy, Holy, Lord God from whom all Holy desires and good works do proceed I beg thou wilt be merciful unto me at this time, Granting that I may become a true Magician and Contemplator of thy wondrous works in the Name of the Father, Son, and Holy Ghost, and being inspired and assisted with thy Holy Spirit I may set forth his praise and Glory Knowing of a Certain, I can perform or do nothing but what is given unto me from above, therefore, in all my Acts, and at all times, I will call upon thy most Holy Name for thine help and assistance.

I Beseech thee O Lord God that thou wilt purge me and wash me and clean me in the Blood of Our Saviour from all my sins and frailties. And that thou wilt henceforward Vouchsafe to keep and defend me from Pride, Lust, Lying, Swearing, Blasphemy, Drunkeness. Sloth, Covetousness, Evil Communications, and all deadly sins and offences, profaneness, and Spiritual wickedness. But that I may lead a Godly, Sober, Constant, Holy, Pure, and Undefiled Life, walking uprightly in thy sight through the Merits of Christ Our Lord and Saviour, Amen."

[121] "Omnipotent and Eternal Lord God who sittest in Heaven and dost from thence behold all the Dwellers upon Earth, Most mercifully I beseech thee to hear and answer the petitions of thine Unworthy servant, which I shall make unto thee through Christ our Lord who liveth and reigneth with thee in the Unity of the Holy Spirit Ever one God World without end, Amen.

Send down O Lord, the Spirit of thy Grace upon us. Enabling us to bring to pass what I now desire. Give me strength and courage to call thy Spirits from their several coasts that they may Commune with me, and truly fulfill my Desires in all things. O Lord put fear far from me. Give me an abundance of thy Grace and faith whereby all things are made possible unto man, put Envy and wicked Phantasms far from my mind and grant me true Zeal, Favour, and an Intensive Spirit of Prayer, that I may offer up a well pleasing Sacrifice unto thee.

I beseech thee O Holy Father, that thou wilt purge me from all uncleanness, both of Flesh, and Spirit that neither the Deceiver, nor any of his Spirits may have power to hurt me in Soul or Body, or any way

---

[229] See also See Scot (1665), p. 221.

hinder the Accomplishment of my Desires, or hurt, or terrify, or affright me in any manner of way, but let me use thy Ministering Spirits and Angels O Lord so as I may thereby have wisdom and knowledge. Grant O Most Merciful God that this which I desire may come to Effect, and that whichsoever of thine Angels I shall call, may Speedily attend to the words and Conjurations of my mouth, and come unto me in the peace of the Lord Christ, Amen.

Lord, I believe help my unbelief, in thee alone is fulness of all things &c. from thee proceedeth Every Good Gift, for thou art Alpha and Omega, to thee therefore be ascribed, is rightly due, all Honour and Glory.

O Blessed and Most Merciful God, who art full of Pity and Compassion, [122] thou hast promised at what time soever a sinner doth repent him of his sins, from the bottom of his heart, thou wilt turn away the remembrance of them from before thy face. I Confess unto thee O Father, most humbly and sorrowfully, that I was born, and hath lived in iniquity and transgression, ever since I came forth from my mother's womb. I have justly merited thine indignation. But do thou O Lord forgive me in the Blood of our Lord Christ, and grant that for the future I may walk in Newness of Life, and Holiness of Conversation, in and through Our Only Lord and Saviour, Jesus Christ. Amen.

O Lord I beseech thou wilt hear and answer in the Wounds of Our Blessed [Saviour], Saying as He Himself hath taught us, saying, Our Father, which art in Heaven, &c. &c.

In the Name of our Lord Jesus Christ, the Father and the Holy Ghost, the Holy Trinity, and Unspeakable Unity, I Call upon thee that thou mayest be my Salvation and Defence, and the Protector of my Body and Soul, and of all my Goods, through the Virtue of thy Holy Cross, and through the Virtue of thy Passion, I Beseech thee O Lord Jesus Christ that thou wilt Bless and Sanctify these Consecrations and Benedictions which I shall utter with my mouth, and offer up and make in thy Most Holy Name, and that thou wilt give me thy Divine Virtue and Strength, that which of thy Angels or Ministering Spirits I shall Invoke, or Conjure may readily appear unto [me], and attend to the words and Conjurations of my mouth. Grant this O Lord, for the Merits of this thy Holy Name, Amen.

Holy, Holy, Lord God of Sabaoth, who shall come to Judge the Quick and the Dead, thou art Alpha and Omega, First and Last, King of Kings, and Lord of Lords, **Ioth Aglanbroth, El Abiel Anathiel Hel Messias Escherie Athanatos Imas.** By these thy Holy Names, by all others, [123] I do call upon thee and beseech thee O Lord Christ. By thy Nativity and Baptism. By thy Cross and Passion. By thy Precious Death and Burial. By thy Glorious Resurrection and Ascension. By the coming of the Holy Ghost. By the Bitterness of thy Soul when it departed from the Body. By thine Angels, Archangels, Prophets, and Patriarchs, and by all sacraments which are made in thine honour. I do worship and beseech thee to accept these prayers, Conjurations and words of my mouth which I shall utter and use, and that being Strengthened, Sanctified and Blessed by the power of thy Holy Spirit, they may by thy Holy Command be Efficacious. And that such of thy Spirits, or Angels, as I shall Invoke may thereunto attend [and readily appear forthwith unto me from their several Coasts]²³⁰ according to the words by one to be pronounced, and then truly fulfill and satisfy all my requests in the Name of the Father, and of the Son, and of the Holy Ghost. Amen.

I Beseech thee by thy Humility and Grace, I Implore thee O Holy **Adonay Vegadona.** And by all thy Holy Names, and by all thine Angels, Archangels, Powers, Dominations and Virtues, and by thy Names with which Solomon did Bind the Devils, and shut them up **Ethrack Elion Agla Goth Ioth Nabroch,** and by all thy Holy Names which are written in this Book, and by the Virtue of them all, that thou Enable me to Congregate all thy Spirits that they may give me true Answers to all my Demands, and that I receive satisfaction in all my requests without hurt in Body Soul or Goods, through our Lord **Jesus Christ** who liveth and reigneth with thee in the Unity of the Holy Spirit, Ever One God World without End, Amen.

O Father Omnipotent, O wise Son, O Holy Ghost the Comforter, and Searcher of all hearts, O ye three persons in One Godhead in Substance, who didst spare Adam and Eve in their sins, and O thou Lord who died for their Sins a most filthy, and ignominious Death, testifying it upon the Cross. O thou Most Merciful God, when I fly unto thee, and beseech thee by all the means I can, By these the Holy Names of thy Holy Son, Alpha et Omega, [124] and all other his Names, Grant me thy Virtue and power, that what I now desire, I may be able to bring to pass through thy assistance of thy Holy Angels that which of thy Spirits soever I do call upon in the Name of the Father, and of the Son, and of the Holy Ghost, may forthwith come unto me, talk and converse, so that I may plainly understand and audibly hear them speak unto me, and that I may plainly understand the words which they shall utter, through the Virtue and Merits of our Lord **Jesus Christ** thy Son who liveth and reigneth with thee in the Unity of the Holy Ghost, Ever One God World without end, Amen.

O Great and Eternal virtue of the Highest which through disposition these being called to Judgement **Vaichron Tetragrammaton Olioram Aoym Messias Sother Emanuel Adonay.** I worship thee, I invocate thee, I implore thee with all the strength of my mind that by thee my present prayers and Conjurations may be Hallowed, and that all the Angels and Spirits which I call from their several Regions and Places, by and in the Virtue of thy several Glorious, Mysterious, Incomprehensible Unspeakable Names may come unto me forthwith and fulfill my will and requests in all things. In the Name of the Father, and of the Son, and of the Holy Ghost.

Fiat. Fiat. Fiat. Amen, Amen, Amen.

In the Name of the Most Glorious God of Paradise of Heaven and of Earth, of the Seas, and of the Infernals by thine Omnipotent help. May I perform this work who liveth and reigneth. Ever One God World without End. Amen. O most Strong and Almighty God, without beginning or ending by thy Clemency and knowledge, I desire that my Questions, Work, and Labour may be fulfilled and truly accomplished through thy worthiness Good Lord, Amen.

---

²³⁰ The contents of the square brackets are part of the original text and not an addition. – Ed.

O Holy, Patient and Merciful God, the Lord of all Wisdom, Clear and Just, I most heartily desire thy Clemency and Mercy, Holiness and Justness to fulfill and perform this my Will and Work, through thy worthiness [125] and blessed Power who livest and reignest Ever one God World without end, Amen.

O Most Merciful Father, have mercy upon me and defend me from all Wicked, Evil and Deceitful Spirits, restrain their power Good Lord from touching, hurting, terrifying, or affrighting me in Body and Soul for thy Great Mercy's Sake. I beg, implore, and beseech thee O my God and rock of my Salvation, my stay and my Guide. But that I beg thy Divine Nature will please and assist that I may become a Contemplator of thy Glorious Works, and may be illustrated [illuminated] with all Divine Wisdom and Knowledge, that thereby, I may bring Honour and Glory to thy Most Blessed Name. Amen.

In Nomine **Orphaniel** Angelo Magno precioso et honorato, Vene in pace.

In Nomine **Zebul** Angelo Majori atque forti et potento, Vene in pace.

In Nomine **Dagiel** Angelo magno principe forte atque potenti, Vene in pace.

In Nomine **Salamla** Angelo potentissima magni et honorato, Vene in pace.

In Nomine **Acimoy** Angelo Magnifortis potentis et honorato, Vene in pace.

In Nomine Pastoris Angelis Sancti et Magni, Vene in pace.

In Nomine popelius Angeli Magni et potentis et principis, Vene in Pace."

IN>--------------<RI

"Samac Salamana Belmai Geragam Raamansin Escherie Miel Egrephas Josanum Sabach Harm Robe Sepha Sother Ramar Semiot Lemaie Pherator Amiphin Gesegon Amen, Amen, Amen."

>------------------<

INRI

[126] Names and Offices of The
Ruling Presiding and Ministering
SPIRITS

Spirits of the Sun Gabriel, Michael, Vionatraba.
Presiding Spirits Pabel Ustael Burchat
Serving or Ministering Spirits Capabili Atel Aniel Magabriel Habudiel

[127] **Spirits of the Moon** Gabriel Michael Madiel	**Spirits of Jupiter** Zadkiel Sachiel Castiel Asasiel
Presiding Spirits Deamiel Janael Sachiel Zaniel	*Presiding Spirits* Suth Rex Maguth Gutriz

Ministering Spirits Habiel Bachanael Corabiel Mael Uvael	*Ministering Spirits* Curaniel Pabiel Hanum Osael Vianiel Janiel Zeubiel Miltiel
Spirits of Mars Samael Friague Guael	**Spirits of Venus** Anael Sachiel Chedu Sitaniel
Presiding Spirits Damael Calzas Arragon Lama	*Presiding Spirits* Corat Tamael Senaciel Turiel Coniel
Ministering Spirits Astagna Lobquin Soneas Jaxel Isiael	*Ministering Spirits* Babiel, Hadie Maltiel Huphaltiel Maltiel Peniel Penael Penat Porno
Spirits of Mercury Raphael Mathlai Tarmiel	**Spirits of Spirits, Saturn** Cassiel Machatan Uriel Balidet
Presiding Spirits Baraborat Jerescue Mitraton Thiel	*Presiding Spirits* Maymon Abumalith Assaibi
Ministering Spirits Reael Jerabel Venabel Abniori	*Ministering Spirits* Bilet Misabis Caimax Ismoli Passron Suquinos Hunabel Cynabat

[128] "Omnipotent and Eternal God who hast ordained the whole Creation for thy praise and Glory, and for the Salvation of Man, I earnestly Beseech that thou wouldst send me one of thy Spirits of the order of **Jupiter**, one of the Messengers of **Zadkiel** whom thou hast appointed governor of thy Firmament at this present time most faithfully, willingly, and readily to shew me these things which I shall ask, Command, or require of Him, and truly execute my desires, nevertheless, O Most Holy God, thy will, and not mine be done, through **Christ** thine only begotten Son our Lord, Amen.

O Lord we place our hope in thee. Doubt not the Righteousness of our heart. Thou lovest the Just, hatest the wicked, be our protector. Thou art our Strength and thou alone can help us, strengthen us with thy Divine Power, we have nothing to fear from Evil Spirits, be in the midst of our hearts and we cannot be frightened.

O Lord, the Almighty Creator of the Air, the Heaven, the Earth and the Water, deign to be with me in this Circle, we are here with humility by the Inspiration of an Eternal Goodness, of a Divine prosperity and abundant charity, may the adverse Spirits be removed far from this place, and may the Angels of peace succour us.

O Lord, Condescend to extend over us thy Infinite Mercy and may these thy Holy Names be ever blessed and protect our operations, this Celestial and Mysterious Circle incloses thy Hallowed Names. O Lord our hope and Sustainer, have mercy upon us and Enable us to bring our Operations to perfection, Amen.

O Lord hearken unto us, let our Exclammations *(sic)* reach even unto thy Greatness O God, who hast reigned throughout all ages, who by thine Infinite Mercy and Wisdom, hast created everything Visible and Invisible. We praise thee, we bless thee, we adore thee, and Glorify thee for ever. Deign to be propitious unto us, we are the work of thy hands, deliver us from the night of Ignorance, which conceals thee from the Unjust who deserve not thy blessing. Enlighten our hearts, with a portion of wisdom, [129] take away from our sense all wicked and criminal desires, be favourable unto us by thy power and

Greatness, and by thy Terrible and Ineffable Name which is **Saday** at which all tremble in the Heavens, in the Air, in the Earth, in the Abyss of <u>waters</u>. Cause that the Spirits of whom we have need may come and shew themselves to us with mildness, that they may be obedient and shew unto us that which we desire. Amen."

INVOCATION

"Spirits whose Assistance I require, behold the Sign and the very Hallowed Names of God, full of power, who with a breath is able to bow everything. Tremble and Obey the power of this our Pentacle. Go out of your hidden Caves and dark places Cease your hurtful occupations to the unhappy Mortals whom without ceasing you torment. Come into this place where the Divine Goodness has assembled us, be attentive to our Orders and Known to our just Demands, believe not that your resistance will cause us to abandon our Operations, <u>nothing</u> can dispense with your obeying us, We Command you by the Mysterious Names, **Elohe Agla Elohim Adonay Gibort.** Amen.

I call upon thee **Zadkiel** in the Name of the Father, and of the Son, and of the Holy Ghost, Blessed Trinity, Unspeakable Unity.

I Invoke and Intreat thee **Zadkiel** in this hour to attend to the words and Conjurations which I shall use this Day by the Holy Names of God **Elohe El Elohim Elion Zebaoth Escherie Jah Adonay Tetragrammaton.**

I Conjure, thee, I Exorcise thee thou Spirit **Zadkiel** by these Holy Names **Hagios O Theos Iseyros Athanatos Paracletus Agla On Alpha et Omega Joth Aglanbroth** [130] **Abiel Anathiel Tetragrammaton -**

יהוה

and by all other Great and Glorious, Holy and Unspeakable Names, the Mysterious Mighty, Powerful, Incomprehensible Names of God that you attend unto the words of my mouth, and send unto me **Pabiel** or other of your Ministering serving Spirits who may shew me such things as I shall demand of him in the Name of the Father, and of the Son, and of the Holy Ghost. Amen.

I Intreat the[e] **Pabiel** by the whole Spirit of Heaven, Seraphim, Cherubim, Thrones, Dominations, Witness, Powers, Principalities Archangels, Angels, by the Holy Great and Glorious Angels **Ophaniel, Tetra, Dagiel, Salimia, Acimoy, Pastor Poti,** that thou come forthwith readily shew thyself, that we may see you, and audibly hear you speak unto us, and fulfill our Desires, and by your Star which is **Jupiter,** and by all the Constellations of Heaven, and by whatsoever thou obeyest, and by thy Character which thou has given, proposed, and confirmed, that you attend unto me according to the Prayers and Petitions which I have made unto Almighty God. And that, thou forthwith sendest unto me one of thy Ministering Spirits, who may willingly, truly and faithfully fulfill all my Desires, and that thou commandest him to appear unto me in the form of a Beautiful Angel, Gently Courteously, Affable, and Meekly entering into Communication with me, and that he neither permitting any Evil Spirit to approach in any sort of way to hurt terrify or affright me, nor deceiving me in any wise. Through the

Virtue of Our Lord and Saviour **Jesus Christ** in whose Name I attend, wait for, and expect thy Appearance.

Fiat Fiat Fiat

Amen. Amen. Amen."

After repeating this powerful Invocation earnestly and with great faith and Devotion the Spirit will be compelled to appear receive him courteously, Bind him with the Bond of Spirits then the Invocant need not fear, but he must take care that he asks nothing but what is lawful and right. His appearance is generally attended with great Splendour.

[131] **Interrogatories**[231]

"Comest thou in peace, in the Name of the Father, Son, and Holy Ghost? *Yes*

Thou art Welcome Noble Spirit, what is thy Name? *Yes*

I have called thee in the name of **Jesus of Nazareth** at whose Name Every knee doth bow both in Heaven, Earth, and Hell, and every tongue shall confess there is no Name like unto the Name of **Jesus** who hath given power unto Man to bind and to loose all things in his most Holy Name. Yea even unto those that trust in his Salvation.

Art thou the Messenger of **Zadkiel**? *Yes.*

Wilt thou Confirm thyself unto me at this time and henceforth reveal all things unto me that I shall desire to know, and teach me how I may, Increase in Wisdom and Knowledge and shew unto me all the Secrets of the Magic Art, and of all Liberal Sciences, that I may thereby set forth the Glory of Almighty God.? *Yes*

Then I pray thee give and Confirm thy Character unto me whereby I may call at all times, and also swear unto me this Oath, and I will Religiously keep my Vow and Covenant unto Almighty God and will courteously receive thee at all times where thou dost appear unto me."

[132] יהוה [והרה]

IHS

Magister   Zadkiel   Pabel [Pabiel]

[133] **Form of a Bond of Spirits**

"**I Pabiel,** Ministering Spirit and Messenger of the Presiding and Ruling Spirit of **Jupiter,** appointed thereunto by the Creator of all, Visibly and Invisible do swear, promise and plight my faith, and unto thee in the presence, and before the Great יהרה [יהוה] and the whole Company and Host of Heaven, and by all the Holy Names of God do swear and bind myself unto thee by all the contents of God's sacred Writ, by the Incarnation, Sufferings, Passion, and Death, By the Resurrection and Glorious Ascension of Our Lord and Saviour **Jesus Christ.** By all the Holy Sacraments, By the Mercy of God, by the Glory

---

[231] Questions that should be addressed to the spirit, with the answer that the spirit should give. – Ed.

and Joys of Heaven, By the Forgiveness of Sin, and hope of Eternal Salvation, By thy Great Day of Doom, By all Angels, Archangels, Seraphim, Cherubim, Dominations, Thrones, Principalities, Powers and Virtues, and all other be blessed and Glorious Company of Heaven, By all the Constellations of Heaven, and by all the Several Powers and Virtues above rehearsed and by whatsoever Else is Holy or binding through, Do I swear and promise and Vow unto thee that I will Come, appear, and haste unto thee, and at all times and places, and in all Hours, Minutes and Days, from this time forward unto thy life's end. Wheresoever thou shalt Call me by my Name, or by my Office, and I will come unto thee in what form thou shalt Desire, either Visibly or Invisibly, and will answer all thy Desires, and give testimony thereof, and let all the powers of Heaven witness it. I have hereunto Subscribed my Hand and Confirm my Seal and Character unto thee. Amen."

Bethor – Pabiel - Sachiel

[134] The aforesaid Bond of Spirits together with the Seal and Character of the Planetary Angel must be written on Virgin Parchment and laid before the Spirit when he appears; at that time The Invocant must not lose confidence but be patient, firm bold and persevering and as aforesaid take care that he requires nothing of the Spirit but with a view to the Glory of God, and the well being of his fellow creatures. Having obtained his Desires of the Spirit, the Invocant may License him to Depart in the following manner.

License to Depart

"For as much as thou comest in Peace and Quietness, and hast answered unto my Petition, I give humble and hearty thanks unto Almighty God in whose Name I called thee and thou camest, and now thou mayest Depart in peace unto thine Orders, and return unto me again at what time soever I shall call thee by thine Oath, or by thy Name, or by thine Order, or by thine Office, which is Granted thee from the Creator, and the power of God be with me and thee, and upon the whole Issue of God Amen.
Glory be to the Father, and to the Son, and to the Holy Ghost."

It would be advisable for the Invocant to remain in the Circle for a few minutes after reciting the Licence, and if the place of Operation be in the open air, let him destroy all traces of the Circle &c. and return quietly to his home. But should the Operation be performed in a retired part of a House, the Circle may remain as it might serve in a like future Operation, but the room or Building must be locked to avoid the intrusion of the Vulgar.

[135] **Plate IV. PENTACLES**

Of The

Seven

PLANETS

[136] **Plate V.** [Seal of the] **Sun**

[137] **Plate VI.** [Seal of the] **Moon**

[138] **Plate VII.** [Seals of the other 5 planets]

[139] The following Invocations of the Seven Planetary Spirits, or Angels must be earnestly recited before the

Appearance of the Spirit whom the Invocant wishes to Invoke using one of the Invocations proper for the Spirit, and so of the rest in addition to the forms of prayer and Invocations before rehearsed.

Invocation of the Spirits of the Sun.

"O ye Heavenly Spirits who have been Created to behold the face of Him who is seated on the Cherubims, I Conjure you in the Name **Saday, Cados, Phaa,** and by the name of the first Light which is the Sun, that you come and Contribute to the success of my Operations. I Beseech you to Employ your power and Virtue in keeping off the Evil Spirits that might overturn the benign Influence of my work by Virtue of **Abiaye Rapdiel Caracazad Amadiel.** *ff.*"

Invocation of the Moon

"Haste ye Sublime and Sublunary Genii who are obedient to the Sovereign Grace Come and Assist in the Operation that I undertake under the Auspicies of the Grand Luminary of the Night, I Invoke you to this purpose be favourable and hear my Entreaties in the Name of Him who Commands the Spirits in the Regions you inhabit **Bileth Missabu Abuzaha.** *ff.*"

Invocation of Mars

"Come Military Warlike Genii who execute the Commands of the Sovereign Ruler of the Universe, Come and assist me in the operation that I undertake, Come I conjure you by the Name **Elibra, Elohim, Saday.** Keep from me all Evil Spirits that my Labours of this Day may not be frustrated I Conjure you by the Mighty names of your Rulers **Damael Lobquin** *ff.*"

[140] Invocation of Mercury.

"Great and Swift Spirits of Mercury, we pray you to hear our humble petition and Supplication. Come to us ye Spirits who preside over the operation of this day, hear favourably the Invocation I now make unto you O ye Heavenly Genii who have power over the wonders that are wrought on this Day. Come and remove the Rebel Spirits, and cause me to succeed in my Operation. *ff.*"

Invocation of Jupiter

"I Conjure you by the Holy Name **Emanuel** all your Heavenly Genii, who second by your Aid the Great Distributor of Health Honour and Riches, Come to my Assistance, reject not the prayer that I make unto you through the Intercession of thy Spirits **Maguth Gutriz** be kind and refuse me not thy powerful Aid. *ff.*"

Invocation of Venus

"Come on the wings of the wind ye happy Spirits, who preside over the workings of the Heart, I Conjure you by the Veneration You have for the Mysterious Name Setchiel, hear favourably the Invocation that I make this Day destined to the wonders of the Lord. Be ready to lend me your Assistance to succeed in what I have now undertaken. *ff.*"

Invocation of Saturn

"I conjure you by the Name of the Spirit, and the Sovereign Creator of all things by the wonderful Names of the Deity to whom thou art Subject **Adonay, Agla, Tetragrammaton, Gaha,** hear me I Adjure you O Mighty Spirit, and grant me your Assistance that I may succeed in my Operations of this Day. *ff.*"

[141] **Plate VIII. Seals and Characters of the Seven Planets With Their Perfumes.**

Och - Michael

Perfume

Saffron, Aloes Balsam of Myrrh or Caurier [Laurier] the sixth part of an ounce added to a grain of Musk and Ambergris pulverized and mixed together into the size of small peas.

[142] **Plate IX. Phul – Gabriel**

Perfume

The Head of a Frog, the eyes of a Bull, a grain of white Poppy, Storax, Loadstone Camphor pulverized with the paste of young Bailey.

Perfume

Euphorbium Bdellium Sal Ammoniac Helebore Roots and a little Sulpher *(sic)* made into paste with the Blood of a Black Cat and the Brains of a Raven.

Phaleg - Samael

[143] **Plate X. Ophiel - Raphael**

Perfume

Mastic of the East Chosen Incense Aloes Powder of Agate pulverized and made into paste with Fox's Blood, and the Brains of two or three Magpies, and made into small Balls.

Perfume

The seed of the Ash Tree, the Wood or shoot of Aloes Storax, Loadstone, and powder of Benjamin and the end of quills mixed together and made into small Balls.

Bethor - Sachiel

[144] **Plate XI. Hagith - Arael**

Perfume

Musk Ambergris, Wood of Aloes Dried Red Roses, Coral, pulverized & made into paste with the Blood of a Pigeon & the Brains of three Sparrows.

Perfume

Grains of Black Pepper, Grains of Hogsbane, Roots of Mandrake, Powder of Loadstone Myrrh of the East, pulverized and made into a paste with the Blood of a Bat and the Brains of a Black Cat.

Aratron - Cassiel

[Part 6. Crystallomancy]

Crystaliomancy *(sic)*

or

The Art of Invocating

SPIRITS

By

The

CRYSTAL

[146] **Preface**

The art of Invocating Spirits by the Crystal was known and practised by the Ancients which all those who read Sacred or profane History may discover. The Sacred Text contains many instances in which Invocation by the Crystal is alluded to, and it is the opinion of many Learned and Eminent Men that the Urim and Thummim of the Holy Scripture was used for a similar purpose as the Crystal is in our day.

As it is nowhere forbidden in Scripture to enquire of and hold Converse with the good Spirits, it is not accounted sinful to Invoke their Spiritual Aid in all matters that are just and lawful. For this purpose whoever wishes to obtain the assistance of these good Spirits, must lead a Religious Life, keeping himself as is were apart from the World, making himself clean and pure, also make frequent Ablutions and prayers for several days before he begins his Operations. Moreover, he must possess great courage, firmness, Confidence and Skill in all he undertakes relative to the Operation he is about to perform. He must be earnest in the recital of the Benedictions, Invocations, &c. for if only carelessness is employed, he or they who do this, only trifle to be trifled with to their cost. For doubtless the All wise and Benevolent Creator implanted in the Heart of Man a desire to search [147] into the Future so a certain extent as for as this life is concerned, at the same time He allowed him lawful and just means to gratify it such as that Transcendent Science of pure Astrology teaches. But Crystaliomancy being of a higher order still, Man is capable by the Assistance of and holding Converse with the Celestial Messengers, of arriving at that knowledge and perfection that will be of the utmost benefit to him in this Life, also assist in fitting him for another and better World.

It will be vain for any one who thinks of gaining any of this World's riches &c. by calling upon these bright Spirits for their assistance, for such would be most assuredly denied them, for it is only to the Wise and prudent that these secrets are revealed. Therefore any one wishing to Experimentalize with unlawful wishes Unchaste or Unholy desires would meet with nothing, but Shame, Confusion and Disappointment.

[148] **Concerning the Rules, Forms, Ceremonies, &c. to be necessarily observed in the Practice of this Art**

The Invocant may if he choose at the commencement of his Operations, have one or two wise, discreet persons as companions to assist him, but he, or they must conform to all the rules and forms necessary likewise consent to all that is required so carry this Operation in effect. Every preparation made for this purpose (during the Increase of the Moon, must be done. The Invocant may perform these Operations at any Season of the

Year providing he finds the Luminaries in fortunate aspect with each other also with the Benefic Planets Jupiter and Venus. When the Sun has reached his greatest Northern Declination is said to be the best time. All the Instruments Apparatus &c. required in the Operation must be entirely new, having never before been devoted to any other purpose, they must be made or provided by the Operator himself or under his immediate supervision and at the proper time as he shall direct. He must be careful to leave no part of the Operation un-performed, for upon the exactness with which it's performed depends the certainty of his success. The Operator must take notice every thing employed in this Art must be duly consecrated before being used. After which he should allow no persons to touch or handle any Instrument &c. particularly the Crystal, except himself or his companions in the Operation. The more sacred they are kept the more fit for that which they are designed. The forms of Consecration may be found in the sequel of this Work.[232]

[149] Concerning the Room Containing the CIRCLE

The Invocant must in order to carry on his Work have a small Room in a retired part of the House such as an Attic, or a low kitchen might be preferred, made clean and neat, having no sumptuous ornaments to divide or distract his attention, also free from the Hurry of Business and from the prying and curious intruder. The floor must be perfectly clean and even so as to receive the lines of the Circle and Characters to be traced thereon.

The Circle may then be drawn seven feet in diameter and, the Holy Names and Characters written therein according to the following Model, with consecrated Chalk or Charcoal. Should not the Invocant have a pair of Compasses of sufficient, r[a]dius to trace the lines of the Circle, He may use a piece of Twine attached to a pin as a centre, and the other end fastened to the Chalk or Charcoal. He may if he choose, in the absence of the above mentioned articles, sprinkle the floor with find sand and then draw the Circle, Characters &c. with the Magic Sword; but the first method mentioned is by far the best, and being the most durable, may by being used carefully, so preserved as to serve in several of the like Operations. The room when not in use must be kept locked up.

The Invocant must be reminded that this preparation also must be made during the increase of the Moon.

[150] Plate I.

[151] Concerning the Apparatus and Instruments used in this Art

The Operator must be provided with a small table covered with a fair white Linen Cloth, also a Chair which should be placed in the Room ready for the Operation. Also the necessary Apparatus for making a fire when required, in order to burn the perfumes and making a fumigation proper to the Planet governing the Operation and the hour in which he would work. Also a Torch, and two wax Candles placed in Gilded or Brass Candlesticks highly polished and Engraven as shown.

The Operator must have a pair of Compasses wherewith to Draw the Circle, also some Twine or Thread, a Knife, a pen-knife, a pair of Scissors. A Magic Sword of pure steel and about two feet and a half in length and about one inch in width and engraven as shown. Also wand of Hazel Wood of a year's growth and a yard in

---

[232] Part 2. – Ed.

length and Engraven as shown. The Operator must also have as Small New Box containing the following Articles: small Vials containing the perfume for each planet, also small bottles containing ink suitable to each planet, (see former part of this work) some paper, parchment, with proper pens of either Raven or Crow's Quill, to write thereon.

To give sacredness, also extra power to the Operation in an Experiment. The operator should be clad in white Linen Garments and white shoes also a girdle of Virgin parchment or highly polished Leather, and fortified with the Twelve Great Names of God written thereon in letters of Gold.

[152] Description of the Crystal

The Invocant must be provided with a crystal of about four inches in Diameter or at least the size of a large orange, properly ground and polished (on a Friday when the Sun gets into his own sign Leo) so as to be free from Specs or Spots, it must be inclosed in a Frame of Ivory, Ebony, or Boxwood, highly polished and around which must written in raised Letters of Gold the Mighty Names of Supreme Majesty Tetragrammaton, Adonay, Emanuel, Agla. Round this Frame are fixed five small Crystals to represent the Animal, Vegetable, Mineral and Astral kingdoms, and the one at the top to represent the B of the Lord. The pillar and Pedestal to which the frame containing the Crystal is fixed may be formed of any suitable wood and design as shown to be gilded, or highly polished, the Name written thereon as aforesaid. N.B. If the Operator cannot do all this himself he must employ therein some discreet and skilful Artist, to do it but he must be present in order to see that no part of the work is neglected or done improperly, and to employ the proper days and hours for such work. When completed it must be duly Consecrated as aforesaid, and then placed in a New Box, or Drawer properly fastened with lock and key to keep it free from Dust, also from the touch and sight of the Vulgar or common people.

The crystal may be used in a Common plain frame, and without the five additional Crystals; but it has not so much virtue & power, for by their Addition & the manner in which the whole is Executed is said to be more efficacious in the Operations.

[153] Plate II.

[154] Consecration of the Ground

Bless O Lord I beseech thee this Ground and place and drive away all evil and Wickedness from this Circle. Sanctify and make it become meet and convenient for thy servant to finish and bring to pass therein all my Desires through Our Lord and Saviour, Amen. Be thou Blessed, Purified and Consecrated in the Name of the Father and of the Son and of the Holy Ghost.

Blessing of the Lights

I Bless in the Name of the Father and of the Son, and of the Holy Ghost. O Holy Holy Holy Lord God, Heaven and Earth are full of thy Glory, before whose face there is a bright shining Light forever. Bless now O Lord these creatures of light which thou hast given for the kindly use of Man, that they by thee being Sanctified, may not be put out or extinguished by the Malice, power, or filthy darkness of Satan. But may shine forth brightly and lend their assistance to this Holy Work through Christ our Lord Amen.

Consecration of the Instruments

O Great God, who art the God of Strength and greatly to be feared. Bless O Lord these Instruments that they may be a terror unto the Enemy and therewith I may overcome phantasms and oppositions of the Devil through thy Influence and help of thy Holy and Mighty Names, **On El Agla Tetragrammaton**, and in the Cross of Christ our Lord, Amen.

[155] Consecration of the Crystal

Eternal God who by thy wisdom hast given and appointed great power in the Characters and other Holy Writings of thy Spirits, and hast given unto them that with them faithfully power thereby to work many things. Bless now O Lord this Crystal formed, framed and written by the hand of mine unworthy servant that being filled with Divine Virtue, Power and Influence by thy Command O Most Holy God it may shew forth its virtue and power to thy praise and Glory. Through Christ Our Lord and Saviour, Amen.

Then say

I Bless and Consecrate this Crystal I the Name of the Father, and of the Son, and of the Holy Ghost.

The Invocant must have the Seal of the Spirit he would Invoke, Also the Pentacle and Character of the Planet governing the Day and hour of Operation, and above all the Grand Pentacle of Solomon[233] the Model of which is given in the former part of this Book, these must be written on Virgin Parchment with proper ink and duly Consecrated in the Aforesaid manner. In Consecrating all the Instruments &c. necessary in this Art. The Invocant must recite the Forms &c. while placing his hands upon the different Articles with his Face turned towards the East.

[156] Plate III.

[157] Having done that he may then place the Table with the Crystal thereon together with a Candlestick containing a lighted wax candle on each side before the Circle. All being ready. Let the Invocant and his companions (if any) enter the Circle in the Day and Hour of Mercury (the Moon increasing) and commence his Operations by earnestly Invoking the Spirit Vassago, as an Experiment in the following manner.

Invocation

"I Exorcise Call upon and Command thee Spirit Vassago by and in the Name of the Immense and Everlasting God **Jehovah Adonay Elohim Agla El On Tetragrammaton** and by and in the Name of Our Lord and Saviour **Jesus Christ** the only Son of the Eternal and true God Creator of Heaven and Earth and all that is in them **Wipius Sother Emanuel Primogenitus Homonsion Bomes Via Veritas Sapientia Virtus Leof Mediator Agnus Rex Pastor Prophetas Sacerdos Athanetos Paracletus Alpha et Omega,** by all these High Great Glorious Royal and Ineffable Names of the Omnipotent God and by His only Son our Lord and Saviour **Jesus Christ** the second essence of the Glorious Trinity. I Exorcise Command and Call upon and Conjure thee Spirit **Vassago** wheresoever thou Art, (East, West,

---

[233] This All powerful Pentacle should be present at all Magical Operations, where the good Angels or Spirits are invoked to appear. – Sibley.

North or South or being bound to anyone under the Compass of the Heavens) that you come immediately from the place of your private abode or residence and appear to me visibly in fair and decent form in this Crystal Stone or Glass. I do again Exorcise and Powerfully Command thee Spirit **Vassago** to come and appear Visibly to me in this Crystal Stone or Glass. I do again strongly bind and Command thee Spirit **Vassago** to come and appear visibly to me in that Crystal Stone or Glass, by the Virtue and power of these Names by which I can bind all rebellious [158] Obstinate and Refractory Spirits **Alla Carital Marihal Carion Urion Spyton Lorean Marmos Agaion Cados Yron Astron Gardeong Tetragrammaton Strallay Spignos Yah On El Elohim** by all aforesaid, I Charge and Command thee Spirit **Vassago** to make haste and come away and appear visibly to me as aforesaid without any further tarrying or Delay in the Name of Him who shall come to Judge the Quick and Dead and the World by Fire."

Amen.

This Conjuration after repeated and the Invocant being patient and constant in his perseverance, and not disheartened nor dismayed by reason of tedious Prolixity or Delay. The Spirit will at last appear. Bind him with the Bond of Spirits, and then you may talk with him &c.

That this is a true Experiment, and that the Spirit halt been obliged to the fellowship and Service of a Magic Artist heretofore is very certain as may appear by this following Obligation the which, the Invocant may if he pleaseth have fairly written on an Abortive[234] and laid before him and discourse with the Spirit concerning it.

[159] Bond of Spirits

I **Vassago** under **Baro** the King of the West, not compelled by command or fear but of my own accord and free will, especially oblige myself by these presents firmly and faithfully and without deceit to J.W.[235] to obey at any time and at any place whensoever and wheresoever he shall call upon me personally to appear in this Crystal Stone or Glass and to fulfil his Commands truly in all things wherein I can by the virtue of all the Names of God especially by those words the most powerful in the Magical Art **Lay Abryca Mura Spron Malgava Ryshin Layagamum Arasin Layson** and by virtue wherewith the Sun and Moon were darkened and my Planet and by the Celestial Characters thereof and principally by this Seal binding most solidly. In witness of which Guilty Person he commanding I have signed this Present Obligation with mine own Seal to which I always stick close.

Vassago

Seal of the Spirit Vassago

[160] After the Invocant has obtained the assistance and the desired Information of the Spirit he may courteously License him to Depart in the following manner.

---

[234] Virgin parchment. – Ed.

[235] The initials of the Operator to whom the spirit was bound. – Ed.

License to Depart

Forasmuch as thou comest in peace and quietness without noise, terror, or hurt to me (or my fellows) and hast answered unto my petition, I give humble and hearty thanks unto Almighty God, in whose Name I called thee and thou camest and now thou **Vassago**, mayest Depart in Peace unto thine Orders and return unto me again at what time soever I shall call thee by thine Oath, or by Name, or by thine Order, or by thine Office which is Granted from the Creator, and the power of God be with me and thee and upon the whole Issue of God, Amen. Glory be to the Father, and of the Son, and to the Holy Ghost.

As all Aerial Spirits are very Powerful, and slow in their appearance, so also is their Departure, and it would be as well for the Invocant not to leave the limits of the Circle for a few minutes after the Licence is recited.

The above powerful Experiment proves the possibility and truth and reality of the existence of Aerial Spirits who may be compelled to appear at the will of the Operator, and be so bound as to become subservient to his Desires provided he asks nothing but what is just and right, which will assuredly be granted if he retains the firm confidence and strict secrecy.

[161] Invocation by the Crystal may be used for the purpose of conversing with, and obtaining the assistance of the Planetary Angels, and as they are not so Obstinate and Refractory as the Aerial Spirits they are more easily invoked to appearance, and being gentle and mild generally in their Demeanour, there is no danger in the Operation of calling them to appear, which they will readily do afterwards at the Will of the Operator, particularly the Angel or Spirit governing the Planet under whose Influence the person desirous of assistance is born. The Invocant must take care that in Invocating any one of these Beautiful Spirits, he must first be earnest in his request and that it is according to the Nature and Office of the Spirit he invokes, for instance if he wish for Honour, Dignity, or Riches, he must perform his Operations in the hour of the Sun on Sunday, and so of the rest which the first part of this Book teaches. The Operator may use the same forms & Ceremonies as for the Aerial Spirits, taking great care that no part of them be neglected, then he may expect success infallibly to follow.

To Conclude, The Invocant must observe the greatest pecularities *(sic)* in the Science of Magic, are the particular Ingredients required, Tools Apparatus &c. Times & Seasons of Conducting the Operation. And Secrecy, for every portion or part must be performed strictly according to the rules given and every Detail with the minutest exactness & Care.

[162] [Part 7. Miscellaneous Examples and Experiments]

[163] **Miscellaneous**

Examples and Experiments

In

Natural, Cabalistic, and Ceremonial

Magic

With the Experiment in all its Details of Raising the Powerful Spirit Oberion

Also the

Measure, Proportion and Harmony of the Human Body

Magic Tables &c

The whole Executed with Illuminated and Coloured

Figures, Circles &c

Concluding with the Art of Fascination &c

1520

[164] **Natural Magic**

CHARMS &c.

To Fascinate Birds.

Mix together the juice of rue and vinegar and steep corn therein, this corn thrown to birds, shall so fascinate them upon eating thereof that they may be easily caught with the hand. In like manner poppy seeds steeped in brandy for twenty-four hours will have the same effect.

To make a Room appear in Flames, or to be filled with Serpents &c.

Take half an ounce of Sal-ammoniac, one ounce of Camphor, and two ounces of Aqua Vitae (or requisite rectified Spirits of Wine) put them in an earthen pot, narrowing towards the top, and set fire to is. The effect will be so immediately alarming that the persons in the room will even fancy their own garments are on fire. But the illusory flames will, nevertheless do no harm.

[165] To make a Room appear full of Serpents. Take the skin of a Snake or Serpent, and in it place a wick of the like skin dried and twisted, fill up the skin with the fat of the Snake or Serpent with which you must mix some aqua vitae, and light it when the sign Scorpio is ascending with the Moon therein, and the room will instantly appear full of Serpents Snakes &c. hissing and writhing about in every direction to the horror and astonishment of the spectators, so perfect will the allusion [illusion] be that they would believe it a reality.

To make the Faces of a party appear Ghastly and Death Like.

I order to perform this strange feat take half a pint of Spirits of wine or strong Brandy, and having warmed it put a handful of salt with it into a Basin, then set it on fire with a lighted piece of paper, and [it] will have the effect of making every one present look, "As if they were newly Risen from their cold Graves." N.B. this can only be done in a close room.

Properties of Herbs &c.

"Anoint thee with the juice of Canabus [cannabis] and Archangel; and before a mirror of steel, call Spirits, and thou shalt see them and have power to bind and to loose them." "The fume of fleniculis[236] chaseth away Spirits" "Take the herb Avisum, and join it to camphire, and thou shalt see Spirits, that shall dread thee. It helpeth much to the achieving of secret things." "Petersilion chaseth away all the Spirits of Riches."

[166] The Ring of Strength

Let the Operator form the Ring of Virgin Gold on Sunday under the influence of the Sun in the Hour of Jupiter during the Increase of the Moon. It must be set with seven precious stones, at equal distances from each other, and the Names of the seven planetary Angels engraven as shown in the above Model. The Precious Stones must be as follows. The Diamond, The Ruby, The Emerald, The Jacynth, The Sapphire, The Beryl and The Topaz. This Ring must be perfumed with the composition of the following Drugs, Musk, Storax, Euphorbium, Incense, Benjamin, Ambergris, Myrrh, during this part of the Operation, the Orations for the Seven days of the Week must be recited with earnestness.

[167] Should there be not sufficient time to complete the Operation, the Operator must wait till the next favourable planetary hour arrives, on the next day of the Sun. Also should he not be able to form this Ring himself, he may employ therein some wise and discreet Artist to assist him, but he must be present in order to see that no part of the Operation be omitted. This ring may be of any convenient size and worn anywhere about the person, or may be made small enough to be worn on the finger where rings are usually worn. The composition of this Ring is attended with much Labour and expense, but the Virtue and power it possesses repays for all, being invaluable and renders the wearer thereof invincible as Achilles; fearing no man.

[168] Charm against Furious Beasts

Repeat earnestly and with sincere faith these words: -
"At destruction and famine, thou shalt laugh, neither shalt thou be afraid of the beasts of the earth."
"For thou shalt be in league with the stones of the field, and the beasts of the field shall be at peace with thee." *Job.* V - 22. 23.

Charm against Troubles in General

"He shall deliver thee in six troubles, yea in seven there shall no evil touch thee."
"In famine he shall redeem thee from death, and in war from the power of the sword."
"And thou shall know that thy tabernacle shall be in peace, and thou shalt visit thy habitation and shalt not err." *Job* V - 19. 20. 26.

Charm against Enemies

Behold God is my salvation; I will trust and not be afraid for the Lord Jehovah is my strength and my song; he is also become my Salvation.

For the stars of Heaven, and the Constellations thereof; shalt not give their light; the Sun shall be darkened in

---

[236] Or 'fieniculis.' Maybe the herb smallage. – Ed.

his going forth, and the Moon shall not cause her light to shine.

"And behold at eventide, trouble; and before the morning he is not: this is the potion of them that spoil us and the lot of them that rob us." *Isaiah* XII - XVII.

Thus also, when we would avoid peril by fire or water we make use of this passage: - "When thou passest through the Waters, I will be with thee; and through the rivers they shall not overflow thee: when thou walkest through the fire, thou shalt not be burned, neither shall the flame kindle upon me." *Isaiah* XLIII – 2.

[169] Charm to bind or Compel a Thief

To bind a thief so that he shall have neither rest nor peace till he return thee thy lost goods, go to the place from whence they were stolen away, and write the name of the person or persons thou suspectest upon fair Virgin Parchment, and put the same underneath the threshold of the door they went out of. Then make four crosses on the four corners or posts of the doorway, and go your ways saying: "Thou thief who hast stolen and taken away (here name the Article or goods) from this place, Abraham by his virtue and the power God gave him call thee back again: Isaac by his power stop thee in the way. Jacob make thee go no farther, but Bring them back again. And Joseph by his power and virtue, and also by the grace and might of the Holy Ghost force thee, to come again into this place, and that neither Solomon let thee nor David bid thee but that thou or the same through Christ Our Lord do cause thee presently and without stay to come again into this place and bring them with thee. Fiat, ffiat, ffiat, *(sic)* Cito, Cito, Cito. In the Name of the Father, and of the Son, and of the Holy Ghost."

Repeat these words three times, and the thief shall not rest nor delay till he return thee thy lost goods.

A Ring of Power to overcome Enemies

Let the character of Saturn (♄) be engraven upon a Magnet or piece of Loadstone in the time of the Moon's increase, and being worn on the right hand no enemy shall overcome the wearer.

[170] Plate II - To Cause Destruction To Enemies

The Above Talisman made on a Tuesday in the Hour of Mars when in an evil Aspect to the Moon and let the inscription in the double Circle be engraven as above shown. From this verse drawn forth the name of the Evil Angel or Messenger of Mischief Mirael מיראל of the Spiritual order of warriors whose name is Engraven in the centre as shown. This Talisman is cast or made of Iron or of Virgin parchment engraving or writing thereon the name of the Enemy whom is to be subverted or destroyed and the effects will soon follow. The wearer must keep this Talisman about him in Secrecy.

[171] A Charm to protect against Thieves

Deus autem transiens per medium, illorum, ibat + Thus sepus + benedictus Deus quotidie prosperus iter facit Deus salutaris noster + Ihus obstinenter occuli eorum ne videant, et dorsum eorum ni curva + Ihus + effundus supra eas irs tua, et furor ire tue comprehendat eos + Irnat + supra inimicas meos formido et pavo in magnitudine brachii fiant eniobiles, quasia Lapis, donec per transeat famulus tuus + quem redemisti + dextera tua magnificata est, in Virtute Domini per crusist inimicus in multitudine virtutis tuae deposuisti omnes adversarious meos + Jhesu + eripe me et ab in surgentibusque in me libera me + Jhesu + custodi me, et de manu peccatoris et ab hominibusque iniquis eripe me + Jhesu + eripe me de opera tibis que iniquitate et a viris sanguine salva me + **Gloria Patri + Authos+ Anostra + Moxio x Bay + Eloy + Apen + Agias + Yskiros.**

The words of these Charms must be repeated with great earnestness and confidence for according to the Vehement Desire of the Operator, so will to the result of the Operation: it is not the mere repeating the words that will ensure success, but a firm trust and sincere faith must accompany them, then the Charm will be efficacious. For according to the learned and the wise in these matters, there is not a Verse, Line, Word, or even a letter in the Holy Scriptures which has not some particular meaning, either offensive or defensive, being read in the original Hebrew.

[172] **Method of Raising and Invocating Spirits**

The various manuscripts relative to the fact of spiritual intercourse all agree in declaring, that those who would invocate Spirits must, for some days previously, prepare themselves to these high and mysterious ceremonies by living in a manner secluded from the rest of the world, being religiously disposed, and at least for three days must live free from sensual gratifications.

The place chosen, must be secluded, solitary, and isolated from the resort of men, where no business is carried on, where no unhallowed eye must enter, and where the pryings of curiosity remain ungratified. For this reason, dilapidated buildings, free from the tread of human footsteps; or in the midst of forests, lonely caves, or rocks by the sea shore, or where the general appearances indicate desolation and darkness. It must be remembered that all and every order of these unearthly Agents are averse to visible appearance, that when they do appear; they make use of the most horrid forms, accompanied by the loudness thunders, and most furious lightnings to affrighten the Invocator, and swerve him from his purpose. The Invocator must accustom himself to see and hear all this, without the least appearance of agitation: for this purpose, he must be a man of undaunted courage, quick foresight, of great firmness and resolution, also possessing great confidence. He must also have two associates with him, who must be well acquainted with Magic Rites, and particularly in dismissing Spirits: for it is far easier to raise than to dismiss or lay a Spirit through the unaccountable antipathy existing by thes[e] invisible [173] agents towards the human race. The place being chosen secure and free from interruption, the Invocant must choose the proper day and hour for working, according to the nature, order, and office of the Spirit he would invoke, not forgetting to raise the good Spirits in the increase of the Moon. He must also be provided with the seals of the Earth, the seals of the Spirit, and the sacred Lamen or Pentacle, above all the Pentacle of Solomon, the Magic Sword, Vestments, and other Instruments necessary for the Operation, the description of which have already been given in the first part of this *Mysterious Book*, the whole of which must be completed in the hour of Mercury. Also he must have the perfume agreeable and proper to the Spirit. Also he must Exorcise or Consecrate the place he would Invocate in after the accustomed manner. He may then proceed to draw the Circle nine feet in diameter: within the outer circle, two concentric circles of a hand's breadth must be made, and the four quarters of the world marked therein by a correct compass. In the midst for divine protection, must be described the great and powerful Names of God **Jehovah, Tetragrammaton, Adonai, Sadai**, and appropriate inscriptions: taking care that the Circles be correctly formed, and duly joined and fortified with sacred crosses within and without; the chalk or charcoal being first properly consecrated. The Lights used upon the occasion must be of wax, and each Candlestick inclosed in a magic pentacle. The sword must be of pure steel, made expressly for the occasion, and, indeed so must all the Instruments and properly Consecrated, and never be devoted to any other purpose. All things being ready, the Invocant with his associates, must enter the Circle in the proper planetary hour, and having entered, must with the [174] sword proceed to consecrate and close the Circle in the accustomed manner, after which he must proceed as he thinks fit to adjure, constrain and force the spirits to visible appearance. In doing which he must be patient not despairing, but determined to bring his will and purpose to the desired effect. After earnestly repeating the Invocation, let the Invocant look round, to see if any spirit does appear, which if he delays, then let him repeat the Invocation three times, and if the Spirit be obstinate, and will not appear, then let the Invocant adjure it with Divine power according to the nature and office of the Spirit: Thus shall he effect his purpose. When the Spirit appears, let the Invocant turn himself towards it, courteously receiving it, and demanding answers to his questions, but if the Spirit shall be obstinate ambiguous, lying, or else refractory, let the Invocant bind it with the Bond of Spirits if necessary, and if you doubt any thing, make without [outside] the circle with the consecrated sword, the figure of a triangle or pentagon, and compel the Spirit to enter it; then having obtained of the Spirit that which you desire, License it to depart with courteous words, giving it command that it do no hurt whatever. And when it is departed, make a short stay in the Circle, and use some prayer giving thanks to God and the good angels; then you may depart. The Invocant must take notice that when he begins his work the Air must be clear and serene, if it be in the day see that the sun shines; if it be in the night, let the Moon be unobscured, or the sky full of Stars, for in foul or close weather the spirit will not be visible, because it cannot receive bodily form or shape from the Elements. After having completed the Ceremonies &c. The Invocant may destroy all traces of the Circle &c. and depart in peace to his own home.

[175] Incantation

To Bind the Ground whereby neither Mortal nor Spiritual Beings can have Power to Approach within a Limited Distance.

Having made your necessary suffumigations and mystic preparations, describe a circle of a hundred feet or more in diameter, or as much more or less as you may think fit; and if you wish to keep all living creatures from within a quarter of a mile or more of your Experiment, make, at the four parts of the same, East, West, North and South, proper crosses, and devoutly pronounce thrice the following Incantation.

"In the Name of the Father and of the Son and of the **Holy Ghost** Amen. I bind all mortal and immortal, celestial and Terrestrial, visible and invisible beings excepts those Spirits whom I have occasion to call, to avoid and quit this space of ground which I now mark, and wherein I now stand, and that with all possible speed and despatch. I bind you to avoid and no longer to tarry, by the unspeakable power of Almighty **God**, by the most high and Mighty name of + **Tetragrammaton** + by the all powerful names + **Agla** + **Saday** + **Jesu** + **Messias** + **Alpha** + **et Omega** +. By all these most high and powerful names, I charge, adjure bind and constrain both mortal and immortal, terrestrial, Celestial, visible, and invisible beings to avoid, quit, and depart this ground, and do request that none of you, except those I have occasion to call at this time, be suffered to come within these sacred limits. These things I request in the Name of the **Father** and of the **Son** and of the **Holy Ghost**, Amen."

Then dig a certain depth at the four parts of the compass, and bury the seal of the earth in each part, and now no power either visible or invisible, shall have power to come near thee, or to interrupt thy proceedings.

[176] Plate III - Experiment
Of Invocating or Raising the Powerful Spirit
OBERION

[177] The Invocant who would raise or Invocate this powerful Spirit Oberion must in the first place, draw out his seal and Character, and the different offices subservient to him, in the first Monday after of full Moon, and in the hour of the Moon, Mars, Mercury, or Saturn; and when these are made, he must repeat the following ceremonial words: -

"O ye Angels of the Sun and Moon I Conjure and pray you, and Exorcise you, that by the virtue and power of the Most High God Alpha and Omega, and by the name that is marvellous **+ El +** and by Him that made and formed you, and by these signs that be here, so drawn forth in these resemblances, and now in the might and virtue of your Creator and in the name of him the most shinning **God** and by the virtue of the **Holy Ghost**, that now, or whensoever that I shall call on **Oberion**, whose image is here pictured, made, or fashioned, and his name that is here written and his Signs here all drawn and graven, written or made, that **Oberion** be compelled now to obey me, and here to appear openly before me, and fulfil my request."

The next day, write or make the name of his first counsellor, Taberyon and on the right side, that of Oberion's character saying,

"I Exorcise thee Taberyon by the power of God, and by the virtue of Heavenly Kings, earthly kings, and infernal kings, and by king Solomon, who bound thee, and made thee subject unto him, and by all his signs and seals, and by the four elements, by which the world is sustained and nourished and by the serpent that exalted in the wilderness. – that thou Taberyon now help to give true council to thy Lord Oberion, that he do show himself instantly unto me and fulfil my request."

This must be said three times each day, and three times each night, over the writings. The third day, in the third hour, write and make the name of his other counsellor Teveyron, with his signs and Characters, and do and say as before rehearsed.

[178] This done, suffumigate your seals and writings with a suffumigation of Saffron, Aloes, Mastic, olibanum, and orpient; and note the fire used for this purpose must be of elder wood, or thorns.

Then choose such a secret and retired place, as has been described & where no human footsteps may interrupt thee make thy Circle of the following form. Note; the ground or floor must be perfectly clear and even in order to trace the lines of the Circle, Characters &c. with much exactness according to the foregoing Model, which being made, and consecrated according to the rules of Ceremonial Magic; let the Invocant & his associates enter the Circle in the Hour of Mercury, closing it properly and guarding it with Crosses &c. as before said, then begin, his Invocations in the following manner on bended kness *(sic)* and with great devotion.

"I Conjure Invocate, and Call upon the Oberion by the Father, the Son and the Holy Ghost, and by Him who said, and it was done: who commanded and it stood fast, who willed, and it was created and by his Son Jesus Christ, in whose name all Heavenly, Earthly and Infernal do bend and obey: and by the unutterable name of Ineffable Majesty + Tetragrammaton + O thou Spirit Oberion I Command thee withersoever thou now art, whether in sea, fire, air, or flood, whether in the air above or in the region beneath, to appear instantly unto me and my fellows, without hurting me or them or any living creature which God has made. This I thrice command thee in the name of the Ineffable Adonai. Amen."

If as the third repetition of this Invocation, the Spirit gives no visible token of his appearance (which generally is accompanied with tremendous noises frightful hissings tumultuous yellings and fearful shrieks) then begin to rehearse the following great bond or incantation and if the spirit were bound in chains of darkness in the lowest pit of the infernal regions, he must appear, when this great Sentence is rehearsed.

[179] Form in which the Spirit Oberion

Usually Appears
[180] The Great and Powerful Incantation[237]

O thou rebellious and fearful spirit prince amongst the fallen angels, **Oberion**, I conjure and bind thee to visible appearance by the following most high, most terrible and mighty Invocation: -

"Hear O ye Heavens, and I will speak saith the Lord and let the sea, the earth - yea, hell and all that is within them contained, mark the words of my mouth: Did not I, saith the Lord, fashion you and make you? Did not I: as an eagle who stirreth her nest fluttereth over her young ones, with her wings and carrieth them on her shoulders? have I not so nourished you, that you were fat, and loaden with plenty? Why have you then so spurned with your heels against me, your Maker? Why have you seemed to coequal yourselves with me? What thereby have you reaped? Have you not purchased instead of that heavenly felicity, hellish perplexity? How have you that fire kindled which doth and shall for ever at my pleasure, burn you in the bottomless pit of perdition? Why are you so unfaithful and disobedient to my most Holy names and words? Know you not that I am God alone and that there I none but me? Am not I the only יהוה. Is it not in my power to kill and make alive - to wound and to heal - to oppress and to deliver? If I whet the edge of my sword, and my hand take hold of it, to do justice against them who disobey my holy name who are able to abide the same? To have their sword, eat their flesh and my sharp arrows of hell fire to be drunk in their blood? Which of you that are disobedient to my name saith the Lord, is able to withstand mine anger? Am not I Lord of Lords, and Omnipotent, and none but I? Who can command the Heavens to smoke, the Earth to fear, the waters to flow, and hell to tremble? Are not the corners of them all in my hands O thou obstinate and stubborn Spirit why hast thou dealt so froward with me (saith the Lord) to urge me to command my faithful servant [181] Michael, my valiant champion, to expel and put thee out of the place where thou wast filled [with] wisdom and understanding, continually beholding my wondrous works? Didst not thou see my glory with thine eyes,

---

[237] This great Call or Invocation is said to be equally powerful in raising any other Spirit. – Sibley.

and did not thy ears hear the Majesty of my voice? Why art thou gone out of the way? Why art thou become an open sepulchre? With thy tongue dost thou deceive my servants, for poison is under thy lips, thy mouth is full of cursing and bitterness and thy feet are swift to shed innocent blood. Is this the obedience thou owest unto me, and the service thou offerest? Verily, for this thy obstinacy, disobedience, pride and rebellion, thou shalt be bound, and most cruelly tormented with intolerable pains and endless eternal perdition."

Then if the Spirit be still rebellious or refractory, make a fire of brimstone and stinking substances, thorns briars &c. Then write the Name of the Spirit in the Virgin Parchment, and burn it thrice, repeating the following adjuration: -

"I Conjure thee creature of God, Fire, by him who commanded and all things were done and by the living God, and by the true God, and by the Holy God, and by Him who made thee and all the elements by his word, by Him who appeared to Moses in fiery bush, and by Him who led the children in a fiery pillar, through the wilderness, and by Him who shall come to judge the World by fire and brimstone, that thou perform my will upon this refractory and disobedient spirit: till he come unto me, and show himself in all things as I shall command him. O Heavenly God, Father and author of all virtues, and the Invisible king of Glory, most strong and mighty Captain of the strong and triumphant arm of Angels, God of Gods, Lord of hosts, which on thy hands the corners of the earth which with the breath of thy mouth makest all things to shake and tremble, which makest thy Angels lightnings, and thy Spirits [182] flames of fire, vouchsafe, I beseech thee O Lord, to send thy Holy Angels into this place of fire, to torment, vex, and persecute this disobedient Spirit, Oberion, and overcome him, as Michael the Archangel overcame Lucifer the prince of darkness, till he come to me, and fulfil all my will and desire. Fiat, fiat, fiat. Amen."

"O thou most puissant prince **Radamanthus**, which dost punish in thy prison of perpetual perplexity, the disobedient Spirits and also the grisly ghosts of men dying in dreadful despair. I Conjure, Bind and Charge thee, by **Lucifer, Beelzebub, Satan,**[238] **Tamanill**, and by their power, and by the homage thou owest unto them; and also I charge thee, by the triple crown of **Cerberus** by **Styx** and **Phlegethon**, by the Spirit **Darantos** and by his ministers, that you torment and punish this disobedient Spirit **Oberion**, until you make him come corporally to my sight, and obey my will and commandment in whatsoever I shall charge or command him to do. Fiat, fiat, fiat. Amen."

These things being rightly performed, the Spirit will be constrained to visible appearance; but it will be in a horrible and ghastly form at first, and attended by terrible convulsions of the elements. This mighty Spirit is chiefly under the dominion of the Sun and Moon, he will then assume the appearance in great pomp and terror, that of a scaly monster, with the face of a woman and a royal crown upon his head, attended by innumerable and countless legions, which will astound and frighten the Invocant if he be not on his guard, also he will be in great danger and peril if the Magic circle be not well made and fortified. But if all the before mentioned rules be followed, he need not fear any harm from this rebellious and Powerful Spirit who <u>must</u> become obedient

---

[238] The first three demonic names were usually edited out of later grimoires to avoid potential prosecution. – Ed.

when thus exorcised. His office is to give Prosperity in Journeys and Voyages, also Riches, Dignity and Honour. [183] After the Spirit has appeared, and performed the will and request, the Invocant must use the utmost caution in quitting the limits of the Magic Circle, for this end, he must devoutly rehearse the following license to Depart.

> "I conjure thee **Oberion** by the visible and holy temple of Solomon, which he did prepare to the most holy God, by all the elements, and by that most Holy Name that was graven on Solomon's Sceptre, that for this time, thou do depart quickly, quietly and peaceably without lightnings, thunder, rain, wind, storm, or tempest, or any noise terror whatsoever; and whensoever I shall call thee, I charge thee that thou do come to me and my fellows without delay or tract of time, not molesting me or any other creature that God hath made to his glory and praise, and the use of man, or without disordering any thing, putting up or casting down anything, or doing any hurt any other way whatsoever, either in thy coming or going, not hurting, troubling, or molesting me or any other creature, neither by thyself, nor [by] any spirit or spirits for thee or at thy procurement, at any time or times, now or hereafter; by the virtue of our **Lord Jesus Christ**, the **Father**, and the **Holy Ghost**, go thy way in peace to the place God halt appointed for thee, and peace be between thee and me. In nomine **Patris + et Filii + et Spiritus Sancti**. + Amen."

The Invocant must repeat Licence three times, and afterwards repeating the Lords prayer, must leave the circle walking backwards. He must then destroy all traces of the circle and remove all Instruments used for the purpose, and return home by a different path from that by which he came. So shall no Spirit have power to harm him, &c. let him on no account neglect any of the foregoing rules for they are essential to his safety.

Such were the mystic rights, ceremonies, &c. used by the ancient and learned in the Art, a study to the sublimity of which modern times afford no parallel as the experiment already evinces, which is here given, not to be put in practice being too powerful for most of the present sceptical generation to attempt. Were they to do so, they would experience the stern realities of these Mighty Spirits who can be invocated to appear with such tremendous powers and such awful attributes, as to cause many persons to shrink back and tremble.

[184] Concerning the Proportion, Measure, & Harmony of the Human Body.[239]

Homo quoniam pulcherrimum absolutissimum que Dei opus, and imago, and minor mundus, ideoque perfectiore compositione, ac suaviori harmonia, sublimiorique dignitate omnes numeros, mensuras, pondera, motus and elementa, coetelaq[ue] omnium illum componetia in se continet ac sustinet, omniaque in covelut in supremo artificis, supremam quandam sortem ultra communem consonantiam quam habent in aliis compositis, consequntur: hinc antiqui omnes, digitis olim numerabant, and digitis numeros indicabant, ex ipsisque humani corporis articulus, omnes numeros mensuras proportiones, ac harmonias inventas fuisse, probare visi sunt. Unde ad hanc corporis commensurationem, sempla, aedes, domos, theatra, insuper and

---

[239] The following Latin passage has little or nothing to do with magic, and consequently has not been translated. It compares the human body with architecture and its ratios, and with the cubit dimensions of the ark. It expounds at length on the geometric figures that can be drawn on the body, such as the triangle, or its division into five parts. – Ed.

navigia and *machinas* and *quodcunque artificii genus*, and *artificiorum aedificiorumque quaecunque sunt partes* and *membra, puta columnas, epistilia, bases, antes, stilobates* and *hujusmodi coeteramomnia partiuntur, alque ex humano corpore deducunt. Quin* and *ipse Deus docuit Noe fabricare area ad humani corporis mensuram, ut qui ipse totam mundi machinam humano corpori Symmetria fabricavit: unde ille magnus, hic vero minor mundus nuncupatur. Hinc microcosmologi nonnulli, humanum corpus per sex pedes, pedem vero per X gradus,* and *gradum quemque per minutias V metiuntur: unde numerantur: IX gradus, qui faciunt minutias C.C.C. quibus aequiparantur totidem cubiti geometrici quibus descripta est arca a Mose: secut enim corpus humanum est in longitudine trecentum minatorum in latitudine quinquaginta in altitudine triginta: sic* and *longitude arcae facit cubitorum trecentorum, latitudo quinquaginta altitudo triginta, ut sit utrobique longitudinis ad latitudinis ad altitudine sesculpa proportio, ad altitudinem deculpa, latitudinis ad altitudinem super partiens duas tertias: parig: modo omnium membrorum commensurationes sunt proportionatae* and *[185] consonantes,* and *cum mundi membris atque archetypi mensures sic convenientes, ut nudum sit in homine membrum, quod non responde at alicui signo, alicui stellae, alicui intelligentiae, alicui divino nomini in ipso archetype Deo tota autem corporis mensura tornatilis est et a rotundiate proveniens ad ipsam sendere dignoscitur.*

Est etiam quadrata mensura corpus proportionatissimum quippe statuatur expassis brachiis in coiunctos pedes erectus homo, quadratum constituet aequilaterum, cuis centrum est in imo pectinis.

Quod si super esdam centro circulus fabricetur per summum caput, demissi brachii quousque extremi digiti circuli illius circumferentiam contingant passique pedes in eadem circumferentia quantum extrema manuum a summo vertice distat, tunc circulum illum super imi pectinis centro ductum in quinque aequas partes dividunt, perfectum que pentagonum constituunt, ipsique pedum extreme tali ad umbilicum relati, triangulum faciunt aequilaterum.

Quod si immotis talis pedes dextrorsum sinistrorsum que in utrumque latus protendantur, & manus ad capitis lineam eleventer, ipsi tunc extremi pedum manumque digiti aequilaterum quadratum dabunt, cuius centrum supra umbilicum in cinctura corporis.

Quod si manibus sic elevatis, taliter pedes, crura pandantur quo homo decimaquarta parte erectae staturae suae brevior sit; tunc pedum distantia ad imum pecten relata, aequilaterum triangulum faciet, and centro in umbilico polito, circumductus circulus manuum pedumque extrema continget.

Quod si manus supra caput quam altissime extendantur cubitus aequabunt verticem: et si tunc irinctis pedibus ita stans homo in quadratum aequilaterum locetur, per extrema manuum et pedum conductum centrum illius quadrati in umbilico erit: quui idem medium est inter summum verticem et genua.

[186] **Plate V.**[240]

[187] *Sed iam ad particulares mensuras perveniamus Circuitus hominis sub alis, medietatem continet suae longitudinis, cuis medium est in imo pectore: abinde vero sursum ad medium pectus inter utrasque mamillas, et a medio pectore in summum verticem utrobique pars quarta: similiter ab imo pectine usque sub genua, et in*

---

[240] This is a rather poor copy of da Vinci's drawing of the ratios and proportions of the human body. – Ed.

de ad extremos talos pars hominis quarta. Eadem est latitudo spatularum ab uno extremo in alterum: eadem est longitudo a cubito in extremum longioris digiti, ideoque hic cubitus dicitur: hinc quatuor cubiti constituunt longitudinem hominis: latitudinem vers quae in spatulis est cubitus unus que vero in cinctura est, pes un cubitum autem constituunt palmi sex pedem vers quatuor: et quatuor digiti palmum: totaque hominis longitudo palmarum viginti quatuor, pedum sex, digitorum sex et nonaginta. Ab imo pectinis ad summum pectoris, pars longitudinis sexta: a summo pectore ad supremam frontem, et radices imas capillorum pars longitudinis septima: corporis robusti et bene quadrati pes, est pars longitudinis sexta: procerioris autem septima: nect potest Varrone et Gellio testibus humanum corpus proceritatem septem pedem excedere. Denique cincturae diameter et quod a restricta manus usque in interiorem plicaturam cubiti spatium est: et quod a pectore usque ad uclasque mamillas sursum ad suprema labra, five deorum usque ad umbilicum est, quodque est inter extrema offium supremi pectoris gulam cingentium, et quod ad planta pedis ad finem lacerti: et exinde in mediam genu rotulam, omnes hae mensurae sibi coequales sunt, et septimam totius altitudinis costituunt. Caput hominis ab imo mento in summum verticem, pars longitudinis octava: to etidem a cubito in finem spatularum: tantus etiam reperitur procerioris hominis cinc turae diameter. Circulus capitis per supremam frotem et imas radices occipitis ductus, facis totius longitudinis partem quintam: tantundem [188] etiam prestat latitudo pectoris, Hominem quadratum et compactum constituunt facies movem, procerum vero decem. In novem itaque portiones hominis longitudine partita, facies a suprema fronte usque in extremum mentum, una est: deinde ab imo gutturis sive supremo pectoris ad summum stomachum altera: abinde ad umbilicum, tertia: ab hoc ad imum femur, quarta: ab illo coxendices ad poplitem constituent duas: abinde usque ad nodum pedis, crura continent duas alias: quae omnes partes sunt octo. Porro arcus a summa fronte ad summum verticem et quod est a mento ad summum pectoris guttur, atque quod a nodo pedis ad imam plantam, haec tria spracia coniuncta constituunt nonam. In latum quoque pectus habet partes duas et utraque brachia septem. Quod vero corpus decem facies constituunt ipsum est proportionatissimum. Hujus itaque primo portio est a summo vertice ad imas nares: abinde ad supresmum pectus secunda et consequenter ad supremum stomachum, tertia, ab eo ad umbilicum, quarta, et inde ad imum pecten quinta, ubi est medium humanae longitudinis, a quo usque in extremas plantas, sunt quinque ualiae partes, quae prioribus juncta, faciut decem integras, quibus proinde corpus omne mensura proportionatissima commensuratur, nam facies hominis ab imo mento ad summam frontem et radices imas capulli est, quata pars una decima. Manus hominis a restricta usque ad extremum longioris digiti, etia pars una: similiter inter utraque mammillarum puncta, pars una: et ab utrisque ad imam gulam, triangulus aequilaterus. Frontis inferioris ab una aure ad alteram, latitudo est partis unius: totius autem pectoris latitudo videlicet a supremo pectore ad ju[n]cturas spatularum, utrobique partis unius: quae facient duas. Circulus capitis transversus ab interstitio superciliorum per supremam potem [189] usque in finem occipitis ubi terminatur capillitium, etiam, partium duarum ab humeris extrinsecus ad juncturas articulorum manus et intrinsecus ab axellis ad confinia palmae digitorum, partes tres: circulis capitis permetiam frontem partium trium. Circulus cincturae tenet partes quatuor in robusto homine in delicatiori corpore, pars tres cum dimidiae seu quantum est a summo pectore in imum pecten. Circulus pectoris per alas ad tergum partes quinque, videlicet quantum longitudinis totius medium asummo vertice ad nodum gulae, sunt totuis altitudinis quae decimaetertiae[que] elevatis in altum brachiis cubitus accedit summo vertici. Caeterium nunc quae adhuc reliquae commensurationes sibi aequales sunt: spectemus.

Quantum est a mento ad summum pectus, tanta est latitudo colli: quantum a summo pectore ad umbilicum, tata est colli circulatio quantum a mento in supremum verticem, tanta est latitudo cincturae: quantum est ab interciliis ad sunt mas hares, tantum a jugulo distat productio menti, quantum que a summis naribus ad mentum tantum ad mentum tantum a jugulo ad imam gulam. Item oculorum ab interciliis ad interiores angulos concavitas, ac summorum narium prominentia and quod ab inuis naribus ad extremum supremi labri interstitium est, haec tria sunt interse aqualia.

[190] The following Talisman must be formed as follows.

Take a piece of Virgin parchment about three inches square and on it Engrave according to the model, it has two faces therefore the words and Characters are to be written on each respective side as shewn, or [on] a plate of Iron highly polished, and of a circular form, (the size immaterial.) may be employed instead of parchment, this plate must be engraven on both sides as shown, the formation and preparation belonging to this Talisman must be made in the day and hour of Mars which is the first hour and the Eigthth *(sic)* hour after sunrise on Tuesday when the Moon is in sextile or Trine to Mars and if possible when both the Luminaries are in fortune aspects with Jupiter, Venus, or Mercury, which every astrologer knows, and which the Ephemeris will teach; all must be done in the Increase of the Moon. If parchment is to be employed, the ink must be consecrated and of the proper colour suitable to Mars and the lines & Characters must be drawn and written distinctly, if Metal is employed it must be engraven in the same manner. When completed the person for whom it is made must retire to a secret place and fumigating it with the Magical suffumigation of the Spirits of Mars which consists of Red Saunders, Frankincense & pepper repeating the orations &c. for Tuesday, as given in a former part of this Work, likewise he may recite one or two passages from the Psalms where David prayed that he might overcome his enemies, also there are numerous passages in the scriptures that might be repeated for the same purpose but firm trust and sincere faith must be employed in repeating these Orations & passages, or but little benefit will be derived. After the Talisman be completed, it must [be] kept clean & suspended from some part of the Body of the wearer and in great Secrecy, or it may be worn on the finger in the form of a ring, the Characters &c. engraven on the inside. It is said to give Victory over every earthly Enemy when rightly formed.

[191] Plate VI - THE IMPERIAL TALISMAN
FOR VICTORY OVER
ENEMIES

[192] Powerful Talisman
For
Secret Love

This Invaluable and Admirable Talisman is copied, and the manner in which it is composed is translated from an ancient Manuscript. Its Virtue and Power have been often proved and verified by the most learned and skilful in the Occult Sciences. This Mysterious Image when formed according to the Rules of Art, has the means of producing that Secret and pure Love in the heart of either Male or Female on whom it acts, that neither Time Distance nor Circumstance can dissolve, and nothing but Death separate.

[193] The manner of composing the Talisman is as follows. Get a plate of Silver of about three inches in diameter put it in the Fire for a few minutes till it is hot enough to receive the essence of the perfumes proper the Planet Venus, which are Valerian, Enrula Campana, Red Coral, Dried Red Roses, Musk and Ambergris, these must all be properly dried and pulverized and the powder sprinkled on the silver plate while it is hot, after which the plate must be polished and engraved according to the following Model. All this Operation must be perform[ed] in the hour of Venus on Friday or Monday, the size of the Talisman is of no consequence. In constructing this Talisman if Silver be not employed, Virgin Copper managed in the same way will serve. All these little materials & Ingredients must be consecrated before being used.

[194] Plate VII.

[195] The Artist is fully aware, that without the assistance of an Invisible power subject to an all wise Creator, a senseless plate of metal engraven with Mysterious Names and Characters is useless - notwithstanding whatever secret or hidden properly it may possess Now as has been said in the former part of this Book that every kind of plant, Mineral, or Metal is appropriated to one or other of the seven planets and each of these Planets governed by a Celestial Angel or Intelligency [Intelligence] under whom are many Heavenly Genii who are permitted to Execute the earnest and lawful demands of the operator according to the Sovereign Will of an Omnipotent God. Such a power governing the Day and Hour of Operation, to give life and virtue thereto, must be invoked visibly or invisibly present at the operation to render the desired aid. The Invocant must have firmness, Courage, patience, and great Faith & Confidence in the success of his operation, and not in any way quake, or tremble, or be dismayed at the presence of these Glorious and Celestial Beings with their Mighty Attributes, for they are harmless. There <u>must</u> <u>be</u> mutual Sympathy existing between the Operator and the wearer of the Talisman, also a small part conducive to success must be taken and submitted to as a cooperation in the Work by the latter. Having begun his Operation at the time stated, let the Operator repeat his Invocation earnestly as follows. After which, the Spirit will appear, if the Invocant be patient and watchful. If he appears not at the first call, or Invocation, it must be repeated, even the third time, but if the Operator be confident he rarely has to repeat this All powerful Conjuration but once, for this Glorious and Celestial being is neither obstinate nor refractory, but become subservient to the Will of the Invocant and he will come either in a Visible or Invisible form.

[196] Invocation

"O Thou Mighty Prince of Love **Lord Abalidoth** who lovest thy Servants and will be loved by them, I pray you to make this Operation successful by granting my desires and give Virtue and Power to this Talisman so that it may not fail in being Efficacious in winning and for Ever sacred Pure and Genuine Love of M.L.K.[241] towards me by the Interposition of these among the heavenly Genii whom you cherish most which are **Raniel Corat Radie Penat** I intreat you to diffuse on my Operation such success as shall be conformable to my intention and redound to your Glory with all suitable acknowledgement O thou fair Angel of God **Anael** Prince of Love be propitious to my Vows that through thy mediation I may hopefully fulfil my Desires by Jesus Christ our Lord, Amen.

---

[241] The 'target' of the operation. – Ed.

Come on the wings of the Zephyrs fair **Anael** and all ye Happy Genii who preside over the workings of the Heart. Come Heavenly **Sarabotes Husaltiel [Hufaltiel] Doremiel Setchiel** hear favourably the Invocation that I make this Day destined to the Wonders of Love. Be ready to lend thy Assistance to succeed in gaining the pure sincere undivided and unchangeable Love of M.L.K. that he or she may feel its powerful influence and be both able and willing to exercise as benign power and virtue to its fullest extent.

I conjure you by the Veneration you have for the Mysterious Name **Setchiel**, O beneficent Genii who preside over the Operation of this Day I conjure you fair **Anael** who rejoicest at these fumigations and smells come to receive them, be favourable and kind unto me Vouchsafe to Bless this Talisman and to Consecrate it so that it may have Power to bind M.L.K and make him or her to Love me with a secret and undying Love.

I again Conjure **Talaroth Miveg Cuphaniel Clearos** that you will come with all your power to scatter and put to flight the Evil Spirits which are hurtful and inimical to good operations cause me to succeed by the Powerful Virtue in what I have undertaken this Day, in the Name of the Father and of the Son and of the Holy Ghost."

[197] The sign of the coming of this fair and beautiful Angel, is a furious west wind mingled with gentle Zephyrs accompanied with invisible and Heavenly music delightful to the ear and thrilling the heart and Soul with enchanting strains of harmony, then follow sweet sounds of the most melodious voices in concert, to which the most accomplished earthly singer with the richest voice affords no parallel or comparison. After these sweet sounds have ceased, there will be a bright and shining light in the midst of which will appear innumerable forms of handsome maidens in the most enticing forms mingling with their presence. Music, Joy, and Beauty. These disappearing, will be succeeded to the astonishment of the Invocant sweeter sounds even than before, heralding the approach of this Mighty and Glorious Spirit who appears with a fair body, mean stature with an amiable pleasant and handsome countenance and of a pure white, and Golden coloured hair, his motion is like a clear star, and when properly and earnestly invoked he will appear willingly in the above form in all the plenitude of Majestic Glory and surrounded by a brilliant light of resplendent beauty which will ravish the senses and fill the soul of the Operator with Delight and wondrous amazement. When this Glorious Angel is summoned to appear visibly, the Invocant must receive him affably and courteously, present unto him his petition written on Virginal parchment, which after he has granted by his presence, License him to Depart in the usual and respectful manner, this will be accompanied with similar sounds to those heard on the approach of this beautiful Spirit. After the Invocant has succeeded so far let Him complete the Talisman[242] according to the Rules of Art omitting nothing, after which let him return thanks unto Almighty God for his permission in allowing these Heavenly beings to assist in the Operation. This Matchless Charm when completed must be worn in Secret in some part of the Dress nearest the heart, its power and virtue is to make the wearer become so lovely charming & fascinating in the eyes of him or her whose heart is stirred up with an unconquerable and Secret Love that he cannot be happy only in the presence of his or her adorned one. All this powerful Operation must be done in secret & at the proper Times.

---

[242] The figures on the outside of the Talismanic Circles are not to be engraved thereon, being only an embellishment. – Ed.

[198] After the Artist has Invoked to visible appearance this Beautiful and Mighty Spirit who from his gentle mild and amicable nature is ever ready to lend his Assistance according to true and earnest desires of the Invocant therefore it would afford an excellent opportunity to have all ready in the operation by the Wheel of Magic (as per example)[243] to further solicit the Aid of this powerful Spirit during his presence and so to blend the two Operations together which would act with a two fold power on the object acted upon and cause this potent Charm to act with certainty and success but the wearer of this infallible Talisman must not lose sight of the fact that all the power which is given in Heaven and on Earth is derived from God alone, who maketh his Angels Ministers for the purpose of executing his Holy Will, therefore he or they who would solicit and Invoke their Aid must bear in mind that it is only by Divine permission according to the strength of our faith and vehemence of our desires that these Glorious and Celestial Intelligences are allowed to leave their bright abodes thus breaking the bonds of natural order and to hold converse with us finite mortals. Therefore it behoves all who desire to [have] the Aid of these Heavenly beings must pray for Protection and Help of God, to whom we must appeal in every time of need, not forgetting to return thanks for every favour and success granted to us.

Whoever wears the Talisman &c. must be reminded that he or she must conform to all the details of the Operation and be willing & ready to comply with whatever request th[at] he has the power to grant for the furtherance and success of the Operations which when combined in the manner aforesaid will have the effect of producing that secret, genuine, and imperishable Love in the heart of the Object on whom the Operator or wearer has fixed his or her choice. Also it will gain the Universal Love and respect of all mankind, and in a great degree ameliorate the feelings of the most Malicious and Inveterate foes of him or her who trusts in it.

[199] Plate VIII – A Charm for Healing
Diseases

[200] The Letters which compose this Charm must be written in a pyramidal form us shown, on Virgin Parchment, with the Quill of a Raven and with Ink formed out of the smoke of a Consecrated Wax Candle in a plain and distinct manner without any regard to ornament colouring &c. of any kind, this Figure may be surrounded with a double Circle and the sentences therein written in a common plain hand with the ink aforesaid, it is said to give more force in the Charm. Let the party who is afflicted of the disease, which he would have cured, wear the Charm hung round his neck during the time that the Moon performs one circuit through the twelve signs of the Zodiacs and let it be performed on the day of the full Moon, and if possible while the Moon is in the Magical signs Sagittarius or Pisces and in a fortunate aspect with Jupiter, Venus, or Mercury. It is necessary that the wearer have a firm and confident faith in the Power of Divine Omnipotence: and the following Oration must be said upon first beginning to wear this Holy Charm, with great earnestness and devotion, and in very difficult cases the Patient should repeat the Oration daily in the same manner.

Oration

"O sweet Lord **Jesus Christ** x the true God, who didst descend from the kingdom of thy Almighty

---

[243] See Part 4. – Ed.

Father being sent to wash away our sins, to release those who were in prison and afflicted, to console the sorrowful and the needy, to absolve and to liberate me thy servant from my affliction and tribulation in which I am placed. So, O Omnipotent Father, thou that didst receive us again, by his expiation, into that Paradise by thy blood. **O Jesu**, *x* obtained, and didst make us equal among Angels and men. Thou, O Lord **Jesus Christ** *x* wert worthy to stand between me and mine enemies, and to establish my peace and to show thy grace upon me, and to pour out thy mercy. And thou, O Lord didst extinguish the anger of mine enemies, which they contained against me, as thou didst take away the wrath of Esau, which he had against Jacob his brother **O Lord Jesus** *x* extend thine arm towards me, and deliver me from my affliction, even as thou didst deliver Abraham from the hands of the Chaldean, and his son, Isaac from the sacrifice, and Jacob from the hand of his brethren, Noah, from the deluge: and even as thou deliveredst the servant Lot; thy servants Moses and Aaron, and thy people Israel, from the hands of Pharaoh, and out of the land of Egypt; David from [201] the hands of Saul, and the giant Goliath; or as thou didst deliver Suzannah from her accusers; Judith from the hands of Holofernes; Daniel from the den of lions; the three youths from the fiery furnace; Jonah from the whale's belly; or as thou deliveredst the son of Canannea who was tormented by the devil; even as thou deliveredst Adam from hell by thy most precious blood; and Peter and Paul from chains. So, O, most sweet Lord Jesus *x* Son of the living God, preserve me thy servant, from my affliction, and mine enemies; and be my assistant, and my blessing. By thy Holy Incarnation. By thy fasting and thirst. By thy labours and affliction, By thy stripes, By thy thorny Crown, By thy drink of gall and vinegar, By thy most cruel Death, By the words which thou spakedst upon the Cross, By thy descent into hell, By thy consolation of thy Disciples, By thy Wonderful Ascension, By the Appearance of the Holy Spirit, By the Day of Judgement, By thy great Gifts, and by thy Holy Names **Adonay** *x* **Eloym** *x* **Aeloym** *x* **Yacy** *x* **Zazael** *x* **Paliel** *x* **Saday** *x* **Yzoe** *x* **Yaras** *x* **Caelphi** *x* **Saday** *x* and by thy Ineffable Name יהוה **Jehovah.** *x* By all these Holy, Omnipotent, and All-powerful names of singular efficacy and extraordinary power, which the elements obey, and at which the devils tremble: O most gratious **Jesu** *x* grant, I beseech thee that this Holy Charm, which I now wear about my person, may be the means of healing my lamentable sickness: so shall the praise thereof be ascribed, O Lord, to thee alone, and thou shalt have all the Glory, **Amen.**"

Fiat   Fiat   Fiat

By making use of the above occult and sacred remedy the most miraculous cures have been heretofore performed: and as there is nothing therein which is in any way derogatory to the power of the Supreme being, or inimical to our fellow-creatures, there certainly can be no harm in making continual use thereof upon every occasion

This admirable Charm is translated from a curious Manuscript of the Twelfth Century.

[202] Another Way

If it were required to perform a cure upon one at a distance, or without the afflicted party's knowledge thereof, let the Charm be written on Virgin Parchment, and then you may perform the cure without their knowledge by scraping out <u>one line</u> of the Charm every day with a new knife, kept for the express purpose; and as scraping out each line, say as follows: -

"So as I destroy the letters of this Charm, **Abracadabra**, so, by the virtue of this sacred Name, my all grief and dolor depart from A. B. In the Name of the Father and of the Son and of the Holy Ghost. In the Name of the Father, I destroy this disease, In the Name of the Son I destroy this disease, and in the Name of the Holy Spirit, I destroy this disease. Amen."

By performing the Operation with strict Confidence and earnestness, Many have healed livers diseases this way, the disease wearing by little and little, away. Therefore keep it a secret, and fear God. (*Ancient Manuscript*)

[203] **Plate IX - Amulet or Charm**
For Amorous Intrigues Friendship &c.

[204] To compose this Amulet or Charm according to the Rules of Art, the following ingrediences are necessary. A piece of fair Virgin parchment about three inches square, or a plate of copper highly polished of the same size, on which must be engraven in the circles, or written in green Ink property consecrated; the perfumes composed as mentioned in the last experiment, to which, must be added a small lock of hair from the nape of the neck, et pubis pudendum of the person who is to wear the charm, also a little menstruous sanguis,[244] and a small quantity of blood drawn from the right hand by piercing gently with a small penknife or needle at the Mount of Venus, a portion of the blood must be mixed with the hair cut very fine and used with the perfumes in suffumigating the Pentacle, if metal be employed the perfume is to be used us mentioned elsewhere The figure in the interior circle of the foregoing Model is a rude representation of the form in which the Spirit usually appears when invoked to aid in the operation, this figure is not to be drawn on the pentacle but in the place thereof, the Names of the parties consenting to the operation, to be written in their own blood and joined by the name Anael between them thus, James-Anael-Jane. The Pentacle of Solomon, or the Character of the Spirit governing the operation may be engraven or written on the reverse side of this Amulet, according to the models already given. This Operation being under the influence of the Planet Venus, must be performed at Sun-rise on Friday, the Moon increasing, and in fortunate aspect to Venus, Jupiter or Mercury.

Now as has been remarked in the preceding Experiments that these plates of metal &c. with their Mysterious characters have no power nor force in themselves, though there may be a latent virtue. It is therefore necessary to Invoke one of those Glorious and powerful Angels, who governs such operation to give vivifying power, force, and virtue to succeed in the operation. For which purpose the Operator must be of a religious frame of mind, intrepid in Spirit, persevering in pursuit, fearless in danger, faithful and patient in waiting, earnest in his desires and confident of success. He may then earnestly commence invoking the Spirit to visible appearance, if he does not appear at the first call, let the Operator after waiting a short time, repeat the Invocation, even the third time if he does not appear. The Spirit generally appears in a visible form at the first call if the air is calm and bright and a cloudless sky, but if the sky is overcast by clouds rain or tempest, or the elements otherwise disturbed, the Spirit may appear but not in a visible form not being able to take form or shape at that time, therefore clear sky serene weather by day or night is requisite for intercourse with those Glorious inhabitants of the Spheres.

---

244 Pubic hair and menstrual blood. – Ed.

[205] **Invocation**

"Happy Spirits and Genii who preside over the softest emotions of the heart, I pray you to hear favourably the Invocation that I make this Day destined to the wonders of pure Love and Sincere Friendship, be ready with the power and virtue you possess through the Sovereign command, will and permission of the Omnipotent and Eternal God whose All-seeing eye searcheth the secret recesses of the heart and reins of his people, lend me your assistance to succeed in what I have undertaken.

I Invoke, and call upon, and Command thee Fair **Anael** prince of Love by the Mighty, Incomprehensible, and Ineffable Names of the great יהוה **Saday El On Adonay Elohim Tetragrammaton** that thou will send unto me **Amabiel** or other of your Ministering Spirits who shall appear visibly to me in the fair and beautiful form of an Angel to give virtue and power and success so this operation and impress upon this mysterious Image that virtue to accomplish the desired effect.

I Invoke again thou powerful Spirit **Amabiel** to appear before me visibly in fair and perfect Form without delay and render unto me thy powerful aid in the Operation of this day.

I again conjure thee Spirit **Amabiel** by the Names of the heavenly Genii **Abalidoth Setchiel Husaltiel [Hufaltiel] Doremiel** that thou immediately appear to me as aforesaid with all your power to scatter and put to flight the Evil Spirits which are inimical to good Operations, cause me by thy powerful virtue to succeed in what I have undertaken this Day which is consecrated to Venus. Therefore, Through the virtue of our Lord and Saviour **Jesus Christ** in whose Name I attend, wait for, and expect thy appearance."

The Invocant need be under apprehension or fear of harm or danger in Invocating this Celestial Intelligence who is Humane, Affable, and kind, and perfectly harmless, and may be invoked to appear in less time & with less trouble than the other Planetary Angels.

[206] After reciting the Invocation, the Invocant must wait with patience the appearance of the Spirit who generally appears at the first call if the Atmosphere be clear and serene, the signs of his coming are similar to those mentioned in the foregoing Experiment viz. a furious west wind which lasts but a few minutes when all becomes calm and quiet, then are heard the most enchanting strains of Heavenly music, accompanied by melodious voices, so powerful rich and sweet - as to charm the ear and feelings with exstacy, *(sic)* these sounds die away in sweet distant murmurings, which are followed by the appearance of innumerable handsome maidens, lovely to behold, being full of Music Joy & Beauty, their stay is short, and again the Elements seem in commotion for a few seconds, when all again becomes quiet. Suddenly a Glorious and shining light, appears in the midst of which a clear star is seen quick in motion which suddenly resolves itself into the form of a beautiful Angel, surrounded by resplendent beams of Angelic Glory and brightness, which so enchant the feelings of the Invocant - as to cause him to fall down and adore the Creator, who has given him by his sovereign will, permission to hold converse with those Glorious Inhabitants of the Celestial Spheres. This beautiful Spirit thus appearing,[245] the Invocant must receive him courteously fearing no harm

---

[245] This Glorious Being sometimes appears on the forms of a beauteous female wish angel's wings, and a regal crown upon her head, her countenance of surpassing loveliness. – Sibley.

from him, for his provence & office is to promote Love between Married persons, Amorous intrigues, and Friendship with all. The Operator must lay the prepared Amulet or charm before this Immortal being, signifying his intention and wish, which will be notified & answered by his presence; duly impressing the Mysterious Image with Power and virtue requisite for the accomplishment and success of the Operation.

After the Invocant has obtained his desires &c. of the Spirit, he may License him to Depart in the same courteous manner as he received him, his departure will be attended with sounds, appearances &c. similar to those which heralded his coming. All being completed, the person who is to wear the charm must sew it up in a new piece of Silk or Cloth of a green colour, and fasten it in the lining of the dress so as not to be seen; & worn day and night next the heart. This being kept a profound secret & having faith, the wearer may secure the Love of his most dearest friends, and the good will and friendship of most of those persons with whom he may come in contact. The Operator should return hearty thanks to God, for his success in the Operation.

[207] **Plate X - Electrum Magicum**

[208] The Electrum Magicum is a compound of all the seven metals in a due order and fit time melted together into one Mass of Metal in which all the Virtues of the Seven Planets are joined together under their influences. In this Electrum, the Operations of the Heavens, and Influences of the Seven Planets are combined and stored up. Therefore the Ancient Persian Magi: and the Chaldaeans found out and performed many wonderful things by its means. The manner in which this Electrum is composed is as follows. Take four half ounces of pure Gold which must be poured through the Antimony, melt it on Sunday in the hour of the ☉ which is the first hour after Sun-rise, when it is well fused, throw purified saltpetre into it, until it emits sparks of all kinds of colours, when it is well purified, pour it into a new vessel, afterwards melt in it, on a Monday in the hour of the Moon ☽ four half ounces of refined silver: purify it with salt of tartar, which has no culinary salt in it, and do not continue the operations beyond their respective planetary hours. On a Tuesday, in the hour of ♂, melt clean pure Iron with potashes, and cleanse it further with pitch or tar. On a Wednesday, in the hour ☿, melt four half ounces of Quicksilver, which purify with pitch. On Thursday, in the hour of ♃, melt three half ounces of Tin; purify it with the fat of a ram. On a Friday in the hour of ♀, take four half ounces of the Virgin Copper, purify it with vinegar and Saltpetre carefully: then strain it through a piece of leather. On the Saturday, in the hour of ♄, melt pure Lead, throw a good deal of pitch or tar upon it, and put it by, and take, in the hour of the Sun Jupiter, Venus, or Mercury, the Moon increasing in Light and in a favourable aspect to one or more of the fortunate planets to meet in the same hour all the Metals together. Put therefore, your purified Lead first into the crucible, afterwards the Tin before it is too hot, then pour the quicksilver into it and stir it about with a hazel stick, then put the copper into it, and give it a strong heat, afterwards the Silver, next the Gold. While all this [is] fusing, throw into it the eighth part of an ounce of mineral steel, also a small portion of perfume peculiar to each planet, viz. Musk, Ambergris, Storax, Benjamin, Euphorbium, Bdellium, Mastic, Incense, Loadstone, Red Roses, Red Coral, Myrrh of the East and grains [of] Black pepper, these perfumes must be pulverized and cast into the crucible while the mass is fusing & properly incorporated with it. After this compound is thoroughly mixed and incorporated & become as one Metal. It must be taken & placed in the crucible & put over the fire which must be fierce till it is all melted, this must be done in [209] the first hour after sun rise on Sunday or Thursday. In order to cast this melted metal in plates, the operator must be

provided with a mould of about three inches in diameter the thickness of the plate is immaterial but of a substance so as not liable to be broken; while pouring the metal into the mould, the operator must repeat the following prayer three times

Prayer.

"O! *x* Tetragrammaton *x* thou powerful God and Father, we praise, love, and pray to thee, we also here are collected laying before thee like poor earth, and ashes. We honour thy Holy and Majestic Name, we pray thee thou will permit thy Glorious Inhabitants of the Spheres to assist and bring to pass the lawful, just, and earnest desires of thy humble servants and that thou wilt empress this Image and Characters thereon, with Divine Power and Virtue, through Our Lord and Saviour Jesus Christ. Amen."

Then sing a song of praise to God such as the *Psalm Te Deum Laudamus* &c. The Latent properties of these Metals when compounded as above described have power and Secret virtue to drive away Evil Spirits and to assist in promoting Health, Honour, Riches, Eloquence, Trade Business, Love and Friendship, Secret Dreams, discovery of Hidden Treasures, Victory over Enemies also to Defend against and moderate chief of the Troubles & inconveniences of Life.

It must not be supposed a person possessing a Mysteries Image composed of this invaluable metal will enjoy any of the above gifts without Divine Aid added to an earnest faith of the possessor, for which purpose a plate of this precious compound must have seven circles engraved upon it in each must be engraven or written a short sentence descriptive of the Wish or desire of the Operator peculiar to the seven planets, according to the following model. The Seals of the Seven Planetary Angels & their Characters must be engraven in the respective circles during which time (at Sunrise) on Sunday the prayer should be repeated with great earnestness, such will be the power & virtue of this admirable Talisman that success generally will attend the operator if the manner composing it be strictly observed. It will not lose its virtue by a change of Masters providing the New Master Agrees & believes with faith & confidence in its Efficacy.

[210] **Plate XI.**

[211] **Magia Campanum**

This bell must be formed of electrum magicum, and fashioned as above shown and according to the rules as before mentioned, round it the words + **Tetragrammaton** + and + **Sadai**+ must be engraven in relief and also the sign and planet under which the operator is born. Also inside thereof the word + **Elohim** - and the clapper **Adonai**. It must be kept in a clean chamber, and not touched or handled but by the operator. When the Celestial Spirits or agents are to be Invoked, make a fire with incense and proper perfumes agreeable to the good Angel to be invoked, then rehearse devoutly an appropriate incantation such as the one already written, naming the Spirit, and ring the bell thrice, when the Spirit will instantly appear before thee, and thou will have thy wishes performed. This must be kept a great secret. This Bell may be of any size & weight. Its virtue & power is when rung, to draw many Spirits and spectres of various kinds, also to drive away all evil Spirits. By an earnest desire for any new undertaking and expressing the same on the inner surface of the Bell in words & characters, the Bell being rung as before, the Spirit governing such and undertaking would appear in any form the Operator wished, by renewing the words & characters Evil Spirits, wild beasts & even men [212] would be driven away at the sound of this instrument, for being made of the Electrum it is more importance than words, although the latter must be expressed earnestly desiring our wish to be gratified. The Operator must take care that he expresses nor desires any thing that is not agreeable, or in accordance with the nature of the Good Spirits he wishes to Invoke, for by doing so, he might be annoyed by the appearance of Evil Spirits &c. instead of the good in that case, he must dismiss by powerful adjurations, ringing the bell three times. Therefore when any of the Celestial Messengers or Glorious Spirits are invoked to appear, the Operator must wait with patience: and be firm, courageous, possessing great confidence trusting in God. When the Spirit appears, he must be received courteously, and without fear, terror or dismay: after the operator has had his desire granted, and his wishes gratified, Let him dismiss the Spirit in the same courteous manner as he received him by ringing the Bell and repeat[ing] the Licence to Depart, which he will do imperceptibly, vanishing as into thin air. It has been said, that if a constellated Plate made of Electrum, after the manner as before described, and placed under a person's pillow at night, [it] will give him extraordinary and beautiful Dreams, and make him hear heavenly Music.

[213] Septem Annulus

Compositio Septem Annulorum is formed as follows: The operator must be provided with the seven virgin Metals which are governed by the seven Planets as have been mentioned in the former part of this Book, they must be pure and unadulterated. On Sunday at Sunrise, having everything ready for the operation as before described, take a sufficient portion of pure Gold and put it in a ladle of Iron over a fierce fire till it is thoroughly melted, during this process cast a small portion of perfume proper to the Sun, and when thoroughly melted & mixed take the ladle containing the melted metal and cast therefrom a ring (the size of the fourth finger) into a mould formed for the purpose, which being done, the ring must be polished and engraven with the Name, Seal, Character and Number of the Planetary Angel who governs the operation on Sunday. While performing the Operation the Operator must devoutly, and with confidence, repeat the Oration, Invocation & Conjuration proper to the Sun (see Talismans), Should there not be sufficient time during the Planetary hour to complete the Operation, the Operator must wait patiently till the next hour of the Sun arrives, and so on till the ring is completed, which, when done must be carefully wrapped up in a piece of Silk of a yellow or gold colour, and kept by itself secretly till it is to be worn on the finger. The same process must be gone through in respect to the other rings on their respective days and in their respective planetary hours, which is always the first hour after sunrise and so on. The Operator must take care that he omits not the reciting of the Orations &c. proper to the planets on their respective days, but carry out the details with much exactness & punctuality in each Operation. The Operator must remember that the remaining six rings are composed of the following Metals, viz. Silver for Monday under the Moon, Iron for Tuesday under Mars, Quicksilver for Wednesday, under [214] Mercury. Tin for Thursday under Jupiter. Copper for Friday under Venus, Lead for Saturn on Saturday. Every operation must be performed during the Increase of the Moon. Each of these rings when made, polished and engraven with the Seals, characters, &c. (on the inside) of the respective planets governing the operations must be kept like the one for Sunday, wrapped up separately, and in secresy, *(sic)* till the wearer thinks proper to wear them. They are intended to be worn as follows only one on each day, viz. the gold one on Sunday, for Health, Honour, and Riches. The silver on Monday, for safety in Travelling by Sea or Land. The Iron for Tuesday, against Enemies, Troubles &c. The Quicksilver for Wednesday, for acquiring Eloquence, Liberty &c. Tin for Thursday, for prosperity in Trade & dealings. Copper for Friday for secret Love and Amorous Intrigues, friendship &c. Lead for Saturday for Discovery of Treasures, remarkable Dreams &c. The secret properties of the Septem Annulorum when properly formed according to the rules of Art, will considerably and their possessor in the common affairs of life, providing he consents to all that is done in their formation and possess an earnest belief in their efficacy. It has been proved that a ring of Virgin Silver made on Monday in the hour of the Moon when in fortunate Aspect with Jupiter has a singular effect in curing fits of Epilepsy by constantly wearing the ring night and Day. The manner of forming this powerful Ring is as follows: if a married person is afflicted; there must be collected a Silver coin such as a shilling or sixpence of each of the opposite sex who are married also, till a sufficient number is collected to purchase a sufficient weight of Virgin Silver ring to form the ring, which must be formed in the same manner as before describe. If the unmarried be afflicted, then the silver coins must be collected of the opposite sex of the same condition, each contributing to the success of the Operation by repeating a short earnest prayer for the recovery of the patient &c. This ring is efficacious in driving away Fits of Melancholy &c. The engraving must be inside.

[215] **Plate XIII – Septem Annulus**

[216] **Plate XIV – [De Fascinatione]**

[217] De Fascinatione atque eins Artificio

Fascinato est ligatio quae ex Spiritu fascinatis per oculus fascinati ad cor ipsius ingressa pervenit. Fascinationis ante instrumentum spiritus est scil vapour quidam purus lucidus subtilis, a cordis calore ex puriou sanguine generatus, hic similes siti radios as per oculos semper emittit radii isti emissi vaporem spiritualem secum ferunt: vapor ille sanguinem, sicut apparet in lippis ac rubentis oculis, eujus radius usque ad obvios spectantis oculos emissus, vaporem una secum corrupti sanguinis trahuit, eujus contagione cogit spectantis oculos morbo simili laborare. Sic pater factus et in aliquem intentus oculus cum forti imaginatione pro snorum radiorum aculeis, qui spiritus vehicula sunt, ipsos in adversas oculos jaculatur: qui quidem lentus spiritus fascinati deverberans oculos, eum a percutientis corde incitatur, percussi praecordia, tanquam regionem propriam fortitus, eum vulnerat et spiritum inficit peregrinus his spiritus. Unde Apuleius: Isti, inquit, oculi sui per meos oculos ad intima delapsi praecordia acerrimum meis medulis commovent incenduim. Scias itaque homines tum maxime fascinari, quando frequentissimo intuitu aciem visus ad aciem dirigentes, oculi oculis reciproce inhiant, radii radiis copulantur et lumina luminibus junguntur, tunc spiritus spiritui jungitur et scintillas defigit, sic fortissimae ligationes, sic amores acerrimi solis oculorum radiis accenduntur etiam vel repentino quodam intuiti, veluti jaculo seu ictu totum corpus penetrante: unde tunc spiritus et sanguis amatorius sic vulnerati, non aliter in amantem et fascinantem feruntur, quam sanguis et spiritus vindictae alicujus caesi prolabuntur in caedentem unde Lucret[ius], de his amatoriis fascinationibus, cecinit:

Yda petit corpus mens unde est sancia amore.

Nanque omnes plerunque cadunt in vuluus, et illam

Emicat in partem sanguis quaque laedimur ictu:
Et si cominus est, hostem ruber occupat humor.

Tanta est fascinationis potentia praesertum quando affectui vapores oculorum subserviunt. Idcirco intuntur fascinates collyriis, unctionibus, alligationibus et hujusmodi, ad spiritum tali vel tali modo afficiendum et corroborandum. Ut ad inducendum amorem collyriis utuntur-venereis ex hyppomane sanguine columbarum vel passerum et ex similibus: Ad inducendum timorem, collyriis utuntur Martialibus, ut ex oculus luporum, hienae et similibus. Ad calamitatem vel aegritudinem utuntur Saturnalibus, Similis de singulis ratio est habenda.[246]

[218] A few remarks on Invocation of the Planetary Angels by the Crystal.

As a full and clear explanation has already been given of the method of Invocating Spirits by the Crystal accompanied by an experiment, it is quite unnecessary to say any more on that head, Therefore those who desire a view of those glorious inhabitants of the planetary world, or to gain any information from them, that is according to their nature to grant, must have a humble faith and trust in God; under such a feeling of earnestness and confidence, it never can be offensive to Him. Because as has been before remarked, a method similar to this was doubtless employed by the ancient when they wished to inquire of the Lord for any special object, or of the Heavenly Messengers for any lawful information of which the scripture affords many proofs. Also the evidence that this practice is not lawful is not to be found in the word of God, on the contrary it is an undeniable fact that the Blessed Jesus, did not forbid the practice of making such enquiries. David asked the Lord "Shall I go up into any of the cities of Judah?" The Lord answered עֲלֵה *olah*, "go up." This and many other answers to the good seers of old. No doubt than then as now, great purity was required, or no answer would be given. Good seers in the Crystal can always read plainly all that is written or revealed therein; but indifferent seers only, perceive a degree of splendour or brightness in the crystal, when any truth was alleged; and a certain darkness of the stone when falsehood was stated. In this way they decided on the credibility of witness &c. Among the many visions and revelations that have appeared in the crystal in our day to good seers of both sexes, leading pure lives and of undoubted veracity, many of the miracles of our Lord and other scriptural events. Also among other questions and answers, have been the following: - "Should we make our supplications in the name of our Lord?" - Answer - "Why, He is our Mediator:" "Are the Catholics right to pray to the Virgin Mary?" In reply, there instantly appeared a vision of the cross, as represented in Plate [XV] in one of the quadrants with the words as in the double circle annexed. By this Vision it was understood, that not to the Virgin Mary, but to Him who suffered on the cross, and in his Name should Christians supplicate. It appears that [it] was Michael an Angel of the Sun, from whom these revelations came, but who does not often appear accept by powerful invocations such as are made by good and faithful persons, such is Daniel and the seers of old who all enquired of the Lord in a similar manner. The Spirits of Jupiter when called to appear in the crystal or make any revelation: the vision is generally accomplished with majestic splendour and such astounding brightness, as to compel the seer or seeress to withdraw his or her eyes therefrom. Such was the manner in which the Prophets, Priests & Seers of the Holy Scriptures obtained their answers, when a question was seriously & faithfully asked. For God by various means reveals his will to mankind.

---

[246] This passage examines the old theory that fascination comes from the eyes as a projected ray. – Ed.

[219] **Plate XV. Vision**
in the
Crystal

[220] **An**
Experiment
To Invoke the Spirit of
VENUS
in the
CRYSTAL

[221] The Method of Invocating Beautiful Spirit in the Crystal differs somewhat from those Experiments performed in invocating the Aerial Spirits and with less trouble and no danger. When the Operation is performed in all its details with much exactness, this Glorious Being will appear in the Crystal Globe in the form of a clear star at first, immediately afterwards it will assume the form of a beauteous female most fascinating to behold and surrounded with green and silver coloured rays so brilliant and glistening as almost to dazzle the eye of the beholder. The signs of the coming of this Glorious Angel are similar to those described in the foregoing experiments. The Operator must be pure in mind and body, expressing his desires earnestly and faithfully, asking nothing but what is lawful and right and not offensive to God nor contrary to the nature and office of the Spirit who is so mild and gentle as to become almost subservient to the human will after being once invoked to appear, particularly by those born under the resplendant Orb governed by this Beautiful Angel. It is presumed that every preparation connected with [this] Experiment is made in that manner as aforementioned elsewhere, which after being completed, the Moon increasing. Let the Operator and the company (if any) surround the Crystal, and commence earnestly Invoking the Spirit as follows.

"I call upon thee **Setchiel** in the name of the Father, and of the Son, and of the Holy Ghost Blessed Trinity Unspeakable Unity. I Invoke and intreat thee **Setchiel** in this hour to leave your bright abode, and come and appear visibly to us in thy glorious form of a Beautiful Angel in this Crystal Stone or Glass ~~and~~ and attend to the words and conjurations which I shall use this Day by the Holy Names of God **Elohe El Elohim Elion Yah Adonay Tetragrammaton**, that you attend to my requests and grant my desires according to the Sovereign Will of Him who is **Alpha et Omega** and by all other Great, Glorious, Holy, Unspeakable, Mysterious, Mighty, Powerful, Incomprehensible Names of the Most High. I again conjure, call upon thee fair Angel of God, **Setchiel**, Prince of Love and friendship, that thou wilt come without delay and appear to me in this Crystal in all the plenitude of thy Virtue and Power and reveal to me by thy wisdom and counsel such knowledge, and answers to my requests that they may redound to thy Honour, and to the Glory of God, and the welfare of mankind. Again I invoke and intreat thee **Setchiel** that you will come with all your power and scatter and put to flight the Evil Spirits which are inimical to this Operation; **Anael Sarabotes Abalidoth Amabiel**. Waiting patiently in the Name of the Father, Son, and Holy Ghost, for thy appearance and aid, which I hope thou wilt give to succeed in this Operation."

The Operator after reciting with great earnestness and devotion the above Invocation, must remain silent for the appearance of the Spirit, which will be in the manner as aforesaid, he must diligently watch for the Spirit as it assumes the human form, and instantly make known his requests in a courteous and becoming manner, the answers will be given in a clear and intelligent manner which there is no mistaking although not given in an Audible Voice. Should the Operator fail in obtaining satisfactory answers to his [222] earnest appeals through any failing, mishap, or negligence of his own, he must repeat the Invocation as before, till he gets his desires granted. The office of this Mild and Gentle Spirit is to u[n]fold the secrets of human nature, and to promote Love and Friendship. After having obtained his desires of the Spirit of Venus, the Invocant may rehearse a short sentence as a dismissal as follows.

> "Blessed and fair **Setchiel** who by the sovereign command, will, and permission of the Omnipotent Creator of the Universe hast appeared in the Crystal and hast answered my requests and petitions for which I return sincere thanks and now thou mayest Depart in peace unto thy abode where peace and contentment reign, and return unto me again and appear in this [crystal] whensoever I shall call thee by thy Name or by thy Office, and the peace of God be with me and thee and with all mankind. Amen. Glory be to the Father and to the Son and to the Holy Ghost."

The truth of this Experiment has been proved by eminent professors of the Occult Science and of undoubted veracity, and who all agree in declaring that the Glorious Spirit of Venus, from its mild, gentle and friendly nature, is more easily invoked than any of the other Planetary Spirits either in the Crystal or out of it, still it is said, that any one wishing to invoke the Spirit governing the Planet under the influence of which he was born can do so with morse [more] certainty & less trouble, even if it were the Spirit of Saturn or Mars.

A certain amount of caution is required in Invocating these Beautiful Spirits in the Crystal lest the Evil Spirits by their craftiness and subtlety may so transform themselves and gain admittance into the Crystal, and thus deceive the Operator into a belief that he is dealing with the Good Spirits if he is not will on his guard. It is not always requisite that the Spirit should always appear in human form in the Crystal, but at all times his presence is manifested by a brilliant display of light and scenery, for surpassing any thing produced by any of the powers of darkness. Not only that, the manifest tokens of the presence of the Good Spirits produce in the mind pure thoughts and feelings, while the other, whatever are the forms assumed, are only so many allurements and temptations, to deceive and betray the unwary. After all, if the Operator be firm sincere, faithful, confident, & persevering with patience, he will obtain that knowledge and assistance of those Bright Celestial Messengers that will render him Wiser, Happier, & Better in this World, and fit for that to come.

[223] **Plate XVI.**

[Part 8. Geomancy]

[225] **The Science**

of

Geomancy

or

The Art of Casting

Celestial

Lots

[226] **Geomancy**[247]

Geomantica ysau[?] est ars qua per sortan reddit nobis judicum ad omnium quaestionem de quaeunque re. Consistit autem sors hujusmodi in punctis, ex quibus deducuntur vita quaedam figura secundum rationum paritatis et imparitatis: qua figurae tandem reducuntur ad figuras coelestes, carum naturas et proprictatus assumentes, juxta signorum and planetarum rationes. Hoc ante inprimis nobis considerandum est quoniam sors hujusmodi in quantum talis, nihil peritatis portendere potest, nisi radicata fuerit in virtute aliqua sublimiori: et hanc duplicem posuerunt hujus scientia anteus: unam quae in Religion et ceremoniis consistit: et ideo voluerunt projectionis punctorii hujus sortis fiery in terra eum digito indicet quare hec sors hinc elemento appropriata est sicut hydromantia igni: et hydromantia aqua: tum, quia arbitrabantur manum projicietis, potissime por terrestres spiritus dirigi atque moueri: et ideo praemitte liqutur sacrae quidam incaname[n]ta et deputationes eum aliis quibusdam ritibus et magicis observationibus hujusmodi spiritus ad hoc allicientes. Alia potastas hanc sortan dirigens ae regens, ipsa est anima projicientis, quando fertur in aliquam magnum egressum sui desiderii. Tunc erim omnis sors habit naturalem obedientiam ad ipsam animiam: et de necessitate habet efficaciam, et movetur ad id quod anima ifssa desiderat. Et hae via est longem verior et purior, ute referet, ubi, vel quomodo puncta projiciantur. Habet itaq[ue] hoc artificium eandem [eadem] radiean eum artificio quaestionum astrologicarum: quae et ipsae non aliter verificari possunt, nisi constanti et recissivo[?] affectu ipsius quaerentis. Nunc ad praxin~~stanti~~ hujus artificii procedamus: et primo secendum[?] est, quod omnes figurae super quibus totum hoc artificium fundatur, duntaxat sedeim sunt: ut hic infra cum suis nominibus annotata vides.

[227] This curious science termed Geomancy is of high antiquity, and was in great repute amongst the ancient Chaldeans, Babylonians, Hebrews, Arabians, and other orientalists. It was a favourite study amongst the Druids, and constitutes a singular feature at the present day in freemasonry, it being the chief study of the Rosie Crucians, and was much practised by that singular race of beings whose secrets are now in the care of that society. In the Holy Scriptures we have frequent mention made of "Casting Lots," which was, no doubt, a species of geomantic divination, and was allowed as a final decision amongst the early Christians. In remote ages, the answers given by the seers as recorded in holy writ, was no doubt given by this species of curious

---

[247] A fuller introduction to geomancy (with details of practice and a history of the art, and without the need to read Latin) can be found in Skinner, *Geomancy in Theory & Practice*, Singapore: Golden Hoard, 2011. – Ed.

knowledge. And in later years, we have had many professors thereof, although not since the seventeenth century: yet few have given the subject the consideration it merited; for there is little doubt but it might in proper hands be brought to such perfection, as to become almost an universal knowledge; and as it does not require so much attention to arithmetical data, as astrology, it becomes far more facile and pleasing on that account.

[228] Plate XVII - A Table of the Sixteen Geomantic Figures

[229] *Quibus vero planetis figurae istae distribuenter, dicamus, ex hoc enim omnis figurarum proprietas atque natura, totiusque artificii indicium dependet. Sunt itaque Fortuna Major atque minor solem referentes: sed prima solem diurnum and in dignitatibus suis constitutum: altera autem nocturnum, vel in minoribus dignitatibus constitutum. Via autem atque populus Lunam referunt: prima ab mitio semper crescentem: secunda plenaim lumine and decrescetem. Acquisitio vero and Letitia Jovis sunt: sed prior Jovem magis fortunatum habet: secunda minus, sed extra detrimentum, Puella and Amissio Veneris sunt: prior fortunata, altera tanquam retrograda, vel combusta. Conjunctio and Albus, utraequae Mercurii figurae sunt, and utraequae bene: sed prima fortunatior; Puer atquae, Rubeus Martem referiit: quarum prior Martem habet benevolum, secunda autem maleficum. Carcer atquae Tristitia utraequae figura Saturni sunt, and malae: sed prima majoris detrimenti. Caput vero and Cauda suas naturas sequuntur. Hic itaque eum sint infallibiles figurarum comparationes, facite ex his signorum aequiparantiam dignoscimus. Habent itaque Fortuna Major and Minor signum Leonis, quod est dom[icilia] Solis. Via autem atquae Populus signum Cancri; quod est Lune. Acquisitio signum Piscium. Letitia vero Sagittarum quae sunt domicilia Jovis. Puella Taurum, Amissio Libram, quae sunt domus Veneris. Conjunctio Virginem, Albus Geminos domus Mercurii; Puer autem and Rubeus Scorpionem, domum Martis. Cancer Capricornum and Tristitia Aquarium domicilia Saturne. Caput vero and Cauda ita distribuuntur, ut Caput adhaereat Capricorne, Cauda vero Scorpioni. Hinc facile triplicatates signorum elicere potes secundum nationem triplicitatum signorum Zodiaci. Constituunt itaque triplicitatem igneam, Puer ultraque Fortuna, ac Letitia: Terram vero [230] Puella, Conjuctio, Cancer, atque Caput: Aeream Albus, Amissio atque Tristitia: Aqueam via. Populus, Rubeus, Cauda atquae Acquisitio. Et hic ordo Secundum rationem signorum sumptus est. Qui vero secundum naturas Planetarum atque ipsarum figurarum triplicitates constituere velit, hic haec observet regulam, ut triplicitatem igneam constituant: Fortuna Major, Rubeus. Puer and Amissio. Aeream Fortuna Minor, Letitia, Puella and Conjunctio. Aqueam Acquisitio, Cauda, Via and Populus. Terream Carcer, Tristitia, Albus atque Caput. Et haec via magis observatur, quam prima, quam secundum signorum rationem constituere docuimus. Hic ordo longem verior est atque rationabilior, quam ille qui vulgo celebratur hujusmodi descriptus. Triplicitatis ignae sunt Cauda, Fortuna Minor, Amissio and Rubeus: Aeree Acquisitio, Letitia, Puer and Conjunctio: Aquae Populus, Via, Albus and Puella: Terree, Caput, Fortuna Major, Carcer and Tristitia: Distribuunt enim issas figuras duodecim signis Zodiaci in tunc modum: Arieti datur Acquisitio: Tauro Fortuna Major cum Minori: Gemellis Letitia: Cancro Puella atquae Rubeus Leoni Albus: Vigini Via: Liberae Corput atquae Conjunctio: Scorpioni Puer: Sagittario Tristitia atquae Amissio: Capricorno Cauda: Aquario Populus: Piscibus Cancer.*

[231] **Triplicities of the Sixteen Geomantic Figures**.

[232] **The**
Method of Casting
The Celestial Lots

"And they gave forth their Lots, and the Lot fell upon Matthias, and he was numbered with the eleven Apostles." – *Acts* 2. 26.

According to the system of the ancients, as the manuscript which has been consulted exemplifies, the diviner, or seer, who wishes to predict by these lots, should procure a quantity of clean <u>earth</u> or clean sand, either of which should be mixed with water, for <u>seven</u> days, in equal portions; which should be done either under the arising of the fortunate <u>constellations</u>, or in the hours of the seven <u>planets</u>; and when this is done, the earth so formed into portions should be mixed together, in a fortunate day and hour. Whereby they affirm that "<u>the universal</u> effect may be more <u>plainly</u> and <u>easily</u> <u>known</u> and <u>declared</u>." Others made their figure in wax tables, but they all declare that the projection on <u>earth</u>, is the surest and most conducive to the discovery of truth; and that the figure should not be made or [233] <u>cast</u> at any time, but that divination should only be made, "<u>when the weather is bright and clear, and neither dark nor windy</u>, for distemperance [intemperance] in the elements, may cause changes in the passions of the souls." They also affirm, that when a figure is made, or judged, "<u>the Moon should be</u> [free] <u>from all impediment</u>, for it the Moon apply to <u>Saturn</u> or <u>Mars</u>, the soul thereby is inclined to lie, and also, that the figure should be made with the most sincere desire to ascertain the truth thereof.

MODERN METHOD [248]

The modern method of casting these celestial Lots, is by making the points either upon paper or a state, with any convenient instrument, either pen, crayon, chalk, pencil, or pointer, whichever may be nearest at hand; and the modern Geomancers affirm that great verity may be found in the art, when thus practised. Although they allow that the <u>ancient</u> method is the more exact. This being seriously thought of and the <u>mode</u> thereof selected, the diviner must proceed to make sixteen lines of points, which points must be made from <u>right</u> to <u>left</u>, contrary to the usual mode of writing; and in so doing he must [234] not count the <u>number</u> of points he makes, but leave that entirely to chance, or the sympathetic impulse which will guide the hand, so as to produce a figure corresponding to the true <u>answer</u> of the event sought after.

The following example will suffice to set this doctrine in easy light.

Example of forming the Points.

[235] The <u>points</u> being made as directed, let them be joined together two and two, leaving the <u>last</u> points unjoined, as in the example, where the first line being even, <u>two</u> points are left; the second line being <u>odd</u>, one point is left; and so of the rest.

This being done, arrange the four figures thus found, in order, from right to left, calling the first No. 1, the

---

[248] "Modern" in the late 18th century.

second No. 2, and so of the others thus: -

Then proceed to take the points of each figure is [as] they stand in a line, and form thereof another figure; thus in the first line of the figure, No. 1, are 2 points; in No. 2, 2 points; in No. 3, 1 point; and in No. 4, 2 points; which collected together, form this symbol: -

Do the same with the <u>lines</u> of the other three figures, which will give the second row of the figures, thus -

Which are termed No. 5, 6, 7, and 8.

[236] These being found, place the whole eight in a line thus: -

And then join each figure to its companion; that is to say - take the number of points in the first and second, third and fourth, and so of the rest, calling two or four points <u>even</u>, and one or three points <u>odd</u>; by which means you find out four other figures, which are placed thus: -

And which correspond to Nos. 9, 10, 11, and 12.

This being done, you have the whole of the figures, which the twelve Geomantic houses, and which cons[t]itute the chief part of the scheme. But there yet remain four other accidental figures, namely, the two <u>witnesses</u>, the <u>judge</u>, and the <u>sixteenth</u> figures.

[237] The witnesses are formed from the 9[th] and 10[th], and the two adjoining figures in the second row, and are these: -

And the judge is formed from out of these two, in like manner and is. The formation of the sixteenth figure, has been hitherto unknown, but it is of the utmost consequence in the formation of the judgement, especially where the answer seems a[m]biguous, and we will therefore give the secret of finding it, which is done by joining together the 1[st] and 15[th] figures (the judge) and out of these extracting the figure in question. The sixteenth figure is: -

We will now place the figure in its proper order, as it will give a clear idea of the process: -

| 8th House. | 7th House. | 6th House. | 5th House. | 4th House. | 3rd House. | 2nd House. | 1st House |

| 12th House | | 11th House. | | 10th House. | | 9th House |

| | Left Witness. | | | | Right Witness | |

| | | Judge | | | 16th Figure, or Final Result | |

[238] The Method of Divining by a figure of Geomancy.

In order to be perfect in the use of Geomancy, it is absolutely necessary that the student should be well acquainted with the Science of Astrology, as it regards the <u>houses</u> and quality of the seven planets; which are made use of in Geomancy, in the same manner, except as far as the symbolical nature of the figures themselves are concerned.

The Nature of the Sixteen Figures of Geomancy

Acquisitio [—] Is the best of the whole sixteen figures, and is a sign of riches, joy, gain, acquisition, profit, and a good end of all enterprises; it is the symbol of good fortune, of honour, renown, and happiness, it denotes long life, fortunate marriages, and success in every undertaking. It is a figure of **Jupiter**, and under the sign **Aries** it is exalted in the first house, and has its fall in the seventh, which is to be judged the same as in Astrology.

[239] **Amissio** — Is an evil figure; being the symbol of loss, and small profit; it is also found to be generally evil in most undertakings, and is an issuing figure. It is under **Venus**, and the sign **Scorpio**, its exaltation is in the 8th, and its fall in the 2nd house.

Fortuna Major — Is the symbol of wealth and rank, of power, honour, and dignity, and of an exceeding great manner. It is singularly good in all matters of gain, and to be preferred to none but acquisitio. It is ruled by the **Sun**, and is under the sign **Aquarius**: its exaltation is in the 11th house, and its fall in the 5th.

Fortunate *(sic)* **Minor** — Is the lesser fortune, it betokens disappointments and but small gain, being an issuing and wasteful figure; yet it is good for dignities, although ill in matters of profit. It is ruled by the **Sun**, and is partially under **Taurus**; its exaltation is in the first house, and its fall in the 7th or western angle.

Letitia — Is the figure emblematical of joy, gladness, fullness of pleasure, [240] and gay delights; endearments, profit, gain, and all favourable things, which it signifies similar to acquisitio. It is a very fortunate symbol wherever found, and productive of success, it is under **Jupiter**, and the sign **Taurus**; it is exalted in the second house, and its fall is in the 8th opposite.

Tristitia — Is the origin or source of sorrow, melancholy, heaviness of heart, lowness of spirits, dolor, grief, malice, and mischief and is extremity unfortunate in all affairs she may signify. She is also the cause of loss, disgrace, and trouble. It is under the evil planet **Saturn**, and in the sign **Scorpio**, and has its exaltation in the 8th and its fall in the 2nd house.

Rubeus — Is another no less vicious and wicked figure, it is the source of war and bloodshed, signifying guilt, deceit and perversion of truth; and intestine [internecine] quarrels animasitico, and discord. It is highly unfortunate in every undertaking; when it is found in the ascendant, Geomancers frequently destroy the figure. It is under **Mars** in the sign of **Gemini**, it is exalted in the 3rd house; and has its fall in the 9th.

Albus — Is a figure formed mainly good and oftentimes conducts to gain; especially in affairs of science and learning. It is under **Mercury**, and the sign **Cancer**. It is exalted in the 6th house, and its fall in the 12th house, which is opposite thereto.

[241] **Conjunctio** — Is a figure of gathering or conjoining; it is a controvertible figure, good with good, and evil with evil; it is a symbol of a funeral, "for it representeth the bier on which dead men are borne." The points being 2 before, 2 behind, and 2 in the centre; it is under **Mercury**, retrograde in **Virgo**. It is a Bicorporal figure, exalted in the 6th house, and has its fall in the 12th house.

Carcer — Is the emblem of a prison, imprisonment, close shut-up places, close vessels, and is amazingly evil, as its name imports, It gives loss in all things, poverty and wickedness, it is also unlucky in every undertaking; it is under **Saturn**, and the sign **Pisces**; it is exalted in the 12th house, and has its fall in the 6th house, or house of evil fortune.

Populus — Is the symbol of a multitude, a congregation, an assembly, a confused retinue. It is generally accounted evil and unpropitious: and generally signifies moving or journeys. It is under the full **Moon** in the sign **Capricorn**, and is exalted in the 2nd house, having the fall in the 8th.

[242] **Via** — Is the figure of quickness and facility; of travelling, removals, journeys, and voyages. It is a wasting and dissipating figure, and unlucky in all matters of gain or profit. It denotes hasty moves and short visits, when found in the scheme. It is under the new **Moon** in **Leo**, and is exalted in the 5th house, having its fall in the 11th.

Caput [Draconis] — Is the symbol of the Dragon's head and is generally accounted as fortunate and propitious in the undertakings. It is good for matters of gain, and in money affairs is well. It signifies something quickly coming on, being an entering figure. It is the Dragon's head in **Virgo,** and is a commixture of **Jupiter** and **Venus** conjoined.

Cauda [Draconis] — Is the symbol of evil and misfortune, disgrace, scandal, slander, poverty and ruin. It wastes the substance, annoys the asker, and hinders the undertaking. It is always and at all times evil. This is the Dragon's Tail in **Sagittarius** formed out of a mixture of **Saturn** and **Mars**.

[243] **Puella** — Is a pleasant and favourable symbol: it signifies fulfilment of wishes, joy and contentment, success in love, and mayy [many] equally propitious wants; it is favourable also in money affairs; it is the sacred emblem of the cross; and is ever found to be a sign of equality, justice, and devotion. It is under the planet **Venus** and the sign **Libra**. It is exalted the seventh house, and has its fall in the ascendant.

Puer — Is the emblem of a drawn sword, and of war, battles, hostility, quarrels, contentions, and discords. It conducts but poorly to gain or profit, being naturally evil and malignant: consequently no success can attend the question where it is a Significator. It is under **Mars** and the warlike sign is **Aries**. The ascendant of England. It is exalted in the first house; and has its fall in the angle opposite.

In the order to judge from the figures, as before observed, the student must learn to be well acquainted with the essential and accidental dignities, stations, aspects, and positions of the geomantic emblems, and be ready in his reference to the twelve celestial houses, by which means, if he be sincere in his wishes, the most astonishing answers may be obtained.

[246] [Talisman of Never ending Love]

[247] The Experiment

As an Experiment for Secret Love is given and performed by the Wheel of Magic, and one of a powerful nature it is intended to be employed in the following Operation thus blending the two Experiments together, the combined influence of which acts with ten-fold power particularly when aided by a Sympathetic feeling in the parties concerned. The manner of performing this Grand Experiment in its united form, which must be strictly carried out according to the rules of Art in every detail with much exactness, as follows. The Operator must have a plate of pure Silver highly polished of about three inches in diameter; of a hexagonal form (thickness immaterial) He must make a suffumigation of the following ingredients. Lavender, Valerian, Red Roses, Red Coral, Musk, Ambergris, these must be mixed with small portions of Hair from the nape of the neck or pudendum of the wearer of the Amulet, the whole must be thoroughly dried and reduced to a powder, then mix with the blood of a pigeon or dove while quite warm: also a small quantity of *sanguis mensis* into a paste of which, form lozenges of the weight of ten grams, dry them thoroughly, then heat the Silver plate quite hot and while in this state grate thereon on both sides a portion of the lozenges so as to produce an agreeable odour, after which, repolish the plate, and engrave it according to the foregoing Model with much care and distinctness, omitting the ornaments or embellishments, which are not required.[250] Should the Operator prefer to make use of a fair Virginal parchment to the Silver plate, he must dissolve five of the Lozenges in pure water with which he must sprinkle the parchment on both sides, and dry it well before [248] a fire composed of Sweet Brier, Sweet Marjoram, or other scented Woods. Then draw the requisite lines and figures with consecrated Ink of a green colour, not omitting to recite the Orations &c. for Friday which are contained in [a] former part of this Book [Part 2] with great earnestness, at this stage of the Operation, the Operator must now use the Philter which has been prepared as aforesaid, by drinking a portion of this powerful potion to his beloved pronouncing his or her Name three times also the Name Aniel, this potion should be taken every time you recite any sentence for spiritual aid. The two Christian Names of the Lover and Beloved must be written in the Blood as for the philter joined together by the Name Aniel, also the two hearts joined together as in the Model. All this Operation must be done in the day and hour of Venus (which the Cabalistic Art teaches.) the Moon increasing, and in fortunate aspect to Jupiter, Venus, or Mercury from the sign Taurus. It really seems vain to endeavour to explain anything more than what has been already said in former Experiments, that a plate of Metal or a piece of

---

[249] Double experiment of great power for secret love in the form of Hercules' node.

[250] The embellishments are what makes this grimoire unique, however they should be ignored from a practical point of view when drawing these figures. – Ed.

parchment with certain figures, or Mysterious Characters, engraven or written thereon, can have any power or life giving principle in them, whatever other latent properties they may possess. But at the expense of repetition we will once more explain, that the Vivifying power and vital principle so necessary in Experiments of this kind, cannot be given to a senseless plate of Metal &c. (they being but visible and earthly agents.) but by Invoking the aid of the good Spirits to impress their divine virtue and power upon them and make them efficacious. For this purpose, let the Operator choose a retired spot in which to perform his Operations, and thereon draw a circle not less than seven feet in diameter in which he and his associates (if any) may enter, it being their fortress and defence against all evil and Malignant Spirits who might assail the Operator and thwart him in his undertaking. Having great courage, confidence, perseverance and patience. All being ready, let him commence by earnestly invocating the fair [249] and beautiful angel Aniel as follows:

Invocation

"O thou fair Angel of God **Aniel** who by Divine Permission and Sovereign Grace of Almighty God hast condescended to leave thy bright abode and appeared in a beautiful form visibly to mortals sinful as they are, I pray you by the interposition of your favourites **Sarabotes, Sausaltiel, Doremiel, Setchiel** to hear favourably my petition that you will once more leave your celestial sphere or send one of your Ministering Spirits to aid me in this operation, impress this Talisman with a double portion of thy mighty power and virtue so that I may secure the pure unchangeable and eternal Love of **A.B**. I again beseech and entreat thee **Aniel** who preside over the workings of the heart to come on the wings of the Zephyrs thou fair and beautiful Angel, Prince of Love, Gentleness and Peace and appear unto me before this circle in all the plenitude of thy Power and Glory and hearken to my request which I now make unto thee in the Name of Him who and by His Almighty Power commanded and it was done. Be propitious to my undertaking impress this mysterious image with Divine virtue and make it efficacious in producing that sincere Love and Affection towards me thy unworthy servant from the heart of the object of my adoration which no earthly power can vanquish and nothing but death can separate or dissolve. I pray that thou wilt extend thy mighty power fair **Aniel** and cause sincere friendship and good-will towards me by all mankind. Come powerful and mighty Spirit **Sarabotes** with all your cohort and scatter and put to flight all [250] evil Spirits that may be inimical to my operations of this day. Cause me to succeed by thy mighty power in what I have undertaken this day destined to the wonders of Love. I invoke intreat and call upon thee **Aniel** once again, to come from thy blest abode or residen[c]e and appear unto me in the form of a Glorious and beautiful Angel without delay or hindrance, notify by thy presence thy power and willingness to hear favourably the prayers and appeals for aid in my operations of this day under the influence of that beauteous orb of Venus the sixth Luminary in the firmament. Be favourable unto me blessed Spirit which will redound to thy glory with all suitable acknowledgement, while I hope for, wait for, and expect thy appearance in the Name of the Father, and of the Son, and of the Holy Ghost **Abalidoth Amabiel Aba Santanael**."

After the powerful Invocation has been once recited, and the Spirit does not appear in a reasonable distance of time, viz. from three to five minutes, repeat the Invocation, even the third time if required. But the Spirit generally appears at the first call, the sign of his coming is similar to those in the former experiments, his appearance is attended with even more splendour, b[e]aming forth with such Angelic Glory as to dazzle the eye of the Operator and entrance his soul with ravishing delight. He must be received courteously and with humility, his nature is so mild gentle and pacific that no danger is to be apprehended at from this Brilliant inhabitant of the spheres the Prince of Love and Friendship, nor from those Spirits which accompany him. When this has been done and his presence duly acknowledged, let him be bound with the Bond of Spirits. The Operator must then present unto him his request written on Virginal parchment together with the prepared Talisman sprinkled with the Philter or Love potion which will be immediately impressed with divine power and virtue according to the wish and design of the Operator. For the more ardent, earnest, and chaste he is in his desires, the stronger will be the golden cord of sympathy and Friendship, and the tighter will be the silken bands of Love and affection which Bind two such loving hearts together. After the operator has obtained his desires of the Spirit he may license to depart in the same courteous manner as he received him, which will be instantly followed by the signs of departure similar to those of his coming. The operator must office all tracts of the Circle &c. after giving humble and hearty thanks unto God for permitting this Glorious Angel to come at his call and to his Operation, giving the required aid to render it successful. This admirable Talisman this prepared, will render the wearer thereof so enchanting in the sight & feelings of his or her adored object as to render a rival impossible. Provided he or she consents and complies with all that is requisite in every detail of the Operation. It must be worn constantly Night & Day near the heart with the strict secrecy & confidence of its efficacy.

[251] [Circle of Anael]

[252] Magical Experiments.

[253] A Safe Way to Secure a House.

Whoso wishes to protect himself against thieves by night or by day, also to secure his House from the same, must proceed as follows: The Charm in Latin against Theft given in a former page of this work must be translated and written on Virgin Parchment, and worn about him constantly, and repeat the words every morning, so shall no theft happen to annoy him personally. Then to bind or secure his house or any particular room containing money or other valuable property; Let him draw a circle of any convenient size on the floor of the room wish consecrated Chalk or Charcoal, and write therein any sentence expressive of his desires to retain the thief (should he enter) similar to the foregoing model, also the Seals and Crosses must not be omitted. Then the Operator must write on Virginal parchment of an Octagonal form these characters e a j, then add the Name Zaziel or other of the Spirits of Saturn together with his planetary Character. Also these numbers 1, 3, 5, ¼, ⅐ in black ink, after this is done he must make a fire of thorns elder wood &c. producing smoke in which the parchment must be held till perfumed, then sprinkle it over with Nightshade three times, deposit it in the earth under the floor so as to conceal it, and retire to rest. This powerful Operation must be performed in the night on Saturday in the Hour of Saturn when [254] he is in evil aspect with the Moon and in her decrease: and if the thieves enter the house they will not be able to leave it till sunrise, unless spoken to by Name.

For Outhouses

The Operator must prepare for the operation at the same time and in the same manner as the foregoing operation with the exception of the Circle (which is not here required). He must write on parchment these Characters d b h. Add the Name of the Spirit this Character as before also these figures ♃, 8, 5, 3, ⅙, ⅐. Perfume as before, then sprinkle the parchment with the juice of hemlock, and place it under the threshold of the entrance, or in some secret corner of the outhouse under the floor or earth, there the thieves must remain till sunrise if they enter, the operator must not omit repeating the words of the Charms he wears about him, as before, for upon the exactness, earnestness & confidence with which any Magical Experiment is performed, much depends the certainty of success. Instances are recorded in which such operations as the above, have been performed according to the Rules of Art by which Depradators have been defeated in their attempts to approach within a limited Distance of a House or premises.

There are several powerful Experiments relating to the secret Influences of Saturn and Mars, by which in the hands of evil disposed or ignorant persons, sometimes much mischief is produced, therefore we will forbear to mention them at present, as it is only to the wise and prudent, such occult secrets are intended to be revealed.

[255] But as prevention is at all times better than a cure, or punishment for crime, we have let our good will reign triumphant, thinking & feeling that we are justified, if we can by any lawful or secret means, which are only to be discovered in the great store house of Nature, perform an Experiment which has the power to defend us or any of our friends from any unlawful act therein which any evil disposed persons may attempt, by keeping them at a distance from us and our premises. As we shall Invoke Divine and Powerful Aid to assist in the Operation we see nothing sinful nor unlawful in performing such Experiment which has for its object the welfare of our fellow men.

To bind the Ground & Premises, whereby neither Mortals nor Spiritual Beings can approach within a limited distance.

This all-powerful Experiment must be performed in the day and hour of Jupiter, by describing a circle of a hundred feet or more in diameter whereby the Dwelling, Garden, Orchard &c. is inclosed if possible, fortify it with Divine Names, Crosses each of which must be written on Virgin parchment and deposited within the circle in the Earth opposite the four Cardinal paints. After suffumigating them with the perfumes proper to the Sun, Jupiter, & Mercury, viz. Saffron, Myrrh, Benjamin, Storax, Mace, Incense &c. in the Day & hour of Mercury. The Moon increasing, and in fortunate Aspect to Jupiter or Venus. The Operator having the Grand Pentacle of Solomon and the pentacles of the Sun & Jupiter before him may commence reciting in the centres of the Circle the following great Bond or Incantation, which must be earnestly repeated in the Day & Hour of Mercury.

[256] Incantation

"In the Name of the Father, and of the Son and the Holy Ghost, Amen. I bind all mortal and immortal, celestial and terrestrial, visible and invisible beings, except those who are my real friend, and are well disposed towards me, to avoid and quit this space of ground, which I now mark, and wherein I now stand, and that with all possible speed and dispatch. I bind you to avoid and no longer tarry, by the unspeakable power of Almighty God by the most high and Mighty Name of + **Tetragrammaton** + by all-powerful names. + **Agla** + **Saday** + **Jesu** + **Messias** + **Alpha** + and **Omega** +. By all these most High and powerful Names, I charge, adjure, bind, constrain both mortal and immortal, terrestrial, celestial, visible, and invisible beings to avoid, quit, and depart this ground, and do request that name of you, except those who are my real friends &c. as aforesaid be suffered to come within these sacred limits. These things I request in the Name of the Father, and of the Son, and of the Holy Ghost, **Amen**."

This powerful Incantation must be recited three times with great earnestness & faith. Then let the Operator dig a depth just outside the circle, of three feet, at the four parts of the Compass, and bury the seal of the Earth in each part, and no power, either visible, or invisible will have power to enter this boundary having a dishonest intention or purpose. The Operator will be still farther defended personally from Fraud or Theft, if he wear the Latin Charm, also the Pentacle of Solomon & repeat the Charm as in former Experiments.

[257] **To find out, Bind, and Compel a Thief to return Lost Goods when stolen.**

To bind a Thief so that he shall have neither rest nor peace till he return thee thy lost goods; go to the place from whence they were stolen away and write down the day, hour and minute if you can when the Goods were stolen and the name of the planet ruling the day, also the name of the suspected thief on virgin parchment and place the same under the threshold of the door he or they went out of. Then make four crosses on the four corners or posts of the doorway. After this is done so far, write down on virgin parchment the following characters ☽ ☉ ʒ ✳ △ ∑ together with the name Samael,[251] then turn round three times and repeat the charm each time, written in page 7 [i.e. page 169] viz, "Thou thief who hast stolen &c." If you hear no news of the thief in 48 hours, as it is most certain you will; then prick the parchment full of holes and hang it up in chimney where the heat of the fire may scorch it, and thief or thieves will be so restless and ill at ease, being discovered, and having no peace, till he or they bring home your goods, throw them privately into your house, or some place belonging to you.

It must be remembered, that unless the goods are actually stolen the above charm will have no effect, for if they are only mislaid, or taken away in jest, or lost through carelessness or neglect, a theft is not committed. To ascertain whether the goods are stolen or not, apply to a skilful Astrologer who will give the required information. This is a grand secret and must be strictly guarded and inviolably kept or little or no success will attend the Operation.

[258] **Hominem Rebus Fascinum Liberare.**[252]

For this purpose a small private Room must be chosen, and a fire made of charcoal thorns and briars, and a little sulphur must be thrown in, taking care to have a ventilator that the carbon may escape.[253] Then fasten the

---

[251] Examine the facsimile of this page for the exact form of the characters. – Ed.

[252] To release a person from an enchantment. – Ed.

[253] Actually the point is to have the sulphur dioxide escape. It is dangerous to burn sulphur in an enclosed space, as it can cause breathing difficulties, and has even been fatal. – Ed.

door and window of the room so that no person can enter or look in, for the person or persons performing the Operation must be calm, quiet and undisturbed, not a word must be spoken during the Operation by the parties concerned. The Operation may now be commenced by cutting some of the afflicted person's hair from the nape of the neck, also the parings of the finger and toenails, clip them small and burn them to powder, put the powder in Sal-Ammoniac, write the suspected parties name backwards on parchment which must be dipped in aqua vitae (water of life) or Spirits of wine place the Sal-Ammoniac with the powder, together with the written parchment in some convenient vessel over a slow fire (composed as aforesaid) then let the afflicted person sit by it and watch it that it catcheth not free, speak no word, and if there is a noise, write down how often it is heard, and affix the sign of the " before each writing, the person offending will then be compelled to come to the house, being so restless, and knock at the door or shutter under some excuse, such as wanting to borrow something or give some information about some person or other, but on no consideration make any reply in any way, but keep your seat, when after a short time the person will appear before you.

This important and powerful Experiment is best performed in the night at the hour of twelve, in the decrease of the Moon she being in Scorpio, and is good aspect to Mercury, but if possibly in evil position to Saturn. Many instances in which this Experiment has proved successful, where the patient has recovered, and ended in the disgrace and punishment of the offender. Keep this secret.

To conceal or hide Money or Treasures so that they may never be stolen or discovered

Take Coriandrum of the second kind, which maketh one to sleep; and join thereto Croco, insgreno, and apio, and grind them together with the juice of hemlock: then make a suffumigation therewith, and suffume the place where thou will hide any treasure in, when the " is joined to the ☉, in the angle of the earth; and that treasure, so hidden, shall never be found, particularly if hidden in the earth, the " being in an earthy sign, and the planet Saturn ruling the hour of concealment.

[259] A Talisman against Enemies

The Operator must observe that every preparation connected with this Admirable Talisman must be made as before mentioned in this Book, and according to the ancients being under the dominion of the Sun and Jupiter. It must be cast of the purest grain Tin in the day and hour of Jupiter when in good aspects to the Sun from the signs a e or i and to the Moon in her increase. The characters &c. must be engraven as in the above model in the day and hour of Mercury and if possible in fortunate aspect to Saturn or Mars. When finished it may be suspended about the neck or any part of the body of the wearer, keeping it a secret from all but him or herself. Its effects are, to give decisive victory over enemies, to defend against their machinations, and to inspire the wearer with the most remarkable confidence. The orations &c. must be said.

[Part 10. Magical Tables]

Magic Tables

or

Scale of Numbers

De unitate & ejus scala [Of the Scale of One and Unity]

The Original World	I Yod	One Divine essence, source of Virtue and Power the Name of God expressed in one simple letter.
Intellectual World	Soul of the World	One Supreme Intelligence the first Creature of the fountain of Life.
Celestial World	Sun ☉	One ruler of the Stars the fountain of light.
Elementary World	Philosopher's Stone.	One Instrument subject, all virtue nature et transmutation, naturalium & transnaturalium.
Minor World	The Heart.	One beginning of Life and lastly E[x]piring.
Infernal World	Lucifer.	One Prince of the Rebellious Angels & Darkness.

[262] Scala Binarii [Scale of Two]

In Archetype	חיה אל	Jah El	Name of God in Two Letters
Intellectual World	Angel	Soul	The intelligent substances of Choler.
Celestial World	SOL	LUNA	Two Great Luminaries
Elementary World	Earth	Water	Two Elements producing Animal Life.
Minor World	Cor: Heart	Brain	Two principles of Life
Infernal World	Behemoth Fletus	Leviathan Stridor dentium	Duo quae comminatur Christus Damnatis.

[263] Scala Ternarii [Scale of Three]

In Archetypo	Pater	שדי Sadai Filius	Holy Spirit	Name of God in three Letters. Three persons in the Divine Essence.
In the Intelligible World	Above Innocents	Middle Martyrs	Low or Beneath Confessors	Three Hierarchies of Angels. Three Degrees of the Blessed.
In the Celestial World	Motion Cardinal Diurnal	Fixed Succedent Nocturnal	Common Cadent Between	Three Quarternions of Signs. Three Quarternions of Houses. Three Lord of the Triplicities
Elementary World	Simple	Composite	Decomposite	Three Degrees of the Elements.
The Minor World	The Head in which groweth the intellects answering to the intellectual World	The Breast wherein the Heart the seat of life is, answers to the Celestial World	The Belly wherein engendereth strength in genital members, answering the Elementary World.	Three Births answering to the Triple World
In Mundo Infernali	Alecto Minos Malefici	Magera [Megera] Aeacus Apostatae	Tesiphone [Ctesiphone] Radamanth[us] Infideles	Tres furiae Infernales. Tres iudices Infernales. Tres Gradus Damnatorum.

[264] Scala Quaternarii ad Ouatuor [Scale of Four]
Elementorum Correspondentiam [Element Correspondences]

Name of God Quadriliterum	יהוה				In mundo Archetypo in de lex prudentia
Four Triplicities of the Hierachies of the Intelligencies	Seraphim Cherubim Thrones	Dominations Powers Virtues	Principalities Archangels angels	Innocents Martyrs Confessors	In mundo intellectuali unde fatalis
Four Principal Angels presiding in Celestial World	מיכאל Michael	רפאל Raphael	ג[ב]ריאל Gabriel	[א]וריאל Uriel	
Four Rulers of the Elements	שרף Seraph	כרוב Cherub	שישחר [תרשיש] Tharsis	אריאל Ariel	
Four Devoted Animals	Lion	Eagle	Man	Calf	
Four Triplicities of The Tribes of Israel	Dan Asa Nephthali	Judah Issachar Zabulon	Manasses Benjamin Ephraim	Reuben Simeon Gad	
Four Triplicates of the Apostles	Mathias Peter James the Gr[ea]t	Simon Bartholomew Matthew	John Philip James the Less	Thaddeus Andrew Thomas	
Four Evangelists	Mark	John	Matthew	Luke	
Four Triplicities of the Signs	Aries Leo Sagittarius	Gemini Libra Aquarius	Cancer Scorpio Pisces	Taurus Virgo Capricornus	In the Celestial World which is from the Law of Nature

[265]

Stella and Planets relating to the Elements	Mars and Sol	Jupiter and Venus	Saturn and Mercury	Fixed Stars and the Moon	
Four Qualities of the Celestial Elements	Lume[n]	Diaphanii	Agilitas	Sodalitas [Soliditas]	
Four Elements	אש Ignis	רוח Air	מים Aqua	עפר Terra	The elementary World, ubi lex generationis & corruptionis
Four Qualities	Heat	Moisture	Cold	Dry	
Four Seasons	Summer	Spring	Winter	Autumn	
Four Cardinal points of the World	East	West	North	South	
Four perfect created ingredients &c	Animals	Plants	Metals	Stones	
Four qualities of Animals	Walking	Flying	Swimming	Creeping	
Plants answering to the four Elements	Seeds	Flowers	Leaves	Roots.	
Quae in Metallis	Gold and Forum [Iron]	Copper and Tin	Quick-Silver	Lead and Silver	
Four Qualities in Stones	Clear and Hard	Light & Transparent	Bright and Congealed	Heavy & Opaque	
Four Elementas hominis	Mind	Spirit	Life or Soul	Body	Minor World

[266]

Four Powers of The Soul	Understanding	Reason	Imagination	Sense	
Four indiciariae Potestates	Faith	Knowledge	Judgement	Experience	
Four Moral Virtues	Quietness	Temperance	Prudence	Fortitude	
Senses answering to the Four Elements	Seeing	Hearing	Tasting & Smelling	Touching	
Four Elements of the Human Body	Spirit	Flesh	Humours	Bones	
Fourfold qualities of the Spirit	Animal Spirit	Life	Creation or Birth	Nature	
Four Humours	Choler	Blood	Phlegm	Melancholy	
Four degrees comprising manner	Force	Nimbleness	Rest	Slowness	
Four princes of the evil Demons in the Elementary World	Iams Samael	Lzazo [Izaza] Ahazel [Azazel]	Iazo Azael	Iazjm Mahazael	In mundo infernali ubi lex irae and punitionis [In the infernal world under the law of punishment]
Quatuor flumina Inferna	Phlegethon	Cocytus	Styx	Acheron	
Quatuor principes Demonorium super Angelos mundi	Oriens	Paymon	Egyn	Amaymon	

[267] Scala Quinarii [Scale of Five]

Name of God in five Letters. Name of Christ in five Letters	אליון אלהים יחשוה	Eleon Elohim Jhesuh				In Archtypo
Five properties of the Understanding	Spirits of the first Hierarchy vocati dii sive full DPL	Spirits of the Second Order dicti Intelligentia.	Spirits of the Third Order vocati angeli qui mittu[n]tur.	Celestium Animal Body	Heroes or Souls of the blessed	In the Intellectual World.
Five erratic Stars ruling	Saturn	Jupiter	Mars	Venus	Mercury	In the Celestial World
Five genera corruptibilii	Aqua	Aer	Ignis	Terra	Mixtis	In the Elementary
Five species of Mixture	Animals	Plants	Metals	Stones	Zo[o]phytes	
Five senses	Tasting	Hearing	Seeing	Feeling	Smelling	In the Minor World
Quinque Tormenta Corporalia [Five Bodily Torments]	Amaritudo Mortificans [Deadly bitterness]	Ululatus Horrisoni [Horrible howling]	Tenebrae Terribiles [Terrible darkness]	Ardour Inextinguibilis [Unquenchable heat]	Foetor Penetrans [Penetrating stink]	In Mundo Infernali [In the Infernal World]

[268] Scala Senarii [Scale of Six]

In Archtypo	[אלוהים] אליחם			[גבור] גבזי		אל	Name of Six Letters
The Intelligible World	Seraphim	Cherubim	Thrones	Dominion	Powers	Virtues	Six Order of Angels who are not of the former order
The Celestial World	Saturn	Jupiter	Mars	Venus	Mercury	Luna	Six Planets zodi[a]cal per Latitudes from the ecliptic
The Elementary World	Quietness	Thinness	Sharpness	Bluntness	Thickness	Motion	Six substantial qualities of the Elements
The Minor World	Intellect	Memory	Sense	Motion	Life	Essence	Six degrees of Man
In Mundo Infernali [In the Infernal World]	Act[e]us	Megalesius	Ormenus	Lycus	Nicon	Minor [Mimon]	Six Demons calamitatum omnium autores [Six Demons responsible for all disasters]

[269] Scala Septenarii [Scale of Seven]

In Archetypo	Ararita אראריתא				Assor Ehel אשר אחל [Asher Eheieh אשר אחיה]			Name of God in Seven Letters
Intelligible World	צפקיאל Zaphkiel	צדקיאל Zadkiel	כמאל [סמאל] Samael	רפאל Raphael	אלהאכי [האניאל] Aniel [Haniel]	מיכאל Michael	גבריאל Gabriel	Seven Angels who stand before the face of God.
Celestial World	שבתאין Saturn	[צרק] רם Jupiter	יסמואר [מאדים] Mars	שמש Sol	נוגה Venus	כוכב Mercury	לבגה [לבנה] Luna	Seven Planets
Elementary World	Lapwing Cuttle fish Mole Lead Onichinus [Onyx]	Eagle Dolphin Whale [Hart] Tin Sapphire	Vulture Pike Wolf Iron Diamond	Swan Sea calf Lion Gold Carbuncle	Pigeon Thymallus Tiger Copper Emerald	Stork Mullet Ape Quicksilver Agate	Owl Aerulus Cat Silver Chrystal	Seven Birds. Planets Seven Fishes. Planets Seven Animals. Planets Seven Metals. Planets Seven Stones. Planets.
Minor World	Right foot Right ear	Head Left ear	Right Hand Right Nostril	Heart Right Eye	Pudendum Left Nostril	Left Hand Bone [mouth]	Left Foot Left Eye	Seven perfect members distributed. Seven foramina capitis planetis distributa
In Mundo Infernali [In the Infernal World]	Gahenna [Hell] גיהנם	[Portae Mortis] Gate of Death וצל מות	[Umbra Mortis] Shadow of Death ירעש תום	Puteus Interitus [Pit of Destruction] באר שחת	Lutum Fecis [Clay of Death] מטהירין	Perditio [Perdition] אכדון	Fouea [Depth of the Earth] שאול [מאול]	Septan habitacula inferoru[m], que discribit Rabbi Joseph Castiliensis, Cabalista in *Horto nucis* [Seven infernal habitations which Rabbi Joseph of Castile, the Cabalist, describes in *The Nut Garden*]

[270] Scala Octonarii [Scale of Eight]

Name of God in eight Letters		Eloha Vedaath אלוה ודעת			Tetragrammaton יהוה ודעת Vedaath				In archetype
Octo Beatorum Praemia [Eight Blessed Rewards]	Haereditas [Inheritance]	Incorrupt-ibilis] [Incorrupt-ibility]	Potestas [Power]	Victoria [Victory]	Visio Dei [Vision of God]	Gratia [Grace]	Regnum [Kingdom]	Gaudium [Joy]	Intelligent World
Octo Coeli Visibiles	Coelum Stellatum	Coelum Saturni	Coelum Jovis	Coelum Martis	Coelum Solis	Coelum Veneris	Coelum Mercurii	Coelum Lunae	Celestial World
Octo qualitates particulares [Eight particular qualities]	Siccitas terrae [dry earth]	Frigidatus aquae [cold water]	Humidatus aeris [moist air]	Caliditas Aenis [ignis] [hot air/fire]	Caliditas Aeris [hot air]	Humiditas aqu[a]e [moist water]	Siccitas ignis [dry fire]	Frigi[di]tas Terrae [cold earth]	Elementary World
Octo Beatorum-gaudia [Eight kinds of blessed men]	Pacifici [Peacemakers]	Esurientes sitientes iustitiam [Those that thirst for Righteous-ness]	Mites [The Meek]	Persecutiupter (sic) iuistia [iustitiam] [Those Persecuted for Righteousness]	Mundi Corde [Pure in Heart]	Misericodes [Merciful]	Pauperes spiritu [Poor in spirit]	Lugentes [Mourners]	In Minor Mundo [In the Minor World]
Octo damnatorum proemia [Eight rewards of the damned]	Carcer [Prison]	Mors [Death]	Judicium [Judgement]	Ira Dei [Wrath of God]	Tenebra [Darkness]	Indignatio [Indignation]	Tribulatio [Tribulation]	Anguistia [Anguish]	Mundo Inferni [Infernal World]

[271] Scala Novenarii [Scale of Nine] [254]

---

[254] A more reliable set of Kabbalistic correspondences can be found in Skinner, *The Complete Magician's Tables,* Singapore: Golden Hoard, 2017. – Ed.

Appendix 1. Contents of all known Manuscripts of Sibley's *Clavis*

All available manuscripts of the *Clavis* have been listed in the following pages with the page numbers of their Chapters and illustrations, so that the contents of each manuscript lines up and can be exactly compared with all others. Gaps are deliberate and represent missing chapters or illustrations rather than the result of wayward formatting. From this table it can clearly be seen that MS 18 is by far the most complete, with a number of additional texts that do not appear in any other versions.

The page numbers of MS 18 in these tables are the page numbers as marked in the manuscript, not the continuous numbering used in this printed edition, although the numbers are effectively the same up to page 108 (with a one page difference from page 80 to 90).

pp.	8. National Library of Israel MS Yar. Var. 18	pp.	1. Weiser MS - Peterson, *The Clavis or Key to the Magic of Solomon*
	Date: 1836 Pages: 265. Scribe: Raphael?		**Date: 1878. Pages: 281. Scribe: ?**
	Frontispiece	16	Frontispiece
title	Clavis or Key to Unlock the Mysteries of Magic	title	The Clavis or Key to Unlock the Mysteries of Magic of Rabbi Solomon
1	Preface	3	Preface
2	Chapter 1 - What disposition those ought to posses	17	[Chap I]. What Dispositions they ought to possess who are willing to participate
2	Chapter 2 - What is the proper place, also Time for the Exercise	20	Chap II. What are the proper Places and Time for the Exercise of this Great Art.
3	Chapter 3 - Of Matters relating to the Operations and method of	23	Chap III. Of Matters relating to the Operations, and the manner of preparing them
6	Chapter 4 – Concerning the Necessary Instruments	30	Chap IV. Concerning the Necessary Instruments.
7	Chapter 5 – Concerning the Influences and Secret Virtues	32	Chap V. Concerning the influences and secret virtues of the Moon, in her
10	Chapter 6 – Of the manner of working the Figures of Talismans	38	Chap VI. Of the manner of working the Figures of Talismans and Characters,
11	Plate I - Grand Pentacle of Solomon	43	The Grand Pentacle of Solomon.
13	Chapter 7 – Concerning the Hours of the Day and Night	44	Chap VII. Concerning the Hours of the Day and Night for the Seven Days of the
14	Chapter 8 – Concerning the Perfumes that are proper	46	Chap VIII. Concerning the Perfumes that are proper for the Seven Planets for
14	Chapter 9 – Concerning the Orations, Invocations and	48	Chap IX. Concerning the Orations, Invocations, and Conjurations for every Day
15	Chapter 10 – Concerning Orations in the Form of Exorcisms to	49	Chap X. Concerning Orations in the Form of Exorcisms, to consecrate all the
	Pentacles		**Pentacles**
17	Pentacle for Sunday under the Sun (intro)	53	Pentacle for Sunday under the Sun
18	Oration, Invocation and Conjuration for Sunday	55	Oration, Invocation and Conjuration
20	Plate II - The Mysterious Cabalistic Names of the Hours of the	60	The Mysterious Cabalistic Names of the Hours of the Day and Night
21	Plate III - The Hours of the Day and Night on Sunday	62	Hours of the Day and Night of Sunday
22	Plate IV – Pentacle for Sunday made under the Sun (image)	63	Pentacle for Sunday under the Sun
23	Plate V – Sun Pentacles	64-68	Sun Pentacles
24	Plate VI – Sun Pentacles	69-73	Sun Pentacles
25	Plate VII – Sun Pentacles	74	Sun Pentacles
26	Description and Use of the foregoing Mysterious Figures or		
28	Pentacle for Monday under the Moon (intro)	75	Pentacle for Monday under the Moon
29	Oration, Invocation and Conjuration for Monday	76	Oration, Invocation and Conjuration
32	Plate VIII – The Hours of the Day and night on Monday	81	Hours of the Day and Night on Monday
33	Plate IX – Pentacle for Monday made under the Moon (image)	83	Pentacle for Monday under the Moon
34	Plate X – Moon Pentacles	84-88	Moon Pentacles
35	Plate XI – Moon Pentacles	89-92	Moon Pentacles
37	Pentacle for Tuesday under Mars (intro)	93	Pentacle for Tuesday Under Mars
	Hours of the Day and Night of Tuesday [missing]	98	Hours of the Day and Night on Tuesday
37	Oration, Invocation and Conjuration for Tuesday	94	Oration, Invocation and Conjuration
40	Plate XII – Pentacle of Tuesday under Mars (image)	100	Pentacle for Tuesday Under Mars
42	Plate XIII – Mars Pentacles	101-105	Mars Pentacles
43	Plate XV – Mars Pentacles	106-110	Mars Pentacles
45	Pentacle for Wednesday under Mercury (intro)	111	Pentacle for Wednesday under Mercury
45	Oration, Invocation and Conjuration for Wednesday	112	Oration, Invocation and Conjuration
48	Plate XVI – Hours of the Day and Night on Wednesday	116	Hours of the Day and Night on Wednesday
49	Plate XVII – Pentacle for Wednesday under Mercury (image)	118	Pentacle for Wednesday under Mercury
50	Plate XVIII – Mercury Pentacles	119-123	Mercury Pentacles
51	Plate XIX – Mercury Pentacles	124-127	Mercury Pentacles
53	Pentacle for Thursday under Jupiter (intro)	128	Pentacle for Thursday under Jupiter
54	Oration, Invocation and Conjuration for Thursday	129	Oration, Invocation and Conjuration
56	Plate XX - Hours of the Day and Night on Thursday	134	Hours of the Day and Night on Thursday
57	Plate XXI – Pentacle for Jupiter on the day of Thursday (image)	136	Pentacle for Thursday under Jupiter
58	Plate XXII – Jupiter Pentacles	137-141	Jupiter Pentacles
59	*Plate XXIII [missing]*	142-145	Jupiter Pentacles
61	Pentacle for Friday under Venus (intro)	146	Pentacle for Friday under Venus
62	Oration, Invocation and Conjuration for Friday	148	Oration, Invocation and Conjuration
64	Plate XXIV – Hours of the Day and Night on Friday	153	Hours of the Day and Night on Friday
65	Plate XXV – Pentacle for Thursday [Friday] under Venus (image)	146	Pentacle for Friday under Venus
66	Plate XXVI - Pentacles of Venus	155-159	Venus Pentacles
67	Plate XXVII - Pentacles of Venus	160-163	Venus Pentacles
69	Pentacle for Saturday under Saturn (intro)	164	Pentacle for Saturday under Saturn
70	Oration, Invocation and Conjuration for Saturday	166	Oration, Invocation and Conjuration
72	Plate XXVIII - Hours of the Day and Night on Saturday	171	Hours of the Day and Night on Saturday
73	Plate XXIX – Pentacle for Saturday under Saturn (image)	173	Pentacle for Saturday under Saturn
74	Plate XXX - Pentacles of Saturn	174-178	Saturn Pentacles
75	*Plate XXXI [missing]*	179-182	Saturn Pentacles
79	Plate XXXII - the Mysterious Ring	187	The Mysterious Ring
	Four Experiments with Specific Spirits		**Four Experiments with Specific Spirits**
80	An Experiment of the Spirit Birto	189	An Experiment of the Spirit Birto
83	Plate XXXIII - Birto - Wyvern with 2 Circles	190	Birto with 2 Circles

	8. National Library of Israel MS Yar. Var. 18		1. Weiser MS - Peterson, *The Clavis or Key to the Magic of Solomon*
85	An Experiment of the Spirit Vassago	195	An Experiment of the Spirit Vassago
88	Plate XXXIV - Seal of the Spirit Vassago	200	Seal of the Spirit Vassago
89	An Experiment of the Spirit Agarese (sic)	201	An Experiment of the Spirit Agares
94	An Experiment of the Spirit Bealpharos	208	An Experiment of the Spirit Bealpharos
96	Plate XXXV - Illustration of Bealphoras		
98	Plate XXXVI - 1. Magister Circle 2. Homo Sacarus Muselo meas	212-213	Magister Circle - Homo Sacarus Musela mea Cherubosea
100	**The Wheel of Magic**	217f	**The Wheel of Magic** [foldout]
101	Wheel of Wisdom	217	The Wheel of Wisdom
102	Key to the Wheel of Wisdom	219	Key to the Wheel of Wisdom
104	Full Directions for Magical Operations.	222	Full Directions for Magical Operations.
	A Secret and Complete Book of Magic Science	231	**A Complete Book of Magic Science**
1	Book of Magic Science	234	Book of Magic Science
3	Plate I - Blessings, Benedictions and Consecrations	236	Benedictions and Consecrations
7	Plate II - (hexagram with eye)		
8	Plate III - Wands & hexagram - Oration, Prayer		
9	Oration, Prayers		
15	Names and Offices of the Ruling, Presiding and Ministering	251	Names and Offices of the Ruling, Presiding and Ministering Spirits
21	Zadkiel		
22	Form of Bond of Spirits	260	Form of Bond of Spirits (Pabiel)
24	Plate IV - Pentacles of the Seven Planets	275	Pentacles of the Seven Planets
25	Plate V - Sun		
26	Plate VI - Moon		
27	Plate VII - Seals of 5 Planetary Angels		
28	Invocations of the Seven Planets		
30	Plate VIII - Seals and Characters of the Seven Planets with their	267	Seals and Characters of the Seven Planets
31	Plate IX - Seals and Perfumes - Moon & Mars	281	*end*
32	Plate X - Seals and Perfumes - Mercury & Jupiter		
33	Plate XI - Seals and Perfumes - Venus & Saturn		
t	**Crystaliomancy or the Art of Invoking Spirits by the**		
1	Preface		
4	Concerning the Room Containing the Circle		
5	Plate I - Circle		
6	Concerning the Apparatus and Instruments used		
8	Plate II - the Mirror		
9	Consecrations and Blessings		
11	Plate III - Instruments: wands, daggers and candles		
14	Bond of Spirits for Vassago		
1	**Miscellaneous Examples and Experiments**		
2	Natural Magic - Charms		
4	Plate I - the Ring of Strength		
8	Plate II - To Cause Destruction to Enemies		
9	Charm against Thieves		
10	Method of Raising and Invoking Spirits		
14	Plate III - Experiment of Invoking or Raising the Powerful		
17	Plate IV - Form in which the Spirit Oberion usually Appears		
18	The Great and Powerful Incantation		
22	Concerning the Proportion, Measure & Harmony of the Human		
24	Plate V - [Human Body and Zodiac]		
29	Plate VI - The Imperial Talisman for Victory over Enemies		
30	A Powerful Talisman for Secret Love		
32	Plate VII - [Talisman for Love]		
37	Plate VIII - A Charm for Healing Diseases		**National Library of Israel MS Yar. Var. 18** (continued)
41	Plate IX - Amulet or Charm for Amorous Intrigues, Friendship	64	Plate XVII - A Table of the Sixteen Geomantic Figures
44	Plate X - Electrum Magicum	67	Triplicities of the Sixteen Geomantic Figures
47	Plate XI - [Planetary Talisman]	68	Method of Casting the Celestial Lots
48	Plate XII - Magia Campanum	80	Experimentum Duplex Magnae Potentiae Amori Secreto forma Nodi Herculi
50	Septem Annulus (Seven Rings)	81	Venus interlace sigil
52	Plate XIII - Septem Annulus	82	The Experiment
53	Plate XIV - De Fascinatione	86	Anael sigil
56	Plate XV - Vision in the Crystal	87	Magical Experiments
57	An Experiment to Invoke the Spirit of Venus in the Crystal	94	A Talisman against Enemies
60	Plate XVI - Anael [Mirror]	95	Magical Tables or Scale of Numbers
61	The Science of Geomancy or the Art of Casting Celestial Lots		

pp.	2. University of Utah, Marriott Library, BF 1601 C53	pp.	3. Adam McLean identified as MS. In Private Collection (with 168 folios)
	Date: **Pages:** 268. **Scribe:** same as No. 7		**Date:** **Folios:** 168 (84 pp). **Scribe:**
	Frontispiece		Frontispiece
title	**Clavis or Key to Unlock the Mysteries of Magic**	title	**The Clavis or Key to Unlock the Mysteries of Magic of Rabbi Solomon.**
1	Preface		[Preface]
17	Chapter 1 - What Disposition they ought to possess who are		Ch 1 What Disposition they ought to possess who are willing to participate in the
21	Chapter 2 - What is the proper places and Time for the		Ch 2 What are the proper Places and Time for the Exercise of this Great Art.
24	Chapter 3 - Of matters relating to the Operations		Ch 3 Of Matters relating to the operations and the manner of preparing them
32	Chapter 4 – Concerning the Necessary Instruments		Ch 4 Concerning the necessary Instruments.
35	Chapter 5 – Concerning the Influences of the Moon		Ch 5 What are the Influences a[nd] secret Virtue the different situations of the
43	Chapter 6 – Of the Manner of working the Figures of		Ch 6 Of the manner of working the Figures of Talismans, Characters, etc according
			The Grand Pentacle of Solomon.
49	Chapter 7 – Concerning the Hours of the Day and Night		Ch 7 Concerning the Hours of the day and Night for the Seven days of the week
51	Chapter 8 – Concerning the Perfumes that are proper for the		Ch 8 Concerning the Perfumes that are proper for the seven Planets for every Day
54	Chapter 9 – Concerning the Orations, Invocations and		Ch 9 Concerning the Orations, Invocations and Conjurations for every Day in the
55	Chapter 10 – Concerning Orations		Ch 10 Concerning Orations in the form of Exorcisms to consecrate all the things
	Pentacles		**Pentacles**
63	Pentacle for Sunday under the Sun	17	Pentacle for Sunday under the Sun
65	Oration, Invocation and Conjuration for Sunday		Orations
73	Mysterious Cabalistic Names of the Hours of the Day and		Cabalistic Names of the Hours
74	Hours of the Day and Night on Sunday		The Hours of the Day
76	Pentacle for Sunday		Pentacles for Sunday under the Sun
77-83	Sun Pentacles		Pentacles
84	Pentacle for Monday under the Moon		Pentacle for Monday under the Moon
85	Oration, Invocation and Conjuration for Monday		Orations
90	Hours of the Day and Night on Monday		Cabalistic Names of the Hours
91	Pentacle for Monday under the Moon		The Hours of the Day
92-94	Moon Pentacles		Pentacles
95-100	Moon Pentacles		
101	Pentacle for Tuesday under Mars		Pentacle for Tuesday under Mars
107	Hours of the Day and Night of Tuesday [missing]		Orations
102	Oration, Invocation and Conjuration for Tuesday		Cabalistic Names of the Hours
108	Pentacles of Tuesday under Mars		The Hours of the Day
109-113	Mars Pentacles		Pentacles
114-118	Mars Pentacles		
119	Pentacle for Wednesday under Mercury		Pentacle for Wednesday under Mercury
121	Oration, Invocation and Conjuration for Wednesday		Orations
125	Hours of the Day and Night on Wednesday		Cabalistic Names of the Hours
126	Pentacle for Wednesday under Mercury		The Hours of the Day
127-131	Mercury Pentacles		Pentacles
132-135	Mercury Pentacles		
136	Pentacle for Thursday under Jupiter		Pentacle for Thursday under Jupiter
138	Oration, Invocation and Conjuration for Thursday		Orations
144	Hours of the Day and Night on Thursday		Cabalistic Names of the Hours
145	Pentacle for Thursday under Jupiter		The Hours of the Day
146-150	Jupiter Pentacles		Pentacles
151-154	Jupiter Pentacles		
155	Pentacle for Friday under Venus		Pentacle for Friday under Venus
157	Oration, Invocation and Conjuration for Friday		Orations
164	Hours of the Day and Night on Friday		Cabalistic Names of the Hours
165	Pentacle for Friday under Venus		The Hours of the Day
166-170	Pentacles of Venus		Pentacles
171-174	Pentacles of Venus		
175	Pentacle for Saturday under Saturn		Pentacle for Saturday under Saturn
178	Oration, Invocation and Conjuration for Saturday		Orations
183	Hours of the Day and Night on Saturday		Cabalistic Names of the Hours
184	Pentacle for Saturday under Saturn		The Hours of the Day
185-189	Pentacles of Saturn		Pentacles
190-193	Pentacles of Saturn		
194	The Mysterious Ring	87	The Mysterious Ring.
	Four Experiments with Specific Spirits		**Four Experiments with Specific Spirits**
201	An Experiment of the Spirit Birto		

	2. University of Utah, Marriott Library, BF 1601 C53		3. Adam McLean identified as MS. In Private Collection (with 168 folios)
209	An Experiment of the Spirit Vassago		An Experiment of the Spirit Vassago who may be called upon to appear in Chrystal
217	Seal of the Spirit Vassago		
219	An Experiment of the Spirit Agares	95	An Experiment of the Spirit Agares.
227	An Experiment of the Spirit Bealpharos	98	Of the Spirit Bealpharos.
237	1. Magister Circle 2. Homo Sacarus Muselomea		Magister Circle - Homo Sacarus Meus Elomeas Cherubosca
242	The Wheel of Magic		The Wheel of Magic
244	**Wheel of Wisdom**		**Wheel of Wisdom**
245	Key to the Wheel of Wisdom		The Key to the Wheel of Wisdom.
			Full Directions for Magical Operations.
	A Secret and Complete Book of Magic Science		**The Complete Book of Magic Science Containing The Method of Constraining**
254	Full directions for Magical Secrets and Operations		
268	*end*		Circles, candlesticks and magical apparatus.
			Names of the offices of the Ruling, Presiding and Ministering Spirits.
			The form of the bond of Spirits given one J.W. 1573.
			The Pentacles of the Seven Planets.
			The Seals and Characters of the Seven Planets.
			Series of circular seals of Olympian spirits.
			The spiral Semaphora for Success in Life / Elaborate circle with various rays
			Crystaliomancy Or the Art of Invoking Spirits By the Crystal.(12 folios)
		168	*end*

476

pp.	4. University of Manchester John Rylands GB 0133 Eng MS 40	pp.	5. The Society of Esoteric Endeavour / Caduceus Books [S.E.E.]
	Date: c. 1825 - c.1835. Pages: 246 Scribe: J.D?		**Date: 1868. Pages: 150. Scribe: Robert T Cross.**
	Frontispiece		
1	**The Clavis of Key to unlock the Mysteries of Magick of Rabby**	1	**Solomon's Clavis or the Key to unlock the Mysteries of Magic**
3	Preface	2	Preface
16	Chapter 1. What Disposition they ought to possess who are willing to	13	1 - What Disposition is required
18	Chapter 2. What are the proper Places and Time for the Exercise of this	15	2 - What are the proper places and times
20	Chapter 3 Of matters relating to the Operation and manner of preparing	17	3 - Of matters relating to the Operations
27	Chapter 4 Concerning the necessary Instruments	24	4 - Concerning the requisite Instruments
29	Chapter 5 What are the Influences and Secret Virtues which the	26	5 - What are the Influences and Secret Virtues
35	Chapter 6 Of the Manner of working the Figures of Talismans,	32	6 - Of the manner of working the Figures of Talismans
40	Grand Pentacle of Solomon	37	Grand Pentacle of Solomon
41	Chapter 7 Concerning the Hours of the Day and Night for the Seven	38	7 – Concerning the Hours of the Day and Night
43	Chapter 8 Concerning the Perfumes that are proper for the Seven	40	8 – Concerning the Perfumes that are proper
45	Chapter 9 Concerning the Orations, Invocation and Conjuration for	41	9 – Concerning the Orations, Invocations for every day of the Week
46	Chapter 10 Concerning Orations in the form of Exorcisms to consecrate	42	10 – Concerning Orations in the form of Exorcisms
	Pentacles		**Pentacles**
51	The Pentacle of the Sun to be made on a Sunday in the Hour of the Sun	46	Pentacle of the Sun
52	Oration, Conjuration and Invocation for Sunday	48	Oration, Conjuration and Invocation for Sunday
55	The Mysterious Cabalistic Names of the Hours of the Day and Night	54	Hours of the Day and Night
54	The Hours of the Day and Night on Sunday		
		55v	Pentacle of the Sun to be made on Sunday in the Hour of the Sun
59-65	Sun Pentacles	56	Sun Pentacles
66-72	Sun Pentacles	57-58	Sun Pentacles
73	Sun Pentacles	58	Sun Pentacles
		59	Pentacle of the Moon
81	Oration, Invocation and Conjuration for Monday	60	Oration, Invocation and Conjuration for Monday
78	Hours of the Day and night on Monday	65	Hours of the Day and night on Monday
77	Pentacle of the Moon made on Monday in the Hour of the Moon	66	Pentacle of the Monday to be made on Monday (image)
84-88	Moon Pentacles	67	Moon Pentacles
89-94	Moon Pentacles	68-69	Moon Pentacles
97	Pentacle of Mars made on Tuesday	70	Pentacle for Mars and Tuesday
98	Hours of the Day and Night of Tuesday	75	Hours of the Day and Night of Tuesday [missing]
100	Oration, Invocation and Conjuration	71	Oration, Invocation and Conjuration for Tuesday
97	Pentacle of Mars made on Tuesday under Mars	76	The Pentacle of Mars to be made on Tuesday (image)
104-108	Mars Pentacles	77	Mars Pentacles
109-115	Mars Pentacles	78-79	Mars Pentacles
116	Pentacle of Mercury to be made on Wednesday	80	Pentacle under Mercury for Wednesday
121	Oration, Invocation and Conjuration	81	Oration, Invocation and Conjuration
119	Hours of the Day and Night	84	Hours of the Day and Night
118	Pentacle of Mercury to be made on Wednesday	85	Pentacle of Mercury to be made on Wednesday (image)
125-129	Pentacles of Mercury	86	Pentacles of Mercury
130-135	Pentacles of Mercury	87-88	Pentacles of Mercury
136	Pentacle of Jupiter to be made on Thursday under Jupiter	89	Pentacle for Thursday under Jupiter
140	Oration, Invocation and Conjuration [139 - with Hebrew table]	90	Oration, Invocation and Conjuration
139	Hours of the Day and Night on Thursday	94	Hours of the Day and Night on Thursday
138	Pentacle of Jupiter to be made on a Thursday	95	Pentacle of Jupiter to be made on a Thursday (image)
143-149	Jupiter Pentacles	96	Jupiter Pentacles
150-155	Jupiter Pentacles	97-98	Jupiter Pentacles
156	Pentacle to be made on Friday under Venus	99	Pentacle of Friday & Venus
161	Oration, Invocation and Conjuration	100	Oration, Invocation and Conjuration
159	Hours of the Day and Night on Friday	103	Hours of the Day and Night on Friday
156	Pentacle to be made on Friday under Venus	104	Pentacle of Venus to be made on Friday (image)
165-169	Pentacles of Venus	105	Pentacles of Venus
170-175	Pentacles of Venus	106-	Pentacles of Venus
176	Pentacle of Saturn to be made on Saturday under Saturn	108	Pentacle for Saturday and Saturn
182	Oration, Invocation and Conjuration for Saturday	111	Oration, Invocation and Conjuration for Saturday
179	Hours of the Day and Night	114	Hours of the Day and Night
176	Pentacle of Saturn to be made on Saturday under Saturn	115	Pentacle of Saturn and Saturday (image)
185-191	Pentacles of Saturn	116	Pentacles of Saturn
192-197	Pentacles of Saturn	117	Pentacles of Saturn
202	The Mysterious Ring many Doctors of the Cabala have made use	118	The Mysterious Ring (image)
	Four Experiments with Specific Spirits		**Four Experiments with Specific Spirits**
204	An Experiment of the Spirit Birto, as hath been often proved at the	122	An Experiment of the Spirit Birto
207	Birto - Wyvern with 2 circles		

	4. University of Manchester John Rylands GB 0133 Eng MS 40		5. The Society of Esoteric Endeavour / Caduceus Books [S.E.E.]
223	An Experiment of the Spirit Vassago	125	An Experiment of the Spirit Vassago
229	Seal of the Spirit Vassago		
209	An Experiment of the Spirit Agares	131	An Experiment of the Spirit Agares
215	[A Experiment] Of the Spirit Bealpharos	134	[An Experiment] of the Spirit Bealpharos
221	1. Homo Sacarus Mus Elomeas Cherbosca 2. Magister Circle	139	1. Magister Circle 2. Homo Sacarus Muselomeas Cherubosea
230v	**Wheel of Magic**	143	**Wheel of Magic**
231	The Wheel of Wisdom	140	The Wheel of Wisdom
232	The Key to the Wheel of Wisdom		
235	Full Directions for Magical Operations	150	*end*
246	*end*		

pp.	6. London University Senate House Library - Harry Price HPF 1/10		9. Library & Museum of Freemasonry (SRIA) MS 2083
	Date: after 1822. Pages: 186. Scribe: 'Raphael'		**Date: 1832. Pages: 172. Scribe: Frederick Hockley.**
	Plate I - Signs, Seals and Magical Tools (frontispiece)		
title	Clavis Resero Arcana Mysteria - Rabbi Solomonis	1	The Keys of Rabbi Solomon
1	Preface		
6	Clavis or Key to Unlock the Mysteries of Magic - What disposition they ought to	3	The Keys of Rabbi Solomon Chapter 1st
8	Chapter II - What are the proper places and times for the exercise of this Great Art	5	Chapter 2nd
9	Chapter 3 - Of matters relating to the Operations and manner of them to be	7	Chapter 3rd
11	Chapter 4 - Concerning the necessary Instruments	12	Chapter 4th
12	Chapter 5 - What are the Influences and Secret Virtues of the Moon in her different	14	Chapter 5th
18	Chapter 6 - Of the manner of working the figures of Talismans	19	Chapter 6th
16	Plate II - Grandis Pentaculum Solomonis	22	The Great Pentacle of Solomon
20	Chapter 7 - Concerning the hours of the Day and Night for the Seven days of the	24	Chapter 7th
21	Chapter VIII - Concerning the Perfumes that are proper for the Seven Planets	25	Chapter 8th
21	Chapter [9] - missing	27	Chapter 9th
22	Chapter 10 - Concerning Orations in the form of Exorcisms to consecrate all things	28	Chapter 10th
	Pentacles	34	**Pentacles**
24	Pentacle for Sunday under the Sun (intro)		
27	Oration, Invocation, Conjuration		
26	Plate IV - Hours of the Day and Night of Sunday	37	Hours of the Day and Night of Sunday
25	Plate III - Pentacle of the Sun (image)	38	The Day of Sunday Under the Sun - - Pentacle of the Sun
29	Plate V - Sun Pentacles	40	Pentacle of the Sunday for Honours and Riches (incomplete)
30	Plate VI - Sun Pentacles	41	Pentacle of Sunday for Honours and Riches (incomplete)
31	Plate VII - Sun Pentacles	42	For Honours & Dignities of Sunday under the Sun (incomplete)
32	Description; Precious Stones	43-54	(A further 9 incomplete Sun Pentacles)
35	Plate VIII - The Pentacle of the Moon (image)	56	The day of Monday Under the Moon. Pentacle... Moon
34	Oration, Invocation, Conjuration	61	Oraison, Invocation and Conjuration
36	Plate IX – The Hours of the Day and Night of the Good Genii ...over Monday	58	The Hours of the Day and Night of Monday (incomplete)
35	Plate XII - Lunae Pentaculum	64	Talisman or Pentacle for travels by Land by Sea (incomplete)
37	Plate X - Pentacles of the Moon	65	Pentacle or Talisman for Love. The Monday under Moon
38, 39	Plate XI - Pentacles of the Moon / Plate XII - Pentacle of the Moon	67	(A further 7 incomplete Moon Pentacles)
42	Pentacle of Mars (intro)	75	The day of Tuesday under Mars. Pentacle of Mars (incomplete)
45	Plate XIV - Hours of the Good Genii who prevail on Tuesday	79	Oraisons, invocations and Conjurations
42	Oration, Invocation, Conjuration (Pentacle of Mars)	81	Pentacle & Talismans (incomplete)
44	Plate XIII - Martis Pentaculum	82	To be fortunate. The Tuesday under Mars (incomplete)
46	Plate XV - Mars Pentacles	84	Talisman for Military expeditions (incomplete)
47-48	Plate XVI & XVII - Mars Pentacles	85-89	(A further 5 incomplete Pentacles of Mars)
51	Pentacle under Mercury	93	The day of Wednesday Under Mercury. Pentacle... (incomplete)
51	Oration, Invocation, Conjuration	97	Invocation, Oration and Conjuration
54	Plate XIX - Hours of the Good Genii who prevail on Wednesday	95	The Hours of the Day and Night of Wednesday (incomplete)
53	Plate XVIII - Mercurii Pentaculum	97	Talisman against Slavery Wednesday Under mercury (incomplete)
55	Plate XX – Mercury Pentacles	99	Talisman for Games of Hazard, Wednesday ... Mercury
56	Plate XXI – Mercury Pentacles	100-107	(A further 7 incomplete Pentacles of Mercury)
61	Plate XXII - Jovis Pentaculum	109	The day of Thursday under Jupiter Pentacle of Jupiter
59	Oration, Invocation and Conjuration for Thursday	114	Oration, Invocation and Conjuration for Thursday
62	Plate XXIII - Hours of the Day and Night on Thursday	111	Hours of the Day and Night on Thursday (incomplete)
65	Plate XXVI - Pentacle of Jupiter	116	Talisman for the game of Hazard Thursday under... (incomplete)
63	Plate XXIV - Jupiter Pentacles		
64	Plate XXV - Jupiter Pentacles	118-127	(A further 7 incomplete Pentacles of Jupiter)
70	Pentacle for Friday under Venus	128	The day of Friday under Venus Pentacle of Venus (incomplete)
69	Oration, Invocation and Conjuration for Friday		
72	Plate XXIV – Hours of the Day and Night on Friday	129	The Hours of the day and Night of Friday (incomplete)
75	Plate XXXI – The Great talisman of Venus	133	Oraison, Invocation and Conjuration
73	Plate XXIX - Venus Pentacles	135	Talisman for Love (incomplete)
74	Plate XXX - Venus Pentacles	136-144	(A further incomplete Pentacles of Venus)
78	Pentacle for Saturday under Saturn	146	The Day of Saturday under Saturn Pentacle of Saturn (incomplete)
83	Plate XXXV - Hours of the Day and Night on Saturday	147	The hours of the day and Night of Saturday (incomplete)
80	Plate XXXII – Pentacle for Saturday under Saturn	148	The Pentacle of Saturn (not drawn)
81	Plate XXXIII - Pentacles of Saturn	152	Oration, Invocation Conjuration of Saturn
82	Plate XXXIX - Pentacles of Saturn	154-165	(A further incomplete Pentacles of Saturn)
87	Plate XXXVI - the Mysterious Ring	166	Mysterious Ring
	Four Experiments with Specific Spirits	168	*end*
88	Plate XXXVII - Experiment of the Spirit Birto		
91	Plate XXXVIII Birto - Wyvern		

	6. Senate House Library Uni of London Harry Price HPF 1/10		
102	An Experiment of the Spirit Vassago		
105	Seal of the Spirit Vassago		
92, 94	An Experiment of the Spirit Agares - Seal of Agares		
96	Plate XXXIX - An Experiment of the Spirit Bealpharos		
100	Plate XL - Magister Circle - Homo Sacarus Mus Elomeas Cherubosca		
107	Plate XLI - The Wheel of Magic		
106	**Wheel of Wisdom**		
108	Key to the Wheel of Wisdom		
110	With Full Directions for Magical Operations		
	Complete Book of Magic Science		
1	Liber Perfectus Magiae Scientiae		
3	Plate I - Blessings, Benedictions and Consecrations		
7	Plate II - (hexagram with eye and wands)		
8	Plate III - Hexagram		
13	Names and Offices of the Ruling Spirits		
19	Plate IV - Form in which the Spirit Pabiel sometimes Appears		
21	Form of Bond of Spirits		
22	Plate V - Pentacula Septem Planetatum		
23	Invocation of the Spirits of the Seven Planets		
25	Plate VI - Seals and Characters of the Seven Planets [& Olympic Spirits]		
26	Plate VII - Seals of the Olympic spirits		
	Crystaliomancy or the Art of Invocating Spirits by the Crystal		
1	Preface - Invocation of the Crystal		
2	Concerning the Room Containing the Circle		
5	Plate I - Circle - Messias Agla		
3	Concerning the Apparatus and Instruments used		
8	Plate II - the Mirror with Angel		
6	Consecrations and Blessings		
11	Bond or Obligation of the Spirit Vassaga (sic)		
	Experimentum Potens Magna in Occult Philosophy Arcanorum		
	Miscellaneous Examples and Experiments		
20	Plate VII - the Talisman or Ring of Strength		
1	Plate I - to Cause Destruction to Enemies		
5	Plate II - To Secure a House from Theft		
23	De Annulis eorum Compositionibus, &c.		
24	Invocation of the Spirit Oberion		
26	Form in which the Spirit Oberion usually appears		
27	The Great and Powerful Incantation		
31	Circle		
18	Plate VI - Imperial Talisman for Victory over Enemies		
7	Plate III - Charm for Healing Diseases		
			6. Senate House Library Uni of London Harry Price HPF 1/10
			(continued)
			Experiments
		12	Double Experiment of Great Power Amori Secreto forma Nodi
10	The Art of Fascination	13	Plate IV - Venus interlace sigil
		23	Angels and spits of Venus sigils
		15	Plate V - To Bind the Ground, whereby neither mortal man nor
34	[Geomancy page begun but not finished]	34	*end*

pp.	10. Ritman Library MS PH 304	pp.	12. Edward Hunter MS (Hell Fire Club publication)
	Date: 1874? **Pages:** 166. **Scribe:** Professional scribe		**Date:** 20th century? **Pages:** 60. **Scribe:** Edward Hunter?
	Signs, Seals and Magical Knife (frontispiece)		
title	Clavis or Key To Unlock the Mysteries of Magic of Rabbi Solomon	1	The Keys of Rabbi Solomon
122-127	Preface to the First Part		
1	Clavis or Key to Unlock the Mysteries of Magic - What disposition they	2	Chapter I - The dispositions required of a person wishing to partake
2	Chapter 2 - What are the proper places and times for the exercise of this	4	Chapter II - Which are the places and times proper and suitable
3	Chapter 3 - Of matters relating to the Operations and manner of them to be	6	Chapter III - Of the matters which serve for the operations
5	Chapter 4th - Concerning the necessary Instruments	10	Chapter 4 - What are the instruments proper and necessary for the
6	Chapter 5 - What are the Influences and Secret Virtues of the Moon in her	12	Chap[ter] 5 -What are the influences and secret virtues of the…Moon
9	Chapter 6 - Of the manner of working the figures of Talismans	16	Chapter 6 - Of the manner of working the figures, Talismans, characters.
11	The Grand Pentacle of Solomon	19	Grand Pentacle of Solomon
10	Chapter 7 - Concerning the hours of the Day and Night for the Seven days	20	Chapter 7 - Of the hours of the day and of the night
13	Chapter 8 - Concerning the Perfumes that are proper for the Seven Planets	21	Chapter 8 - Of the proper perfumes suitable to the seven Planets
13	Chapter 9 – Concerning the Orations, Invocations, and conjurations	22	Chapter 9 - Of the Oraisons, invocations, and conjurations
14	Chapter 10 - Concerning Orations in the form of Exorcisms to consecrate	23	Chapter 10 - Of the Oraisons in form of exorcisms, to Consecrate all
	Pentacles		**Pentacles**
17	Pentacle of the Sun	25	The Pentacle of the Sun for Sunday
19	Oration, Invocation, Conjuration	27	The Pentacle of the Sun for Sunday [pages 26-27 exactly repeated in
17	The Hours of the Day and Night of Sunday	29	Oraisons, Invocations, and Conjurations of the Sun for the day of Sunday
18	The Mysterious Cabalistic Names of the Hours of the Day and Night	31	The names mysterious and Cabalistic of the hours of the Day, and of the
21	Pentacle of the Sun x 2 (for Honour & Riches)	33	Pentacle of the Sun [for] Sunday
22	Sun Pentacle	34	Sun Pentacles for Honours and Riches
23	Sun Pentacle	35	Sun Pentacles against the Dead, unclean animals, and all spirits to obey
24-28	Sun Pentacles	36	Explanation of the following Talisman
28	Precious Stones	38	Observations on the following Talismans
29	The Pentacle of the Moon made on Monday	40	Pentacle of Monday, under the Moon
31	Oration, Invocation, Conjuration	42	Oraison, Invocation and Conjuration
30	The Hours of the Day and Night on Monday	41	Hours of the Day and Night of the day of Monday
33	Talisman for Travelling by Sea or Land made on Monday	44	Of the Moon, Pentacle or Talisman, for Love
34-37	Pentacles of the Moon	45	Another Talisman [for Love], to have familiar Spirits
		47	[Pentacle] against the Perils of Travel…under the Moon; of familiar
39	Pentacle of Mars Made on Tuesday	48	Pentacle of Mars, for the Day of Tuesday
41	Plate XIV - Hours of the Day and Night	49	Hours of the Day and Night of Tuesday
41	Oration, Invocation, Conjuration (Pentacle of Mars)	50	Composition of Perfumes for Mars, Oraisons, Invocation, Conjuration
42	Mars Pentacles	51	Pentacles of Mars to be successful in military Enterprises
43-46	Mars Pentacles	53	Precious Stones affected to Mars; Trees affected to Mars
		54	Pentacles of Mars] against fires
49	Pentacle of Mercury to be made on Wednesday	55	The Day of Wednesday under Mercury; Pentacle of Mercury
48	Oration, Invocation, Conjuration	57	Composition of Perfumes for Wednesday,; Invocation; Oraison;
51	Hours of the Day and Night	56	Hours of the Day and Night of Wednesday
52-56	Mercury Pentacles	59	Pentacles and Talismans for Wednesday
		60	Precious Stones affected to Mercury; Trees affected to Mercury
			[Incomplete - unfinished by the scribe]
57	The Pentacle of Jupiter to be Made on Thursday		
58	Oration, Invocation and Conjuration for Thursday		
60	Hours of the Day and Night of Jupiter		
61-65	Pentacles of Jupiter		
67	The Pentacle of Venus to be made on Friday		
68	Oration, Invocation and Conjuration for Friday		
69	The Hours of the Day and Night of Venus		
70-78	Elaborate- Pentacles of Venus		
82	Orations, Invocations and Conjurations		
81	Pentacle of Saturn to be made on Saturday		
83	Hours of the Day and Night under Saturn		
85-86	Pentacles of Saturn		
89	The Mysterious Ring		
	Experiments with Specific Spirits		
91	The Experiment of the Spirit Birto		
103	An Experiment of the Spirit Vassago		

	10. Ritman Library MS PH 304		
106	Seal of the Spirit Vassago		
95	An Experiment of the Spirit Agares		
98	Of the Spirit Bealpharos		
108-109	To help a person under Witchcraft, to find out a thief, etc		
101	Magister Circle - Homo Sacarus Mus Elomeas Cherubosca		
110	The Wheel of Magic		
111	**Wheel of Wisdom**		
113	Key to the Wheel of Wisdom		
116	Full Directions for Magical Operations		
129	**Complete Book of Magic Science (FH)**		
133	Blessings, Benedictions and Consecrations		
135	[hexagram with eye]		
137	Hexagram		
143	Names and Offices of the Ruling, Presiding and Ministering Spirits		
151	Pentacles of the Seven Planets		
153	Invocation of the Spirits of the Seven Planets		
156	Seals and Characters of the Seven Planets [& Olympic Spirits]		
161	The Imperial Talisman for Victory over Enemies		
163	Talisman for Love		
165	Talisman with 7 stars		
166	The Spiral Semaphora for Success in Life		
167	*end*		

Appendix 2. Mélusine and the Wyvern

This intriguing story tells of the beautiful Mélusine, the result of the marriage of the King of Scotland and his fairy wife. The King of Scotland was the first to fall foul of the fairy wife's prohibition against seeing her in the bath. In her youth Mélusine entombed her father in a mountain leaving her mother heartbroken. The deed displeased her mother and as punishment Mélusine was condemned to transform into a serpent from the waist down every Saturday.

Another story tells of Raymond of Poitou coming across Mélusine in the forest of Coulombiers in Poitou in France. He was struck by her beauty and proposed marriage. Just as her mother had done, she laid a condition on her suitor: that he must never enter her bedchamber on a Saturday. One day he broke the promise and saw her in the form of a part-woman, part-serpent, but after pleading with her, she forgave him. When, during a disagreement, he called her a "serpent" in front of his court, she assumed the form of a dragon or wyvern, provided him with two magic rings, and flew off, never to return. This is suggestive of the two circles (or rings) flanking a wyvern in the Birto invocation.

The King of Luxembourg also claimed descent from Mélusine. Some generations later, Jacquetta was born in 1416 to Peter of Luxembourg and Margaret de Baux.[255] Jacquetta at the age of 17, married the recently widowed and much older John Bedford of Lancaster, Duke of Bedford. The Duke of Bedford was the younger brother of Henry V; so was in the line of succession to the throne. Upon reaching her new home Jacquetta discovered her husband's interests in alchemy and magic, and his library with a significant collection of rare books on these subjects. This was possibly her introduction to the magical world. It is rumoured that the Duke prized his wife's innate abilities for communicating with the spirit world, especially because she was young, pure and virginal.

As you read through story of her early life, one realises that the magical world had opened several doors for Jacquetta: her ancestral connection to Mélusine; her possible meeting with Joan of Arc; and her marriage to an aristocrat with royal blood who had a strong interest in alchemy, magic and with a large library which probably included access to grimoires and other magical texts.

Her first marriage however was short lived, and the Duke of Bedford died in September of 1435, making his young wife the sole heir and leaving her most of his estate. Jacquetta soon married Sir Richard Woodville, and moved to the country with her new husband, and lived there for many years and had several children. Elizabeth Woodville was the

---

[255] It is possible that Jacquetta may have met Joan of Arc since her uncle, John of Luxembourg, held Joan of Arc for four months from the English. Whether she met Joan of Arc or not, she may have been inspired by Joan's spiritual or magical abilities.

first born daughter of Jacquetta, Duchess of Bedford and Sir Richard Woodville 1st Earl Rivers.

In 1464, the recently victorious King Edward IV surprised everyone by declaring that he had secretly taken a bride, the beautiful Elizabeth Woodville. Elizabeth was a most unlikely bride, being already a widow with two sons, and so rumours sprang up that the deep love between King Edward and Elizabeth must have been assisted by magic. It is believed that the wedding took place in Northamptonshire, on Mayday, 1st of May 1464.

When the War of Roses began, the Woodvilles initially supported the Red Rose, but the tables turned, when the victorious King Edward IV met the beautiful Elizabeth on his way back from the war, fell in love and married her rapidly.

Rumours of magic, witchcraft and astrology followed Jacquetta and her Queen daughter throughout their lives. There was enough for Jacquetta to be accused twice of witchcraft. Both times she managed to reach out to her royal connections and was acquitted. It is not therefore impossible that Edward IV and his queen Elizabeth Woodville may well have witnessed or participated in the evocation of Birto, relying upon the magical abilities inherited from Jacquetta and the ancestral Mélusine. The use of an image of the wyvern then becomes understandable.

The association with magic does not end there, as Elizabeth Woodville's daughter married Henry VII (1485-1509) who kept a secret room for the practice of magic that was not discovered until the reign of Elizabeth I.

A modern day referent to the story of Mélusine can be seen on the Starbucks logo, which shows her with a split serpent/mermaid tail.

Bibliography

Manuscripts

See the Introduction for a survey of the extant manuscripts of the *Clavis,* also Appendix 1 for an analysis of their comparative contents.

For Morrisoneau *Key of Solomon* (text-group RS) manuscripts by Rabbi Solomon see:

Wellcome MS 4656

Wellcome MS 4657

Wellcome MS 4660

Wellcome MS 4661,

Wellcome MS 4670 [256]

Other *Key of Solomon* manuscripts include:

Aubrey MS 24

Additional MS 10862

Lansdowne MS 1202

Lansdowne MS 1203

Sloane MS 1307

Wellcome MS 3203

Wellcome MS 4668

Wellcome MS 4669

Wellcome MS 4665

Sources of Four Experiments

Wellcome MS 2842

Sloane MS 3847, ff. 124v, 125v

Sloane MS 2848, f. 10

---

[256] Printed in Skinner & Rankine (2008).

Books

Abano, Peter de. *Heptameron, or the Magical Elements* in Agrippa, H. C. *Fourth Book of Occult Philosophy*, revised edition ed. Stephen Skinner. Berwick: Ibis Press/Nicolas-Hays, 2005.

Abraham of Worms, *aka* Abraham of Wurzburg. *The Book of the Sacred Magic of Abramelin the Mage*. (trans. and ed.) S. L. MacGregor Mathers. London: Watkins, 1898; 2nd edition 1900; rpt. New York: Causeway, 1974; New York: Dover, 1975.

Abraham of Worms, Georg Dehn, (ed. and trans.) Steven Guth. *The Book of Abramelin*. Lake Worth: Ibis, 2006.

Agrippa, H. C. *De Occulta Philosophia libri tres*. Koln, 1533. ed. Vittoria Perrone Compagni. Leiden: Brill, 1992.

Agrippa, H. C. *Fourth Book of Occult Philosophy*, (ed.) Stephen Skinner. Berwick: Ibis Press/Nicolas-Hays, 2005. [Contains: *Of Magical Ceremonies; Heptameron; Of the Nature of such Spirits; Arbatel of Magick; Of the Magick of the Ancients; Of Geomancy; Of Astronomical Geomancy*.]

Agrippa, H. C. *Three Books of Occult Philosophy*. (Trans.) James Freake [Dr John French]. (ed.) Donald Tyson. St Paul: Llewellyn, 1993.

Almond, Philip. *England's First Demonologist: Reginald Scot & The Discoverie of Witchcraft*, New York: Tauris, 2011.

Anon. *Grimorium Verum*. Memphis [Paris?]: Chez Alibeck l'Egyptian, 1517 [1817?].

Anon. *Les Clavicules de Salomon*, Paris: Chamuel, 1892.

Anon. *Les Véritables Clavicules De Salomon, Suivies du Fameux Secret du Papillon Vert*, Memphis [probably Paris]: Chez Alibeck l'Egyptien, n.d. [18th century - first edition printed in French; a later edition 19th century]

Baker, Jim. *The Cunning Man's Handbook*. Avalonia, Glastonbury, 2014.

Barrett, Francis. *The Magus, or Celestial Intelligencer; being a Complete System of Occult Philosophy*. London: 1801; rpt. New Hyde Park: University Books, 1967; rpt. York Beach: Samuel Weiser, 2000.

Bennett, Chris. *Liber 420: Cannabis, Magickal Herbs and the Occult*. Walterville: Trine Day, 2018.

Butler, E. M. *Ritual Magic*. Cambridge: Cambridge University Press, 1949; rpt. 1979.

Butler, E. M. *The Myth of the Magus*. Cambridge: Cambridge University Press, 1948.

Casaubon, Meric. *A True & Faithful Relation of What Passed for Many Yeers Between Dr. John Dee and some Spirits...*, 1659; Facsimile London: Askin, 1974; Rpt. with extensive corrections from the original MS as *Dr John Dee's Spiritual Diaries (1584-1608)*, (ed.) Stephen Skinner. Singapore: Golden Hoard, 2011.

Cecchetelli, Michael (transl.). *Crossed Keys.* n.p.: Scarlet, MMXI. [Includes: *Le Dragon Noir* and *Enchiridion of Pope Leo III*].

Ch'ien, Kineta (trans.). *The Great Grimoire of Pope Honorius.* Seattle: Trident, 1998.

Conjurer's Magazine. 3 Volumes, London, 1792-1794.

Conybeare, F. C. 'The Testament of Solomon,' in *Jewish Quarterly Review* XI, 1898-1899, pp. 1-45.

Cross, Robert T. (*aka* Raphael). *The Art of Talismanic Magic: Being Selections from the Works of Rabbi Solomon, Agrippa, F. Barrett etc.* 1879, rpt. Chicago: De Laurence Scott, 1916.

Davies, Charles Maurice. *The Great Secret,* London: Redway, 1896.

Davies, Owen. *Popular Magic: Cunning-folk in English History,* Hambledon Continuum, London, 2003.

Davies, Owen. *Grimoires: a History of Magic Books.* Oxford: Oxford University Press, 2009.

De Givry, Emile Grillot. *Picture Museum of Sorcery, Magic, and Alchemy,* (trans. Courtney Locke from *Le Musee Des Sorciers, Mages Et Alchemistes,* Paris, 1929). New Hyde Park: University Books, 1963.

Debus, Alan. 'Scientific truth and the occult tradition: the medical world of Ebenezer Sibly (1751-1799)' in *Medical History,* 1982, Vol. 26, pp. 259-278.

Dee, John, Meric Casaubon (Preface) and (ed.) Stephen Skinner. *Dr. John Dee's Spiritual Diaries (1583-1608).* Singapore: Golden Hoard, 2011. *See also* Casaubon (1659).

Dehn, Georg. See Abraham of Worms (2006).

Driscoll, Daniel. *The Sworn Book of Honorius the Magician.* New Jersey: Heptangle, 1977.

Dumas, François Ribadeau. *Grimoires et Rituels Magiques.* Paris: Pre au Clercs, 1980; Paris: Belfond, 1998. [Includes: *Le Livre des Conjurations du pape Honorius, Enchiridion de Sa Sainteté le pape Léon III, Le Dragon Rouge, La Poule Noire, Le Génie et Le Trésor du Vieillard des Pyramides, La Chouette Noire, Le Rituel de haute magie.*]

Dumas, François Ribadeau. *Le Grand et le Petit Albert.* Paris: Belfond, 1978.

Fanger, Claire (ed.). *Conjuring Spirits: Texts and Traditions of Medieval Ritual Magic.* Gloucestershire: Sutton Publishing and Pennsylvania State UP, 1998.

Fanger, Claire (ed.). *Invoking Angels: Theurgic Ideas and Practices, Thirteenth to Sixteenth Centuries.* Pennsylvania: Pennsylvania State University, 2012.

Fanger, Claire. 'Covenant and the Divine name: Revisiting the *Liber iuratus* and John of Morigny's *Liber florum*' in Fanger, Claire (ed.). *Invoking Angels: Theurgic Ideas and*

Practices, Thirteenth to Sixteenth Centuries. Pennsylvania: Pennsylvania State University, 2012.

Foreman, Paul. Francis Young (ed. and transl.). *The Cambridge Book of Magic: a Tudor Necromancer's Manual.* Cambridge: Texts in Early Modern Magic, 2015. [Contains Cambridge University MS Add 3544.]

Foster, Michael. 'Thomas Allen (1540-1632), Gloucester Hall and the Survival of Catholicism in Post-Reformation Oxford' *in Oxoniensis,* 46, 1981, pp. 99-128

Garner, Bryan (Fra. Ashan Chassan). *Gateways through Stone and Circle.* Nephilim, 2013.

Garner, Bryan (Fra. Ashan Chassan), Foreword by Stephen Skinner. *Gateways through Light and Shadow.* Portland: Azoth, 2016.

Godwin, Joscelyn. *The Theosophical Enlightenment.* New York: State University, 1994.

Gollancz, Herman (ed.), Stephen Skinner (ed.). *Sepher Maphteah Shelomoh (Book of the Key of Solomon),* York Beach: Teitan, 2008.

Hamill, John & R. A. Gilbert. *The Rosicrucian Seer: Magical Writings of Frederick Hockley.* Wellingborough: Aquarian, 1986; rpt. York Beach: Teitan, 2009.

Harms, Daniel and Joseph Peterson. *The Book of Oberon: a Sourcebook of Elizabethan Magic.* Woodbury: Llewellyn, 2015.

Hedegård, Gösta. *Liber Iuratus Honorii.* Stockholm: Almqvist and Wiksell, 2002.

Heydon, John. *Theomagia,* 3 vols., London, 1662-1664.

Heydon, John. *El Havareuna,* London, 1665.

Hockley, Frederick & Alan Thorogood (Ed.). *Clavis Arcana Magica.* York Beach: Teitan, 2012.

Hockley, Frederick & Alan Thorogood (Ed.).*The Pauline Art of Solomon.* York Beach: Teitan, 2016.

Hockley, Frederick & Dan Harms (Ed.). *Experimentum, Potens Magna in Occult Philosophy,* SEE, 2012.

Hockley, Frederick & Dietrich Bergman (Ed.). *A Complete Book of Magic Science.* York Beach: Teitan, 2008.

Hockley, Frederick & R. A. Gilbert (Intro.). *Invocating by Magic Crystals and Mirrors.* York Beach: Teitan, 2010.

Hockley, Frederick & Silens Manus (Ed.). *Occult Spells: a Nineteenth Century Grimoire.* York Beach: Teitan, 2009.

Hockley, Frederick & Silens Manus (Intro.). *Abraham the Jew on Magic Talismans.* York Beach: Teitan, 2011.

Hockley, Frederick. *The Metaphysical and Spiritual Philosophy of the Spirit Eltesmo.* York Beach: Teitan, forthcoming.

Hockley, Frederick, *see also* Porter, John.

Howe, Ellic. *Urania's Children, the Strange World of the Astrologers.* London: Kimber, 1967.

James, Geoffrey. *Angel Magic: the Ancient Art of Summoning and Communicating with Angelic Beings.* St. Paul: Llewellyn, 1997.

Karr, Don (ed.) and Kalnit Nachshon (trans.). *Liber Lunae, the Book of the Moon & Sepher ha-Levanah.* Volume 7, SWCM. Singapore: Golden Hoard, 2011.

Karr, Don and Stephen Skinner. *Sepher Raziel: Liber Salomonis,* Volume 6, SWCM. Singapore: Golden Hoard, 2010.

Kieckhefer, Richard. 'The Devil's Contemplatives: the *Liber Iuratus,* the *Visionem* and the Christian Appropriation of Jewish Occultism,' in Fanger, Claire (ed.). *Conjuring Spirits,* Sutton Publishing, 1998.

Kieckhefer, Richard. *Forbidden Rites: a Necromancer's Manual of the Fifteenth Century.* Stroud: Sutton, 1997, rpt. University Park: Pennsylvania State University Press, 1998.

Kiesel, William. *Magic Circles in the Grimoire Tradition.* Richmond Vista: Three Hands, 2012.

King, B. J. H. (trans.). *The Grimoire of Pope Honorius III.* Kettering: Sut Anubis, 1984.

King, Francis. *Magic: the Western Tradition,* London: Thames & Hudson, 1984.

King, Francis. *Ritual Magic: 1887 to the Present Day.* London: NEL, 1973.

King, Francis. *The Flying Sorcerer.* Oxford: Mandrake, 1992.

King, Francis. *The Magical World of Aleister Crowley,* New York: Coward, McCann & Geoghegan, 1978.

King, Francis & Isabel Sutherland. *The Rebirth of Magic.* London: Corgi, 1982.

King, Francis & S. L. MacGregor Mathers & R. A. Gilbert. *Astral Projection, Magic, and Alchemy: Golden Dawn Material,* London: Spearman, 1972.

King, Francis & Stephen Skinner. *Techniques of High Magic,* Singapore: GHP, 2016.

Klaassen, Frank. 'English Manuscripts of Magic, 1300-1500: a Preliminary Survey,' in Fanger, Claire (ed.). *Conjuring Spirits: Texts and Traditions of Medieval Ritual Magic.* Gloucestershire: Sutton Publishing and Pennsylvania State UP, 1998.

Kuntz, Darcy (ed.). *Ars Notoria: the Magical Art of Solomon...Englished by Robert Turner.* London, 1656, rpt. Sequim: Holmes, 2006.

Láng, Benedek. *Unlocked Books: Manuscripts of Learned Magic in the Medieval Libraries of Central Europe*. University Park: Pennsylvania State University Press, 2008.

Lecouteux, Claude. *Le Livres des Grimoires*. Paris: Imago, 2008.

Leitch, Aaron. *Secrets of the Magical Grimoires*. Woodbury: Llewellyn, 2005.

Madziarczyk, John. *A Sorcerous Anthology: Magical and Occult Writings from the Publications of Robert Cross Smith*. Seattle: Topaz, 2017.

Madziarczyk, John & Ebenezer Sibley. *The Station of Man in the Universe, Ebenezer Sibly on the Spirit World and Magic*, Lulu, 2018.

Macdonald, Michael-Albion. *De Nigromancia of Roger Bacon*. Gillette, New Jersey: Heptangle, 1988.

Marathakis, Ioannis. 'A Source of the Key of Solomon: the Magic Treatise or Hygromancy, or Epistle to Rehoboam' in Lycourinos, Damon (ed.). *Occult Traditions*, Colac: Numen, 2012, pp. 108-120.

Marathakis, Ioannis. *The Magical Treatise of Solomon or Hygromanteia*. Volume 8, *SWCM*. Singapore: Golden Hoard, 2011.

Margalioth, Mordecai (ed.). *Sepher ha-Razim: a Newly Recovered Book of Magic from the Talmudic Period, Collected from Genizah Fragments and Other Sources*. Jerusalem: Yediot Achronot, 1966. [Hebrew]

Mathers, S. L. MacGregor, & Crowley, A. (ed.). *The Book of the Goetia of Solomon the King*. Foyers: SPRT, 1904.

Mathers, S. L. MacGregor. (trans.), Francis King (ed.). *The Grimoire of Armadel*. London: Routledge, 1980.

Mathers, S. L. MacGregor. (trans.). *The Book of the Sacred Magic of Abramelin the Mage*. London: Watkins, 1900.

Mathers, S. L. MacGregor. (trans.). *The Key of Solomon the King (Clavicula Salomonis)*. London: Redway, 1889; London: Kegan Paul, 1909; rpt. Maine: Samuel Weiser, 2000.

Mathews, John. *The Rosicrucian Enlightenment Revisited*. Hudson: Lindisfarne, 1999.

Mathiesen, Robert. 'The Key of Solomon: Towards a Typology of the Manuscripts,' in *Societas Magica Newsletter*, Spring 2007, 17:1, pp. 3-9.

McCown, Chester C. *The Testament of Solomon*. Heft 9. Leipsig, 1922.

McIntosh, Christopher. *The Devil's Bookshelf: a History of the Written Word in Western Magic from Ancient Egypt to the Present Day*. Wellingborough: Aquarian, 1985.

McLean, Adam (ed.). *A Treatise on Angel Magic*, Edinburgh: Magnum Opus Sourceworks, 1982; rpt. Grand Rapids: Phanes Press, 1990; rpt. York Beach: Weiser, 2006.

McLean, Adam (ed.). Fiona Tait, Christopher Upton & J. H. W. Walden (trans.). *The Steganographia of Johannes Trithemius*. Book I & III. Edinburgh: Magnum Opus, 1982.

McLean, Adam (ed.). *The Magical Calendar*. Edinburgh: Magnum Opus, 1979, rpt. Grand Rapids: Phanes, 1994.

Mora, Pierre (trans.) *Les Véritables Clavicules de Salomon*. Paris: Daragon, 1914.

Murtaugh, Stephen. Authentication of "The Secret Grimoire of Turiel" in comparison with Frederick Hockley's "A Complete Book of Magic Science," 2013.

Paracelsus, Robert Turner (trans.), Stephen Skinner (ed.). *The Archidoxes of Magic*. London, 1655; London: Askin, 1975; rpt. Berwick: Ibis, 2004.

Parkins, John. *Book of Miracles,* London, 1817; rpt. Delhi: Facsimile, 2018.

Peterson, Joseph (ed.). *Grimorium Verum*. California: CreateSpace, 2007.

Peterson, Joseph. (ed.) and Ebenezer Sibley and Frederick Hockley. *The Clavis or Key to the Magic of Solomon*. Florida: Ibis, 2009 rpt. 2012.

Peterson, Joseph. (ed.). *Liber Juratus* aka *Liber Sacer*. Lake Worth, Ibis, 2016.

Peterson, Joseph. (ed.). *The Lesser Key of Solomon: Lemegeton Clavicula Salomonis*. York Beach: Weiser, 2001.

Plaingiére. *Grimorium Verum*. [Paris?], 1780.

Porta, Giambattista della. *Magia Naturalis*, 1558.

Porter, John, Frederick Hockley (scribe), Colin Campbell (ed.). *A Book of the Offices of Spirits,* York Beach: Teitan, 2011.

Rankine, David and Paul Harry Barron. *The Book of Gold: a 17th Century Magical Grimoire…using the Biblical Psalms of King David*. London: Avalonia, 2009.

Rankine, David. *The Book of Treasure Spirits: a grimoire of Magical Conjurations*. London: Avalonia, 2009.

Rankine, David. *The Grimoire of Arthur Gauntlet*. London: Avalonia, 2011.

Rudy, Gretchen. *The Grand Grimoire*. Seattle: Trident & Ars Obscura, 1996.

Scarborough, Samuel. 'Frederick Hockley: A Hidden Force behind the 19th Century English Occult Revival' in *Journal of the Western Mystery Tradition*, No. 14, Vol. 2, 2008.

Scheible, Johann. *Das Kloster*. 12 Vols. Stuttgart, 1845-49.

Scot, Reginald. *Discoverie of Witchcraft*. London, 1584, 1661, 1665; rpt. London: Elliot Stock, 1886. [Especially Book xv, Chapter i-iv, pp. 376 *et seq.*]

Shah, Sayed Idries. *The Secret Lore of Magic: the Books of the Sorcerers*. London: Muller, 1957.

Sibley, Ebenezer, *see also* Peterson, Joseph. *Clavis.*

Sibley, Ebenezer. *Uranoscopia, or the Pure Language of the Stars Unfolded,* London, 1780.

Sibley, Ebenezer. *A New and Complete Illustration of the Occult Sciences,* London, 1784.

Sibley, Ebenezer. *A New and Complete Illustration of the Celestial Science of Astrology: or, the art of foretelling future events and contingencies by the aspects...* London, 1784-1788, rpt. 1817.

Sibley, Ebenezer. *Key to Physic and the Occult Science of Astrology,* London, 1792, 1794, 1814.

Sibley, Ebenezer. *The Medical Mirror, or a treatise on the impregnation of the human Female,* London, c. 1796.

Simon. *Papal Magic: Occult Practices within the Catholic Church.* New York: Harper, 2007. [*The grimoire of Pope Honorius III.*]

Skinner, Stephen and David Rankine. *The Practical Angel Magic of John Dee's Enochian Tables,* Vol. 1, *SWCM.* London: Golden Hoard, 2004.

Skinner, Stephen and David Rankine. *The Keys to the Gateway of Magic,* Vol. 2, *SWCM.* London: Golden Hoard, 2005.

Skinner, Stephen and David Rankine. *The Goetia of Dr Rudd,* Vol. 3, *SWCM.* London: Golden Hoard, 2007.

Skinner, Stephen and David Rankine. *The Veritable Key of Solomon,* Vol. 4, *SWCM.* Singapore: Golden Hoard, 2008.

Skinner, Stephen and David Rankine. *The Grimoire of St Cyprian: Clavis Inferni,* Vol. 5, *SWCM.* Singapore: Golden Hoard, 2009.

Skinner, Stephen and David Rankine. *The Cunning Man's Grimoire,* Vol. 9, *SWCM.* Singapore: Golden Hoard, 2018.

Skinner, Stephen and David Rankine and Harry Barron (trans.). A *Collection of Magical Secrets.* London: Avalonia, 2009.

Skinner, Stephen. *Complete Magician's Tables.* London/Singapore: Golden Hoard, 2006; rpt. Llewellyn, Woodbury, 2007, 2011. Fifth expanded ed., Golden Hoard, 2015, 2017.

Skinner, Stephen. *Techniques of Graeco-Egyptian Magic.* Singapore: Golden Hoard, 2014.

Skinner, Stephen. *Techniques of Solomonic Magic.* Singapore: Golden Hoard, 2015.

Skinner, Stephen. *Geomancy in Theory and Practice.* Singapore: Golden Hoard, 2011.

Smith, Robert Cross. *The Straggling Astrologer.* London, 1824.

Smith, Robert Cross. *The Astrologer of the Nineteenth Century.* London: Wright, 1825, rpt. Delhi: Isha, 2013.

Smith, Robert Cross. *Manual of Astrology.* London: Arnold, 1828.

Smith, Robert Cross. *The Familiar Astrologer*. London: Bennett, 1831.

Smith, Robert Cross. *Raphael's Lady-Witch*. London: Wright, 1831.

Smith, Robert Cross. *Book of Fate*. London: Foulsham, 1887.

Sommers, Susan Mitchell. *The Siblys of London: A Family on the Esoteric Fringes of Georgian England,* Oxford: OUP, 2018.

Symon, Jon. *The Sacred Magick of the Angels or Talismanic Intelligencer*. Hamilton: Acorn, 1861, rpt. 1970s.

Thomas, Keith. *Religion and the Decline of Magic*. New York: Scribner, 1971.

Thompson, C. J. S. *The Mysteries and Secrets of Magic*. London: Lane, 1927.

Thorndike, Lynn. 'Traditional Medieval Tracts concerning engraved Astrological images,' in *Mélanges Auguste Pelzer*. Louvain: Université de Louvain, 1947, pp. 217-274.

Thorndike, Lynn. A *History of Magic and Experimental Science*, Volumes I-VIII. New York: Columbia University Press, 1923-1958.

Trithemius, Johannes. *Steganographia*. Frankfort, 1606, 1621. [See also McLean (1982).]

Turner, Robert. *Ars Notoria*. London, 1657.

Véronèse, Julien. 'God's Names and their Uses in the Books of Magic attributed to King Solomon' in *Magic, Ritual, and Witchcraft,* Vol. 5, No. 1, Summer 2010.

Véronèse, Julien. 'Les Anges dans *l'ars Notoria*: Révélation, processus visionnaire et Angélologie,' in *Mélanges de l'École Française de Rome,* 114, no. 2, 2002, pp. 813-884.

Véronèse, Julien. 'Magic, Theurgy, and Spirituality in the Medieval Ritual of the *Ars Notoria*' in Fanger, Claire (ed.). *Invoking Angels: Theurgic Ideas and Practices, Thirteenth to Sixteenth Centuries*. Pennsylvania: Penn State University, 2012.

Véronèse, Julien. 'La transmission groupée des textes de magie "salomonienne" de l'antiquité au Moyen Âge: *textes et représentations, VIe-XIVe siècle*, S. Gioanni et B. Grévin. Rome: EFR, 2008, pp. 193-223.

Waite, A. E. *The Book of Black Magic and of Pacts,* Privately Printed, Edinburgh, 1898; rpt. York Beach: Samuel Weiser, 1972.

Waite, A. E. *The Book of Ceremonial Magic*. New York: University Books, 1961.

Waite, A. E. *The Secret Tradition in Goetia*. London: Rider, 1911.

Wentworth, Joshua (trans.). *The Authentic Red Dragon (Le Véritable Dragon Rouge)...The Black Hen translated from the French Edition,* 1521; rpt. York Beach: Teitan, 2011.

Index